The Handbook of
Family-School Intervention

The Handbook of
Family-School Intervention

A Systems Perspective

MARVIN J. FINE
University of Kansas

and

CINDY CARLSON
University of Texas, Austin

Editors

ALLYN AND BACON
Boston   London   Toronto   Sydney   Tokyo   Singapore

Library of Congress Cataloging-in-Publication Data

The Handbook of family-school intervention : a systems perspective /
  edited by Marvin J. Fine and Cindy Carlson.
     p.   cm.
  Includes bibliographical references and index.
  ISBN 0-205-13024-0
  1. Problem children—Counseling of—United States. 2. Problem
families—Counseling of—United States. 3. Family psychotherapy-
-United States. 4. Home and school—United States. I. Fine,
Marvin J. II. Carlson, Cindy
LC4802.H36 1992
371.7'13—dc20   91-436
                                              CIP

Printed in the United States of America
10 9 8 7 6 5 4 3 2   95 94 93 92

Contents

PART III EXCEPTIONALITY: THE INTERRELATIONSHIP OF FAMILY, SCHOOL, AND CHILD DEVELOPMENT

PART IV   SYSTEMIC APPROACHES TO FAMILY PROBLEMS

PART V   MODELS OF INTERVENTION

PART VI   PROFESSIONAL ISSUES AND FUTURE DIRECTIONS

Preface

The burgeoning field of family therapy, based in systems theory, has had a dramatic impact on the conceptualization and treatment of individual psychopathology. There has also been an exciting and productive extension of the family systems orientation into school-based interventions. This includes a greater awareness of the "power" of the family in creating or maintaining school-related problems of children and a greater appreciation of the interfacing of the family and school systems in treatment.

Adoption of a "family systems" orientation dramatically changes our perspective on the etiology of school-related problems. The essence of a family systems orientation is that the "problem" that a child or adolescent is experiencing is best understood when viewed as an adaptation of that individual to the interactive relationships within the family. Moreover, the behavior patterns of individuals are viewed as a function of circular and reciprocal processes within relationships such that the "cause" of the behavior cannot reasonably be determined to exist within either relationship partner. Rather, behavior is viewed as existing within a relationship, a "whole" that is distinct from the contribution of the individuals.

Systems theorists also view systems and subsystems as interrelated; thus, dysfunctional behavior patterns learned within the family would be expected to "carry over" to closely related settings such as the school and, reciprocally, from the school to

the family. In short, from the systems perspective, the etiology and maintenance of the school-related problematic behavior is not considered to be child based but rather is considered to be based contextually in the immediate and extended sets of relationships in which the child is embedded.

Family systems theory also has implications for assessment and intervention with troubled children. Given that the etiology of problems is viewed as based in the relationships of individuals, assessment practices shift from the individual child to evaluation of the relationships in which the child participates. Congruently, from a systems perspective, interventions that are targeted to the relationships of the child are generally considered to be most effective. Thus, systems practitioners frequently involve families in school-based problems and involve schools in family-based problems.

There are many levels and dimensions of family involvement in relation to what initially appears to be a school-based problem with the child. First-level interventions are preventive in nature, such as parent education classes, that serve the purpose of increasing the effectiveness of parents and establishing a collaborative relationship between home and school. Second-level interventions provide indirect services to the child through consultation with school personnel helping them understand the child's behavior in a "different" way, which may be based on knowledge of the family, such that more supportive behaviors on the part of the school can emerge.

A third level of intervention is the direct involvement of parents and family members with school personnel to collaborate in understanding and modifying both home and school patterns as they pertain to what was initially defined as a child problem. The use of family-school meetings is an example of this type of intervention. A fourth level of intervention is direct services to the family (i.e., family therapy). Although there continues to be debate as to the appropriateness of school mental health professionals being involved in family therapy, and the resources for such services are customarily limited, such activities are indeed occurring within the schools. Systems thinking can also extend to schoolwide interventions. In fact, many systems-oriented practitioners argue that the most effective interventions occur hierarchically at one system level higher than the emergence of the problem. Thus, for example, if several classroom teachers are experiencing difficulty integrating handicapped children into the regular classroom, a schoolwide program directed toward changing attitudes and beliefs of teachers as well as providing curricular and classroom management support would be consistent with a systemic orientation.

A systems orientation highlights the regularities and interrelatedness of patterns of behavior within a social context, such as the family. However, any examination of the family must not only hold a lens to the organization of systemic properties but also be sensitive to the unique characteristics of each family. The relationships that characterize families will differ as a reflection of sociocultural norms and as a reflection of the unique individual developmental needs of family members. Research consistently finds that parent-child relationship patterns differ by socioeconomic status and ethnic variation. Similarly, the unique charcteristics of a particular family member, such as a handicapped child, will alter the "universal" patterns of family relationships and organization.

In summary, a systems perspective compels us to look beyond the individual to the regularities and forces in the context in which the individual's behavior is embedded. Context includes both the patterns of transaction that occur within the context and the beliefs that organize these patterns. Social context can also be construed ecologically to consist of multiple system levels, some immediate and others more distant. The most salient proximal contexts of the child will be the family and, with increasing age, the classroom and peer group. These immediate contexts of the child are strongly influenced by the social values and norms of the larger social context of the neighborhood or cultural group with which the family identifies.

This book adopts a systems perspective and applies it to the treatment of children's school-based problems. The chapters that follow are intended to provide the reader with a good theoretical foundation in systems theory applied to schools and to special problem children and families, as well as provide the reader with models of the practical application of systems theory to school-based intervention. Part I (Chapters 1–3) presents a theoretical overview. Part II (Chapters 4–7) explores the impact of the sociocultural context on family relationships and the family-school interface. Part III (Chapters 8–11) examines the impact of a special child on the family system. Part IV (Chapters 12–16) applies the systems orientation to the troubled families and children. Part V (Chapters 17–25) provides multiple models of family and family-school intervention. The book concludes with Part VI (Chapters 26–28), which gives a consideration of professional issues, including the efficacy of family systems treatment.

In Part I, three chapters provide complementary views of systems theory. In the first chapter, Marvin J. Fine presents a systems-ecological perspective for viewing and intervening in children's school-based problems. In Chapter 2, Cindy Carlson presents three models for intervening with families in the schools and discusses the implications for family assessment that each model presents. The models discussed include the structural, cognitive-behavioral, and solution-oriented approaches. Jeanne M. Plas, in Chapter 3, provides a historical view of the origins of systems theory, which provides the reader with both a sense of the context of this theoretical perspective and an appreciation of its distinctiveness.

Variations in family functioning as reflections of ethnic identity is the focus of Part II. In Chapter 4, Robbie J. Steward and Sadye Logan clarify myths and assumptions regarding the black family, with particular attention to the home-school relationship, and provide clear recommendations for interventions with this minority group. Man Keung Ho, in Chapter 5, provides important information on the diversity of the Asian-American population as well as some of the cultural consistencies that influence the school behavior of children. Implications for treatment are clarified with a case study. In Chapter 6, Meredith Buenning, Nona Tollefson, and Fred Rodriguez elaborate the cultural background factors that contribute to the school achievement patterns of the fastest growing minority group in the United States—the Hispanic population—and provide treatment recommendations. The section concludes with Chapter 7, in which Larry L. Grimm carefully delineates the distinctiveness of the Native American culture and provides a "cultural network model" of counseling that transcends the conventional boundaries of group or family counseling.

Special child populations are high-

lighted in Part III. A proactive, early intervention, family-systems approach to working with preschool children is described in Chapter 8 by Kathleen D. Paget. Her chapter directly targets the demands placed on educational professionals with the passage of Public Law 99–457, the amendment to the Education for All Handicapped Children Act. Robert L. Marion, in Chapter 9, discusses the impact of a mentally retarded child on the family system and clarifies the unique demands placed on the family with the subsequent developmental stages of the child. In Chapter 10, Robert-Jay Green provides a unique ecological-somatic model for understanding child underachievement and learning disorders within the family context. Regarding implications for treatment, Green proposes that clinicians view the family as the primary classroom experience of the child. This section concludes with Chapter 11 by Reva Jenkins-Friedman presenting a systemic view of the families of gifted children. She also provides a systemic perspective on intervention with the difficulties of underachievement and disabling perfectionism in gifted children.

Part IV presents a systemic perspective for viewing problems of school-aged children that are frequently encountered by mental health professionals in the schools. In Chapter 12, Cindy Carlson describes the family processes associated with single-parent and steparent families that can impact upon the school performance of children. Marla R. Brassard and Ilia M. Appellániz examine the abusive family from an ecological-systemic orientation and provide a theoretically consistent assessment and treatment approach in Chapter 13. In Chapter 14, Raymond Tricker and John Poertner focus on substance abuse as a problem of multiple interactions within and between systems and provide a treatment approach that focuses on the family as a framework for prevention and intervention. Research and theory regarding the role of the family system in childhood depression is the topic of Chapter 15, authored by Kevin D. Stark and Catherine Simmons Brookman. A case example is used to clarify a school-based family systems treatment. In Chapter 16, Nicholas C. Aliotti provides a family systems perspective on school phobia, contrasts this with a psychoanalytic perspective, and links the family systems analysis through several case studies to a strategic family intervention plan via several case studies.

Multiple models of family intervention, all of which are consistent with systems theory, are provided in Part V. Several traditional "schools" of family therapy are represented in these chapters: the Bowen Family Systems model (Chapter 17 by Edward W. Beal and Lynn S. Chertkov); structural family therapy (Chapter 18 by Marion C. Fish and Sashi Jain); and the structural-strategic model (Chapter 19 by Robert N. Wendt). In addition, several emergent systems-based treatment models are described. These include Ron Kral's Chapter 20 on Solution-Focused Brief Therapy, a therapeutic model that has emerged from the work of Steven de Shazer at the Milwaukee Brief Therapy Center, and Chapter 21 on the language-systems model, a treatment model that has emerged from the work of the Galveston Family Institute in Houston, Texas. Authors are Lyle J. White, Mary Lue Summerlin, Victor E. Loos, and Eugene S. Epstein.

In addition to descriptions of general models of family therapy, several alternative treatments or treatment perspectives are discussed. In Chapter 22, an ecosystemic approach is described by Don-David Lusterman. Following this chapter, Marvin J. Fine and Jim Jennings link the traditions of family therapy and parent education in Chapter 23. A schoolwide divorce prevention and intervention program is described in Chapter 24 by colleagues at the Newton Public Schools in Newton, Massachusetts, Susan R. Berger, Rohna Shoul, and Susan Warschauer. Finally, this section of the book ends with a chapter that discusses the often difficult task of actually implementing a family systems treatment program in the schools. Chapter 25 is written by a group of social workers and psychologists, Marlene Merrill, Robert Clark, Cheri Varvil, Carey Van Sickle, and Laura McCall, who have successfully implemented and maintained a family systems-based intervention program for the past eight years.

In Part VI, the perspective returns from applications of family systems practice in the schools to the broader issues of professional practice. In Chapter 26, John P. Quirk, Marvin J. Fine, and Linda Roberts discuss the professional and ethical issues that are raised by family-school systems interventions. This chapter not only examines specific ethical dilemmas but also examines the "goodness-of-fit" between family systems interventions and schools. Yvonna S. Lincoln, in Chapter 27, critically examines the limitations inherent in the adoption of general systems theory as a model for the delivery of services in schools. She argues persuasively for an alternative service delivery model based in social constructivism. Since the practice of psychology is embedded in scientific inquiry, the book concludes with Chapter 27, by Agnes Donovan, who reviews the research on the efficacy of family systems interventions with children experiencing school problems. Her review indicates that family approaches hold promise in the treatment of school-related problems but also highlights the need for additional investigation.

The chapters in this book, as a whole, represent a rich diversity of perspectives and approaches. Although a systems orientation was integral to the organization of the book, noteworthy across the chapters is a sensitivity to the importance of family structure and family relationships in the life of the student, and an explicit valuing of enhanced family-school relationships. Although it remains unclear the degree to which school-based professionals can put in place the organizational changes necessary to sustain optimally the systemic perspectives described in this volume, it is the conviction of most systems thinkers that small changes have a ripple effect throughout larger systems. May this book inspire small changes.

ACKNOWLEDGMENTS

The completion of this book, as perhaps with all endeavors, has a unique history. We wish to thank each of the authors for his or her contributions to this book and for their patience with the publication process. We also appreciate Grune and Stratton for their initial support of this work prior to the demise of their publishing company. In addition, we thank Mylan Jaixen, executive editor at Allyn and Bacon, for his faith in this product. And finally, we thank one another for tolerance, patience, inspiration, and the friendship that grows from these.

M. J. F.
C. C.

List of Contributors

Nicholas C. Aliotti
Family Enrichment Center,
La Mesa, California

Ilia M. Apellániz
University of Massachusetts, Amherst

Edward W. Beal
Oak Leaf Center, Bethesda, Maryland

Susan R. Berger
Newton Public Schools, Newton,
Massachusetts

Marla R. Brassard
University of Massachusetts, Amherst

Catherine Simmons Brookman
University of Texas, Austin

Meredith Buenning
Littleton Public Schools, Colorado

Cindy Carlson
University of Texas, Austin

Lynn S. Chertkov
Oak Leaf Center, Bethesda, Maryland

Robert J. Clark
Topeka Public Schools, Kansas

Agnes Donovan
Teachers College, Columbia University

Eugene S. Epstein
Center for Social Theory,
Bad Wimpfen, West Germany

Marvin J. Fine
University of Kansas

Marian C. Fish
Queens College, City University of
New York

Robert-Jay Green
California School of Professional
Psychology—Berkeley/Alameda

Larry L. Grimm
Prescott Neurological Clinic,
Prescott, Arizona

Man Keung Ho
University of Oklahoma

Shashi Jain
City University of New York

Reva Jenkins-Friedman
University of Kansas

Jim Jennings
The Family Tree, Overland Park,
Kansas

Ron Kral
School District of Elmbrook,
Brookfield, Wisconsin

Yvonna S. Lincoln
Vanderbilt University

Sadye L. Logan
University of Kansas

Victor E. Loos
Deer Park Independent School
District, Deer Park, Texas

Don-David Lusterman
Private Practice, Baldwin, New York

Robert L. Marion
University of Texas, Austin

Laura J. McCall
East Central Kansas Cooperative in
Education, Baldwin City, Kansas

Marlene A. Merrill
Harvey County Special Education
Cooperative, Newton, Kansas

Kathleen D. Paget
University of South Carolina

Jeanne M. Plas
Peabody College of Vanderbilt
University

John Poertner
University of Kansas

John P. Quirk
Indiana University of Pennsylvania

Linda Roberts
Kansas City Public Schools, Kansas

Fred Rodriguez
University of Kansas

Rohna Shoul
Newton Public Schools, Newton,
Massachusetts

Kevin D. Stark
University of Texas, Austin

Robbie J. Steward
University of Kansas

Mary Lue Summerlin
Deer Park Independent School
District, Deer Park, Texas

Nona Tollefson
University of Kansas

Raymond Tricker
Oregon State University

Carey A. Van Sickle
Topeka Public Schools, Kansas

Cheri D. Varvil
Topeka Public Schools, Kansas

Susan Warschauer
Newton Public Schools, Newton,
Massachusetts

Robert N. Wendt
University of Toledo

Lyle J. White
Southern Illinois University,
Carbondale

1

A Systems-Ecological Perspective on Home-School Intervention

MARVIN J. FINE
University of Kansas

MENTAL HEALTH professionals and educators have historically been aware of the impact that home and school systems can have on each other in the life of a child. Awareness of this impact has led to a number of theoretical positions and interventions described in the literature that reflect attempts to understand and intervene with children and families and in consideration of the school setting. This chapter is a consolidation and an extension of ideas on a systems-ecological perspective and continues to make the case that viewing a child's difficulty in a systems-ecological context can generate a number of potentially successful and lasting interventions (Apter, 1982; Fine & Holt, 1983; Green & Fine, 1979; Pfeiffer & Tittler, 1984; Swap, 1978, 1984; Mannino & Shore, 1984; Hansen, 1984; Dowling & Osborne, 1985; Lusterman, 1985; Schaefer, Briesmeister, & Fitton, 1984).

A systems-ecological perspective seems particularly well suited to helping professionals who are dealing with across-systems problems and are attempting to understand a child in a particular setting as well as understand the interrelationship of the child with different settings. Whether school-based or community-based, these professionals typically have a psychological orientation and an appreciation of the range of influences on child behavior, including the importance of teacher-classroom and home-family variables. Also, while at times having a direct service involvement, these professionals are often able to assume a consultative orientation, which Rhodes (1970) referred to as the "single most important tool in the ecological model" (p. 50).

WHAT IS MEANT BY THE TERM SYSTEMS-ECOLOGICAL?

From the onset the reader should be aware that there is a tremendous linguistic diversity and conceptual complexity surrounding the attempts by theoreticians and practitioners to understand and

This chapter is an expanded version of an earlier publication by the author entitled, Intervention from a systems-ecological perspective. *Professional Psychology: Research & Practice* 1985, *16*, 262–270. Copyright 1985 by the American Psychological Association. Adapted by permission of the publisher.

intervene from a systemic perspective. There are many strange "bedfellows" whose differences may at times appear to overshadow their similarities and unifying themes. Any textbook on family therapy should immediately impress the reader with the diversity of approaches by people who, for the most part, think of themselves as systemically oriented.

Thinking and Intervening Systemically

In general, from a systemic perspective, individuals are viewed within the context of their relationships and interactions with others rather than being understood mainly on the basis of their individual psychological development. Families can be understood as groups of people who have some connectedness to each other and who learn how to behave and function in relation and in response to each other. There is a reciprocity of behavior so that we cannot think of one person impacting on a second person without also appreciating the interplay between the two individuals. An understanding of any individual requires that we understand the context within which his or her behavior occurs and the reciprocal influences among all of the persons who are in any way connected to the situation.

The behavior an individual exhibits that is of concern to others, such as a child's acting out in school, is understood as serving some purpose for the child within that system. The behavior is not merely seen as a manifestation of an inner psychic disturbance, nor is it understood in a narrow behavioral sense as something a person is doing in anticipation of reinforcement. The behavior and the interactions of the child with others becomes a window that we can look through to understand the child's place in the system and the various roles, relationships, and behavior patterns that characterize the child, specific

settings, and other persons within that system.

A change in any part of a system is likely to influence other parts of the system. Some of those changes are directly observable and some are in terms of structural relationships. Take as an example the situation where a counselor helps a set of parents to become more consistent and contingent in their response to their young child who has a history of testing the limits. Let us assume that the child subsequently becomes less of a limit tester and more compliant with parental requests. From a systemic perspective, a number of things may have happened, including a probable strengthening of the parental subsystem, a clearer hierarchical delineation of the role of parents versus the role of children, and changes of specific communication patterns within the family.

Let us further assume that what was getting in the way of the parents being firm and consistent with their child were some confused beliefs they held about loving parents always being kind and supportive of children and the importance of children somehow learning from their experiences rather than being actively directed by parents. These perceptions and beliefs on the part of the parents were important components of that family system because they connected to not only parental behavior but to the meaning ascribed by the parents to the behavior of their child and themselves. As a result of the parent counseling they received, the parents now believe that children benefit from parental firmness and that, indeed, parental firmness and consistency are hallmarks of how loving and responsible parents relate to their children. The parents have shifted to a different framework out of which to exercise their parenting skills and to develop their relationship with their child.

The described patterns of change illustrate how "single" changes can reverberate throughout the system with other aspects of the system becoming realigned. In addition, what occurred in the example was not simply a change of behavior on the part of the child as a result of the parents being more consistent and contingent but also what is referred to as a "second-order change" (Weeks & L'Abate, 1982); this means that, in fact, the system has changed. The parents now view their child's behavior from a different and more normal, developmental perspective and as a statement by the child of his need for firmer and more consistent parental guidance. What the counselor would hope is that given a new set of skills along with a different way of perceiving themselves in the parenting role, the parents will continue to behave in ways that support healthier and more functional family relationships.

The term *second-order change* was used in this example to represent a change in the system. Many of the changes that professionals have attempted to bring about within families or in terms of a child's school adjustment fall under the category of "first-order change," which essentially means "more of the same" (Weeks & L'Abate, 1982). For example, consider a disruptive child in a classroom who is viewed by the teacher as a negativistic youngster who demands attention and derives gratification from disturbing others. The teacher's historic attempts to manage the child have been somewhat punitive in nature, in essence, attempting to make the "cost" of the misbehavior more than the child is willing to bear. The consultant who helps the teacher to develop a more sophisticated behavior management program built around the teacher's existing perceptions would be likely to support the teacher's maintaining her perception of the child as "bad." Even if the more sophisticated procedures actually worked to change the behavior, the child may continue to be seen as a bad child whose behavior is now under control. A more positive reframing of the child's behavior that would help the teacher to develop a positive and proactive stance toward the child would be likely to lead to a second-order change; that is, the change within the system of which the child is a part.

It should be noted that there may be situations in which first-order change or intervention is appropriate (L'Abate, Baggett, & Anderson, 1984). An example would be a child with a reading problem and a need for a more sophisticated remedial reading program. But in many situations it is a particular view that defines the problem in self-limiting terms.

Helping parents or teachers to modify their perceptions and beliefs about a situation in which they are a part so that they will approach that situation from a new perspective could be thought of as representing a paradigm shift (Kuhn, 1962). When a mental health professional begins thinking in more systemic terms, considering the reciprocal interplay of the individuals within that system as opposed to a more linear perspective such as "Johnny makes noises to attract attention," then that mental health professional has engaged in a paradigm shift. From that moment on, human events are perceived and understood in a different way. Within a systemic framework the notions of cause and effect are interactive and basically circular. What is cause and what is effect cannot be neatly partialed out because of a kind of continuous loop in which the child and his or her behavior interact with others and the setting.

The systemic position is quite phenomenological and relativistic in relation to notions of objectivity. What is *real* is what people experience as being *real*. Plausible hypotheses that can serve some functional purpose are as *real* as the mental health professionals' conclusions, based ostensibly on some objective criteria such as counting pre- and postintervention behaviors. This way of thinking opens the doors for some creative interpretations or reframings of behavior by the mental health professional and the use of techniques that support the involved persons in understanding their behavior and the behavior of others in more useful ways.

It is beyond the scope of this chapter to do a comparative analysis or detailed description of the different schools within the rubric of systemic approaches. Many of the differences will be illustrated in subsequent chapters. Two approaches that will be mentioned because of their utilization within the systems-ecological perspective being discussed include the structural and strategic approaches to understanding and intervening with problem relationships.

Structural and Strategic Interventions

Both structural and strategic interventions are based on a systemic understanding of relationships (Fraser, 1982; Stanton, 1981; Nichols, 1984). There is a recognition by the therapist or consultant that the involved persons in a given situation are connected to each other in reciprocally interactive ways, that there is a structure to the relationships, and that there is a homeostatic quality to the system that resists change. As one reads the literature, it seems clear that at times structural and strategic interventions are quite different in orientation, yet at other times there is considerable overlap. People who intervene strategically do so out of an awareness and consideration of the structure of relationships, and those who are mainly concerned with the structural aspects of a family may also elect to use strategic interventions to precipitate change.

Structural Approach

The structural viewpoint is concerned with the structure of relationships as reflected in how the system is organized (Minuchin & Fishman, 1981). What boundaries exist between the parent and

child subsystems? In what roles are family members cast? Is there a "good child," a "parental child," a "sick child," and how are relationships acted out in conjunction with these roles? Are certain family members in an alliance with or coalition against other family members?

Alliances can be understood in terms of triangulations of relationships. As an example, one parent may side with the symptomatic child against the other parent. There are other variations, such as both parents joining in a scapegoating view of the child as being the main problem in the family and as a masking of their own relationship difficulties. Such triangulations can extend from home to school, with a not uncommon configuration being that of the parent and child versus the school. Such triangulations reflect dysfunctionality in the system and serve the purposes of detouring effective solutions and maintaining dysfunctional patterns (Umbarger, 1983).

Intervention will typically attempt to shift key aspects of the system, such as drawing clearer boundaries between the parent and child subsystems, or breaking dysfunctional alliances, or helping the involved persons to establish more appropriate patterns of behavior. Depending on how tightly dysfunctional the system is, it may be possible simply to give certain people information and to encourage specific behavior changes.

There is evidence that teachers seek consultation mainly because of a lack of knowledge or skill rather than lack of objectivity (Gutkin, 1981). Both parents and teachers may respond to suggestions by the consultant on different ways of interacting with the child that in fact represent structural shifts. A series of school-family meetings that include the parents, child, and school personnel can reveal important information on how persons interact and the interrelational roles that they play (Fine & Holt, 1983; Aponte,

1976). As the respective members of both the immediate family and school systems interact, there may actually be an enactment of some of the dysfunctional patterns. For example, a child may comment that a particular teacher is treating him unfairly and the parents may immediately jump to the child's defense, carrying the argument forward with the teacher. The school personnel and parents then get into an argument while the child sits back and the real issues of his behavior and effective ways of managing him get ignored. The consultant needs to be quick to observe patterns that may reflect such enactments, and then to incorporate this understanding into an intervention plan.

The consultant is in a position to encourage important structural changes within the family-school meeting that can potentially extend into both home and school. One example involved a situation where parents and teachers were seemingly in conflict over a child. Notes and phone calls from school to home had only served to exacerbate the parents' and school's view of each other in oppositional terms. As the family and educators came into the meeting room, it was noted by the consultant that the family seated itself quite separately from the teachers and with the child snuggly nested between both parents. The teachers and assistant principal were clustered somewhat apart from the family, with the consultant across the desk from both subgroups. It was evident that the battle lines had been drawn. As the discussion proceeded, it was also observed that the child was inappropriately outspoken and in other ways was assuming too much power in the meeting. At one point the consultant interrupted the child and emphasized that some important decisions would have to be made by the responsible persons, namely the parents. The parents and teachers were then asked to move closer together, with the child now left a little more on the fringe. The consultant in-formed the child that it would be useful for him to listen carefully to what was being discussed so that he might have a chance later to contribute his ideas. This comment by the consultant seemed to have headed off a beginning move by the parents to want the child to be more central in the discussion because it was "his right." The parents seemed satisfied that the consultant had indicated that the child would be included later.

This meeting progressed fairly well with the animosity between parents and teachers becoming substantially reduced as they were actually able to converse in a face-to-face way. One interesting event occurred as the parents and teachers began to deal more objectively with some of the events that had precipitated the meeting. The student began to interrupt, which irritated the parents. The consultant suggested that the parents reiterate to their son that he would have a chance to contribute his ideas and reactions later, but that he needed to be a silent observer at this time. The parents turned to their son and quite firmly instructed him to sit quietly, and then the meeting proceeded.

The case required additional meetings in order to finally work out some agreements between home and school concerning expectations for child behavior, and for there to be adequate followup by both home and school. The description, though, of what went on at the one family meeting illustrates the concerns of the consultant with structural aspects of relationships and with the attempts to realign those relationships. In this instance realignment included strengthening the parental subsystem and promoting a positive collaboration between home and school.

Strategic Approach

The strategic approach is typically more problem-solving oriented than the structural approach and is willing to use a wide range of strategies, many of which are somewhat indirect, in order to induce change (Fisch, Weakland, & Segal, 1982; Haley, 1976, 1980; Stanton, 1981).

The strategic therapist views behavior in a systemic way, with cause and effect being circular and as simply points in a dysfunctional sequence of events. The assumption is that the involved persons are behaving in ways that perpetuate the "problem." The therapist's job is to break dysfunctional sequences and, in effect, solve the "problem." Solving the problem is mainly understood as alleviating symptoms (Foley, 1986; Nichols, 1984).

The responsibility for therapeutic change lies within the therapist's capacity to initiate some specific strategies aimed at producing certain changes. This kind of thinking on the order of selecting what will work has given therapists and consultants the go-ahead to use a wide range of interventions, including some that might be found quite manipulative by therapists of other orientations.

Papp (1981) defined a paradoxical intervention as "One that, if followed, will accomplish the opposite of what it seemingly intended to accomplish" (p. 246). From this position, strategic therapists are likely to offer a range of interpretations and directives. For instance, a child who has continued her misbehavior despite direct attempts by teachers or parents to get her to stop might be instructed by the therapist to continue acting out. The therapist might add some other elements, such as having the child predict how many times in the next week she will misbehave, or suggesting that, given the child's obvious inability to change, for her to try to change would be potentially hurtful in some way.

In one case, a child agreed to misbehave a certain number of times in the week following contact with the consultant. The child had actually insisted that he would not misbehave. But instead of accepting the child's intent, as teachers typically had done in the past, the consultant insisted that rapid change would not be "good" for the child and that he might not be capable of self-control without additional help. This led to an agreement for three outbursts in class. The child did not exhibit any outbursts the following week but instead of praising the child, the consultant suggested a relapse. The explicit rationale was that the child was probably not ready to be a "good kid" and get compliments but still needed to annoy the teacher. The child continued to be well behaved in class and the teacher was able to respond in a positive way to the child.

This is an example of a "win-win" situation, typical of many strategic interventions. If the child had continued misbehaving, then it would have seemingly confirmed the consultant's interpretations. By being well behaved, the child could act as if he had beaten the consultant.

Reframing behavior is an extremely important strategy. It allows the strategic therapist to change people's views of what is going on from a negative to a positive. Essentially, reframing can change people's view of the realities of a situation. An example might be a consultant turning to the child at a family-school meeting and commenting that he appreciates the child's continual testing of limits because it is the child's way of communicating to parents and teachers that they need to work together in a more consistent fashion. This kind of interpretation given to the child and in front of the parents is again likely to create a "win-win" situation. That is, if the child continues misbehaving, then it is interpreted as a message to parents and teachers that more is needed from them by way of consistency. And if the child, in order to thwart the consultant's interpretation, chooses to "get better," this again becomes a "win" situation because of the improvement in behavior.

There are a number of excellent references on strategic intervention that go into greater detail on the theory and clinical application of paradoxical and other techniques (Madanes, 1981, 1984; Weeks & L'Abate, 1982). In addition, Chapter 20 in this book presents several case studies utilizing strategic interventions.

It may be useful for school-based consultants to consider an integration of structural and strategic interventions. Stanton (1981) has described the integration of these two approaches within a family therapy context, and Fine (1984a) has essentially extrapolated from the Stanton article to describe such an integration as used by consultants in educational settings.

The structural approach is usually more straightforward and comprehensible to the involved persons and therefore might be implemented initially. But as resistance to change is noted, then the consultant could consider the use of more strategic interventions. Eventually, as constructive changes occur, the consultant can return to a more explicit focus on structural aspects of the system.

The described home-school conference becomes an excellent opportunity for the consultant to implement such an integration. In actively orchestrating the conference, the consultant can utilize both structural and strategic interventions as deemed appropriate.

Plas (1986) has described a school-based systemic methodology that seems to utilize both structural and strategic techniques in some creative ways. The reader is referred to her book to consider in greater detail a model generally complementary to the systems-ecological position being developed in this chapter.

Ecological Considerations

As reflected in a surge of publications (Plas, 1986; Aponte, 1976; Fine & Holt, 1983; Pfeiffer & Tittler, 1984; Fine, 1984a; Mannino & Shore, 1984; Apter, 1982; Swap, 1978, 1984), systemic thinking extends quite easily to the school context. It is that appreciation of the school and home as behavioral settings that brings in the ecological dimension to the term being used in this chapter: "a systems-ecological perspective." This growing sensitivity to the effects of home and school and home-school relationships on the life of the child has prompted a call for greater parent involvement in education and the assumption by educators of a family orientation (Anderson, 1983; Gilmore, 1974; Lombard, 1979; Pfeiffer & Tittler, 1984; Fine, 1984b; Conoley, 1987).

The historical use of the term *ecological* is in relation to the natural environment. We think of the "ecology" as the collection of reciprocal and interrelated forces around us. We consider climate, habitat, life organisms, food chains, water and other natural resources, and how these factors interact with, influence, and are influenced by the existence of "man" and technology.

Bringing an ecological perspective to the school would consider child-based, teacher-based, and environment-based variables all interacting (Apter, 1982; Bronfenbrenner, 1979). The earlier discussion of "structural" interventions offered some examples of ecological modifications. The child's developmental status, attitudes, and motivations interact with teachers' attitudes and behavior, within a setting that has physical, social, and cognitive elements.

An ecological perspective encourages us to become aware of the match or mismatch of an individual to his or her environment. Rhodes (1970), for example, argued that emotional disturbance was "a function of the reciprocity between the individual and his special environments" (p. 43). He goes on to elaborate:

Disturbance is constituted from a reverberating circuit between the disturbing individual and various significant individuals within the environmental settings such as home, classroom, etc. The disturbance resides in the agitated exchange which takes place between individual and environment. Each contributes to the process. This exchange takes place both at the behavioral level and at the psychodynamic level. The so-called disturbed individual and his surrounding resonators are "in it together." It is their disturbing exchange which creates the problem.

It follows from this view of disturbance that the environment must be given attention equal to that shown to the individual who has been singled out as "disturbed." (Rhodes, 1970, p. 44)

Regarding "disturbing children," once the system establishes a labeling and procedural framework, children get defined and treated accordingly (Hobbs, 1975). For example, when a school decides on a separate room for the emotionally disturbed or behaviorally disordered, the identification-labeling-treatment process occurs within that framework. Individual or group therapy, teacher consultation, and use of transitional settings are less likely to occur as treatment modes. "Least restrictive environment" as per PL 94–142 comes to match the established options, which are usually very few. When one or two classes are filled with disturbing children, more classes are added.

When we think along the lines of "Susie might do better in a highly structured versus open classroom," or "Mark would be less likely to get in trouble if he were sitting away from the traffic flow in the class," we are now thinking in ecological terms. The books on classroom management by Emmer, Evertson, Sanford, Clements, and Worsham (1989) and Evertson, Emmer, Clements, Sanford, and Worsham (1989) are ecologically oriented in their focus on the importance of the classroom environment, seating arrangements, traffic patterns, the ways in which rules get implemented, and the organization of in-

struction. The writings of Swap (1978, 1984) and Apter (1982) are especially important contributors to ecological considerations.

Bronfenbrenner's (1979) ecological framework is useful in furthering our understanding of the child in his or her environment. The term *microsystem* refers to the relationship among persons and environment in an immediate setting such as the classroom, home, or playground. The term *mesosystem* refers to the interrelationship among the various microsystems of which the child is a part. Children may behave differently in different settings. Not only may home and school behavior vary but a child's behavior may vary from classroom to classroom in a departmentalized curricular structure. The attempts to find out why a child seems to get along and function better in one environment over another is a practical example of an ecological inquiry.

The *exosystem* considers the specific social structures and institutions of society such as transportation, government agencies, and mass media, whereas the *macrosystem* is the overall cultural and institutional patterns of which the other systems are parts. This includes the economic, political, legal, social, and educational systems.

Anderson (1983) has identified professional activities that can occur in each of the systems within the total ecological framework of the schools. However, the locus of activity for most community-based and school-based consultants, such as clinical psychologists, school psychologists, counselors, and social workers, is likely to be the micro- and mesosystems. These are the systems within which the consultant has easiest access and can achieve some leverage for producing change. But it may be that for greater and more lasting change, the exo- and macrosystems will need to change.

The term being used, "a systems-ecological approach," may appear redundant, but it is intended to underscore the systemic nature of the child in and across specific settings, and the scope of settings and reciprocal influences in which the child is involved. It also underscores the selective and strategic utilization of interventions that derive from both an awareness of the impact of behavioral settings and from contemporary family therapy. The goal of such interventions is most frequently to modify the systemic-ecological structures and patterns that have been supportive of the "problem." Actually, the locus of intervention may vary in terms of individuals (including the person with the "problem"), so as to include any or all the involved family and school personnel. In some instances persons such as the bus driver, custodian, or school cook might even be included in the intervention program.

SYSTEMS-ECOLOGICAL INTERVENTION

The following points will briefly summarize what a systems-ecological perspective can mean and *not mean* in relation to school-based intervention. These ideas derive from numerous writings on ecological psychology and family therapy (including Apter, 1982; Cook & Plas, 1984; Cullinan, Epstein, & Lloyd, 1983; Haley, 1976; Hobbs, 1975; Madanes, 1981; Minuchin & Fishman, 1981; Rhodes, 1970; Rhodes & Paul, 1978; Swap, 1984; Fine, 1984a, 1984b; Fine & Holt, 1983; and Lusterman, 1985). Many school consultants probably use a systems-ecological orientation without calling it that. They may think in terms of "understanding the total picture." What is sometimes missing, however, is an appreciation for the reciprocal and interactive nature of the child and his or her environment and the range of possible interventions.

1. It should be noted at the onset that there is no "standard operating procedure" for a systems-ecological perspective, as contrasted, for example, with the basic behavior modification paradigm. Rather, a systems-ecological perspective is just that—a perspective involving a mental frame-of-reference and a familiarity with a wide range of techniques and interventions that can be used selectively. The paradigm used, however, is one that considers the importance of systemic relationships and behavioral settings. As stated by Swap (1984), "Ecological solutions are eclectic. . . . the ecological model encourages us to look at systems; the child in several contexts" (p. 141). This also includes the interfacing of settings and systems.

2. A systems-ecological approach is not synonomous with "family therapy." Contemporary family therapy stresses the systemic nature of the family, and from this view a number of therapy-based interventions have emerged, illustrating strategic techniques and methods of altering individual behavior and the family structure. Some of these concepts and techniques are applicable to a clinician who may choose to consult with a teacher, have some short-term conferences with a family, or enact a therapy program with the child. Family therapy of a short-term nature is only one option, and most often, *not* the primary treatment of choice from a systems-ecological viewpoint; this is because family therapy per se has often focused on the family, not the interfacing of family with school, or the ecological realities for the child in school.

3. A systems-ecological approach attempts to view the child's behavior contextually and in interaction terms. "What happens when Billy does . . ." is more relevant than "Why does Billy do. . . ." The sequence of events that precede the undesirable behavior can give a picture of how behavior generates and escalates, and can even lead to a contagion within a set-

ting. An understanding of the characteristic sequencing of events opens the door to considering ways of disrupting the sequence. The foregoing is similar to the behavioral concern with the relationship of stimulus and consequent events to the pinpointed behavior. However, some of the relationships of events are inferred as opposed to being taken concretely, which would be more the case in a behavioral approach.

The importance of interactive patterns necessitates that the consultant ask questions that reveal patterns and interactions. A number of writers (Tomm 1985; Selvini-Palazoli, Boscolo, Cecchin, & Prata, 1980; Cecchin, 1987) have addressed this issue. Understanding relationships in dynamic rather than static terms requires a focus on the sequencing and pattern of interactions, where cause and effect are seen as circular.

4. Assessment is understood as a dynamic, not static, process. It considers the child interacting with others within specific settings and is concerned with patterns of interaction. Although components of settings might be studied, such as classroom seating or traffic patterns, or parental discipline style, such components are only fully understood in dynamic and reciprocally interactive terms.

The specific tools of assessment invite a heuristic set of possibilities, including direct observation within the classroom and/or home, observation of what occurs during a planned parent-teacher-child meeting, and the use of rating scales and interviews. The measurement of "personality" in purely psychodynamic terms adds little to understanding the patterns of interaction, the child's social "pulls" and "pushes," and the reciprocal impact of child and behavioral setting.

Some assessment instruments that purport to capture the child's perceptions of the family or of his or her place in school only offer clues as to what might be happening interactively. They can help us to generate hypotheses to be checked out through observations or ratings of interactive patterns. Multiple ratings, such as both parents and teacher rating the child, and the child rating parents and teacher, come closer than single measurements to disclosing a picture of what might be happening interactively.

5. A systems-ecological approach is concerned with the match or mismatch of the instructional environment to the child. The child's learning style and developmental readiness for certain learning and socialization experiences need to be considered. Numerous structural components of a classroom can be varied, as described earlier in this chapter. The opportunity is present for modification of such classroom variables as seating, pace and content of instruction, size and extent of assignments, nature of teacher-child interactions, small-group versus individual or self-managed instruction, specific teacher control techniques, and the classroom itself. Schools actively resist moving a child out of a classroom in which he or she has major difficulties to another regular classroom that seems to be a better match. Moving the child to a "special" setting is more acceptable since it implies the problem is in the child, not in the original teacher-managed environment. The writings mentioned earlier that stressed ecological considerations (Swap, 1978, 1984; Emmer et al., 1989; Evertson et al., 1989; Apter, 1982) can be particularly helpful to school and family consultants.

6. A systems-ecological approach is cognizant that the child exists in overlapping systems and that changes in one system can influence other systems. For example, a child who is typecast as a "bad" child at home may make good progress at school as a result of some planned school interventions. The feedback to the home may alter the parents' view of the child and subsequently their behavior toward the

child. The child, in turn, may be ready to extend his or her newly established good behavior pattern into the home.

Parent-teacher-child conferences can be a vital source of new information, and perceptions of the child's problem and can alter the systems-ecological environment within which the child exists. Being able to reframe the child's behavior and the reaction of people to the child from a negative to a positive interpretation can be useful in influencing the system. An important goal for the consultant is to help create an ecological and systemic harmony between home and school. Not only does this result in a supportive consistency for all concerned, especially the child, but it reduces the likelihood of destructive triangulations or coalitions that are self-defeating. An example would be the parents siding with the child against the school.

7. A systems-ecological approach recognizes that a system seeks stability and may resist change as a result of a homeostatic balance being achieved. This not only means that the school or home, to name the two most prominent systems the child lives in, may exercise "forces" to maintain the status quo but one system may attempt to influence the other to assume a similar structure in relation to the child. An example would be at a parent-teacher conference where the parents describe the child as being mischievous and irresponsible. The parents present themselves as consistently beleaguered by the child and having to resort to spanking as a final but temporarily successful control technique. The parents attempt to project this view onto the school situation, and if the teacher accepts this view of the child, the two systems are now aligned in a collusive way.

The corollary can occur when the school attempts to extend its view and definition of the child and the child's problem to the home. A fairly common example is when the school attempts to involve the parents in a home reinforcement program tied in with both homework and with school-based child behaviors. By accepting their role in this program, the parents have allowed the home system to shift in the direction of alignment with that of the school. In many instances such an alignment and cooperation is constructive. But there may be instances where it is advisable to keep home and school separate and where the parents ought not be involved in an extension of the school program into the home. The consultant has an extremely important role to "traffic cop" communication and interactions in order to maintain a functional rather than dysfunctional resolution of the problem.

8. Intervening from a systems-ecological perspective requires a particular way of viewing the child and his or her problem rather than the automatic use of certain techniques. Indeed, as a result of the view of what is occurring from a systemic paradigm, techniques might be used that borrow from behavior modification, multimodel therapy, family therapy, group dynamics, instructional technology, and many other frames of reference. The goals of intervention would be to decrease the reciprocal negative impact of the child's behavior on the environment, to shift aspects of the child's environment so that the function of "bad behavior" decreases, and to create structures within the child's environment that are conducive to healthy development. As described earlier in this chapter, a particular intervention may appear "behavioral," but from a systemic perspective the consultant can understand how that intervention affects subsystem boundaries, hierarchies of relationships, and the roles of different persons in the situation.

9. A systems-ecological approach recognizes that the standard operating procedures in a situation may have exacerbated a "problem" and in fact may have defined the problem. Examples

would be the use of certain labels that represent a static view of the child and that in turn establish a stimulus value to the child that influences child-environment interactions. The choice of interventions may need to be something novel or different, or a creative variation of an existing procedure. (The concepts of first- and second-order changes were discussed earlier.) The most useful aspect of a particular intervention may be a creative reframing of the child's behavior so as to modify the parents' or teacher's perceptions of the child and to stimulate their willingness to attempt different approaches. Sometimes a greater acceptance and tolerance of the child can occur without the need for the parents or teacher to formulate a new "plan of attack."

10. As stated earlier, a systems-ecological approach lends itself to a consultative model. The school psychologist or social worker, for example, is in a position to take into account the broad spectrum of interactions that influence and are influenced by the child. The consultant is able to initiate conferences involving teachers and parents and even the child (Aponte, 1976; Fine & Pitts, 1980; Fine & Holt, 1983). In such meetings the consultant is in a position to orchestrate what occurs, functioning alternatively as a traffic cop, interpreter of events, and homework giver. These sessions are opportunities for an enactment of dysfunctional patterns and establishment of healthier ways of interacting and problem solving (Minuchin & Fishman, 1981). The consultant can assist all the involved persons to avoid the traps of self-fulfilling labeling and the use of historically unsuccessful strategies.

At times, the consultant will offer information, shift the focus on specific members of the group meeting, use a paradoxical intervention, or choose to sit passively so as to let "things" happen. The consultant is in a position to head off the frequent fantasy of one-session solutions and to structure for continued involvement of the relevant individuals.

In direct contact with the teacher(s), specific aspects of how the environment matches the child can be considered. Again, information giving, strategic interpretations of data (i.e., sometimes the use of reframing and useful fictions), and altering some classroom variables can occur.

The "joining" function of the consultant (Minuchin & Fishman, 1981) is considered important since he or she is presumably better able to influence change when seen as part of the involved group rather than as an outsider. This calls for a modification of the model of consultation that depicts the consultant as an outsider with clear-cut boundaries between his or her involvement and the consultee's ownership of the problem.

CASE STUDY

The case of Larry exemplifies intervention from a systems-ecological perspective. Following the presentation of the case there will be further discussion of important aspects of the intervention program.

Larry, a physically large 15-year-old young man, was transferred from one state hospital to another in order to be close to his parents. His mother, who was on her third marriage, saw herself as inadequate and in need of a strong husband. Larry's "incorrigibility" was used as proof of her ineptness as a parent. Larry was eventually admitted to a group home in the community and entered junior high school where he was considered learning disabled, mildly retarded, and emotionally disturbed. The LD label was the most convenient one in terms of available programs.

Shortly after enrollment his teachers panicked. Larry had refused some assignments, pounded his desk, and glared at the teacher. Given his institutional background and sheer bulk, it was feared that he might attack a teacher.

The consultant had some familiarity with Larry's background. Although any of the three labels could be justified via usual school criteria, it seemed more important to define Larry to school personnel in terms that would reduce their anxiety and offer them some functional direction to go with Larry. His aggressive stance was framed as "the way he's learned to behave in order to keep away people who were making frustrating demands on him." His blurting out of epitaphs such as, "like hell," "shit no" and his subsequent inability to express himself verbally in complete sentences were described as examples of "trained institutioned behavior" rather than examples of psychotic or irrational behavior. In essence he was presented as a person with limited coping skills who had been taught to act stupid and crazy.

Through a series of meetings with school personnel, some of which included Larry, the school was assured that Larry had never attacked a teacher although he had been in fights with peers and had a history of minor theft, vandalism, truancy, and running away. Those sessions were opportunities for Larry's behavior to be reframed from "crazy" to "faulty social learning," and for the teachers to share successful incidents.

Larry was involved in individual counseling. After a few sessions, he became more aware of how his "crazy" behavior scared people, made them think he belonged in an institution, and would in short order get him back into the institution. The counseling was less "insight" oriented and more social-relations training oriented. Some simple diagramming was used to show the circular connecting of behaviors and reactions and to illustrate what was

actually happening between Larry and his teachers. He also received some brief training in completing sentences, asking for help, thanking teachers for help, and verbalizing his frustration with academic tasks. This training was also framed in relation to how one person's behavior can pull a certain behavior from another person to which the first person then reacts. The school staff spent time with Larry, spelling out their availability but also asserting clear limits regarding his behavior.

The group home parents also received consultative services and were able to view Larry's behavior not as "crazy" but as the result of poor learning experiences. They already were keying in on how Larry was provoking other boys in the home but seemed able to control his behavior when it served his needs. However, since the group home was on a behaviorally based point system, the house parents were inclined to think of their boys' successes or failures as reflected in the gaining or losing of points. Their own sense of success seemed tied in with the point gains of the boys. They were helped to see Larry's behavior differently during the times he was losing points. These times were reframed as testing periods by him to establish whether or not he would be asked to leave the home. In this light it was seen as important that Larry have periods of failure. The house parents were able to take on a more therapeutic posture regarding Larry because of the reframing.

Counseling also occurred with the mother and her new husband. They both expressed some frustration over Larry's "problem" and seemed to feel impotent as change agents. For the mother this was a continuation of her historic role and a way of pulling in "rescuers." Their parenting skills were strengthened via specific communication training. Also, with an improved marital adjustment, the mother's need to have an "uncontrollable" child diminished.

Larry continued to make progress in

school, made the football team, and over the next few years became accepted in the school setting as a "normal" boy with learning problems rather than "the crazy kid from the state hospital." He still presented management problems from time to time but the teachers were considerably more confident and effective in dealing with him.

When Larry was no longer a problem in the school setting and had become a leader in the group home, consideration was focused on reentering him into his family. By that time a younger brother had been identified by the parents as incorrigible and the family was once again in an uproar around that boy's problems. This seemed to be a replay of the mother's earlier experiences with Larry and signaled growing marital problems. Larry chose the option of staying in the group home until graduation.

Discussion of Larry's Case

An important key to intervention was to define Larry as experiencing socialization problems rather than psychological problems and to view the help he needed as mainly educational rather than psychiatric. This way of framing the situation demystified the problem and identified an appropriate role for the school. An additional strategy by the consultant was to identify the state hospital as the "persecutor," Larry as the "victim," and the school as the "rescuer." This helped to create a positive "let's help each other" relationship between Larry and the school, with the state hospital seen as the "bad guy." This way of triangulating relationships represented a constructive shift from the initial view by school personnel of themselves as victimized by both the state hospital and Larry.

Larry's case illustrated several important aspects of a systems-ecological intervention. A key goal was to create a better match of Larry with his educational setting. To this end, multiple and strategic interventions occurred, as orchestrated by the consultant. Intervention included individual teacher consultation, group sessions with several teachers (sometimes including Larry), and individual counseling and social-skills training sessions with Larry. Consultation with the group home parents also occurred, as did therapy for the parents. Reframing was a major technique used by the consultant but one also needs to consider the "joining" aspect of the consultant's role.

When the consultant arrived, several of the teachers were already frightened and concerned enough about Larry to begin questioning whether he belonged in a public school. The consultant was able to pick up very quickly on their concerns and was able to "join" with them as he humorously described his own anxiety on first meeting the physically formidible Larry.

Through multiple contacts with teachers, the consultant conveyed a "we're in this together" attitude that encouraged the others to view him as an involved colleague but also as an expert and leader. The consultant avoided communicating the impression of being psychologically distanced from Larry and the teaching staff and also avoided appearing as an advocate for Larry against the school system.

The success of the case seemed related to the consultant's success in helping key people to redefine Larry and themselves in relation to Larry. Each of the three important systems in Larry's life—school, family, and group home—were all actively involved and were able to view each other in a supportive and collaborative fashion. Larry himself also has to be considered an important catalyst to the positive changes in the systems. By learning and exhibiting new behaviors, he subsequently "pulled" more positive behaviors from people and reinforced their changing perceptions of him. The circular and reciprocal aspects of interpersonal behavior began to work on his behalf.

The termination of the case occurred

at a point where Larry was able to make some proactive decisions for himself, and, in doing so, reinforced people's perceptions of him as a more stable and rational person.

SUMMARY

A systems-ecological framework for home-school intervention requires an appreciation of the reciprocal influences of settings, persons, and patterns of interaction. "Disturbed" or "problem" behavior of a child is considered to be a symptom of a dysfunctional system, including the "fit" of the setting(s) to the child.

Mental health professionals, whether school or community based, can utilize this frame of reference to precipitate helpful changes that have the potential to be lasting. Taking on a consultative role can enhance the flexibility and maneuverability of the mental health professional in orchestrating interventions. This broadly understood consultative role can allow the mental health professional to meet with many of the involved persons (teachers, family members, identified child, etc.) as needed, on a one-to-one or group basis. This allows for varied creative strategies to affect change in the system and settings of which the child is a part.

The goal of intervention is to decrease dysfunctional and increase functional aspects of those systems; achieving this goal might require creating a better fit between the child and the learning environment, assisting home and school to assume a different and more productive view of themselves and the child, altering structural components such as strengthening the parent subsystem, and fostering a collaborative relationship between home and school.

Not considered in this chapter are a number of ethical and professional issues that have been discussed in previous publications (Fine, 1984a; Fine & Holt, 1983). Chapter 26 will focus on potential ethical and professional problems embedded in the use of a family-systems orientation.

References

Anderson, C. (1983). An ecological developmental model for a family orientation in school psychology. *Journal of School Psychology, 21,* 179–189.

Aponte, H. J. (1976). The family-school interview: An eco-structural approach. *Family Process, 15,* 303–311.

Apter, S. J. (1982). *Troubled children: Troubled systems.* New York: Pergamon Press.

Bronfenbrenner, U. (1979). *The ecology of human development: Experiments by nature and design.* Cambridge, MA.: Harvard University Press.

Cecchin, G. (1987). Hypothesizing, circularity, and neutrality revisited: An invitation to curiosity. *Family Process, 26,* 405–413.

Conoley, J. C. (1987). Schools and families: Theoretical and practical bridges. *Professional School Psychology, 2,* 191–203.

Cook, V. J., & Plas, J. M. (1984). Intervention with disturbed children: The ecological viewpoint. In M. Fine (Ed.), *Systematic intervention with disturbed children.* New York: Spectrum Publications.

Cullinan, D., Epstein, M., & Lloyd, J. (1983). *Behavior disorders of children and adolescents.* Englewood Cliffs, NJ: Prentice-Hall.

Dowling, E. T., & Osborne, E. (Eds.) (1985). *The family and the school—A joint systems approach to problems with children.* London: Routledge and Kegan Paul.

Emmer, E. T., Evertson, C. M., Sanford, J. P., Clements, B. S., & Worsham, M. E. (1989). *Classroom management for secondary teachers* (2nd ed.). Englewood Cliffs, NJ: Prentice-Hall.

Evertson, C. M., Emmer, E. T., Clements, B. S., Sanford, J. P., & Worsham, M. E. (1989). *Classroom management for elementary teachers* (2nd ed.). Englewood Cliffs, NJ: Prentice-Hall.

Fine, M. J. (1984a). Integrating structural and strategic components in school-based consultation. *Techniques, 1,* 44–52.

Fine, M. J. (1984b). Parent involvement. In J. E. Ysseldyke (Ed.), *School psychology: The state of the art.* Minneapolis, MN: National School Psychology Inservice Training Network.

Fine, M. J., & Holt, P. (1983). Intervening with school problems: A family systems perspective. *Psychology in the Schools, 20,* 59–66.

Fine, M. J., & Pitts, R. (1980). Intervention with underachieving gifted children: Rationale and strageties. *Gifted Child Quarterly, 24,* 51–55.

Fisch, R., Weakland, J. H., & Segal, L. (1982). *The tactics of change: Doing therapy briefly.* San Francisco: Jossey-Bass.

Foley, V. D. (1986). *An introduction to family therapy* (2nd ed.). Orlando, FL: Grune & Stratton.

Fraser, J. S. (1982). Structural and strategic family therapy: A basis for marriage or grounds for divorce? *Journal of Marital and Family Therapy, 8,* 13–22.

Gilmore, G. E. (1974). School psychologist-parent contact: An alternative model. *Psychology in the Schools, 11,* 170–173.

Green, K., & Fine, M. J. (1979). Family therapy: A case for training school psychologists. *Psychology in the Schools, 17,* 241–248.

Gutkin, T. B. (1981). Relative frequency of consultee lack of knowledge, skill, confidence, and objectivity in school settings. *Journal of School Psychology, 19,* 57–61.

Haley, J. (1976). *Problem solving therapy.* San Francisco: Jossey-Bass.

Haley, J. (1980). *Leaving home: The therapy of disturbed young people.* New York: McGraw-Hill.

Hansen, J. C. (Ed.) (1984). *Family therapy with school related problems.* Rockville, MD: Aspen.

Hobbs, N. (1975). *The futures of children.* San Francisco: Jossey-Bass.

Kuhn, T. (1962). *The structure of scientific revolutions.* Chicago: University of Chicago Press.

L'Abate, L., Baggett, M. S., & Anderson, J. S. (1984). Linear and circular interventions with families of children with school related problems. In J. Hansen (Ed.), *Family therapy with school related problems.* Rockville, MD: Aspen.

Lombard, T. J. (1979). Family-oriented emphasis for school psychologists: A needed orientation for training and practice. *Professional Psychology, 10,* 687–696.

Lusterman, D. D. (1985). An ecosystemic approach to family-school problems. *The American Journal of Family Therapy, 13,* 22–30.

Madanes, C. (1981). *Strategic family therapy.* San Francisco: Jossey-Bass.

Madanes, C. (1984). *Behind the one-way mirror: Advances in the practice of strategic therapy.* San Francisco: Jossey-Bass.

Mannino, F., & Shore, M. (1984). An ecological perspective on family intervention. In N. O'Connor & B. Lubin (Eds.), *Ecological approaches to clinical and community psychology.* New York: Wiley.

Minuchin, S., & Fishman, H. C. (1981). *Family therapy techniques.* Cambridge, MA: Harvard University Press.

Nichols, M. (1984). *Family therapy: Concepts & methods.* New York: Gardner Press.

Papp, P. (1981). Paradoxes. In S. Minuchin & H. C. Fishman (Eds.), *Family therapy techniques.* Cambridge, MA.: Harvard University Press.

Pfeiffer, S. I., & Tittler, B. I. (1984). Utilizing the multidisciplinary team to facilitate a school-family systems orientation. *School Psychology Review, 12,* 168–173.

Plas, J. M. (1986). *Systems psychology in the schools.* New York: Pergamon Press.

Rhodes, W. C. (1970). *The emotionally disturbed student and guidance.* Boston: Houghton Mifflin.

Rhodes, W. C., & Paul, J. (1978). *Emotionally disturbed and deviant children: New views and approaches.* Englewood Cliffs, NJ: Prentice Hall.

Schaefer, C. E., Briesmeister, J. M., & Fitton, M. (Eds.) (1984). *Family therapy techniques for problem behaviors of children and teenagers.* San Francisco: Jossey-Bass.

Selvini-Palazoli, M., Boscolo, L., Cecchin, G., & Prata, G. (1980). Hypothesizing-circularity-neutrality: Three guidelines for the conductor of the session. *Family Process, 19,* 3–12.

Stanton, M. D. (1981). An integrated structural-strategic approach to family therapy. *Journal of Marital and Family Therapy. 7,* 427–439.

Swap, S. M. (1978). The ecological model of emotional disturbance in children: A status report and proposed synthesis. *Behavior Disorders, 3,* 186–196.

Swap, S. M. (1984). Ecological approaches to working with families of disturbing children. In W. O'Connor & B. Lubin (Eds.), *Ecological approaches to clinical and community psychology.* New York: Wiley.

Tomm, K. (1985). Circular interviewing: A multifaceted clinical tool. In D. Campbell &

R. Draper (Eds.), *Application of systemic family therapy: The Milan approach.* Orlando, FL: Grune & Stratton.

Umbarger, C. C. (1983). *Structural family therapy.* Orlando, FL: Grune & Stratton.

Watzlawick, P., Weakland, J. H., & Fisch, R. (1974). *Change.* New York: Norton.

Weeks, G., & L'Abate, L. (1982). *Paradoxical psychotherapy.* New York: Brunner/Mazel.

Wendt, R. N., & Zake, J. (1984). Family systems therapy and school psychology: Implications for training and practice. *Psychology in the Schools, 21,* 204–210.

2

Models and Strategies
of Family-School Assessment
and Intervention

CINDY CARLSON
University of Texas, Austin

THE FAMILY AND SCHOOL SYSTEMS have long been acknowledged as the primary socializers of children. Although both systems have a major impact on children, it is acknowledged that the family's influence is more pervasive, continuous, and personal than that of the school (Okun, 1984). Children are significantly socialized by the family regarding the acquisition of knowledge and cognitive strategies, rules for behavior, and motivational forces such as self-efficacy, self-esteem, self-monitoring, and attributions for success (Hess & Holloway, 1984). Moreover, problems within the family frequently place children under significant emotional stress, which, in turn, interferes with school performance. Numerous school-related problems of children have been associated with dysfunctional family processes. These include peer relational difficulties and conduct disorders (Patterson, DeBarsyshe, & Ramsey, 1989), depression (Stark & Simmons-Brookman, this volume), hyperactivity (Barkley, 1981), school phobia (Aliotti, this volume), and substance abuse (Tricker & Poertner, this volume).

Similarly, many types of distressed or dysfunctional family environments have been associated with school performance difficulties. These include families characterized by divorce, single parenthood, and remarriage (Carlson, this volume, 1985, 1987); violence and discord (Emery & O'Leary, 1982; O'Leary, 1984); child physical and/or sexual abuse (Brassard & Apellaniz, this volume); and parental psychopathology (Baldwin, Cole, & Baldwin, 1982). In summary, numerous research studies have demonstrated that children with various types of school behavior and learning problems tend to come from homes or schools that are disadvantaged or deviant in some respect (see review by Rutter, 1985).

Despite consistent evidence that the family plays a critical role in the optimal development and subsequent school performance of children, assessment practices, particularly within the school setting, remain primarily child centered (Carlson & Sincavage, 1987, 1988). As noted by Conoley (1987), "It is a mistake to believe that what is done for convenience (i.e., focus assessment on the single child or classroom) represents the way the world really works. In fact, the world is captured more by the assumptions related to ecological theory than by prevailing theories of individual differences" (p. 192).

Current conceptualizations of the family and the family-school interface reflect a widespread acceptance of the explanatory power and complementarity of systems theory and ecological theory. At the core of a systems orientation is the concept that elements exist in a state of organized and active communicative interrelatedness and interdependence within a bounded unit (e.g., the child, family, classroom, school), such that the activities of one element cannot help but have a direct or indirect influence on the other elements of the system, resulting in a whole (relationship or milieu) that is greater than the elements (Koman & Stechler, 1985).

At the core of an ecological orientation are the following concepts: (1) systems are nested hierarchically, (2) hierarchically lower system levels are autonomous but are also controlled to some degree by higher system levels, and (3) the quality of the interface or communication flow between systems is a key factor in the development of the members of the system (Bronfenbrenner, 1980). Furthermore, membership in each system, which reflects a unique whole, is different for the child. Ecological theory thus supports a concern with assessment and intervention in multiple systems, such as the family, school, and peer group, while emphasizing assessment and intervention at the interface of these systems.

The compatibility of these two theories has led some scholars to integrate the ecological and systems perspectives (Fine, this volume; Lusterman, 1985, this volume; Plas, 1986). An ecosystemic orientation has significant implications for the methodology required for assessment of children's problems in the school setting. First, a child's dysfunctional behavior is viewed as meaningless without a view to the systemic context in which it is embedded. Second, systems theory implies a *relational* versus *individual* focus to assessment and intervention.

At face value, assessment of the context in which behavior is embedded implies that the multiple systemic contexts of the child should be assessed, including the family, classroom, and peer systems. However, the ecosystemic context of the child is complex and resources for comprehensive assessment are scarce. Rather, the initial focus of assessment should be the systemic locus of the child's problem. The locus of the problem concerns for whom the problem is an issue currently (Aponte & VanDeusen, 1981). Elaborated by Aponte and VanDeusen (1981), the *primary* locus of the problem is the system or systems that are engaged in the essential and habitual generation and maintenance of the problem. Within the primary locus system(s) are *problem bearers,* who have been blocked in carrying out some necessary function and thus are experiencing failure, and *participant components,* those persons being stressed by their relationship with the problem bearer(s).

The *secondary* locus of the problem is the system or systems that form the habitual, but not essential, environment of the problem. The actions of persons in the secondary locus system serve as the active environment for the problem. The secondary system may accommodate and therefore reinforce the problematic behavior patterns and structure of the primary locus system, but the problem would continue to exist whether the secondary systems were present or not.

Finally, the *tertiary* locus refers to the passive environment of the problem in which the problem patterns are set, but are only incidental. Aponte and VanDeusen (1981) use the metaphor of a theatrical play to clarify the roles of the primary, secondary, and tertiary ecosystemic locus of the problem, with the primary locus being the actors in the play, the secondary locus equivalent to the stagehands, and the tertiary locus similar to the audience. Thus, a primary goal of an ecosystemic assessment is the determination of which system(s) generate and maintain the child's problem and the nature of the relationship between systems.

Thus, a second key implication of the ecosystemic approach to assessment is a relational focus. A relational focus demands attention to and techniques for evaluating the *interactions* of elements within the systems and between systems. This is in contrast with traditional assessment techniques that focus on individual variability. Moreover, a systemic assessment focus is in contrast with a strictly ecological approach that examines individual variability across multiple systems. Thus, assessment techniques that permit examination of behavior and perceptions within and across relationships are most appropriate.

It is the purpose of this chapter to provide several models and strategies for assessing the family system and its interface with the school system. Although an ecosystemic perspective is accepted as the valid foundation for the chapter, the emphasis will be on assessment of the family system. As school-based personnel have the least experience with assessment of this system, the family system is acknowledged to have the most pervasive influence on the child, and, therefore, to be the most frequent primary locus of problems. Although it is beyond the scope of the chapter to discuss treatment, it is assumed that a primary purpose of assessment is to provide direction for intervention. Thus the assessment models and measures to be discussed in this chapter have been selected based on their compatibility with

systems theory and their clear connection with a well-developed model of treatment.

In the first part of the chapter, three models of intervention will be applied to family assessment: systemic-structural, cognitive-behavioral, and solution-oriented. Next, an overview of different strategies or methods of capturing relational phenomena in the family will be presented. Methods to be discussed include the interview (with family, school personnel, family and school), observation, and self-report measures (with whole family, parents, child). Finally, a concluding section will integrate the approaches and methods into a recommended family-school assessment framework.

MODELS OF FAMILY ASSESSMENT/INTERVENTION

Systemic-Structural Model

The systemic model of assessment and intervention presented here is based on the structural family therapy approach (Minuchin, 1974; Minuchin & Fishman, 1981; Minuchin, Montalvo, Guerney, Rosman, & Schumer, 1967; Minuchin, Rosman, & Baker, 1978). Although developed for family systems, schools and families share several fundamental organizational similarities that enhance the applicability of this model to schools. Schools and families are functionally and structurally similar (Conoley, 1987; Fisher, 1986; Plas, 1986). Both the family and school systems exist primarily to socialize children and include such functions as nurturance; education; learning rules and consequences; and provision of safety, food, and shelter. Structurally both systems are open, which means that each survives by maintaining a delicate equilibrium or continuity while faced with continuous demands for adjustment from outside its boundaries (Conoley, 1987).

Structurally, schools and families are also organized hierarchically, often with males in positions of authority, and with the effects of stress at higher levels of the hierarchy felt at lower hierarchical levels. Like families, schools are comprised of various overt and covert subsystems. Rigid covert alliances in schools, as in families, can create organizational distress (Fisher, 1986). Finally, both family and school systems possess a well-articulated belief or value system, which influences the nature of their transactions.

The basic premises of the systemic model are that (1) systems are organized and (2) they operate through transactional patterns. Transactional patterns refer to invisible rules and operational routines that define how the interdependent, subordinate parts relate to each other and how they influence the larger system. The term *structure,* a key focus of assessment in this model, refers to the relatively enduring transactional patterns that organize the components of the system into a somewhat stable relationship. Systems are organized hierarchically, with the various subsystems reflecting differentiated roles within the system. The system's hierarchical organization is determined by both universal and idiosyncratic constraints. For example, the universal organizational pattern in schools would place the principal at the top of the hierarchy; however, the degree to which power at the top is shared with other roles (e.g., counselor, assistant principal) is likely to reflect individual competencies and personalities. The universal organizational pattern in families would place the parent subsystem in charge.

From the structural perspective, there is not a "correct" hierarchical organization. Rather, the factors that are critical to successful system operation include (1) clarity and agreement among members

regarding the desired hierarchy, (2) adequate power or force of members to carry out operations within their designated hierarchical position, and (3) a match between hierarchical position and assigned purpose within the system. The absence of these criteria are illustrated in the following dysfunctional family patterns: (1) parents have widely discrepant rules for their children or fail to agree on who is in charge, (2) a parent is assumed to be hierarchically in charge of the family but lacks the power to behave authoritatively, and (3) a child has the force to dominate the family (or classroom) but this capacity does not match the child's purpose (i.e., to be socialized by adults) within the system. An initial focus of assessment, then, is the *power hierarchy* within the family and school systems. According to Haley (1987), child problems most frequently derive from confused hierarchy, which is evident in the patterns of interaction surrounding rule establishment, rule clarity, monitoring, rule enforcement, consistency, and follow-through.

Closeness, distance, and information exchange between members of the family, between school personnel related to the problem child, and between the family and school are the second key targets of assessment. Parameters of closeness and distance can be observed by noting physical contact, amount of verbal communication, communication content (e.g., support or criticism, mind reading, talking for another person), pronoun use (e.g., *we* versus *I*), distribution of gaze, personal physical spacing (as evident in seating), and emotional space (as evident in tolerance of individual differences in thoughts and feelings). The closeness and distance between family members is equivalent to an assessment of the *boundaries* of the system from a structural perspective. Critical to adequate system functioning is a structure that permits the accomplishment of the differentiated roles of the subsystems (i.e., autonomy), yet provides the necessary information, resources, and emotional support (i.e., cohesion) to accomplish functions.

Although endless variations of workable system structures may exist, the adequacy of a system's organization is strongly related to the clarity of *boundaries* or rules regarding participation in different roles (Haley, 1987). Boundaries serve to protect the differentiation of the family system such that autonomy and cohesion can be reciprocally operative. Systems or relationships within and between systems that have overly intrusive boundaries, with low levels of differentiation between subsystems, are labeled *enmeshed*, whereas overly rigid boundaries that promote excessive autonomy between systems or subsystems are termed *disengaged*. Child problems associated with enmeshed systems typically involve a compromise to the development of competence, independence, mastery, and control of impulses; disengaged systems are associated with child problems involving limited monitoring or nurturance, such as conduct disorders (Hoffman, 1981).

A third focus of assessment, which combines the elements of power and boundary, is the *identification of pathological triangles* within and across systems. Haley (1987) notes that most child problems involve both a malfunctioning hierarchy and a pathological triangle. Bowen (1978) is credited with first observing dysfunctional triangular arrangements in families. He observed that triangles emerge when the tension is intolerable between two members of a system, and a third member (often the symptomatic child) is brought in to diffuse it. Four pathological triadic arrangements, which represent rigid coalitions or alliances of two or more members against a third, have been implicated:

1. *Triangulation*, in which two members vie for the allegiance of the third member
2. *Coalition*, in which two members join in alliance against a third member
3. *Detouring-attacking*, in which two members in covert conflict detour their conflict by scapegoating a third party
4. *Detouring-supportive*, in which two members in covert conflict detour their conflict by overprotection of a third member (Umbarger, 1983)

In the detouring-attacking triangle the third party is typically viewed as "bad," whereas in detouring-supportive triangles the third party is typically viewed as "sick."

A fourth target of systemic assessment is the discrete, time-limited *sequences of behavior* that constitute a particular transaction, especially transactions that surround the identified problem of the child in the family and school settings. The goal of the assessment is to identify the feedback loops that are operating in a homeostatic manner to maintain the child's problem. *Feedback loops* refer to the communication pathways across boundaries within the system that signal to members their degree of conformity or discrepancy from the overall purpose of the system. Feedback loops that promote stability, equilibrium, and a reduction of behavior inconsistent with system goals are termed constancy or *deviation-countering* loops. Feedback loops that promote growth, diversity, change, or an increase in activity are termed variety or *deviation-amplifying* loops. Both types of feedback are essential to functional systems. Over-reliance on one type of feedback loop may exacerbate a child difficulty and point to the need for an intervention that disrupts the ineffective feedback loop and replaces it with an alternative action (Hoffman, 1981).

The *perceptions or beliefs* that system members have developed regarding their role and function and the meaning of the child's problem behavior is the final target of assessment in the systemic-structural model. Although the systemic-structural model has not articulated the interface of cognition and behavior as well as the cognitive-behavioral model (to be discussed subsequently), challenging the perceptions of reality that system members hold is noted as an important class of interventions that facilitate changing the interactions underlying the symptom (Minuchin, 1974). Perceptions and beliefs regarding the child's problem can be determined by listening to the descriptions of the problem as provided by system members.

In summary, the systemic-structural model can be used to assess the family system, the school system, or the family-school relationship. An assessment from this perspective is typically based on an observation of the interactions within or between the family and school system. Hypotheses regarding expected patterns can be gleaned from interviews that focus on the transactional processes surrounding the child's problem; however, most mental health professionals operating within the structural framework claim that it is only by observing the transactional reality of systems that hypotheses can be confirmed. This assumption supports meetings with the whole family, meetings with the group of involved school personnel, and family-school meetings as mechanisms for observing interaction patterns.

When confirming hypotheses regarding the systemic dynamics underlying the child's problem, observation should focus on a determination of the following:

1. The functionality of the existing hierarchy
2. The quality of boundaries between dyads within each system, between subsystems (surrounding each whole system), and between systems
3. The existing alliances or coalitions within and across systems
4. The capacity (i.e., power, resources, flexibility, and responsiveness) of systems, subsystems, and members to carry out their role and function
5. The perceptions or meanings system members have created for their function and for the child's problem behavior

Cognitive-Behavioral Model

It is a basic premise of the cognitive-behavioral approach that members of a system in their complex interactions with one another actively interpret and evaluate each other's behavior and that their emotional and behavioral responses to one another are influenced by these interpretations and evaluations (Epstein, Schlesinger, & Dryden, 1988). Although these cognitive mediation principles have their roots in the theory and practice of individual therapy, they have recently been applied to family systems (Epstein, Schlesinger, & Dryden, 1988). Moreover, it has been proposed that family (and other system) members' behavior toward each other will change only if their views of themselves and others change (Barton & Alexander, 1981).

It is assumed, therefore, that the content of an individual's perception of his or her interactions with other persons affects both the intensity of his or her emotional distress regarding the relationship and his or her behavioral responses toward the other parties. The therapeutic goal thus becomes providing system members with new information that will impel them to new emotional and behavioral reactions in order to maintain cognitive consistency. It is proposed that attributional shifts are necessary to change behaviors among related persons, but also that in turn these cognitive changes are unlikely to persist without subsequent behavior changes that are consistent with more positive attributions (Barton & Alexander, 1981; Epstein, Schlesinger, & Dryden, 1988). Thus, assessment and intervention must be focused on both system members' cognitions and dysfunctional behavioral patterns within the cognitive-behavioral model.

The cognitive-behavioral model applied to disturbed family systems assumes that family members tend to attribute problems in other members to stable negative traits (e.g., lazy, manipulative, hyperactive). Change is not viewed as possible because these negative traits are perceived as stable and within the person. Furthermore, negative attributions about other system members are often juxtaposed with negative self-attributions regarding one's ability to change or control relationships with the other party (Epstein, Schlesinger, & Dryden, 1988).

There are at least three sources of external events within the family upon which individual cognitions can be built: (1) behaviors by other family members toward the self (e.g., father criticizes child), (2) the combined effects of several members' behaviors toward self (e.g., father criticizes child and mother defends), and (3) observations the self makes about relationships among other family members (e.g., child notices parents are frequently in conflict).

At least four types of cognitions may occur as family members appraise each other: (1) cognitions about self (e.g., I am stupid), (2) cognitions about self in relation to each other family member (e.g., child sees mother as approachable but father as unapproachable), (3) cognitions about relationships among subgroups of other family members (e.g., child sees parents' marriage as troubled), and (4) cognitions about the self in relation to a subgroup of other family members (e.g., child concludes that he or she is the cause of marital distress) (Epstein, Schlesinger, & Dryden, 1988).

The second thrust of the cognitive-behavioral model is the behavioral component. The cognitive-behavioral approach is based on a premise that distress among family or family-school systems derives not only from distorted appraisals but also from actual dysfunctional behavioral exchanges (Epstein, Schlesinger, & Dryden, 1988). The traditional behavioral deficits and excesses associated with family distress include deficits in the skills of communication, assertiveness, negotiation, and problem solving, and excesses of aversive behaviors, such as criticism, physical aggression, and nagging (see Patterson, 1982). Applying behavioral theory to family systems, Epstein, Schlesinger, and Dryden (1988) note that family members have two types of behavioral response options available to them: respond to one other family member or respond to subgroups (e.g., parental unit) within the family. From this perspective, the opportunity for the development of dysfunctional behavioral patterns increases exponentially as the number of members of a system increases, a factor that may be of particular importance in remarried family systems (see Carlson, 1985).

In assessing system dysfunction from the cognitive-behavioral model, as previously noted, both cognitions and dysfunctional behavioral patterns must be assessed. Beginning with the cognitive component, three major types of cognition are considered important. These include (1) *beliefs* each member has about the nature of relationships in the system and the individual functioning of system members, (2) *attributions* system members make about the causes of the problem, and (3) *expectancies* about the likelihood that certain events will occur in the future under certain circumstances.

In general, persons develop beliefs about relationships based on experiences with relationships, which can come from various sources, such as family of origin, past and current romantic and friendship relationships, and cultural representations of successful relationships (e.g., representations in the media). Expectancies derive in part from past experiences with other system members. When accurate, expectancies enhance the certainty and predictability of relationships; when inaccurate, expectancies may create self-fulfilling prophecies. Based on the beliefs one holds about relationships in general and expectancies developed about relationships in particular, individuals enter each interaction with family members with a set of preconceived notions that may guide their behavior toward the other person, create emotional distress for the individual (if the belief and expectancy are discrepant), and produce selective attention to salient aspects of the interaction. Causal attributions are the inferences persons made regarding the determinants of their positive and negative interactions. As noted earlier, negative and stable attributions about others tend to bias family members' perceptions of and emotional responses to one another, thus exacerbating distress in relationships.

The assessment of beliefs, expectancies, and attributions can occur with self-report or interview methods of data collection. Although no standardized family measures have been published that directly evaluate these cognitive mediators, many measures are available that capture perceptions of family relationships (Grotevant & Carlson, 1989). In the absence of cognitive behaviorally based formal instruments, mental health professionals can assess family and school system cognitions by means of an interview and with informal observations of spontaneously reported beliefs, expectancies, and attributions by system members in their interactions with one another (Epstein, Schlesinger, & Dryden, 1988).

Assessment of behavior dysfunction, the second component of the model, calls for the systematic observation and recording of concrete instances of the problem behavior, followed by a functional analysis of the environmental contingencies surrounding the behavior. Behavioral data can be collected through observation of family interaction patterns in a family or family-school interview; through questioning regarding frequencies, antecedents, and consequences of the problem behavior in individual interviews; and through logs of behavior (participant observation) recorded by family members at home or by school personnel in relevant school settings. Behavioral family therapists tend to take a more linear than systems view of problem formulation, focusing on the contingent control of one member's behavior by another.

In summary, the cognitive-behavioral model of family-school assessment assumes that system members' beliefs, expectancies, and attributions regarding their relationships and the problem child will mediate their behavior toward the child and toward others in relationship with self and the child. Inaccurate, negative, and stable attributions of others are characteristic of distressed systems. Behavioral changes cannot be undertaken without a change in the interfering cognitive mediators held by family members, and subsequent behavioral changes must be consistent with expanded cognitions in order to maintain both cognitive and behavioral changes. The focus of a cognitive-behavioral family-school assessment, then, is a determination of (1) the stable and negative cognitions regarding the identified problem child held by persons in relationship with the child and (2) the associated dysfunctional behavioral interactions.

Solution-Oriented Model

The solution-oriented model of assessment and intervention presented here reflects the recent refocusing of brief therapists from problems to solutions (de Shazer, 1982, 1985, 1988; Kral, 1986; O'Hanlon & Weiner-Davis, 1989; O'Hanlon & Wilk, 1987). Influential forerunners to the solution-oriented model were Milton Erikson (e.g., see Haley, 1973), the problem-solving strategic formulations of Jay Haley (1987), and the brief therapy approach of the Mental Research Institute (Watzlawick, Weakland, & Fisch, 1974). Briefly summarized, key assumptions of these early strategic problem-focused frameworks were as follows:

1. Problems consist of repeated, undesirable behaviors in the present.
2. The occurrence of all behavior is continually shaped, maintained, and changed primarily by ongoing reinforcements in the particular behaving individual's system of social interaction.
3. People's attempted logical "solutions" to the problem often contribute most to the problem's maintenance and exacerbation.
4. Given this conception of problems and their resolution, the therapist must be an active agent of change who considers what the most strategic change in the solutions might be.
5. Work only for small change. A change anywhere in the cycle will change the entire sequence of behavior surrounding the problem, and thus have a "ripple effect" within the system.

In summary, the forerunners of solution-oriented therapy focused on "problems," how difficulties get to be problems, and how to solve problems.

de Shazer (1985) has challenged the assumption that the solutions to problems are closely related to the nature of the problems presented. Based on his practice and research, de Shazer (1985) has concluded "that the process of solution, from one case to another, is more similar than the problems each intervention is meant to solve" (p. xv). Thus, a successful intervention need not fit the problem; rather, it need only fit the problem situation in such a way that a solution evolves. In short, a thorough diagnosis of the problem is not essential to the solution. In order to prompt solutions to problems, rather than diagnosis of problems, expectations of change and solution are developed with the clients. The clinical implications of the solution-oriented approach, articulated by O'Hanlon & Weiner-Davis (1989), are as follows:

1. Clients have the resources and strengths to resolve complaints.
2. Change is constant; thus, the therapist uses verbal and nonverbal mechanisms to give the impression that it would be surprising if the presenting complaint were to persist.
3. The therapist's job in assessment and intervention is to identify and amplify change.
4. It is usually unnecessary to know a great deal about the complaint in order to resolve it.
5. Symptoms do not serve functions for individuals, relationships, families, or other systems; thus, it is not necessary to know the cause or function of a complaint in order to resolve it.
6. A small change is all that is necessary; a change in one part of the system can affect change in another part of the system.
7. There is no single "correct" or "valid" way to live one's life; therefore, clients, not therapists, identify the goals to be accomplished.
8. There may be more or less "useful" viewpoints to solving problems;

therefore, therapists may shift perceptions of the situation.

9. Since change is the goal, focus on what is possible and changeable rather than on what is impossible and intractable.
10. Rapid change or resolution of problems is possible.

The primary method of assessment in the solution-oriented model is the interview. The solution-oriented model of family-school assessment/intervention assumes that systems possess the resources to solve their own problems but "get stuck" in the "doing" and "viewing" of the problem such that problem solving is impeded. It is assumed that therapists assisting in problem resolution also get stuck when the focus of assessment remains either history or the problem. Thus, solution-oriented therapists use the assessment interview as an opportunity to search for solutions to the complaint, which will be evident in exceptions to the problem presented by the members of the family or school, less pathological views of the problem presented by the interviewer, and the reported resources and strengths of family members for solving or keeping problems from developing, for example, in other aspects of their life or with other children.

Consistent with the assumptions of the solution-oriented model, a cooperative or collaborative, rather than expert, relationship between the therapist and family is established in the assessment interview. In the assessment interview, the therapists and distressed system(s) negotiate a solvable problem and search for solutions. The interview session is also viewed as intervention. Through the use of solution-oriented interviewing techniques (discussed later in the chapter), clients can experience significant shifts in their thinking about situations in the course of the interview. These cognitive shifts permit persons to leave the interview free to act in more productive

ways. Intervention plans or tasks assigned at the end of an interview simply serve to reinforce a change that has already occurred in the interview session (O'Hanlon & Weiner-Davis, 1989). The assumptions of this model, which support the ripple effect of small change, suggest that the interview could be conducted with as few or as many persons related to the problem. In reality, however, it would appear optimal to develop solutions with those system members who represent the primary locus system (Aponte & VanDeusen, 1981) and/or who are "complaining" (White, Summerlin, Loos, & Epstein, this volume).

Intervention in solution-oriented therapy consists of three things (O'Hanlon & Weiner-Davis, 1989):

1. Change the "doing" of the situation that is perceived as problematic.
2. Change the "viewing" of the situation that is perceived to be problematic.
3. Evoke resources, solutions, and strengths (typically from other areas of competence within the client or system) to bring to the situation that is perceived as problematic.

Changing the "doing" has been termed a *complaint pattern intervention* and changing the "viewing" a *context pattern intervention* (O'Hanlon & Weiner-Davis, 1989).

In summary, the solution-oriented model of family-school intervention de-emphasizes the role, function, and origins of children's problems within family or school systems; rather, it emphasizes the resources and capacities of all systems to change. Since the origins of the problem are of little relevance within this model, assessment is no longer the search for causes of the problem but rather the search for exceptions to the problem and the identification of resources possessed by system members in other aspects of their lives that might be brought to bear upon the identified problem. In contrast to most therapy models, the solution-oriented model is noteworthy for the emphasis on collaboration between therapist and client.

Summary

Three models of systems-oriented assessment and intervention have been discussed. The models share some assumptions and are distinguished by others. For example, all three models share a focus on present transactional and perceptual reality, yet each model focuses its lens on a different aspect of the problem. The cognitive-behavioral model focuses on the cognitions and dyadic behavioral sequences that control the performance of the problematic behavior. The systemic-structuralists attend to these same processes of behavior and cognition; however, the emphasis in on the larger organization or structure that is created by repeated dyadic behavioral transactions. The solution-oriented model, in contrast with both the structural and cognitive-behavior models, remains less concerned about the systemic variables maintaining the problem; rather, it seeks to discover the variables that control when the problem does not occur. A summary of the differences in the focus of assessment across the three models appears in Table 1.

The different perspectives from which systems can be viewed suggest that different strategies for assessing dysfunctional systems might also be necessary. Next, we will turn to a discussion of available strategies for assessing family systems.

METHODS AND STRATEGIES OF FAMILY ASSESSMENT

Three principal methods used in psychological assessment are applicable to the assessment of family and school systems and their interface. These include in-terview, observation, and self-report methods. Within each of these broad categories numerous variations exist. It is beyond the scope of this chapter to discuss these assessment methods in depth; rather, we will briefly describe these methods, discuss their strengths and limitations, and show how these methods interface with the models presented. For further discussion of family assessment issues, the interested reader is referred to Carlson (1987, 1991) and Grotevant and Carlson (1989).

Interviews

The interview has been considered to be the most useful assessment method within the family therapy tradition. Preference for this strategy has emerged as a result of the emphasis in systems theory on the role of here-and-now transactional patterns in the maintenance of problem behavior. From a systems perspective, the primary goal of an interview is to gather information in a way that clarifies the behavioral transactions and cognitions within the family or school system that serve as the supportive context for the child's dysfunctional behavior in school and thus points to solutions for breaking that pattern.

System theorists differ in viewpoint on which members of the system(s) must attend the interview for an adequate assessment of the child's presenting problem. Structural family theorists contend that an assessment interview with the whole family or the family and school conjointly is essential to clarifying patterns of interaction (e.g., Aponte, 1976; Minuchin, 1974). Brief problem-oriented and solution-oriented therapists, in contrast, believe that patterns can be discerned and changed with a single-member focus to assessment and intervention (e.g., Fisch, Weakland, & Segal, 1982). Family therapists using the cognitive-behavioral model have not clearly stated either a theoretical or empirical rationale for who should attend the interview (Epstein, Schlesinger, & Dryden, 1988). However, as Haley (1987) asserts, the way in which the child's problem is examined is the beginning of intervention. Thus, a whole family interview or a family-school conjoint meeting enhances not only the validity of an assessment of the family or family-school context but also serves to "frame" the situation as a contextual, not individual, problem.

Guidelines for conducting a family or family-school interview will vary depending on the model of intervention that is

TABLE 1 Comparison of family assessment/intervention models

Dimension	Systemic-Structural	Cognitive-Behavioral	Solution-Oriented
Sources of problems	Dysfunctional organizational patterns	Negative and stable cognitions	Rigid problem-solving behavior
Temporal perspective	Assessment/treatment focus on the present	Assessment/treatment focus on the present	Assessment/treatment focus on the present
Role of insight	Insight is not necessary for effective change	Insight is necessary for effective change	Insight is not necessary for effective change
Role of behavior and perception	Behavioral interactions influence perception	Perception and behavior have reciprocal impact	Perception influences behavioral actions
Primary focus of assessment	Transactional behavior patterns	Linear dyadic behavior and individual cognitions	Exceptions to the problem in behavior or perception
Target system level of assessment	Whole system with attention to subsystems	Individual in relation to other individuals and subsystems	Individual
Methods of assessment	Observation (informal) and interview	Observation (formal), interview, self-report	Interview
Role of assessment	Circular process of assessment-intervention-assessment	Linear process with assessment leading to diagnosis and intervention	Simultaneous process with assessment-intervention
Theory of change	Change transactional patterns maintaining the symptom; secondarily change perceptions	Change negative cognitions, which sets the stage for behavioral change, which maintains altered cognitions	Change the behavior and perceptions of the problem; evoke resources from areas of competence
Role of therapist	Directive: Provides new meanings and prescribes behavior	Expert Consultative: Provides rational evidence for new cognition changes	Collaborative Consultative: Co-constructs goals, and provides multiple new meanings and behavior change options
Therapeutic modality	Experiential education	Education	Language

guiding the interviewer. Excellent guidelines for conducting an interview in the structural framework are provided by Haley (1987), with a step-by-step elaboration of Haley's method by Weber, McKeever, and McDaniel (1985). This theory, as previously noted, emphasizes the role of present system transactions versus past history in problem formation and maintenance; a therapeutic goal of problem resolution while altering structures that support the problem; and a brief, action-oriented intervention. Therefore, a key focus of the interview is to create a situation (enactment) in which system members can interact with one another such that the interviewer can observe and evaluate the transactions. Familiarity with structural family therapy theory will enhance the interviewer's competence in assessing the meaning of transactions. Recommended readings include Aponte (1976), Minuchin (1974), Minuchin and Fishman (1981), Minuchin, Rosman, and Baker (1978), Haley (1987), Umbarger (1983), Stanton (1981), and Aponte and VanDeusen (1981).

In contrast with the structural framework for conducting interviews, the solution-oriented interview, with its emphasis deriving a solution versus an understanding of the transactions surrounding the problem, is not concerned with an illustration of the problem in present transactional reality. The solution-oriented interview has been described by Kral (1986), O'Hanlon and Weiner-Davis (1989), Lipchik and de Shazer (1988), and Tomm (1987a, 1987b). Interview components include:

1. Joining
2. A brief description of the problem with an emphasis on facts or events, not subjective feelings, cognitions, or past history
3. Questioning
4. Normalizing and depathologizing

5. Negotiating a concrete (behavioral) goal of change (O'Hanlon & Weiner-Davis, 1989)

Questioning, a critical stage of the solution-oriented interview, is designed to clarify the goals of the client while refocusing attention toward change. Questions thus focus on (1) exceptions to the problem (e.g., "When don't you have this problem?", "What is different then?"); or (2) if clients are unable to report any exceptions, in the future, without the problem (e.g., "If I could wave a magic wand and remove this problem, how would your life be different?"); or (3) if clients are unable to respond to either of the above questions, asking facts (not cognitions) about the problem, (e.g., "If I had a video camera in your home/classroom, what would I see?") (O'Hanlon, 1988). It is important to note that questions regarding "why" the problem exists are avoided. Rather, the focus of questioning is on the positive and on what is working (Kral, 1986). As previously noted, solution-oriented interviewing is viewed as an intervention as well as an assessment.

A family system or family-school interview within the cognitive-behavioral framework, in contrast with the solution-oriented interview, is more heavily focused on the diagnostic end of the diagnosis-intervention continuum. The primary purpose of a cognitive-behavioral interview is to determine the cognitions mediating the behavior of participants engaged in the problem (Epstein, Schlesinger, & Dryden, 1988). To identify cognitions, it is recommended that the interviewer probe for automatic thoughts (expectancies and attributions) by adapting individual cognitive therapy techniques such as inquiring about the specific behavioral interaction that took place, as well as the accompanying mood state(s) and stream-of-consciousness thinking process. Similarly, when the interviewer notices a shift in mood or behavior during the interview, he or she should inquire about relevant associated cognitions. Therapists will also be able identify expectancies and attributions with attention to the spontaneous statements of family members and school personnel. Beliefs can be identified in two ways. First, the interviewer can look for repeated themes within the family or school systems. Second, the interviewer can follow a line of questioning that probes the implications of successively elicited automatic thoughts (e.g., "If that were so, what would that mean?") (Epstein, Schlesinger, & Dryden, 1988).

The interview method of family assessment has both strengths and limitations. The interview is perhaps the most efficient means of obtaining both objective data about family transactional patterns and subjective data about perceptions and feelings of family members. On the other hand, the interview is subject to multiple sources of error. One source of error derives from family members whose reports of events may be inaccurate or intentionally falsified, particularly in front of other family members or school personnel. Moreover, reports of subjective data may be biased by social desirability or lack of insight. These sources of error, however, tend to be of little concern to systems-oriented therapists primarily because with their emphasis on the here-and-now and their view that assessment and intervention are simultaneous and recursive, versus sequential and linear processes, the biases in the reports of family or school members simply become grist for intervention. A second, perhaps more serious, source of interview error derives from the exclusive reliance on the clinical skill and judgment of the interviewer. The limitations of clinical judgment versus statistical prediction have been well documented (Meehl, 1954).

Clinical methods, such as the interview technique, have been considered essential for obtaining information when adequate objective measurement techniques are not available (Anastasi, 1982). Currently, the lack of coherence across theorists regarding the essential family processes to evaluate, as well as the lack of psychometrically validated objective measures, assures that the interview will remain a key family assessment method. Furthermore, the systems-oriented models of family treatment that merge the treatment stages of diagnosis and intervention expand the traditional view of the interview as an assessment device to a primary mode of intervention.

Observation

Observation has increasingly become the method of choice for identifying dysfunctional patterns of family and family-school interaction among family researchers and clinicians. The move toward observation methods has been stimulated by early criticism of the validity of family self-report methods (Straus & Brown, 1978), empirical evidence for the relatively low correspondence between what people say they do and their actual behavior (Gottman, 1979), and research that successfully differentiates distressed from nondistressed families when interaction patterns are the criteria (Gottman, 1979; Minuchin, Rosman, & Baker, 1978; Patterson, 1982). Observation is frequently characterized as requiring fewer inferences, and, therefore, as providing a more objective view of system functioning than other assessment methods. In reality, observation methods vary in type, methodological rigor, level of inference required, susceptibility to bias, and both the type and quality of data they yield. Informal observation procedures, in which no systematic coding scheme is used, have been found to yield no greater than chance levels of discrimination between distressed and nondistressed families (Conger, 1981). Formal observation schemes, in contrast, which provide systematic monitoring and recording of behavioral events, can provide a precise description of interactive patterns that can be the key for identifying how a child's problem behavior is elicited, maintained, and organized within the family or classroom system (Cairns & Green, 1979; Patterson, 1982).

Formal observation methods can be categorized as (1) *naturalistic* (i.e., behavior is observed as it naturally occurs in the environment), (2) *analogue* (i.e., behavior is observed in a controlled environment designed to elicit behavior of interest), and (3) *participant* (i.e., family members monitor their own or another member's behavior) (Wilson, 1986). Coding schemes that derive from the behavioral tradition emphasize naturalistic observation (e.g., see Patterson, 1982). The family therapy tradition has tended to use analogue observation with families assigned discussion tasks focusing on family decision making, revealed differences, or unresolved conflicts in a clinic setting (e.g., see Watzlawick, 1966). The correspondence between naturalistic and analogue observations is currently undetermined, and thus it cannot be presumed (Wilson, 1986). Participant observation has infrequently been used by systems-oriented family therapists; however, it is a common procedure for collecting behavioral data within the cognitive-behavioral model (Epstein, Schlesinger, & Dryden, 1988). Greater use of this method for assessing the whole family context has been encouraged (Margolin, 1987).

Several behavioral observation codes are noteworthy for their significance in the school setting. For elementary school-aged children and their families, the Family Interaction Coding System (FICS) (Reid, 1978), designed to measure prosocial and aversive behavior within the family, is the most carefully developed and researched. Patterson (1982) provides an excellent guide to the coding system, results of research, and treatment implications. For adolescent family systems, the Defensive and Supportive Communication code, which discriminates delinquent from normal families, may be useful (Alexander, 1973a, 1973b). An advantage of this coding system is that it is simple relative to most behavioral coding schemes. In addition, Alexander has developed a family problem-solving treatment program that blends systems theory and behavioral theory; thus, data derived from the coding can be readily linked with treatment (Barton & Alexander, 1981).

Formal observation procedures have the advantage of significantly enhanced reliability and validity, and have been the assessment method of choice of behaviorally oriented therapists. The disadvantage of formal observation methods rests in the cost of data collection and analysis, or, in the case of participant observation methods, the compliance and reliability of the participant observers. However, Patterson (1982) has found that parents are quite reliable observers of their children. In contrast with the favored role of formal observation techniques with behaviorally oriented clinicians, family systems-oriented therapists have favored informal observation, generally of the whole system within an interview (or analogue) situation, to establish hypotheses regarding communication patterns underlying individual symptomatology.

Informal observations, based on the systemic-structural approach, would focus informal observation on repeated patterns of transaction within the family that were reflective of the underlying structure of the family and that appeared to support or maintain the symptomatic behavior. Patterns of behavior reflective of inverted power hierarchies, covert and rigid alliances between family members, enmeshed or disengaged dyadic relationships, and/or a lack of organization and resonance within the family are common foundations for children's behavior problems. The obvious advantage of informal observation is that it is cost effective and utilizes the profound information-processing capacities of humans to integrate and organize data. The disadvantage, of course, is the reliance on clinical judgment and the lack of reliability that is characteristic of informal assessment methods.

One solution to enhancing the reliability of informal observation is the use of clinical rating scales of family dynamics. Rating scales provide a method of objectifying observations of family interactions such that prediction, treatment evaluation, and communication among professionals may be enhanced. Rating methodology takes advantage of the complex information-processing capabilities of the interviewer/rater to abstract and synthesize relevant pieces of information to arrive at a summary judgment. As such, given the complexity of family dynamics, this method may be particularly useful for assessment of complex systems.

Numerous clinical family rating scales have been developed (for a comprehensive review see Carlson & Grotevant, 1987a, 1987b; and Grotevant & Carlson, 1989). Particularly useful are rating scales derived from a clear theoretical base but also with accompanying self-report measures. These permit a multimethod family evaluation to be completed within an integrated theoretical framework. Family rating scales that are consistent with systems theory and that have complementary self-report measures include the following: the Beavers-Timberlawn Family Evaluation Scale and Family Style Scale (Beavers, n.d.); the McMaster Clinical Rating Scale (Epstein, Baldwin, & Bishop, 1982); the Family Assess-

ment Measure Clinical Rating Scale (Skinner & Steinhauer, 1986); and the Clinical Rating Scale for the Circumplex Model of Family Functioning (Olson & Killorin, 1985).

The primary advantages of clinical rating scales for evaluating family functioning are their communicative value and, if completed with more than one rater, their check on the reliability of clinical judgment. Disadvantages of rating scales include their susceptibility to numerous rater errors, as well as the fact that their communicative value is limited by the "shared reality" across professionals of the meaning of the rated constructs (Carlson & Grotevant, 1987a). Thus, clinical rating scales are most likely to be useful in a school or clinical setting that adheres to a clear and consistent theoretical approach to assessment and intervention with families.

In summary, formal observation methods can be expected to identify reliable specific behavioral contingencies that may underlie problematic behavior of the child. These methods are favored by cognitive-behavioral therapists. Informal observation methods, guided by the therapists' model of problem development and resolution, have been the choice of most family system therapists. Unless informal observation is systematic, however, it may provide meaningless information. One solution to increasing the objectivity of informal observation methods is the use of clinical rating scales for codifying family interaction patterns. Although this method is common in family research settings, it has not appeared to be used widely in clinical practice. Perhaps family systems therapists who view observation, hypothesizing, and challenging as a circular process of assessment-intervention find observation errors to be irrelevant as they are clarified with the system's response to intervention (Fishman, 1983, de Shazer, 1982).

Self-Report Methods

In contrast to observation models, which assess overt behavior, self-report methods are useful for assessing the interior or insider perspective of family relationships. This assessment method evaluates the subjective conditions within the family context, and, as such, is particularly compatible with the cognitive-behavioral model. The use of self-report methods has a long history of use in the diagnosis of children within the schools, and therefore fits easily within accepted school psychological practices.

Self-report methods include both objective and projective measures. Objective measures of family functioning consist primarily of paper-and-pencil questionnaires. Questionnaires of family functioning can be differentiated by the target of assessment: whole family, marital subsystem, parent-child subsystem, or sibling relationship. Regarding these family system assessment targets, the greatest test development has been in the measurement of whole family, marital, and parent-child relationships. Although research clearly documents the importance of the marital relationship to child symptomatology (O'Leary, 1984), existing measures of the marital relationship, which frequently include questions regarding the couple's satisfaction with their sexual relationship, are generally considered inappropriate for the school setting, given the cultural norm of family privacy, and therefore will not be discussed further in this chapter. For information on marital measures, the interested reader is referred to Filsinger (1983) and Straus and Brown (1978).

Many family psychologists argue that measures of whole family functioning are most consistent with the theoretical premise of systems theory; that is, the whole is greater than the sum of the parts. Thus, the recent decade has witnessed the development of numerous objective self-report measures of whole family functioning. Although various standardized family assessment measures are available, research on the validity of existing measures, particularly with regard to differential prediction of child symptomatology, remains seriously limited (Grotevant & Carlson, 1989). Instrument selection must currently be governed by available relevant criteria, including data on psychometric validation, ease of use (e.g., item length, reading level of questions, instructions for administration and interpretation of scores), appropriateness for the setting, and the expected utility of the measure for the purpose identified.

An additional limitation of objective self-report measures of whole family functioning for school-related assessment is that most measures are constructed with reading levels appropriate for the age range of early adolescent to adult. Only one questionnaire for school-aged children has been published (i.e., Children's Version of the Family Environment Scale [Pino, Simons, & Slawinowski, 1984]), and its psychometric properties are uncertain (Grotevant & Carlson, 1989). Thus, objective self-report data about the family milieu must be obtained primarily from parents and adolescents within the family. The capacity of younger children to report reliably on whole family processes with questionnaires has not been adequately investigated. Rather, clinicians are limited to evaluating the subjective perceptions of younger children regarding their family with projective methods or with questionnaires that examine the children's perceptions of their parents (versus whole family).

Measures of the parent-child relationship typically fall within the socialization-versus-systems-theory framework. Although parent self-report measures of child functioning are far more numerous, attention to the bidirectional influence of the child on the parents has encouraged the development of child reports of parent functioning too. Parent reports tend to emphasize parenting values and styles, whereas child reports of parenting tend to focus on parent behavior versus attitudes (Grotevant & Carlson, 1989). A few measures have been developed that permit the identification of the viewpoints of both the parent and child within the same theoretical framework. Reciprocal parent-child measures include the Family Assessment Measure-Dyadic Scale (III) (Skinner, Steinhauer, & Santa-Barbara, 1983, 1984) and the Parent Acceptance-Rejection Questionnaire (Rohner, 1984) (described in Grotevant & Carlson, 1989). It is only with parent and child versions of the same measure that relationship reciprocity (highlighted in the cognitive-behavioral model previously discussed) can be measured.

The limited psychometric development of the majority of existing objective self-report family and parent-child measures suggests that these measures be used with caution, particularly in situations involving the educational placements (see Carlson, 1991). However, the field of family assessment has progressed rapidly, providing school-based clinicians with an array of new assessment options. Although it is beyond the scope of this chapter to review all available family and parent-child self-report measures, several that appear to be particularly useful in the school setting will be briefly described. For a comprehensive discussion of family assessment, the interested reader is referred to Filsinger (1983) and Grotevant and Carlson (1989).

Measures of the whole family systems that appear to have particular utility for school-related assessment include: Family Environment Scale (FES; Moos & Moos, 1986), Family Adaptability and Cohesion Evaluation Scale III (FACES III; Olson, Portner, & Lavee, 1985), Family Assessment Measure III (FAM III; Skinner,

Steinhauer, & Santa-Barbara, 1984), Family Process Scales (Form E) (FPS; Barbarin & Gilbert, 1979), and Structural Family Interaction Scale—Revised (Form A) (SFIS—R; Perosa, 1986). Each of these self-report measures of whole family functioning is consistent with family systems theory. Furthermore, each measure has been psychometrically evaluated and, if necessary, revised to enhance its psychometric properties.

To date, the FES has been most widely used in research and clinical studies. The FAM-III has the advantage of including three forms: a whole family, dyadic, and self in the family form; this permits a multilevel assessment of the family across similar constructs, as well as the opportunity to identify the reciprocal viewpoints of parties within a dyadic relationship. An advantage of the SFIS—R (Form A) is its theoretical basis in structural family theory, which makes it most useful for practitioners who conduct family interventions within this framework. Only the FES and the SFIS—R have published studies that evaluate the discriminant validity of their measure for differentiating families with children exhibiting school problems, and no comprehensive study has been completed. Thus, these measures of family functioning can provide evidence of family problems, a direction to further assessment, but the link between identified family difficulties and the school-based problems of children must remain a hypothesis to be tested with additional assessment and intervention methods. As noted earlier, whole family self-report measures are appropriate for completion by parents and adolescents.

In addition to measures of the whole family environment, measures of the parent-child relationship can be particularly important in the school-based assessment of children. Parent-child measures that are recommended based on careful review (see Grotevant & Carlson, 1989) include

Parent as a Teacher Inventory (PAAT; Strom, 1984), Parenting Stress Index (PSI; Abidin, 1983), Parent Perception Inventory (PPI; Hazzard, Christensen, & Margolin, 1983), and Parent Acceptance-Rejection Questionnaire (PARQ; Rohner, 1984). The PAAT and PSI are completed only by parents; the PPI is completed only by children; and the PARQ contains equivalent forms for both parents and children. With the exception of the PARQ, these measures are designed primarily for elementary school-aged children and their parents; however, an adolescent version of the PSI in being validated (Abidin, 1989).

The advantage of the PAAT is its focus on education; that is, the parents' view of their role in assisting the child in cognitive development. The strength of the PSI is its strong theoretical foundation in attachment theory, temperament theory, and stress theory such that a bidirectional view of parents' health with the parents' view of the difficultness of the child, in conjunction with their perceived overall life stress, can be integrated in measurement. The advantage of the PARQ is the availability of parent and child forms as well as the availability of translations of this measure in many languages, as it has been used primarily in cross-cultural research. The PPI is one of the few psychometrically sound child reports of parental behavior; it is based on social learning theory.

For family assessments with younger children, using a parent report or child report of parenting behavior may be the objective measurement of choice. In addition, both a whole family and parent-child measure may be considered appropriate, as these measures derive from distinct theoretical traditions with the whole family measures primarily assessing system properties in the family, whereas the parent-child measures assess parenting capacity or style. In short, whole family measures and parent-child measures are distinct and

complementary. For additional information on these measures, see Grotevant and Carlson (1989).

In summary, self-report measures of family and parent-child functioning can provide an assessment of the insider or subjective reality of family members that is objective, is cost effective, and fits easily within the norms of traditional psychological assessment. Multiple measures of whole family functioning and parent-child relationships have been developed. Unfortunately, few have been standardized or normed such that use for clinical decision making is advisable. Furthermore, few of these measures have been validated using school-related criteria. A final shortcoming of the state of the art in objective family assessment methods is the lack of measures for completion by elementary school-aged children. The developmental progression of children's conceptions of family remains an empirical question to be investigated. Currently, practitioners are limited to the use of projective techniques for capturing younger children's subjective reality of whole family relationships.

Given the lack of objective self-report measures for middle childhood, clinicians frequently use projective techniques to obtain the subjective evaluations of children regarding their family. The most popular projective method used in schools is the Kinetic Family Drawing (Burns & Kaufman, 1970; Reynolds, 1978). Although an advantage of this measure is its clear manual and scoring system, the focus of the test as a measure of individual child psychopathology leaves it lacking as a measure of family system properties. More promising projective measures for evaluating family relations include the Family Relations Test—Children's Version (FRT; Bene & Anthony, 1978) and the Family Apperception Test (FAT; Sotile, Julian, Henry, & Sotile, 1988).

The FRT, based in psychoanalytic

theory, is a measure of the intensity of a child's thoughts and feelings toward family members, as well as his or her estimates of their reciprocal feelings. Consideration of Piagetian cognitive development theory is employed in the FRT with a younger and older child version and greater complexity of emotions possible for selection in the older child version. The test consists of the placement of items (emotions), each printed on a separate card, onto the figure(s) that the child associates with the item. In contrast, the FAT is based on responses to pictorial stimuli, similar to the Thematic Apperception Test, with scoring designed to assess family system variables. The 21 stimulus cards depict common family activities, constellations, and situations, and are designed to elicit wideranging projective associations regarding family process and structure, as well as affect concerning specific family relationships.

Both measures have been used with children as young as six years old. The commonly acknowledged disadvantages of projective techniques are their lack of normative data and lack of standarized administration and scoring procedures, particularly at the final integrative and interpretive stages (Anastasi, 1982); however, the FAT and FRT have attempted to meet this criticism with clear administration and scoring procedures, as well as preliminary evidence of psychometric reliability and validity.

SUMMARY AND DISCUSSION

Assessment of individual psychopathology and intellectual functioning has an enduring history within the field of psychology and in the practice of psychology in the educational setting. Child assessment practice within schools has expanded within recent decades from a singular focus on intraindividual variables to a consideration of classroom environmental variables, a shift primarily reflective of the widespread acceptance within psychology of the explanatory power of behavioral theory. Despite consistent evidence that the quality of parenting and functioning within the family significantly influences the academic performance and social adjustment of children in school, expansion of traditional child-focused assessment to the other relevant systems of the child, such as the family system, has not occurred.

Multiple explanations for the continuation of child-focused assessment practices appear plausible. First, the relationship between families and schools has weakened. The family-school relationship in recent decades has become increasingly characterized by separation, which has been promoted by desegregation busing and maternal employment, and by differentiation of roles and functions, promoted by the professionalization of education (Lightfoot, 1978). In addition, increased national attention to civil rights has strengthened the rights to privacy of the child and family such that informal communication and collaboration are unintentionally discouraged. Thus, although the education and socialization of children are interrelated functions, socialization has become increasingly viewed as the domain of the family, whereas schools are viewed as responsible for education.

Second, the prevalent psychological theory of recent decades—behavioral theory—emphasized the role of contingent patterns of reinforcement in the *immediate* context of the individual (i.e., the classroom). Reinforcement patterns established within distal contexts were not expected to be operative within proximal contexts. Behavioral theory also limited the scope of child assessment by ignoring the impact of cognitive maturation on the acquisition of social patterns and the impact of emotion on social learning. Thus, for school-related problems, evaluation of the immediate classroom context was viewed as sufficient to explain the origin and maintenance of symptomatology.

Third, school mental health resources are limited and have been further strained by the demands placed on schools by the requirement associated with passage of the Education for All Handicapped Children Act in 1975. Completing ecologically comprehensive and valid assessments for every child referred for special services becomes a low priority in the face of inadequate resources. Finally, until recently, measures for assessing the family social milieu were not available.

Although assessment of the family context has not been characteristic of traditional psychological assessment of the child, barriers to the incorporation of analysis of family processes and strengths appear to be disintegrating. First, national opinion and social policy reflect alarm regarding the lack of parent involvement in education and the ability of families to socialize children without assistance from other social institutions (e.g., Edelman, 1987). Second, the most recent amendment of the federal legislative initiative regarding the Education of All Handicapped Children (PL 99–457) reflects the increasing emphasis on the involvement of family systems. Noteworthy in this legislation is the requirement that the strengths and needs of families with handicapped infants and toddlers be evaluated in order to develop a treatment plan. As noted by one expert, "It would be difficult, if not impossible, for professionals to ignore this clear mandate that the family be included in the process of developing a treatment plan" (Gallagher, 1989, p. 390).

Next, the increasing popularity of systems theory and ecological theory has broadened the perspective of psychologists regarding the meaning of the context of behavior such that multiple contexts and the relationships between contexts are now

viewed as salient to the etiology and treatment of childhood disorders. Moreover, recent advances within developmental psychology highlight the role of emotion in children's learning and development (Harris, 1989) and the impact of early relationship disturbance on subsequent social and cognitive functioning (Sameroff & Emde, 1989). These empirical and theoretical advances argue for the uniqueness of the family social context. Patterns of behavior learned within the family can be expected to differ in strength from patterns learned within the school context in that these patterns (1) reflect preconscious learning, (2) reveal strong emotional bonds, and (3) endure over time.

Finally, as evidenced by recent publications (e.g., Grotevant & Carlson, 1989), the field of family assessment has demonstrated remarkable growth and development in the past decade.

Research consistently finds that the quality of parenting and functioning within the family significantly influences the academic performance and social adjustment of children in school. Therefore, identifying family processes that may underlie or maintain the school-related difficulties of children is important in order to determine the most effective treatment and the prognosis for success. When chronic family dysfunctional processes are present, and these support the symptomatology of the child, brief, school-based, child-oriented treatments are unlikely to be successful.

In this chapter, many methods of family assessment have been discussed, including family or parent interviews, observations of family process, self-report measures obtained from parents and children regarding their family functioning or parent-child relationship, and projective devices. Each method has strengths and limitations; each method focuses the assessment lens on a distinct aspect of the family. Observation and interviews provide methods of examining the family from an outsider's perspective, a view that is frequently at odds with the insider viewpoint (i.e., the subjective reality of family members). Family members' subjective reality is best assessed with self-report or interview methods. Most family researchers and clinicians recommend that an assessment of the family include measurement of both the insider and outsider perspective (e.g., Grotevant & Carlson, 1989).

The goal of assessment is the careful selection of treatment. Three modalities of treatment, considered to be applicable to intervention with families in the school setting, have been discussed in this chapter. The systemic-structural approach to family assessment and intervention represents a "traditional" family therapy perspective. The advantage of this approach is its emphasis on larger system patterns of interaction and organization.

A second intervention approach, the cognitive-behavioral model, represents the first efforts in the field to integrate cognitive-behavioral theory and therapy, typically applied to individual treatment, with family systems theory. The familiarity of most school mental health professionals with behavioral and cognitive-behavioral intervention strategies suggests this model may be particularly accessible. The advantage of the cognitive-behavioral model is its elaborate delineation of the role of family members' negative and stable cognitions in maintaining dysfunctional behavior patterns.

The third intervention model discussed, the solution-oriented model, is not well integrated with family systems theory; however, this approach has been successfully practiced within the school setting with individual children, teachers, and parents (Kral, 1986), used in family-school meetings (Carlson & Hickman, in press), and applied to clinical intervention with families (de Shazer, 1982). The advantage of this model of intervention is its brief

orientation and emphasis on the positive, including strengths, solutions, and collaboration, versus the more frequent school orientation toward pathology, problems, and blame. In summary, just as there are multiple choices available to the clinician in the selection of family assessment methods, these three models represent but a few of the available family intervention choices.

Although the assumptions underlying the structural, cognitive-behavioral, and solution-oriented treatment models are quite distinct, in practice the models appear to be complementary. The solution-oriented model provides a mode of intervention that is most similar to existing school consultation approaches, and therefore is likely to (1) be most easily implemented in the school setting and (2) provide a feasible initial focus to family intervention. If change is not forthcoming with the solution-oriented model, however, the structural approach offers a mechanism by which the existing underlying organizational dysfunction of the larger system (family, school, or family-school relationship) can be identified and altered. The cognitive-behavioral model strongly complements both the solution and structural approaches. Both the structural and solution-oriented models purport to change family members' perceptions of the problem. The cognitive-behavioral model provides clear direction regarding the types of perceptions that are most strongly related to the child's problem behavior and, therefore, most critical to change in conjunction with alterations of the behavioral patterns related to the symptom.

In summary, the critical role of the family in children's school success and failure suggests that when children are experiencing difficulty in school, an evaluation of family strengths and limitations is as critical as a comprehensive evaluation of the individual child. Moreover, increasing focus on family assessment, family support, and family involvement in education is congruent with federal legislation and social policy initiatives, which strongly influence school practice. A multimethod approach to family assessment has been recommended to provide assessment data on both the observed patterns of interaction within the family that maintain the problem behavior and the subjective reality or cognitions of family members regarding self and the identified problem child. Assessing both the behavioral patterns and stable cognitions of family members is viewed as critical to linking the family assessment with intervention.

Three approaches to working with families, that were deemed appropriate to the school setting, were discussed. Although distinct in theoretical assumptions, all three interventions seek to ameliorate the symptomatic behavior of the child, in as brief a period as possible, by changing both the cognitions and behavioral patterns of family and school system members that appear to be most integral to the etiology and maintenance of the child's problem in school.

References

Abidin, R. R. (1983). *Parenting Stress Index (PSI)*. Charlottesville, VA: Pediatric Psychology Press.

Abidin, R. R. (1989). *Determinants of parenting behaviors*. Invited address presented at the annual meeting of the American Psychologial Association, New Orleans.

Alexander, J. F. (1973a). Defensive and supportive communication in family systems. *Journal of Marriage and the Family, 35*, 613–617.

Alexander, J. F. (1973b). Defensive and supportive communication in normal and deviant families. *Journal of Consulting and Clinical Psychology, 40*, 223–231.

Anastasi, A. (1982). *Psychological testing* (rev. ed.). New York: Macmillan.

Aponte, H. J. (1976). The family-school interview. *Family Process, 15*, 303–310.

Aponte, H. J., & VanDeusen, J. M. (1981). Structural family therapy. In A. S. Gur-

man & D. P. Kniskern (Eds.), *Handbook of family therapy* (pp. 310–360). New York: Brunner/Mazel.

Bagarozzi, D. A. (1985). Dimensions of family evaluation. In L. L'Abate (Ed.), *The handbook of family psychology and therapy: Vol. II* (pp. 989–1105). Homewood, IL: Dorsey.

Baldwin, A. L., Cole, R. E., & Baldwin, C. P. (1982). Parental pathology, family interaction, and the competence of the child in school. *Monographs of the Society for Research in Child Development, 47* (5, serial no. 197).

Barbarin, O. A., & Gilbert, R. (1979). *Family process scales*. Ann Arbor, MI: Family Development Project.

Barkley, R. A. (1981). Hyperactivity. In E. J. Mash & L. G. Terdal (Eds.), *Behavioral assessment of childhood disorders* (pp. 127–184). New York: Guilford.

Barton, C., & Alexander, J. F. (1981). Functional family therapy. In A. S. Gurman & D. P. Kniskern (Eds.), *Handbook of family therapy* (pp. 403–443). New York: Brunner/Mazel.

Beavers, W. R. (n.d.). *Beavers-Timberlawn Family Evaluation Scale and Family Style Evaluation Manual*. (Available from the Southwest Family Institute, Dallas, TX, 75230.)

Bene, E., & Anthony, J. (1978). *The Family Relations Test*. Windsor, England: NFER-Nelson.

Bertalanffy, L. von (1956). General systems theory. *General Systems Yearbook, 1*, 1–10.

Bowen, M. (1978). *Family therapy in clinical practice*. New York: Jason Aronson.

Bronfenbrenner, U. (1980). *The ecology of human development*. Cambridge, MA: Harvard University Press.

Burns, R. C., & Kaufman, S. H. (1970). *Kinetic family drawings (K-F-D): An introduction to understanding children through kinetic drawing*. New York: Brunner/Mazel.

Cairns, R. B., & Green, J. A. (1979). How to assess personality and social patterns: Observations or ratings? In R. B. Cairns (Ed.), *The analysis of social interactions: Methods, issues, and illustrations* (pp. 209–226). Hillsdale, NJ: Erlbaum.

Carlson, C. I. (1985). Best practices in working with single-parent and step-families. In A. Thomas & J. Grimes (Eds.), *Best practices in school psychology* (pp. 43–60). Kent, OH: National Association of School Psychologists.

Carlson, C. I. (1987). Family assessment and intervention in the school setting. In T. R.

Kratochwill (Ed.), *Advances in school psychology* (Vol. VII). Hillsdale, NJ: Erlbaum.

Carlson, C. I. (1991). Assessing the family context. In R. Kampaus & C. R. Reynolds (Eds.), *Handbook of psychological and educational assessment of children. V. II: Personality behavior, and context* (pp. 546–575). New York: Guilford.

Carlson, C. I., & Grotevant, H. D. (1987a). A comparative review of family rating scales: Guidelines for clinicians and researchers. *Journal of Family Psychology, 1,* 23–47.

Carlson, C. I., & Grotevant, H. D. (1987b). Rejoinder: The challenges of reconciling family theory with method. *Journal of Family Psychology, 1,* 62–65.

Carlson, C. I., & Hickman, J. (in press). Family consultation in schools in special services. In C. A. Maher & R. E. Greenberg (Eds.), Effective teams and groups: Vital contributions to special needs students [Special issue]. *Special Services in the Schools, 6.*

Carlson, C. I., & Sincavage, J. M. (1987). Family-oriented school psychology practice: Results of a national survey of NASP members. *School Psychology Review, 16*(4), 519–526.

Carlson, C. I., & Sincavage, J. M. (1988, August). *Survey of family-oriented school psychology practice.* Paper presented at the annual meeting of the American Psychological Association, Atlanta, GA.

Conger, R. D. (1981). The assessment of dysfunctional family systems. In B. B. Lahey & A. E. Kazdin (Eds.), *Advances in clinical child psychology* (Vol. 4) (pp. 199–243). New York: Plenum.

Conger, R. D. (1983). Behavioral assessment for practitioners: Some reasons and recommendations. In E. E. Filsinger (Ed.), *Marriage and family assessment* (pp. 137–152). Beverly Hills: Sage.

Conoley, J. C. (1987). Schools and families: Theoretical and practical bridges. *Professional School Psychology, 2,* 191–203.

Cowan, P. A. (1987). The need for theoretical and methodological integrations in family research. *Journal of Family Psychology, 1,* 48–50.

Cromwell, R. E., & Peterson, G. W. (1983). Multisystem-multimethod family assessment in clinical contexts. *Family Process, 22,* 147–171.

de Shazer, S. (1982). *Patterns of brief family therapy.* New York: Guilford.

de Shazer, S. (1985). *Keys to solution.* New York: Guilford.

de Shazer, S. (1988). *Clues: Investigating solutions in brief therapy.* New York: Norton.

Edelman, M. W. (1987). *Families in peril: An agenda for social change.* Cambridge, MA: Harvard University Press.

Emery, R. E., & O'Leary, K. D. (1982). Children's perceptions of marital discord and behavior problems of boys and girls. *Journal of Abnormal Child Psychology, 10,* 11–24.

Epstein, N., Baldwin, L. M., & Bishop, D. (1982). *McMaster Clinical Rating Scale.* (Available from Brown/Butler Family Research Center, Providence, RI.)

Epstein, N., Schlesinger, S. E., & Dryden, W. (1988). Concepts and methods of cognitive-behavioral family treatment. In N. Epstein, S. E. Schlesinger, & W. Dryden (Eds.), *Cognitive-behavioral therapy with families* (pp. 5–48). New York: Brunner/Mazel.

Filsinger, E. E. (Ed.) (1983). *Marriage and family assessment.* Beverly Hills: Sage.

Fisch, R., Weakland, J. H., & Segal, L. (1982). *The tactics of change.* San Francisco: Jossey-Bass.

Fisher, L. (1986). Systems-based consultation with schools. In L. C. Wynne, S. H. McDaniel, & T. T. Weber (Eds.), *Systems consultation: A new perspective for family therapy* (pp. 342–356). New York: Guilford.

Fishman, H. C. (1983). Reflections on assessment in structural family therapy. In B. Keeney (Ed.), *Diagnosis and assessment in family therapy.* Rockville, MD: Aspen.

Furman, W., & Buhrmester, D. (1985). Children's perceptions of the qualities of sibling relationships. *Child Development, 56,* 448–461.

Gallagher, J. J. (1989). A new policy initiative: Infants and toddlers with handicapping conditions. *American Psychologist, 44*(2), 387–391.

Gilbert, R., & Christensen, A. (1985). Observational assessment of marital and family interaction: Methodological considerations. In L. L'Abate (Ed.), *The handbook of family psychology and therapy: Vol. II* (pp. 961–988). Homewood, IL: Dorsey.

Gottman, J. (1979). *Marital interaction: Experimental investigation.* New York: Academic Press.

Grotevant, H. D., & Carlson, C. I. (1989). *Family assessment: A guide to methods and measures.* New York: Guilford.

Haley, J. (1973). *Uncommon therapy.* New York: Norton.

Haley, J. (1987). *Problem-solving therapy* (rev. ed.). San Francisco: Jossey-Bass.

Haley, J. (1980). *Leaving home.* New York: McGraw-Hill.

Harris, P. L. (1989). *Children and emotion.* New York: Basil Blackwell.

Hazzard, A., Christensen, A., & Margolin, G. (1983). Children's perceptions of parental behaviors. *Journal of Abnormal Child Psychology, 11*(1), 49–60.

Hess, R. D., & Holloway, S. D. (1984). Family and school as educational institutions. In R. D. Parke (Ed.), *Review of Child Development Research, Vol. VII: The Family* (pp. 179–222). Chicago: University of Chicago Press.

Hoffman, L. (1981). *Foundations of family therapy: A conceptual framework.* New York: Basic Books.

Huston, T. L., & Robins, E. (1982). Conceptual and methodological issues in studying close relationships. In L. H. Brown & J. S. Kidwell (Eds.), Methodology: The other side of caring [Special issue]. *Journal of Marriage and the Family, 44*(4), 901–925.

Jasnowski, M. L. (1984). The ecosystemic perspective in clinical assessment and intervention. In W. A. O'Connor and B. Lubin (Eds.), *Ecological approaches to clinical and community psychology* (pp. 41–56). New York: Wiley.

Johnson, O. G. (1976). *Tests and measurements in child development: Handbook, Vols. I & II.* San Francisco: Jossey-Bass.

Koman, S. L., & Stechler, G. (1985). Making the jump to systems. In M. P. Mirkin & S. L. Koman (Eds.), *Handbook of adolescents and family therapy* (pp. 1–20). New York: Gardner.

Kral, R. (1986). *Strategies that work: Techniques for solution in the schools.* Milwaukee, WI: Brief Therapy Center.

Lightfoot, S. L. (1978). *Worlds apart: Relationships between families and schools.* New York: Basic Books.

Lipchik, E., & de Shazer, S. (1988). Purposeful sequences for beginning the solution-oriented interview. In E. Lipchik (Ed.), *Interviewing* (pp. 105–117). Rockville, MD: Aspen.

Lusterman, D. D. (1985). An ecosystemic approach to family-school problems. *American Journal of Family Therapy, 13,* 22–30.

Maccoby, E. E., & Martin, J. A. (1983). Socialization in the context of the family: Parent-child interaction. In F. M. Hetherington (Ed.), *Handbook of child psychology: Vol. 4. Socialization, personality and social development* (pp. 1–102). New York: Wiley.

Margolin, G. (1981). The reciprocal relationship between marital and child problems. In J. P. Vincent (Ed.), *Advances in family intervention assessment and theory: An annual compilation of research (Vol. 2).* Greenwich, CT: JAI Press.

Margolin, G. (1987). Participant observation procedures in marital and family assessment. In T. Jacobs (Ed.), *Family interaction and psychopathology* (pp. 391–426). New York: Plenum.

Markman, H. J., & Notarius, C. I. (1987). Coding marital and family interaction: Current status. In T. Jacobs (Ed.), *Family interaction and psychopathology* (pp. 329–390). New York: Plenum.

Meehl, P. E. (1954). *Clinical versus statistical prediction: A theoretical analysis and a review of the evidence.* Minneapolis: University of Minnesota Press.

Minuchin, S. (1974). *Families and family therapy.* Cambridge, MA: Harvard University Press.

Minuchin, S., & Fishman, H. C. (1981). *Family therapy techniques.* Cambridge, MA: Harvard University Press.

Minuchin, S., Montalvo, B., Guerney, B., Rosman, B., & Schumer, F. (1967). *Families of the slums.* New York: Basic Books.

Minuchin, S., Rosman, B., & Baker, L. (1978). *Psychosomatic families.* Cambridge, MA: Harvard University Press.

Moos, R. H., & Moos, B. S. (1986). *Family Environment Scale manual* (rev. ed.). Palo Alto, CA: Consulting Psychologists Press.

Nunnally, J. C. (1978). *Psychometric theory* (2nd ed.). New York: McGraw-Hill.

O'Hanlon, W. H., & Weiner-Davis, M. (1989). *In search of solutions: A new direction in psychotherapy.* New York: Norton.

O'Hanlon, W. H., & Wilk, J. (1987). *Shifting contexts: The generation of effective psychotherapy.* New York: Guilford.

Okun, B. F. (1984). Family therapy and the schools. In J. C. Hansen (Ed.) & B. F. Okun (Vol. Ed.), *Family therapy with school related problems* (pp. 1–12). Rockville, MD: Aspen.

O'Leary, K. D. (1984). Marital discord and children: Problems, strategies, methodologies and results. In A. Doyle, D. Gold, & D. S. Moskovitz (Eds.), *Children in families under stress. New Directions for Child Develop-*

ment, No. 24 (pp. 35–47). San Francisco: Jossey-Bass.

Olson, D. H. (1977). Insiders' and outsiders' views of relationships: Research studies. In G. Levinger & H. Rausch (Eds.), *Close Relationships: Perspectives on the meaning of intimacy.* Amherst: University of Massachusetts.

Olson, D. H., & Killorin, E. (1985). *Clinical Rating Scale for the Circumplex Model of marital and family Systems.* (Available from Family Social Science, University of Minnesota, St. Paul, MN 55108.)

Olson, D. H., Portner, J., & Lavee, Y. (1985). *FACES III.* (Available from Family Social Science, University of Minnesota, St. Paul, MN 55108.)

Patterson, G. R. (1982). *Coercive family process.* Eugene, OR: Castalia.

Patterson, G. R., DeBarsyshe, B. D., & Ramsey, E. (1989). A developmental perspective on antisocial behavior. *American Psychologist, 44,* 329–335.

Perosa, L. M. (1986). The revision of the Structural Family Interaction Scale. Unpublished manuscript.

Perosa, L. M., Hansen, J., & Perosa, S. (1981). Development of the Structural Family Interaction Scale. *Family Therapy, 8,* 77–90.

Peterson, G. W., & Cromwell, R. E. (1983). A clarification of multisystem-multimethod assessment: Reductionism versus wholism. *Family Process, 22,* 173–178.

Pino, C. J., Simons, N., & Slawinowski, M. J. (1984). *Chidren's Version/Family Environment Scale.* Palo Alto, CA: Consulting Psychologists Press.

Plas, J. M. (1986). *System psychology in the schools.* Elmsford, NY: Pergamon.

Reid, J. B. (Ed.) (1978). *A social learning approach to family intervention: Vol. 2. Observation in home settings.* Eugene, OR: Castalia.

Reynolds, C. R. (1978). A quick-scoring guide to the interpretation of children's kinetic family drawings (KFD). *Psychology in the schools, 15*(4), 489–492.

Roberts, G. C., Block, J. H., & Block, J. (1984). Continuity and change in parents; child-rearing practices. *Child Development, 55,* 586–597.

Rohner, R. P. (1984). *Handbook for the study of parental acceptance and rejection* (rev. ed.). Storrs: Center for the Study of Parental Acceptance and Rejection, University of Connecticut.

Rutter, M. (1985). Family and school influences on behavior development. *Journal of Child Psychology and Psychiatry, 26,* 349–368.

Sameroff, A. J., & Emde, R. N. (Eds.) (1989). *Relationship disturbances in early childhood.* New York: Basic Books.

Skinner, H. A., & Steinhauer, P. D. (1986). *Family Assessment Measure Clinical Rating Scale.* (Available from Addiction & Research Foundation, Toronto, Ontario, Canada.)

Skinner, H. A., Steinhauer, P. D., & Santa-Barbara, J. (1983). The Family Assessment Measure. *Canadian Journal of Community Mental Health, 2,* 91–105.

Skinner, H. A., Steinhauer, P. D., & Santa-Barbara, J. (1984). *The Family Assessment Measure: Administration and interpretation guide.* (Available from Addiction & Research Foundation, Toronto, Ontario, Canada.)

Sotile, W. M., Julian, A., Henry, S., & Sotile, M. O. (1988). *Family Apperception Test manual.* Charlotte, NC: Feedback Services.

Standards for education and psychological testing. (1985). Washington, DC: American Psychological Association.

Stanton, M. D. (1981). Strategic approaches to family therapy. In A. S. Gurman & D. P. Kniskern (Eds.), *Handbook of family therapy* (pp. 361–402). New York: Brunner/Mazel.

Straus, M. A., & Brown, B. W. (1978). *Family measurement techniques: Abstracts of published instruments, 1935–1974* (rev. ed.). Minneapolis: University of Minnesota Press.

Strodtbeck, F. L. (1954). Husband-wife interaction over revealed differences. *American Sociological Review, 16,* 468–473.

Strom, R. (1984). *Parent as a Teacher Inventory manual.* Bensenville, IL: Scholastic Testing Service.

Tomm, K. (1987a). Interventive interviewing: Part I. Strategizing as a fourth guideline for the therapist. *Family Process, 26*(1), 3–14.

Tomm, K. (1987b). Intervention interviewing: Part II. Reflexive questioning as a means to enable self-healing. *Family Process, 26*(2), 167–184.

Umbarger, C. C. (1983). *Structural family therapy.* New York: Grune & Stratton.

Watzlawick, P. (1966). A structured family interview. *Family Process, 5,* 251–271.

Watzlawick, P., Fisch, R., & Segal, L. (1982). *The tactics of change.* San Francisco: Jossey-Bass.

Watzlawick, P., Weakland, J., & Fisch, R. (1974). *Change: Principles of problem formation and problem resolution.* New York: Norton.

Weber, T., McKeever, J. E., & McDaniel, S. H. (1985). A beginner's guide to the problem-oriented first family interview. *Family Process, 24*(3), 356–364.

Wilson, C. C. (1986). Family assessment in preschool evaluation. *School Psychology Review, 15,* 166–179.

3

The Development of Systems Thinking: A Historical Perspective

JEANNE M. PLAS

Peabody College of Vanderbilt University

The man forcing himself up the country hillside was 66 years old; he looked tired. "But no," he muttered aloud to no one in particular, "It's not that I'm so tired, really. The true problem is that my heart is so sore. I feel like someone is giving it a twist—and most of the life is slowly being wrung out of me."

It was the spring of 1844, and Ian Foerster's son—his only son—was in trouble. Thomas, Lisbeth, and their three daughters lived just across the hill in the next parish, and from all indications it looked like their once happy home was coming apart. Ian knew—in a way that people sometimes just sense these things—that if his boy's family could not get life and love back into it, the last years of his own life were going to be painful and without hope of a peaceful dying.

But what had gone wrong? What were the reasons for such a once happy family to have become so miserable? Who and what were to blame?

During most of the intense conversations he had shared with his father, Thomas blamed Lisbeth and their eldest daughter Harriet. Lisbeth was "willful" and "becoming more so with each passing year." Harriet was not "accomplished" and took too much of her mother's time and too often her mother's side in the family arguments. Harriet blamed the twins, Alberta and Ariel, 10 years younger than herself, whining, clinging, and constitutionally argumentative as far as the eldest girl was concerned. The twins seemed to oscillate emotionally between their mother and father, and between moments of extreme reticence or the most astounding weeping and flailing about.

Lisbeth blamed Thomas. That was clear—very clear. "Yet, for *what*," Ian wondered, as he trudged across the hill yet one more time to honor his son's request "to have a look" and "to have a talk with Lisbeth and the girls."

Ian believed that *someone* was doing something "bad wrong" in that house. But who? Who was really to blame? As he hurried along into the chilly twilight, Ian was sickened by his own agitation and seemingly useless ruminations. Was Thomas going to have to put Lisbeth out? Who would care for the girls? How could his son get by without a wife? But, if nothing changed at all, how could these children be raised straight and true in such a house? What was happening to cause this once beautiful family to come apart? And how could it all get fixed?

In 1968, after 20 years of thoughtful consideration, Ludwig von Bertalanffy, mathematician, social theorist, and originator of general systems theory, told us that "the system problem is essentially the problem of the limitations of analytical procedures in science" (1968, p. 19). The problem that the heartsick Ian had faced over 100 years earlier had essentially been the same: a failure of exclusively analytical thought processes to be adequate to the task of understanding family system dynamics. In other words, Ian had adopted the problem-solving method that dominated the thinking of his times. That method, now often referred to by a variety of titles such as *Newtonian, classical, mechanistic, Cartesian, analytic,* and *positivist,* assumes that the world in which we live, the world that contains the problems we try to solve, operates in much the same fashion as does a machine. Everything in Ian's world, including the family, was assumed, then, to contain a structure with fixed and movable parts that were responsible for the shift or application of energy that was "driven" in order to accomplish work efficiently. If his son's family was "falling apart," it was because some *part* was malfunctioning. Someone wasn't carrying his or her share of the load. Or, someone was putting too much pressure on certain parts of the system that could not bear such a load. And so forth.

Problem solving within this model involves a systematic search for the part or parts that are damaged, weak, or missing, and thus responsible for the inefficient shift of energy from one part of the system to another or, in a worst case scenario, for the cacophony of grating noise that is created when the machine is totally breaking down as the parts jam into one another, crack, break, and eventually stop moving. This mechanistic perspective dominated the world view of European and American laypersons and scientists from the seventeenth century until just yesterday.

WORLD VIEWS

Human beings are relatively new to the business of scientific investigation of themselves and the world in which they live. While astronomy has been around for centuries, most of the other sciences are scarcely more than 100 to 300 years old. While relatively short, the amount of time spent in scientific investigation *has* been sufficient to provide us the opportunity in this century to form the astounding idea that *all such systematic investigation is predicated on a belief that we already know what the world is like.* Science proceeds with guidance from a prevailing world view (i.e., a set of beliefs concerning the nature of the world and the way it "works").

Sarason (1981) has acknowledged that one of his professional challenges has been to get his students to understand that they, indeed, *have* a world view. He wants his students to accept that we don't possess a set of accurate understandings about the way things really "are"; we only have a "view." He has noted that the term *world view* is intimidating for some, "associated with erudite minds (e.g., Hegel, Kant, Herder, Marx, Vico) with a proclivity for obscure writing. Less erudite people, regardless of their place and status in society, would rather believe they possess no world view or possess one that is so undifferentiated as not to be dignified by scrutiny or a pretentious sounding label" (p. 49). Happily, Sarason's lament was not nearly so characteristic of the 1980s as it was of the 70s. Many people these days, especially many psychologists, are beginning to find the concept of world view to be scientifically and personally useful.

Many of us are now beginning to understand that the very questions we ask—either personally or in scientific and applied psychology—emerge from a particular world view that is responsible for validating them as well as creating them. In Ian Foerster's time, the prevailing world view would have made it impossible for someone to ask whether the "fact" that electrons whirl about at some distance from a nucleus means that theoretically (and in fact) a tabletop contains more space than matter. If such a question had been even partially fabricated by someone in the early nineteenth century, others who shared the prevailing world view would have invalidated it, undoubtedly providing very uncomplimentary labels for the kind of person who could devise such a question.

As we approach the twenty-first century, we are beginning to get a purchase on the idea that today's most basic truths may well be tomorrow's falsehoods. We operate within a best-guess framework as far as the world is concerned. Developments in science and philosophy have shown the inadequacy of most world views to "stand the test of time." Therefore, we reason that we, too, probably do not own the truth, but rather work within a perspective, possessing only a conventional set of habits about how to go about looking at life.

Each of us is heir to a prevailing world view and a personal one. The prevailing view is one that is owned by all those who share our sociocultural history and location. To a great extent, Western people in our day share a particular set of beliefs concerning the world. For example, among other things, we believe that there is such a thing as subatomic reality, the existence of God cannot be proven to the satisfaction of everyone, and people are capable of destroying themselves and the entire species. Although these ideas only represent a way of looking at things, we believe them to contain immutable truth.

The personal world views that we possess also contain strong beliefs, but these assumptions are more specific. For example, if you are a U.S. citizen and a Republican from New York City, it is likely that you know (i.e., believe) that work

effort and talent are almost always rewarded, that less government is better government, and that New York City traffic problems cannot ever really be solved, only managed.

Preferring the German word for world view, *weltanschauung*, Sarason (1981) wrote:

> One does not choose to have a weltanschauung. It emerges and develops over a lifetime. It may change in certain respects but rarely in regard to its origins and bases, which remain silent and axiomatic. . . . A weltanschauung is not motivated; it is received, imbibed, a kind of given, a basic outline within which motivation gets direction. (p. 47)

Given Sarason's understanding, it is easy to see that personal world views are a bit more mutable than is the prevailing world view we have imbibed. Over time, a Republican may turn to the Democratic party or a northerner may come to adopt the assumptions more often found in the South. In contrast, it is unlikely that the prevailing world view, the more general fabric of assumptions with which we create beliefs concerning the nature of reality, will change to a great degree across our lifetimes. For example, it is unlikely that those who have received the current Western world view will ever come to assume that the existence of God will be proven (one way or another) to the satisfaction of all who live. But whether such views change or not, of importance for the discussion of the history of systems thinking that follows is the understanding that a world view of some sort is always in place, operating in such a way as to stimulate the creation of certain kinds of knowledge while eliminating the possibility of other kinds of knowledge ever being formed.

World Views: A Historical Perspective

John Dewey and Arthur Bentley (1949) have provided one of the best historical introductions to the significant prevailing world views that have guided philosophical and scientific investigation throughout the development of Western civilization. Their historical understandings provide an excellent introduction to the currently emerging world view that relies heavily on systems thinking. Dewey and Bentley talk about the self-actional, interactional, and transactional views that have dominated Western scholarship and thinking.

The self-actional way of looking at things originated with the early Greeks; Aristotle was its most articulate proponent. This world view dominated Western thinking from about the fourth century B.C. until about the seventeenth century A.D. The self-actional world view assumes that things act under their own powers and behave according to their individual natures. They can hardly do otherwise. It was widely and strongly assumed for almost twenty centuries, for example, that a chair remained stationary because it was the nature of the chair—and of most material bodies—to be at rest. If a rock were held in the hand, then dropped, people believed that it would fall to Earth of its own power because its nature was to be at rest upon the Earth. The rock, and all things, moved themselves back in natural directions when disturbed in an unnatural way. People did not question these ideas. They scarcely knew they held them. That is the way the prevailing world view operates. It forms the background from which thought takes shape.

As the seventeenth century came to a close, Sir Isaac Newton successfully promulgated ideas that eventually resulted in a radical change in the prevailing world view. He called the Western world's current assumptions to attention and offered a set of contrasting assumptions that came to dominate thinking for the next 200 years or so. The interactional view that we associate so closely with Newton supposes

that thing is balanced against thing in causal interdependence. The chair that remains stationary in your dining room does so because it is in interdependent balance with forces around it that are trapping it there. Newton asked the world to consider the roles of such factors as atmospheric friction and gravity when considering the chair. It is not that it is the "nature" of the chair to be at rest, he said. Rather, the chair would be in motion if it were not that it was in causal balance with other natural phenomena. (Indeed, he mused, an object outside the Earth's atmosphere might travel on indefinitely if nothing were to stop it or change its course.)

This way of thinking developed in tandem with the machine. It fits beautifully with a model of the world as machine. This is the world that the heartsick parent, Ian Foerster, lived in and solved problems in. This mechanistic, causal world is the one each reader of this book is heir to. The immutable, pervasive ideas that are at its core are those that we are forced to apply to the task of establishing an introductory grasp of the newly emerging world view— the systems view. And sometimes, for any given person, the older received ideas are not adequate to the task of creating or recognizing the newer models of thought.

Dewey and Bentley referred to the emerging view as the "transactional" view in an early attempt to distinguish it from the interactional. They talked about this new way of thinking in terms of a new language that would cease relying on words that split things into artificial parts in an effort to understand the whole. A fundamentally important characteristic that distinguishes this new way of thinking about the world is that unlike the previous two prevailing world views, this one does not rely on the idea of causality as a major tool for making sense out of the world.

The self-actional view gave a lot of attention to the role of causality by assuming that things caused their own actions. While God was the ultimate overseer, everything was the source of its own movement and growth. Likewise, the interactional view was predicated on the notion that causality was central to the way things work in the world. All things are balanced in causal interdependence with other things. For every action there is a reaction; one must always consider a phenomenon in relation to its reciprocal. For example, within an interactional perspective, an observer might see that when you provoke me (cause) I yell (effect), and when I yell (cause) you withdraw (effect), and so forth. Complicated causal chains represent the way things work. And things work very much like a machine works.

Within the newly emerging systems world view, the focus has shifted from attention to what-causes-what to an appreciation for the whole—the system that is assumed in this world view to be different from the mere sum of its parts. An important point here is that within a pure systems view, the "parts" of a system recede in importance. In fact, many systems thinkers now assume that when one is focusing on parts and the way they cause certain effects, one cannot be looking at the system itself (cf. Plas, 1986).

TWENTIETH-CENTURY CONTRIBUTIONS TO THE EMERGING SYSTEMS PERSPECTIVE

What are the factors that have precipitated the transition from the mechanistic world view to the systems view? What has prompted the Western world to begin to change its collective mind (once again) about the basic nature of reality?

Clearly, there has been no Newton, no single person who is substantially responsible for the radical shift in collective perspective. Rather, the causes seem to be multiple. Important sources can be found in early to mid-twentieth-century politics, physics, biology, scientific psychology, and general systems theory and cybernetics.

Sociopolitical Sources

Although there have been multiple transformations within the kind of thought that supports emerging sociopolitical trends in the world today, the one that seems to be most important for a discussion of the history of systems thinking has been the growing reaction to and abandonment of classical positivism—the philosophical world view that concentrates exclusively on observables, assuming that only knowledge gained through sense perceptions can be valid. Auguste Comte is the early nineteenth-century father of positivism, a part of the prevailing nineteenth-century world view that was nicely compatible with the mechanistic notions that were dominating the conduct of science during those days.

Comte believed that biological, physical, and social development was naturally slow, systematic, and progressive. In other words, he assumed that if natural processes of all kinds were not interfered with they would develop in an orderly way in a positive direction. Most of us received this orientation during our enculturation into the society in which we live. We grew up assuming that if things are allowed to develop naturally, progress results. Along with everyone else we assumed that over time things were getting better. Thus, most Western people growing up in the 1920s and 30s assumed, without really thinking about it, that human beings would discover more and more useful knowledge in the years to come. We would figure out how to avoid wars. More material wealth would inevitably become available for everyone. And so forth.

Comte's general orientation to things can be thought of as an anticipatory conservatism. Proper development will naturally occur if the slow, inevitable processes of change are allowed to operate undisturbed. Everything we do today creates a brighter tomorrow. "Progress is our most important product." Comte believed that the motto, *order and progress,* best exemplified the spirit of positivism and he once wrote that he would always be proud that he was the author of that motto (Lenzer, 1975).

The fundamental classic positivist notions that have been called into question during the latter part of the twentieth century include:

1. Objects, "things," need to be the primary unit of study; if something cannot be seen, touched, or heard, it doesn't exist.
2. Developmental change will always yield progress (i.e., something good) if interference does not occur.
3. All "good" progress is slow, incremental, and linear.

As you will see throughout this book, these positivist notions are being replaced these days by ideas that suggest that a more useful unit for study is the relationship rather than the related objects; progress is not necessarily always linear; and that some kinds of enduring change are sudden (e.g., total system changes represented by conversion, revolution, some types of family intervention).

While a discussion of the sociopolitical events that have encouraged the development of a new way of thinking are beyond the scope of this chapter and book, obviously the realization of the potential of nuclear war has forced us to recognize and reevaluate the assumption that progress is inevitable or even that it is our "most important product," and thus a necessary component of the good life.

Physics

Some of the earliest and most startling contradictions of the mechanistic world view have been developed in this century within the field of physics where investigation of reality at the subatomic level has forced the development of radically new theories and philosophies. Chief among these has been a reevaluation of the relationship of the observer to that which is observed and a radical shift away from the belief that the "object" or "thing" is the basic "building block" of reality.

When one is attempting to study phenomena that are too small to be perceived through human senses, the relationship of the investigator to that which is to be studied is complicated and crucial. A relationship between the observer and observed is formed such that the phenomena that become available for study are represented by that relationship. In addition to this complicating dynamic, the old laws of Newton were found to be invalid for applications at the subatomic level, in great part because the solid, material bodies that formed the building blocks of Newton's world and the Newtonian world view cannot be found at the nuclear level of reality. Theoretical physicist Fritjof Capra has described the consequences of this in the following way:

> In contrast to the mechanistic Cartesian view of the world, the world view emerging from modern physics can be characterized by words like organic, holistic, and ecological. It might also be called a systems view, in the sense of general systems theory. The universe is no longer as a machine, made up of a multitude of objects, but has to be pictured as one indivisible, dynamic whole whose parts are essentially interrelated and can be understood only as patterns of a cosmic process. (1982, pp. 77–78)

As developments in modern physics have proceeded, many physicists and other thinkers stimulated by these radically new ideas began to focus attention on relationship rather than object, whole rather than part, change rather than cause.

Biology

The contributions of Gregory Bateson, the biologist - psychologist - anthropologist - theoretician, to the newly emerging world view have been enormous. Within the group of twentieth-century thinkers (across a variety of academic disciplines) who made substantial contributions to the development of systems thinking, Bateson stands out as the one most often consulted and most often quoted. Although his primary identity was as a biologist (Bateson, 1979), the readers of this book will probably be most familiar with his pioneering work in family therapy at the Palo Alto Veterans Center in the 1950s. That work will be described a little later in this chapter during a discussion of the contributions of scientific psychology to the evolution of systems thinking. At this point, a brief look at Bateson's biological contributions is in order.

Bateson's most important contributions in biology have been theoretical. He forces a reevaluation of Darwin's theories by offering a new way of looking at the importance of "context" for the development of an individual and a species. While as yet only partly defined according to Bateson, the idea of context, for him, overlaps with the idea of meaning so that mind and nature are twin aspects of the same phenomenon. Obviously, there is much wholism in his view. Bateson wrote:

And "context" is linked to another undefined notion called "meaning." Without context, words and actions have no meaning at all. This is true not only of human communication in words but also of all communication whatsoever, of all mental process, of all mind, including that which tells the sea anemone how to grow and the amoeba what he should do next. (1979, p. 15)

Bateson believes that we cannot really understand biological processes without understanding what "communication" is truly all about—those processes that all living things participate within when transmitting information within and across individuals and species. As a result of this intense focus on communication, Bateson came to the conclusion that we had to reevaluate the role of language in understanding. Language not only represents the world view in force at any given time, it *is* that world view. Therefore, an inspection of language usage and meaning is crucial for all who wish to think in terms of systems as they attempt to ask and answer questions within their field of interest. Although many others have made this point, Bateson's voice has been a strong one in convincing other theorists to give the role of language primacy when they are thinking about how to develop or use a systems point of view.

Another contemporary theoretician who has made important contributions to a systems orientation within biology is Humberto Maturana (1975; Maturana & Varela, 1980). The original work (with Varela) that stimulated his theoretical interest in systems thinking involved research on communication processes occurring between the retina and brain in the frog. Later, he developed the idea that living systems, when perturbed in specific ways, could leap very quickly to new levels of organization and thus transformation (cf. Prigogine, 1980). He was able to develop his theory and research results as a consequence of insisting on looking at the system as a whole and concentrating on the role of communication processes rather than "things."

Psychology

The roots of systems thinking run deep within the history of psychology. Psychology is the youngest of the major scientific disciplines, just over 100 years old. Because of its youth, its history has been influenced by some of the more contemporary general philosophies and theories; indeed, much of the history of psychology reflects the struggle inherent in the move from the prevailing Newtonian world view to the newer systems view.

Shortly after the turn of the century, Max Wertheimer and his younger colleagues, Wolfgang Köhler and Kurt Koffka, developed what has come to be called *gestalt psychology* (labeled by the German word meaning "whole" or "shape"). Through a series of ingeniously designed studies, the three researchers showed that human beings do not perceive the world as a thing-in-itself. We are dependent on the nature and limitations of our neural organization as we try to make sense out of the world. This idea is a forerunner of a notion now so prevalent within some interpretations of systems psychology—the idea that it is not useful to think of the practitioner and researcher as being completely and functionally separate from the client or the object of study.

This early gestalt idea leads smoothly into the assumption that physical and social reality are "constructed." Reality is as influenced by the person who is perceiving it as it is by what is "actually out there" (cf. Berger & Luckmann, 1972). The observer becomes part of the system that is under investigation. (And most often, the psychological scientist-practitioner's choice of words for describing what is going on represents that relationship.)

Köhler later produced other important gestalt work during an extended stay in the Canary Isles. His famous experiments with chimpanzees involved a series of problem-solving challenges relative to how the chimps might reach bananas that had been placed out of reach but within retrievable distance if sticks lying within the area were to be put together for retrieval purposes. Köhler's work was hailed as a demonstration of the "existence" of insight learning in higher primates. The conclusion was that trial-and-error learning was the method of choice for higher primates, including human beings, only when all the parts of a puzzle were missing. If all parts of a possible solution are available, Köhler claimed, human beings (and chimpanzees) will "restructure the field" rather quickly. "Insight learning" will occur. This idea provided an important impetus for the development of concentrating on the whole, the field, the context (i.e., the system).

During the 1940s, a group of psychologists known as the transactional functionalists (e.g., Ames, 1960; Cantril, Ames, Hastorf, & Ittelson, 1949) produced further groundbreaking work in the area of visual perception that showed that we cannot know the "object" independent of the involvement of the relationship between the observer and that which is observed. The majority of the famous visual illusion experiments that have become a classic part of introductory psychology courses were devised by this group.

Again, the important contribution to the development of systems thinking that was produced by this work was the demonstration that the *relationship* between the one who is doing the looking and that which is seen is inescapably implicated in the phenomenon that is available for investigation. The thing-in-itself cannot be known. What we bring to the perceptual experience influences the "reality" we can know. In addition, the transactional functionalists made much of the context surrounding and supporting the events of perception. The environment becomes part of the system that needs to be understood if we are to understand human behavior.

At the Palo Alto Veterans Hospital in the 1950s, Gregory Bateson and his colleagues (Bateson, Jackson, Haley, & Weakland, 1956; Bateson, 1972) created a psychotherapeutic approach that focused on the family rather than the identified patient, on the system rather than the individual. Out of this grew Bateson's now legendary work on the double-bind theory of schizophrenia. Bateson contended that schizophrenia was a "failure" of communication within the family rather than a "disease" that resided within an individual. He showed that family communication patterns were remarkably similar across all schizophrenic families with whom his group was working at the time. These patterns involved an emphasis on double messages that negated each other (each on a different level of communication). For example, a schizophrenic family member might be told that he or she would be unlovable if caught exhibiting a certain behavior, but if that behavior were not to be exhibited the family member ought to consider himself or herself a failure.

Bateson began to see that communication (often exclusively language based) was the "stuff" of which the family was made and the "stuff" of which schizophrenia was made. One of his most important contributions to systems theory has been the suggestion that communication patterns can be considered functionally representative of the system. That is, *if you are looking for the system, look for the patterns of communication*. This approach is not linear in that action does not proceed in a direct fashion through causal links. Rather, there are feedback loops. The whole is greater than the sum of its parts; the family is different than the mere collection of its members.

In the 1960s and early 70s, several groups began to translate Bateson's ideas into innovative approaches to family therapy (cf. Selvini-Palazzoli, Cecchin, Prata, & Boscolo, 1978; Hoffman, 1981). Exciting developments then began to occur in other therapeutic settings such as the community and school. The chapters that follow provide an excellent overview of the state-of-the-therapeutic-art using a systems perspective. To some degree, either consciously or unconsciously, the approaches reported in this book are indebted to the pioneering work of Gregory Bateson, who believed that a full understanding of a symptom such as schizophrenia could only be achieved if one were to study the system that expresses it. In the case of schizophrenia, that system is composed of family communication patterns.

General Systems Theory and Cybernetics

From 1940 through the early 1960s, Ludwig von Bertalanffy, biologist, mathematician, and theoretician, developed *general systems theory,* an approach that attempts to understand what organization, itself, is all about. von Bertalanffy was interested in organization wherever it is to be found, whether in a cell, a human being, a family, or the Milky Way. Thus, he referred to his work as *general* systems theory since he believed that the principles that governed organization were similar or redundant across all aspects of existence. von Bertalanffy defined this body of thought in a variety of different ways over the years. A definition typical of the way he might have phrased it is that GST is a science of wholeness, a general theory of organization, that seeks to formulate principles that are valid for systems in general regardless of the type of elements or type of forces (energy) within them. Obviously, a meta-goal for von Bertalanffy was the creation of a unified science. He believed that the scientific differentiation that had proliferated during the eighteenth and nineteenth centuries (under the dominance of the Newtonian world view) would eventually be replaced by a single science that was concerned with organization wherever it was deemed to be of scientific interest. This new science would be a systems science.

As mentioned earlier in this chapter, von Bertalanffy believed that the major difficulty facing the systems scientist lay in the impossibility of understanding a system when trying to apply analytic thought processes—and such processes are just the ones that we have been enculturated to bring to bear in our problem-solving situations. Like Bateson, he encouraged systems theorists to discard deductive and inductive reasoning processes that tend to identify parts rather than wholes and tend to result in the development of causal chains as explanatory devices. Reasoning through analogy (sometimes called abduction) seemed to him to be at least a beginning response to the problem. When one uses analogical reasoning, there is a search for patterns, a search for redundancies.

von Bertalanffy's work was very technical as well as abstract. In addition, he often relied on mathematical situations as examples. As a result, until recently his work has not been widely read by those scientists (across all disciplines) who were not theoretically inclined and already persuaded by the possibilities inherent in a systems approach. Lately, more and more scientists and interventionists are turning to von Bertalanffy's writings and are finding them relatively easy to grasp in many ways. The difference in readability now as opposed to 30 years ago lies in the readers' more general acquaintance with these ideas. Most people are now able to bring a more adequate background to a reading of this work than people were able to do during the time that the work was actually proceeding.

von Bertalanffy, Bateson, Margaret Mead, and others were among those who were initially interested in the ideas emerging in the 1940s from the new field called *cybernetics*. A cybernetic system is a self-regulating system. In a cybernetic relation, an output signal (information) acts on an input signal (information) so as to modify future output. A "homing" device is an example of applied cybernetics. Another example is the cruise control mechanism you may have in your automobile. A cybernetic system is distinguished from a classical machine by the nature of the communication feedback processes that are involved. Thus, a cybernetic system seems to have some of the properties of an organic system.

Today, a new field concerned with the cybernetics of cybernetics is promising to have great applicability to systems work across all disciplines (cf. von Foerster, 1973). Within this frame of reference, the observer becomes part of the system in ways that are reminiscent of the earlier gestalt psychology and modern physics work presented earlier in this chapter. Within this model, however, the role of language becomes even more important. The circumscribed system of primary importance is one that is created through a communication system that involves a cybernetic device of some sort and an observer.

A good example is a computer and its user. Together, they create a system that can be understood through investigation of the communication patterns present as the total system (machine and user) sets about the business at hand. The system feeds on itself in a recursive way. (Brad Keeney is a current spokesperson for this point of view relative to psychological intervention. His focus is the family and he sees the relationship of cybernetics system to "user" to be much like that of family to therapist.)

Today, a few people think in terms of

general systems theory as originated by von Bertalanffy when they refer to systems theory. Nonetheless, in many indirect ways, GST has made important contributions to this newly emerging world view and some think of it as the formal beginning of this approach toward understanding reality.

THE HISTORY OF SYSTEMS THINKING AND CURRENT APPROACHES IN PSYCHOLOGY

As mentioned in the previous two introductory chapters, the array of systems approaches that follow are at times vastly different with respect to theoretical approach and intervention techniques. Reasons for this differentiation lie within the history of the development of systems thinking and the nature and function of world views.

In the 1990s we are at the cusp as the Newtonian, mechanistic world view is being replaced by a new way of thinking about the world. As yet, this emerging world view has not reached a satisfying stage of development. Some themes are present; others lag developmentally behind. It is clear to most, however, that systems thinking is going to be an important component of the newly emerging world view. In fact, many think that the term, *systems view,* will become the most accurate label for the set of assumptions that will come to dominate the general way of Western thinking.

What the complete set of assumptions will be can only be conjecture at this point. We await further developments. As a result, current psychological assessments and interventions that are based on a systems perspective are bound to differ quite radically in theory and practice as each relies on a somewhat different set of assumptions about the nature of a system, its organization, and its characteristic processes.

As we have seen, certain processes have been emphasized within some disciplines, while other disciplines seem to have neglected them in favor of concentrating on other issues. For example, some approaches eschew causality in order to concentrate on patterns; others search for multiple causes in order to represent more fairly the contributions of a greater number of parts relative to the whole.

Each of the approaches that follows represents an excellent example of a particular interpretation of systems thinking, given the current state of development of the overall world view. Each of the authors in this collection would respond in a somewhat different way to Ian Foerster's troubles with his son's family all those years ago. Although the differences across writers would be substantial, each would, nonetheless, share a tendency to abandon the classical search for a primary cause, a single person or a single dynamic upon which to rest blame. Each would focus on the nature of the system rather than on understanding the pathological dynamics of an identified patient.

In many cases, the theory supporting a given approach that follows will be easily traced to one of the historical roots presented here. In other cases, the connections will be less clear as the originator of the approach relies on assumptions that are more deeply hidden within the history of psychology (or another discipline) and have not yet received warranted attention. In some cases, an author's assumptions are more uniquely his or her own, representing very contemporary thinking, and as such may constitute a very original theoretical contribution that will be adequately evaluated only in years to come. Indeed, all the work contained in this volume will be subjected to scrutiny in years to come as we struggle to understand our intellectual future and the possibilities it creates for scientific-professional psychology.

Thus, the reader of this volume is in an excellent position to catch a glimpse of psychology's future. No doubt much of that future will be created by—and constrained by—systems thinking. Much of what is most exciting and potentially very useful in contemporary psychology is represented in the chapters to come. Much of it is very new. Yet, as we have seen here, history has prepared the way. Systems thinking has had its roots across the variety of scientific fields that human beings have labored in for some time now. Yet, these ideas are very different ideas from those that have previously dominated our way of thinking. They need careful consideration. Such consideration can be found in the pages that follow.

References

Ames, A., Jr. (1960). *The morning notes of Adelbert Ames, Jr.* New Brunswick, NJ: Rutgers University Press.

Bateson, G. (1972). *Steps to an ecology of mind.* New York: Ballantine.

Bateson, G. (1979). *Mind and nature: A necessary unity.* New York: Dutton.

Bateson, G., Jackson, D. D., Haley, J., & Weakland, J. (1956). Toward a theory of schizophrenia. *Behavioral Science, 1,* 251–264.

Berger, P. L., & Luckmann, T. (1972). *The social construction of reality.* Garden City, NY: Doubleday Anchor Books.

Bertalanffy, L. von (1968). *General systems theory.* New York: George Braziller.

Cantril, H., Ames, A., Hastorf, A. H., & Ittelson, W. H. (1949). Psychology and scientific research. III. The transactional view in psychological research. *Science, 110,* 517–522.

Capra, F. (1982). *The turning point: Science, society, and the rising culture.* New York: Simon & Schuster.

Dewey, J., & Bentley, A. (1949). The knowing and the known. Republished in R. Handy & E. C. Harwood (Eds.), *Useful procedures of inquiry.* Great Barrington, MA: Behavior Research Council, 1973.

Foerster, H. von (1973). Cybernetics of cybernetics (physiology of revolution). *The Cybernetician, 1,* 31–43.

Hoffman, L. (1981). *Foundations of family therapy: A conceptual framework for systems change.* New York: Basic Books.

Keeney, B. P. (1983). *Aesthetics of change.* New York: Guilford Press.

Lenzer, G. (Ed.) (1975). *Auguste Comte and positivism: The essential writings.* Chicago: University of Chicago Press.

Maturana, H. (1975). The organization of the living: A theory of the living organization. *International Journal of Man-Machine Studies, 7,* 313–332.

Maturana, H., & Varela, F. J. (1980). *Autopoiesis and cognition: The realization of the living.* Dordrecht, Netherlands: D. Reidel Publishing.

Plas, J. M. (1986). *Systems psychology in the schools.* New York: Pengamon Press.

Prigogine, I. (1980). *From being to becoming: Time and complexity in the physical sciences.* San Francisco: W. H. Freeman.

Sarason, S. B. (1981). *Psychology misdirected.* New York: The Free Press.

Selvini-Palazzoli, M., Cecchin, G., Prata, G. & Boscolo, L. (1978). *Paradox and counterparadox: A new model in the therapy of the family in schizophrenic transaction.* New York: Jason Aronson.

4

Understanding the Black Family and Child in the School Context

ROBBIE J. STEWARD
University of Kansas

SADYE L. LOGAN
University of Kansas

BEING VIEWED as the only means for both social and economic advancement, the pursuit and acquisition of formal education have traditionally been strongly encouraged within black families and communities across the United States (Ho, 1987). For blacks, education symbolizes hope for a better future. However, such hopefulness is not reflected in the statistics depicting actual levels of education attained.

In 1978, of the 24.4 million blacks in the United States, 52.4 percent of black adults had not completed high school; 9.7 percent had attained less than five years of any formal education; and only 7.2 percent were college graduates (Bureau of the Census, 1979). Those who had attained higher levels of education were found to experience unemployment more often and make less money than white counterparts (Smythe & Smythe, 1976). Black college graduates have been found to be unemployed as frequently as white males who

had not graduated from high school (Langer, Gersten, Green, Eisenberg, Herson, & McCarthy, 1974; National Urban League, 1978). Even when both parents are present and working, as in 52 percent of all black families, only 56 percent of the median white family income is attained. Similar results were found when incomes of middle-class black families were only 81 percent of that of white peers (National Urban League, 1978).

For many blacks, education may or may not provide a better lifestyle than parents or grandparents, for there are seemingly no guarantees. However, it does seem certain that education will not provide a lifestyle quite equal to that of white peers. The message appears clear: No matter how hard one works, equity for U.S. blacks remains elusive for many.

The above reality alone would more than likely be a major contributor to apathy and hopelessness existing within some black communities today. On one hand, black children are exposed to early teaching and media purporting education as the way—the hope for a better future. On the other hand, they are also able to observe the results of failed attempts of those around them as well as the limited monetary and status gains experienced by those who have been successful in moving through school. Educational institutions could realistically be perceived as entities to be approached with skepticism and challenge, but to approach nonetheless. This approach-avoidance conflict existing within the relationship between many black students and the school system and the resulting academic and adjustment difficulties (particularly predominantly white school systems) would seem "natural" given the proliferation of contradictory information in daily reality.

As with all students, black students' academic failures can occur for many other reasons than that presented above. However, the purpose of this chapter is to increase readers' understanding of the unique experience of black students within the predominantly white school system and to provide suggestions for intervention in the face of academic and adjustment problems that black students might experience in moving through such a system.

THE BLACK STUDENT AND THE SCHOOL SYSTEM: A HISTORICAL OVERVIEW

Prior to the 1900s, a poor quality of education, educational failure, and school dropouts within the black community were not viewed as problems. This was primarily due to the fact that the social, economical, and political ecological realities for black families during that time were vastly different than they are today. For example, although black heads-of-households were relegated to the lowest level of the job market, it was possible for most to earn a living and take care of a family without the benefits of an education. But times have changed. This change began with the impact of the Industrial Revolution and became increasingly more evident with the current explosion of scientific and technological advances that impact all aspects of our lives in significant ways. But more importantly, technological change in the area of information is viewed by some as deskilling (Hill, 1987). This dire view is based on the Bureau of Labor Statistics forecast that in 1990 there would be four times as many new jobs for janitors, fast-food workers, and waitresses (1.2 million) as compared to 250,000 jobs for computer analysts and programmers (Hill, 1987). The implications are obvious. Future high school and college graduates must be highly prepared educationally to compete effectively for these scarcer and better jobs. Of equal importance, however, is the need for high-level interpersonal skills that are necessary prerequisites to obtaining a job as well as maintaining effective on-job relationships (Jones & Jones, 1970).

Comer (1985) points out that the period extending from 1865 to 1915 was diametrically different for black Americans than for European and Asian immigrants due to political freedom. This important factor served to shape the life changes of blacks. Essentially, blacks were denied access to economic, political, and educational opportunities. This period also paralleled the course of the Industrial Revolution, which caused a dramatic shift in the job market. Workers were viewed as being displaced from the farm to the factory and needing at least a modicum of education to secure and maintain a job.

The lack of consistent economical, political, and educational opportunities for blacks resulted in a segmented black America: the "haves" and the "have nots." The "haves" in black America are generally referred to as *upwardly mobile* and in the middle- to upper-income bracket. During the beginning of the twentieth century and beyond, this segment of black America experienced a sense of togetherness, pride, organization, and purpose through participation in the black church and other social and fraternal organizations within the black community. Further, these families were financially solvent, experienced a sense of well-being, and provided a nurturing environment in which children were able to take advantage of educational opportunities and be better prepared to participate in the labor market. As a result, they were better equipped to prepare their children to participate more effectively in subsequent generations.

The "have nots" constitute a disproportionate number of black Americans who are generally referred to as the *working poor* and the *underclass*. In addition to the debilitating effects of enslavement, the problems and needs of this segment of the black population were further exacerbated by a closed opportunity structure and a nonnurturing environment. For example, this segment of black America was least prepared to utilize the strong social network within the black community as well as the insufficient jobs and educational opportunities within the larger society.

Research and experience have shown that the aforementioned political and economic realities of the black experience in the U.S. society have had an inverse impact on the educational achievement of black Americans. To fully appreciate the impact of these ecological realities on black access, achievement, status, and other educational concerns, it is necessary to examine the interactional process between black educational achievement and such salient factors as poverty, racism, and the black family.

Poverty

The debilitating effect of poverty is shaping the life experience of nearly 12.5 million children and their parents; half of all black children are poor (Children's Defense Fund, 1985). Evidence shows that children raised in poverty are likely to experience a number of psychosocial stressors (Jones, 1981). At greatest risk are children born into one-parent households, particularly to teenage women. These parents cannot afford adequate daycare and often children are left for extended time with little or no supervision. The home environment may contain little or no educational or sensory stimulation and life experiences usually do not extend beyond the block where they live. Therefore, when these children attend school, they are at risk for school failure.

However, despite the recognition today that they are not "culturally deprived" (implying that they lack any sense of social structure and culture) but are "culturally different" from mainstream U.S. values, norms, and behaviors, schools still vie this diversity as a deficit to be changed rather than strengths upon which to build (Coalition of Advocates for Students, 1985). Children are expected to adapt quickly or be written off as failures. Often, children are further penalized if they speak with a black dialect. This difficulty not only creates problems in understanding the teacher but also invariably leads to being evaluated negatively or testing lower. According to available evidence, teachers are also biased against poor children and (1) expect less of them academically, (2) reinforce their low self-esteem and acting-out behavior, and (3) instill in them a sense of failure and feelings of inferiority (Brookover, Beamer, Efthim, Hathaway, Legatte, Miller, Passalacqua, & Tornatzky, 1982). According to the Children's Defense Fund (1985), poverty is a greater child killer than traffic accidents and suicides combined. The results are social and psychological problems for children at home as well as in school.

Racism

Racism is perhaps the most devastating social reality impacting the life changes of
black families and children. As indicated
earlier, blacks have historically been excluded and devalued as human beings in
U.S. society. For example, as recently as
the 1940s, blacks were still subjected to a
range of human degradation as extreme as
lynching and as pervasive in nature as separate toilet and drinking facilities (Comer,
1985). These conditions have had a devastating impact on the black psyche. Essentially, the consequences of racist social
policies and programs have handicapped a
significant portion of the black community.

Examples of these handicaps are reflected in all aspects of black life, but for
our purposes the focus will be especially on
the educational system. The numerous
education reform reports consistently
agree that racial discrimination remains a
serious hindrance to quality education for
black children. The general profile evolving from these reports depicts a discouraging portrait of such discrimination (Children's Defense Fund, 1985):

- Some 80 percent of the black children in this country are educated in
  less than 4 percent of the school districts.
- Only 8.5 percent of all teachers are
  minorities.
- Black children tend to start out on
  par with white children in regard to
  intellectual endowment and psychosocial support, but drop below
  grade-level expectation by latency
  age and continue to fall further behind as they get older.
- The national dropout rate for blacks
  in high school is nearly twice that of
  whites.
- At the high school level, blacks are
  suspended three times as often as
  whites.

It has been noted that the official policies
and practices in the nation's educational
system have resulted in significant resegregation of the schools, which perpetuates
the aforementioned profile as well as a
tracking and sorting system where whites
are relegated to upper-level courses and
blacks to lower-level courses (Coalition of
Advocates for Students, 1985).

Hard questions are being asked
about discrimination and differential
treatment of children in the educational
system. Within this context it has been
noted that public education has changed
drastically since the Supreme Court de-
clared that the doctrine of "separate but
equal" had no place in the education of the
nation's children; however, concerns are
being raised from all segments of society
about the quality of public education.
Although the evidence suggests that
schools, more than ever before, are more
diverse in terms of representation of race,
language, culture, and levels of physical
and mental disabilities, it further suggests
that the majority of these children are of
low socioeconomic status and the education of nearly all of them may be characterized as inferior (Coalition of Advocates for
Students, 1985).

These findings are not encouraging.
However, it is imperative that these statistics be examined within a context. Logically, explanation may be sought from a variety of perspectives. It is suggested here
that these problem areas be viewed in an
ecological context, which also includes a
deeper understanding of the black family.

The Black Family and
Community Life

In order to understand the black child,
one not only needs an appreciation of his
or her family and community life but also
an understanding of black child development. It is suggested here that in order to
obtain such a perspective, two broad-based

assumptions must be adopted about the black family and the black community.

Assumption 1: Black families are not homogenous nor do they have a uniform set of experiences. There is no such entity as *the* black family. Black families represent a diverse mixture of ethnic groups and cultures, with the majority being descendants of enslaved Africans from West Africa. Within this context, the diversity within and among black families may be viewed in terms of values, personal characteristics, lifestyles, religious influences, regional influences, socioeconomic status, level of acculturation, family size and structure, and age. These rich differences among black families have evolved out of a unique sociocultural and economic background. As indicated earlier, this unique background includes an African as well as a mainstream or Euro-American cultural heritage, coupled with the experience of slavery and a continuous manifestation of institutional racism, as evidenced in structural unemployment, neighborhood and housing patterns, and numerous forms of subtle human degradation.

Traditional research on black family life has consistently attempted to perpetuate the notion of a lower-class subculture in which the standards of behavior are assumed to be a normative and a generic representation for black culture. Essentially, black Americans have evolved a set of beliefs, values, attitudes, and standards of behavior that were necessary to survive in a hostile environment (Chestang, 1972). It is within this functionally adaptive context that current researchers are acknowledging the strong, intact, resilient kinship system of blacks that existed in urban and rural communities from slavery until a few years before the great depression (Hill, 1972; Genovese, 1974; Gutman, 1976).

Contemporary studies on black families continue to describe viable functional systems (Billingsley, 1968; Geisman, 1973;

McAdoo, 1978; Stack, 1974). However, it is important to acknowledge that numerous black families are experiencing a great deal of external as well as internal stress. It is these systemic strains that help to create diversified family forms and proactive coping devices. The following proactive devices have been described by Hill (1972) and further elaborated on by other researchers (Gary, Beatty, Berry, & Price, 1983; McAdoo, 1978; Royce & Turner, 1980): (1) strong kinship bond, (2) strong work, (3) adaptability of family roles, (4) strong achievement orientation, and (5) strong religious orientation.

Assumption 2: Black communities and neighborhoods are not homogenous entities. Billingsley (1968) has utilized the concept of ethnic subsociety to describe the black community. This concept underscores the diversity that exists within black communities in terms of social class, region, and place of residence. Essentially, the day-to-day existence of black families is carried out in diverse neighborhoods, ranging from the affluent to varying stages of decay and deterioration. In a sense, black communities reflect a variety of lifestyles and experiences for the inhabitants based on the availability or lack of resources. Despite what researchers have referred to as lack of cohesiveness within black communities, there appears to be a degree of strength that is inherent on two broad levels.

First, there is the tendency to informally adopt children and to incorporate nonfamily into the family household (Billingsley, 1968; Hill, 1972). Second, there is a pervasive assumption that people are doing the best they can. In short, the community residents care about each other and will lend a helping hand. This caring is reflected in the supportive network of black self-help organizations. Thus, it is important to be able to conceptualize the black community as a valuable source of support for children and families.

In summary, the black community provides the people with the roots of their existence. Interdependence among community members for emotional and physical support as well as an education in life is expected (Solomon, 1976). When all is well emotionally and financially and members are adequately fulfilling perspective roles, as in all family systems, homeostatis is maintained with little effort and all members benefit regardless of need. But, in the face of crises and/or increases in dysfunctional/nonfunctioning membership, adjustments are made that well may be detrimental to the well-being of the entire black family unit. Such negative consequences could also contribute to the potential for academic failure of the black student.

THE IMPORTANCE OF A CONCEPTUAL FRAMEWORK

In counseling students from black families, it is most important to recognize the intricate and sometimes complicated bond that exists between the black student, his or her family, and the broader environment. We believe that to appreciate fully and recognize those qualities that are culturally unique in black families, those qualities that black families share with mainstream America as well as qualities of the impinging environment, an expanded context is required.

Conceptually, the ecological framework allows for this broader context. Such a framework focuses on the social process of interaction and the transactions between the factors impacting the growth and development of the black child (Figure 1) and the child's environment (including but not limited to the school, family, and community; see Figure 2) (Gordon, 1969). This perspective also encourages multiple interventions within systems.

According to Germaine (1973), practitioners stand at the interface not only to the child and school but to family and school and to community and school. As many other practitioners do, the authors believe that in order to understand the work effectively with black families, educators and practitioners must be willing to expand the context in which teaching and treatment occur and to broaden the definition of their roles (Aponte, 1979; Bennett, 1975; Stein, 1974). Those significant others in the lives of the black child must be cognizant of the effects various external systems have on the child and his or her family. They, too, must join and work with systems other than the school

PRACTICE PRINCIPLES AND CONCEPTS USEFUL FOR EFFECTIVE INTERVENTION WITH BLACK FAMILIES

As a practitioner working with black students and families, it is most important to recognize the intricate and sometimes complicated bond that exists between the black student and the absent family unit. It is imperative to remember that the practitioner is privy to only part of the complete story when only the student is present, and to make any assumptions based on past experience with other black students or students in general could be detrimental to the development of a positive relationship with the student or the family. This would not only fail to assist in productive change but may well impair students' abilities to perform academically.

Because black students and family units are strongly interdependent, an important first step in assessing the reasons for a client's presence is to arrange, with the client's awareness, a session with will-

The Person (The Black Child)

- Incorrect racial self-identification
- Individual life-cycle tasks
- Quality of self-image
- Coping style, including trust level and hope in life
- Developmental milestone
- Personality characteristics
- Boundaries
- Values, beliefs, and attitudes

←——— Transaction (Process) ———→

The Social Environment

- School and other institutions
- Mass media
- Stresses and demands
- Quality and type of social networks
- Societal and/or cultural norms, values, and attitudes
- Historical milieu (racist experiences)

The Sibling System

- Life-cycle needs
- Personality characteristics
- Child-parent relationship
- Peer relationships
- Relationship to extrafamilial world
- Boundaries

The Parental System

- Life-cycle needs
- Spousal or partner relationship
- Parent-child relationship
- Boundaries
- Personality characteristics
- Attitude, values, and beliefs

The Family System

- Economic, social, and educational level of the family
- The extended family
- Culture, emotions, and intellectual quality of the home
- Power structure
- Communication (values, beliefs, attitudes)
- Boundaries
- Interpersonal relationship
- Degree of individuation
- Acceptance of separation and loss
- Problem-solving capacity

The Family Life Cycle

- Stage
- Cultural factors
- Needs and problems

FIGURE 1 Factors impacting the education of black children
Adapted from Logan (1989).

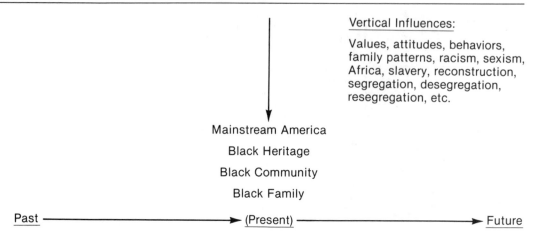

Vertical Influences:

Values, attitudes, behaviors, family patterns, racism, sexism, Africa, slavery, reconstruction, segregation, desegregation, resegregation, etc.

Mainstream America

Black Heritage

Black Community

Black Family

Past —————————————→ (Present) —————————————→ Future

Horizontal Influences:

Life-cycle events, the economy, education, polity, acute and chronic illness, early death, lack of nurturing, etc.

FIGURE 2 An ecological framework for viewing black families
Adapted from Logan (1989).

ing key people in the student's daily life. These individuals might be of assistance in clarifying and understanding the presenting problem, as well as serving as some assistance in bringing about change in the improvement of current academic performance and emotional well-being.

In the case where the family has been referred, it would be critical to have the individual responsible for the referral present, or at least some message from him or her that clearly states the reasons for this action. (Often black clients find themselves shuffled from agency to agency, and between professionals without ever knowing the reasons.) Although all members present at this particular session may not be present in the following session, this initial session could assist in:

1. Overriding any natural tendency on the practitioner's part to immediately develop assumptions about reasons for black students' academic or emotional adjustment difficulty based on previous personal and/or professional experience

2. Providing the practitioner with the opportunity to assess the extent of students' support network

3. Providing the practitioner with the opportunity to observe the students' interaction with significant others

4. Giving the practitioner the opportunity to offer interest in becoming a part of the family unit and developing a collaborative relationship in the best interest of the student

5. Allowing the practitioner to make some assessment of the extent to which he or she can become a member of the student's family system

6. Identifying the student's strengths and weaknesses as perceived by the student, family members, and other attenders

7. Developing an understanding of the student's future goals as perceived by the student, family members, and other key support members.

Afterwards, information may be gathered about the student's self-perceptions and other-perceptions, as well as the perceptions of others about the student. The presence and the absence of certain people would provide the practitioner with information about the existing support network, and all present would be validated for attending and encouraged to continue in their support. Such an introductory session would allow the practitioner to identify more accurately targets of intervention: the student, the family system, the surrounding community, or various combinations of the three. By inviting the possibility of a complete picture into the initial session, the practitioner can receive a picture comprehensive enough to increase effectiveness in assisting the client. However, practitioners must be prepared personally as well as professionally in order to take on such a large task.

First, practitioners must be genuine in the expression of concern about a client's cause for being present and sincere in committing to working with the client toward identified goal(s) (Carkhuff, 1969; Vontress, 1970; Wiltmer, 1971). Black clients have historically had a negative relationship with the field of mental health, and may often justifiably harbor feelings of distrust (Patterson, 1973; Russell, 1970; Tolson, 1972). This initial distrust also has a tendency to increase sensitivity to incongruence between facial expression, body language, behavior, and what is actually said. More merit is given to what is seen by the client as opposed to what is said by the practitioner. Any deceit on the part of the practitioner may immediately be detected by the client and sever even the slightest possibility for the development of a working relationship.

Such deceit may well be unintentional. Practitioners may have good intentions, but be unaware of prejudicial or stereotypical thinking and relay such messages in the process of "helping" clients. A practitioner then may be perceived as incompetent and services would terminate prematurely.

Second, practitioners must be proficient in being process oriented and relational as well as content oriented and directive in the relationship with a black client (Smith, 1985). During initial sessions it is critical that the interpersonal rules for interaction be identified and adhered to by the practitioner; violation of such rules will slow or hinder the process of becoming a part of the family system. An example might be the rule that traditional black families have of giving esteem to elders by maintaining formal titles of Mr., Mrs., or Miss before first or last names. Doing differently without being given permission would be seen as disrespectful and generate additional mistrust. One long-standing rule used to clarify rules within another culture: When in doubt, ask! This is preferable to making a false assumption, acting on it, and losing the client as a consequence.

Process skills would also play a major role in clarifying rules by identifying who speaks to whom, relaying what, and in what manner. Such would be very important in increasing each client's awareness of personal impact and the relationship to the problem. However, on the other hand, being aware of information and being comfortable sharing such information as expert would be essential in assisting in problem solving in areas of survival and support. Often knowledge about other assistance or contacts within the environment is essential. For example, telling parents that a child should not be responsible for maintaining a household or caring for younger siblings would be a major mistake that could lead to termination. (This would be the result of focusing on content only.)

Being process oriented would aid the practitioner in recognizing parental overload and identifying the need for help. This, in turn, could result in identifying other resources for assistance in some areas that might alleviate some of the family pressures. Knowing when to be process oriented as opposed to content oriented is highly dependent on the practitioner's skill level in following the client's lead as needs are presented. Competency in doing so is crucial.

Third, practitioners must be able to (1) respond spontaneously, (2) use "normal" vocabulary, (3) be brief, (4) be to the point, and (5) remain relatively present oriented (Stikes, 1972). Given that black families usually approach counseling when they are in crisis and have immediate needs, counseling that focuses on the past or that presents deep-seated roots of present behavior using psychological jargon would benefit none. Practitioners must be able to follow clients and attend to what is presented.

Fourth, practitioners must be aware of black family dynamics (Lewis & Lewis, 1970), particularly those related to academic achievement (Greenberg & Davidson, 1972):

1. Parents maintain a quality of communication that tends to stimulate the child's problem-solving ability, independence, and productivity.
2. There are frequent occurrences of the expressions of warmth, interest, affection, and encouragement.
3. Close family ties exist.
4. There is maintenance of some structure and order for the child.
5. Goals of performance are established.
6. Control mechanisms are used, including giving assistance when requested or when the need is perceived.

Practitioners must also be effective in identifying such dynamics behaviorally within the context of each unique family system and use this information in evaluating the plan of action mutually developed by both the practitioner and client.

Fifth, practitioners must have some realistic understanding of the negative environmental factors that impact the lives of black people in the United States on a daily basis. It is important that those involved in the lives of black children not assume a color-blind perspective. Such does not allow for an appreciation of those distinguishing qualities and experiential conditions of ethnically different students that influence their learning styles, intellectual endowments, cognitive perceptions, and classroom behavior. Gay (1975) states that for those black children labeled as school failures, the problem is more a result of conflicting messages about how and what children should learn as well as the difficulties involved in making the transition from "home living" to "school living." Racism must be acknowledged as a real force within predominantly white America today, and not only an issue of the past.

Using all of the above skills, practitioners must then be able to assess the psychological status of the identified client (student), the psychological status of the family system, the extent of the cooperation and influence of the community support network, and the contribution of the academic environment to the client's present academic and/or adjustment difficulties.

DEVELOPING INTERVENTION STRATEGIES

After the initial assessment, a practitioner can more clearly identify the point(s) of necessary intervention to rectify a client's difficulty in comfortably fitting into the unique system of the academic environment. Intervention could occur at one or all of the following possible levels: the student, the family, the community, and/or the school system. In order to illustrate student difficulties at each of these levels and possible intervention strategies, examples of student issues and sample therapeutic responses by the practitioner are presented next.

Even when the black family is consistently engaging in all of the previously mentioned supportive behaviors and the student is academically prepared, difficulty in adjusting to a nonresponsive predominantly white environment can lead to academic failure. Consider the following case study.

CASE STUDY 1

Sheila, a 17-year-old junior, is a new student who has recently moved to the area. Her parents have called you, the practitioner, in order to schedule an appointment because of their concern about Sheila's failing grades and difficulty adjusting to the new school. They are particularly concerned because Sheila's previous cumulative GPA was 3.85 (and she scored 27 on the ACT). All three of them will attend the first session.

Intervention Step #1: Assess the academic environment.

Before the session, you approach Sheila's teachers in order to gather some information about Sheila's behavior in the classroom and attain a sense of the teachers' and students' reactions and responses to Sheila in the classroom. She is described as attractive, well-dressed, very poised, and initially very capable of articulating her re-

sponses to questions and her ability to ask provocative questions that result in much class discussion. Her grades had always been within the top 5 percent in all of her classes but have consistently dropped after mid-semester, as she has become less and less interactive. She appears to be a loner. No effort had been made to find out reasons for the behavior change.

Intervention Step #2: Conduct the interview.

After scheduling the initial session, Sheila and both parents attend. The following information is attained: Sheila's relationship with her parents is warm and supportive. Her parents are both very successful, upwardly mobile professionals who have recently attained better positions. (The present school has less than a 2 percent minority population. This composition is reflective of the surrounding community where Sheila and her family have recently moved.) Sheila is an only child and has attended only private black schools. Although she has lived in predominantly white neighborhoods, her connection with the black middle-class community had been strong.

Both sets of grandparents are college graduates from predominantly black institutions and continue to live in the city from which Sheila's family has recently moved. Sheila's parents received undergraduate degrees from predominantly black institutions, however, received graduate degrees from a well-known predominantly white university.

The decision to move was made only after much deliberation, but has been very difficult for them all. Sheila hesitantly admits that she was presently experiencing some reactions from others that she had never experienced prior to this semester. She had not mentioned it to her parents before, being respectful of their difficulty in making the adjustment to the new environment.

Intervention Step #3: Enlist the support of the school system.

Rubovitz and Maehr (1973) found that black gifted achievers receive less attention and are least supported and most criticized in the classroom, even when compared to their nonachieving and nongifted black counterparts. Therefore, one key intervention strategy would be to engage in some collaborative efforts to assist Sheila in developing some sense of belongingness in the academic environment (especially given the lack of responsiveness by most of the teachers you have approached). An example might be to approach teachers and staff regarding Sheila's difficulties in order to enlist their support in assisting in her adjustment into the new school environment. It is especially important that this is presented as your interest in developing a collaborative relationship with you, the practitioner, and Sheila in order to generate alternative strategies to make the academic experience easier for her.

Intervention Step #4: Assist the family.

Another focus of intervention would be to identify minority (black, in this case) organizations and social networks in the surrounding community. This would serve as a means of assisting the family in making a smoother psychological transition from the home community to the new environment.

Intervention Step #5: Assist the student.

It is apparent in this case that Sheila is experiencing difficulty in accepting the reality of racism and not being accepted by peers. Offering her the opportunity to discuss experiences and to assist in developing some strategies for identifying and dealing with both blatant and subtle racism would provide her with the necessary sup-

port until an adequate support network has been established.

There are many creative ways of attending to Sheila and her family. However, initially it is most important to acknowledge that the problem of racism is real and that there are some effective means of dealing with those who are hurtful regardless of the reasons.

In conclusion, academic failure is not always the result of lack of academic preparedness, but due to environmental influences. Black students learn more from the school system than reading, writing, and arithmetic. In addition to these skills, black students must acquire those that contribute significantly to the ability to cope effectively within future predominantly white environments.

The strong interdependence between the black student and the family unit is not always apparently beneficial to individual members when viewed by outsiders; in fact, it may be detrimental to the growth and development of the child. During periods of crisis or when there is an increased membership of dysfunctional/nonfunctional individuals, family members are required to make necessary adjustments for the good of the whole. Homeostatis may be maintained, sometimes at the expense of individual members.

The student, at such times, must assume additional responsibilities ordinarily reserved for adults, in addition to other daily responsibilities. Fair or not, this is a reality for many black students and making those oft-times burdensome adjustments can result in receiving high praise from family unit members because of exemplified loyalty to the family unit. This would be particularly true if praise were being received from elders who are held in high esteem in the community. When optimal family unit functioning is maintained and the family unit's priority is to care for its own at all costs, the outcome can be very expensive for the black student, especially if the school system is not structured to accommodate such crisis periods. Consider the following case study.

CASE STUDY 2

Susan has been referred to you because of an increased number of absences, which has resulted in a drastic drop in GPA since Susan has missed several homework assignments and scheduled tests. An initial session with Susan and her visiting grandmother is scheduled. Her grandmother states that she is a representative of the parents. Both are very glad that an interest was expressed in Susan. The grandmother congratulates you for being so nice to do so. Every attempt made by you to focus on Susan and school is met with how proud she and the family are of Susan, especially how she helps the family.

Susan has recently moved from her hometown in order for her parents to seek better job opportunities. Her father had been laid off from his old job. Susan is the third eldest daughter of five children. Her younger siblings are in preschool. Her two eldest sisters have moved from home, are married and have children of their own. However, recently one has had to move back home with two children due to marital problems. She is pregnant and very sick, and is unable to work. The doctor has recommended that she do very little or the baby's life could be jeopardized.

Susan's grandmother has come from out of town (hometown) to help take on some of the additional load, but has to return soon. Susan says that she will miss her grandmother a great deal. When grand-

mother leaves, Susan will assume a large amount of the responsibility for childcare and cleaning. She may have to take a part-time job in order to help make ends meet until her sister is able to get some financial assistance.

Both parents work in positions that most likely pay minimum wage. Neither was able to come. Susan's father also has an additional part-time job. The family is praying that something will come through very soon. The hour ends and very little that you really wanted to accomplish during the introduction session was addressed.

Intervention

It is important to acknowledge any negative reactions related to thinking about the unfairness of a child being overburdened with adult responsibilities. This scenario could be commonplace in the black family because (1) children are perceived as financial assets (Bullock & Rodgers, 1975); (2) it is acceptable to ask children to "bear much" in the name of family as a strategy of developing discipline and the emotional "hardening" necessary to survival (Billingsley, 1968; Grier & Cobles, 1968; Martin & Martin, 1978; Shimkin, 1978); and (3) emphasis is on taking care of those within the family who are needy, especially in the case when no real sense of community has had time to develop (Martin & Martin, 1978; Shimkin, 1978).

Engaging in judgment and struggling with the unfairness of the situation only results in inaction; however, it is action that Susan needs.

1. Relay the important message of "I care" to Susan and at least one key family member. This is very important.
2. Since you are aware of Susan's family system and the parents' willingness but inability to come in for a meeting, it would be important to schedule another session with Susan alone in

order to ask the information that was missed.

3. In addition to asking Susan how she would think such additional responsibilities would interfere with academic performance, it would be beneificial to brainstorm together to give you a clearer perception of Susan's perception and how the two of you might intervene in order to best benefit her.

4. Generate creative ways in which you can assist Susan and her family by working with teachers and the school system to:
   a. allow Susan to know assignments far in advance of the due date.
   b. identify ways Susan can verify reading assignments (i.e., by writing summary papers).
   c. identify contact people (other students) who could bring in assignments during absences.
   d. identify students who would be able and willing to serve as tutor for coursework where Susan is weak.
   e. help Susan's family create a sense of community (i.e., by identifying possible free childcare options and contacting local churches to see who might be available to visit Susan's sister during the day or bring a meal).

5. Positively reinforce all of Susan's efforts to continue school in spite of added responsibilities.

6. If prayer is seen as an option, encourage and validate Susan in doing so (Larsen, 1976).

7. Remember that the family system is in crisis and intervention strategies at this point should be immediate. Focusing on Susan's future in terms of vocational training, college, career, and so on is secondary. Focusing on Susan's past would be inexcusable. Intervention should include behaviors that will assist her in getting through the present semester.

With Susan's permission, periodically send a letter to her family reflecting concern for the family situation, explaining how you have worked to restructure coursework requirements in respect for their present difficulties, and addressing Susan's strengths, positive qualities, and progress. This will assist busy family members in staying abreast of what is happening in their child's life. (It is important to note that, in this case, without any intervention the probability for failure increases significantly.)

Sometimes a family is totally unavailable and unresponsive to all efforts of contact on the part of the school system personnel and practitioner. The following example is not as positive or as optimistic as the previous two examples. Students may be failing or exhibiting some disciplinary problems and be asked or required to appear without the support of parent(s) or any school personnel representative. Although the prognosis in this case is poorer than in the other examples presented, maintaining some level of optimism is critical. The practitioner's interest in the student must be established with sincerity and some level of optimism must be maintained. Attempts to understand all of the issues that the student presents, the expression of genuine interest in those issues, and consistent validation of any attempts by the student to play the academic game may be the only hope for this student's academic future. Consider the following case study.

CASE STUDY 3

A teacher has referred John, a 12-year-old sixth-grader, and his mother (a single parent) to you for disciplinary reasons and poor academic performance. John is reported to disrupt class consistently by talking disrespectfully and abusively to other students and the teacher, who has made several attempts to contact John's mother without success. John began this behavior at the beginning of the year in a teasing manner, but has escalated this behavior into full-blown abuse. The principal has also attempted to contact John's mother with little success. When a contact is made and an appointment is set, she fails to come in. Now the telephone has been disconnected. A letter has recently been sent recommending contact with the counselor.

John and his teacher arrive one day after a fight breaks out in class due to John kicking another student. The teacher appears angry and leaves immediately. John states that he does not know why his mother does not respond. Rumor has it that John's mother is an alcoholic and is presently unemployed.

Intervention Step #1: Address the student as a person.

In this case, it is critical to first connect with John in some personal way that does not directly address the reasons for his presence. This strategy addresses John as a person and not as one who is a problem or who has a problem. In doing so, you will most likely be providing an unique experience that he may need in order to alter his abusive interaction style. An example of an opening statement might be: "Hello, John. A lot seems to be going on between you and your teacher right now, but before we get to that, tell me a little about yourself. What kinds of things do you like to do for fun? What do you do when you're not in class?"

This line of questioning would hopefully lead to the opportunity for you to express more interest in John as a person, as well as find some common ground of interest. It is also important that you look for strengths within the child or within his family. These strengths can be built on and used as a positive force in moving beyond feelings of hopelessness.

Intervention Step #2: Address the current situation.

Next, it is critical to address John's feelings about having to be in the office, his reasons for the meeting, and his reasons for the disruptive behavior. Information gathered here would serve as a vehicle to understanding John's side of the story and also serve as a reality check of John's perceptions.

Intervention Step #3: Address the future.

Depending on what happens as a result of Step #2, short- and long-term goals of your relationship with John could be established in terms of future meetings. It is important that you relay the message of wanting to be an ally, and not an adversary.

Intervention Step #4: Address the teacher.

Set up appointments with teachers who interface with John and allow them to express their perceptions about the cause of the behavior, to get a sense of what has been tried to stop the behavior, and to provide some insight about John's relationships with classmates in general. This serves two purposes: (1) it provides teachers the opportunity to share and (2) it enlists their support in attending to John's lack of fit to the school system at the current time.

Intervention Step #5: Attend to the family.

Even though letters fail to elicit responses from John's mother, a home visit may be another viable alternative in order to enlist her support. There could be many reasons why a single, unemployed, parent may have difficulty attending an appointment, and to assume disinterest without investigation may be in error. Even in cases where parents do not respond, contact with parents should be maintained in order to relay the status of their child, the problem, and progress made.

Continued interaction with the student and home visits may result in the identification of other family and/or community members who may be willing to act as support in place of the parents. In cases where there is some parental response, you may enlist the support of available community resources to assist the family in receiving whatever additional help necessary. In these cases it is important to remember that the more comprehensive the intervention strategies, the more likely a successful outcome will occur.

CONCLUSION

Given that most practitioners' training does not include instruction in cross-cultural treatment, that most mental health professionals have had very little contact with those outside of their own culture of origin, and that most trainees are from white middle-class backgrounds, it would seem imperative to encourage professionals to engage in some additional activities to decrease the ignorance about other groups and, as a result, to appreciate better the culturally differences. The authors recommend the following:

1. Engage in self-examination in areas of values, biases, and prejudicial thinking and increase awareness of the negative impact of these on others (Rosen & Frank, 1962; Sager, Brayboy, & Waxenberg, 1972).

2. Courageously challenge yourself as well as the system to become more accepting of ethnic and racial differences.

3. Commit to expanding your knowledge base in cross-cultural issues and multicultural education (Lewis & Lewis, 1970; Rousseve, 1965; Vontress, 1969).

4. Recognize that although racial and ethnic differences do exist, attention to individual differences is crucial to the development of the therapeutic relationship.

These must occur in order to assure a more responsible mental health profession, a healthier and more productive society, and consequently a better future for us all.

References

Aponte, H. (1979). Family therapy and the community. In M. Gibbs & J. Lachenmeyer (Eds.), *Community psychology: Theoretical and empirical approaches*. New York: Gardner Press.

Bennett, J. (1975). *The new ethnicity: Perspectives from ethnology*. St. Paul: West.

Billingsley, A. (1968). *Black families in white America*. Englewood Cliffs, NJ: Prentice-Hall.

Bowen, M. (1976). Theory in the practice of psycho-therapy. In P. Guerin (Ed.), *Family therapy: Theory and practice*. New York: Gardner Press.

Brookover, W., Beamer, L., Efthim, H., Hathaway, D., Legatte, L., Miller, S., Passalacqua, J., & Tornatzky, L. (1982). *Creating effective schools: An in-service program for enhancing school learning climate and achievement*. Holmes Beach, FL: Learning Publications, Inc.

Bullock III, C., & Rodgers, H. (1975). *Racial equality in America: In search of an unfulfilled goal* (pp. 172–173). Santa Monica, CA: Goodyear.

Bureau of the Census, Statistical Abstract of the U.S.: 1979. (1979). Washington, DC: Government Printing Office.

Carkhuff, R. R. (1969). *Helping and human relations, Vol. 1: Selection and training*. New York: Holt, Rinehart, and Winston.

Chestang, L. (1972). *Character development in a hostile environment.* Chicaco: University of Chicago, School of Social Service Administration.

Chestang, L. (1976). The black family and black culture: A study of coping. In M. Satomayor (Ed.), *Cross-cultural perspectives in social work practice & education.* Houston: University of Houston, Graduate School of Social Work.

Children's Defense Fund. (1985). *Black and white children in America: Key facts.* Washington, DC: Government Printing Office.

Clark, C. (1972). Black studies or the study of black people. In R. Jones (Ed.), *Black psychology.* New York: Harper & Row.

Coalition of Advocates for Students. (1985). *Barriers to excellence: Our children at risk.* Boston: City Municipal Government.

Cole, B. P. (1983). The state of education for black Americans. *Education 84/85, annual editions.* Guilford, CT: Dushkin.

Comer, J. P. (1985). Empowering black children's educational environments. In H. P. McAdoo and J. L. McAdoo (Eds.), *Black children: Social, educational, and parental environments.* Beverly Hills: Sage.

Delgrado, A. (1982). On being black. In F. Yamamoto and L. Evan (Eds.), *Effective psychotherapy for low income and minority patients.* New York: Plenum.

Gary, L., Beatty, L. A., Berry, G. L., & Price, M. D. (1983). Stable black families: Final report. In *Mental Health Research and Development,* edited by Institute for Urban Affairs and Research. Washington, DC: Howard University Press.

Gay, G. (1975). Cultural differences important in education of black children. *Momentum,* pp. 30–33.

Geisman, L. L. (1973). *555 families: A social-psychological study of young families in transition.* New Brunswick, NJ: Transaction Books.

Genovese, E. (1974). *Roll Jordan Roll.* New York: Pantheon.

Germaine, C. (1968). Social study: Past and future. *Social Casework, 49,* 403–409.

Germaine, C. (1973). An ecological perspective in casework practice. *Social Casework, 54,* 323–330.

Gordon, W. E. (1969). Basic constructs for an integrative-generative conception of social work. In G. Hearn (Ed.), *The general systems approach: Contributions toward a holistic conception of social work.* New York: Council on Social Work Education.

Greenberg, J., & Davidson, H. (1972). Home background and school achievement of black urban ghetto children. *American Journal of Orthopsychiatry, 42,* 803–810.

Grier, W., & Cobles, P. (1968). *Black rage.* New York: Basic Books.

Gutman, H. (1976). *The black family in slavery and freedom: 1750–1925.* New York: Pantheon Books.

Haskins, J. (1974). *Witchcraft, mysticism & magic in the black world.* New York: Doubleday.

Hill, R. B. (1972). *Strengths of black families.* New York: Emerson-Hall.

Hill, R. B. (1987). Building the future of the black family. *American Visions, 2*(6), 16–25.

Ho, M. (Ed.) (1987). Family therapy with black Americans. In *Family Therapy with Ethnic Minorities.* Beverly Hills: Sage.

Jones, F. (1981). External cross-currents and internal diversity: An assessment of black progress, 1960–1980. *Daedalus, 110*(2), 71–101.

Jones, M. H., & Jones, M. C. (1970). The neglected client. *Black Scholar, 1,* 35–42.

King, J. (1976). African survivals in the black American family. *Journal of Afro-American Issues, 4,* 153–167.

King, J. (1979). African survivals in the black American family: Key factors in stability. In G. Henderson (Ed.), *Counseling ethnic minorities.* Springfield, IL: Charles Thomas Publisher.

Langer, T. W., Gerten, D. J., Green, E. I., Eisenberg, J. G., Herson, J. J., & McCarthy, E. D. (1974). Treatment of psychological disorders among urban children. *Journal of Consulting and Clinical Psychology, 42,* 170–179.

Larsen, J. (1976). *Dysfunction in the evangelical family: Treatment consideration.* Paper presented at the meeting of the American Association of Marriage and Family Counseling, Philadelphia.

Lewis, M. D., & Lewis, J. A. (1970). Relevant training for relevant roles: A model for educating inner-city counselors. *Counselor Education & Supervision, 10,* 31–38.

Logan, S. (1989). Assessing black family forms. In S. Logan, E. Freeman, & R. McRoy (Eds.), *Social work practice with black families.* New York: Longman.

McAdoo, H. (1977a). *The impact of extended family variables upon the upward mobility of black families: Final report.* Washington, DC: Department of Health, Education and Welfare,

Office of Child Development, Contract no. 90-C-631(1). December.

McAdoo, H. (1977b). Family therapy in the black community. *Journal of American Orthopsychiatric Association, 47,* 74–79.

McAdoo, H. (1978). The impact of upward mobility of kin help pattern & the reciprocal obligations in black families. *Journal of Man & Family, 4,* 761–776.

Martin, E., & Martin, J. (1978). *The black extended family.* Chicago: University of Chicago Press.

National Urban League (1978). *The state of black America 1977.* New York: Author.

Patterson, L. (1973). The strange verbal world. *Journal of Non-white Concerns, 1,* 95–101.

Rosen, H., & Frank, J. D. (1962). Negroes in therapy. *American Journal of Psychiatry, 119,* 456–460.

Rousseve, R. J. (1965). Counselor education & the culturally isolated: An alliance for mutual benefit. *Journal of Negro Education, 4,* 395–403.

Royce, D., & Turner, G. (1980). Strengths of black families: A black community perspective. *Social Work, 25,* 407–409.

Rubovitz, P., & Maehr, J. (1973). Pygmalion black and white. *Journal of Personality, 23,* 210–218.

Russell, R. D. (1970). Black perception of guidance. *Personnel & Guidance Journal, 48,* 721–728.

Sager, C. J., Brayboy, T. L., & Waxenberg, B.R. (1972). Black patient—White therapist. *American Journal of Orthopsychiatry, 42,* 415–423.

Shimkin, D. (1978). *The extended families in black societies.* The Hague: Mouton Publishers.

Smith, E. M. J. (1985). Ethnic minorities: Life stress, social support, and mental health issues. *The Counseling Psychologists, 13,* 537–539.

Smythe, M., & Smythe, H. (1976). *Black-American reference book.* Englewood Cliffs, NJ: Prentice-Hall.

Solomon, B. (1976). *Black empowerment.* New York: Columbia University Press.

Stack, C. (1974). *All our kin.* New York: Harper & Row.

Staples, R. (1976). *The black family: Essays & studies: Vol. 2.* Belmont, CA: Wadsworth.

Stein, K. (1974). *Systems theory, science, & social welfare.* Metuchen, NJ: Scarecrow Press.

Stikes, C. S. (1972). Culturally specific counseling—The black client. *Journal of Non-White Concerns, 1,* 15–23.

Tolson, N. (1972). Counseling the disadvantaged. *Personnel & Guidance Journal, 50,* 735–738.

U.S. Department of Education (1987). *Schools that work: Educating disadvantaged children.* Washington, DC: Author.

Vontress, C. E. (1967). Counseling negro adolescents. *School Counselor Journal of Negro Education, 38,* 266–275.

Vontress, C. E. (1969). Cultural differences: Implications for counseling. *Journal of Negro Education, 37,* 266–275.

Vontress, C. E. (1970). Counseling blacks. *Personnel & Guidance Journal, 48,* 713–720.

Wiltmer, J. (1971). Effective counseling of children of several American sub-cultures. *School Counselor, 19,* 49–52.

5

Asian-American Students: Family Influences

MAN KEUNG HO
University of Oklahoma

ASIAN-AMERICANS are often perceived as sharing the same or similar characteristics, but they actually are comprised of many diverse groups: Chinese-, Japanese-, Korean-, and Filipino-Americans, and Samoans, Guamanians, Hawaiians, and other Pacific Islanders. Other groups include recent immigrants and refugees from Vietnam, Thailand, Cambodia, Laos, and Indonesia; persons from India, Pakistan, and Ceylon; and children of mixed marriages where one parent is Asian (Marishima, 1978). There are obvious language, historical, social, and economic differences. Generational status (new immigrants versus third and fourth generation) among groups and individuals should not be overlooked.

Asian-American students can present some difficulties that require assistance from mental health professionals and indicate the need for counseling or at least consultation with the family and others. Before initiating counseling or other interventions with Asian-American students, professionals need to develop an ecosystemic understanding of the Asian-American students and their families and to appreciate their individuality.

An ecosystem viewpoint considers individuals in relation to their immediate family and in consideration of the broader cultural, ethnic, and ecological context. The interplay of the family, with its ethnic ties in the public schools, and the helping agency person is especially important. Relevant ecosystemic viewpoints have been presented by Fine (this volume), Lusterman (1985), and Mannino and Shore (1984). The importance of considering family's ethnicity when offering professional services has been underscored in the family therapy literature (McGoldrick, Pearce, & Giordano, 1982).

ECOSYSTEMS: UNDERSTANDING ASIAN-AMERICAN STUDENTS AND THEIR FAMILIES

Population

The Asian-American population has doubled since 1970, now comprising about 2 percent of the total U.S. population (3.5 million), and continues to increase. The population distribution of Asian-Americans in 1970 and 1980 is shown in Table 1.

TABLE 1   Asian-Americans in the United States, 1970 and 1980

Year	Chinese	Filipino	Japanese	Korean	Vietnamese	Samoan	Guamanian
1970	435,062	343,060	591,290	70,000[a]	N.A.[b]	N.A.	N.A.
1980	806,042	774,652	700,974	354,593	261,729	41,948	32,158

Source: U.S. Bureau of the Census, "U.S. Summary," Characteristics of the Population: 1980, Vol. 1, (Washington, DC: U.S. Government Printing Office, May 1983), pp. 9–20.
[a]Estimated
[b]N.A. = not available

In 1970 the most populous Asian-American group was the Japanese (591,290), followed by the Chinese (435,062) and the Filipinos (343,060). In 1980, however, the Chinese were the most numerous (806,042), followed by the Filipinos (774,652) and the Japanese (700,974). The Koreans showed a five-fold increase from an estimated 70,000 in 1970 to 354,593 in 1980. Other Asian groups identified by the U.S. Census, but who are not included in Table 1, are the Asian-Indians (361,531) and the native Hawaiians (166,814).

The Immigration Act of 1965 and the U.S. policy on refugees that resulted from the Vietnamese War are primarily responsible for the rapid Asian-American population increase in this country. Most Asian-Americans live in West Coast and East Coast urban areas and in Hawaii. There was a concentrated effort by the U.S. government to scatter recent Southeast-Asian immigrants throughout the country. The majority were resettled in California (135,308), Texas (36,198), and Washington state (16,286).

Socioeconomic Issues

Selected socioeconomic characteristics of Asian-Americans are provided in Table 2.

Asian-American families are more likely than either black or white families to have children under age 18. One out of every ten Asian-American households is headed by a female whose spouse is not present. Asian-American households that are headed by women are less likely to include children than households headed by black and Hispanic women. Asian-Americans make up the smallest proportion of people without a high school diploma and the largest proportion of those with at least one college degree.

Despite comparatively high national unemployment rates, a relatively large proportion of Asian-Americans are part of the labor force. Asian-American women are less likely to be employed outside the home than men. The median income of an Asian-American household is $2,000 above the national average. Proportionally, Asian-Americans own fewer homes than their white counterparts.

Historical Influences

The Chinese were the first immigrants from Asia to arrive in the United States during the 1840s. Their immigration from China was encouraged by the social and economic unrest in China at that time and by overpopulation in certain provinces (DeVos & Abbott, 1966). During this period, there was a demand in the United States for Chinese to help build the transcontinental railroad. However, a diminish-

TABLE 2 Selected socioeconomic characteristics of racial and ethnic groups in the U.S., 1980 (Percentages)

Characteristics	Ethnic and Racial Groups			
	White	Black	Asian and Pacific Islanders	Hispanic
Family Type				
Families with children under 18 years	49.4	61.0	61.5	67.8
Female-headed households; no husband present	11.1	37.3	10.9	19.8
Female-headed households with children under 18 years	56.1	68.8	56.5	72.6
Education				
Persons 25 years or older with less than high school degree	31.3	49.4	25.8	56.7
Persons 25 years or older with at least a college degree	17.2	8.4	32.5	7.6
Employment				
Persons 16 years or older in labor force	62.2	59.2	66.3	63.4
Unemployed persons 16 years or older	5.8	11.7	4.8	9.1
Females 16 years or older in labor force	41.5	48.4	45.0	39.1
Income				
Median income	$20,840	$12,618	$22,075	$14,711
Persons living below poverty level in 1979	9.4	30.2	13.9	23.8
Persons who own homes	67.8	44.4	51.5	43.5

Source: U.S. Bureau of the Census, *1980 Census Population Supplementary Reports PHC 80-S1-1— Provisional Estimates of Social, Economic, and Housing Characteristics: States and Selected Standard Metropolitan Statistical Areas* (Washington, D.C.: U.S. Government Printing Office, 1982), pp. 47, 100.

ing labor market and fear of the "yellow peril" made the Chinese immigrants no longer welcome. Chinese men were robbed, beaten, and murdered, especially if they tried to compete with whites in the mining districts of western states.

This anti-Chinese sentiment culminated in the passing of the Federal Chinese Exclusion Act of 1882, the first exclusion act against any ethnic group. This racist-immigration law was not repealed until 1943, as a gesture of friendship toward China who was an ally of the United States during World War II. The Immigration Act of 1965 finally abolished national-origin quotas; "old-timer" immigrants were characterized as primarily uneducated peasants, unskilled laborers, and men. Post-1965 immigrants have been well-educated, urban families (Lai, 1980).

Early Japanese immigrants came to the United States from 1890 to 1924, after the Chinese exclusion laws. They left a rapidly industrializing country as "contract laborers" for the plantations in Hawaii. Legislation similar to the anti-Chinese acts was passed against the Japanese. Anti-Japanese prejudice culminated in the forced removal in 1942 of over 110,000 Japanese, 75 percent of them American citizens, to guarded relocation centers. Unlike the Chinese, Japanese immigrants were allowed to start families, employing the "picture bride" (bride selected by photograph) method of marriage. Consequently, the acculturation process of their American-born children occurred much earlier than for immigrant Chinese children. Hence, in general, the Japanese are more acculturated than the Chinese, even though the Chinese have been in this country for a longer time.

The Filipino population in the United States grew most rapidly after the Immigration Act of 1965. As a result of the Spanish-American War and the Treaty of Paris (1899), the Philippines at one time was actually a possession of the United States until the Tydings-McDuffie Independence Act conferred commonwealth status on the Philippines. Filipinos then became aliens for the purpose of U.S. immigration. The earliest Filipino immigrants were unskilled laborers or students who were encouraged by the U.S. colonial government to attend U.S. colleges and universities (Melendy, 1980).

Immigrants who came in the 1960s were mostly young professionals, both men and women. Many of them experienced difficulties in obtaining U.S. licenses to practice their profession. The majority of the surviving early Filipino immigrants are now retired, living in cheap hotel rooms and small apartments. They experience health-care problems, limited recreational opportunities, and physical and psychological isolation.

The number of Korean immigrants just prior to the Immigration Act of 1965 was slightly over 7,000 (Kim, 1980). A high proportion of them were Christians, because American missionaries in Korea played a major role in their immigration. Kim (1980) estimated that 90 percent of the Korean immigrants have been here less than 15 years—since the Immigration Act of 1965 went into effect in 1968. The largest Korean community, with a population over 150,000, is in Los Angeles. Generally, Korean post-1968 immigrants have had to endure less hostility and structural discrimination than the early Chinese and Japanese immigrants.

The Pacific Islanders include groups such as Samoans, Tongans, Guamanians, and a small number of Tahitians and Fijians. Samoan immigration began to increase in 1951 when the U.S. Navy closed its island base. Guamanian immigration was facilitated by the 1950 Organic Act, which conferred U.S. citizenship on inhabitants of the territory of Guam. Because of their ties with the church of Jesus Christ of Latter-Day Saints, many Tongans have settled near Salt Lake City, Utah. The Pacific Islanders as a group are relatively few in number and have no visible strong ethnic community in the United States today.

Southeast Asians from Cambodia, Laos, and Vietnam came to this country primarily as refugees. Statistics of 1980 indicate 415,238 Indochinese are in this country, 78 percent of which are from Vietnam, 16 percent from Cambodia, and 6 percent from Laos. The majority of them have settled in California, Texas, and Washington (Montero & Dieppa, 1982). Cambodia, Laos, and Vietnam were part of the old French colonial empire and were lumped together as French Indochina. Cambodian culture was influenced by India, whereas the people of Laos are mainly ethnic Thai. The Vietnamese culture was heavily influenced by

China. The exodus of Vietnamese refugees began in 1975 with the fall of Saigon and U.S. withdrawal from the country. The first wave of refugees were mostly well-educated professionals. A second wave was admitted to this country after 1975 and consisted of less-educated people. The latter group has experienced more difficulty than the first group in adjusting to the United States.

Racism and Discrimination

The designation of Asian-Americans as a minority group that has experienced prejudice and discrimination is misunderstood by many who fail to assess accurately the status of Asian-Americans and to conceptualize racial discrimination. Asian-Americans have had a history of exploitation and racism in the United States (Lyman, 1977). Federal legislation has often restricted Asian immigration or, as in the case of the 1924 Immigration Act, prohibited their immigration entirely. Asian immigrants were placed in the category of "aliens ineligible for American citizenship." Alien land laws completed the nightmare in that "aliens ineligible for citizenship" were denied the right to own property. Antimiscegenation laws, which prohibited interracial marriages, were passed. More than 110,000 Japanese-Americans were relocated in detention camps during World War II.

Restrictions against Asian-Americans covered many other areas of life as well. Employment and housing opportunities were limited, and the full use of public and private facilities was denied. Such structural, social, and psychological constraints relegated Asian-Americans to second-class status.

Gains in civil rights and civil liberties occurred only after World War II. Today, Asian-Americans are often considered "model" minorities (Asian American Advisory Council, 1973), but many still face discrimination and prejudice (Kim, 1978).

Asian-American Culture

School counselors should focus on understanding the cultural values, belief systems, and societal norms of American culture as well as Asian traditional culture. In an attempt to understand Asian-American students and to work effectively with this unique ethnic group, Ho (1976) lists seven salient cultural values operating among Asian-Americans. These indigenous cultural values are described below.

1. *Filial piety.* The respectful love of parent is the cornerstone of morality and is expressed in a variety of forms. *Oya-KoKo,* a Japanese version of filial piety to parents, requires a child's sensitivity, obligation, and unquestionable loyalty to lineage and parents. An Asian child is expected to comply with familial and social authority, even to the point of sacrificing his or her own desires and ambitions.

2. *Shame as a behavioral influence.* Shame (*tiu lien* in Chinese) and shaming are used traditionally to help reinforce familial expectations and proper behavior within and outside of the family. Should an individual behave improperly, he or she will "lose face" and may also cause the family, community, or society to withdraw confidence and support. In Asian societal structures, where interdependence is very important, the actual or threatened withdrawal of support may shake a person's basic trust and cause him or her considerable anxiety at the thought of facing life alone

3. *Self-control.* Self-discipline is another concept highly valued by Asian-Americans. The value *enryo* requires a Japanese individual to maintain modesty in behavior, be humble in expectations, and show appropriate hesitation and un-

willingness to intrude on another's time, energy, or resources. To *Yin-Nor* for a Chinese is to evince stoicism, patience, and an uncomplaining attitude in the face of adversity, and to display tolerance for life's painful moments.

4. *Middle-position virtue.* In training children, Asian parents emphasize a social norm that cultivates the virtues of the middle position, in which an individual should feel neither haughty nor unworthy. Middle-position virtue is quite different from perfectionism and individualism, which are highly valued by middle-class white Americans. Asian-American emphasis on middle position brings an individual in step with others instead of ahead or behind others. Thus, it fosters an individual's sense of belonging and togetherness.

5. *Awareness of social milieu.* As Asian's concern for the welfare of the group is also related to his or her acute awareness of social milieu, characterized by social and economic limitations and immobility. The individual is highly sensitive to the opinions of peers and allows the social nexus to define his or her thoughts, feelings, and actions. In the interest of social solidarity, the Asian subordinates himself or herself to the group, suppressing and restraining any disruptive emotions and opinions. Despite an individual's wealth and social status, compliance with social norms (which provide him or her with social esteem and self-respect) is strictly observed.

6. *Fatalism.* Constantly buffeted by nature and by political upheaval over which they had little control, Asian-Americans adopted a philosophical detachment. This resignation allowed people to accept their fate with equanimity. Other than trying to philosophize or to ascertain underlying meaning in life events, the Asian met life pragmatically. It is unfortunate that this pragmatic adaptability, the very factor that contributed to success

in the United States, later became a serious handicap. The Asian-Americans' continuing silence only let them fall further behind in an alien U.S. culture that encouraged and, indeed, demanded aggressiveness and outspoken individualism. This fatalistic attitude of Asian-Americans has partly contributed to their unwillingness to seek outside professional help. Unfortunately, the Asian's pragmatic adaptability is often misconstrued as resistance by some mental health and social service providers.

7. *Inconspicuousness.* Fear of attracting attention was particularly acute among the thousands of Asian immigrants who came to the United States illegally. Experiences with racist segments of U.S. society further convinced the Asian immigrant of the need for and value of silence and inconspicuousness. Fear and distrust still linger today among the descendants of early immigrants. It is understandable why Asians are extremely reluctant to turn to government agencies for aid, even in cases of dire need. Asian-Americans' silence and inconspicuousness tend to make them verbally passive members in politics, group work, and community activities.

Family Structure and Influences

The cohesive extended network of the traditional Asian-American family is structured and prioritized with male dominance and parental ties paramount. A male child has distinct obligations and duties to his parents that assume a higher value than obligations to his siblings, children, or wife. Sibling relationships are considered next in priority and are frequently acknowledged through cooperative adult activities. Concepts and teachings, such as working hard, responsibility, family obligations, and collaboration, pervade parent-child relationships. Members of the older generation are responsible for transmitting guidelines for socially acceptable behavior, educating younger people in how to deal with life events, and serving as a source of support in coping with life crises (Coelho & Stein, 1980). A traditional Asian-American family becomes the primary caretaker of its members' physical, social, and emotional health.

The traditional Asian-American family structure provides stability, interpersonal intimacy, social support, and a relatively stress-free environment for its members (Hsu, 1972). However, the process of immigration and cultural transition exerts a severe blow to these families. Relatives and close friends are often no longer available to provide material and emotional support to needy members. The traditional hierarchical structure and rigidity of family roles often make the expression and resolution of conflicts within the nuclear family very difficult. Little or no interpersonal interaction outside of the nuclear family, in turn, forces greater demands and intense interaction *within* the nuclear family. This can leave members highly vulnerable and with many unresolved conflicts.

Discrepancies in acculturation between husband and wife and between parents and children negatively affect the decision making and functioning of a family. An individual's acceptance of and compliance with western values such as individualism, independence, and assertiveness (especially in attitudes related to authority, sexuality, and freedom of choice) make the hierarchical structure of a traditional Asian-American family dysfunctional.

While an Asian-American family undergoes several stages in its attempt to help its members, different families may have different service needs and help-seeking patterns. Generally, there are three types of Asian-American families in the United States (Ho, 1987):

1. *Recently arrived immigrant families.* Initial request for services by this type of family tend to be predominantly requests for information and referral, advocacy, and other concrete services such as English-language instruction, legal aid, and childcare. Due to cultural differences, unfamiliarity with mental health resources, and language barriers, these families seldom seek personal or psychological help.

2. *Immigrant-American families.* These families are characterized by foreign-born parents and American-born children and a great degree of cultural conflict between them. They usually require help in resolving generational conflicts, communication problems, role clarification, and renegotiation.

3. *Immigrant-descendant families.* The families usually consist of second- (Japanese *Nisei*) or third- (Japanese *Sansei*) generation American-born parents and their children. They speak English at home and are acculturated to western values. They can seek help from mainstream human service agencies, mental health centers, and private practitioners with some degree of comfort.

Problems and Adjustments of Asian-American Students

In addition to the normal problems and adjustment that every student must face in a school environment, Asian-American students face additional problems with cultural conflict (Yao, 1985). Jones (1982) believes that many forms of culture conflict are really manifestations of cultural racism. Although there is nothing inherently wrong in acculturation and assimilation, he believes that "when it is forced by a powerful group on a less powerful one, it constitutes a restriction of choice; hence, it is no longer subject to the values of natural order."

Sung (1987) found that young Chinese students exhibited anxiety over the inability to reconcile the Western values of independence with their feelings of filial piety and family obligation. They also reported feelings of social isolation and feelings of passivity in schools and in social situations.

In an attempt to combat social isolation and gain a feeling of belonging and acceptance, an Asian-American student is forced to find reference groups in the United States. He or she may identify entirely with traditional Asian culture, or reject Asian culture as old fashioned and dysfunctional. He or she may adopt U.S. values exclusively, or become bicultural. Unfortunately, regardless of what value system a student adopts, there are potential adjustment problems.

ECOSYSTEMIC INTERVENTION WITH ASIAN-AMERICAN STUDENTS AND THEIR FAMILIES

School counselors or other mental health professionals who work with Asian-American students need to have firsthand knowledge of how this unique ethnic minority group has traditionally responded to psychological and counseling services. It is also advisable for professionals to be familiar with traditional help-seeking behaviors of Asians. MoKuau (1987) has warned that a student's orientation to the process of help seeking and the "fit" between traditional paradigms and those utilized by providers may be critical to successful process and outcome.

Studies indicate that Asian-Americans seeking counseling services were more severely disturbed than Caucasians (Okimoto, 1975). There is a tendency for Asian-Americans to somatize so that stress and tension are frequently turned into physical complaints (Sue & Sue, 1971). In personality measures, Asian-American students have indicated more feelings of isolation, loneliness, anxiety, and emotional distress than Caucasians (Sue, Ino, & Sue, 1983).

In spite of their many psychological and counseling needs, Asian-American students do not generally turn to school counselors for assistance. Literature on minority counseling indicates that western modes of service delivery have not been effective (Bromerly, 1987). Low utilization and early termination of services by Asian-American students support this premise (Sue, 1981).

Implications for Professionals

The foregoing discussion cautions professionals concerning the need for knowledge and sensitivity when intervening with Asian students and their families. Particular concern with the indications of help seeking and accepting behavior by the Asian-American students and families needs to be considered.

Although family structure and function may vary, the professional can apply existing frameworks (e.g., Minuchin & Fishman, 1981) to understand the nature of a given family. In particular, the concept of "joining" becomes very important in working with a family system that tends to view "outsiders" with suspicion and apprehension.

The professional's caring and empathic posture remains vital as a vehicle for communicating a respectful attitude toward the family. The focus on helping the individual child needs to occur in consideration of the implications of change for the family, and in terms of how the family can accept and support such changes. The following case example illustrates counseling with Asian-American students employing an ecosystemic approach.

CASE STUDY

According to a report by two teachers, Vin Tran, an 11-year-old Vietnamese fifth-grader, was experiencing school problems. His problems included failure to turn in homework, tardiness, poor concentration, daydreaming, and sudden and frequent temper tantrums. The teachers were puzzled because Vin normally was a "model" student.

Vin's problem began about two months ago. He had been a quiet student but exhibited no language difficulty, and he seemed well acculturated. Two teachers talked to Vin separately, attempting to find out the causes of his sudden change of behavior. Vin refused to volunteer any information and became teary when pressed with further questions. The teachers then referred Vin to the school counselor for consultation.

The school counselor had a positive rapport with Vin because he had once helped with two Vietnamese students who had a mild school adjustment problem. When the counselor saw Vin in her office, Vin kept his head down and avoided looking at her. The counselor empathized by commenting that Vin must be troubled by something unusual. He said he intended to do his homework and promised to do better in the future. He volunteered no other information. The counselor responded that she was more concerned about Vin's total well-being than just his homework. She also told him that she understood and respected his difficulty in talking about his feelings at this moment. She asked if he would object if she arranged a meeting with his parents. Vin tearfully nodded his head and said, "You can talk to mom." The counselor agreed.

Mrs. Tran, Vin's mother, was anxious and apologetic when she met with the counselor. Mrs. Tran spoke English fairly well and volunteered that she understood Vin had not been doing well at school and that he was also having behavioral problems at home. The counselor empathized by stating that Mrs. Tran must be puzzled, as the school personnel were, about Vin's sudden change of behavior.

Mrs. Tran apologized again saying she had not been "much of a mother" to Vin the last few months after her husband had moved out to live in an apartment with another Vietnamese woman. The counselor responded by saying that it must be difficult for her to cope with this new change. Mrs. Tran replied that since her husband moved out, she had been sleeping and eating poorly. Also, she had to take additional medication for her colitis problem. Vin's mother felt that the turmoil at home and her bad physical and emotional health had contributed to her son's tardiness at school. She also commented that she too had been wanting to talk to the school counselor to get her advice on how to handle Vin's behavioral problems at home. The counselor suggested some single-parenting skills, and Mrs. Tran promised that she would try to implement them and that Vin would improve at school.

Two weeks after the counselor's interview with Vin's mother, no apparent improvement was evidenced in Vin's school performance and behavior. The counselor called Mrs. Tran for another appointment.

Again, Mrs. Tran was apologetic to the counselor about the lack of improvement in Vin's school behavior and her behavioral management of him at home. "If it were not for my husband, I would never be able to handle Vin at home," volunteered Mrs. Tran. The counselor inquired if Mr. Tran had returned home and lived with the family again. Mrs. Tran replied that her husband had not moved back home, but that he would come regularly and promptly if she called on him for disciplinary assistance whenever she got into conflict with Vin. Mrs.

Tran also suggested that Mr. Tran might not be a good husband, but that he was a very good, responsible father. "Vin minds only his father," volunteered Mrs. Tran. The counselor responded, "Vin misses his father and you (Mrs. Tran) miss your husband." Mrs. Tran cried and avoided eye contact with the counselor.

After Mrs. Tran left the meeting, the counselor realized the ecosystemic factors that contributed to Vin's negative change of school performance and to his mother's lack of motivation and effort in carrying out the school counselor's suggestions for single parenting. Mrs. Tran was saddened by her husband's rejection of her and by the disharmony at home. She missed her husband and needed him very much to be the head of the household. The only way she could manage to see him was to call on him to discipline her son. This opportunity provided the only hope and function to reunite the family. As much as Mrs. Tran wanted to see Vin's behavior improve, she was not willing nor ready to forego the only opportunity to see her husband and possibly reunite the family.

Vin's acting-out behavior also served a function: to repair his parents' marriage and to reunite the family. Had his behavior improved, his mother would have no excuse to call on his father and he would not see his father as often. The counselor's intervention so far had been linear (i.e., helping the mother to change her son's behavior). The counselor realized now that the new intervention needed to be circular or ecosystemic and involve the father.

To safeguard the father from losing face over moving out of the home, living with another woman, and contributing to his son's misbehavior, the counselor contacted the father for an individual interview.

Mr. Tran was frail but gentle. He was a school teacher in Vietnam but could only secure janitor work in this country. He spoke English fairly well but with great hesitancy. The counselor acknowledged his interest in assisting his son. Mr. Tran readily recognized his son's problem and he apologized for the trouble his son had caused the school.

The counselor appealed to Mr. Tran for his cooperation in assisting his son. Mr. Tran related that he had done his best to help Vin whenever his wife called on him, and he solicited the counselor's suggestions. The counselor explained to Mr. Tran the dynamics behind his son's problems and validated Mr. Tran's behavior and positive intention toward his son.

In further discussion, the counselor made suggestions for ensuring a proper father-son relationship while the father was not living at home. Mr. Tran agreed to a conference with both his son and his wife present. The meeting took place three days later. The purpose of the conference was for Mr. Tran to reassure his son that despite his separation from his wife, he still cared for him and wished to maintain a good relationship with him. Mr. Tran suggested that he and Vin see each other twice a week, once at Vin's mother's home and once outside of the home. Mr. Tran also informed his wife that he would no longer rush in to resolve the mother-son conflicts when his wife called. He told Mrs. Tran he had yet to make a final decision regarding his marriage despite the fact that he no longer lived with the other woman.

Mrs. Tran was ambivalent about Mr. Tran's decision, but she agreed to comply with the plan for the sake of Vin's school performance and behavior. Vin was also ambivalent about the new plan but was delighted that he would be seeing his father twice a week.

The counselor met with the family two more times during the next three-week period. The teachers and Mrs. Tran reported that there was a marked positive change in Vin's behavior and that Mr. Tran had been visiting Vin at home more than once a week. Vin's parents eventually began marital therapy to improve their marriage.

SUMMARY

Counseling and other interventions with an Asian student require that professionals have an ecosystemic understanding and appreciation of the student's individuality, sociopolitical background, culture, and family influences. The interplay of the student and his or her family with public school officials and all helping professionals is especially important. Professionals should be particularly sensitive to the help-seeking and help-receiving behaviors of the ethnic minority client.

As the case study shows, assisting a student requires that helping professionals consider how the entire family will accept and support changes, and examine the implications these changes have for both the student and family. A caring, nonassuming, and empathetic attitude is essential for any professional working with an Asian student and family.

References

Asian American Advisory Council. (1973). *Report to the governor on discrimination against Asians.* Seattle: Author.

Bromerly, M. (1987). New beginnings for Cambodian refugees or further disruptions. *Social Work, 32,* 236–239.

Coelho, G., & Stein, J. (1980). Change, vulnerability, and coping: Stresses of uprooting and overcrowding. In G. Coelho (Ed.), *Uprooting and development.* New York: Plenum Press.

DeVos, G., & Abbott, K. (1966). *The Chinese family in San Francisco.* DSW dissertation, University of California, Berkeley.

Ho, M. (1976). Social work with Asian Americans. *Social Casework, 57,* 195–201.

Ho, M. (1987). *Family therapy with ethnic minorities.* Beverly Hills: Sage.

Hsu, F. (1972). *American museum science book.* Garden City, NY: Doubleday.

Jones, J. (1982). *Prejudice and racism* (p. 166). Reading, MA: Addison-Wesley.

Kim, B. (1978). *The Asian Americans: Changing patterns, changing needs.* Monclair, NJ: Association of Korean Christian Scholars in North America.

Kim, H. (1980). Koreans. In S. Thernstrom et al. (Eds.), *Harvard encyclopedia of American ethnic groups* (pp. 601–606). Cambridge, MA: Harvard University Press.

Lai, H. (1980). Chinese. In S. Thernstrom et al. (Eds.) *Harvard encyclopedia of American ethnic groups* (pp. 217–234). Cambridge, MA: Harvard University Press.

Lusterman, D.-D. (1985). An eco-system approach to family-school problems. *The American Journal of Family Therapy, 13,* 22–30.

Lyman, S. (1977). Chinese secret societies in the occident: Notes and suggestions for research in the sociology of secrecy. In S. Lyman (Ed.), *Tha Asian American in North America.* Santa Barbara, CA: ABC-Clio.

Mannino, F., & Shore, M. (1984). An ecological perspective on family intervention. In N. O'Conner & B. Lubin (Eds.), *Ecological approaches to clinical and community psychology.* New York: Wiley.

Marishima, J. (1978). The Asian experience: 1850–1975. *Journal of Ethnic and Special Studies, 3,* 8–10.

McGoldrick, M., Pearce, J., & Giordano, J. (Eds.) (1982). *Ethnicity and family therapy.* New York: Guilford Press.

Melendy, H. (1980). Filipinos. In S. Thernstrom et al. (Eds.), *Harvard encyclopedia of American ethnic groups* (pp. 354–362). Cambridge, MA: Harvard University Press.

Minuchin, S., & Fishman, H. (1981). *Family therapy techniques.* Cambridge, MA: Harvard University Press.

MoKuau, N. (1987). Social worker's perceptions of counseling effectiveness for Asian American clients. *Social Work, 32,* 331–335.

Montero, D., & Dieppa, I. (1982). Resettling Vietnamese refugees: The service agency's role. *Social Work, 27,* 74–82.

Okimoto, D. (1975). *Asian key person: Survey on drug abuse.* Task Force Report of Seattle King County Drug Commission, Seattle.

Sue, D. (1981). *Counseling the culturally different: Theory and practice.* New York: Wiley.

Sue, S., & Sue, D. (1971). Chinese American personality and mental health. *Amerasia Journal, 1,* 36–49.

Sue, S., Ino, S., & Sue, D. (1983). Nonassertiveness of Asian-Americans: An inaccurate assumption. *Journal of Counseling Psychology, 30,* 581–588.

Sung, B. (1987). *The adjustment experience of Chinese immigrant children in New York City.* New York: Center for Migration Studies.

Yao, E. (1985). Adjustment needs of Asian immigrant children. *Elementary School Guidance and Counseling, 21,* 222–227.

6

Hispanic Culture and the Schools

MEREDITH BUENNING
Littleton Public Schools, Colorado

NONA TOLLEFSON
University of Kansas

FRED RODRIGUEZ
University of Kansas

A POPULATION IN TRANSITION

The population of the United States is changing, gradually but profoundly. Today, we are a nation of 240 million people, about 50 million (21 percent) of whom are black, Hispanic, or Asian. Although federal and private projections vary, they all point in the same direction: Soon, after the turn of the century, one out of every three Americans will be non-white (Hodgkinson, 1986b, p. 4).

The average white American is 31 years old, the average black American is 25, and the average Hispanic American is 23; white Americans are moving out of their childbearing years just as blacks are moving into them (Hodgkinson, 1986b, p. 16). In this decade, minorities of all ages constitute 20 to 25 percent of our total population; the percentage of minorities among school-aged youth is over 30 percent. The conclusion for U.S. education is inescapable: U.S. public schools are now and will continue to be heavily enrolled with minority students, and an increasing number of minority students will be eligible for college (Hodgkinson, 1986a).

Although there is growing recognition of the importance of such demographic change, there is also apprehension that this society's major education institutions are not responding quickly enough in developing policies that will maximize the contributions made by the escalating numbers of minorities in the population. This chapter will discuss the challenges to the school posed by one minority group—Hispanic students. The culture of Hispanics and the culture of U.S. schools will be described and interventions will be introduced that may mediate the potential conflict between the schools and the Hispanic culture.

DEMOGRAPHICS OF THE HISPANIC POPULATION

Hispanic Americans are the nation's fastest growing major subpopulation. The nation's Hispanic population grew by 30 percent between 1980 and 1987, a rate of increase five times that of all other racial and ethnic groups combined, according to a report by the U.S. Bureau of the Census. The report, which uses new estimating methods designed to produce a more accurate count, also found a sharp rise in the number of school-aged Hispanics over the past five years. The number of such children, ages 5 to 19, increased by 14 percent from 1982 to 1987, from 4.69 million to 5.35 million. According to the study, the number of Hispanic children under age 5 also increased during that period, from 1.7 million to just under 2 million, as did the number of Hispanics in the prime child-bearing years, ages 20 to 29, increased from 3.13 million to 3.39 million.

The total number of Hispanic Americans reached 18.8 million in 1987, up from 14.6 million counted in the 1980 census. During the same period, the non-Hispanic population rose from 212 million to 220 million, a 6 percent increase. Hispanic youth are a rapidly growing group with a high incidence of poverty, a high dropout rate, and a low level of educational attainment.

Poverty

The poverty rate for Hispanic families in 1986 was about two-and-a-half times that of non-Hispanic families. Just under 25 percent of Hispanic families lived below the poverty line last year, compared with 10 percent of non-Hispanic families. The number of impoverished Hispanic families headed by single women increased from 426,000 in 1981 to 528,000 in 1986. But because of the increase in the total Hispanic population, the percentage of such families decreased slightly, from 53.1 to 51.2 percent.

Dropouts

In 1987, the median number of years of schooling completed by Hispanics 25 years

of age or older was 12.0. For the total non-Hispanic population in the same age group, the median number of years of schooling was 12.7. The percentage of Hispanics age 25 or older who had completed four years of high school was 51 percent in 1987. The percentage completing four or more years of college was 9 percent. The percentage of Hispanics age 25 or older who had completed fewer than five years of schooling was 12 percent, compared with 2 percent for non-Hispanics in that age group.

Not only do Hispanics drop out at a higher rate than other groups but they drop out of school earlier. Thus, Hispanic dropouts typically have lower educational attainment than do other dropouts.

Educational Attainment

Hispanics as a group have lower academic achievement than whites (Carter & Segura, 1979; Argulewicz & Sanchez, 1982; Hernandez, 1973; Kaufman & Kaufman, 1983; Sattler, 1982; Plisko, 1983, 1984; Grant & Snyder, 1984). Hispanic students are overrepresented in special education classes, compared to their incidence in the general population (Wright & Santa Cruz, 1983; Maheady, Towne, Algozzine, Mercer, & Ysseldyke, 1983; Brosnan, 1983); they also have poorer reading skills. Hispanics typically exhibit a reading achievement lag of approximately two grade levels by the time they reach sixth grade (Hoffer, 1983).

Hispanic students who complete high school enter college at about the same rate as do whites. In 1981, more than 26 percent of whites, 20 percent of blacks, and 17 percent of Hispanics age 18 to 24 years old were enrolled in college (U.S. Bureau of Census, 1983, No. 373). Though high school completion and college attendance are on the rise, very few Hispanics complete baccalaureate programs within the traditional four-year period. Furthermore,

Hispanics are nearly twice as likely as whites to attend two-year colleges, and half as likely to attend universities (Olivas, Brown, Rosen, & Hill, 1980, p. 118).

EXPLANATIONS FOR THE ACHIEVEMENT PATTERNS OF HISPANICS

No single factor or set of factors has achieved wide support in explaining why Hispanics do poorly in school. The absence of consistent data on language usage, quality of schools attended, quality and quantity of programs to teach English to Spanish speakers, and differences in experiences of different Hispanic groups preclude drawing conclusions with certainty. Nevertheless, several possible factors have been linked, some more strongly than others, to the school achievement of Hispanics.

Family socioeconomic background, English language ability, and nativity seem to be important factors. Families with higher incomes and higher levels of education generally have children who themselves do better educationally than their less advantaged counterparts. Knowledge of English increases the rates of high school completion and college entrance. According to one study (Fligstein & Fernandez, 1982, p. 38), Hispanics who are English-monolingual approximate the high-school degree completion rate of whites. Although no set of demographic factors satisfactorily explains the lower levels of educational attainment among Hispanics, researchers have advanced a cultural conflict theory to explain the achievement patterns of Hispanics.

Cultural Conflict

Researchers have hypothesized that the academic achievement problems of His-

panics are a result of culture or value conflict between home and school/society (Argulewicz & Sanchez, 1982; Ballesteros, 1976; Kagan & Knight, 1979; Sattler, 1982; Knight, Kagan, Nelson, & Gumbiner, 1978; Kagan & Madsen, 1971; Laosa, 1982; Rist, 1972; Trueba, 1983; Ramirez & Castaneda, 1974; Carter & Segura, 1979). Hispanic students may be caught between a home culture that advocates compliance with authority, field-sensitive behaviors, and cooperation, and a school culture that values independence. Low achievement may be a manifestation of the conflict. This premise has been most frequently identified as the *cultural gap, cultural conflict,* or *cultural mismatch theory.*

As an explanation for the academic deficits of Hispanic students, the cultural conflict theory has the properties of a systems theory. It assumes that the education of Hispanics is, like any system, not understandable by a study of its parts (school or student) in isolation. Carter and Segura (1979) proposed an "interaction of cause and effect among three important variables—the school, the social system, and the Hispanic subcultural group" (p. 7).

Carter and Segura (1979) organized the factors most consistently used to understand the educational deficits of Hispanic students into three subgroups. Besides the interactionist theory that they favor, they identified the cultural deprivation theory and the structural environmentalist position. The cultural deprivation theory attributes the achievement deficits to deficient skills, values, and attitudes of the Hispanic population, including those of the youth, their parents, and the larger minority community. The proposed solution has consisted of compensatory-remedial programs that have attempted to change the child rather than the school.

The second group of theorists blame the schools for the low academic achievement of Hispanics. Among the schools' failures are continued isolation and de facto segregation of Hispanic youth, refusal to allow children to use the language with which they are most comfortable, lack of emphasis on reinforcement and rewards, low teacher expectations, and the use of curriculum and materials that are not compatible with the minority child's culture.

Today's educators frequently support the cultural deprivation theory when searching for the reasons for the educational deficits of Hispanic children. Carter and Segura (1979) specified four components of this frequently cited theory:

1. The academic difficulties of Hispanics are a result of home socialization patterns.
2. School personnel need to overcome the failure of Hispanics through remedial programs.
3. The schools' main function is to Americanize foreigners.
4. The schools' curriculum and underlying values represent the cultural characteristics needed to succeed.

We suggest four alternative hypotheses that are congruent with the interactionist theory proposed by Carter and Segura (1979):

1. The lower academic achievement of Hispanics is related to an interaction and conflict between the socialized values of school/society and home.
2. These academic difficulties will not be solved without studying the interaction.
3. The function of education is to encourage cultural pluralism—allowing each student to retain his or her unique values, while encouraging the modification of only those behaviors that significantly interfere with school success and cannot be accommodated through the school curriculum.

4. The schools' policies and practices should be flexible enough to allow for varying attitudes, values, and learning styles without sacrificing a student's success in school.

Thus, in order to obtain a good fit or match between the culture of the school and the Hispanic culture, sometimes the school will need to make changes and sometimes the students will need to adapt. As with any system, the interactions between groups are of ultimate importance and need to be considered.

Cultural Background of Hispanics

Rarely is it debated that there are significant differences between the cultural values and attitudes of many Hispanics and whites. Hispanics have been resistant to assimilation, hesitating to be absorbed into the majority culture. They have tended to retain the values of the Hispanic culture rather than accept those more typical of white (Ramirez & Castaneda, 1974).

Ramirez and Castaneda (1974) describe these values as falling into four major clusters: (1) identification with family, community, and ethnic group; (2) personalization of interpersonal relationships; (3) status and role definition in family and community; and (4) Mexican Catholic ideology. Included in cluster 2 are mutual dependence, cooperative behaviors, and a need for affiliation and help. Separation of sex roles and the importance of being well behaved and well educated socially are stressed in cluster 3. Authoritarian beliefs based on parents and other adults as representatives of God are included in cluster 4. Ramirez and Castaneda (1974) summarize the value orientation as follows:

Socialization in traditional Hispanic culture results in individuals who are strongly identified with their families and ethnic group, sensitive to the feelings of others, oriented towards cooperative achievement, respectful of adults and social convention, and who expect to receive close guidance from adults. (p. 48)

Cultural differences between Hispanics and whites have been consistently reported in the areas of human relationship styles, cognitive styles, and responses to authority figures. Researchers have observed that Hispanics are more cooperative and less competitive than whites (Kagan & Knight, 1979; Kagan, Knight, Martinez, & Santana, 1981; Kagan & Madsen, 1971; Knight & Kagan, 1982; Knight, Kagan, & Buriel, 1982, Kagan, 1977). As a group, Hispanics have also been found to be more field dependent or field sensitive than whites (Buriel, 1975; Ramirez & Price-Williams, 1974; Kagan & Zahn, 1975). Because competitive and field-independent behaviors are advocated in school, a conflict between the culture of home and school may result.

Culture of the School

It is generally accepted that academic achievement is related to cognitive, affective, and social variables. The importance of affective variables, specifically locus of control orientation and cognitive style preference, in explaining differences in achievement is widely supported in the research literature. Students with an internal locus of control and a field-independent cognitive style have higher achievement patterns than do students with an external locus of control and a field-dependent cognitive style. The relationship between internality and achievement has been established across grade levels (Kennelly & Mount, 1985; Sherris & Kahle, 1984), ability levels (Johnson & Kanoy, 1980; Swanson, 1980), and cultures (Kishor, 1983; Maqsud, 1983).

Field independence, like locus of orientation, has been shown to be related

to achievement across a wide range of educational experiences. Field-sensitive students are described as being more influenced by personal relationships and by praise or disapproval from authority figures than are field-independent students who have the higher achievement patterns.

In a study of 480 first- and third-grade students, Saracho (1984) found a significant relationship between field independence/field dependence and achievement for first-graders. Blaha (1982) found field independence to be the single best prediction of reading achievement for economically disadvantaged fifth-graders attending urban elementary schools. In a similar study, Garner and Cole (1986) found achieving seventh-grade students from families with lower SES scores had significantly higher scores for internal and field-independent measures. Buenning and Tollefson (1987) found that cognitive style preference was the factor that differentiated high-achieving white and Hispanic students from lower-achieving students. High achievers in this group of fifth- through eighth-graders were less traditional in their attitudes toward authority and more field independent than were lower achievers.

In addition to ability, cognitive style preference, and locus of control orientation, academic achievement appears to be related to social factors in the school environment. Research evidence indicates that cooperative learning rather than competitive or individualistic procedures encourage positive academic and social outcomes among boys and girls from different ethnic groups (Johnson, Johnson, & Maruyama, 1983). Skon, Johnson, and Johnson (1981) found that children with high ability benefited as much from interacting with children with moderate or low ability as they did from interacting with children with high ability. Stainback,

Stainback, and Froyen (1987) found that placing disruptive students with well-behaved students led to fewer disruptive behaviors. These authors attributed the decrease in disruptive behaviors to appropriate behavioral models and peer pressure. Reviews of 28 field projects and related studies concluded that cooperative grouping increased mutual concern among students (Slavin, 1980), and that there was a tendency for students who worked together to like one another (Madden & Slavin, 1983).

Although research illustrates the benefits of cooperation, U.S. schools adopt a competitive, individualistic approach to learning. Parker (1985) and Lew, Mesch, Johnson, and Johnson (1986) describe U.S. schools as places where students learn in isolation, competing with each other for the rewards of schools and grades. The individualistic approach to learning is highlighted by Johnson and Johnson (1985), who estimate that students work together at most 10 to 20 percent of the time.

INTERVENTIONS

Steps need to be taken to address the problems of low achievement and high dropout rates among Hispanic students. This section will introduce interventions designed to reduce the conflict between the socialized values of school/society and the Hispanic home/students. The goal of these interventions is to encourage cultural interaction and understanding between the two systems and to make modifications in the educational program, when necessary, to provide a better match between home and school. Four levels of intervention will be discussed: the teacher preparation level, the school organization level, the school instructional level, and the interpersonal level.

Teacher Preparation Level

Justiz and Darling (1980) argue for the need to adopt a multicultural perspective in teacher education. Such a perspective, they contend, must be acquired early in a person's preparation program, if the teacher is to function in a culturally pluralistic school. These authors specify four conditions that must be met in a teacher preparation program for teachers to develop a multicultural perspective: (1) a culturally heterogeneous student population, (2) a culturally heterogeneous faculty, (3) a commitment by faculty to respect and to appreciate the ways of others, and (4) the "intrusion" of multicultural concepts into the curriculum and the classroom.

Too frequently, students who are preparing to be teachers do not have the opportunity to meet and to become acquainted with black, Hispanic, or Asian students either in their teacher education classes or in the student teaching environment. Although most prospective teachers are introduced to multicultural concepts, opportunities to interact with and observe black, Hispanic, and Asian teachers need to be provided for teachers in training. Teacher preparation programs need to seek out culturally pluralistic schools so that first-year teachers have the basic cultural understanding necessary to function effectively in these schools.

School Organization Level

A systems approach to improving the educational attainment of Hispanic students may require fundamental changes in the organization and culture of the school. Interventions at the school organization level can help to reduce the cultural conflict between home and school.

The importance of a school culture that emphasizes achievement for all students has been expressed most clearly by what has become known as the *effective schools movement.* After five to ten years of process product research, this movement has identified teacher and school factors that impact favorably on educational achievement.

Studies indicate that increases in student achievement are positively correlated with a schoolwide commitment to learning, the actions of teachers, and the interactions between students and teachers. Characteristics of effective schools include high expectations for students and teachers, strong leadership, positive school climate, high levels of student on-task behavior, materials at the appropriate difficulty level for students, a strong emphasis on academics in the curriculum, ongoing evaluation, and an atmosphere that emphasizes the recognition and understanding of cultural differences (Rankin, 1979; Good, 1979; Brophy, 1979).

More specifically, characteristics have been found to identify effective urban schools, a setting where most Hispanic students are found. High levels of parent involvement and a school climate conducive to learning have been cited (Edmonds, 1979; Brookover, 1981). Furthermore, researchers have recognized additional variables that have helped children to achieve who have had histories of failure. They include not allowing cultural, family, and sex differences to influence teacher expectations, and a teacher/pupil relationship that is warm, encouraging, and personal rather than businesslike and demanding (Stallings, 1979; Evertson, 1980).

In many ways, the effective schools movement is now inseparable from the back-to-basics movement. In calling for order and discipline, basic skills, and increased testing, the two movements are mutually reinforcing. There can be little doubt that the effective schools formula has achieved its widespread popularity partly because of these similarities. The danger is that the mission of social justice of the effective schools movement is being diluted. The recent education reform reports proposed something like an effective school agenda when their authors called for increased time-on-task, a greater emphasis on the basic skills, and tougher discipline. But the reports largely ignored the special needs of the poor or ethnic minorities and of inner-city youth. Many policy makers seem to believe that traditional bureaucratic approaches to schooling, which have worked poorly in the past, can now produce academic success for all students (Stedman, 1987).

In concentrating on the basics and testing, the current reform movement ignores the cultural nature of schooling. The typical school remains a white, middle-class institution whose language and world view are alien to members of different cultures and classes. Historically, the indifference or outright hostility of the schools toward groups not part of the mainstream has contributed to their academic failure.

We encourage educators committed to increasing the educational achievement of Hispanic students to emphasize the "effective school" variables that have the greatest chance of closing the gap between the system or culture of the school and the system or culture of the Hispanic child. Some of the variables are strong leadership, high expectations for Hispanic students to learn, more emphasis on academic coursework, and greater opportunity for cultural understanding through the employment of Hispanic teachers and involvement of Hispanic community members in the school.

Effective bilingual programs have been identified through similar procedures as those used in the effective schools research. Carter and Chatfield (1986) described three effective bilingual programs. Effectiveness was measured by school achievement and in all cases both limited

English-proficient (LEP) and English Only (EO) poor children did well academically. A "positive school social climate" was found in these schools, which included the following characteristics: high expectations for all students, a strong academic focus, teacher's rejection of the cultural deprivation hypothesis as an explanation for the academic deficiencies of the students, and high staff morale where teachers felt ownership of the system and believed it would work.

Carter and Chatfield (1986) analyzed characteristics unique to one of these schools. The school served one of the poorest populations in Cula Vista, California, and most of the minority students were Hispanic. They found a multiethnic staff, with 10 of the 19 teachers non-Anglo and 7 Hispanic. Six of the teachers were fully certified bilingual teachers. The Bill of Rights of the school was as follows: "Each person has a right: To be treated with kindness. To tell his/her side of the story or give her/his views. To be safe and healthy. To have an orderly environment. To use and own property, and to be different" (p. 215).

Although school staff were aware of students' home life, this factor was not blamed for their school problems. The community and school were intertwined, with community members (e.g., senior citizens) volunteering to help at school, and school resources used to aide the community. Bilingual education was provided and 70 percent of the students participated. Some participants were Spanish speakers learning English, and others were English speakers learning Spanish. Team teaching occurred in this program, with one teacher instructing in Spanish and the other in English.

Garcia (1986) reported information from the Significant Bilingual Instructional Features Study (SBIF). In this study, 58 classrooms were identified that were nominated by parents, students, and

school staff and that also had very high rates of student involvement in academic tasks. Unique instructional features of these schools included: (1) English was used only 60 percent of the time or less for instruction and (2) use of minority cultural referents during instruction and demonstration of a respect for the rules and values of these cultural groups increased a feeling of trust between students and teachers.

Too frequently, Hispanic students enroll in vocational rather than academic courses that place lesser demands for language competence and verbal problem-solving skills. Morgan (1983), in an analysis of the achievement patterns of Hispanic students attending public schools and catholic schools, found that Hispanic students gain in verbal achievement in private schools. He attributed the gain, in part, to the fact that private schools typically have fewer vocational offerings and, consequently, Hispanic students must enroll in academic courses. Valdivieso (1986) also notes that "Catholic schools in central cities can shape ambitions and motivate students to aspire because such schools offer a limited, academically rigorous curriculum, rooted in a sense of community, nurturance, discipline, and esteem" (p. 196). The point to be made here is that all schools need to work to develop that sense of nurturance and that insistence on achievement that promotes attainment of knowledge and skills.

School quality, discrimination by school professionals against Hispanics, and teachers' self-fulfilling prophecies of low achievement for Hispanics have historically played a role in "pushing" Hispanics out of school. For example, Hispanics in the Southwest have long been discriminated against in the public school systems. They have been segregated from non-Hispanic origin children and punished for using Spanish, even in casual conversations. They have attended schools that are poorly staffed and equipped. In fact, a 1987 report by the National School Desegregation Project stated, "Racial segregation of Black students in the public schools changed little from 1980 to 1984, but Hispanic students became much more segregated. Both situations reflect long-term trends." These trends can be altered through the organizational strategies cited in this section.

School Instructional Level

The culture and organization of the school sets the tone of the school, but it is the school staff as individuals who work with students. Effective schools stress achievement, and teachers in these schools help students to develop the skills needed for the achievement. Teaching strategies can help to bring the culture of the school closer to that of the Hispanic student.

Cognitive Style Strategies

There are differences in the problem-solving behaviors encouraged in Anglo and Hispanic homes. The Anglo culture stresses independence and analytic problem solving more than does the Hispanic culture, and these are the skills that are also stressed in school. Thus, Anglo children have the advantage of the home and the school teaching and reinforcing the same types of problem-solving behaviors. Hispanic students as a group do not live in families where the adults in the family manipulate language and solve problems as part of their daily lives (Valdivieso, 1986). Teachers have the choice of helping students develop the necessary language and problem-solving skills or of accommodating the students by making fewer demands for language competence and problem solving. If Hispanic students are to achieve in schools, teachers, counselors, and school psychologists must insist that students be taught and that they learn the problem-solving skills stressed in school.

Although children with field-independent problem-solving skills are more academically successful in school, this success should not result in the belief that field-independent behaviors and teaching strategies that encourage them are inherently superior. Rather, field-independent children may experience a better "match" between their style and the typical school's curriculum and objectives. Another way to meet the problem-solving and cognitive style preferences of Hispanics is to modify teaching strategies to accommodate them.

Ramirez and Castaneda (1974) noticed relationship preferences when studying the cognitive styles of school-aged children. With regard to relationship to peers, field-independent children prefer to work independently and compete in a task-oriented manner. In contrast, field-dependent or field-sensitive children like to work cooperatively toward a common goal and are more sensitive to the feelings and ideas of others. When relating to teachers, field-independent children prefer formal task-oriented interactions and have little desire for the teacher's help. Children with a field-sensitive orientation are more interested in a personal relationship with the teacher, want to be like the teacher, and seek more guidance and help from the teacher.

In an attempt to increase the match between the curriculum and the characteristics of Hispanic students, Contreras (1985) listed teaching strategies that are congruent with the preferences of field-sensitive students. They include encouraging expression of feelings, allowing students to work cooperatively, personalizing the curriculum by relating the content to the ethnic and cultural experience of the student, humanizing the information by presenting it in a story form that emphasizes human characteristics, and presenting concepts globally.

Cooperative Learning Strategies

Studies have demonstrated that Hispanic children tend to be more motivated by altruism or group enhancement goals, whereas white children have stronger competitive motives (Kagan, 1977). Thus, cooperative learning would appear to provide a good match between the culture of the Hispanic student and the instructional methodology of the school. In addition, cooperative learning has been found to be beneficial for all children.

Roger and David Johnson, researchers at the University of Minnesota, have completed more than 80 research studies on cooperative learning. They concluded, "Children who learn cooperatively— compared to those who learn competitively or independently—learn better, feel better about themselves and get along better with each other" (Kohn, 1987, p. 53). In 21 of their 26 controlled studies, they found cooperation resulted in higher achievement than competition. In addition, their studies have demonstrated that prejudice is reduced when students from different ethnic backgrounds learn cooperatively.

To promote cooperative learning, Johnson and Johnson advocate projects that create "positive interdependence" on each other (Kohn, 1987). Specific ideas include developing a group product that is given a group grade. Members specialize in a part of an assignment and the teacher assigns "interconnected roles." For example, one person may record ideas, another may check to see that people are completing their parts, and another may verify that they are collaborating. No one is allowed to take responsibility for the group. To avoid this and to ensure that all have learned to use materials equally well, the teacher selects students at random to answer questions and take a test for the group.

Johnson, Johnson, and Maruyama (1983) have examined the research on cooperative learning and concluded that cooperation is the key variable in promoting positive interpersonal relationships in desegregated settings. More specifically, their meta-review of studies on this topic concludes that "cooperation without interpersonal competition promotes greater interpersonal attraction . . . than do interpersonal competition, individualistic efforts, and cooperation with interpersonal competition" (p. 38). They further conclude that in "many classrooms throughout North America highly individualistic and often subtly competitive learning procedures are being used in desegregated and mainstreamed classrooms. . . ." (p. 38). The results of this review indicate that cooperative learning procedures should be used in these classrooms.

Two skills necessary for successful academic performance are (1) active processing of new knowledge during the acquisition phase of learning and (2) competence in demonstrating knowledge once it is attained (Lambiotte, Dansereau, Rocklin, Fletcher, Hythecker, Larson, & O'Donnell, 1987). These skills can probably best be acquired in a cooperative setting. Group discussion, study groups, and team projects provide the opportunity for students to acquire these skills. Knowledge acquisition is facilitated when students have opportunities to ask questions, elaborate, give oral summaries, and check on the accuracy of other summaries (Yager, Johnson, & Johnson, 1985).

Webb (1985) also stresses the importance of the type of verbal interaction that occurs in the group. Stating the correct answer is less beneficial than explaining why a correct answer is the correct answer. Giving an explanation is helpful to the student who knows the correct answer because it forces the speaker to clarify and reorganize the information. For the student who does not know the answer, it provides the opportunity to hear a different explanation, ask questions, and restructure information.

TUTORING AND COOPERATIVE TEAM LEARNING. In Walberg's (1983) review of theories and research on adaptive instruction, both tutoring and student-team cooperative learning approaches are viewed as instructional innovations that can adapt learning environments to students' learning and behavioral styles. A meta-analysis reported in 1982 by Cohen, Kulik, and Kulik concluded that tutoring frequently has an educationally as well as statistically significant effect on student achievement and attitudes toward subject matter.

Efforts to reorganize school practices so as to initiate and facilitate tutoring and other cooperative learning approaches can have a positive impact on students' achievement and attitudes. Cooperative team learning appears prominently in recommendations in both the desegregation literature and effective schools research.

TEAM ASSISTED INDIVIDUALIZATION. Slavin (1983) and his colleagues at Johns Hopkins University have developed a modified student teaming approach using programmed materials to advance individualization of instruction. Called Team Assisted Individualization (TAI), the approach is intended to reap the achievement benefits of providing instruction appropriate to the needs and skills of individual students by reducing the time and management costs of programmed instruction and increasing the amount of direct instruction teachers can deliver as part of an individualized program. Working in small, heterogeneous teams, students handle the routine management and checking required for individualization, and the teams are rewarded based on the number and accuracy of units completed by all team members. Field tests using TAI for

mathematics instruction have resulted in positive improvements in interracial attitudes and in students' achievement.

Interpersonal Level

At the interpersonal level, interventions are needed that will reduce cultural conflict by promoting interactions between teacher and student and student and student. Allport (1954) identified four conditions that lead to improved race relations: (1) cooperation across racial lines, (2) equal-status roles for students of different races, (3) contact that permits students to learn about each other as individuals, and (4) communication of unequivocal teacher support for interracial contact.

After reviewing a set of 19 studies, Slavin (1985) concluded that when the conditions outlined by Allport were present, friendship between students from different ethnic groups improved. Other writers (Miller, Brewer, & Edwards, 1985) contend that Slavin's view is too optimistic. They argue that too often school interventions that are supposed to promote cooperation do little to reduce category-based interactions. For them, emphasis on category membership as a distinctive or salient feature of a group will reduce any lasting effect of the group. Here, it seems essential to adhere to Allport's third condition—contact that permits students to interact as individuals rather than as representatives of racial/ethnic groups. Providing the time and the environment for students to interact with each other as individuals may promote the cognitive dissonance necessary to cause both individuals to restructure their views of a racial/ethnic group.

Allport's condition of unequivocal teacher support for interracial contact may be what is lacking in some classrooms. Schools set up very clear norms for academic and social behavior, and if the norms are that students of like ability interact and students from the same racial/ethnic groups interact, then parents, teachers, and students must work together to modify these expectations.

The following interventions are not a template for addressing all of these interpersonal issues; rather, they are illustrative of ways to develop positive relationships between Hispanics and whites in schools.

1. Teachers need to learn as much as they can about Hispanics.
   a. Individuals differ in cultural dimensions such as language, skills, degree of acculturation, and ethnic identification. Be aware of Hispanic family values and culture.
   b. Be aware of the social forces affecting the Hispanic, such as socioeconomic status, unemployment/underemployment, and lack of educational opportunities.
   c. Try to understand the student's background. What obstacles are in the student's path? How can a skilled professional help? Know the community in which you work in order to understand the environmental forces that surround students. It would certainly be ideal if the staff member lived in the community in which he or she works.
   d. The Hispanic family may be one of the most influential socializing agents for a child. If the family cannot participate in the school setting, the views and opinions of the family should be discussed since they will influence the student.
   e. Be aware of the cultural conflicts that a Hispanic may be facing. Accepting all Anglo values can alienate the Hispanic from his or her

family. Likewise, if Hispanic students accept only "traditional" values, this may cause the student and/or parent to deal poorly with American social institutions.
   f. Be aware of the benefits and barriers of working with someone from your own ethnic group or from a different ethnic group.
   g. Circulate—talk to students and family members in other places besides school.
2. Teachers need to be aware of biases and stereotypes.
   a. Be aware of personal biases of cultural and racial stereotypes. It is important to be familiar with proper terms that the individual may use to address himself or herself (i.e., Mexican-American, Chicano, Latino, Hispanic).
   b. Counselors, social workers, and educators should realize that they may unconsciously possess stereotypes, perceptions, or expectations that are detrimental to Hispanic students.
3. Teachers should encourage a feeling of trust between themselves and Hispanic students.
   a. Develop a personal relationship with the students and/or family member. A relationship of trust and helping may transcend cultural differences. It is helpful to understand, respect, and appreciate the Hispanic experience, as well as the historical contributions to this society.
   b. Provide encouragement, emotional support, and positive reinforcement. Just being interested in the student and his or her family and being interested enough to follow-up may serve this purpose.

Ancillary school personnel can also play an important role in the lives of

Hispanic students. Counselors, school psychologists, and social workers will be called on to work with Hispanics with low achievement and, in many cases, with these students' teachers. Consequently, these school persons need to have knowledge about the Hispanic culture and to be aware of any stereotypical views that they hold about Hispanics. It is important that human service workers maintain a high level of cultural awareness by attending staff-development programs and by maintaining professional contacts with the Hispanic community. It is equally important that they maintain an effective referral system. The counselor, psychologist, and social worker may be a Hispanic student's only contact with the larger services available in the community.

Just as human service workers must be aware of their views of Hispanics and their culture, they must assist all members of the school to understand and respect difference between the Hispanic and Anglo cultures. Too frequently, schools attempt either to mold students into stereotypical behavior or to make them "melt" into the mainstream and "act like whites." Neither response is appropriate. Human service workers can help teachers to recognize Hispanic preference for cooperative learning and to implement this type of learning environment. They can also assist teachers in developing strategies for facilitating independence—an important skill for success in school.

Finally, human service workers must adapt and promote the attitude that all students are unique and should be treated as individuals. Although Hispanic students may share a common culture, each is unique. All school personnel must remain sensitive to the pressure, sometimes subtle and sometimes not so subtle, that teachers and students can exert on students to "fit in." To be different in appearance, in language usage, and in values from the dominant culture may cause students to feel out of place and out of control, and these feelings may in turn hinder achievement. It is the adults in the school environment who can set a norm of respect, and it is human service workers in their role as child advocates who can encourage the setting of the norm.

References

Allport, G. W. (1954). *The nature of prejudice.* Reading, MA: Addison-Wesley.

Argulewicz, E. N., & Sanchez, D. T. (1982). Considerations in the assessment of reading difficulties in bilingual children. *School Psychology Review, 11,* 281–289.

Ballesteros, O. A. (1976). *The effectiveness of public school education for Mexican-American students as perceived by principals of elementary schools of predominantly Mexican-American Enrollment.* San Francisco: R & E Research Associates.

Blaha, J. (1982). Predicting reading and arithmetic achievement with measures of reading attitudes and cognitive styles. *Perceptual and Motor Skills, 55,* 107–114.

Brookover, W. B. (1981). *Effective secondary schools.* Philadelphia: Research for Better Schools, Inc.

Brophy, J. E. (1979). Teacher behavior and student learning. *Educational Leadership, 37,* 33–38.

Brosnan, F. (1983). Overrepresentation of low-socioeconomic minority students in special education programs in California. *Learning Disability Quarterly, 6,* 517–525.

Buenning, M., & Tollefson, N. (1987). The cultural gap hypothesis as an explanation for the achievement patterns of Mexican-American students. *Psychology in the Schools, 24,* 264–272.

Buriel, R. (1975). Cognitive styles among three generations of Mexican-American children. *Journal of Cross-Cultural Psychology, 6,* 417–429.

Carter, T., & Chatfield, M. (1986). Effective bilingual schools: Implications for policy and practice. *American Journal of Education, 95*(1), 200–232.

Carter, T. P., & Segura, R. D. (1979). *Mexican Americans in school: A decade of change.* New York: College Entrance Examination Board.

Cohen, P. A., Kulik, J. A., & Kulik, C. (1982). Educational outcomes of tutoring: A meta-analysis of findings. *American Educational Research Journal, 19,* 237–248.

Contreras, M. (1985). *Hemispheric learning and the Hispanic student.* Paper published in EDRS.

Edmonds, R. (1979). Effective schools for the urban poor. *Educational Leadership, 37,* 15–24.

Evertson, C. M. (1980). *An overview of research: Classroom organization and effective teaching project.* Austin, TX: Research and Development Center.

Fligstein, N., & Fernandez, R. M. (1982). *The causes of Hispanic educational attainment, patterns and analyses.* Paper prepared for the National Commission on Employment Policy. Chicago: Opinion Research Center.

Garcia, E. (1986). Bilingual development and the education of bilingual children during early childhood. *American Journal of Education, 95*(1), 96–121.

Garner, W. C., & Cole, E. G. (1986). The achievement of students in low-SES settings. An investigation of the relationship between locus of control and field dependence. *Urban Education, 21,* 189–206.

Good, T. L. (1979). Teacher effectiveness in the elementary school. *Journal of Teacher Education, 30,* 52–64.

Grant, W. V., & Snyder, T. D. (1983–84 edition). *Digest of education statistics.* Washington, DC: U.S. Government Printing Office.

Hernandez, N. G. (1973). Variables affecting achievement of middle school Mexican-American students. *Review of Educational Research, 43*(1), 1–39.

Hodgkinson, H. L. (1986a). The patterns in our social fabric are changing. *Education Week,* May 14.

Hodgkinson, H. L. (1986b). Today's numbers, tomorrow's nation—Demography's awesome challenge for schools. *Education Week,* May 14.

Hoffer, K. R. (1983). Assessment and instruction of reading skills: Results with Mexican-American students. *Learning Disability Quarterly, 6,* 458–467.

Johnson, B. W., & Kanoy, K. W. (1980). Locus of control and self-concept in achieving and underachieving bright elementary students. *Psychology in the Schools, 17,* 395–399.

Johnson, D. W., Johnson, R., & Maruyama, G. (1983). Interdependence and interpersonal attraction among heterogeneous and homogeneous individuals: A theoretical formulation and meta-analysis of the research. *Review of Educational Research, 53,* 5–54.

Johnson, R. T., & Johnson, D. W. (1985). Student-student interaction: Ignored but powerful. *Journal of Teacher Education, 36*(4), 22–26.

Justiz, M. J., & Darling, D. W. (1980). A multicultural perspective in teacher education. *Educational Horizons, 58,* 203–205.

Kagan, S. (1977). Social motives and behaviors of Mexican-American and Anglo-American children. In J. L. Martinez (Ed.), *Chicano psychology* (pp. 45–96). New York: Academic Press.

Kagan, S., & Knight, G. (1979). Cooperation-competition and self-esteem: A case of cultural relativism. *Journal of Cross-Cultural Psychology, 10*(4), 457–467.

Kagan, S., Knight, G., Martinez, S., & Santana, P. E. (1981). Conflict resolution style among Mexican children: Examining urbanization and ecology effects. *Journal of Cross-Cultural Psychology, 12,* 222–232.

Kagan, S., & Madsen, M. (1971). Cooperation and competition of Mexican, Mexican-American, and Anglo-American children of two ages under four instructional sets. *Developmental Psychology, 5*(1), 32–39.

Kagan, S., & Zahn, C. L. (1975). Field dependence and the school achievement gap between Anglo-American and Mexican-American Children. *Journal of Educational Psychology, 67,* 643–650.

Kaufman, A. S., & Kaufman, N. L. (1983). *Kaufman assessment battery for children: Interpretative manual.* Circle Pines, MN: American Guidance Service.

Kennelly, K. J., & Mount, S. A. (1985). Perceived contingency of reinforcements, helplessness, locus on control, and academic performance. *Psychology in the Schools, 22,* 465–469.

Kishor, N. (1983). Locus of control and academic achievement: Ethnic discrepancies among Fijians. *Journal of Cross-Cultural Psychology, 14*(3), 297–308.

Knight, G. P., & Kagan, S. (1982). Siblings, birth order, and cooperative-competitive social behavior: A comparison of Anglo-American and Mexican-American children. *Journal of Cross-Cultural Psychology, 13*(2), 239–249.

Knight, G. P., Kagan, S., & Buriel, R. (1982). Perceived parental practices and prosocial development. *The Journal of Genetic Psychology, 141,* 57–65.

Knight, G. P., Kagan, S., Nelson, W., & Gumbiner, J. (1978). Acculturation of second- and third-generation Mexican American children. *Journal of Cross-Cultural Psychology, 9*(1), 87–97.

Kohn, A. (1987). It's hard to get left out of a pair. *Psychology Today, 21*(10), 53–57.

Lambiotte, J. G., Dansereau, D. F., Rocklin, T. R., Fletcher, B., Hythecker, V. I., Larson, C. O., & O'Donnell, A. M. (1987). Cooperative learning and test taking: Transfer of skills. *Contemporary Educational Psychology, 12,* 52–61.

Laosa, L. M. (1982). School, occupation, culture, and family: The impact of parental schooling on the parent-child relationship. *Journal of Educational Psychology, 74,* 791–827.

Lew, M., Mesch, D., Johnson, D. W., & Johnson, R. (1986). Components of cooperative learning: Effects of collaborative skills and academic group contingencies on achievement and mainstreaming. *Contemporary Educational Psychology, 11,* 229–239.

Madden, N. A., & Slavin, R. E. (1983). Mainstreaming students with mild handicaps: Academic and social outcomes. *Review of Educational Research, 53,* 519–569.

Maheady, L., Towne, R., Algozzine, B., Mercer, J., & Ysseldyke, J. (1983). Minority overrepresentation: A case for alternative practices prior to referral. *Learning Disability Quarterly, 6,* 448–546.

Maqsud, M. (1983). Relationships of locus of control to self-esteem, academic achievement, and prediction of performance among Nigerian secondary school pupils. *British Journal of Educational Psychology, 53,* 215–221.

McClintock, C. G. (1974). Development of social motives in Anglo-American and Mexican-American children. *Journal of Personality and Social Psychology, 29,* 348–354.

Miller, N., Brewer, M. B., & Edwards, K. (1985). Cooperative interaction in desegregated settings: A laboratory analogue. *Journal of Social Issues, 41*(3), 63–79.

Morgan, W. R. (1983). Learning and student life quality of public and private school youth. *Sociology of Education,* pp. 187–202.

Olivas, M. A., Brown, G. H., Rosen, N., & Hill, S. (1980). *The condition of education for Hispanic Americans.* Washington, DC: National Center for Education Statistics.

Parker, R. E. (1985). Small-group cooperative learning—Improving academic, social gains in the classroom. *NASSP Bulletin, 69,* 48–57.

Plisko, V. W. (Ed.) (1983 edition). *The condition of education.* Washington, DC: U.S. Government Printing Office.

Plisko, V. W. (Ed.) (1984 edition). *The condition of education.* Washington, DC: U.S. Government Printing Office.

Ramirez, M. III, & Castaneda, A. (1974). *Cultural democracy, bicognitive development, and education.* New York: Academic Press.

Ramirez, M. III, & Price-Williams, D. (1974). Cognitive styles of children of three ethnic groups in the United States. *Journal of Cross-Cultural Psychology, 5,* 425–433.

Rankin, S. (1979). A conversation with Stuart Rankin. *Educational Leadership, 37,* 74–77.

Rist, R. (1972). Social distance and social inequality in a ghetto kindergarten classroom: An examination of the "cultural gap" hypothesis. *Urban Education, 7,* 241–262.

Saracho, O. N. (1984). Young children's academic achievement as a function of their cognitive styles. *Journal of Research and Development in Education, 18*(1), 44–50.

Sattler, J. M. (1982). *Assessment of children's intelligence and special abilities* (2nd ed.). Boston: Allyn and Bacon.

Sherris, J. D., & Kahle, J. B. (1984). The effects of instructional organization and locus of control orientation on meaningful learning in high school biology students. *Journal of Research in Science Teaching, 21*(10), 83–994.

Skon, L., Johnson, D. W., & Johnson, R. (1981). Cooperative peer interaction versus individual competition and individualistic efforts: Effects on the acquisition of cognitive reasoning strategies. *Journal of Educational Psychology, 73,* 83–92.

Slavin, R. E. (1980). Cooperative learning. *Review of Educational Research, 50,* 315–342.

Slavin, R. E. (1983). *Team assisted individualization: A cooperative learning solution for adaptive instruction in mathematics.* Paper presented at an invitational conference on Adapting Instruction to Individual Differences, Pittsburgh.

Slavin, R. E. (1985). Cooperative learning: Applying contact theory in desegregated schools. *Journal of Social Issues, 41*(3), 45–62.

Stainback, W., Stainback, S., & Froyen, L. (1987). Structuring the classroom to prevent disruptive behaviors. *Teaching Exceptional Children, 19*(4), 12–16.

Stallings, J. A. (1979). *The process of teaching basic reading skills in secondary schools.* Menlo Park, CA: SRI International.

Stedman, Lawrence C. (1987). It's time we changed the effective schools formula. *Phi Delta Kappan,* pp. 215–224.

Swanson, L. (1980). Cognitive style, locus of control, and school achievement in learning disabled females. *Journal of Clinical Psychology, 30,* 964–967.

Trueba, H. (1983). Adjustment problems of Mexican and Mexican-American students: An anthropological study. *Learning Disability Quarterly, 6,* 395–415.

U.S. Bureau of the Census (1983). *Current population survey.* Washington, DC: U.S. Government Printing Office.

Valdivieso, R. (1986). Hispanics and schools: A new perspective. *Educational Horizons, 64*(4), 190–197.

Walberg, H. (1983). *Instructional theories and research evidence.* Paper presented to an invitational conference on Adapting Instruction to Student Differences, Pittsburgh.

Webb, N. M. (1985). Verbal interaction and learning in peer-directed groups. *Theory into Practice, 24*(1), 32–39.

Wright, P., & Santa Cruz, R. (1983). Ethnic composition of special education programs in California. *Learning Disability Quarterly, 6,* 387–394.

Yager, S., Johnson, D. W., & Johnson, R. T. (1985). Oral discussion, group to individual transfer, and achievement in cooperative learning groups. *Journal of Educational Psychology, 77,* 60–66.

7

The Native American Child in School: An Ecological Perspective

LARRY L. GRIMM

Prescott Neurological Clinic, Prescott, Arizona

IT IS NAIVE to suggest that the Indians of North America (or, as they are more appropriately referred to, Native Americans) represent a single unified group, as there are many distinctive features that differentiate the numerous and varied tribes; however, there are many commonalties and it is upon this premise that this chapter is written. The shared issues addressed are by and large related to traditional values. The long history of cultural, psychological, and physical genocide stems from a lack of appreciation and respect of a value system that differs from that of the dominant culture. A thorough discussion of shared traditional values is necessary in order to appreciate fully the motivating forces, the sources of conflict and misunderstanding by the dominant culture, and the basis for maximizing the likelihood of successful interventions with children and families.

Socrates suggested that "before you teach, know your human subjects" (Bryde, 1971, p. 1). Since Native Americans are members of what is believed to be the oldest race, it seems reasonable that a thorough knowledge of these people is commonplace. Unfortunately, this is not the case; perhaps James Fenimore Cooper was correct in his assessment, "who shall fathom the mind of the noble red man" (Bryde, 1971, p. 1). This certainly appears to be the case when examining how the dominant culture of the United States has coexisted with the Indians of North America, but for the most part has not fully understood or appreciated them. This misunderstanding has resulted in a long history of cultural, psychological, and physical threats, which many have referred to as genocide.

HISTORY OF GOVERNMENT INVOLVEMENT

The history of government interference in the lives of Native Americans is predicated on the simple premise that these individuals are incapable of taking care of themselves and are in need of custodial care until fully acculturated (Szasz, 1974). George Washington and Thomas Jefferson viewed them as culturally inferior and advocated government involvement with social, religious, and economic practices (Fate, 1978).

Beginning in 1819, Congress regularly appropriated $10,000 a year to support Christian missionary teachers, of various denominations, in an effort to "remake the Indian culture on the Anglo-American model" (Young, 1977, p. 1). The intent of this schooling effort, along with the judicious bribery of tribal leaders, was to assimilate or remove natives in an attempt to ultimately ensure the peaceful acquisition of Indian land. This process gradually failed as chiefs reacted militantly and centralized the control of their respective tribes, which resulted in increased unity and even greater resistance. Even though these acculturation efforts were resisted, the battle took its toll on the health of Native Americans (Young, 1977).

Under the jurisdiction of the War Department, Native Americans were treated as wards of the government, which resulted in an eventual breakdown of the authority of tribal leadership. In 1849, Congress shifted control of Indian affairs from the War Department to the newly formed Department of Interior, which placed Indian affairs in the realm of domestic business. By 1921, assessment of the effectiveness of the Department of Interior was in question, as reflected by health conditions on certain reservations with a birth rate 26 percent higher than the national average and a death rate 163 percent higher (Young, 1977). At the same time, education was viewed as inadequate, with poorly funded programs staffed by inadequately trained and poorly motivated teachers and administrators.

In 1926, President Coolidge's Secretary of the Interior, Hubert Work, requested the privately endowed Institute for Government Research (which later became the Brookings Institute) to investigate these allegations. This investigation resulted in the published reports entitled *The Problem of the Indian American,* published in 1928 by Lewis Meriam and colleagues. The Meriam Report, as it later was referred to, was the first critical ex-

amination of Indian affairs. The findings included low income, poor health, overall high death rate particularly among infants, appalling living conditions, poor nutrition, inadequate sanitary facilities, and a lack of a broad educational policy within the educational system (Szasz, 1974; Thompson, 1978; Young, 1977).

In 1930, approximately 90 percent of all Native American school-aged children were enrolled in school, whether bureau boarding schools, mission schools, or public schools. The largest proportion of children were enrolled in bureau boarding schools. These schools were characterized by compulsory attendance, overcrowding, militaristic rules, harsh discipline, a curriculum that consisted largely of vocational training, insufficient food, and improper treatment of illnesses (Szasz, 1974; Thompson, 1978). Moreover, due to limited funding and inadequate staffing, preadolescents were required to staff the shops, work in the garden, and help in the kitchen (Szasz, 1974). The boarding schools and urban relocation were part of an intentional policy of removing Native Americans from the influence of their culture (Green, 1983).

Specific to the issue of boarding schools, the Meriam Report recommended that education be the primary focus of the Indian Bureau. Further, education should be at all levels in order to enhance community ties. Public day schools on the reservation should serve a dual function as community centers. Recommendations for boarding schools included presenting Indian culture, developing a curriculum that is adaptable and flexible, upgrading physical conditions, and making provision for adequate personnel through improved training standards and increased salaries (Szasz, 1974; Thompson, 1978; Young, 1977).

In response to this report, Congress passed the Indian Reorganization Act of 1934, commonly referred to as the Indian

New Deal. This act empowered the Commissioner of the Office of Indian Affairs to make suitable provisions for the training of Indians along with the requirement of suitable services to include education, public health, and necessary social services. Also in 1934, Congress passed the Johnson O'Malley Act, which allocated federal monies for Native American children to attend public day schools. Although well intended, many public school administrators were more concerned with the federal dollars than providing appropriate education (Szasz, 1974).

During the administrations of Hoover and Roosevelt, the Meriam Report provided guidelines to Commissioners of Indian Affairs, each in turn. Collier, then Commissioner of Indian Affairs, resigned in 1945 and with his resignation neither the bureau or Congress were any longer in the mood for reforms. In 1950, The Hoover Commission, as well as the Booz, Allen, and Hamilton Reports, suggested that the federal government should abandon its historic role as trustee and advocate for the Indian people. This recommendation was based largely on the recognition of widespread failures to accomplish its intended purpose. In response to public sentiment in the late 1960s regarding civil rights, Education Directors Marburger and Zellers reconsidered the recommendations of the Meriam Report (Szasz, 1974; Thompson, 1978).

In 1969, the report of the Senate Special Subcommittee on Indian Education, entitled "Indian Education: A National Tragedy, A National Challenge" (more commonly referred to as the Kennedy Report), formally revisited the Meriam Report and examined the extent to which recommended change had occurred. The findings were appalling, with a scant few of the goals realized in the 35-year period (Szasz, 1974).

In 1977, President Carter's Commission on Mental Health found that in general the nation's minorities and rural populations were at increased risk for psychological and emotional distress (President's Commission on Mental Health, 1977). In response, Congress passed the Indian Child Welfare Act of 1978, which focuses on the prevention of serious emotional or physical damage to children, families with problems, or children "at risk" within these families. Specific applications of this act to Native Americans are with issues of personal safety and cultural genocide (with the continued practice of removing children from their families and kinship system) in order to attend boarding schools, and with foster placements (Red Horse, 1982).

SCHOOLING OF NATIVE AMERICANS

The history of government interventions with Native American children, particularly with respect to relocation efforts such as boarding schools and foster placement, has weakened families by removal of children from their family structure (Unger, 1977). Although the stated policy is one of assimilation, the results have been a disruption of normal family life and eventual cultural genocide. Parents are robbed of the full responsibility of parenting, which in effect stifles their maturing and as a result may perpetuate this continued practice (Unger, 1977). This continued practice of removing children from their family structure serves only to alienate children from their family, and parents in turn no longer know their own children. Such separation is bound to have an adverse effect on the family system and increase the likelihood of significant emotional problems, which often results in impaired academic performance and increased possibility of psychological problems that may last well in to adulthood (Unger, 1977; Metcalf, 1975).

Conflicts

The adverse effects of this process are greatest with ethnic groups that resemble the dominant culture the least, with those who are uprooted from their family structure, and with the disruption of traditional social supports (Yates, 1987). Children of disrupted families, chiefly among those who are not well grounded in traditional values or not fully acculturated, tend to be passive and less responsive than those from either traditional or fully acculturated families (Boggs, 1965). Parents in disrupted homes are less likely to interact and be involved with their children. This is exacerbated when children, through separation, have assimilated and parents have not, leaving them to feel abandoned and devalued (Yates, 1987).

Spilka (1966) posits that the schooling process contributes to feelings of alienation by virture of the abrupt shift in cultural values emphasized by the family in early years to the school's exclusive focus on the values of the dominant culture.

Although cultural conflict is quite prevalent and pervasive, the effects may not be readily apparent in the first few years of school as Native American children appear to be assimilating the dominant culture's values. Notwithstanding the likelihood that assimilation may have taken place to some extent, it is extremely more plausible that this response pattern is indeed quite superficial, which is commonly associated with a brusque shift in cultural standards (Krush, Bjork, Sindell, & Nelle, 1966). Further, attempts to match the values of the prevailing group are commonplace among children who are socially deprived (Zigler, 1983).

Academic Problems

Unfortunately, school experiences often accentuate, rather than lessen or resolve, feelings of alienation and identity prob-lems among Native American children and youth (Saslow & Harrover, 1968). The frequent result is a disproportionate incidence of academic, behavioral, and emotional concerns.

A sense of alienation and accompanying identity problems are fostered by a stripping away of values held to be important and replacing them with values that are largely incompatible with traditional values (Saslow & Harrover, 1968). Again, this begins with the earliest schooling experiences and the effects often go unnoticed, as early childhood development is largely at a normal rate, even somewhat advanced with the classification of shapes and colors (Spellman, 1968; Silk & Voyet, 1970). Development continues at a normal rate until verbal expectations increase, at which time measured IQ performances decrease. Academic achievement remains largely commensurate with the national average through third grade, at which time performance begins to diminish.

The beginnings of academic problems continue and escalate through adolescence. This reversal and downward trend in academic performance is recognized as the "crossover phenomenon" (Saslow & Harrover, 1968; Jessen, 1974). The trend or tendency is that the higher the grade level placement, the greater the disparity with the national average or expectation in academic performance (Zintz, 1960).

At an earlier time, failing to recognize the effects of this "crossover phenomenon," roughly 75 percent of Native American children were felt to be retarded (Anderson, 1936). Currently, in light of continued high rates of academic failures, it is not surprising that there is an overall dropout rate of 60 percent among children attending boarding school and a lower rate with those attending public day schools.

Accompanying this disproportionately high dropout rate is an alarming incidence of special education placements that greatly exceed the national incidence figures. At present, 33 percent are classified as learning disabled and 19 percent as mentally retarded; 20 to 25 percent experience significant emotional disorders (Ramirez & Hockenberry, 1980; Beiser, 1972; Goldstein, 1974). This probable overidentification and accompanying disproportionately high incidence of special education placement is likely attributed to a host of related factors. Two of the most critical factors are extremely high incidences of otitis media and inadequate prenatal and postnatal nutrition. Although these factors definitely mediate academic performance, more pronounced influences are cultural and language differences, both of which are largely incompatible with mainstream academic standards, as well as a general lack of sensitivity of assessment techniques (Bryde, 1971; Yates, 1987).

Language and Cognitive Differences

Academic problems are largely language based and may take the form of problems with auditory processing (discrimination, association, sequencing, or memory), verbal expression, or reading (John-Steiner & Osterreich, 1975; Lombardi, 1970; Trimble, Goddard, & Dinges, 1977; McShane, 1980). In contrast, strengths are often found with visual processing (spatial organization and memory of visual patterns), language patterns that are typified by verbal descriptions that are rich in visual detail, and the use of graphic metaphors (Kleinfeld, 1973). Even though these are decided strengths, they represent cognitive styles that are in many ways incompatible with the prevailing curriculum.

Although Native American children have many language opportunities in an atmosphere rich in oral language tradition, the language structure differs greatly. Languages that are visually mediated, as is the case with most of the vast number of Native American languages, tend to limit the ability to understand and make abstract verbalizations (John-Steiner & Osterreich, 1975). Moreover, languages that rely heavily on graphic visualizations and abstractions through metaphors are structured quite differently from English. The verb forms of Native American languages depend on shape; however, according to Carroll and Casagrande (1958), form-based languages do not readily lend themselves to verbal abstractions. As might be expected, Blanchard (1983) reports that Native American children's facility of English language is the poorest of any ethnic group.

Yates (1987) suggests that although Native American children have decided cognitive strengths, these are in areas that are not typically stressed in school. This mismatch creates academic dissonance that results in increased emotional problems, depression, helplessness, alienation, and behavioral problems. Although this appears to be a tenable hypothesis, school climate also plays an important role in diminished academic performance. Kleinfeld (1973) found that Native American children had enhanced performance on selected subtests of the Wechsler Intelligence Scale for Children when the examiner communicated nonverbal acceptance and warmth. Bryde (1971) generates the effects of acceptance and warmth to improved overall academic performance.

Academic problems are attenuated by a sense of alienation, which Spilka and Bryde (1966) define as a general condition in which values, mutually agreed upon goals, and means do not regulate behavior. The results are feelings of powerlessness, normlessness, meaninglessness, social isolation, and self-estrangement. This condition is more prevalent among adolescents in boarding schools, plaguing approximately 75 percent of them. These strong feelings of alienation exacerbate identity problems so common in adolescence (Erikson, 1963). Kleinfeld and Bloom (1977) posit that identity-related issues are at the core of most emotional problems among adolescents, particularly between the ages of 15 and 19 years. Academic problems are not the only negative consequence of this scenario, however; socioemotional concerns also abound.

SOCIAL CONCERNS

Alcohol and drug abuse in Native Americans is at an extremely high rate, with alcohol consumption among teenagers at 50 percent, as compared to 20 percent nationally (Jensen, Strauss, & Harris, 1977; Cockerham, 1975), and an alcoholism rate two to three times the national average (Beiser & Attneave, 1982; Goldstein, Oetting, Edwards, & Garcia-Mason, 1979). The incidence of substance abuse is at 22 percent, with an average of 9 percent (Beiser & Attneave, 1982; Goldstein et al., 1979). Adolescent males tend to resort to alcohol abuse, drug abuse, and delinquency, whereas females generally resort to alcohol abuse, suicide attempts, and unwanted pregnancies.

Alcohol abuse takes its toll with a high rate of accidents, suicides, delinquency, and related health problems. Alcohol is associated with 75 percent of the accidents and 80 percent of the suicide attempts among adolescents (Cohen, 1982). Suicides occur at twice the national average, with the largest incidence in late adolescence to early adult years (Unger, 1977).

Forslund and Meyers (1974) reported that 12 percent of the Native American adolescents make court appearances (compared to a national average of 2½ percent); these are mostly for alcohol-related misdemeanors or petty offenses. Curiously, when court appearances are controlled for alcohol, there is no significant difference between Native American adolescences and their counterparts (Forslund & Meyers, 1974).

The extremely high rate of foster placements, ranging from 5 to 20 times the national average (Mindell & Gurwitt, 1977; Buler, 1977), with 85 percent of these with non-Native American families (Mindell & Gurwitt, 1977), gives the impression of a similarly high rate of maltreatment, which is not the case. The rate of maltreatment is 6.5 per 1,000 with boys and 2.7 per 1,000 with girls, which is quite low when contrasted with 13 per 1,000 with black children and 15 per 1,000 for white children (Nagi, 1977; Oakland & Kane, 1973).

Maltreatment of Native American children is seldom in the form of physical abuse, as physical punishment is disdained by most Indian groups. Neglect, or, as is more often the case, perceived neglect comprises most cases of maltreatment (Nagi, 1977). The high rate of out-of-home placements is not directly related to documented cases of maltreatment, but rather to the policy of custodial care and acculturation. Removal of children from their homes and communities is not entirely the result of government intervention, as the Mormon church has played a key role in providing foster placements.

Despite relocation efforts, Native American children comprise a larger segment of the population, as represented by an average age of 17.3 years as compared to 29.5 years with the total population (Wallace, 1972). Roughly 326,000 children are school-aged, which comprises an extremely large proportion (Lazarus, 1982). The larger percentage of children is directly related to the birth rate that is roughly twice that of the national average.

However, the high birth rate is also associated with an infant mortality rate that exceeds that of any other ethnic group. The death rate among children and adolescents is two to three times the average incidence rate, with the majority of deaths occurring in infants and young children (Yates, 1987).

Native Americans have remained remarkably resilient in the face of long-standing adversity, which speaks to their adaptive skills and viability as a people. Exemplifying their resilience is the population level, which has steadily increased from approximately 220,000 in 1900 to between 1 and 2 million (U.S. Bureau of Census, 1980). These numbers represent a diverse group of people, with 478 distinct tribes recognized by the federal government and another 52 tribes not so recognized (Lazarus, 1982). Of these tribes, 180 are land based on reservations or reserves. Roughly one-third of the total number reside on reservations, one-third live off the reservation (mostly in urban areas), and the remaining one-third alternately spend time on and off the reservation (U.S. Bureau of Census, 1980).

The median annual income among Native American families is well below the poverty level, with an annual income of $13,678.00 and an even lower level on some reservations. The overall unemployment rate is approximately 40 percent, with rates as high as 75 to 90 percent on some reservations (U.S. Bureau of Census, 1980). Economically speaking, this is a severely disadvantaged population.

Accompanying these adverse economic conditions are a number of health problems. The disability rate ranges from four to six times the national average. Disabilities among children are related to inadequate nutrition, a high prevalence of hepatitis B infection, and otitis media. Diabetes and alcohol-related complications are the most common debilitating conditions among adults (Wallace, 1972; Association on American Indian Affairs [AAIA], 1986).

VALUE CONFLICTS

A preponderance of child, adolescent, and family problems are associated with a self-defeating stance that occurs when one finds it difficult to embrace the values of the dominant culture, even though to do so seemingly is the only path to success (Unger, 1977). Alienation and weakened identities, along with a general lack of economic means, result in a devalued ethnic self-image, hostility toward the dominant culture, and an absence of initiative (Saslow & Harrover, 1968). Bryde (1971) asserts that the clash of values is central to the legacy of government interference, the current state of affairs, and the ineffectiveness of typical child and family interventions.

Much of the misunderstanding that has precipitated the current situation with Native Americans is centered around a lack of appreciation and respect for traditional values. A word of caution is in order prior to such a discussion of traditional values. When one examines those values that are held in common across all tribal groups, much of the distinctiveness associated with each tribe, and for that matter with individuals, is lost at the risk of making such generalizations. Furthermore, this is a discussion of traditional values that are very much a part of the background of all Native Americans, but may not be adhered to by all, particularly those who have fully assimilated into the dominant culture. These values are largely held today among the more traditional individuals (i.e., those who reside on reservations) and to a lesser extent by those living off the reservation.

In determining the extent to which these values are practiced by individuals, it is necessary to ascertain whether they currently live on a reservation, the proximity of their family to the reservation, and how long they have lived off the reservation (Little Soldier, 1985). Although these traditional values are associated with an older way of life still largely practiced on reservations today, Red Horse and Red Horse (1981) suggest that even among urban Native Americans these values are still very much a part of their fabric, especially with respect to family ties. This discussion will highlight a number of separate domains that address respect for children and elders, cooperation and harmony, and family and kinship ties.

Respect for Children

Children, by and large, are accorded the same degree of respect as adults, within the context of a horizontal class structure (Blanchard, 1983; Pelletier, 1970). Children are viewed as autonomous equals and thus parents choose not to interfere in their lives (Ishisaka, 1978). This begins with an acceptance of basic impulses of children, in that infants are nursed when hungry, toddlers are allowed to eat and sleep whenever they choose, and toilet training is not attempted until a child can walk, talk, and understand some words (Saslow & Harrover, 1968). Erikson (1963) says of the Pine Ridge Sioux, "The developmental principle in this system holds that a child should be permitted to be an individualist while young" (p. 67).

Gill (1982) acknowledges a high degree of importance placed on childhood as a period of development and the soberness with which the responsibility for a child's welfare is assumed. Parents elect not to interfere in their child's development, thus allowing the child to make his or her own decisions. Children are given instruction and counsel, and are then shown respect and allowed to make their own decisions (Ishisaka, 1978). Children are given responsibility and authority to make their own decisions (Pelletier, 1970; Unger, 1977). Among Native Americans, noninterference in the lives of children is a sign of acceptance, whereas in contrast the values of the dominant culture interpret this archetype as indulgence or neglect (Pelletier, 1970).

Disciplinary Measures

In keeping with the respect accorded to children, disciplinary measures typically do not involve corporal punishment, as this is believed to do more harm than good (Niethammer, 1977). Gentleness is the rule with disobedient children, although some degree of harshness exists. The Papagos, of the southwest desert region, believed that children under 10 years old should be disciplined little so they would not have to experience suffering. Parents seemed undisturbed by a child's inappropriate behavior, ignoring rather than rebuking them. Expectations of children were greater among the plains Indians, such as the Cheyenne, with appropriate behavior being rewarded with love and warmth, whereas unacceptable behavior resulted in rejection and loneliness.

Many tribes, such as the Crow, Menominee, and Iroquois, poured water down the nose or splashed some on the face of disobedient or bawling children. The Fox and Winnebago tribes often had children reflect and fast for one meal when disobedient. Navajo and Quinault rebuke or shame older children who are disobedient. Few tribes revert to physical punishment and when doing so it is usually in the form of a light whipping by a community disciplinarian (e.g., the Sampoil) or a designated family member such as the mother's brother (e.g., the Tewa). The threat that a "bogey man" will carry away disobedient children is common with the Zuni and the Hopi (Neithammer, 1977).

Although Native American children

are disciplined, they are not accustomed to the typical structure of school. Loud talking, verbal reprimands, and physical punishment are viewed as ill-mannered. Patience and politeness are expected to allow for individual expression, and confrontations are perceived as rude interruptions. The typical result of this interchange is a display of shyness, or a disinterest in school. Native American children are accustomed to working without obvious structure and tend to work better when no one is directly "in charge." Even though they may at times acquiesce to the obvious structure of school, the prevailing attitude is that "we were here first and we will outlast you" (Pelletier, 1970; Bryde, 1971).

Respect for Elders

Traditional values are emphasized with children. Although such values are taught throughout the year by a variety of means, they are formally instructed by the grandfather's stories and by modeling on the part of grandparents regarding how to interact with the physical environment and within the social system (Pelletier, 1970). Respect for the wisdom of their elders is stressed and children are instructed not to question their elders or to look directly in their face, which is viewed as disrespect (Philips, 1972). The Cheyenne believe that the mores are safe as long as there is respect for the elders (Light & Martin, 1985). In addition, a number of indirect means are employed that include tone of voice, gesture, innuendo, laughter, and silence (Bryde, 1971).

The obvious implications of this pattern of early instruction for the schooling process is learning by observation, as opposed to a direct display of curiosity by interacting verbally and questioning. These differences in learning styles give the uninformed the impression of diminished capacity (Little Soldier, 1985).

Another common response pattern that is oft misunderstood is the dropping of one's head as a sign of respect and compliance to an elder; however, this is perceived by non-Native Americans as passivity and a lack of self-confidence (Little Soldier, 1985).

Although the transition from childhood to adulthood is often marked by "rights of passage" rituals or ceremonies, the maturing process is far more gradual, as even young children are given responsibilities, such as caring for infant siblings (Niethammer, 1977). Again, respect for the position of children is witnessed by the autonomy, the level of responsibilities, and the impact on the kinship system. Native Americans hold that not only does the community shape the child but the child shapes the community (Unger, 1977). Respect for children is consistent with the prevailing attitude of cooperation and harmony with the environment.

Cooperation and Harmony

Importance is placed on cooperation and harmony with the environment and with others. Competition is not discouraged, as is popularly believed; rather, intraindividual competition is encouraged as is competition with others, so long as no one is hurt, emotionally or physically, in the process (Bryde, 1971; Krush et al., 1966).

Specifically, this sense of cooperation and harmony surfaces in a system of reciprocity, which in many tribes is quite well defined and enforced (Bryde, 1971). Reciprocity has its roots in the early days when day-to-day physical survival depended on hunting and gathering. Although everyone initially concerned themselves with the survival of their immediate family, the next level of concern was for other kin and their survival. Although physical survival remains an issue in many instances, it is not as pressing a threat as psychological survival. This established network of support is by no means any less important today (Bryde, 1971).

The obvious implications in the school are realized immediately with a general lack of individual competition and a reliance on the peer structure, which are incompatible with traditional instructional and counseling approaches. Another outgrowth of this pattern is the open borrowing or even apparent theft of items within the classroom. *Apparent borrowing or theft* is a more appropriate term, because it really does not exist since there is no individual ownership among Native Americans, as everything belongs to everyone (Bryde, 1971).

Present Orientation

Another feature of harmony with one's environment is contentment to live in the present. Short-term present-oriented goals are consistent with this orientation; however, deadlines and long-range planning are markers for the future, which may not be realized (Little Soldier, 1985; Krush et al., 1966). This unhurried present orientation allows time to reflect patiently (Little Soldier, 1985). Although less stressful, the impressions of this orientation are of laziness or irresponsibility (Bryde, 1971). Similarly, the time to reflect is perceived as mental slowness (Little Soldier, 1985).

Traditional Family Structure and Values

Value Conflicts Affecting Family Relationships

Contributing concerns associated with cultural and identity conflicts are ongoing problems of poor nutrition and health, high unemployment, substandard housing, and high mortality rate. All of these stressors increase the likelihood of individual mental health problems, resulting in marked maladjustment with increased morbidity, mortality, alcohol abuse, homicide, and suicide (Goldstein, 1974). Although directly there is an increased risk for individual maladjustment, the repercussions are felt throughout the family unit.

The clash of values, whether direct or indirect, is ultimately felt the strongest within the family (Unger, 1977). Families as well as extended family relationships serve as the core of Native American tribal groups (Unger, 1977). The continuity of religion and kinship affiliation increases the likelihood of a stable childbearing environment (Goldstein, 1974). Disrupted or altered kinship ties, particularly of well-differentiated traditional families, poses a threat to parent-child relationships (Boggs, 1965). Goldstein (1974) suggests that continued changes in subsistence, residence, education, and religion result in marked changes in affiliation and interaction between family members.

The absence of clearly defined values, either traditional or those of the dominant culture, poses a threat to parental confidence in child rearing. This disruption produces a profound and perhaps long-lasting impact on children, as culture determines personality (Boggs, 1965).

Extended Family Ties

Extended family relationships are an integral aspect of Native American tribal groups, but they are not structured the same as European models of extended families with three generations living in the same household (Red Horse & Red Horse, 1981). Family relationships extend beyond the three generations of parents, children, and grandparents, to include anyone of blood relationship, however distant. Kinship is extended to all who belong to the larger extended family unit, which is referred to as a *clan*.

Native American extended families

are a horizontal extension of several households, irrespective of proximity, that share critical cultural components. This "village network" is strongest on reservations, but elements are found to some degree off the reservation in urban areas (Red Horse & Red Horse, 1981).

Within the framework of the "village network" is the concept of transactional field, in which all social transactions take place. The family represents the primary arena for cultural orientation and socialization. This practice usually involves the elders maintaining regular contact and responsibility for the grandchildren. Although this is commonplace on the reservation, it continues to be the family pattern with the overwhelming majority of urban families (Red Horse & Red Horse, 1981).

The obligation to the family system follows an interesting pattern. In the dominant culture, with increasing age there is a linear relationship with increased independence of the originating family unit, whereas the relationship among Native Americans is curvilinear. Mutual interdependence increases with age, as does a sense of family obligation, pattern maintenance responsibility, and dependence on mutuality of familial relationships. Typically throughout the life span there is a balance of interdependence and dependence, without hampering individual self-reliance (Red Horse & Red Horse, 1981).

Family responsibilities extend to all aspects of daily living. Reciprocity is a central responsibility to members of a clan and is necessary for physical survival and psychological support. Knowing that the larger community shares in the responsibility of meeting one's needs leads to greater confidence and peace of mind. Traditionally, all rejoice in an individual's accomplishments and share the disappointment of failures. A built-in support system is in place that extends beyond the immediate family to the clan and, in some cases, to all Native Americans (Bryde, 1971; Niethammer, 1977).

Tribal groups have developed well-defined and somewhat institutionalized roles within the clan structure (Saslow & Harrover, 1968). Exemplifying this structure is the matrilineal and often matrilocal organization of many tribes. Within this framework, the family unit is centered around the mother (Niethammer, 1977). All of the sisters on the mother's side are referred to as "mother" and are responsible for "true" motherly functions, including physical care, training, rewarding, punishing, and nursing (Bryde, 1971; Niethammer, 1977). Membership in the clan is held through one's mother. Even though the clan structure is quite large, one cannot marry anyone who holds membership in either the mother's or father's clan. When a young man marries, he is expected to leave his parents' band and go live with his bride and her family, of which her mother is the head. The wife holds the power within kinship ties, whereas the husband's power extends beyond the family (Downs, 1972).

In many tribes, such as the Navajo, the terminology with respect to kinship ties is quite complex, which speaks to the importance placed on extended family ties (Downs, 1972). Likewise, the structure is often quite well defined, such as with the Navajos where daughters and fathers maintain an indirect relationship through the mother/wife, both having a direct relationship with the mother/wife. Sons, however, enjoy a direct relationship with both mother and father (Downs, 1972).

The Hopi and Tewa define a distribution of responsibility within the extended family for the purposes of child rearing. Primary relationships that involve authority and control are the direct responsibility of the mother, as these are matrilineal and matrilocal people. Primary disciplinary powers are the responsibility of the mother's brothers. The father and his siblings are responsible for mutual aide and affection (Saslow & Harrover, 1968).

The tight structural organization of the community enforces social conformity among families. Social control is achieved through gossip, public ridicule, social ostracism, and historically through the use of witchcraft (Saslow & Harrover, 1968). The structure of family affiliations and interactions, though quite well defined, meets its greatest challenge when children enter school. Parents view school with mixed feelings as they realize that although an education is necessary for their children's survival in the dominant culture, it also poses a threat to cultural values (Saslow & Harrover, 1968).

INTERVENTIONS WITH CHILDREN AND FAMILIES

Problematic Concerns Related to Interventions

Prior to a discussion of guidelines for intervention with Native American children and families, it must be remembered that the non-Indian world is believed to be threatening and hostile. Nothing makes a Native American angrier than actions that are perceived as attempts to assimilate him or her into the dominant culture (Bryde, 1971).

Since kinship relations are valued, children are likely to view non-Indian help as meddlesome (Trimble, 1976; Bryde, 1971). As such, referrals may prove ineffective for this reason, as well as for the lack of voluntariness on the part of the child. Quite typically, when Native Americans need help they go for advice to one they can trust (Bryde, 1971). They tend to be quite sensitive to the need for trust and understanding in relationship building (Trimble, 1976). The trusted individual is usually considered to be a wise elder.

Often it may be enough to be in the presence of a wise elder, without a word spoken by either party, in order to benefit. When the wise one speaks, he or she is listened to and the listener takes and applies needed council often without a word spoken in return (Bryde, 1971).

Effective interventions begin with a genuine respect and love for Native American children (Bryde, 1971). Out of this position of genuine love, one can begin to increase individual awareness of traditional Native American values and thereby be in a better position to empower Native American students to utilize viable resources within their system to achieve personal self-fulfillment. It is necessary to assess the extent to which traditional values are ascribed to, as well as the values of the dominant culture. Realizing this stance helps to determine the likelihood and even the extent of cultural dissonance (Red Horse, 1982).

Fully enculturated (those adhering firmly to traditional values) or acculturated (those fully embracing the values of the dominant culture) children tend to be plagued with fewer culturally related problems. The greatest degree of conflict is with children that are caught between the two value systems, not well grounded in either culture. Assessing the value structure of a child also serves to ascertain the extent to which social support is available and usually accessed (Red Horse, 1982).

It is important to understand and appreciate the individual child's goals, motivations, and resources. Obviously it is not possible in this chapter to address the plethora of individual issues, but it is worthwhile to examine some common needs. These typically include self-acceptance, acceptance from others, and self-fulfillment.

Self-acceptance is a view of self in the context of the social system; namely, acceptance from family members and others in the Native American community.

Acceptance from others in a traditional sense is predicated on the extent to which one adheres to traditional values. Self-fulfillment from a traditional position might be summed up as "one who offers good advice and will help others when possible" (Bryde, 1971, p. 6). Traditional views of self are in the context of the larger group, which again is consistent with the spirit of cooperation and harmony. These needs or personal goals are seemingly not unique to Native American children until viewed in light of the traditional value structure.

Native American children often feel uncomfortable when they are the focus of attention; thus, individual therapies are likely to prove ineffective. Working through groups of peers is less threatening and is consistent with the prevailing attitude of cooperation and harmony. This approach may be more effective when no one individual is singled out; rather, all peers are encouraged to help one another and grow (Bryde, 1971).

Model for Counseling Native Americans

In this light, Red Horse and Red Horse (1981) advocate a "cultural network model" of counseling with Native Americans that transcends the conventional boundaries of group counseling. In this model, the peer group is integrated into the existing extended family system and community organizations. The peer group thereby becomes an extension of the family system, whereby all initial interventions take place. This process utilizes a combination of group work, cultural imperatives, and community standards of practice to reinforce the traditional value orientations characteristic of Native American extended families.

The guiding premise of this model is that families with strong traditional and structural integrity remain more cohesive and adaptable. Problems arise or are exacerbated when there is a disruption of traditional values. Interventions take place through the traditional transactional field of the family system. In doing so there is the potential for positive role model identification, where bonds are recaptured with the traditional values adhered to on the reservation. Relationships are recovered with dispersed members of the extended family. Also, there is a critical identification with traditional values.

Strong extended family relationships provide the structural fabric for the "cultural network model." In addition to working through the family system, a decided advantage of this approach is that it lessens the intrusiveness of helping professionals. Trust in professional involvement is enhanced, therapy goals are seen as more realistic when viewed in light of traditional expectations, and the helping professional is perceived as nonjudgmental.

Within this context, Red Horse (1982) further emphasizes four domains that need to be addressed when working with Native American families. The first is the *spiritual* aspect of the family system. In order to bring about behavioral change, there is a need to encourage harmony and congruence of mind, body, and spirit. Also, the use of traditional spiritual leaders, who possess rigorous training in cultural ways, is encouraged, particularly with those whose value system is more traditional or middle ground.

A second aspect to be addressed is that the strong sense of *group identity* among Native Americans produces a closed system that seemingly is impermeable to outsiders. Understandably, Native Americans prefer human services from other Native Americans or at least from those who follow the principle of immersion, whereby there is a conscious effort to appreciate and even join in family dilemmas in order to decrease social distance.

Again, it is important to remember that extended family relationships among Native Americans portray a symbolic sense of community through pure extended family ties. It is also significant that fictive relationships are common among bicultural families. Penetration of the family system is enhanced by treating the spiritual aspects of the family integrity with respect and dignity (Red Horse, 1982). This approach is consistent with Friesen's (1974) recommendation to encourage constituents, rather than work against the kinship structure.

A third phase is that of *picturing*, which is an active process in which family members assess group cohesiveness using symbolic cultural norms to revitalize familial integrity. To assist in this process, it is helpful to involve a number of cohorts within the context of the therapy session. Suggested individuals to include would be someone knowledgeable in Native American family development and process, another who intimately understands typical family scenarios (such as an elder), and, where appropriate, a spiritual leader (such as a medicine man).

The final aspect is joining or *mending fractured family systems*. This is accomplished by reconstituting the extended family in a manner compatible with traditional Native American value orientations. Again, the need to join or mend fractured families stems from the realization that by and large all of the problems experienced by Native American children are related to a conflict of their traditional values and the prevailing values of the dominant culture.

CONCLUSION

School personnel should make every effort to lessen the dissonance experienced by many Native Americans. Begin by recognizing the importance of the extended family and by respecting the parents, grandparents, aunts, and uncles as the child's "first teachers." The school should clearly be an extension of the home, not making any conscious effort to undermine traditional values (Biglin & Pratt, 1973). All interventions (counseling or curricular) are enhanced by a thorough understanding of traditional Native American values. The quality of all such interventions, as well as the classroom climate, will greatly be enhanced by not only a genuine respect for traditional values but also an incorporation of these values into the school setting.

Briefly stated, these values may be summed up to include a genuine respect for the dignity of childhood, an emphasis on modeling as an important instructional mode, recognizing the utility of cooperation to facilitate learning in a spirit of unity and harmony, and an unhurried "present" orientation that creates a comfortable atmosphere in which to appreciate the value of the moment. All of this is set in the secure context of well-defined extended family relationships.

Appreciation of the traditional value system of Native Americans is a necessary requisite for family/school-based interventions. A lack of respect for the values of Native Americans has resulted in a long history of genocide, in an attempt to replace traditional values with those of the dominant culture. This continued practice will only be met with resistance and hostility, yielding ineffective and counterproductive results at best.

There is a need to recognize and appreciate the value system of Native Americans and work through this system. More directly, there is a need to understand the individual Native American in light of this context in order to effect meaningful and lasting change.

References

Anderson, F. N. (1936). A mental-hygiene survey of problem Indian children in Oklahoma. *Mental Hygiene, 20,* 472–476.

Association on American Indian Affairs. (1986). *Program of activities.* New York: Author.

Beiser, M. (1972). Etiology of mental disorders: Social-cultural aspects. In B. Wolman (Ed.), *Manual of Child Psychopathology* (pp. 150–188). New York: McGraw-Hill.

Beiser, M., & Attneave, C. L. (1982). Mental disorders among Native American children: Risks and risk periods for entering treatment. *American Journal of Psychiatry, 139,* 193–198.

Biglin, J. E., & Pratt, W. (1973). *Indian parent involvement in education.* Las Cruces, NM: ERIC Clearinghouse on Rural Education and Small Schools.

Blanchard, E. L. (1983). The growth and development of American Indian and Alaskan native children. In G. J. Powell (Ed.), *The psychosocial development of minority group children* (pp. 115–130). New York: Brunner/Mazel.

Boggs, S. T. (1965). An interactional study of Ojibwa socialization. *American Sociological Review, 21,* 191–198.

Bryde, J. F. (1971). *Indian students and guidance.* New York: Houghton-Mifflin.

Buler, W. (1977). The destruction of American Indian families. In S. Unger (Ed.), *The destruction of American Indian families* (pp. 1–13). New York: Association on American Indian Affairs.

Carroll, J. B., & Casagrande, J. B. (1958). The function of language classifications in behavior. In E. E. Maccoby, T. M. Newcomb & E. O. Hartley (Eds.), *Readings in social psychology* (3rd ed.) (pp. 18–31). New York: Holt, Reinhart & Winston.

Cockerham, W. C. (1975). Drinking attitudes and practices among Wind River Reservation Indian youth. *Journal of Student Alcoholism, 36,* 321–326.

Cohen, S. (1982). Alcohol and the Indian. *Drug Abuse and Alcoholism Newsletter, 11,* 1–3.

Downs, J. F. (1972). *The Navajo.* New York: Holt, Rinehart & Winston.

Erikson, E. H. (1963). *Childhood and society* (2nd ed.). New York: W. W. Norton.

Fate, M. J. (1978). *Special needs of handicapped Indian children and Indian women's problems.* Washington, D.C.: Bureau of Indian Affairs, North American Indian Women's Association.

Forslund, M. A., & Meyers, R. E. (1974). Delinquency among Wind River Indian Reservation youth. *Criminology, 12,* 97–106.

Friesen, J. W. (1974). Education and values in an Indian community. *The Alberta Journal of Educational Research, 20,* 146–156.

Gill, S. D. (1982). *Native American tradition.* Belmont, CA: Wadsworth.

Goldstein, G. S. (1974). The model dormitory. *Psychiatry Annals, 4,* 85–92.

Goldstein, G. S., Oetting, E. R., Edwards, R., & Garcia-Mason, V. (1979). Drug use among Native American young adults. *The International Journal of Addictions, 14,* 855–860.

Green, H. J. (1983). Risks and attitudes associated with extracultural placement of American Indian children: A critical review. *Journal of the American Academy of Child Psychiatry, 22,* 63–67.

Ishisaka, H. (1978). American Indians and foster care: Cultural factors and separation. *Child Welfare, 57,* 299–307.

Jensen, G. F., Strauss, J. H. & Harris, V. W. (1977). Crime, delinquency, and the American Indian. *Human Organization, 36,* 252–257.

Jessen, M. (1974). An early childhood program for American Indians. *Contemporary Education, 45,* 278–281.

John-Steiner, V., & Osterreich, H. (1975). *Learning styles among Pueblo children: Final report.* (DHEW-NIE Grant, HEW: NE-G-00-3-0074). Albuquerque: University of New Mexico.

Kleinfeld, J. S. (1973). Effects of nonverbally communicated personal warmth on the intelligence test performance of Indian and Eskimo adolescents. *Journal of Social Psychology, 91,* 149–150.

Kleinfeld, J. S., & Bloom, J. (1977). Boarding schools: Effects on the mental health of Eskimo adolescents. *American Journal of Psychiatry, 134,* 411–417.

Krush, T. P., Bjork, J. W., Sindell, P. S., & Nelle, J. (1966). Some thoughts on the formulation of personality disorder: Study on an Indian boarding school population. *American Journal of Psychiatry, 122,* 868–876.

Lazarus, P. J. (1982). Counseling the Native American child: A question of values. *Elementary School Guidance and Counseling, 17,* 83–89.

Light, H. K., & Martin, R. E. (1985). Guidance of American Indian children: Their heritage and some contemporary views. *Journal of American Indian Education, 25,* 42–46.

Little Soldier, L. (1985). To soar with the eagles: Enculturation and acculturation of Indian children. *Childhood Education, 61,* 185–191.

Lombardi, T. P. (1970). Psycholinguistic abilities of Papago Indian school children. *Exceptional Children, 36,* 485–493.

McShane, D. (1980). A review of scores of American Indian children on the Wechsler Intelligence Scales. *White Cloud Journal, 1,* 3–10.

Metcalf, A. (1975). From school girl to mother: The effects of education on Navajo women. *Social Problems, 23,* 535–544.

Mindell, C. E., & Gurwitt, A. (1977). *The placement of American Indian children: The need for change.* Paper presented at the meeting of the American Academy of Child Psychiatry, Washington, DC.

Nagi, S. Z. (1977). *Child maltreatment in the United States.* New York: Columbia University Press.

Neithammer, C. (1977). *Daughters of the earth: The lives and legends of American Indian women.* New York: Collier Books.

Oakland, L., & Kane, R. L. (1973). The working mother and child neglect on the Navajo Reservation. *Pediatrics, 51,* 844–853.

Pelletier, W. (1970). Childhood in an Indian village. *Northian, 3,* 20–23.

Philips, S. U. (1972). Participant structures and communicative competence: Warm Springs children in community and classroom. In C. B. Cazden, V. P. John, & D. Hymes (Eds.), *Functions of language in the classroom* (pp. 370–394). New York: Teacher's College Press.

President's Commission on Mental Health. (1977). *Preliminary report.* Washington, DC: U.S. Government Printing Office.

Ramirez, B. A., & Hockenberry, C. M. (1980). *Special education policies for American Indian and Alaska native exceptional children.* Reston, VA: Council for Exceptional Children.

Red Horse, J. (1982). Clinical strategies for American Indian families in crisis. *Urban and Social Change Review, 2,* 17–19.

Red Horse, J. G., & Red Horse, Y. A. (1981). *A cultural network model: Perspectives from an urban-American Indian youth project.* (Report No. RC 014 678). Minneapolis, MN. (ERIC Document Reproduction Services, No. ED 248 997).

Saslow, H. L., & Harrower, M. J. (1968).

Research on psychosocial adjustment of Indian youth. *American Journal of Psychiatry, 125,* 224–231.

Silk, S., & Voyet, G. (1970). *Cross cultural study of cognitive development on the Pine Ridge Indian Reservation.* (Pine Ridge Research Bulletin, No. 11, DHEW Publication HSM 80-69-430). Washington, DC: Indian Health Service.

Spellman, C. M. (1968). *The shift from color to form preference in young children of different ethnic backgrounds.* Austin: University of Texas, Child Development Evaluation and Research Center.

Spilka, B. (1966). *The Sioux Indian school child: A tentative perspective for education.* Denver: University of Denver, Psychology Department.

Spilka, B., & Bryde, J. F. (1966). *Alienation and achievement among Oglala Sioux secondary students.* Denver: University of Denver, Psychology Department.

Szasz, M. (1974). *Education and the American Indian: The road to Self-Determination, 1928–1973.* Albuquerque: University of New Mexico Press.

Thompson, T. O. (Ed.). (1978). *The schooling of Native America.* Washington, DC: American Association of Colleges for Teacher Education and The Teacher Corps, United States Office of Education.

Trimble, J. E. (1976). Value differences among American Indians: Concerns for the concerned counselor. In P. Pederson, J. Draguns, W. Conner, & J. Trimble (Eds.), *Counseling across cultures* (pp. 65–81). Honolulu: University Press of Hawaii.

Trimble, J. E., Goddard, A., & Dinges, N. G. (1977). *Reviews of the literature on educational needs and problems of American Indians, 1971–1976.* (Report No. DHEW Contract 300-76-0436). Seattle, WA: Ba Helle Memorial Institute, Social Change Center.

Unger, S. (Ed.). (1977). *The destruction of American Indian families.* New York: Association on American Indian Affairs.

U.S. Bureau of Census. (1980). *1980 Statistical Abstracts.* Washington, DC: U.S. Government Printing Office.

Wallace, H. M. (1972). The health of American Indian children. *Health Service Reprints, 87,* 867–876.

Yates, A. (1987). Current status and future directions of research on the American Indian child. *American Journal of Psychiatry, 144,* 1135–1142.

Young, M. (1977). *Captives within a free society*. American Indian Policy Review Commission's Tentative Final Report. Washington, DC.

Zigler, E. F. (Ed.). (1983). *Children, families, and government: Perspectives on American social policy*. Cambridge: Cambridge University Press.

Zintz, M. V. (1960). *Indian research study, final report*. Albuquerque: University of New Mexico.

Proactive Family-School Partnerships in Early Intervention

KATHLEEN D. PAGET
University of South Carolina

We need to look at new approaches to families. We need to recognize the resilience of the American family, even though it may be different from ours, and we need to realize that we are not going to be able to have one approach or one program or one set of parents' meetings or one manual that fits every parent. (Vincent, 1985, p. 35)

Promoting proactive partnerships between families and schools is an art. As illustrated by the above quote, no standard set of techniques can ever be developed to apply to all situations. Recent demographic changes reveal the myth of a "typical" American family and challenge us to embrace a respect for diversity (Vincent & Salisbury, 1988). With such diversity, interactions between school personnel and families must be characterized by a reciprocal responsivity to the complexities of one another's situations and by a rhythm calibrated to one another's needs. In short, the chemistry must be there.

Historically, parent-school relations have been uni-directional rather than reciprocal, and conflictual rather than re-sponsive. During colonial times, parents were active in efforts to improve their children's schools, but received little from the school in return (Kagan, 1987). Since the passage of the Education of All Handicapped Children's Act in 1975, parents have been "involved" in numerous facets of their children's education, but have felt they were more on the receiving than the giving end of the information flow (Goldstein & Turnbull, 1982; Hocutt & Wiegerink, 1983). Admittedly, parents now desire a mutually balanced role for themselves and other members of their families when interacting with school personnel.

The importance of family-school partnerships to the quality of a very young child's early education cannot be overstated. A confluence of developmental, ecological, and behavioral principles has long suggested that services to infants, toddlers, and their families are not appropriate without concomitant services to families (Belsky, 1981; Bronfenbrenner, 1979; Dunst, 1985; Garbarino, 1983). It goes without saying that when the home-school interface is strong, the children involved are likely to benefit (Bronfenbrenner, 1979; Garbarino, 1983). In fact, the family is such an important influence on young children's development, that school systems should be considered supplemental to family systems rather than families being perceived as adjunctive to schools (Farkas, 1981).

The recent passage of Public Law 99–457 (The Education of the Handicapped Act Amendments of 1986) affords school personnel numerous opportunities to engage in exchanges with families of very young children. Within the Preschool Grant Program for children three through five years of age, parent involvement and all due process rights therein are an "allowable cost" rather than paid services targeting the child only. Within the Early Intervention Program for handicapped infants and toddlers birth through two years of age, the family system as a whole is emphasized, with the Individualized Family Service Plan (IFSP) structuring an assessment of family strengths and needs as they relate to the young infant or toddler. The IFSP must be evaluated with parents at least once a year and reviewed every six months or more often when appropriate.

Case management procedures and interagency collaboration also are mechanisms for more frequent and regularly scheduled communication between schools and families. Although the acknowledgment of the family as a system is more explicit in the legislation for infants and toddlers than for preschool-aged children, it is the belief of this author that services to families birth onward should be conceptualized in systemic terms. Thus, throughout the information that follows, the word *families* will appear instead of *parents*. This shift is expressed as part of a movement away from "parent involvement" as we knew it under Public Law 94–142 to "family support," as we will come to know it under Public Law 99–457

(Kagan, 1987; Turnbull & Summers, 1986).

The purpose of this chapter is to provide a framework for operationalizing opportunities for family-school partnerships, with families of infants, toddlers, and preschoolers who have impairments comprising the focus of discussion. In the spirit of normalization, the principles and strategies also apply to families of all children who attend school. The chapter begins with a discussion of partnership from a systemic perspective, moves to an explication of principles that guide successful partnerships, and proceeds to specific strategies for linking school and family subsystems. In addition, innovative school-based programs that are creatively developing linkages for families are discussed.

A SYSTEMS PERSPECTIVE ON PARTNERSHIPS

Just as families comprise uniquely configurated subsystems (e.g., sibling, extended family, marital, parental), so are school systems composed of component parts. Each school system operates in its own unique fashion based on the interrelationships among these components (Plas, 1986). Individuals available as resources to families comprise professional/paraprofessional and administrative/direct service subsystems and include principals, teachers, psychologists, exceptional education coordinators, teacher aides, counselors, social workers, school board members, the school district administration, secretaries, and bus drivers. With this many available resources, opportunities abound for multiple and mutually respectful relationships that create strong family-school partnerships (cf. Garbarino, 1983). Use of the term *school personnel* rather than *school professionals* conceptually and semantically broadens the diversity of individuals within the school system with whom families should feel free to have contact.

From a systemic perspective, recognition is given to the interplay of variables that occurs when families and school personnel interact. In Barsch's (1969) words, "What would at first glance appear to be a relatively mechanical, simple encounter is in truth a very complex situation" (p. 12). Contributing to the complexity are the following:

1. Varied social, economic, educational, ethnic, racial, and religious backgrounds of families and school personnel
2. Past experiences of parents in interacting with schools and professionals
3. Past experiences of school personnel in interacting with parents
4. The level of interpersonal communication skill possessed by parents and school personnel
5. Their respective beliefs about schooling, parenting, and handicapping conditions
6. Their expectations and stereotypes
7. Their personal and professional value systems (Seligman, 1979)

The complexity is also explained well by Bandura's (1978) reciprocal determinism model, whereby the individuals in a partnership are understood as bringing to it elements of each person's characteristics, beliefs, training, and experiences; the current and previous environments within which each person has functioned; and each person's interactional patterns with significant environments. Bandura's model offers a proactive framework within which to view partnerships in that each person's behavior has the potential to influence (change) the environments in which he or she functions. Because of its

emphasis on person-environment interactions within all relevant settings, the reciprocal determinism model is aligned closely with what other writers have termed "a systems perspective" (e.g., Turnbull & Turnbull, 1986), "systemic communication" (Plas, 1986), or "systems thinking" (Christenson, Abery, & Weinberg, 1986).

From the vantage point of systemic communication and reciprocal determinism, when differences exist between families and professionals, much potential exists for positive change and strong partnerships. In fact, Plas (1981) states that "strength is available to the process if the individuals are not of one mind. There is creative energy to be tapped within the tensions created by oppositional frames of reference" (p. 75). Thus, the mere existence of differences may set the stage for positive communication if the individuals involved enter situations with a view toward facilitating the creation of a solution that finds no one gaining at the expense of another's loss.

In contrast to a win-win philosophy, there often is a win-lose element in interactions. When family-school relationships become problematic, there is a tendency to place the blame on one or the other party, by defining the problem as existing in either the school personnel or the family. If school personnel take the position that families are responsible for the problems that arise in interactions, then they are likely to believe it is families' responsibility for ameliorating the problems. Dunst, Trivette, and Deal (1988) put it this way:

The dilemma and predicament that professionals get themselves into when working with families is thinking about things as right or wrong, black or white, night or day. Anytime one thinks about things in an either-or fashion, sooner or later the professional will see him or herself as right and the family as wrong and try to convince or even coerce the family into doing what the help giver considers appropriate or right. (p. 61)

Presumably, the same is true when families see school personnel as the cause of a difficulty. Under these conditions, differences become conflicts because the individuals involved take sides and create oppositional encounters (Dunst, Trivette, & Deal, 1988).

From a reciprocal determinism and systemic perspective, the quality of communication is representative of an interactive system rather than individual people (Bandura, 1978; Bertalanffy, 1968; Plas, 1986). That is, the locus of communication is viewed as residing in the *interactions* between people, not within people. Thus, when problems arise, the emphasis is on changing interactional patterns and deflecting attention away from placing blame for the problem on one person or another. Instead of focusing on the issue of blame, one is free to explore the variables that may contribute to the difficulty in communication. This sense of freedom lends itself to perspective taking and provides professionals and families the opportunity to see how the problem appears to themselves and each other.

Sometimes it is relatively easy to identify the variables that contribute to a particular problem, such as when parents cannot participate regularly in school meetings because they have no telephone or transportation (Turnbull & Turnbull, 1986). In other cases, the variables may be less obvious and more difficult to identify and address, such as in situations where there is a clash of beliefs between the parent and a person within a school. The important point is that the parties involved work together to explore and resolve the problem. By engaging in the process of mutual problem solving, both parties have the opportunity to express and try to fulfill

their needs. Furthermore, a willingness to share responsibility for communication difficulties maximizes the probability that families and school personnel work toward mutual solutions in a nonthreatening and nondefensive manner.

PRINCIPLES OF PROACTIVE PARTNERSHIPS

Dunst and Trivette (1987, pp. 451–453) delineate 12 principles that have implications for the manner in which school personnel develop, implement, and evaluate their communication patterns with families. Taken collectively with a systems perspective, the principles enhance the likelihood that relationships will be proactive and empowering. Deriving their principles from the help-seeking literature (e.g., Fisher, Nadler, & DePaulo, 1983; Gross & McMullen, 1983), Dunst and Trivette suggest the following for school personnel:

1. *Be both positive and proactive.* This principle suggests the need for a sincere sense of caring, warmth, and encouragement when offering or responding to requests. An important outcome of this is freedom of self-expression felt by families.

2. *Offer rather than wait for help to be requested.* School personnel who are sensitive to family members' verbal, nonverbal, and paraverbal messages are likely to be perceived by the family as more responsive to their needs. When this occurs, the likelihood of a strong partnership is enhanced.

3. *Engage in help-giving acts in which locus of decision making clearly rests with the family.* This includes decisions about needs, goals, options for carrying out interventions, and whether or not to accept the services offered by the school. Thus, to be maximally effective, the ability to refuse services must be explicitly recognized by

the school, the decision sanctioned, and the opportunity for future interactions left open as an option, not a demand. The involvement of families in partnerships with school personnel is likely to be stronger if this principle is applied and families are involved on a voluntary basis.

4. *Offer aid and assistance that is normative in terms of the family's own culture.* Nonnormative help frequently is demeaning and conveys a sense that the family has an inferior status or is incompetent (Hobbs, Dokecki, Hoover-Dempsey, Moroney, Shane, & Weeks, 1984). Thus, in our interactions with families whose culture or socioeconomic status is different from our own, we must not imply deviance or deficits. Rather, understanding a family's culture and social network may be key to partnership.

5. *Offer aid and assistance that is congruent with the family's appraisal of their problems or needs.* Without this as a guiding principle, families may be resistant to professional recommendations, which they perceive to be inaccurate and intrusive.

6. *Offer aid and assistance in which the response costs of seeking and accepting help do not outweigh the benefits* (Gross & McMullen, 1983). From families' points of view, services that are offered in ways that promote self-esteem, a sense of control, competence, and adequacy are more likely to be seen as personally cost effective.

7. *Offer help that can be reciprocated and sanction the possibility of "repaying" the helpgiver.* Reciprocity is a method of reducing indebtedness and enhancing self-esteem. Professionals who encourage a payback system of some kind bolster family members' sense that they have as much to give as to take. This principle embodies the spirit of partnership as a mutual relationship among individuals of equal status.

8. *Enhance the self-esteem of the recipient and help the individual experience immediate success in solving a problem or meeting a need* (Nadler & Mayseless, 1983). This is accom-

plished by using a family's existing strengths as a basis for helping them solve small problems and experience immediate success before tackling more difficult problems and needs. Self-esteem enhancement of family members is likely to lead to responsive behaviors and motivation, and thus, is key to formation of partnerships with reticent or "resistant" families and maintenance of partnerships with all families.

9. *Promote the family's use of natural support networks and neither replace or supplant them with professional services* (Hobbs et al., 1984). According to Hobbs (1975), help-giving efforts are empowering if they strengthen normal socializing agents (relatives, neighbors, friends, etc.) and promote a sense of competence and well-being among all members of the family's social network. Thus, school personnel should both (a) respond to requests from families regarding the support of identified network members and (b) initiate assistance to families in identifying new network members who are, as yet, untapped resources.

10. *Convey a sense of cooperation and joint responsibility (partnership) for meeting needs and solving problems* (Hobbs et al., 1984). Exchanges that promote participatory decision making and shared responsibility set the occasion for the family to feel valued, important, and "an equal."

11. *Promote the acquisition of effective behavior that decreases the need for help, thus making the person more capable and competent.* This type of help "enables the recipient to become more self-sustaining and less in need of future help" (Brickman, Kidder, Coates, Robinowitz, Cohn, & Karvza, 1983, p. 19), thus promoting independence and problem-solving capabilities. Especially as a result of initiatives related to interagency coordination within Public Law 99–457, parents of young children with special needs will be in contact with innumerable human service professionals. Thus, it behooves professionals to en-

franchise and empower parents as their children's best advocates.

12. *Help the family not only see that problems have been solved or needs met but that the family member(s) functioned as active, responsible agents who played a signficant role in improving his or her own life* (Bandura, 1982). According to Brickman and colleagues (1983), "It is the recipient's own belief in (himself or herself) as a causal agent that determines whether the gains made will last or disappear" (p. 32). Thus, parents and other family members should perceive *themselves* as responsible for producing and maintaining the abilities to meet their own needs and those of the child.

Turnbull and Summers (1986, p. 303) make four additional recommendations that serve as additional guidelines for promoting partnerships. These authors emphasize the following for service providers:

• Individualize our responses, respect families' preferences, and provide an array of options for participation from which families can choose.
• Make certain that our recommended interventions do not upset the delicate balance of the entire family system, by ensuring that what we ask is both important and efficient and by recognizing the legitimate interests of all family members.
• Recognize the competing responsibilities of families, support them in setting priorities according to their values, and help focus attention on the positive contributions that a child with a disability makes to meeting family needs.
• Be supportive of families as they move through the life cycle.

Synthesis of these recommendations and principles suggests that school personnel must reexamine their ability to (1) offer preferences for involvement to families, (2) identify demands and expectations placed on families, (3) implement effective help-giving strategies, (4) express respect of alternative family relationships and emerging family systems, and (5) encourage families to provide feedback regarding the services they receive.

It is particularly important that these principles be applied artfully with parents of very young children, given the possibility that such parents have not had prior contact in a parental role with school personnel, feel more deferential to professional judgment than more experienced parents, experience stress during the transition to public school, are beginning to confront issues of stigma, and are seeking their own ideology to guide decision making (Barber, Turnbull, Behr, & Kerns, 1988). Possessing a conceptual grasp of the principles and feeling confident in implementing them are two different processes. Thus, implementation strategies are discussed in the next sections.

STRATEGIES FOR RECOGNIZING NEEDS OF FAMILY SUBSYSTEMS

Although it is unlikely that all subsystems within a family would be equally involved in a young disabled child's education, it is essential that school personnel approach the family from a systemic perspective. In doing so, the complexities of a family's situation emerge naturally and an optimal number of significant others are communicating with the school and with each other. With respect to the complexity of family systems and subsystems, Winton (1986) states, "Perhaps the most important guiding principle in . . . designing intervention with families is to be able to direct one's focus to certain aspects of the system, while at the same time making sure to acknowledge what parts of the system are being ignored and why" (p. 249).

In the spirit of the above quotation, the following is a discussion of methods for including family subsystems in family-school interactions. The reader is wise to bear in mind that this particular conceptualization of subsystems is somewhat arbitrary and is done for purposes of clarification. Each family is comprised of its own unique configuration of subsystems, with the forms of interaction across subsystems varying from one family to the other.

The Marital Subsystem

Researchers agree that the birth of an infant impacts husband-wife relationships although the exact nature of the impact is likely to vary from one family to the next (Crnic, Greenberg, Ragozin, Robinson, & Basham, 1983). When developing partnerships with parents, school personnel must be sensitive to the implicit and explicit needs of the parents as marital partners. Turnbull and Turnbull (1986, p. 51) suggest the following:

- If couples indicate they do not have much time alone, encourage them to consider activities they may wish to engage in separately from their child or children.
- Provide information on community respite care or childcare services parents may access when they choose to spend time separate from their child or children. Informal arrangements may be preferred between couples interested in reciprocating childcare.
- Consider the time and energy "costs" of home interventions. Questions may be asked, such as, "Will this home program interfere with evening time with your husband or wife?" "Are there alternatives that might work better?"

- Seek ways to offer flexible scheduling or alternatives if a planned school activity conflicts with an activity a couple has planned.

The Parental Subsystem

Research evidence underscores the need for school personnel to promote partnerships by responding to each parent's needs rather than approaching parents as a homogeneous pair (Brotherson, 1985; Gallagher, Cross, & Scharfman, 1981). Fathers and mothers may share many of the same concerns, but they each also may have concerns and challenges that are uniquely their own. For single parents, it is important to understand their needs without overinterpreting their single-parenthood status as the cause of all obstacles encountered.

To maximize opportunities to involve parents, Turnbull and Turnbull (1986, pp. 54–55) suggest the following for school personnel:

- Assist mothers and fathers in identifying alternative activities that accommodate the needs of their young child with an exceptionality. For example, although a father may not be able to play softball with his physically disabled son, together, they can collect softball cards of their favorite players.
- Provide and encourage visiting opportunities at school for both mothers and fathers. Send a letter home at the beginning of the year (with quarterly reminders) of the school's visiting policy, which should reflect flexibility, responsivity, and accessibility to families. Individual visits could be supplemented by regular visiting days for groups of parents.
- Develop flexible scheduling to accommodate both working parents for IEP, IFSP, evaluation, or parent-teacher conferences. School policy may dictate the times for some conferences, but staff could

change their schedule on parent-teacher conference days to work from noon to 8:00 P.M. rather than 8:00 A.M. to 4:00 P.M. Provide opportunities for another conference if one parent is unable to attend. For a single-parent family, provide flexible scheduling and opportunities for the parent to attend with a friend, relative, or other advocate.

• Aid both fathers and mothers in locating information to provide them with necessary knowledge. Both parents may have a great need for a variety of information pertaining to (1) their child's exceptionality, (2) aspects of a particular exceptionality, (3) legal issues and policies relating to rights and benefits, and (4) consent issues. Each parent may have a need for different information. In addition to professional literature, parents may benefit from reading the personal experiences of other parents. Develop a library, allowing parents and other family members opportunities to check out materials.

• Provide parents with the opportunity to discuss with other parents their concerns, successes, and experiences in raising a child with an exceptionality. One strategy is to establish father, mother, or parent support groups. Another strategy is to arrange "mentor" relationships between "experienced" parents who would agree to spend time with parents who are new to these circumstances.

The Sibling Subsystem

Many young children with exceptionalities live in families with brothers and sisters who are younger or older, handicapped or nonhandicapped. Many variables make the sibling subsystem a particularly unique one that exerts considerable influence within a family constellation (cf. Paget, 1988). In fact, data exist to suggest that by one year of age, children spend as much time interacting with their siblings as with their mothers or fathers (Lawson & In-

gleby, 1974). Research has indicated that siblings may be very effective in training programs and that such training may result in benefits for the entire family (Simeonsson & Bailey, 1986; Brody & Stoneman, 1986; Hannah & Midlarsky, 1985). Thus, school personnel must be aware of the importance of this subsystem within some families and encourage sibling participation in family-school partnerships. Turnbull and Turnbull (1986, pp. 56–57) make the following suggestions:

• Include siblings, when appropriate, in intervention planning and ask them to attend the IEP or IFSP conference. If a sibling chooses to assume an active part in the education and training of the child with an exceptionality, and it is advantageous to both, make opportunities available for siblings to have a role. Allow opportunities to participate in a variety of ways and to the extent that the sibling chooses.

• Provide information or resources to siblings who would like more information about exceptionality (e.g., Powell & Ogle, 1985). This could be part of the parent resource library and coordinated by a special education teacher, social worker, school psychologist, or counselor. Make someone available if a sibling would like someone to talk to. A specific source of information for siblings is a newsletter, *Sibling Information Network,* published through the Department of Educational Psychology, University of Connecticut, Storrs, CT 06268.

• Arrange a time for siblings to observe their brother or sister in the special classroom. This could give siblings an opportunity to observe the successes of their brother or sister, as well as observe the methods and procedures that are used. Important caveats, however, are that some siblings will indicate a personal need not to be associated with their brother or sister in a school setting and that observation of classroom settings should be done when a knowledgeable adult is available to respond to questions and comments.

• Allow siblings to obtain information and discuss their feelings and fears in a safe environment, thus providing the opportunity to share experiences. A sibling support group could be conducted by a teacher, principal, social worker, psychologist, or counselor, as well as PTA members who are siblings of a person with an exceptionality.

The Extrafamilial Subsystem

Accumulating evidence suggests the roles played by extended family and community (e.g., neighborhood) members serve to modify family interactions and stress levels and facilitate intervention efforts (Bronfenbrenner & Crouter, 1982; Crnic et al., 1983; Hobbs, 1975; Vadasy, Fewell, Meyer, & Greenberg, 1985). Especially relevant to family-school partnerships are findings that absence of support and dissatisfaction with existing relationships are associated with resistance to professionally prescribed intervention plans (Dunst, 1986; Dunst, Trivette, & Deal, 1988). Without satisfactory social support, a family's unmet needs, isolation, and frustration may result in school personnel becoming just another aversive group to avoid.

Families are likely at times to want the presence of a support person during their interactions with school personnel. These requests are entirely consistent with Hobbs's (1975) notion regarding the importance of strengthening existing social networks. Turnbull and Turnbull (1986, p. 60) make additional recommendations for school personnel so as to promote a family's sense of social support:

• Ask the parents if there are any friends or relatives who would like more information about exceptionality and what type of information they want. The same checkout resource library made available to parents and siblings could also be made available to others.

• Consider conducting a grandparent or other extended family member support group. This group could give relatives an opportunity to share their concerns and successes with others in similar situations. It could be organized by the school social worker, psychologist, counselor, or possibly a PTA volunteer who is a grandparent or an extended family member of a child with an exceptionality.

When considering specific strategies for involving family subsystems in partnerships with schools, it becomes clear that a wide-angled, systemic view of intra- and extrafamilial subsystems is necessary to meet the unique needs of families. It is imperative that school personnel, together with the family, discern which subsystems within the family *and* school to mobilize so as to promote the most effective partnerships possible. It is conceivable, for example, that a mother may want her neighbor, who provides respite service for her child to be present, as well as the school's bus driver, who has a particularly good relationship with her child.

With a broad scope on the multitude of possibilities for partnership, school personnel will likely be more responsive to the special requests made by families. Thus, although policy mandates a minimum structure for conferences such as IEP and IFSP meetings, there is no reason why constraints need to be placed on the selection of additional individuals that family members choose to be involved.

RECOGNITION OF FAMILY PREFERENCES FOR INVOLVEMENT

An overlooked strategy for enhancing the likelihood of effective family-school partnerships is to evaluate early in the school year the variety of ways that families wish to be involved. A continuum of strategies, anchored by formal opportunities at one end and informal opportunities at the other, provides a wide range of possibilities. Although we often conceptualize planned conferences (e.g., IEP/IFSP meetings and review) as the primary forum for communication, other opportunities abound to set the stage for open exchanges of information:

- Unplanned conferences
- Family handbook
- Handouts for specific situations
- Newsletters
- Letters
- Written notes
- Photo notes
- Log books
- Progress reports
- Written and telephone messages
- Special activities (e.g., special lunches, field days for students and parents, school-improvement projects)

A collection of opportunities is likely to be essential to meet the unique needs and preferences of families. In this regard, some researchers have found that informal contact is often *preferred* by parents to more formalized contact (Turnbull, Winton, Blacher, & Salkind, 1983; Powell, 1987; Winton & Turnbull, 1981) and often is a good precursor to more formal meetings.

Two major characteristics of informal contact desired by parents are that it be frequent and that information be shared in a "give-and-take" fashion. Thus, systematic opportunities must be created for families to respond to the information provided by the school to ensure a reciprocal and active role for the family in the communication process. A log book on a child's school experiences could be formatted in such a way as to provide space for regular entries by school personnel *and* responses by family members. In addition, newsletters may be written jointly by school personnel and family members, or such newsletters could be a forum for expression by a family-to-family support group. Informal conversation, or "kitchen talk," is also an important element of a support group's experience (Powell, 1987). The operative issue is that a variety of communication models needs to be offered to families, with efforts made to proactively meet the needs of each family member rather than reactively confront unmet needs later.

A matrix for conceptualizing and recording such opportunities appears in Figure 1. Although not intended to be exhaustive, the matrix illustrates that many simple, innovative strategies may be implemented, and numerous individuals involved, given the requisite flexibility, creativity, and motivation to enhance the information flow with families. School personnel may wish to consider developing record forms based on the matrix, with such forms structured to include information regarding (1) the names of school personnel who would facilitate the interactions and (2) the frequency with which the forms would be completed and reviewed. In the spirit of reciprocity, direct communication with family members is essential to assess their preferred forms of involvement. Thus, the matrix in Figure 1 also can be used as a menu of opportunities from which family members select their preferences.

Additional resources for evaluating needs and preferences of families are provided by Turnbull and Turnbull (1986) and Farkas (1981). These sources include a variety of excellent checklists unique to school boards, principals, teachers, and families to self-examine, evaluate, and discuss school policies and practices related to serving families. The unique features of these checklists are (1) their provision of collective viewpoints and individual per-

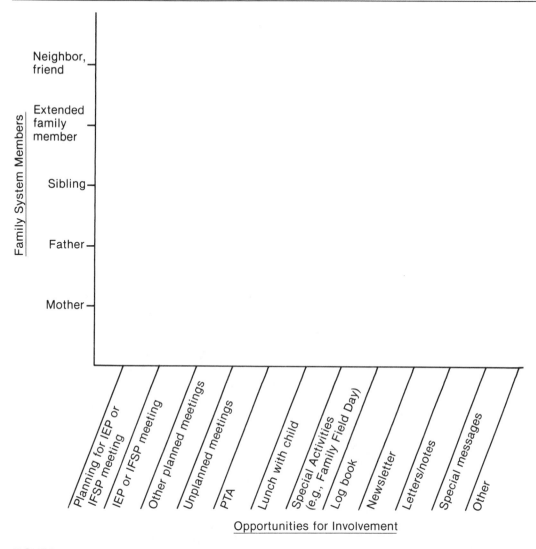

FIGURE 1 Plan of proactive partnerships

spectives on various aspects of home-school communication, (2) their emphasis on both the content and process of communication, and (3) their utility as mechanisms for enhancing communication among key individuals within a school. Because of their innovativeness, specificity, and comprehensiveness, these checklists are excellent departure points for future instrument development in this area. Pe-

rusal of these checklists quickly illustrates their utility for positively enhancing family-school partnerships, through individual interviews or "consciousness-raising" group activities. During the process of generating options for involvement, school personnel must remember to apply the help-giving principles delineated earlier and present the option of *no involvement* to families. If the family so chooses, the door may be left open for involvement at a future point in time.

INNOVATIVE SCHOOL-BASED PROGRAMS

Although school-based family support programs are not plentiful in number, several model programs do exist. The following are selected examples (cited in Kagan, 1987) of family support efforts functioning in conjunction with public schools. Developed for all interested families, these programs serve as useful departure points for programmatic options that possess a normalizing spirit for families of young children with impairments.

• *New Parents as Teachers.* Operating in Missouri school districts, this program provides information and services to any family with a child under three years of age. Families are assisted in providing a home environment that aids child development. The schools offer services to parents before the child is born and continue providing support until the child reaches age three. Multiple services include drop-in childcare, home visitor programs, a lending library, newsletters, joint parent-child activities, information and referral systems, parent support and education groups, and a "warm-line."

• *Peralta Year-Round School.* Serving a multiethnic community in California, the Peralta School operates on a year-round schedule. The schedule and other policies were developed *by* parents to meet *their* needs. After-school services are provided for children of working parents, evening parent education and support groups are maintained, and a networking line and information and referral services are provided.

• *Parent Education Resource Center* (PERC). Operating in Utah, PERC is a re-

source center that lends books, tapes, educational toys, and filmstrips on child development and parenting to families. PERC also sponsors many workshops for families, using representatives from community health, mental health, social and family service agencies, and the PTA.

• *Parents in Touch.* In Indianapolis, Indiana, this program promotes the direct participation of parents in the education of their children and strengthens communication and cooperation between home and school. There is a coordinated system of parent-teacher conferences, workshops, DIAL-A-TEACHER, home visits, and a parent line offering recorded messages.

Characteristics common to these programs are proactive accessibility, flexibility, and responsivity to family needs and concerns. Interested readers are encouraged to consider ways to adapt and combine elements of innovative programs to meet their needs in their respective employment settings. Additional descriptions of exemplary programs appear in publications such as the newsletter of the Family Resource Coalition.

FUTURE DIRECTIONS

As long ago as 1917, John Dewey wrote, "A being which can use given and finished facts as signs of things to come, which can take given things as evidence of absent things can, in that degree, forecasts the future" (p. 21).

Activities related to family-school partnerships have no "given and finished" facts. Though there are traditional practices, these "old habits" need not guide the ways in which we serve young children and their families in the future. Given the changing composition of the American family, flexible and responsive family support must be a central part of all early intervention services. Legislative initiatives, research findings, and best practices combine to create a platform for this to occur.

Recognition of the changing needs of families and children is only one of many prerequisites to the development of proactive family-school relationships. The translation of awareness into appropriate services cannot occur until that recognition has been assimilated into the policies and programs within school systems.

Administrative policies must be examined and, if necessary, changed to encourage the development of individualized strategies for family support and participation. During this reexamination process, we need to create more informal opportunities for communication and relax our approaches to formalized contact. Attention should also be given to the language we use to describe what we offer, such that *parent involvement* is replaced by *family support,* and *committees, conferences,* and *task forces* are reconceptualized in the reciprocal spirit of terms such as *quality circles* (Peters & Austin, 1985).

We need to create forums for families to provide feedback regarding the quality of services they are receiving and the impact of school policies and practices on their lives. Through individual or group interviews with families, we could "walk through" the entire IEP or IFSP process and glean much information regarding what kinds of services have what kinds of impacts on which kinds of children in which kinds of families (cf. Shonkoff, Hauser-Cram, Krauss, & Upshur, 1988). Certainly, our ultimate goal is high-quality, responsive services; partnerships inspired by new approaches to families are the medium for realizing that goal.

References

Bandura, A. (1978). The self system in reciprocal determinism. *American Psychologist, 33,* 344–351.

Bandura, A. (1982). Self-efficacy mechanism in human agency. *American Psychologist, 37,* 122–147.

Barber, P. A., Turnbull, A. P., Behr, S. K., & Kerns, G. M. (1988). A family systems perspective on early childhood special education. In S. L. Odom & M. B. Karnes (Eds.), *Early intervention for infants and children with handicaps* (pp. 179–198). Baltimore: Paul H. Brookes.

Barsch, R. H. (1969). *The teacher-parent relationship.* Reston, VA: The Council for Exceptional Children.

Belsky, J. (1981). Early human experiences: A family perspective. *Developmental Psychology, 17,* 3–23.

Bertalanffy, L. von (1968). *General systems theory: Foundation, developments, applications.* New York: Braziller.

Brickman, P., Kidder, L. H., Coates, D., Robinowitz, V., Cohn, E., & Karvza, J. (1983). The dilemmas of helping: Making aid fair and effective. In J. D. Fisher, A. Nadler, & B. M. DePaulo (Eds.), *New directions in helping: Vol. 1. Recipient reactions to aid* (pp. 18–51). New York: Academic Press.

Brody, G. H., & Stoneman, Z. (1986). Contextual issues in the study of sibling socialization. In J. J. Gallagher & P. M. Vietze (Eds.), *Families of handicapped persons* (pp. 197–218). Baltimore: Paul H. Brookes.

Bronfenbrenner, U. (1979). *The ecology of human development: Experiments by nature and design.* Cambridge, MA: Harvard University Press.

Bronfenbrenner, U., & Crouter, A. C. (1982). Work and family through time and space. In S. B. Kamerman & C. D. Hayes (Eds.), *Families that work: Children in a changing world* (pp. 39–83). Washington, DC: National Academy Press.

Brotherson, M. J. (1985). *Parents' self-report of future planning and its relationship to family functioning and stress in families with disabled sons and daughters.* Unpublished doctorial dissertation, Department of Special Education, University of Kansas.

Christenson, S., Abery, B., & Weinberg, R. (1986). An alternative model for the delivery of psychological services in the school community. In S. N. Elliott & J. C. Witt (Eds.), *The delivery of psychological services in the school* (pp. 349–392). Hillsdale, NJ: Erlbaum.

Crnic, K., Greenberg, M., Ragozin, A., Robinson, N., & Basham, R. (1983). Effects of stress and social support on mothers of premature and full-term infants. *Child Development, 54,* 209–217.

Dewey, J. (1917). *Creative intelligence: Essays in the pragmatic attitude.* New York: Holt.

Dunst, C. J. (1985). Rethinking early intervention. *Analysis and Intervention in Developmental Disabilities, 5,* 165–201.

Dunst, C. J. (1986). *Measuring parent commitment to professionally-prescribed child-level interventions.* Unpublished paper, Family, Infant and Preschool Program, Western Carolina Center, Morganton, NC.

Dunst, C. J., & Trivette, C. M. (1987). Enabling and empowering families: Conceptual and intervention issues. *School Psychology Review, 16,* 443–456.

Dunst, C. J., Trivette, C. M., & Deal, A. (1988). *Enabling and empowering families: Principles and guidelines for practice.* Cambridge, MA: Brookline Books.

Farkas, S. C. (1981). *Taking a family perspective. A principal's guide for working with families of handicapped children.* Washington, DC: Family Impact Seminar. Philadelphia, PA: Temple University Press.

Fisher, J. D., Nadler, A., & DePaulo, B. M. (Eds.) (1983). *New directions in helping: Vol. 1. Recipient reactions to aid.* New York: Academic Press.

Gallagher, J. J., Cross, A., & Scharfman, W. (1981). Parental adaptation to a young handicapped child: The father's role. *Journal of the Division for Early Childhood, 3,* 3–14.

Garbarino, J. (1983). *Children and families in the social environment.* Hawthorne, NY: Aldine Publishing.

Germain, C. D., & Gitterman, A. (1980). *The life model of social work practice.* New York: Columbia University Press.

Goldstein, S., & Turnbull, A. (1982). Strategies to increase parent participation in IEP conferences. *Exceptional Children, 48,* 360–361.

Gross, A. E., & McMullen, P. A. (1983). Models of the help-seeking process. In B. M. DePaulo, A. Nadler, & J. D. Fisher (Eds.), *New directions in helping: Vol. 2. Help-seeking* (pp. 45–70). New York: Academic Press.

Hannah, M. E., & Midlarsky, E. (1985). Siblings of the handicapped: A literature review for school psychologists. *School Psychology Review, 14,* 510–520.

Hobbs, N. (1975). *The futures of children: Categories, labels, and their consequences.* San Francisco: Jossey-Bass.

Hobbs, N., Dokecki, P. R., Hoover-Dempsey, K. V., Moroney, R. M., Shayne, M. W., & Weeks, K. H. (1984). *Strengthening families.* San Francisco: Jossey-Bass.

Hocutt, A., & Wiegerink, R. (1983). Perspectives on parent involvement in preschool programs for handicapped children. In R. Haskins & D. Adams (Eds.), *Parent education and public policy* (pp. 211–229). Norwood, NJ: Ablex.

Kagan, S. L. (1987). Home-school linkages: History's legacies and the family support movement. In S. L. Kagan, D. R. Powell, B. Weissbourd, & E. F. Zigler (Eds.), *America's family support programs* (pp. 161–181). New Haven, CT: Yale University Press.

Kagan, S. L., & Schraft, C. M. (1983). Developing parent commitment to public education: New directions for the 1980's. In R. L. Sinclair (Ed.), *For every school a community: Expanding environments for learning* (pp. 24–38). Boston: Institute for Responsive Education.

Lawson, A., & Ingleby, J. D. (1974). Daily routines of preschool children: Effects of age, birth order, sex, social class, and developmental correlates. *Psychological Medicine, 4,* 399–415.

Miller, N. B., & Cantwell, D. P. (1976). Siblings as therapists: A behavioral approach. *American Journal of Psychiatry, 133,* 447–450.

Nadler, A., & Mayseless, O. (1983). Recipient self-esteem and reactions to help. In J. D. Fisher, A. Nadler, & B. M. DePaulo (Eds.), *New directions in helping: Vol. 1. Recipient reactions to aid* (pp. 167–188). New York: Academic Press.

Paget, K. D. (1987). Systemic family assessment: Concepts and strategies for school psychologists. *School Psychology Review, 16,* 429–442.

Paget, K. D. (1988). Early intervention: Infants, preschool children, and families. In J. C. Witt, F. M. Gresham, & S. N. Elliott (Eds.), *Handbook of behavior therapy in education.* New York: Plenum Press.

Peters, T., & Austin, N. (1985). *A passion for excellence.* New York: Random House.

Plas, J. M. (1981). The psychologist in the school community: A liaison role. *School Psychology Review, 10,* 72–81.

Plas, J. M. (1986). *Systems psychology in the schools.* New York: Pergamon.

Powell, D. (1987). Life in a parent support program: Research perspectives. *Family Resource Coalition Report, 6(3).*

Powell, T. H., & Ogle, P. A. (1985). *Broth-*

ers and sisters: A special part of exceptional families. Baltimore: Paul H. Brookes.

Seligman, M. (1979). *Strategies for helping parents of exceptional children.* New York: Free Press.

Shonkoff, J. P., Hauser-Cram, P., Krauss, M. W., & Upshur, C. C. (1988). Early intervention efficacy research: What have we learned and where do we go from here? *Topics in Early Childhood Special Education, 8,* 81–93.

Simeonsson, R. J., & Bailey, D. B. (1986). Siblings of handicapped children. In J. J. Gallagher & P. M. Vietze (Eds.), *Families of handicapped persons* (pp. 67–80). Baltimore: Paul H. Brookes.

Turnbull, A. P., & Summers, J. A. (1986). From parent involvement to family support: Evolution to revolution. In S. M. Preschel, C. Tingey, J. E. Rynders, A. C. Crocker, & D. M. Crutcher (Eds.), *New perspectives on Down Syndrome* (pp. 289–305). Baltimore: Paul H. Brookes.

Turnbull, A. P., & Turnbull, H. R. (1978). *Parents speak out: Views from the other side of the two-way mirror.* Columbus, OH: Charles Merrill.

Turnbull, A. P., & Turnbull, H. R. (1986). *Families, professionals, and exceptionality* (pp. 142–143). Columbus, OH: Charles Merrill.

Turnbull, A. P., Winton, P. J., Blacher, J. B., & Salkind, N. (1983). Mainstreaming in the kindergarten classroom: Perspectives of parents of handicapped and nonhandicapped children. *Journal of the Division of Early Childhood, 6,* 14–20.

Vadasy, P. F., Fewell, R. R., Meyer, D. J., & Greenberg, M. (1985). Supporting fathers of handicapped young children: Preliminary findings of program effects. *Analysis and Intervention in Developmental Disabilities, 5,* 125–137.

Vincent, L. J. (1985). *Family relationships. Equals in this partnership: Parents of disabled and at-risk infants and toddlers speak to professionals* (pp. 33–34). Washington, DC: National Center for Clinical Infant Programs.

Vincent, L. J., & Salisbury, C. L. (1988). Changing economic and social influences on family involvement. *Topics in Early Childhood Special Education, 8,* 48–59.

Winton, P. (1986). The developmentally delayed child within the family context. In B. K. Keogh (Ed.), *Advances in special education, Vol. 5: Developmental problems in infancy and the preschool years* (pp. 219–255). Greenwich, CT: JAI Press.

Winton, P., & Turnbull, A. P. (1981). Parent involvement as viewed by parents of preschool handicapped children. *Topics in Early Childhood Special Education, 1,* 11–19.

9

The Mentally Retarded Child in the Family

ROBERT L. MARION

University of Texas, Austin

APPROXIMATELY 3.4 MILLION children are born in the United States each year (U.S. Bureau of the Census, 1982). Of that number, about one-third are born with some impairment or disabling condition. Limiting the childbirth statistics to the area of mental retardation has even greater significance. In the United States approximately 2,100 infants are born each week who are either mentally retarded or who will become mentally retarded at some point in their lifetime.

Down Syndrome, one of the most common birth defects and the most prevalent physical cause of mental retardation in the United States, is still found to occur in about 1 out of every 1,000 births. The Down Syndrome category of mental retardation alone has relevance to the societal impact of mental retardation when figures concerning birth rates are examined. For instance, the chance of a woman, between ages 20 to 24, giving birth to a Down Syndrome child is about 1 in 1,500. The chances have increased to about 1 in 100 when the woman is age 40 or above. Mental retardation can truly be said to touch the lives of many in the United States. Historical accounts have documented this fact not only in the United States but also in previous societies.

The causes for the handicapping condition of mental retardation that affects the lives of so many individuals and families has been defined by many professionals from the fields of medicine, psychology, rehabilitation, and special education. Although there has been greater consensus about the causal factors of mental retardation than any other handicapped group, this category of handicapped individuals is not homogeneous either by causation or degree. Rather, numerous causal factors have resulted in heterogeneous classifications and populations.

Indeed, the various causal factors (e.g., genetic disorders, toxic agents, infectious diseases, and environmental factors) have resulted in such heterogeneous populations of mentally retarded persons that these individuals have, in turn, heavily impacted the two systems deemed most responsible for the education and nurture of children. The two systems, families and schools, have often been confused and frustrated in their efforts to serve this population, and have frequently been at odds concerning the course of action to be taken with their mentally retarded charges. Both entities have now been linked together even more closely through legislation and court decisions. However, these linkages have not been achieved without some cost to each of the participating systems.

CHANGING FAMILIES AND SCHOOLS

Marion (1981) recorded how the merits and/or failures of each Mainstream American entity has been perceived by the general public. It was reported that some family experts had pointed to the increase in the divorce rate, the rapid growth of single-parent families, the spiraling rise of teenage pregnancies, and the absence of mothers in the home as contributing factors to the disintegration of the American family system. As proof of the adverse effects of the forced or voluntary absence of the female figure in U.S. households, Marion referenced the large numbers of troubled, abused, illegitimate, and handicapped children that were viewed by some family experts as the consequences of the demise of the family unit (Bronfenbrenner, 1977; Hobbs, 1975; Clark, 1974, Shane, 1973).

Marion (1981) also reported that proponents of the family system were equally as strong in their defense of the American family. He found that many positive thinkers rejected any suggestion that the family was disintegrating. Rather, they believed that the American family was in good health but less mobile than its predecessor and that the extended family concept was higher percentage-wise in the 1970s than in the eighteenth and nineteenth centuries. Others were firmly convinced that the ability of the American family to adapt to other systems was proof that the family was alive and well and not dying. Finally, it was argued that changing family functions

actually enhanced the wellness of the family since members had more free time and energy to minister to other individuals within the family circle (Bane, 1977; Vincent, 1966; Parsons, 1955).

Schools, the other comparable childcare system, have not been without its stages of duress or periods of success. Early educational advocates stressed the value of a good education if individuals wished to advance in an industrial U.S. society. The *Brown* court decision of 1954 and the post-Sputnik legislation also served to enhance this perception of the value of education. At later junctions in history, others utilized the belief that "knowledge is power" to further strengthen the role of education in an individual's quest for social and economic status.

During the Civil Rights decade of the 60s, Myrdal (1962), Jensen (1969), Coleman (1966), and others directly equated equality of education and access to education opportunity to the quality of life enjoyed by U.S. citizens. This ideology about schools was advanced as a possible remedy for the lack of social and economic advancement by minorities (Cohen, 1970). Compensatory education, civil rights legislation, and favorable court decisions continued to support this contention of education during the 1960s.

This activity ushered in the Golden Age of Special Education in the 1970s. Societal attitudes toward handicapped people broadened, thanks to the work of concerned professionals in the field and the well-organized efforts of committed advocacy groups and citizens. Bolstered by the progressive legislation of the 1970s (i.e., PL 94–142) and favorable court decisions (i.e., *Penn.* v. *PARC*, 1972), educational opportunities for the handicapped have continued to expand through the 1980s and into the 1990s.

Education has not always enjoyed a tranquil relationship with its public during its existence as a childcare entity. As early as 1846, schools feuded with parents and complained of the general apathy of parents and the public. Harsh and unflattering criticism was directed toward the schools concerning consolidation of small districts into large centralized systems following mass immigration between 1880 and 1930 (Roper, 1977).

Similar outbursts of frustration concerning the school's ability to produce enough capable scientists and mathematicians accompanied the launching of Sputnik in the late 1950s. Other opponents of schools decried the alienation of the poor and culturally different within the school system of the 1960s (Hickerson, 1966; Coleman, 1966; Glazer & Moynihan, 1963). The credentialing methods of the schools were also attacked as Hurley (1969) and Miller (1967) criticized the schools for becoming labeling and sorting factories where students were credentialed by race, creed, socioeconomic status, and handicap.

School reformers appeared again in the late 1970s. Some sought a return to the 3 Rs—reading, writing, and arithmetic— whereas others demanded that entire school systems be replaced (Gallup, 1973; Passow, 1976; Brown & Task Force, 1975). Finally, educational reform movements of today are seeking solutions to a dwindling human capital market. They are actively pursuing contemporary answers to the education and training of under- and un-educated minorities, young mothers in need of childcare assistance, one million high school dropouts annually, and over 2 million graduates who are functionally illiterate. Although the business community has attempted to help with its "adopt a school" and "scholars on loan" programs, the demand for school reform persisted during the decade of the 1980s (*Business Week*, 1988).

If reform was called for in Mainstream American Education (MAE), certain conditions also existed within the subsystem special education (SED), which called for additional accommodation with families whose mentally retarded children occupied places within the greater system (MAE) and the subsystem, special education (SED).

The first linkage between the systems was effected by the fact that children with mental retardation are exceptional children or children with differences having the same needs as their peers but also having needs particular to their exceptionality or handicap (Cruickshank, 1967). The second linkage between families and schools was assured through the passage of PL 94–142 or the Education of All Handicapped Children Act of 1975. This legislation gave the rights of a free and appropriate public education to all handicapped children, including children with mental retardation. The final tie was effected through the enactment of Public Law 99–457. Its passage extended the rights and privileges of PL 94–142 downward and encompassed handicapped children from birth to two years of age. The net effect of these major pieces of legislation has been to bring the family and the school together in a co-equal partnership from the birth of the child through 21 years of his or her life.

CRISES PERIODS WITHIN THE DEVELOPMENTAL STAGES

Despite the protective legislation covering the education and treatment of handicapped children, parents are not insulated from the shock and the accompanying reactions when they are told that they have become parents of a mentally retarded child. From the moment of delivery, parents are concerned about the condition and health of their child. When parents hear the words, "You have a healthy baby," they are relieved and excited. Often those most desired words are not heard by parents. Instead, they may be dismayed to learn that their baby is retarded or has Down Syndrome. When those words are heard, many parents have retreated into a state of shock, confusion, and pain.

The strong feelings that overcome parents following the birth of the mentally retarded infant is tied to the loss that they feel has occurred. It can be equated to the loss of a loved one. Many parents are confused because they do not understand what the terms *mental retardation* or *Down Syndrome* mean. Some may have an image of the child with a protruding tongue, strange looking eyes, and thick hands. Others, more sophisticated in the field of mental retardation, might have a need to be told about the level of retardation suffered by the child. Still others may not have any idea about the concept of mental retardation and have a desperate need for information about the condition (Marion, 1981). Whatever the situation, the birth of an infant with mental retardation into a family unit can be considered a nonnormative and a stressful event. It has been referred to as the first crisis period in the lives of families with exceptional children (Barraga, 1966).

Not only do parents have negative reactions to the birth of a mentally retarded child but the shock reverberates throughout the family system. Since the family is comprised of members in dynamic interaction to one another, the birth of a child with mental retardation has the potential to disrupt the functioning of all family members and to cause the unit to fall into disequilibrium (Ross, 1964; Fleck, 1967). The emotional give and take of family relationships expressed through the roles of family members have been acknowledged to be central to the mental health of the family (Ackerman, 1966; Ferber & Beels, 1972).

Moreover, the family has grown to be a system not just through the interaction of its members but also through the relationship of the family with the society at large (Burgess, 1926). In other words, the family unit can be changed as a direct result of societal forces (i.e., mores, customs, public opinion) that demonstrably impact upon its function.

Certainly the birth of an infant with mental retardation has an eventful impact on the family. Moreover, when there is suspicion of a handicap or when questions arise concerning the nature of the disability, the diagnosis and treatment of the handicap has been the cause of the second crisis period in the lives of families with mentally retarded children (Barraga, 1966). Thus, whichever crisis period is dominating the attention of the family, it can be said that stress has been introduced into the family circle. In either crisis period, the birth or the diagnosis and treatment of the child with mental retardation, stress has been found to be the one constant variable introduced into the family circle.

In the crisis period surrounding the birth of a mentally retarded child, the emotional stress that parents are feeling is manifested by expressions that are not usually a natural part of their personality. During this crisis period, it has been reported that parental reactions have been guilt (Murray, 1981; Marion, 1981; Hannam, 1975), denial (Roos, 1977; Wikler, Wasaw, & Hatfield, 1981), and grief and sorrow (Wright, 1976; Koslow & Cooper, 1978; Ohshansky, 1963). These feelings should be expected from parents who have a retarded child. The justification for these feelings are lodged in the fact that parents have a desire to attain immortality. With so much ego at stake, parents have the basic impulse to deny the imperfect child. The ambivalence of their feelings is reflected in their urge to destroy the mentally retarded infant or in their desire to love the imperfect child (Marion, 1981).

Parents have also been known to experience strong feelings of guilt due to these love-hate feelings. The sorrow reaction evolving into grief and mourning can be better understood within the concept of the loss of a loved one. Parents are mourning the loss of the child-that-might-have-been—a normal child turned mentally retarded.

Since professionals and parents are alike in their lack of haste to label children, often the term *developmentally delayed* has given both parties a reprieve from the harsh reality of the label *mental retardation.* This has been particularly true in the case of the mildly retarded child who often does not exhibit distinguishable physical characteristics at birth. Therefore, when children are very young, observed developmental delays are not forcefully remediated in all cases or are not seriously regarded by some parents and professionals in the hope that the child will achieve normal development in later stages.

In the ensuing controversy that follows the diagnosis and treatment of many mentally retarded children, parents have often sought answers and information concerning the child with mental retardation. They have searched for answers to explain why the child with mental retardation was born to them and why their child is defective. Parents have a need for facts to explain their circumstances and the dilemma that surrounds the family. Parents are confused and stress becomes a constant companion as they and other family members attempt to gain a proper perspective of the effect of the child with mental retardation.

The attending psychologist who works with these families should have a firm commitment to effecting change in the family system when treatment is begun. Initially the therapist must accept the premise that at birth and upon the diagnosis of the handicap, the child with mental retardation will have an effect on the entire family system. Within this context, the therapist must have an understanding of two important concepts at the onset of family therapy: (1) the family with a mentally retarded child has a problem that will affect the family functioning over the lifespan of the family unit and (2) it is important to determine the "age" of the family when they enter therapy. Age of the family is determined by the length of time that a family has been together and the place of its members in the family life cycle (Ehly, Conoley, & Rosenthal, 1985).

Recognizing that the birth of a mentally retarded child and/or the subsequent diagnosis of mental retardation will affect the family functioning at these crises stages, the psychologist should seek to intervene during the disorganization period of family functioning immediately following the crisis. During this interval, therapists can have a greater impact on the family if they concentrate on the major subsystems of the family with the mentally retarded child: the spouse relationship, the parent-child relationship, and the sibling relationship (Minuchin, 1974). Also, effectiveness will be increased if their efforts to work with the family are conducted through family perspectives that include family function, family structure, and family life cycle (Skrtic, Summers, Brotherson, & Turnbull, 1983).

The family life circle has certain transition junctures that seem to cause additional stress in the lives of families (Carter & McGoldrick, 1980; Skrtic et al., 1983). The third stage of the family life cycle described by Carter and McGoldrick has within it the elements that correlate to the crises precipitated by the birth and the subsequent diagnosis and treatment of the mentally retarded child. This stage is referenced to the family with young children. The entry of young children with mental retardation into the family circle has qualified these families for this level.

At this level of the life cycle, especially when the infant is very young, parents are expected to make necessary adjustments in the family system so that the new arrival is included. Also, they have to take on parenting roles so that family functions and family culture can be transmitted within the family unit. These required adaptations are given added significance for families when viewed through the eyes of the greater community. In the United States, society has delegated to the family the responsibility for providing a socially supported group pattern for the male and female to care for the young and given them the responsibility for nurturing their young (Ackerman, 1966). At this stage, then, families not only have the task of reorganizing their lives but are also expected to socialize the young child with mental retardation.

Psychologists will have to try several forms of intervention when working with families with mentally retarded children. First, therapists should have conferences with parents to allow them to vent the full range of emotions outlined earlier. During these times parents have one fundamental need—to be helped. The psychologist must have the sensitivity to recognize the intensity of the various emotions that the spouse subsystem is feeling about the child-that-never-will-be. They will have to work with parents in helping them to recognize that they can have ambivalent feelings, such as the urge to destroy the imperfect child, or can be filled with love for their infant. Therapists should be prepared to assist parents with the strong guilt feelings that accompany these love-hate emotions.

Therapists should also expect periods of mourning and depression that may vary in intensity and duration. For some parents the pain of the birth of a mentally retarded infant has struck deeply and has overwhelmed them. Others have not been as incapacitated by the event but still have a need for assistance until they can once

again begin working to reestablish equilibrium in the family circle.

Additionally therapists should also have continuing meetings with the parents and family members to define the nature of the mental retardation. Different levels of mental retardation should be discussed in layman terms so that the family has a realistic picture of the child. The terms *educable* (EMR), *trainable* (TMR), and *severely/profoundly* (S/PMR) *mentally retarded,* together with their acronyms, should be clearly defined and information exchanged with parents especially as they relate to the future of the child.

Parents and other immediate family members should be made to understand that the different levels of intelligence will have an effect on the ability of the child in school, in day-to-day activities, and in later life. Most assuredly, parents should be given an explanation about what constitutes the categories in which their child will eventually find himself or herself. For instance, the intelligence factor will have great significance between being labeled EMR (IQ between 69–52), TMR (IQ between 54–36), or S/PMR (IQ between 39–19). Therapists will have to help the family resolve the sorrow and grief that often accompany this information.

Psychologists must also be prepared to face the anger of parents as they attempt to hold others and themselves responsible for the child's mental retardation. Families with a diagnosed child as well as those with a prior knowledge of the retardation of their child now have to face the harsh reality that the child will be a life-long problem for which all the family subsystems will have to make an adaptation.

As the infant continues to grow and thrive, parents and other family members must be prepared for the changes that will occur in the family circle because of the needs of the mentally retarded child. Understanding that medical, emotional, economic, and professional stress factors have the capacity to immobilize the interactions of family members, the therapist will have to align parents and family members with voluntary organizations that will assist them in reducing disruptions within the family unit. Therefore, the aid of parent groups from local chapters of advocacy organizations such as the Association of Retarded Citizens will have to be sought for the support that only those who have had direct exposure to the condition of mental retardation can give to others in like circumstances. In this situation parents and family members have an opportunity to exchange information, receive moral support, and, above all, see for themselves that it is possible to live with the affected child. This can be accomplished through various groups that have been formed at different age levels to assist parents and other family members, including the retarded child (i.e., teenage groups).

The psychologist has other opportunities to influence the quality of life enjoyed by parents with mentally retarded young children. Working with the physician, the therapist is strategically positioned to support the fellow professional's efforts to encourage parents to enroll their young charges in preschool programs. Preschool programs help parents see their child's future. Preschools assist in the social, physical, emotional, and intellectual development of the child and provide respite care for the youngster. All of these activities have the potential to be catalysts for positive change in the three subsystems of the family that must interact in order for a successful return to equilibrium to occur.

Of particular importance to the therapist at this juncture is the role reorganization and new role complementarity that must take place among the three family subsystems. The key principle of the transition process at this stage is centered on the acceptance of new members into the system comprised of the subsystems: spouse, parent-child, and siblings. The psychologist, then, not only has to direct his or her energy toward creating more efficient interactions within the spouse relationship but has to display equal facility for working within the parent-child and sibling relationship of the family. Thus, the role reorganization and new role complementarity factors will have to weigh heavily in the therapist's approach when working with other family members concerning the entry and maintenance of the mentally retarded in the family.

The psychologist who wishes to attend families of mentally retarded children during the preschool stage will have to recognize that the family of age is still in the third stage of its life cycle. It is still orienting the child into the family unit and is now seeking the accommodation of its members into their new roles. During the preschool years the therapist should also be prepared to address the stress that accompanies the role complementarity process as the family seeks to regain its equilibrium.

The mentally retarded child's delayed development occurring at this time can have a significant impact on the family during this stage of the family's life cycle. School psychologists will have to assist parents in handling altered role expectations. For example, fathers might need help in dealing with their diminished or nonexistent role as playmate or model for their moderately or severely mentally retarded child (Gallagher, Cross, & Scharfman, 1981). Mothers, on the other hand, might need assistance as they seek to adjust their roles from breadwinners to homemakers to ensure the nurturing of their mentally retarded child (Wikler, 1983).

In counseling parents, therapists would be well advised to concentrate their energies on the problems of uncertainty about the child's education, continuing medical complications often associated with the condition, and the practical and emotional impact of these complications on everyday life (Stagg & Catron, 1986). Psychologists will have to offer ego-supportive counseling to assist the family with a number of stresses arising from these issues. One such issue is to assist families in managing the major problem of isolation and loneliness. Parents, especially mothers, have complained bitterly about the restricted social contacts that accompany the presence of the mentally retarded child in the family (Gabel & Kotsch, 1981; Birenbaum, 1972; Farber, 1968). Ross (1964) also spoke of the widening of the social distance between families with mentally retarded children and friends. He stated:

It is totally impossible to achieve any degree of empathy for the state of the mentally defective for we cannot suspend our higher mental processes or temporarily cancel everything we learned. Because of its nature, mental retardation offers some peculiar characteristics and problems. . . . (p. 100)

Attending psychologists must be particularly mindful of this felt difference in families with mentally retarded children. Their loneliness will be manifested not only within the family circle but also without. Visiting patterns are visibly affected since not only do parents make less visits outside the home but fewer friends visit homes of parents with mentally retarded children (Stagg & Catron, 1986). Therapists will have to recognize the warning signs that signal the onset of sadness caused by this loneliness and will have to closely monitor their relationships with parents to prevent any steep descent into depression.

Psychologists should be alerted that social network members are not necessarily present to alleviate the need for professional services (Gourash, 1978). The two influences of family network sources that are unlikely to be in place have been

referred to as (1) buffering the experiences of stress, thus obviating the need for help; and (2) precluding the necessity for professional help through the provision of instrumental and affective support (p. 516). Therefore, in addition to ego-supportive counseling, therapists will have to continue to encourage parents to maintain contact with parent groups so that they realize that there are "others like us out there."

Siblings are also affected by loneliness that is felt within the family circle. Crnic and Leconte (1986) have reported that siblings of mentally retarded children have more opportunities for contacts with medical and educational service providers and less chance for social contacts with their peers due to the presence of the mentally retarded sibling within the family unit. Also, the affected siblings have to endure unfavorable comments caused by cultural attitudes related to the stigma frequently attached to the condition of mental retardation (Goffman, 1963).

Furthermore, the presence of a mentally retarded child can have an effect on the self-esteem of nonhandicapped siblings. The embarrassment and resentment that unaffected siblings may feel have sometimes resulted in a lowered self-concept of those siblings. Psychologists will have to work with unaffected siblings to provide them with coping skills to adapt to the stresses that befall them within the family.

Rather than focusing on a deficit model of coping, therapists should have a working knowledge of more positive-based models that can help to alleviate the stresses that normal siblings might be feeling from living with a mentally retarded child. Psychologists will have to use such positive models as proposed by Crnic, Friedrick, and Greenberg (1983) or Folkman, Schaefer, and Lazarus (1979). Folkman and associates utilized five types of coping resources to temper the adverse effects of stress caused by living with a handicapped individual: health-energy-morale, problem-solving skills, social network supports, utilitarian resources, and general and specific beliefs. Crnic and colleagues' (1983) model is specifically geared toward familial adaptation to retarded children and has provisions for sibling interactions. Thus, recognizing that this is a family problem, therapists should be working with all members to achieve equilibrium in the family.

PRESCHOOL AND FAMILIES

In reviewing what has happened to families with preschoolers, much of what was cited earlier has focused on meeting the affective needs of family members. However, families do not exist in a vacuum but also interact with other systems. One of the most prominent systems with which collaborative interaction by the family has been institutionalized has been the school system. Prior to 1975, much of the formal schooling process began at ages five or six when young children entered kindergarten. With the passage of The Education of All Handicapped Children Act of 1975, or Public Law 94–142, handicapped children have been afforded the opportunity to begin school at age 3 and to continue until they reached the age of 22. In 1986, the provisions for educational services and equal educational opportunities for young handicapped children were extended downward to ages zero to two with the passage of Public Law 99–457.

Both of these pieces of major legislation have stipulated that extensive parental and family involvement is necessary in order for both entities to conform to the intent of the law. Therefore, zero to two legislation has mandated that a family

service plan be included so that a full range of services can be provided to families with young handicapped children.

Families with mentally retarded children have had some choices in the area of preschooling for their children. Basically, young mentally retarded children have been served by three approaches—home-based, center-based, or home-center-based programs. In other words, early intervention activities are carried out in the home, the center, or in combination home-center programs. Families with mentally retarded children have accessed all of these types of preschool programs (Trohanis, Cox, & Meyer, 1982). The entry of their mentally retarded children into preschool can be deemed as another crisis period in the lives of parents and the family.

This crisis period should not be taken lightly by the school psychologist. First, this crisis period is arriving earlier in the lives of the family with mentally retarded children. Some families are still contending that developmental delays will eventually be outgrown and become history. Other parents and family members have had to acknowledge that the youngster is retarded. They are seeking schooling situations that will not only provide the child with needed skills to advance through the developmental stages but will also give family members an opportunity to proceed onward through the third stage of the life cycle. In this instance, the psychologist will not have to preclude the use of any of the more familiar and frequently used methods of parent involvement. On the contrary, the therapist has the option of including any intervention methods previously used with parents within the context of family intervention.

An example of how the psychologist can be involved in assisting a family with a mentally retarded preschooler to address a life-cycle issue is demonstrated by the following case study.

CASE STUDY 1

The Smith family unit is comprised of two parents, a 19-year-old daughter (Melissa), a 16-year-old son (John), and a 3-year-old Down Syndrome girl (Anne) with medical problems. Melissa has assisted the mother in the care of the retarded sibling while balancing a close relationship between the mother and the young retarded child. The father has been working late hours at the office since the birth of Anne due to loss of family income when the mother was forced to quit her job to care for Anne. The marital relationship between the spouses is still good, although some distance between the two has occurred. As a result, the mother has become more attached to the siblings than to the spouse. The family is about to experience another change since Melissa has decided to marry and move to another state.

The marriage is consummated and Melissa moves away with her husband. When this occurs the mother forms a stronger emotional attachment with Anne, who has returned her attention and justified her need to be wanted as a parent. Another shift is occurring as John is now moving well into adolescence. The family structure now has weak boundaries between Anne and the mother (overly attentive), distance between the father and Anne, and between the spouses.

The psychologist who has intervened with this family wants to encourage more contacts (social activities) between the parents to narrow the distance between the two spouses, provide other sources of emotional satisfaction for the wife, and work with the mother to permit distance between Anne as the family experiences a life-cycle transition. The therapist discourages increased contact between Anne and the mother through concentrated mother-child activities. If allowed, this would only tend to make an atypical family structure even more inflexible. The mother-retarded child dyad would move closer together and make separation more difficult when developmentally appropriate to do so. Recognizing the consequence of such action, the psychologist continues to intervene with the Smith family in the directions indicated to return the family to equilibrium.

TRANSITION TO K–12 SCHOOLS

The transition from the less regimented infant-parent and young toddler programs to the more structured world of public schooling has presented problems for both schools and parents. Matriculation from noncategorical to schools operating under PL 94–142 guidelines has been a particularly sensitive issue. A factor that has strongly influenced school-family interaction during this time span has been the fourth crisis period faced by families with mentally retarded children.

As noted previously, parents of educable mentally retarded (EMR) children may have views that differ appreciably from those of parents of trainable (TMR) or severely/profoundly (PMR) retarded children. Again, as Barsch (1969) indicated, the psychologist who is working with parents of an EMR child has probably met an adult who is experiencing the pain of living with a labeled child for the first time. In contrast to that adult, parents of a TMR or PMR child have lived with the realization that their child is mentally retarded before beginning interactions with the K–12 system. In the case of all levels of severity, the question of transition to school has become a formidable step for parents with mentally retarded young children.

THE MENTALLY RETARDED CHILD IN SCHOOL

Together with their frustrations and traumas surrounding the transition process, parents and families of a MR child now have to contend with a new environment and system. The receiving systems, the school districts, have to prepare for working with children from families with members who might still be harboring feelings of sorrow, guilt, ambivalence, denial, anger, and other emotions in varying degrees. Moreover, it is conceivable that the trauma of entering their mentally retarded child into the structured environment of the school may have the danger of causing parents and families to regress to earlier periods of conflict from which they previously had emerged.

ELEMENTARY SCHOOL INTERVENTION

The school stage has truly been perceived as a crisis period for parents and families of mentally retarded children. The anxieties of families has been heightened by both school and family issues. School issues have often had their origins in the labels that schools have applied to mentally retarded children. Schools have generally determined the level of participation by children with mental retardation by categorizing them as educable (EMR), trainable (TMR), and severe/profoundly (S/PMR) mentally retarded.

The EMR child has the capacity to (1) acquire academic skills at the primary and late elementary grade levels, (2) obtain vocational skills to the level where the child can be partially or totally self-sufficient as an adult, and (3) develop the social skills necessary to survive as an independent citizen in society.

Schooling for a TMR child is usually provided in self-contained classrooms with instruction directed toward the teaching of daily living skills. Academics are limited to a functional vocabulary of sight words (i.e., *stop, bus, walk*) and simple number concepts. In secondary schools, the emphasis is on vocational preparation for unskilled employment (i.e., maintenance, cafeteria service) and sheltered workshop employment (Heward & Orlansky, 1980).

Training for a S/PMR child has generally been limited to language skills and to self-help skills (eating, drinking, toileting, and dressing). Severely/profoundly mentally retarded individuals may have a tendency to be self-abusive, may have trouble in meeting their self-care needs, or may have a need for around-the-clock supervision and care. The severity of these needs have previously caused schools to steer away from attempts to educate S/PMR children in public school systems. However, the passage of PL 94–142 has forced schools to renew their efforts to include and to educate S/PMR children in the public schools.

One of the school issues that has dominated the thinking of families with mentally retarded children at the elementary level has been the question of mainstreaming, or the placement of mentally retarded children in regular classrooms with nonaffected peers. Although schools have emphasized that the mainstreaming approach is not for all handicapped students, parents of mentally retarded children have often insisted that the mainstreaming approach is best for their child. Families with EMRs, TMRs, and S/PMRs have all had a problem with the mainstreaming question. The following case study illustrates the effects of this common problem on family hierarchy and structure.

CASE STUDY 2

Robert, a severely retarded boy of six years old, has been mainstreamed into a regular public school first grade. His parents are concerned about his adjustment to regular first grade after having spent two years in a special preschool program. The mother believes her son has not learned anything during his first four months in public school. She feels that this reflects a lack of interest and preparation on the part of both the teacher and the administrator of the school.

The mother visited both the teacher and the principal the previous June to discuss Robert's coming to school in the fall. In spite of this, both professionals seemed to have made a poor effort to prepare for Robert, even though special education classes for severely mentally retarded students were new to the campus.

The father was reluctant to have Robert enter public school, because he felt that the boy was not ready. He is also worried that Robert's presence in the elementary school will cause problems for his older sister, Kate, who is 9 years old.

The parents had to make major family lifestyle adjustments in order for Robert to attend public school. But at the end of four months, their efforts seem wasted. Public school seems to not be providing benefits either to their son or to his family.

Unlike the father, the principal and the teacher had not anticipated any problems in enrolling Robert in their school. They assumed that their usual methods for easing new special children into the first grade would be sufficient. Although they had no experience in dealing with the specific challenges that a child with a severe disability presented, they felt confident that they could learn how to deal with these problems when the child actually arrived on the scene, and that it was best not to set up a "self-fulfilling prophecy" by making elaborate special preparations.

Both the administrator and teacher are surprised and unprepared for the amount of time and energy required to get the special services personnel organized to work with Robert. By November neither had found answers to the problem. They finally concede that the problem is too great for them and assure the mother that they will be better prepared next year.

The school psychologist is faced with a family for whom a conflict of views were represented concerning whether Robert was ready for mainstreaming into first grade. The parents, as decision makers, represent divergent views concerning what is beneficial for their son. The father is uncomfortable with his son and prefers to set him apart in a special program where he would not compromise the family's acceptance in the community. On the other hand, the mother is determined to include Robert in as many activities in the school, in the community, and in the family life as possible.

First, the therapist ascertains where it is best to enter the family's hierarchy. She decides how to interface with both decision makers in the hopes of achieving the goal of successful mainstreaming for the child. It is important that the parents not perceive the therapist as a decision maker. Thus, she decides to hold separate conferences with each parent since the boundaries between them are quite rigid. Following individual conferences with the spouses, the psychologist then holds a family conference so that family goals may be addressed.

The family is encouraged to recognize that mainstreaming involves change and that change arouses anxiety in persons who are affected, especially when those concerned know it is going to be managed in new and unfamiliar circumstances. The therapist continues individual conferences with each parent to assist him and her in resolving further problems that might arise in the mainstream educational setting (i.e., IEP conferencing).

Also, family adjustment problems are addressed. This family has structurally weak mother-child and rigid father-child boundaries. The therapist does not encourage substantially more contact between the mother and Robert; rather, initially the therapist seeks to promote more social contact between the father and Robert. Later, the psychologist will work toward full family contact between all subsystems with the greater community. Working in this fashion, the therapist attempts to rebalance this family.

Another major school-related problem has been the issue of adjustment by families with mentally retarded children to the label given by the school to their child.

CASE STUDY 3

Charles is a 10-year-old EMR child who does not exhibit any outward signs of mental retardation and is the only child in a two-parent family. He has above-average social skills but below grade level academic problems.

His mother denies that he is retarded and is waiting on him to "get well." She is very close to Charles and spends a lot of time working with him on his school work. Her attitude concerning his handicap is being passed on to Charles and he also refuses to believe that he is retarded. The father is a college graduate and he too hopes that the retardation is a temporary condition. He is not close to Charles but relies heavily on his wife for direction in the rearing of the boy. However, the boy scored a 64 on the Weschler Intelligence test, with the cutoff score for mental retardation being 69.

Charles is not a student who can be easily categorized and has been the subject of numerous meetings between school staff and the family. The special education teacher has decided that the mother is denying that Charles is retarded and is not accepting the truth about the boy's condition. After several unsuccessful conferences with the parent, she referred the family to the school psychologist.

In this case, the psychologist has to work to correct the mother's feeling that Charles's retardation is a temporary condition. Information is provided not only to the mother but also to the father. Additional discussions about mental retardation and concerning mainstreaming and regular class placement will have to be held until parents understand the condition. The therapist's interface is directed toward both parents since the parents are the decision makers, with the husband in total support of his wife's decision. Attitudinal change intervention by the psychologist focuses on the mother since her attitude toward the handicapping condition is being instilled in Charles. Moreover, structurally the boundaries between the mother and the son are weakened (overly close). Thus, any more contact between the mother and son through intense mother-child activities are discouraged. Continued contact of this nature would make the family structure more rigid. The therapist, however, does suggest that the father spend more time with his son and commits to meeting with the family as needed to continue the discussions.

The previous two case studies have considered school-family problems that have had a significant effect on the performance of the elementary school-aged mentally retarded child. These problems have occupied dominant positions in the hierarchy of stress factors for families with mentally retarded children.

There is yet another significant problem that continues to exist between the family of a retarded child and the schools. This last important issue revolves around the behavior of mentally retarded children and the concurrent problem of proper discipline. It should be stressed that the behavior and discipline problems of mentally retarded children are not restricted to the elementary school years. On the contrary, these problems persist throughout the school years and beyond. They are included here and will be further discussed when addressing the problems of adolescence or secondary school-aged mentally retarded students. An example of how behavioral problems can affect family-school functioning is shown in this case study.

CASE STUDY 4

Irene, a single parent (through the death of her spouse) in her mid-30s, has two children, ages 5 and 10. The 5-year-old boy, Thomas, is moderately retarded, having moderately delayed speech and motor skills, becoming withdrawn in the company of strangers, and having adopted a habit of pouting and crying whenever he does not get his way in family activities. Irene worries anxiously about Thomas's behavior. His 10-year-old sister, Maria, is well behaved and doing exceptionally well in school, academically and socially.

Irene has guilt feelings about leaving Thomas in a daycare center but is denied other choices due to the death of her husband. His death meant that she has to work in order for the family to survive since they are not geographically located near any extended family members. The mother is reluctant to enforce any rules because of Thomas's handicap and because she feels guilty about leaving him alone in the daycare center while she works.

Lately, Irene has discovered that the child pouts and falls crying to the floor when he wants Maria's toys or possessions. These actions affect Thomas's work and behavior at school because the special education teacher has noticed that the boy pouts and cries when confronted with an assignment that he dislikes. After several meetings with the special education teacher, Irene is referred to the school psychologist.

The school psychologist empathizes with Irene over the need to work due to the loss of her spouse. As a part of raising Irene's self-esteem, the therapist emphasizes her positive qualities of care and love for Thomas in order to help Irene keep from getting further emotionally entangled with her child. The family's functions are already impaired due to Thomas's actions and Irene's feelings of guilt. Thus, a more intense relationship between the mother and the retarded child will further unbalance the system. Rather, the psychologist stresses the need for Irene to behave toward Thomas as normally as possible. Furthermore, the therapist assures the mother that Thomas's reactions are not necessarily a departure from normal sibling rivalry problems.

The psychologist provides Irene with some behavioral suggestions that will modify Thomas's behavior in the family circle. The therapist instructs Irene in the following activities to implement at home:

1. Teach the parent behavior modification techniques that will assist her in modifying the undesired social skills of the retarded child.
2. Encourage the parent to attend a parent's group where additional behavior modification techniques are taught.
3. Assist the parent to enter into a home-school behavior management program with the child's teacher.

Additional meetings are then held by the psychologist to deal with family roles. Since the boundaries are weak between Thomas and the parent (overly protective), the therapist works with Irene to inform her of activities that will distance her from being overly close to the child (i.e., parent group meetings with other parents in similar circumstances). Also, the psychologist intervenes with the parent concerning her strong feelings about the death of her husband. Irene had not been afforded the opportunity to grieve for the loss of her husband before being forced back into the world of work. This was causing emotional stress in the mother with the resulting guilt feelings concerning the child.

Information is shared with Maria about Thomas's condition. This has a remediating effect on Maria's desire to retaliate against the younger child. Also, shared information about the parent's economic state alleviates any hostile feelings toward Thomas. Finally, information shared with all family members about the financial state of the family will help Irene better execute her role as the chief executive in the family hierarchy. It will also have a needed healthy effect on the family functioning behavior-wise in all the subsystem relationships.

Behavior problems associated with mentally retarded children do not cease for families when the children move into adolescence. Indeed, the problems manifest themselves in such ways that the adolescent phase has been deemed another crisis stage in the lives of families with mentally retarded children. Related problems can be found in some of the concerns that confront families with mentally retarded children during this time frame. During this stage, nonhandicapped teenagers are facing the following developmental tasks:

1. Accepting one's changing body and learning to use it effectively
2. Achieving a satisfying and socially accepted sex role
3. Achieving more mature relations with agemates
4. Achieving emotional independence from parents and other adults
5. Preparing for an occupation and economic independence
6. Preparing for marriage and family life
7. Developing a workable philosophy (Duval, 1962)

In attempting to meet the above tasks, the experiences of mentally retarded teenagers can be expected to be decidedly different from their nonhandicapped peers. This in turn will have the effect of causing stress in the lives of parents and family members. One instance of stress and concern can be equated to the onset of puberty. This is a period punctuated by concerns such as the commencement of menstruation in a female, the beginning of masturbation by the male, plus the coupling of parental concerns about the child's sexuality. As difficult as the period is for the nonhandicapped, this stage often leaves the beleaguered mentally retarded adolescent and his or her family in a state of confusion.

CASE STUDY 5

Carl, age 15, is the oldest of two children in a two-parent family. He has been labeled moderately retarded and has been functioning on a high level for a trainable mentally retarded adolescent. Carl is attending public school in a mainstreamed setting where he has all academic classes with other disabled classmates. He has physical education and art and music classes with nonhandicapped peers. One day during physical education class the assistant instructor, while checking for late arrivals, surprised Carl, as he found him masturbating in the restroom. In talking with the youth, the teacher discovered that this practice has been going on for about six months. Carl indicated that he has been following and copying the lead of several of his fellow classmates. The parents were alerted and the following reactions were elicited.

The father is lackadaisical considering the act, preferring to label the action as Carl is "growing up." Carl's mother is visibly upset and voices her wish to have the teenager sterilized to prevent this situation from leading to a more dangerous intimate "expression of affection."

The family is governed by the father, who makes most of the decisions for the family. His wife has always acquiesced to his will and has established close ties to the son. The marriage is stable, although some distance exists between the spouses.

The psychologist works closely with the family to establish whether the family structure will become maladaptive in this situation should the father make the decision alone. By contacting the father directly, the therapist acknowledges that he understands the uniqueness of the family structure. However, the psychologist is alert to the possibility that the family could fall further into disequilibrium if other family members are not allowed an entry into the problem-solving conferences that could eventually lead to a resolution of the crisis. Should the mother maintain a resolute stance in this case, a challenge to the established leadership pattern could be forthcoming.

Thus, the therapist discourages the father's inclination to shrug off the incident as a "rite of passage that boys pass through." The psychologist then provides the parents with information concerning the "why" of Carl's behavior. A discussion ensues concerning the inappropriateness of the teenager's behavior in a public building. Next, the therapist encourages the father to allow the mother to participate in the intervention process. The psychologist exercises caution and sensitivity to allow the decision-making machinery of the family to fall completely into place. This may result in closing the distance between the two parents.

In individual counseling with Carl, the psychologist communicates that masturbation is a normal sexual expression regardless of its frequency and at what age it is done. However, the therapist conveys to Carl that any direct sexual behavior involving the genitals should take place only in privacy. The psychologist takes extra precautions in making certain that the teenager understands the difference between the privacy of the home versus the privacy of the restroom.

Next, the psychologist meets with the mother. While not acknowledging that her solution is the only answer to the problem, the therapist empathizes with her emotions and feelings due to her concern about the teenager's sexual habits. Communication with the husband is encouraged by the psychologist to alter the distance between the two adults. The mother is also provided with information concerning the sexual behavior of the mentally retarded. At all times, the therapist tries to communicate to the parent an acceptance of the child's sexual behavior. The mother is assured that the appearance of the behavior is not bad. Moreover, the psychologist answers additional questions posed by the mother as she seeks a solution for Carl and his sexual habits as a part of the retarded adolescent population.

Finally, the family is treated as a unit while acknowledging initially that the father has the final authority for the family decision in this family. Moreover, the therapist thinks about intervening beyond the individual or dyads (Montalvo & Haley, 1973; Haley, 1976). For example, in this case to provide the mother only with information that might change her operating procedures with the adolescent might have a beneficial effect on the mother-child dyad initially. However, this individual intervention strategy might be sabotaged by the father. His opposition to any shift in power between the two spouses could be personified by his reliance on the "old way" of handling problems in the household. The end result of this action would be that the conflict would arise between the parents and would create an impossible situation for Carl. This would have the effect of widening the distance between the spouses, closing the distance between the mother and child, and moving the system into an unbalanced state.

Therapists must offer parents and family members understanding as they face the threatening situation of watching the handicapped child become an adult. Much support and information is needed in order to keep families from getting "stuck" in the fourth stage of the life cycle of families (Farber, 1959).

Another crisis in the lives of families with mentally retarded teenagers is also initiated during the fifth life cycle of the family (Marion, 1981; Kotsopoulous & Matathia, 1980). The issue of vocational preparation has presented parents and families with immense problems. It is occurring when the parents and families of mentally retarded adolescents are faced with the problem of making vocational choices. Nonimpaired teenagers find this to be a difficult time; it is an even more stressful situation for mentally retarded persons and their parents, who must face the problem of choosing an appropriate career.

Difficulties revolve around the questions of employment and training. Is immediate employment available or must training be provided? Is the job dead-end or is there an opportunity for advancement? Will the worker's job satisfaction correlate to the employer's? These and other questions should be addressed from a continuum that reaches from a sheltered workshop context to an independent worker concept. This issue is illustrated next.

CASE STUDY 6

Don, aged 16, is moderately retarded and has few chores to do around the home. His mother has tried to get him to clean up his room and after himself. She also has continually nagged him about his laziness since he was 5 years old. However, lately he has been getting up or leaving the house whenever the scolding begins. Don is also having problems lately at the vocational training program he attends. He is not even trying to meet his goals, and the instructor thinks that Don is lazy.

The father is resigned to the fact that Don will never take care of himself. These differences of opinions have created a great deal of distance between the parents. In fact, the father has threatened that he will have no choice but to leave home if something is not done to change Don's behavior. The wife, on the other hand, acts as though the adolescent's behavior is normal for a retarded teenager and has more concern about Don finishing vocational school and finding employment.

The parents have been sent to the school psychologist by the teacher since she felt that the problem was beyond her professional competence. The mother feels closer to the son than she does to the father. The father, at present, does not feel close to either the adolescent or the mother. Moreover, the boundaries have been made more rigid by Don's lack of participation in family activities and his reluctance to become involved in learning a vocation in anticipation of becoming self-sufficient. The father has withdrawn and possibly is feeling some failure as a parent. The mother has not withdrawn but also has low self-esteem concerning her parenting skills.

When entering the family life cycle of this family, the psychologist is cognizant that the family does not have decision-making responsibilities clearly assigned to either parent. Therefore, the therapist works with the family to reestablish lines of authority and assists the parents in not becoming overly intrusive in Don's life. The psychologist also promotes activities that will strengthen the boundaries between the spouse relationship and the father-son dyad. One such activity is the formation of a contractual agreement that is geared toward the performance of each family member. The goal of the contracts is written so that each family member has provisions to fulfill in order for discipline to be improved and for the terms of the contract to be completed.

The therapist also counsels with the parents to assist them in changing the spouse relationship. They are encouraged to expand their social activities together and to maintain a better social relationship with the son. The parents also receive counseling assistance concerning vocational planning for Don to improve the quality of life that he might enjoy in the future. It is important for the parents to learn to set realistic goals for their son. This posture is consistent with Maslow's (1954) hierarchy of needs. Based on this philosophy, the therapist exchanges information with the parents, explaining the placement in vocational education classes, and mediates disputes between curriculum areas (Marion, 1981).

Psychologists should be responsive to the wish of parents that their teenagers reach their potential. However, parents and psychologists may have differing views on that potential. Parents may have the perspective of the three Rs or may set unrealistic academic goals for their teenager. Therapists should have an understanding of these concerns. Parents whose youngster has suffered the pains of the "dummy room" label may suffer from a lack of direction. Psychologists can be prepared to suggest that the youth and parents might follow a course that will produce a functional young adult. The curriculum of the Adult Performance Level (APL) competency-based diploma plan (Marion, 1978) might have the capacity to meet this desire of parents and families of EMR, TMR, and some S/PMR teenagers.

This endorsement of a change in the vocational education program by parents and psychologists will have to be mediated at the ARD (Admission, Review, or Dismissal) meeting or screening team session. Both parents and vocational educators might have reservations to share about the entry of the TMR youth into the program. Helping persons will have to reconcile these differences as well as those shared by the teenager in the best interests of the youth. Sometimes sheltered workshop situations or vocational programs for handicapped youths are the least restrictive alternatives.

The transition process in the fifth life cycle has often produced a crisis in the lives of families with a mentally retarded child. The fifth life cycle phase is distinguished by the launching of children from the family nest (Carter & McGoldrick, 1980). Turnball, Turnbull, Summers, Brotherson, and Benson (1986) have a similar stage (four) in their life-cycle model that is equated to the same activities. This stage has significant implications for the family since it concludes the education and training of the mentally retarded youth in the K–12 public school system.

Earlier, it was stated that PL 94–142 provided for the education of handicapped children and youth ages 3 through 21 years of age. Then the passage of PL 99–457 extended that limit from 0 to 2, giving handicapped youth and children the opportunity to be educated for 22 years.

The last issue pertaining to families with mentally retarded children that will be discussed in this chapter will be the transition problem of parents accepting a multitude of exits from and entries into the family system (Carter & McGoldrick, 1980). This has great importance in the lives of families with mentally retarded children and youth. Turnbull and associates (1986) have listed issues encountered in this life cycle by parents and children undergoing this transition phase.

Adulthood (Ages 21 and Older)
Planning for possible need for guardianship
Addressing the need for appropriate adult residence
Adjusting emotionally to any adult implications of dependency
Addressing the need for socialization opportunities outside the family for individual with exceptionality
Initiating career choice or vocational program
Possible responsibility for financial support
Addressing concerns regarding genetic implications
Introducing new in-laws to exceptionality
Need for information on career/living options
Clarify role of sibling advocacy
Possible guardianship

It can be seen that the successful movement of mentally retarded youths into adulthood will demand responsible attention to the needs of the young disabled adult by schools and families. This has not occurred according to Turnbull and colleagues (1986). Instead, sending schools and receiving agencies generally have chosen not to participate in planning for the transition of young mentally retarded adults until the student who is preparing to exit the schools is well underway in the transition period.

Turnbull and colleagues (1986) gave evidence of the reluctance of a receiving agency to participate fully in the transition process. They described the experiences of a forward planning family. This family was, and rightfully so, concerned enough about the future of their teenager that they attempted to begin the transition process while the youth was still in high school. The response of the receiving program was summed up succinctly by the agency. They stated that since the youngster was only 15 years old, their institution preferred not to become involved in long-range planning for a successful transition to the world of work. In this case, they elected to wait for several years and then at a later age the student would have the opportunity to apply for admission. The bottom line to the story was the fact that the youth was not assured that he would qualify for admission to the desired vocational training program. He would have to meet the criteria of the vocational training program for admission.

This scenario has probably been repeated many times in the lives of families with mentally retarded children. It represents the transition problem faced by a great number of families with young mentally retarded youths. Thus, families (especially parents) with mentally retarded youth have reasons to feel the burnout phenomenon identified by Hagen (1981). Although Hagen applied the psychological, social, intellectual, psychoemotional, and introspective burnout syndrome to professionals, Schell (1981) felt that parents were prone to suffer the same symptoms when they were attempting "to provide help and assistance often from birth to death" (p. 5).

These stress factors are exacerbated when parents and families encounter resistance from schools and outside agencies. When their mentally retarded children have problems gaining admission to career-enhancing vocational education programs (Marion, 1981), such a loss again has the effect of placing a continued drain on family resources. Being denied such an opportunity has meant that families have had to continue to support that young adult since he or she has not acquired the skills to become competitive in the world of work. EMRs and TMRs are not immune from this treatment. Severe/profoundly retarded youths have always been considered high risks for vocational programs. Such treatment has had the effect of creating stumbling blocks that have often caused families to become "stuck" in this phase. In turn, this outcome has also affected the mentally retarded individuals' chances to achieve independent living status. Most importantly, the self-worth of the mentally retarded youth has been dealt a harsh blow.

Psychologists, then, are faced with family situations that are of multiple dimensions. Parents are concerned about what will happen to their young mentally retarded adult when they are deceased. Economic problems are becoming increasingly important in their thinking as they calculate family resources to continue their support of the mentally retarded offspring throughout the life cycle. Finally, their relationships with nonhandicapped siblings may be affected by the nondevelopment of the mentally retarded sibling and the financial drain on resources.

Therapists also might need to counsel the nonhandicapped siblings within the family system. Many siblings are resentful of the fact that the retarded sibling's continued presence might mean diminished opportunity for their social activities and personal growth. Moreover, nonhandicapped siblings might have concerns about the parents' lack of time and attention that is being given to them.

Finally, therapists have to work with the mentally retarded individual who is poorly equipped to obtain an entry to independent living. Since the worth of a person in U.S. society is often determined by his or her ability to hold a job, these mentally retarded youths will be poorly equipped to obtain employment and to sustain themselves in independent living. Braginsky and Braginsky (1975) spoke to the loss of self-concept that occurs when a person suffers from the inability to hold a job and the high cost when a person wears a label. The label and the lost prospect of un- or underemployment has served to create a serious issue for the parents and the family during this stage. Thus, all family functions and all family relationships will have been affected (i.e., parent-child, sibling-sibling, and spouse-spouse)

The family with a mentally retarded child will have moved through six crisis periods and will have attempted the transition through four of the life-cycle stages. In our discussions of the possible situations and circumstances that might face families with mentally retarded children and youth, some past issues have not been examined and were not given the depth of discussion, as this chapter allowed that the focus be given only to the school-family relationship. For instance, the institutionalization of mentally retarded children, a factor of considerable stress to families with mentally retarded children, was not examined. Rather, it was omitted due to the focus on the public school and independent living relationship that would involve most school psychologists.

CONCLUSION

School-based intervention in combination with home efforts have served to increase parent participation in the education of their children. Much of the previous parent and family involvement occurred only at the elementary school level. Thus, one challenge of the future that must be faced by parents and families with mentally retarded children is centered around the transition of youth from school to the world of work or to sheltered work environments and community living. The other challenge has arisen from the concept of mainstreaming mentally retarded children into the regular school curriculum.

The apprehensions and expectations of parents and families will have to be explored and resolved by parents and schools in a co-equal relationship if mentally retarded students are to be truly prepared for integration from the family-school environment into the school environment and finally into the society at large. In the meantime, schools and families will have to continue their joint efforts

to ensure that individuals with mental retardation are allowed to participate freely in the U.S. society and to develop, to the fullest extent possible, the necessary skills and knowledge to assure the success of their endeavors.

References

Ackerman, N. (1966). *Treating the troubled family.* New York: Basic Books.

Bane, M. J. (1977, August 21). Is the American family dying out or just technology stunned? *San Angelo Standard Times,* p. 21.

Barraga, N. (1966). *Parental needs versus affiliate services.* Paper presented at the Texas State United Cerebral Palsy Conference, Fort Worth.

Barsch, R. (1969). *The parent-teacher partnership.* Arlington, VA: Council for Exceptional Children.

Birenbaum, A. (1972). The mentally retarded child in the home and the family life cycle. *Journal of Health and Social Behavior, 12,* 55–65.

Braginsky, D. D., & Braginsky, B. M. (1975). Surplus people: Their lost faith in self and the system. *Psychology Today, 9*(3), 66–72.

Bronfenbrenner, U. (1977). To nurture children. Conversation with Burt Kruger Smith, Hogg Foundation for Mental Health, University of Texas, Austin.

Brown, B. F., & Task Force. (1975). *The adolescent, other citizens and their high schools: A report to the public and the professional.* New York: McGraw-Hill.

Burgess, E. W. (1926). The family as a unity of interacting personalities. In G. D. Erickson & T. P. Hogan (Eds.), *Family therapy: An introduction to theory and technique.* Monterey, CA: Brooks/Cole.

Business Week (1988, Sept. 19). America's schools still aren't making the grade, pp. 129–136.

Caplan, G. (1970). *The theory and practice of mental health consultation.* New York: Basic Books.

Carter, E. A., & McGoldrick, M. (1980). *The family life cycle: A framework for family therapy.* New York: Garner Press.

Clark, M. (1974). Troubled children: The quest for help. *Newsweek 4*(8), 52.

Cohen, D. K. (1970). Immigrants and the schools. In E. Gordon (Ed.), *Review of education-*

al research (pp. 13–28). Washington, DC: American Research Association.

Coleman, J. (1966). *Equality of educational opportunity.* Washington, DC: Department of Health, Education and Welfare, U.S. Office of Education.

Crnic, K. A., Friedrick, W. N., & Greenberg, M. T. (1983). Adaptation of families with mentally retarded children: A model of stress, coping and family ecology. *American Journal of Mental Deficiency, 88,* 125–138.

Crnic, K. A., & Leconte, J. (1986). Understanding sibling needs and influences. In R. R. Fewell & P. F. Vadasy (Eds.), *Families of handicapped children.* Austin, TX: Pro-Ed.

Cruickshank, W. M. (1967). The development of education for exceptional children. In W. M. Cruickshank & G. O. Johnson (Eds.), *Education of exceptional children and youth* (2nd ed.). Englewood Cliffs, NJ: Prentice-Hall.

Duval, E. M. (1962). *Family development.* Philadelphia: Lippincott.

Ehly, S. W., Conoley, J. D., & Rosenthal, D. (1985). *Working with parents of exceptional children.* St. Louis, MO: Times Mirror/Mosby College Publishing.

Farber, B. (1959). Effects of a severely mentally retarded child on family integration. *Monograph Sociological Research Child Development, 24.*

Farber, B. (1968). *Mental retardation: Its social context and social consequences.* Boston: Houghton Mifflin.

Ferber, A., & Beels, C. (1972). What family therapists do. In A. Ferber, M. Mendelsohn, & A. Napier (Eds.), *The book of family therapy.* Boston: Houghton Mifflin.

Fleck, S. (1967). An approach to family pathology. In G. D. Erickson & T. P. Hogan (Eds.), *Family therapy: An introduction to theory and techniques.* Monterey, CA: Brooks/Cole.

Folkman, S., Schaefer, C., & Lazarus, R. S. (1979). Cognitive processes as mediators of stress and coping. In V. Hamilton & D. W. Warburton (Eds.), *Human stress and cognition.* New York: Wiley.

Gabel, H., & Kotsch, L. S. (1981). Extended families and young handicapped children. *Topics in Early Childhood Special Education, 1,* 29–35.

Gallagher, J., Cross, A., & Scharfman W. (1983). Parental adaptation to a young handicapped child: The father's role. *Journal of the Division for Early Childhood, 3,* 3–14.

Gallup, G. H. (1973). Fifth Annual Gallup poll of public attitudes toward education. *Phi Delta Kappan, 38–51.*

Glazer, N., & Moynihan, P. (1963). *Beyond the melting pot: The Negroes, Puerto Ricans, Italians and Irish.* Cambridge, MA: MIT Press.

Goffman, E. (1963). *Stigma.* Englewood Cliffs, NJ: Prentice-Hall.

Gourash, N. (1978). Help seeking: A review of the literature. *American Journal of Community Psychology, 6,* 499–517.

Hagen, M. (1981). "Burnout." Teachers and parents. *Views, 1,* 4–6.

Haley, J. (1976). *Problem-solving therapy.* San Francisco: Jossey-Bass.

Hannam, C. (1975). *Parents and mentally handicapped children.* Middlex, England: Penguin Books.

Heward, W. L., & Orlansky, M. D. (1980). *Exceptional children.* Columbus, OH: Charles E. Merrill.

Hickerson, N. (1966). *Education for alienation.* Englewood Clifts: NJ: Prentice-Hall.

Hobbs, N. (1975). *The futures of children.* San Francisco: Jossey-Bass.

Hurley, R. (1969). *Poverty and mental retardation: A causal relationship.* New York: Vintage Books.

Jensen, A. R. (1969, winter). How much can we boost I.Q. and scholastic achievement? *Harvard Educational Review, 39.*

Kaslow, F. W., & Cooper, B. (1978, January). Family therapy with the learning disabled child and his/her family. *Journal of Marriage and Family Counseling, 4,* 41.

Kotsopoulous, S., & Matathia, P. (1980). Worries of parents regarding the future of their mentally retarded adolescent children. *International Journal of Social Psychiatry, 26*(1), 53.

Marion, R. L. (1978, April). Conversation with mother of learning disabled child. Austin, TX: SCAC.

Marion, R. L. (1981). *Educators and exceptional children.* Rockville, MD: Aspen.

Maslow, A. H. (1954). *Motivation and personality.* New York: Harper & Row.

Miller, S. M. (1967). *Breaking the credential barrier.* Address before American Orthopsychiatric Association, Washington, DC. New York: Ford Foundation Reprint.

Minuchin, S. (1974). *Families and family therapy.* Cambridge, MA: Harvard University Press.

Montalvo, B., & Haley, J. (1973). In defense of child therapy. *Family Process, 12,* 227–244.

Murray, J. (1981). Parental plegia. *Psychology in the Schools, 18,* 201.

Myrdal, G. (1962). *An American dilemma.* New York: Random House.

Oshansky, S. (1963). *Casework services for parents of handicapped children.* New York: Family Service Association.

Parsons, T. (1955). The American family: Its relation to personality and to the social structure. In T. Parson & R. F. Bales (Eds.), *Family socialization and interaction process.* New York: The Free Press.

Passow, A. H. (1976). *Secondary education reform: Retrospect and prospect.* New York: Teachers College Press.

Pennsylvania Association for Retarded Citizens (PARC) v. Commonwealth of Pennsylvania. 343 F. Suppl. 279 (E.D.Pa., 1972), Consent Agreement.

Roos, P. (1977). Parent of mentally retarded people. *International Journal of Mental Health, 6*(1), 96.

Roper, D. (1977). Parents as the natural enemy of the school system. *Phi Delta Kappan, 12,* 239–242.

Ross, A. O. (1964). *The exceptional child in the family.* New York: Grune and Stratton.

Schell, G. C. (1981). The young handicapped child: A family perspective. *Topics in early childhood special education* (pp. 1–3, 37–44). Rockville, MD: Aspen.

Shane, H. (1973). Looking to the future: Reassessment of educational issues of the 1970s. *Phi Delta Kappan, 5,* 326–327.

Skrtic, T. M., Summers, J. A., Brotherson, M. J., & Turnbull, A. P. (1983). Severely handicapped children and their brothers and sisters. In J. Blacher (Ed.), *Severely handicapped young children and their families: Research in review* (pp. 215–246). New York: Academic Press.

Stagg, V., & Catron, T. (1986). Networks of social supports for parents of handicapped children. In R. R. Fewell & P. F. Vadasy (Eds.), *Families of handicapped children* (pp. 279–296). Austin, TX: Pro-Ed.

Tronhanis, P. L., Cox, J. O., & Meyer, R. A. (1982). A report on selected demonstration programs for infant intervention. In C. T. Ramey & P. L. Tronhanis (Eds.), *Finding high risk and handicapped infants* (pp. 163–192). Baltimore, MD: University Park Press.

Turnbull, A. P., Turnbull, H. R., Summers, J. A., Brotherson, M. J., & Benson, H. A. (1986). *Families, professionals and exceptionality: A special partnership.* Columbus, OH: Charles E. Merrill.

U.S. Bureau of the Census (1982). *Characteristics of American children and youth: 1980.* (Current Population Reports, P-23, No. 114). Washington, DC: Government Printing Office.

Vincent, C. E. (1966). Family spongea: The adaptive function. *Journal of Marriage and the Family, 28,* 29–36.

Wikler, L. (1981). Chronic stresses of families of mentally retarded children. *Family Relations, 30,* 281–288.

Wright, L. (1976). Chronic grief: The anguish of being an exceptional parent. *The Exceptional Child, 23,* 160.

Wright, L., Wasaw, M., & Hatfield, E. (1981). Chronic sorrow revisited: Parent vs. professional depiction of the adjustment of parents of mentally retarded children. *American Journal of Orthopsychiatry, 51,* 63.

10

"Learning to Learn" and the Family System: New Perspectives on Underachievement and Learning Disorders

ROBERT-JAY GREEN

California School of Professional Psychology—Berkeley/Alameda

THE PURPOSE of this chapter is to weave together various scattered strands of thinking from different disciplines into a coherent conceptual framework in the area of school achievement and the family. An ecological model is proposed for understanding child and adolescent achievement problems. Four dimensions of a family's learning environment are suggested: family communication deviances, family structure, family attributions, and family achievement values. The metaphor of the family as the "primary classroom" is offered as a way to think about learning styles across home and school contexts. Some treatment guidelines are also suggested.

THE DEFINITIONAL PROBLEM

Since the passage of Public Law 94–142, The Education for All Handicapped Children Act of Congress (Office of Education, 1976), the emphasis of much theory and research in the area of school underachievement has been on children's learning disabilities (LD). In order to familiarize readers with the central ideas in the field of underachievement, the major definitional issues are reviewed below.

Underachievement is defined as a discrepancy between the child's *potential to achieve* in school and his or her *actual achievement*. Underachievement can result from any one or combination of the

Reprinted from Volume 15, Number 2, pages 187–203, of *Journal of Marital and Family Therapy.* Copyright 1989, American Association for Marriage and Family Therapy. Reprinted with permission.

following five child variables: (1) information-processing deficits (e.g., difficulties in perceiving, comprehending, storing, categorizing, retrieving, or coordinating information); (2) attentional deficits; (3) passive opposition to school tasks; (4) performance anxiety; or (5) lack of motivation and effort.

Learning disability is a subcategory of underachievement and includes disorders

in one or more of the basic psychological processes involved in understanding or in using language, spoken or written, which . . . may manifest itself in imperfect ability to listen, think, speak, read, write, spell or do mathematical calculations. Such disorders include conditions such as perceptual handicaps, brain injury, minimal brain dysfunction, dyslexia, and developmental aphasia. Such terms do not include children who have learning problems which are primarily the result of visual, hearing, or motor handicap, emotional disturbance, or environmental, cultural, or economic disadvantage. (Office of Education, 1976)

The *Diagnostic and Statistical Manual* of the American Psychiatric Association (DSM-III-R) includes learning disabilities under the Axis II category *Specific Developmental Disorders*. These disorders all involve what is termed a "significant impairment" in the development of skills not accounted for by the child's age, IQ, or inadequate schooling. Under Specific Developmental Disorders, DSM-III-R lists three subtypes of *Academic Skills Disorders* (arithmetic, expressive writing, reading); three subtypes of *Language and Speech Disorders* (articulation, expressive language, receptive language); *Developmental Coordination Disorder;* and a "Not Otherwise Specified" subtype.

The ultimate decision to place children into LD classes is made by a school's Committee on the Handicapped, which is usually composed of a school administrator, school psychologist, special education teacher, speech pathologist, and one or both parents. Many of the tests used to assess learning disability are unstandardized, and no typical battery of tests has won the allegiance of the field at large. In order to receive LD class placement, a child must show a "significant discrepancy" between scores on tests of intelligence (IQ) and achievement tests. Keogh (1982) reports that out of 408 studies, over 1400 different diagnostic methods had been used to select LD children (including 40 different IQ tests and 79 different achievement tests). Only a small minority (estimated at about 5 percent) of LD cases show demonstrable neurological dysfunction, although LD theories typically presume some underlying neurological deficit (Hagin, Beecher, & Silver, 1982).

LD has been attributed to genetic, biochemical, neurological, behavioral, motivational, attributional, and information-processing deficits, and some of these causal models overlap (Bryan, 1988; Das, Mulcahy, & Wall, 1982; Kolligian & Sternberg, 1986). This theoretical heterogeneity breeds lack of consensus on definitional criteria, even though all of these definitions share the premise that LD is caused by factors *intrinsic* to the child. The case-by-case determination of LD and related special class placement frequently involve considerable subjective judgment and sometimes community politics.

The LD exclusionary criterion "not due to emotional disturbance" is particularly difficult to operationalize in practice. Often, it is impossible to discriminate between LD (which presumes a neurological cause of underachievement, even in the absence of positive findings from neurological examination) and emotional/behavioral problems. Many of the so-called "emotional disorders" on Axis I of DSM-III-R (Attention-Deficit Hyperactivity Disorder, Conduct Disorders, Oppositional Defiant Disorder, Overanxious Disorder, Identity Disorder, and Undifferentiated

Attention-Deficit Disorder) are accompanied by school underachievement.

In addition, studies of the social competence of LD children consistently show that they are less popular and more rejected by their classmates, less skilled in social communication, have lower self-esteem in the achievement domain, and are less competent in the areas of social perception, empathy, and interpretation of nonverbal social cues (Bryan, 1988). Follow-back studies of adjudicated male delinquents and adult schizophrenics reveal poorer premorbid school records (Bower, 1960; Pickar & Tori, 1986). Some theorists believe that the emotional and interpersonal difficulties of LD children stem from the same inferred source (information-processing deficits) as their learning problems: "social problems resemble learning problems; that is, a child may have difficulty reading people, as the child has difficulty reading text" (Bryan, 1988, p. 346). Moreover, in everyday practice, many children diagnosed as LD are also labeled "emotionally disordered."

It is also important to keep in mind that the criteria for "achievement" (or underachievement) are *socially defined and labeled* by specific persons who base their judgments on cultural standards and values within a given school district. Thus, performance defined as underachievement by some parents and school systems would not be considered problematic in other contexts. Furthermore, many children fitting the behavioral criteria for LD class placement come from economically deprived backgrounds and have had inadequate schooling. The LD exclusionary criterion "not due to environmental/cultural/economic disadvantage" is impossible to rule out in these cases.

In view of the above definitional problems, it seems premature to create artificial boundaries around information-processing, neurological, motivational, emotional, and socioeconomic components of achievement or LD problems. These four aspects or a subset seem so intertwined in many cases that a multiaxial approach to definitional criteria seems most appropriate at this time. Except for cases of measurable neurological impairment, mental retardation, pervasive developmental disorders (e.g., autism), visual or hearing handicaps, and other organic dysfunctions, it is arbitrary to assume that the causes of LD are *purely* intrinsic to the child (Coles, 1988).

AN ECOLOGICAL MODEL

It seems that the most useful framework for understanding achievement or its lack (whether LD or otherwise) is a more general ecological-somatic model. This model takes into account presumed genetic or physiological vulnerability and response proclivities, and places them within an interactional framework. Examples pertinent to this model include Wynne's (Wynne, 1971; Wynne & Cole, 1983) framework for schizophrenia spectrum disorders; Thomas, Chess, and Birch's (1968) concept of fit between children's genetically based temperament and the child-rearing environment; Sameroff's (1975, 1979) transactional/cognitive framework for infants at risk; Minuchin, Rosman, and Baker's (1978) framework for psychosomatic disorders; and Engel's (1980) biopsychosocial medical model.

Especially relevant here is Feldman's (1986) genetic/familial/cultural theory for understanding the phenomenon of child prodigies and the development of human abilities (based on an intensive study of six prodigies and their ecosystems). Feldman's brilliant insights into the prodigy phenomenon, and into the systemic nature of the developmental process he calls *co-incidence,* can be extrapolated to apply equally well to underachievers, LD children, average achievers, and above average students:

It is the fortuitous convergence of highly specific individual proclivities with specific environmental receptivity that allows a prodigy to emerge. This is an infrequent and unlikely event. The convergence is not simply between two unitary, looming giants—an individual and an environment—but between a number of elements in a very delicate interplay: it includes a cultural milieu; the presence of a particular domain [of achievement] which is itself at a particular level of development; the availability of master teachers; family recognition of extreme talent and commitment to support it; large doses of encouragement and understanding; and other features. . . . (p. 12)

As Gardner (1983) has argued, family/cultural factors determine which out of many "multiple intelligences" will be valued and amplified and which will be left to lie dormant. He cites an example from the Caroline Islands where a 12-year-old boy is selected by the community on the basis of talent to become a master sailor—an unlikely event in the United States. Contrariwise, persons with the potential to become musical prodigies (or master family therapists) are unlikely to fulfill that potential in the Caroline Islands. In a related vein, ecological factors such as socioeconomic status powerfully influence the identification and long-term prognosis of U.S. children's learning disorders. LD children from higher social classes are significantly more successful in the long run than those from lower classes (O'Connor & Spreen, 1988).

This ecological model points to processes of mutual amplification (for better or worse) between genetic talent or vulnerabilities on the one hand and social factors on the other (Green, 1990). In such a process, biological, psychological, familial, and social network factors are in a process of changing one another such that characteristics of each system and its many levels are increased or reduced together. The whole suprasystem induces and responds to changes in its parts. This general framework applies equally well to such diverse phenomena as children's underachievement, LD, general "giftedness," special learning abilities, and high achievements in the lives of eminent adults (Feldman, 1986; Frey & Wendorf, 1985; Goertzel & Goertzel, 1962; Wendorf & Frey, 1985; Wynne, 1971, 1976; Wynne, Singer, Bartko, & Toohey, 1977).

Achievement problems are best conceptualized as being on a continuum—from those subtypes that are exclusively biologically caused and only marginally responsive to environmental factors, to those that seem more purely socially determined and shaped (Owen, Adams, Forrest, Stolz, & Fisher, 1971). In between these two extremes are the bulk of cases in which presumed polygenetic factors (attentional predispositions, perceptual styles, memory, temperament) may show a wide range of outcomes depending on the constraints they impose and depending on characteristics of the interactional milieu. Given varying degrees of genetic vulnerability, and depending on the unique characteristics of the "achievement ecology," some genetic vulnerabilities may remain inconsequential. In other cases, they may emerge as problems and endure at relatively fixed levels over time (through a *symptom maintenance cycle*); or they may progressively improve or deteriorate over time (through a *beneficent or vicious spiral*). Improvement, deterioration, or stability of symptoms are a function of the whole ecological context of which the child's mind-body is a part.

In the next sections of this chapter, four aspects of family interaction pertinent to underachievement will be discussed: family communication deviances, family structure, family attributions, and family achievement values. At the chapter's conclusion, some hypotheses will be proposed for linking these four family dimensions to the five characteristics of child underachievers (information-processing deficits, attention deficits, opposition to school tasks, performance anxiety, and lack of motivation/effort). The main question before us is: What aspects of family interaction are likely to co-create, co-maintain, or co-amplify a child's poor performance in the school context?

FAMILY COMMUNICATION DEVIANCES

Previous Studies of Parental Communication Deviances and Adult Thought Disorders

In extensive research studied by Wynne, Singer, and their associates, family *communication deviances (CD)* have been defined as oddities of spoken language that impair the establishment and maintenance of a shared focus of attention in communication (Doane, 1978, 1985; Singer, Wynne, & Toohey, 1978). In CD, the speaker leaves the listener confused as to what is meant in a speech or confused about what to focus on in a dialogue. In the scoring manual designed to measure CD, the following categories are included:

1. *Commitment Problems* (the speaker fails to commit to a definite idea)
2. *Referent Problems* (the speaker leaves you wondering what is being talked about)
3. *Language Anomalies* (the speaker constructs sentences or uses words oddly, or uses idiosyncratic-private terms whose meaning is unclear)
4. *Disruptions* (speeches or nonverbal behaviors that are irrelevant or tangential to the topic under discussion and therefore disrupt the task focus of the dialogue)
5. *Contradictory, Arbitrary Sequences* (the speaker gives incompatible ideas, retracts or denies ideas given, or uses peculiar logic)

The reader is referred to Singer and Wynne (1966) for the original scoring manual and to Ditton, Green, and Singer (1987) for a list of categories in Singer's 1973 revised manual.

A large number of earlier studies utilizing the CD scoring manual have shown that high parental CD is associated with offsprings' diagnoses of schizophrenia and of borderline conditions, whereas low parental CD is associated with offsprings' normality (Singer, Wynne, & Toohey, 1978; Doane, 1985). These high parental CD findings have been especially strong for offspring who show more chronic and cognitively disorganized (thought-disordered) subtypes of schizophrenia, when compared to more organized subtypes (e.g., paranoids) (Rund, 1986; Sass, Gunderson, Singer, & Wynne, 1984). Furthermore, longitudinal studies and adoptive studies in the United States and Europe show that high parental CD is predictive of later schizophrenia spectrum disorders in offspring (Goldstein & Strachan, 1987; Tienari, Lahti, Sorri, Naarala, Moring, Wahlberg, & Wynne, 1987).

Put simply, confusing and disorienting styles of parental communication are reflected in the confused and disoriented thought processes of schizophrenic offspring. Related studies have shown that offsprings' and spouses' performance of cognitive tasks in an experimental situation is impaired during and immediately following interactions filled with high CD-type communication (Blakar, 1981; Carter, Robertson, Ladd, & Alpert, 1987; Mossige, Petterson, & Blakar, 1979; Reiss, 1981; Rund, 1986; Shapiro & Wild, 1976; Solvberg & Blakar, 1975). Lastly, Waxler (1974) found that schizophrenic offsprings' performance on a cognitive task improved after interaction with normal offsprings' parents (who presumably were low in CD).

Communication Deviance and Learning Disability

Based on the above CD research, Ditton, Green, and Singer (1987) theorized that *high parental CD would be present whenever offspring exhibit persistent problems in information processing, language usage, and/or focusing attention*—including both childhood learning disabilities and adult schizophrenia spectrum disorders:

> Learning disabled students may find it difficult to attend to, focus on, or complete tasks in school partly because they have not learned these basic cognitive skills in the family setting. Some parents may fail to orient the child to the task, or may not maintain a shared focus of attention long enough for the youngster to understand the relevant aspects of the task. Over time, the parents' inability to teach the child how to focus and how to attend may affect the child's conceptual development. (p. 78)

This hypothesis received strong support in a study of 30 families of students placed in LD classes (for reading and writing difficulties) and 30 families of average-achieving students. Based on blind ratings of parents' communications when instructing their children, 87 percent of LD students' parents showed high levels of CD, and 77 percent of average students' parents showed low levels of CD (chi-square = 16.99, R = .43, *p* < .0001).

Communication Deviance and Underachievement

An intensive search of the literature revealed four other studies that investigated CD-related aspects of communication and children's cognitive functioning in the school setting. Hassan (1974) looked at transactional and contextual "disqualifications" in marital interactions (using a scoring system derived largely from Singer's CD manual). Her subjects were parents of five groups of index offspring (schizophrenic, delinquent, "mildly disturbed," ulcerative colitis, and normals). The "mildly disturbed" group consisted of 12 families, 10 of whom presented underachievement as a complaint. These parents scored higher on transactional disqualification than did parents of normal or ulcerative colitis offspring (but lower than parents of schizophrenic or delinquent offspring). Overall, Hassan's results suggest a moderate degree of parental communication deviance problems in her mildly disturbed (largely underachieving) group.

The remaining three studies looked at parental communication in relation to children's *cognitive/academic problem-solving ability* in school (as assessed through teacher and peer ratings). These three reports, by Fisher and Jones (1980), Wynne, Jones, and Al-Khayyal (1982), and Jones, Wynne, Al-Khayyal, Doane, Ritzler, Singer, and Fisher (1984), were from the University of Rochester Risk Research Program begun in 1972. The children were 7- and 10-year-old males considered at risk for psychopathology because one of their parents had previously been hospitalized with a psychiatric disorder.

Fisher and Jones found that (on a "Consensus Family Rorschach" task) higher scores on combined mother and father CD, higher scores on whole family nonacknowledgment, and lower scores on a composite variable termed "clear communication" all were associated with poorer academic problem solving by the child. Wynne, Jones, and Al-Khayyal found that mothers' healthy communication (a variable derived from CD concepts) was positively related to higher ratings on academic problem solving. Jones and associates determined that families scoring high on CD and low on healthy communication across three experimental tasks (parents' individual Rorschachs, parents' individual TATs, and family consensus Rorschach) had children showing the poorest cognitive/academic performance ($p <$ .0001).[1]

Summary and Implications of CD Research

Based on the research reviewed in this section, it seems that a child's ability to orient to school tasks, grasp task "sets," stay focused on relevant dimensions of such tasks, and organize and sustain goal-directed behavior in academics is a skill developed and maintained in the family setting where the child "learns how to learn." To the degree that the family is characterized by confusing and disorienting communication (communication deviances), the child's ability to think and perform in the school setting may be compromised.[2]

FAMILY STRUCTURE

The Underorganized Family

Over twenty years ago, in studies of families of severely delinquent, lower socioeconomic-class boys, Minuchin and colleagues described the socialization processes in *the underorganized family* and related these processes to the child's learning difficulties in school (Minuchin, Chamberlin, & Graubard, 1967; Minuchin, Montalvo, Guerney, Rosman, & Schumer, 1967). These clinical researchers described the following characteristics of the underorganized family's structure:

1. Parental styles of control that are global and erratic such that clear and consistent behavioral contingencies (rules) for rewards and punishments are lacking
2. Disciplinary responses based on the parents' moods
3. Resolution of conflict by escalating

threats and counterthreats rather than discussions leading to closure
4. An overall deficit of communication through words and logic, which are replaced by intensity of physical action and sound
5. A communication style in which members do not expect to be listened to, so resort to yelling
6. An extreme focus on hierarchical relatedness and immediate compliance by the use of force, rather than long-term solutions and cognitively mediated responses
7. Communication filled with disconnected interruptions and abrupt topic changes

In school, these delinquent children showed an inability to focus their attention, a disruptive communication style that precluded taking in new information, and behavior focused on eliciting authoritarian/proximal control by the teacher rather than on classroom tasks.

A number of controlled studies lend support to Minuchin and associates' clinical impressions above. Owen and colleagues (1971) rated the families of LD children as more disorganized and unstable than the families of normal controls. Kohn and Rosman (1974) found a relationship between disorganized family structure and children's poorer task orientation in early elementary school children who had worse academic achievement. A dissertation by Perosa (cited in Spacone & Hansen, 1984) found that fathers of LD children were somewhat disengaged, neglectful, and distant. In a study of underachieving students in group counseling, Gurman (1970) found that their parents described themselves as ineffective and inconsistent in discipline, and the children felt their parents were indifferent.

The most systems-oriented of studies on this topic used Olson's Family Adaptability and Cohesion Scales (FACES) in a study comparing three groups of predominantly white, middle-class families (Amerikaner & Omizo, 1984). Children in the three groups were either LD, emotionally disturbed, or normal offspring. On adaptability, mothers and fathers in both the LD and emotionally disturbed groups scored in the chaotic range, whereas parents of normals scored significantly more functional (largely in the flexible range). Also, on cohesion, mothers and especially fathers of both LD and emotionally disturbed groups scored significantly lower than parents of normals. These results from Amerikaner and Omizo (1984) demonstrate similarities between families of LD and of emotionally disturbed children—both tend to be chaotic, disorganized, and less cohesive than families of normals.

The Overorganized Family

In contrast to the tendency toward chaotic disengagement in the underorganized family, the polar opposite family structure (overorganized, tending toward rigid enmeshment) may sometimes contribute to another set of achievement problems. Whereas the underorganized structure seems to be associated with child attentional deficits and conduct disorders that interfere with learning, the overorganized structure is sometimes associated with symptoms of obsessional worry, performance anxiety, procrastination, passive-negativism, or oppositional behavior in reference to academic tasks.

The overorganized family is characterized by parental intrusiveness, overinvolvement, and overprotective restrictiveness. In these families, the parents tend to be too involved and too controlling of the child's school performance—taking over, cajoling, pressuring, demanding, and dominating. The child may be perceived as "lazy" or as "weak and in-

competent." Parental attempts to control these problems (especially if these attempts are punitive and escalating) tend to backfire and to maintain or exacerbate the problem. In many cases, the parents are unified and overly involved in the child's school performance. However, in other cases, one parent seems too involved while the second parent is peripheral.

Various other clinicians and researchers have described similar patterns of overinvolvement and overprotectiveness in some of the families of underachievers or LD children (Day & Moore, 1976; Humphries & Bauman, 1980; Kaslow & Cooper, 1978; Kohn & Rosman, 1974; Silverman, Fite, & Mosher, 1959; Staver, 1953). In their review, Spacone and Hansen (1984) likened the family interactions of LD students and other underachievers to the psychosomatic family patterns described by Minuchin, Rosman, and Baker (1978)—enmeshment, overprotectiveness, rigidity, and lack of conflict resolution.

However, while some overorganized, rigid families have an overprotective parental style as described above, others seem to have a more authoritarian-punitive style (Dornbusch, Ritter, Leiderman, Roberts, & Fraleigh, cited in Henderson, 1987). In either case, the parents take too much responsibility for the child's school performance and, complementarily, the child rebels or takes on too little responsibility for achievement.

Sibling Relations and Underachievement

The general literature on sibling relationships suggest that rivalry, unity, identification, and "de-identification" between siblings are the most salient variables (Bank & Kahn, 1982; Minuchin et al., 1967; Schachter, 1985). Siblings explicitly or implicitly compete and compare themselves in the areas of school and nonacademic achievements. Siblings tend to specialize their achievement identities in areas prized by the parents. A child who believes he or she is inferior to a sibling in some sphere of achievement may choose to "specialize" in another area. Such a parceling out of identities may be subtly reinforced by parents.

Schachter (1985) described the process of sibling *de-identification* in well-functioning families and families that were clinic-referred (for behavior or learning problems or both). The most typical pattern consisted of a four-member *tetrad* (or quadrangle) in which two siblings differed markedly in personality (de-identification) and each identified with a different parent (split-parent identification). As expected, this pattern was more frequent in same-sex/first-pair siblings in clinic-referred families (89.5 percent) than for opposite-sex/first-pair siblings (60 percent). Schachter speculates that de-identification diminishes intense sibling rivalry, thus preserving equilibrium and harmony for all family members.

Based on this theory, we would expect children who do poorly in school to have higher achieving siblings, despite equal ability (especially if the members of the pair are close in age, same-sex, and a first-born pair). Furthermore, we would expect that de-identification on achievement would frequently reflect cross-generational coalitions, each sibling being aligned with a different parent (a "quadrangulation").

Overall, there has been little controlled research in the area of sibling relationships and achievement. One clinical report suggested that rivalry is higher among underachievers and their siblings (e.g., Silverman, Fite, & Mosher, 1959). An extremely well-designed study by Owen and associates (1971) showed that the family emotional climate was more negative for the LD child than for his or her sibling. Parents were less accepting, less affectionate, and more pressuring toward the LD child.

FAMILY ATTRIBUTIONS

Interpersonal Attributions and Person Perception

Family members attribute varying degrees of intelligence, inability, laziness, industry, and creativity to one another in particular areas (Laing, Phillipson, & Lee, 1966). Attribution theory looks at how *interpersonal perceptions* and consequent *interpersonal attributions* affect child performance. Labels such as "stupid," "bright," "musical," and so on may be applied to a child. Similarities with other successful or unsuccessful family members or extrafamilial persons may be ascribed.

Such attributions may undermine or support the child's school achievement by creating a self-fulfilling prophecy (Rosenthal & Jacobson, 1968; Watzlawick, 1984). In this process, the child enacts and embodies those characteristics that are attributed to him or her by others. Through positive feedback loops, a cycle is created whereby parental attributions and child characteristics are reciprocally amplified (Alexander & Dibb, 1977; Shapiro, 1969; Stierlin, Levi, & Savard, (1971).

Such attributions may or may not be in accord with test data (e.g., IQ), actual performance (school grades), or the views of others (e.g., school personnel, therapists) (Pollner & McDonald-Wikler, 1985; Shapiro, Fisher, & Gayton, 1974; Wendorf & Frey, 1985). Inappropriately negative family attributions and low expectations in the achievement area seem associated with lowered motivation in the child at school. Inappropriately positive attributions and excessively high expectations may equally undermine a child's achievement motivation. Unable to live up to such expectations, the child may rebel or give up altogether.

The Source of Attributions and the Function of the Symptom

The source of "distorted" interpersonal attributions has not been studied experimentally. However, a large amount of clinical literature suggests that one or both parents' conflicts in the area of achievement may fuel negative parental attributions and the process of projective identification (Grunebaum, Hurwitz, Prentice, & Sperry, 1962; Holder, 1977; Klein, Altman, Dreizen, Friedman, & Powers, 1981a, 1981b; Miller & Westman, 1964; Sperry, Staver, Reiner, & Ulrich, 1958; Stierlin, 1974; Vogel & Bell, 1968).

Stierlin (1974) describes how such unresolved parental conflicts may be conveyed to the child as parental pressure to fulfill the parents' own unrealized aspirations. Alternatively, a child may be given the mission to fail in school in order to protect a parent from feeling competitively inadequate. Also, a child may be given an impossible mission in which a parent, or two conflicting parents, convey incompatible directives about achievement. In the latter situation, the child may be pressured to fulfill vicariously the parents' own unrealized ambitions; simultaneously, however, the parents may undermine the child's efforts.

These theories about the source of negative attributions sometimes propose that the child's school failure serves a homeostatic (morphostatic) function for the family—a positive stabilizing function (Holder, 1977; Klein et al., 1981a, 1981b; Miller & Westman, 1964; Sperry et al., 1958). Johnson (1988) and Colapinto (1988) have recently criticized the notion of an Identified Patient whose school failure serves a homeostatic, myth-preserving, positive function for the family. Johnson believes that the idea of a family-created,

Identified LD Patient implicitly blames the family for causing a symptom that is actually biologically caused. However, based on an ecological-somatic model, LD is hypothesized to have both biological *and* interactional roots.

The lessening of LD symptoms could have destabilizing effects on the family, regardless of its partly biological origins (Green, 1988). Thus, for example, a parent who has organized his or her life meaningfully around the care of an LD child may unwittingly participate in problem-maintenance simply out of habit, or out of an unconscious fear that change will leave a void or create new problems.

Causal Attributions

Additional research has been done on the topic of causal attributions (i.e., how family members *explain the causes of successes or failures* in the domain of achievement). The manner in which parents generally explain the causes of their own and their children's performance may influence the child's tendency to persist or give up on a particular learning task. Such causal attributions vary along continua such as:

1. Internal versus external locus of the cause (Who or what is responsible for the person's performance level, and how much control does the person have over his or her performance?)
2. Stability versus transience of the causal factor (What impact on the individual's performance will the causal factor have in the future?)
3. Widespread versus limited influence of the causal factor (How many different kinds of performance situations might be similarly affected?)

Research suggests that children's causal attributional styles converge with their parents' (Seligman, Peterson, Kaslow, Tanenbaum, Alloy, & Abramson, 1984).

Thus, parents' feelings of helplessness and sense of failure in their own lives may be reflected in children's passivity and perceived helplessness in the face of achievement demands in school (Anderson, 1983; Campis, Lyman, & Prentice-Dunn, 1986; Dweck & Licht, 1980). In these situations, the parents view the child's failure as being beyond his or her control; that is, the cause is considered internal/stable/widespread or external (Kistner, White, Haskett, & Robbins, 1985; Klein et al., 1981a). In a vicious cycle, such parental styles of explaining failure may contribute to a child's learned helplessness, diminished sense of efficacy, lack of effort, and eventual failure, which in turn reinforce the parent's failure-inducing attributions.

FAMILY ACHIEVEMENT VALUES

Families differ in the extent to which they value education and educational institutions. Parents may devalue academic achievement explicitly in words or implicitly by example. They model a set of achievement values through their own work successes and failures; intellectual, cultural, and recreational activities; relations with school authorities; and level of involvement with school activities (Freund & Cardwell, 1977; Gurman, 1970; Henderson, 1987; Klein et al., 1981a, 1981b; Vogel & Bell, 1968; Wynne & Green, 1985).

Klein and colleagues (1981a, 1981b) discuss how parental values based on subcultural factors (ethnicity, SES) may negatively affect the child's motivation in school by undervaluing or overvaluing school achievement. In this regard, McGoldrick and Rohrbaugh (1987) found that American ethnic subcultures differentially valued success and education—American Irish, Black, Italian, Greek, Hispanic and Wasp families tended to place less emphasis on success than American-Asian and Jewish families. Also, O'Connor and Spreen (1988) found that LD children from lower SES families had poorer occupational and educational achievement in adulthood when compared with LD children from higher SES families (in which high achievement presumably was emphasized to a greater degree).

Klein and associates (1981a, 1981b) also note the frequency with which underachievers' parents disparage education and show disregard for school authority, often unfairly blaming the teachers and school system for the child's learning difficulties. The child is sometimes encouraged to defy school teachers and ignore assignments. Thus, parents may model an anticonformist/antischool rebelliousness that their children then imitate (Wynne & Green, 1985). Moreover, in the fields of early childhood and school-aged education, there is substantial evidence of a strong association between supportive/active parental involvement in the child's school-related activities (a sign of placing high value on education and achievement) and higher levels of child school performance (Henderson, 1987).

SUMMARY: LINKS BETWEEN CHILD UNDERACHIEVEMENT AND FAMILY INTERACTION

The ecological-somatic model assumes that the vast majority of achievement problems are at least partially caused or maintained by factors in the family context, as well as by characteristics of the school and larger social systems. A number of hypotheses, linking characteristics of the underachieving child to characteristics of the family, can be derived from this review and used as a guide for future clinical work and research:

1. Information-processing deficits of the child may be maintained or amplified by high levels of family communication deviances.
2. Child attention deficits in the school context may be maintained or amplified by an underorganized/chaotic family structure with a disruptive, interruptive style of family communication.
3. A child's passive opposition and/or performance anxiety in relation to school tasks may be maintained or amplified by an overorganized, rigid family structure in which parents intrusively pressure the child to perform, frequently combined with inappropriately high parental expectations and attributions about the child's ability to perform.
4. A child's lack of academic motivation and effort in school may be maintained or amplified by the family's:
   a. inappropriately negative interpersonal attributions about the child's ability and motivation
   b. causal attributions that assign responsibility for the child's success or failure to factors outside of the child's control
   c. sibling de-identification in which the I.P. both selects and is cast into an inferior achievement identity compared to siblings of equal or lesser ability
   d. overt values, or parental modeling of values, that minimize the importance of education, school authorities, achievement, and intellectual/cultural pursuits.

These hypotheses should be held open to confirmation or disconfirmation as data in a case warrant. Not all subtypes of underachievement can be traced to these patterns alone. Neurological, nutritional, socioeconomic, school-related, peer-related, drug-related, or transitional (e.g., parental divorce) factors can be prepotent.

In many cases, the symptom picture is mixed. A child who is labeled LD may show information-processing, attentional, behavioral, and motivational problems. In such a case, we might find high family CD, an underorganized structure, and values deemphasizing the importance of academic success. In addition, such a child may have a genetic predisposition to the information-processing and attentional aspects of the problem. Thus, the assessment of underachievement and family interaction always must be multidimensional in order to grasp adequately the complexity of these phenomena.

EPILOGUE: TREATMENT IMPLICATIONS

All poorly achieving children should undergo a complete psychoeducational and neurological assessment at the outset of treatment. Likewise, in all cases, the clinician *must* work closely with school personnel and parents in developing, implementing, and maintaining a suitable educational plan at school, or the treatment may be doomed (Wynne & Green, 1985). Conjoint family-school consultation sessions are sometimes useful in working out a cooperative educational plan (Aponte, 1976). However, sometimes it is best for the therapist to play a go-between role, meeting with members of the school and family separately and coaching them to support each other's efforts (Colapinto, 1988; Freund & Cardwell, 1977; Lusterman, 1985). Although traditional family therapy can be used alone in some rare cases, neglecting the family-school interface is usually a fatal error for the treatment (Colapinto, 1988; Fish & Jain, 1985; Freund & Cardwell, 1977; Friedman, 1973; Margalit, 1982; Okun, 1984; Ziegler & Holden, 1988).

With elementary school children, we are exploring some innovative methods of family evaluation based on the CD research. We directly observe the parents' teaching skills and the child's learning skills as enacted in a *family learning task*, which can be taped for review. This method is presented to the family as a way to assess the child's "thinking style." First, without the child present, the clinician explains to the parental couple, or the primary-care parent, the nature of the task they (or he or she) will be participating in with the child. Examples are supervising the successful completion of a grade-level homework assignment from school, instructing the child verbally in how to recreate an "etch-a-sketch" design that the parent has been given (but cannot show), doing a Rorschach Arrangement Task (adapted from Ditton, Green, & Singer, 1987) a consensus Thematic Apperception Test (TAT), or a consensus Rorschach (as used in Wynne, Jones, Al-Khayyal, 1982).

Then, the child is brought into the room and the clinician assesses:

1. How well parents orient their child to the task
2. How well they maintain the task set throughout the interaction
3. How clearly they convey information via language during the instruction period, including their ability to assume the child's frame of reference
4. How they structure, set limits, reinforce, and correct the child
5. How well they acknowledge the child's communications and clarify misunderstandings
6. How they summarize and end the learning interaction
7. How the child derails the instructional process (e.g., by not paying attention visually or auditorially, by starting the task without understanding the instructions, by not asking for clarification when the parents' communication is confusing, by disrupting the task with extraneous remarks or behaviors, by seeking excessive help from the parents without sufficient independent effort first, and so on)

The goal is to assess *in vivo* the family's communication patterns, structure, attributions, and achievement motivations in a teaching/learning interaction. Then, based on this assessment of how a family's teaching/learning style could be improved, parents of these younger children can be asked to start tutoring their child in specific subjects at home because of their child's special learning needs. This framing seeks to remove all blame from parents, who could not have acquired these "remedial teacher" skills previously (Steinert, Campbell, & Kiely, 1981).

We help the parents become better tutors through modeling/demonstrating the tutor role with their child in front of the one-way mirror, role-play practice, review and feedback (using audiotapes or verbal report) of the parents' tutoring at home, and immediate intervention during *tutoring enactments* between parent and child in conjoint sessions.

These parent-training techniques are didactic-experiential and are somewhat similar in form to filial therapy techniques with young children (Guerney, 1964; Stollak, 1981). Like Minuchin, Rosman, and Baker's (1978) "family lunch sessions," the tutoring enactments bring the problem into the therapy room so that new solutions can be tried. Of course, not all parents are suited to function as home tutors, either because they lack personal organization or basic academic skills (e.g., English literacy), or because they are already too enmeshed with the child. In some cases, a peripheral parent can do the tutoring to rebalance the system.

In clinical work and research, it is helpful to think of the *family as the primary classroom* experience in a child's education. This metaphor underscores aspects of family interaction that may be contributing to a child's achievement difficulties in school. In using the metaphor, parents are viewed as the child's primary *teachers*, such that:

1. Parents' communication styles and family interaction patterns are the family's *teaching methods*.
2. Family hierarchy, structuring, and limit setting are the parents' *classroom management techniques*.
3. Family activities and recurrent topics of conversation are subjects in the family's *curriculum*.
4. Siblings are *classmates*.
5. Positive attributions, social reinforcements, and achievement modeling are the ways parents *motivate students to learn*.
6. Objects enriching the home are the family's *educational materials* (toys, books, chemistry sets, pets, magazines, computers, television, etc.).

This analogy helps clarify how the child's cognitive style and behavior at school may be coherent with family patterns, and it highlights six core areas for change.

References

Alexander, B. K., & Dibb, G. S. (1977). Interpersonal perception in addict families. *Family Process, 16,* 17–28.

Amerikaner, M. J., & Omizo, M. M. (1984). Family interaction and learning disabilities. *Journal of Learning Disabilities, 17,* 540–543.

Anderson, C. A. (1983). Motivational and performance deficits in interpersonal settings: The effect of attributional style. *Journal of Personality & Social Psychology, 45,* 1136–1141.

Aponte, H. (1976). The family-school interview: An eco-structural approach. *Family Process, 15,* 303–311.

Bank, S. P., & Kahn, M. D. (1982). *The sibling bond.* New York: Basic Books.

Blakar, R. M. (1981). Schizophrenia and family communication: A brief note on follow-up studies and replications. *Family Process, 20,* 109–112.

Bower, E. M. (1960). School characteristics of male adolescents who later became schizophrenic. *American Journal of Orthopsychiatry, 30,* 712–729.

Bryan, T. (1988). Discussion: Social skills and learning disabilities. In J. F. Kavanagh & T. J. Truss (Eds.), *Learning disabilities: Proceedings of the national conference.* Parkton, MD: York Press.

Campis, L. K., Lyman, R. D., & Prentice-Dunn, S. (1986). The parental locus of control scales: Development and validation. *Journal of clinical child psychology, 15,* 260–267.

Carter, L., Robertson, S. R., Ladd, J., & Alpert, M. (1987). The family Rorschach with families of schizophrenics. *Family Process, 26,* 461–474.

Colapinto, J. (1988). Avoiding a common pitfall in compulsory school referrals. *Journal of Marital & Family Therapy, 14,* 89–96.

Coles, G. (1988). *The learning mystique: A critical look at "learning disabilities."* New York: Pantheon Books.

Das, J. P., Mulcahy, R. F., & Wall, A. E. (Eds.) (1982). *Theory and research in learning disabilities.* New York: Plenum.

Day, J., & Moore, M. (1976). Individual and family psychodynamic contributions to learning disability. *Psychiatric Hospitals Journal, 8,* 27–30.

Ditton, P., Green, R. J., & Singer, M. T. (1987). Communication deviances: A comparison between parents of learning disabled and normally achieving students. *Family Process, 26,* 75–87.

Doane, J. A. (1978). Family interaction and communication deviance in disturbed and normal families: A review of research. *Family Process, 17,* 357–376.

Doane, J. A. (1985). Parental communication deviance and offspring psychopathology. In L. L'Abate (Ed.), *Handbook of family psychology and therapy (Vol. II).* Homewood, IL: Dorsey Press.

Dweck, C. S., & Licht, B. (1980). Learned helplessness and intellectual achievement. In J.

Garber & M. E. P. Seligman (Eds.), *Human helplessness*. New York: Academic Press.

Engel, G. (1980). The clinical application of the biopsychosocial model. *American Journal of Psychiatry, 137,* 535–544.

Feldman, D. H. (1986). *Nature's gambit: Child prodigies and the development of human potential.* New York: Basic Books.

Fish, M. C., & Jain, S. (1985). A systems approach in working with learning disabled children: Implications for the school. *Journal of Learning Disabilities, 18,* 592–595.

Fisher, L., & Jones, J. E. (1980). Child competence and psychiatric risk: II. Areas of relationship between child and family functioning. *Journal of Nervous & Mental Disease, 168,* 332–337.

Freund, J. D., & Cardwell, G. F. (1977). A multi-faceted response to an adolescent's school failure. *Journal of Marital & Family Therapy, 3*(2), 49–57.

Frey, J., III, & Wendorf, D. J. (1985). Families of gifted children. In L. L'Abate (Ed.), *Handbook of family psychology and therapy.* Homewood, IL: Dorsey Press.

Friedman, R. (1973). *Family roots of school learning and behavior disorders.* Springfield, IL: Charles Thomas.

Gardner, H. (1983). *Frames of mind: The theory of multiple intelligences.* New York: Basic Books.

Goertzel, V., & Goertzel, M. G. (1962). *Cradles of eminence.* Boston: Little, Brown & Co.

Goldstein, M. J., & Strachan, A. M. (1987). The family and schizophrenia. In T. Jacob (Ed.), *Family interaction and psychopathology.* New York: Plenum.

Green, R. J. (1988). The "biological reframe": A response to Johnson's views on psychoeducation. *Journal of Marital & Family Therapy, 14.*

Green, R. J. (1990). Family communication and children's learning diabilities: evidence for Coles's theory of interactivity. *Journal of Learning Disabilities, 23,* 145–148.

Grunebaum, M. G., Hurwitz, I., Prentice, N. M., & Sperry, B. M. (1962). Fathers of sons with primary neurotic learning inhibitions. *American Journal of Orthopsychiatry, 32,* 462–472.

Guerney, B. (1964). Filial therapy: Description and rationale. *Journal of Consulting Psychology, 28,* 304–310.

Gurman, A. S. (1970). The role of the family in underachievement. *Journal of School Psychology, 8,* 48–53.

Hagin, R. A., Beecher, R., & Silver, A. A. (1982). Definition of learning disabilities: A clinical approach. In J. P. Das, R. F. Mulcahy, & A. E. Wall (Eds.), *Theory and research in learning disabilities.* New York: Plenum.

Hassan, S. A. (1974). Transactional and contextual invalidation between the parents of disturbed families: A comparative study. *Family Process, 13,* 53–76.

Henderson, A. (1987). *The evidence continues to grow: Parent involvement improves student achievement (an annotated bibliography).* Columbia, MD: National Committee for Citizens in Education.

Holder, V. (1977). The adult literacy campaign. *Family Process, 16,* 514–516.

Humphries, T. W., & Bauman, E. (1980). Maternal child rearing attitudes associated with learning disabilities. *Journal of Learning Disabilities, 13,* 54–57.

Johnson, H. (1988). Biologically based deficit in the identified patient: Indications for psychoeducational strategies. *Journal of Marital & Family Therapy, 13,* 337–348.

Jones, J. E., Wynne, L. C., Al-Khayyal, M., Doane, J. A., Ritzler, B., Singer, M. T., & Fisher, L. (1984). Predicting current school competence of high-risk children with a composite cross-situational measure of parental communication. In N. F. Watt, E. J. Anthony, L. C. Wynne, & J. E. Roff (Eds.), *Children at risk for schizophrenia: A longitudinal perspective.* New York: Cambridge University Press.

Kaslow, F. W., & Cooper, B. (1978). Family therapy with the learning disabled child and his/her family. *Journal of Marital & Family Therapy, 4,* 41–49.

Keogh, B. K. (1982). Research in learning disabilities: A view of status and need. In J. P. Das, R. F. Mulcahy, & A. E. Wall (Eds.), *Theory and research in learning disabilities.* New York: Plenum.

Kistner, J., White, K., Haskett, M., & Robbins, F. (1985). Development of learning-disabled and normally achieving children's causal attributions. *Journal of Abnormal Child Psychology, 13,* 639–647.

Klein, R. S., Altman, S. D., Dreizen, K., Friedman, R., & Powers, L. (1981a). Restructuring dysfunctional parental attitudes toward children's learning and behavior in school: Family oriented psychoeducational therapy (Part I). *Journal of Learning Disabilities, 14,* 15–19.

Klein, R. S., Altman, S. D., Dreizen, K.,

Friedman, R., & Powers, L. (1981b). Restructuring dysfunctional parental attitudes toward children's learning and behavior in school: Family-oriented psychoeducational therapy (Part II). *Journal of Learning Disabilities, 14,* 99–100.

Kohn, M., & Rosman, B. L. (1974). Social-emotional, cognitive and demographic determinants of poor school achievement: Implications for a strategy of interventions. *Journal of Educational Psychology, 66,* 267–276.

Kolligian, J., & Sternberg, R. J. (1986). Intelligence, information processing and specific learning disabilities: A triarchic synthesis. *Journal of Learning Disabilities, 20,* 8–11.

Laing, R. D., Phillipson, H., & Lee, A. R. (1966). *Interpersonal perception.* New York: Springer.

Lusterman, D. D. (1985). An ecosystemic approach to family-school problems. *American Journal of Family Therapy, 13,* 22–30.

Margalit, M. (1982). Learning disabled children and their families: Strategies of extension and adaptation of family therapy. *Journal of Learning Disabilities, 15,* 594–595.

McGoldrick, M., & Rohrbaugh, M. (1987). Researching ethnic family stereotypes. *Family Process, 26,* 89–99.

Miller, D. R., & Westman, J. C. (1964). Reading disability as a condition of family stability. *Family Process, 3,* 66–76.

Minuchin, S. (1974). *Families and family therapy.* Cambridge, MA: Harvard University Press.

Minuchin, S., Chamberlin, P., & Graubard, P. (1967). A project to teach learning skills to disturbed, delinquent children. *American Journal of Orthopsychiatry, 37,* 558–567.

Minuchin, S., Montalvo, B., Guerney, B., Rosman, B., & Schumer, F. (1967). *Families of the slums.* New York: Basic Books.

Minuchin, S., Rosman, B. L., & Baker, L. (1978). *Psychosomatic families.* Cambridge, MA: Harvard University Press.

Mossige, S., Petterson, R. B., & Blakar, R. M. (1979). Egocentrism and inefficiency in the communication of families containing schizophrenic members. *Family Process, 18,* 405–425.

O'Connor, S. C., & Spreen, O. (1988). The relationship between parents' socioeconomic status and education level, and adult occupational and educational achievement of children with learning disabilities. *Journal of Learning Disabilities, 21,* 148–153.

Office of Education (1976). Assistance to states for education of handicapped children, notice of proposed rulemaking. *Federal Register, 41,* (No. 230), 52404-52407. Washington, DC: U.S. Government Printing Office.

Okun, B. F. (1984). *Family therapy with school related problems.* Rockville, MD: Aspen.

Owen, F. W., Adams, P. A., Forrest, T., Stolz, L. M., & Fisher, S. (1971). Learning disorders in children: Sibling studies. *Monographs of the Society for Research in Child Development, 36,* (4, Serial No. 144).

Pickar, D. B., & Tori, C. D. (1986). The learning disabled adolescent: Ericksonian psychosocial development, self-concept and delinquent behavior. *Journal of Youth & Adolescence, 15,* 429–440.

Pollner, M., & McDonald-Wikler, L. (1985). The social construction of unreality: A case study of a family's attribution of competence to a severely retarded child. *Family Process, 24,* 241–254.

Reiss, D. (1981). *The family's construction of reality.* Cambridge, MA: Harvard University Press.

Rosenthal, R., & Jacobson, L. (1968). *Pygmalion in the classroom: Teacher expectations and pupil's intellectual development.* New York: Holt, Rinehart & Winston.

Rund, B. R. (1986). Communication deviances in parents of schizophrenics. *Family Process, 25,* 133–147.

Sameroff, A. J. (1975). Early influences on development: Fact or fancy? *Merrill-Palmer Quarterly, 21,* 217–293.

Sameroff, A. J. (1979). The etiology of cognitive competence: A systems perspective. In R. G. Kearsley & I. E. Sigel (Eds.), *Infants at risk: Assessment of cognitive functioning.* Hillsdale, NJ: Lawrence Erlbaum.

Sass, L. A., Gunderson, J. G., Singer, M. T., & Wynne, L. C. (1984). Parental communication deviance and forms of thinking in male schizophrenic offspring. *Journal of Nervous & Mental Disease, 172,* 513–520.

Schachter, F. F. (1985). Sibling de-identification in the clinic: Devil versus angel. *Family Process, 24,* 415–427.

Seligman, M. E. P., Peterson, C., Kaslow, N. J., Tanenbaum, R. L., Alloy, L. B., & Abramson, L. Y. (1984). Attributional style and depressive symptoms among children. *Journal of Abnormal Psychology, 93,* 235–238.

Shapiro, L. N., & Wild, C. M. (1976). The product of the consensus Rorschach in families of male schizophrenics. *Family Process, 15,* 211–224.

Shapiro, R. J., Fisher, L., & Gayton, W. F. (1974). Perception of cognitive ability in families of adolescents. *Family Process, 13,* 239–252.

Shapiro, R. L. (1969). The origin of adolescent disturbances in the family: Some considerations in theory and implications for therapy. In G. H. Zuk & I. Boszormenyi-Nagy (Eds.), *Family therapy and disturbed families.* Palo Alto, CA: Science & Behavior Books.

Silverman, J. S., Fite, M. W., & Mosher, M. M. (1959). Clinical findings in reading disability children—Special cases of intellectual inhibition. *American Journal of Orthopsychiatry, 29,* 298–314.

Singer, M. T., & Wynne, L. C. (1966). Principles for scoring communication defects and deviances in parents of schizophrenics: Rorschach and TAT scoring manuals. *Psychiatry, 29,* 260–288.

Singer, M. T., Wynne, L. C., & Toohey, M. L. (1978). Communication disorders and the families of schizophrenics. In L. C. Wynne, R. L. Cromwell, & S. Matthysse (Eds.), *The nature of schizophrenia.* New York: Wiley.

Solvberg, H. A., & Blakar, R. M. (1975). Communication efficiency in couples with and without a schizophrenic offspring. *Family Process, 14,* 515–534.

Spacone, C., & Hansen, J. C. (1984). Therapy with a family with a learning-disabled child. In B. Okun (Ed.), *Family therapy with school related problems.* Rockville, MD: Aspen.

Sperry, B., Staver, N., Reiner, B. S., & Ulrich, D. (1958). Renunciation and denial in learning difficulties. *American Journal of Orthopsychiatry, 28,* 98–111.

Staver, N. (1953). The child's learning difficulty as related to the emotional problem of the mother. *American Journal of Orthopsychiatry, 23,* 131–140.

Steinert, Y. E., Campbell, S. B., & Kiely, M. (1981). A comparison of maternal and remedial teacher teaching styles with good and poor readers. *Journal of Learning Disabilities, 14,* 38–42.

Stierlin, H. (1974). *Separating parents and adolescents.* New York: Quadrangle.

Stierlin, H., Levi, L. D., & Savard, R. J. (1971). Parental perceptions of separating children. *Family Process, 10,* 411–427.

Stollak, G. E. (1981). Variations and extensions of filial therapy. *Family Process, 20,* 305–309.

Thomas, A., Chess, S., & Birch, H. (1968). *Temperament and behavior disorders in children.* New York: New York University Press.

Tienari, P., Lahti, I., Sorri, A., Naarala, M., Moring, J., Wahlberg, K. E., & Wynne, L. C. (1987). The Finnish adoptive family study of schizophrenia. *Journal of Psychiatric Research, 21,* 437–445.

Vogel, E. G., & Bell, N. W. (1968). The emotionally disturbed child as the family scapegoat. In N. W. Bell & E. F. Vogel (Eds.), *A modern introduction to the family* (rev. ed.). New York: The Free Press.

Watzlawick, P. (1984). Self-fulfilling prophecies. In P. Watzlawick (Ed.), *The invented reality.* New York: Norton.

Waxler, N. (1974). Child and parent effects on cognitive performance: An experimental approach to the etiologic and responsive theories of schizophrenia. *Family Process, 13,* 1–22.

Wendorf, D. J., & Frey, J., III (1985). Family therapy with the intellectually gifted. *American Journal of Family Therapy, 13,* 31–38.

Wynne, L. C. (1971). Family research on the pathogenesis of schizophrenia: Intermediate variables in the study of families at high risk. In P. Doucet & C. Laurin (Eds.), *Problems of psychosis.* Amsterdam: Excerpta Medica.

Wynne, L. C. (1976). On the anguish, and creative passions, of not escaping double binds: A reformulation. In C. E. Sluzki & D. C. Ransom (Eds.), *The double bind: The foundation of the communicational approach to the family.* New York: Grune & Stratton.

Wynne, L. C., & Cole, R. E. (1983). The Rochester risk research program: A new look at parental diagnoses and family relationships. In H. Stierlin, L. C. Wynne, & M. Wirsching (Eds.). *Psychosocial intervention in schizophrenia.* New York: Springer-Verlag.

Wynne, L. C., & Green, R. J. (1985). A truant family. In S. Coleman (Ed.), *Failures in family therapy.* New York: Guilford.

Wynne, L. C., Jones, J. E., & Al-Khayyal, M. (1982). Healthy family communication patterns: Observations in families "at risk" for psychopathology. In F. Walsh (Ed.), *Normal family processes.* New York: Guilford.

Wynne, L. C., Singer, M. T., Bartko, J. J., & Toohey, M. L. (1977). Schizophrenics and their families: Recent research on parental communication. In J. Tanner (Ed.), *Developments in psychiatric research.* London: Hodder & Stroughton.

Ziegler, R., & Holden, L. (1988). Family therapy for learning disabled and attention-deficit disordered children. *American Journal of Orthopsychiatry, 58*, 196–210.

Endnotes

1. It should be noted that the children in the studies by Fisher and Jones (1980), Hassan (1974), Jones and colleagues (1984), and Wynne, Jones, and Al-Khayyal (1982) were not assessed for LD. Hence, their findings that CD was associated with poorer achievement in general might be masking a more specific association between CD and LD. Additional research, comparing LD and non-LD/underachievers, is needed to see whether parental CD predicts only to LD or to all forms of underachievement.

2. It is possible that parental CD may also be genetically based and should be viewed as a form of LD or subclinical LD. If such were the case, the association between parental CD and child LD found by Ditton, Green, and Singer (1987) would simply mean that the same underlying genetic variable was being measured in different ways over two generations in families. However, even if it were proven that parental CD and child LD shared a common genotype, parental CD may still be a necessary social stressor for the child's genetic vulnerability to reach problematic proportions. In such a case, the parents' genetic makeup would be exerting both an hereditary and an interactional influence on the development of LD in the next generation (Green, 1990). Clearly, longitudinal-adoptive studies—similar in design to those now being conducted on schizophrenia in Finland (Tienari et al., 1987)—will be necessary to determine the separate and combined contributions of genetic and familial factors in LD etiology.

11

Families of Gifted Children and Youth

REVA JENKINS-FRIEDMAN
University of Kansas

Down through the ages almost every culture has had a special fascination about its most able citizens. Although the areas of performance in which one might be recognized as a "gifted" person are determined by the needs and values of the prevailing culture, scholars and lay persons alike have debated (and continue to debate) the age-old issue of "what makes giftedness." What factors cause some individuals to perform so well in their respective fields of endeavor that they gain recognition by their peers, the teachers, or the culture at large? (Renzulli, 1979, p. 3)

Working effectively with families of gifted students rests on understanding the phenomenon of exceptional ability within social and familial contexts. Although gifted individuals have been noted throughout recorded history, systematic support and nurturance, particularly within public school settings, is relatively recent.

This chapter will highlight recent aspects of the field's history to provide a framework for understanding families of children and youth with exceptional ability. Using research findings, a "gifted" family will be constructed from a systems perspective. Issues unique to the families of gifted youngsters will form the basis for identifying dysfunctional elements and working with these families in school settings.

UNDERSTANDING GIFTEDNESS: A BRIEF HISTORY

Over the past 4,000 years, we have seen tremendous changes in the ways in which giftedness has been conceptualized, identified, and supported: from divinity to ordinary behavior, from debilitating to nonneurotic, from inexplicable to highly understandable and measurable. Every new development in understanding intelligence has had a salutary effect on the field of gifted child research (Grinder, 1985). For a more complete discussion of the history of the field, the reader is referred to *The Gifted and Talented: Developmental Perspectives* (Horowitz & O'Brien, 1985).

For example, beginning in the early part of the twentieth century, noted psychologist Lewis M. Terman developed much of the current knowledge base in the field of gifted child education through his landmark research on children with extraordinary intellectual aptitude (New-land, 1976). Terman's longitudinal study of nearly 1,500 youngsters (IQ 140+) dis-pelled many of the "genuis = neurosis" beliefs popular at the time (Terman, 1954). His *Genetic Studies of Genuis* fostered more positive attitudes toward and nurtur-ing of bright children. Programs such as Leta Hollingworth's Terman Classes at the Speyer School (White & Renzulli, 1987) and districtwide offerings began to appear in Cincinnati and Los Angeles (1916), Urbana (1919), and Manhattan and Cleve-land (1922) (Newland, 1976).

The impact of Terman's work is mixed. First, it led to a dramatic increase in systemic offerings for bright children. However, he contributed substantially to defining giftedness solely in terms of in-telligence test scores. This is an especially controversial issue (Sternberg, 1986). Fur-thermore, intelligence tests have been criti-cized for being insensitive to factors that seems to influence adult achievement, such as patterns of highly specific abilities, creative and productive thinking (e.g., originality, inventiveness), and nonintel-lective factors (e.g., perseverance, concen-tration, self-efficacy) (Jenkins, 1978; Ren-zulli, 1979).

In this country as well as abroad, the last 15 years have been marked by an in-creasing abundance of public policies designed to protect the rights of gifted children and to legitimize gifted child education (Kitano & Kirby, 1986). At present, nearly every state in the union has a public plan and guidelines for defining, identifying, and educating its most able youngsters. Gifted child education is man-dated in over 25 states, paralleling other federal legislation for handicapped chil-dren (Houseman, 1987).

Criticisms notwithstanding (cf. Ren-zulli, 1979), the definition is the bulwark of public policies in this country. Its adoption has led to mushrooming numbers of school enrichment programs and teacher education programs on the graduate level, some special education funds, and in-creased public awareness.

Impacts of public policies are already visible in school programs and on families. The numbers of organizations sponsoring conferences for parents of bright children, special publications, and research-based articles have grown dramatically over the past decade. The increase in the numbers of due process hearings for gifted students are an outgrowth of mandated policies, with accompanying pressure on school personnel regarding accountability in methods and tests used in identifying stu-dents.

Concomitant with the increase in states' policies and district programs has been increased demands on the limited time of professional staffs to evaluate (and reevaluate) the intellectual ability of poten-tially gifted youngsters and to consult col-laboratively with teachers in developing appropriate educational opportunities for their gifted students.

Even more critical to the cognitive and emotional development of bright stu-dents is the school psychologist's ability to help families deal constructively with the challenges associated with raising a bright child, and the degree to which giftedness is embedded in social/familial contexts. It is this last issue to which we turn our atten-tion in the sections to follow.

DESCRIBING "GIFTED" FAMILIES FROM A SYSTEMS PERSPECTIVE

It is universally acknowledged that families play a key role in the positive educational and social growth of gifted children. Qual-ities that have been named as important for gifted children to actualize their poten-tials include healthy parent-child interactions (Morrow & Wilson, 1964), shaping values and attitudes (Goertzel & Goertzel, 1962; Parker & Colangelo, 1979), freedom to choose friends, and freedom to make decisions relating to educational opportunities (Bloom, 1985).

In two reviews of research on parents and families of bright youngsters, the writers are critical of this substantial body of literature (Dettmann & Colangelo, 1983; Frey & Wendorf, 1985). They point out that generalizations about families of gifted students have come largely from two sources: univariate studies and anecdotal reports.

Hackney (1982) asserts that the lack of family systems-based research on gifted children limits understanding giftedness, determining the degree to which the impact of the family is random or orchestrated, and alleviating related problems. In the sections that follow, I will draw on the small but growing body of systems-oriented research on families of gifted children, as well as integrating the findings of relevant univariate studies from a systems perspective.

Qualities of a Healthy "Gifted" Family System

In study after study, the profile of these families is the epitome of a self-actualizing family system (Frey & Wendorf, 1985). The various family subsystems, rules, and complementarity of roles create an open, flexible environment that acknowledges the unique qualities of all family members and nurtures their cognitive and emotional growth.

Family Subsystem

Mutually supportive relationships, appropriate degrees of closeness, flexibility, and open expression of thought and feelings characterize the family with at least one child participating in a gifted education program (Cornell, 1983a, 1983b; Frey & Wendorf, 1985). This pattern is strongly associated with higher overall child adjustment, self-esteem, and academic self-concept, as well as fewer discipline, self-control, and anxiety issues (using data from child self-reports and teacher observations). When compared to families with no identified children, "gifted" families more highly value recreational, intellectual, and cultural pursuits, although not in the context of an achievement or competitive framework (Cornell & Grossberg, 1987).

The well-functioning families of gifted children are successful families, reporting a high degree of achievement in both the previous and present generations. These families expect their children to be bright and are not surprised when a family member qualifies for placement in a gifted education program (Frey & Wendorf, 1985).

Parental Subsystem

"Participatory exploration" typifies the way in which these parents structure family interactions, whether resolving conflict (Frey & Wendorf, 1985) or managing planning tasks (Cornell, 1983b). The contributions of each family member are solicited, valued, and incorporated by other family members into discussions. Parents are democratic yet clear leaders in family discussions. They are flexible, adapting their approaches according to their children's ages. In one study, the researchers commented that even experimental tasks employed to assess family functioning were used as teaching opportunities, linked by the parents to current family issues.

Couples handle differences easily and do not appear to feel threatened by conflicting opinions. However, this finding needs to be somewhat qualified, since marital adjustment was used in several studies to select families for further study (cf. Karnes & Shwedel, 1987).

Cornell (1983a, 1983b) found that one topic of difference between parents was likely to be perceptions of their children as gifted. Mothers tended to be more liberal in their definitions of giftedness (as special learning abilities) than fathers (as prodigy or genuis) and thus were more likely to perceive their children as gifted. In contrast, fathers tended to verbalize negative attitudes about their children's abilities and to reject the gifted label.

Looking more closely at the father-child relationship, Karnes and Shwedel (1987) discovered that fathers whose preschool children were identified as gifted reported significantly more involvement with the children in activities such as reading and hobbies and placed a high value on oral language. Finally, they displayed significantly more unconditional positive regard for their children. Fathers of nongifted youngsters spent an average of two-thirds less time in reading activities with their children, valued psychomotor activities over language development, and emphasized dependence on the father as the authority figure rather than encouraging independence.

These findings become important when comparing parental perceptions of their children as gifted or possessing special abilities to the children's personality adjustment. Positive labeling on the part of parents has been found to be associated with taking pride in a child's accomplishments, healthier child personality adjustment, and more intimacy in parent-child relationships, whether or not the child is formally identified (Cornell, 1983a).

The importance of parental perceptions on the actualization of potential is further supported in an investigation of the research linking ability and birth order. In his analysis of archival and biographical data of eminent persons (e.g., presidents, prime ministers, and Nobel laureates), Albert (1980) concludes that parental interests and values combine with family position to accentuate the child's abilities: "He becomes the child who gets an intense socialization in those family interests and traditions" (p. 88).

Further support for the key role played by the parental system are the recent case histories of 120 young eminent persons (Bloom, 1985) and case studies of six prodigies (Feldman & Goldsmith, 1986). According to these researchers, the talent area is almost like a language spoken in the home. Parents routinely provide materials (e.g., musical instruments, typewriters) and lessons in the talent area they value (and often are proficient in, themselves). They are adept "talent scouts," and can recognize a "gifted" response from their child. Often they alert the school that their child is exceptional.

Sibling Subsystem

Among nonproblem "gifted" families, sibling interactions are congruent with the parental subsystem interactions. There is little or no competition for parental approval, and no jealousy or resentment of the gifted label among siblings. Any teasing or antagonism appears to be under the parents' control. When the siblings under study are adolescents, there is a high degree of comaraderie, even with only one identified sibling (Frey & Wendorf, 1985).

However, this picture changes somewhat when we look more closely at the relationship between identified and nonidentified siblings. Cornell & Grossberg (1986) discovered that, among nonproblem families, when the parents report not thinking of the (nonidentified) sibling as gifted, there are repercussions for that child. This group of nonidentified siblings appears to be less well adjusted, and more anxious and neurotic than their siblings. They evidence a lower self-esteem and more defensiveness in their presentation of self, and show less drive to pursue and develop their abilities than their identified siblings. The researchers hypothesize that these nonidentified children might be recipients of negative messages about self-worth from the family system.

In its early stages, labeling appears to be most beneficial to the self-image of the gifted sibling, encouraging cooperation and communication, perhaps as a result of self-enhancing comparisons. In a study of 27 pairs of labeled and unlabeled siblings, Grenier (1985) discovered increased competition and diminished cooperation on the part of unlabeled siblings; in short, labeling damaged the sibling relationship. She noted, however, that these results were mitigated by perceptions of positive treatment by the parents and by the increase in the age difference between the siblings.

Over time, the negative effects of labeling seem to reverse, at least from the perspective of the unlabeled sibling. Five years after identification of their sibling, unlabeled youngsters report greater happiness regarding the gifted child's participation in special education programs and more openness in family communication about the gifted label and program participation. In fact, they perceive fathers as being happier about the label than the fathers report (Colangelo & Brower, 1987). In contrast, the identified sibling is more uneasy regarding family valuing and perceptions. The authors speculate that the gifted child might be the victim of self-generated unrealistic views of the effects of the label on the family. However, they fail to take into consideration that the gifted sample was late adolescents (mean age = 19); thus some of the perceptions could be attributed to developmental issues.

Rules and Complementarity

Labeling seems to impact the quality of family interactions. Well-functioning families of gifted children interact cooper-

atively with a minimum of conflict and maximum freedom for personal expression (Cornell & Grossberg, 1987).

The family environment of gifted children differs significantly from their nonidentified peers in the degree of overt control orientation. There appears to be a relative lack of value placed on set rules and procedures in the family and more emphasis on teaching in all phases of family life. This is reflected, for example, in observations of parental behavior supporting questioning as legitimate rather than as rebellious (Frey & Wendorf, 1985). Karnes and Shwedel (1987) also noted that fathers of young gifted children highly value their children asking unusual questions.

Behaving in adult ways at a young age—making decisions, managing time, acting independently—distinguishes transactions among families of bright children. Case studies and histories offer many instances of bright young people making key decisions about education in their talent area: setting performance standards, deciding to move away from home at young ages to pursue advanced training, evaluating the quality of their instruction—even choosing their teachers (Bloom, 1985; Feldman & Goldsmith, 1986). This can lead to an imbalance of power in the family, particularly when there is only one labeled gifted child. Cornell (1983b) found a tendency in these families for the parents to focus on the gifted child, relinquish control of family interactions, and instead to process to the child's direction, ideas, and decisions.

Summary

"Idealization" is the theme that distinguishes healthy families of bright children. At its most positive, giftedness is an organizing force, shaping the family's corporate personality and structuring family relations to actualize the potential of every family member. Issues can emerge for these families when only one sibling is identified as intellectually gifted, especially if the parents do not actively value the unlabeled sibling.

Personal Experiences

My work with families of gifted children echoes the pattern emerging in the research literature. Well-functioning families are extremely nurturing of their bright children, encouraging each member to develop unique abilities. Labeling is confirmatory rather than reorganizing. Often the parents are bright and/or creative in their own right. They expect their children to be interested, active, and involved in life. Like parents of handicapped children, they are eager to learn about their child's "special condition." They apply the information they learn to their lives as well as to the lives of their children. These parents become informed consumers of educational services and focus on complementing the school program rather than supplanting it.

Issues Affecting "Gifted" Family Systems

Peterson (1977) identifies negative ways in which the presence of a gifted child can affect the family. She speculates that making the gifted child the focal point of the family leads to inappropriate comparisons among siblings and fosters competition. Siblings' jealousy could thus be fueled by highlighting the "special" activities that are part of the gifted child's enrichment program. In such a family environment, she asserts that nonidentified children are less likely to view themselves as successful.

Ross (1979) speculates that the degree to which the gifted child has an adverse impact on the family is directly related to the perceived discrepancy between the gifted child's intellectual capacity and that of other family members. However, from his analysis of eminent politicians and scientists, Albert (1980)

concludes that giftedness is a family organizer. Combined with values and goals, it can "pull together diverse personal and interpersonal factors to make a more coherent organization of a child's and family's transactions" (p. 93).

The foregoing conflicting speculations and hypotheses make more sense when examined from a systemic framework. Based on his clinical work with families of gifted children, Hackney (1981) identifies five areas in which issues might arise: family roles, parents' self-view, family adaptations, neighborhood/community issues, and family/school interactions.

Family Roles

Establishing and maintaining clear boundaries between child and adult roles is a key feature of healthy "gifted" families. However, because bright children often act and sound like adults, parents can find themselves blurring role distinctions. In addition, in the Bloom (1985) and Feldman and Goldsmith (1986) studies, extraordinarily bright children were often called upon to act as adults regarding decisions affecting their talent development. Some "spillover" to family interactions is natural, but can be detrimental to the family and parental subsystems.

Parents' Self-View

Particularly in the early years following labeling, parents report an overpowering sense of responsibility to "do right by" their gifted child. This might include fears regarding their adequacy to raise a gifted child or feelings of guilt that they are neglecting their gifted child's growth. To the degree that parents feel inadequate, family interactions can be adversely affected. Conflict resolution is hampered, and one parent often becomes more peripheral with respect to discipline and/or school achievement (Frey & Wendorf, 1985). Parents sometimes compensate for their feelings by placing excessive performance pressure on themselves and their children, which can negatively affect performance in school and stimulate psychological problems.

Family Adaptations

Lifestyle changes often accompany talent development. Bloom (1985) points out that many families of world-class tennis players, Olympic swimmers, and pianists either moved or divided the household to facilitate the gifted youngster's receiving an appropriate education. Feldman & Goldsmith (1986) describe the incredible efforts of families who undertook to manage their prodigy's education outside of the domain of public education, juggling as many as ten different teachers per week.

It is easy for changes such as these to unbalance family relationships, particularly among siblings. For example, consider Feldman and Goldsmith's (1986) observations of one of their musical prodigies rehearsing a recently composed piece with an orchestra: During a break, the child's younger brother began playing the piano—at least as well as his identified sibling. When the mother was asked what she planned to do with a second extremely talented child, she replied that she had no more energy left to nurture the talent development of her younger son.

Neighborhood/Community Issues

Finding settings where the family and its talented members can interact with intellectual peers can be challenging. Hackney (1981) observes that perceived lack of "neighborhoods" (i.e., referent groups) can encourage families to begin a cycle of withdrawal, insularity, and elitism.

Family/School Interactions

Labeling magnifies the responsibilities of both the home and school. Their roles can seem more critical. To the extent that the family system is fully functional, partnerships can be complementary. However, parents can easily lose objectivity about their child, becoming inappropriate advocates, obsessing about their child, and criticizing the school program rather than complementing its goals.

Summary

Issues that affect the family systems of bright children can be categorized into internal and external concerns. Internal concerns encompass the ways in which the family integrates changes associated with labeling the family member. The external category covers the ways in which the family system connects to its environments of community and school.

Personal Experience

A "gifted" family who I see on a regular basis illustrates how the issues described above can distort the family system.

CASE STUDY 1

The Jones family has two sons, ages 6 and 10. The older child is gifted intellectually and kinesthetically. To support their child's emerging talents, the parents have oriented their work schedules around their child's needs, driving two or three times a week to a nearby city for gymnastic practices, attending meets, and arranging for additional private lessons. The mother continually questions whether the school is appropriately challenging her son because he manages to do his homework in school. She telephones the school's gifted education teacher weekly to discuss her son's progress. The parents discourage their son from playing with the children in his neighborhood because they're "not his equals." The child typically retreats to the computer room in their home on the rare occasions when he has free time. Although their younger child shows signs of talent similar to his older brother, the parents have decided that they haven't the time or energy to nurture his abilities too.

WORKING WITH FAMILIES OF GIFTED YOUNGSTERS: A SYSTEMS PERSPECTIVE

There is abundant literature on methods of education for parents of gifted children; however, the bulk of these methods is school centered. They assume that the school is responsible for the intellectual and affective development of the gifted child. In this framework, parents are passive recipients of information, not teachers or facilitators of their child's growth. School counselors and psychologists are responsible for educating parents relative to the available services and reassuring them that their child's needs can best be met through expertly trained school personnel (Dettmann & Colangelo, 1980).

A far more useful framework for working with parents is a partnership approach (Dettmann & Colangelo, 1980; Fine, 1977; Fine & Pitts, 1980). This paradigm recognizes that all parties have knowledge and expertise that can be beneficial to the child's growth at home and school. School psychologists provide information, help parents understand the issues affecting their child, and encourage parents to make joint decisions regarding their child's educational needs.

A collaborative relationship becomes crucial when dealing with gifted children having problems in school. A systemic orientation aids in the contextual understanding of a child's behavior and assists in "normalizing" the child's position within the school and family systems (Fine & Holt, 1983). Its emphasis helps the child to make a more appropriate school adjustment. Its use of techniques such as triangulation to assess problems and develop interventions has the potential to be particularly effective with sensitive and articulate youngsters who might manipulate family and school systems.

Two categories of problems affecting bright children are receiving increased attention in the literature: underachievement and disabling perfectionism. In this section, I will sketch the family systems surrounding each problem area and suggest methods for working with families in school-based settings.

Problems in School: Underachievement

Definition

Underachievement has been analyzed in the main from psychodynamic perspectives and behavioral frameworks (Fine & Pitts, 1980; Rimm, 1986). Schools, families, and gifted children themselves have been named as causal factors (Whitmore, 1980).

In their review of research on underachieving gifted students, Dowdall and Colangelo (1982) point out that this variability of definitions makes the concept nearly meaningless. However, they note, "The underlying theme of almost all the definitions is that there exists a discrepancy between potential (what a student ought to be able to do) and actual performance (what the student is actually demonstrating)" (p. 179).

For example, Whitmore (1980) focuses on children's behavior in school. She names four syndromes leading to underachievement among gifted students: learning disabilities, behavioral disorders, neurological handicaps, and paralyzing perfectionism. In contrast, Rimm (1986) targets family dynamics as the central force in underachievement. She names three groups of contributing factors: control patterns, imitation, and counteridentification. Clark (1979) divides underachievers into two general categories: chronic and situational.

Dowdall and Colangelo (1982) conclude that the construct is complex and diverse in its causes and manifestations. They attribute some of the variability to the degree of inclusiveness established a priori by particular researchers. In their review of intervention programs, they note that the most promising ones adopt a systems orientation, combining counseling, classroom modifications, and intensive case study work (cf. Whitmore, 1980).

A Systems-Based Conceptualization

In their analysis of the underperformance syndrome, Fine and Pitts (1980) describe a system wherein a bright child might "hide" low self-esteem resulting from skill deficiencies or perceptual motor problems through verbal "defense tactics" (p. 52) such as intellectualizing and rationalizing events to redefine them in favorable ways. They hypothesize that the family system might support underachievement through the parents inadvertently "adultizing" their verbally precocious child or maintaining the child as a problem to mask deeper relational problems in the marital subsystem. They suggest a reciprocal pattern wherein the gifted child provokes a negative reaction, develops a pseudo self-sufficiency, and then denies responsibility for the rejecting behavior of others.

Problems in School: Disabling Perfectionism

Definition

Disabling perfectionism seems to affect bright students who are highly suc-

cessful in school. Undoubtedly, there are many individuals whose high standards and striving for excellence is healthy and productive. However, for some gifted students, performance never quite meets expectations. These individuals, labeled as neurotic perfectionists, are distinguished from their normal peers in four categories (Hamachek, 1978): goals, focus, attitude/style, and task initiation. Thus, normal perfectionists set reasonable, realistic goals for performance (based on knowledge of strengths and weaknesses); focus positively on tasks, concentrating on strengths; are relaxed yet careful; and begin tasks emotionally charged, excited, and clear about what needs to be accomplished. In contrast, neurotic perfectionists demand higher standards that are impossible to attain; try to avoid doing something wrong, concentrating on deficiencies; are tense and deliberate; and begin tasks anxiously, confused, and emotionally drained.

Understanding Disabling Perfectionism

In our recent study of disabling perfectionism among bright adolescents (Jenkins-Friedman, Bransky, & Murphy, 1987), we found a pattern of irrational beliefs regarding performance standards and discrepancies between actual and idealized self-perceptions characterizing these children. Although our study was limited to the school context, we found a positive relationship between these internal indicators and disabling perfectionistic behaviors observed by teachers.

Some of the key behaviors were congruent with those associated with underachievement: counter self-sufficiency, inappropriate standard setting, and blurring the adult and child roles. In addition, these children appear to be less able to delay gratification (e.g., making desires into demands for performance), highly rigid in standard setting (e.g., unable to permit themselves to perform at an average level in any activity), and emotionally immature (e.g., overgeneralizing).

Strategies for Intervention

The goals of intervention are to reduce the child's debilitating behaviors and to support the child in developing a set of more constructive patterns. I have found two sets of strategies applied within a systems context to be effective: direct methods and indirect methods. The first set of methods involves teaching children and their parents about the conditions supporting the issue at hand, practice, and encouragement for change. Indirect methods refer to those techniques developed for working with resistance and reactance.

A Systemic Framework for Intervention

Systemically oriented psychologists advocate creating a close working relationship between the home and school to understand the ecology of the contexts in which particular patterns occur (Fine, 1984). A systems-based intervention would typically involve a series of meetings, including the child, parents, building administrator, school psychologist, classroom teacher, and gifted program specialist (Fine & Pitts, 1980; Rimm, 1986). Having all concerned parties meeting face to face helps to reduce communication confusion, establish common goals, and set guidelines for collaborative work. Concretizing issues, expectations, and intervention plans, conducting followup meetings, and designating a key individual to manage an intervention program will contribute to the success of this approach.

Fine and Pitts (1980) emphasize the importance of the parents and teachers maintaining a strong parental posture. They assert that a strong "good parent" position is likely to be psychologically reassuring to the child, although on a social level the child's reaction might be negative. They caution to expect sabotages as part of the reframing process, and to anticipate that relational conflicts might surface in the course of the intervention process.

Direct Strategies: Upstream Helping

For the past seven years, we have been working with gifted education program teachers and their students to develop and test a three-phase self-reflexive model for empowering bright students to understand and to use their potential (Culross & Jenkins-Friedman, in press). The first phase is *knowledge* about giftedness and related issues. The second, *self-awareness* or *personal relevancy*, emphasizes applying the information to the gifted student's life and experiences. The final and most crucial aspect, *empowerment*, focuses on helping youngsters act effectively (and in accordance with insights generated in phases one and two) in future social and academic situations.

For children experiencing problems associated with disabling perfectionism, we have identified focusing on issues such as setting realistic goals, making appropriate attributions, dealing constructively with success and failure, and managing time effectively. In a systems-oriented approach, the school psychologist, teacher(s), and relevant family members would meet together to learn about the topic (knowledge), share their perceptions of the particular issue as it affects them, and reflect on the ways in which the school and family systems support related behaviors (self-awareness). All would practice more constructive strategies (empowerment) and meet to share feedback.

Strategies for Second-Order Change

The homeostatic qualities inherent within systems make resistance to change an expected reaction. "In a sense the system may need to be unbalanced in order for change to occur" (Fine, 1984, p. 46). In these situations, cognitive/rational approaches such as the one sketched above need to be supplemented. Two techniques we have used successfully are paradoxical suggestions and reframing (Ellis, 1985; Fay, 1978). Both methods help persons in each subsystem experience their patterns in ways that permit change. The strategies are associated with brief therapy approaches, which is more compatible with the limitations of therapeutic intervention in public school settings. Both methods often employ humor, multiple levels of meaning within the same event, and bisociation (juxtaposing two seemingly incompatible frames of reference to spark a creative solution). These approaches appeal to children whose cognitive functioning is sophisticated (Jenkins-Friedman, Bransky, & Murphy, 1987).

Personal Experience

Paradoxical therapy is based on the assumption that in order to change behaviors based on irrationality and illogicality, the therapy must be more irrational and illogical than the client. It is based on the hypothesis: "When you voluntarily practice a symptom that occurs spontaneously, you reduce the spontaneous occurrence of that symptom" (Fay, 1978, p. 21). We employed it in the following case study.

CASE STUDY 2

Carol, a gifted fifth-grader, was taking longer and longer to complete her assignments in school and at home. According to Carol, none of her work was ever quite up to her (exacting) standards until she had revised it many times. Her (unchecked) perfectionis-

tic behavior was causing her to experience severe anxiety attacks and other stress symptoms. In addition, she was falling behind her less-able classmates because she was taking so long to complete her work. Her teacher's and parents' attention only increased Carol's behavior; likewise, working on time-management plans, task analyses, contracting, and goal setting exacerbated the situation.

To change both the behavior for which Carol was rewarded, as well as the context for her behavior, the following plan was used: Carol, her teacher, and her parents, met. All agreed that Carol would work for only 15 minutes on any independent assignment at home or at school. Time for recreation, not for high-quality work, was the new, "illogical" focus of the intervention plan.

For the first week, Carol protested strongly and completed no work. However, the strictly enforced time limits began to change the focus of her attention from being the best student to being the fastest one in the class. Her parents and teacher similarly began to recast their roles from promoting perfection to rewarding task completion.

A naturally self-competitive child, Carol eventually announced that she liked playing "beat the homework clock." Her teacher and parents made sure to refocus their reactions so as to support this emerging pattern. Within a few months, the group met again to process what had transpired and to continue to adapt their strategy to encourage appropriate standard setting.

CONCLUSION

The meaning of giftedness and its impact on the family system have been explored in this chapter. Understanding the gifted child's needs, motivations, and behaviors from a systems perspective provides a means to integrate data from the different systems within which the gifted child operates. The paradigm also allows school psychologists to perceive more accurately the impact on the child of events occurring in these various systems, and to design more effective intervention approaches.

"In this respect, we believe a family/systems approach to gifted children provides educators, counselors, therapists, parents and teachers with many more alternatives in meeting the needs of this very special population" (Frey & Wendorf, 1985, p. 807).

References

Albert, R. A. (1980). Family positions and the attainment of eminence: A study of special family positions and special family experiences. *Gifted Child Quarterly, 24*(2), 87–95.

Bloom, B. S. (Ed.) (1985). *Developing talent in young people.* New York: Ballantine Books.

Clark, B. (1979). *Growing up gifted* (2nd ed.). Columbus, OH: Charles Merrill.

Colangelo, N., & Brower, P. (1987). Labeling gifted youngsters: Long-term impact on families. *Gifted Child Quarterly, 31*(2), 75–78.

Colangelo, N., & Dettmann, D. F. (1983). A review of research on parents and families of gifted children. *Exceptional Children, 50*(1), 20–27.

Cornell, D. G. (1983a). The family's view of the gifted child. In B. M. Shore, F. Gagne, S. Larivee, R. H. Tali, & R. E. Tremblay (Eds.), *Proceedings of the Fourth World Conference on Gifted Education: Face to face with giftedness* (pp. 39–50). New York: Trillium Press.

Cornell, D. G. (1983b). Gifted children: The impact of positive labeling on the family system. *American Journal of Orthopsychiatry, 53*(2), 322–334.

Cornell, D. G., & Grossberg, I. N. (1986). Siblings of children in gifted programs. *Journal for the Education of the Gifted, 9*(4), 253–264.

Cornell, D. G., & Grossberg, I. N. (1987). Family environment and personality adjustment in gifted program children. *Gifted Child Quarterly, 31*(2), 59–64.

Culross, R. R., & Jenkins-Friedman, R. On coping and defending: Applying Burner's personal growth principles to working with gifted/talented students. *Gifted Child Quarterly,* in press.

Dettmann, D. F., & Colangelo, N. (1980). A functional model for counseling parents of gifted students. *Gifted Child Quarterly, 24*(4), 158–161.

Dowdall, C., & Colangelo, N. (1982). Underachieving gifted students: Review and implications. *Gifted Child Quarterly, 26*(4), 179–184.

Ellis, A. (1985). *Overcoming resistance: Rational-emotive therapy with difficult clients.* New York: Springer.

Fay, A. (1978). *Making things better by making them worse.* New York: Hawthorn.

Feldman, D. H., & Goldsmith, L. T. (1986). *Nature's gambit.* New York: Basic Books.

Fine, M. J. (1977). Facilitating parent-child relationships. *Gifted Child Quarterly, 21,* 487–500.

Fine, M. J. (1984). Integrating structural and strategic components in school-based intervention: Some cautions for consultants. *Techniques: A Journal for Remedial Education and Counseling, 1,* 44–51.

Fine, M. J., & Holt, P. (1983). Intervening with school problems: A family systems perspective. *Psychology in the Schools, 20,* 59–66.

Fine, M. J., & Pitts, R. (1980). Intervention with underachieving gifted children: Rationale and strategies. *Gifted Child Quarterly, 24*(2), 51–55.

Frey, J., & Wendorf, D. J. (1985). Families of gifted children. In L. L'Abate (Ed.), *The handbook of family psychology and therapy* (pp. 781–809). Homewood, IL: The Dorsey Press.

Goertzel, V., & Goertzel, M. G. (1962). *Cradles of eminence.* Boston: Little, Brown.

Grenier, M. E. (1985). Gifted children and other siblings. *Gifted Child Quarterly, 29*(4), 164–167.

Grinder, R. E. (1985). The gifted in our midst: By their divine deeds, neuroses and test scores we have known them. In F. D. Horowitz & M. O'Brien (Eds.), *The gifted and talented: Developmental perspectives* (pp. 5–35). Washington, DC: American Psychological Association.

Hackney, H. (1981). The gifted child, the family, and the school. *Gifted Child Quarterly, 25*(2), 51–62.

Hackney, H. (1982). Effects of the family: Random or orchestrated? *Journal for the Education of the Gifted, 6*(1), 30–38.

Hamachek, D. D. (1978). Psychodynamics

of normal and neurotic perfectionism. *Psychology: A Journal of Human Behavior, 15,* 27–33.

Horowitz, F. D., & O'Brien, M. (Eds.) (1985). *The gifted and talented: Developmental perspectives.* Washington, DC: American Psychological Association.

Houseman, W. (1987). *The 1987 state of the states gifted and talented education report.* Council of State Directors of Programs for the Gifted.

Jenkins, R. C. W. (1978). The identification of gifted students through peer nomination. Unpublished doctoral dissertation, University of Connecticut.

Jenkins-Friedman, R., Bransky, T. S., & Murphy, D. L. (1987). *The school psychologist as Prometheus: Identifying and working therapeutically with gifted students 'at risk' for disabling perfectionism.* Paper presented at the annual meeting of the American Psychological Association, New York.

Karnes, M. B., & Shwedel, A. (1987). Differences in attitudes and practices between fathers of young gifted and fathers of young non-gifted children: A pilot study. *Gifted Child Quarterly, 31*(2), 79–82.

Kitano, M. K., & Kirby, D. F. (1986). *Gifted education: A comprehensive view.* Boston, Little, Brown.

Morrow, W. R., & Wilson, R. C. (1964). Family relations of bright high-achieving and under-achieving high school boys. *Child Development, 35,* 1041–1049.

Newland, T. E. (1976). *The gifted in socioeducational perspective.* Englewood Cliffs, NJ: Prentice-Hall.

Parker, M., & Colangelo, N. (1979). An assessment of values of gifted students and their parents. In N. Colangelo & R. T. Zaffran (Eds.), *New voices in counseling the gifted* (pp. 408–414). Dubuque, IA: Kendall-Hunt.

Peterson, D. C. (1977). The heterogeneously gifted family. *Gifted Child Quarterly, 21*(3), 396–411.

Renzulli, J. R. (1979). *What makes giftedness? Reexamining a definition.* Ventura, CA: National/State Leadership Training Institute on the Gifted/Talented.

Rimm, S. B. (1986). *Underachievement syndrome: Causes and cures.* Watertown, WI: Apple Publishing.

Ross, R. (1979). A program model for altering children's consciousness. *Gifted Child Quarterly, 23*(11), 109–17.

Sternberg, R. J. (1986). A triarchic theory of intellectual giftedness. In R. J. Sternberg & J. E. Davidson (Eds.), *Conceptions of giftedness.* New York: Cambridge University Press.

Terman, L. M. (1954). The discovery and encouragement of exceptional talent. *American Psychologist, 9*(6), 221–230.

White, W., & Renzulli, J. S. (1987). A forty year follow-up of students who attended Leta Hollingworth's school for gifted students. *Roeper Review, 10*(2), 89–94.

Whitmore, J. R. (1980). *Giftedness, conflict, and underachievement.* Boston: Allyn and Bacon.

CHAPTER

12

Single Parenting and Stepparenting: Problems, Issues, and Interventions

CINDY CARLSON

University of Texas, Austin

THE LIVING ARRANGEMENTS of children have dramatically changed within the past two decades. Whereas in 1960, 88 percent of children were living with two natural parents, currently only 56 percent of children live with both biological parents. For every 10 Caucasian children in a classroom, it can be anticipated that at least half will have experienced life in a single-parent family, and 1 or 2 are currently living in a stepfamily.

Statistical projections suggest that white children may spend, on average, as many as 6 of their first 18 years in a single-parent home. For black children, 8 or 9 of every 10 children will have resided in a single-parent home and spend, on average, 11 of their first 18 years without two parents (Hernandez, 1988). Single parenting is most prevalent among blacks, more prevalent among American Indians and Hispanics than among whites, and least prevalent among Asians (Laosa, 1988). The antecedents of single and stepparenting vary by ethnic group. Of all white children, over 75 percent result from marital separation or divorce. In contrast, the most frequent precursor of single parenting for blacks is out-of-wedlock births; for Hispanics, it is marital separation, but not

divorce (Laosa, 1988). These data suggest that white children, then, will be most likely to experience remarriage by a parent.

Three demographic trends are primary in accounting for the increase in single-parent and stepfamily homes: (1) a substantial rise in the number of births occurring to unmarried mothers, (2) the continuing high rate of divorce, and (3) the associated increase in the proportion of divorced women with children who remarry (Hernandez, 1988).

The never-married single-parent home is considered to be at greatest risk. Both black and white children living with a never-married mother are more likely to live with a younger mother (less than 25 years old), who has not graduated from high school (50 percent of white births, 40 percent of black births), with an annual family income of less than $10,000 (77 percent white, 80 percent black). This low annual income persists despite the fact that for both blacks and whites, 34 percent of children living with never-married mothers have at least one additional adult relative in the home.

Divorce is the second major demographic variable that affects the living arrangements of children. Although the dramatically increasing divorce rate observed from 1965 to 1979 has begun to level off, it is still predicted that 60 percent of all children will experience a divorce. The transition from a two-parent to a single-parent family, when caused by divorce, is usually accompanied by significant related socioenvironmental changes including income instability, lowered income, and changes in employment, residence, and school (McLanahan, 1983). These changes must be considered in the context of the substantial emotional confusion and loss that accompanies the loss of a parent or spouse (Wallerstein & Kelly, 1980).

Furthermore, when single parenting is the result of divorce, the likelihood of remarriage is higher than for separated or never-married mothers. Therefore, children in postdivorce single-parent homes can be expected to continue to experience more major transitions than their intact family peers.

The resources available to children in single-parent homes, regardless of antecedent, are consistently fewer than in two-parent families. Without exception, across median income groups, the annual incomes of single mothers were less than half, and more frequently one-third to one-fourth, the income of married couple families (Laosa, 1988). Economic adversity has multiple implications. Directly family income can affect the physical health of the child and mother. In addition, socioeconomic status is related to parental behavior toward children, teacher and peer attitudes and behavior, social and educational opportunities, environmental stimulation and attention, and child-rearing styles and expectations.

Indirectly, the social and economic support available to the biological parent in both single-parent and remarried family systems has been found to be positively related to the quality of the parent-child relationship (Hetherington, 1987; Hetherington, Cox, & Cox, 1982; Kanoy, Cun-ningham, White, & Adams, 1984; McLanahan, 1983; Wallerstein, 1986). Contrary to the experience of custodial single mothers, both noncustodial and custodial fathers typically maintain or improve their standard of living following divorce (Hetherington, 1989).

The availability of resources to children improves significantly with remarriage and more closely parallels intact families (Hernandez, 1988). It is estimated that 80 percent of divorced women and 85 percent of divorced men remarry (Clingempeel, Brand, & Segal, 1987). Furthermore, remarriages tend to occur relatively soon following divorce, with a median interval of three years. Remarriage rates are highest and most rapid for younger women with children and lower levels of education (Norton & Glick, 1986). The increasing numbers of children residing for some period of time in more than one home have caused scholars to label these families as *binuclear;* that is, having two parent-based centers (Ahrons & Wallisch, 1987).

Although remarriage typically reduces the economic stress of the single-parent family, and may increase the social support of the custodial parent, it again sets in motion the necessity of a reorganization of family roles, affectional ties, and possible changes in residence, school, and neighborhood. Furthermore, the divorce rate for remarriage is higher than first marriages, thus children of divorce are likely to experience multiple marital transitions, household rearrangements, and geographic moves. The patterning and timing of these multiple transitions may be critical to the long-term adjustment of children (Hetherington, Hagan, & Anderson, 1989).

It is clear from the preceding discussion that a focus on the family types of single parent and stepparent presents a deceptively simple and static view of complex family relationships that are embedded within a socioeconomic milieu, are influenced by multiple variables, and are in continuous transformation over time. Children's responses to chronic economic strain, or to the loss or gain of a parent and related family members, will be more characterized by diversity than predictability. Thus, in the subsequent section complementary theoretical frameworks are provided to organize our understanding of the complex processes associated with the multiple transitions characteristic of single-parent and stepparent family systems.

THEORETICAL FRAMEWORKS

Systems theory, family developmental life-cycle theory, ecological-developmental theory, attachment theory, and stress and coping theory provide complementary frameworks for consideration of single-parent and remarried families.

Systems Theory

At the core of systems theory is the concept that elements exist in a state of active communicative interrelatedness and interdependence within a bounded unit, such as the family. The interrelatedness of elements assures that the behavior or attitudes of one element or family member cannot help but have a direct or indirect influence on the other elements or persons in the system. The distinctiveness of elements, which may be reflected in such attributes as age, gender, and temperament, contributes to the unique and idiosyncratic organization and personality of each family system. The distinctiveness of the elements of systems is also reflected in their different functions or roles. System elements are often organized by function.

Furthermore, systems with adequate complexity are organized hierarchically such that higher-order subsystems or system components exert control over lower-order components. Family systems are universally hierarchically and functionally organized, with parents or other adults in control of and performing the function of nurturance of children. Critical to well-functioning systems is clear boundaries between the subsystems. Clear boundaries are characterized by an adequate flow of information and resources to preserve the essential interrelatedness of elements of the system but also an adequate blockage of information such that the differentiation of system elements is protected from unnecessary intrusion that would compromise its functioning.

The properties of boundary, role, and hierarchy are evident in the repeated interactional or communication sequences between members of the system. From the systems perspective, child dysfunction is reflective of a system with properties and organization that do not optimally support the development of the child. The implication of systems theory for binuclear family systems is that the adjustment of the child will be influenced by the roles, organization, and repeated patterns of transaction between all members within and between related households.

Family Developmental Life-Cycle Theory

A shift in system organization is often reflective of necessary adaptation to either extrafamilial or intrafamilial growth or change. Family developmental life-cycle theory provides a framework for viewing the necessity of systems change over time. Family developmental life-cycle theory, like individual developmental life-cycle theory (e.g., Erikson, 1950), proposes that families face different tasks at progressive stages of development. Normative family life-cycle stages are characterized by changes in the status of family members and particularly by first events for the family (e.g., marriage, birth of a child, child enters school). With each new stage of family development, a reorganization of family roles and subjective experience is required for the optimal growth of family members (Carter & McGoldrick, 1980; 1989). Failure to reorganize the family system when faced with a major developmental life-cycle transition is hypothesized to result in symptomatology of a family member (Terkelsen, 1980).

Single-parent and remarried family systems have unique or paranormative family life-cycle stages that are super imposed upon the universal family life cycle (Carter & McGoldrick, 1980, 1989; Beal, 1980). The completion (often simultaneously) of multiple family life stages, both the normative and the paranormative, within a single family life-time space increases the complexity and difficulty of family reorganization. For example, if two divorced parents remarry within two years following their respective divorces and integrate families with children at multiple age levels, the remarried family will be challenged with simultaneously negotiating the family life-cycle stages of marriage; reorganization of parenting roles; establishment of relations with the noncustodial parent, family, and new extended family members; establishment of sibling relationships, and parenting at multiple child-development stages. Developmental adjustment may additionally be compounded by a move to a larger house in a new neighborhood of city.

Empirical support for the distinctiveness of the life cycles of single-parent and remarried families has been provided by Hill (1986), who found that the timing and duration of stages, transitions between stages, and length of time to make transitions are increased for single-parent and remarried family systems. For the practitioner, the family life-cycle framework provides a useful normative reference for the type of challenges facing single-parent and remarried families, and a means for evaluating the degree of adaptation and direction of family reorganization that is essential for restabilization of the system.

Ecological-Developmental Theory

Family transitions do not occur within a vacuum but rather occur within a social context that may enhance or reduce the resiliency of family members' coping. A framework for understanding the interface of family and social context is provided by an ecological-developmental theory, which conceptualizes the development of children as occurring simultaneously within multiple, nested social environments or systems (Bronfrenbrenner, 1979). These have been identified as (1) *microsystem* (interpersonal relationship settings, e.g., family, school, peer group), (2) *mesosystem* (the connections between two microsystems, e.g., the family-school link), (3) *exosystem* (settings that may impinge on the child but in which he or she is not an active member, e.g., parent's employment), and (4) *macrosystem* (cultural consistencies in the lower system levels, e.g., urban).

Ecological-developmental theory both points to the critical role of multiple system levels on the adjustment of children but, perhaps more important, states that the *quality of the interconnections between systems* will be as critical a determinant of child functioning as within-system variables. Applied to binuclear family systems, ecological theory underscores both the impact of multiple ecological levels in the adjustment of children and underscores the importance of well-functioning system linkages such as the relationship between family and school, family and family, and family and broader social support.

The critical role of system linking in single-parent and remarried family systems has been well articulated by Jacobson (1987), who claims single-parent and stepparent families should be characterized as "linked family systems" because the child is the "link" who is being influenced and influencing multiple households. As the key link, the child is the major channel of communication, overt and covert, between systems. Jacobson's concept of children as the "links" between family systems is generalizable to the family-school relationship.

Attachment Theory

The theoretical frameworks provided to this point center on the family as an organized communicative system with roles, tasks, and boundaries. However, the distinguishing characteristic of family relationships is emotional ties. Family transitions most commonly involve a dramatic alteration of family affectional bonds. It is this author's contention that a primary source of the distress that often accompanies family transitions is the consequent disruption of strong emotional bonds in family dissolution and their replacement with more tenuous emotional bonds in remarriage.

Attachment theory provides a theoretical framework for understanding the impact of disruptions of emotional bonds on the parent-child system and subsequent child-developmental outcomes. Attachment is defined as "any form of behavior that results in a person attaining or maintaining proximity to some other clearly identified individual who is conceived as better able to cope with the world" (Bowlby, 1988, pp. 26–27), with the expression of attachment behavior most evident when the organism is under stress. Although attachment behavior is most obvious in early childhood, it can be observed throughout the life cycle in intimate relationships. The key feature of attachment behavior, present irrespective of age, is the intensity of the emotion that accompanies it and the kind of emotion that is aroused between the attached person and the attachment figure. When the relationship goes well, the attached person experiences joy and security; when the relationship is broken, anxiety, anger, and jealousy are aroused.

Attachment is viewed as being at the root of the parent-child relationship. Parents, through responsiveness to their children, provide a secure base for the child from which he or she can venture forth into the world of school, peers, and individual exploration. Numerous empirical studies have verified the predictive validity of a secure parent-child relationship on multiple subsequent child-developmental outcomes, ranging from social competence to cognitive problem solving (e.g., see Bretherton & Waters, 1985). Children who are insecurely attached to a caregiver demonstrate consistently less well-organized developmental functioning in settings beyond the family. Furthermore, research has demonstrated that the security of parent-child attachment is vulnerable to family stress and changes in the romantic relationships of parents (Egeland & Farber, 1984).

It is expected that single-parent homes, with their vulnerability to multiple stressors and changes in adult romantic partnerships, and stepparent homes, with the introduction of new nonbiological intimate relationships, both have the potential for undermining the emotionally rooted secure attachment base of children with their parents. In divorce, children feel threatened by losing significant attachment figures. For example, statistics indicate that noncustodial fathers dramatically reduce their involvement with their biological children, particularly daughters, following divorce, with a further decrease when either parent remarries (Hernandez, 1988).

In remarriage, secure biological parent-child relationships are threatened by the addition of an intimate attached relationship, primarily between adults, which may in reality alter patterns of interaction or may be perceived by children as threatening the biological parent-child relationship. When children lack secure attachment figures, or when their secure attachments are threatened, their anxiety and anger can be expected to find expression both within the family and in the domains beyond the family toward which the child is oriented to master.

Fulmer (1983), for example, has observed that many of the behavior disorders exhibited by children in single-parent families could be viewed as "collusion mischief" in which the child's anxiety was heightened by the single-parent's apathy, depression, or expressed helplessness, and the child's misbehavior served to "impel" the parent to take action on behalf of the child. Thus, attachment theory provides a theoretical framework for understanding the emotionally based, clinical responses of children to family transitions.

Stress and Coping Theory

The family disruption and reorganization inherent in single-parent and stepfamily systems present children with a significant number of changes with which to cope. Rutter (1979) has reported that when children experience only a single stress, it carries no appreciable risk. When children are exposed to a series of stressors or several concurrent stresses, however, the adverse effects increase multiplicatively, not additively.

Hetherington (1984) argues that a critical mediator of the adverse effects of multiple stressors is the degree of control available to the child over life events. Given that the changes experienced by children in the transitions to single-parent and remarried family systems are changes initiated by adults and most likely perceived by children to be primarily of benefit to the adults, a high perceived level of control over events seems unlikely for children.

Stolberg and Anker (1983) lend empirical support with data that find that extent of environmental changes benefit children in intact families but have an adverse affect on postdivorce children. These researchers further found that as the extent of environmental change increased for the divorced group, children perceived themselves and their parents to be less able to control their world. Thus, cognitive-behavioral strategies that permit children increasing control over their environments are likely to assist children in single-parent and stepparent families with the greater number of environmental changes to which they are likely to be required to adapt.

Five complementary theoretical frameworks have been presented that clarify our understanding of the complexity and range of child-development outcomes associated with single-parent and stepparent families. In the remainder of the chapter these theoretical frameworks will guide discussion of the specific characteristics of the single-parent and stepparent family system. This will be followed by a discussion of intervention implications at the family-school interface. For each family type, definitional issues, system properties, associated child outcomes, mediating variables, and family tasks will be examined.

SINGLE-PARENT HOMES

Definitional Issues

A single-parent family has been defined as one in which someone raises children alone without the household presence of a second parent or parent substitute (Weiss,

1979a). Over 90 percent of single-parent homes are headed by mothers (Hernandez, 1988). Within the definition of single-parent families, variations exist differentiated primarily by the route to single parenthood. Divorce or marital separation is the most common antecedent (70 percent), followed by never-married parents (25 percent and increasing), and death of a spouse (7 percent) (Weiss, 1979a).

Although structurally equivalent, the variations in the antecedent events producing the single-parent family result in considerably different family environments for parents and children (Carlson, 1985, 1987a; Rutter, 1983; Weiss, 1979a). Single-parent homes created by death of a spouse demonstrate the least adverse effects upon children, never-married single-parent homes are consistently found to produce developmental risks for children, and postdivorce single-parent families fall somewhere between widowed and never-married single-parents on risk factors.

System Properties and Adaptations

Single-parent homes are notable for the necessity of accomplishing the same functions or roles as the biologically intact family but with fewer adult participants (Carlson, 1985, 1987a). All families must complete the role-based survival tasks of economic support, childcare, child socialization, and housekeeping, as well as the companionship roles of recreation, leisure, emotional support, and sexual satisfaction (Rollins & Galligan, 1978). The role overload inherent in the single-parent family structure assures a degree of stress and strain on family members, particularly the single parent. For example, research has found that single employed mothers, when compared with other mother groups, spend the least amount of time in personal care (including rest and sleep) and recreational activities (Sanik & Maudlin, 1986).

The "undermanned" structure of the single-parent family demands reorganization of the system to permit a minimal level of acceptable accomplishment of family tasks. Children in single-parent homes are often called upon to assume some of the burden. The advantage of this system reorganization is that it is convenient, is biologically based, may enhance the developmental potential of children, establishes a "cooperative" family environment, and reduces the role strain of the single parent. Children in single-parent homes do, in fact, express greater independence and emotional sensitivity than their peers in intact homes and are more likely to be involved in decisions typically restricted to the parental subsystem, such as how to spend the family income (Weiss, 1979b).

The potential risks of more egalitarian role sharing within the single-parent family are either excessive or developmentally inappropriate role demands on the child or the blurring of generational boundaries that may accompany a more egalitarian relationship between parent and child. If role demands are excessive for the child's developmental status or unique characteristics (see Glenwick & Mowrey, 1986), the child may experience stress, anger, or depression; may lack the family support essential for development in arenas beyond the family; or may exhibit precocious or pseudomature development as characteristic of the "parentified child" (Minuchin, 1974). Thus, critical to the success of internal role restructuring is the establishment of the clear, consistent, and developmentally appropriate parent-child relationship boundaries and expectations.

An alternative to internal role sharing in the single-parent family is the use of social support external to the family. Social support has been consistently found to be positively related to single-parent family health (Hanson, 1986). A variety of social support network options for single-parent families have been identified. These include use of family of origin, a spouse equivalent, extended friendships, and organized social support (e.g., daycare, paid housekeepers) (McLanahan, Wedemeyer, & Adelbaum, 1981; Greif, 1985).

Although utilization of external social support can be considered essential to the well-being of the single-parent family, costs may also be engendered with each type of social support. Family of origin ties can undermine the authority of the single parent (see Dell & Appelbaum, 1977). Spouse equivalent social support may lack the commitment essential for family security and at worst may risk physical and sexual abuse of children. Extended friendship networks require considerable emotional energy and time to maintain. Organized social support, of course, is a financial burden. Therefore, single fathers are most likely to use organized social support (Greif, 1985).

The most negative child outcomes are associated with avoidance of social support. These "insular" single parents are at high risk for child abuse (Wahler, 1980). Although social support typically has been related to single-parent family health, in recent research Hetherington (1989) found that social support had no positive effect on mothers who were either psychologically at risk or without stress. Thus, it would appear that only moderately stressed single mothers are able to benefit from social support.

In summary, the undermanned structure of the single-parent family requires the adjustment of internal roles and the utilization of external social support for optimal functioning. The ability of the single parent to organize internal and external social support is a critical key to successful functioning. Single mothers who are exhausted by full-time employment, worried by inadequate financial support, emotionally bereft of friendships and leisure time are vulnerable to depression and less than optimal in parenting their children. However, it appears important to bear in mind that "it takes money to make money." The single parents with the least available resources also appear least able to utilize social support. This suggests that differentiated intervention strategies are necessary for single parents.

Child Outcomes and Mediating Variables

The child-development outcomes associated with single-parent homes have been well summarized in previous reviews and are found to be significantly different for boys and girls (Carlson, 1987a; Emery, 1988; Hetherington, Hagan, & Anderson, 1989). Briefly, rearing in a single-parent home has been associated academically with lower cognitive functioning, lower school achievement, lower achievement motivation, and a "feminine" cognitive style.

Findings regarding lowered academic performance are stronger for boys than girls, and most applicable to postdivorce single-parent homes (Emery, 1988). Regarding social and personality effects, single-parent homes are associated with a less secure masculine style, greater difficulty with self-control, lower moral development and maturity, and higher rates of antisocial and delinquent behavior in boys. For girls, negative effects of single-parent child rearing are seldom obtained; however, a few studies have found that early maturing girls in single-parent homes may be at some risk for early sexual activity (Hetherington, 1972).

Results regarding self-esteem have been inconsistent across studies for both boys and girls; lower self-esteem appears to be strongly associated with parental conflict regardless of family structure (Emery, 1988). As noted earlier, rearing in a single-parent home has been clinically identified with "growing up a little faster," the implications of which have not been adequately investigated empirically (Weiss, 1979b).

Although finding adverse effects associated with single parenting for boys is consistent across many studies, in reality the range of child adjustment is quite diverse. Although children in postdivorce single-parent homes are two to three times more likely to have contact with a mental-health professional, this is still reflective of only 13 percent of children, indicating that at least 85 percent cope without professional assistance (Emery, 1988). Furthermore, academic performance differences between intact and single-parent homes are seldom large in magnitude, leading several researchers to speculate that effects are mediated through disruptive behavior in school (Emery, 1988; Guidabaldi, Peery, & Cleminshaw, 1984).

Thus, multiple variables mediate the child-development outcomes associated with single-parent homes. These variables include child gender, child temperament and personality, parent psychological well-being, parenting competence and style, coparental relationship, child's relationship with the noncustodial parent, socioeconomic status, and social support.

Investigators concur that measures of parent-child processes relate more strongly to child outcomes than single-parent status (Hetherington, Cox, & Cox, 1982). High-quality single mothering can compensate for loss of the father, whereas low-quality fathering can negatively influence children's development in intact homes (Biller, 1982). It has been argued, however, that when one parent is absent, the remaining parent will have a more intense effect upon the child (Hetherington, Cox, & Cox, 1982). An authoritative parenting style, one that includes adequate control and supervision with adequate nurturance and warmth, is associated with child competence in single-parent homes (Santrock & Warshak, 1979). Single mothers who err in the direction of an authoritarian style of child rearing are also more likely to have competent children; however, permissive single mothering is associated with behavior problems.

Authoritative parenting is emotionally demanding; that is, it produces physiological arousal in the parent (Patterson, 1982). Thus, the psychological well-being of the single-parent provides the foundation for capacity to parent competently. Empirical support has been provided by Kanoy and colleagues (1985), who found that divorced mothers' self-concept predicted the quality of mother-child interaction, father-child interaction, ex-spouse relationship, and children's self-esteem. Unfortunately, single-parent mothers often report lower self-esteem, lower personal efficacy and control, and less optimism about the future when compared with married, never-divorced mothers (McLanahan, 1983). Long-term single mothers report higher rates of depression, psychosomatic symptoms, and loneliness than married or remarried mothers (Wallerstein, 1986). Thus, one critical mediator of children's competence in single-parent homes is the quality of the parent-child relationship, which is determined, in part, by the emotional well-being of the single parent.

The parent-child relationship, however, is bidirectional. Several child characteristics have been found to ease or exacerbate parenting in single-parent homes. Gender is one of the most consistently differentiating variables, as previously noted, with boys residing in single-parent homes exhibiting higher rates of behavioral, academic, and interpersonal difficulties than boys in intact or remarried homes, or than girls in single-parent homes.

There is some evidence that school-aged children adapt better in the custody of the same-sex parent (Camara & Resnick, 1988; Santrock & Warshak, 1979;

Zill, 1988). Many reasons have been offered for the difficult single-parent mother-son relationship. Boys are biologically predisposed to higher rates of activity and aggressive behavior and have been found to display higher rates of acting-out behaviors in the custody of both fathers and mothers than girls (Hetherington, Hagan, & Anderson, 1989).

Relations among male siblings in single-mother homes have also been found to be more antagonistic than in other family structures (Hetherington, Hagan, & Anderson, 1989). Patterson (1986) provides an illuminating illustration of the contribution of siblings to fighting within the family. Perhaps not surprisingly, then, single mothers are vulnerable to child-management difficulties, particularly with aggressive sons (Patterson, 1982). In addition to difficulty with authoritative parenting, however, it has been proposed that boys in single-parent homes are more likely to be exposed to parental conflict than girls, and marital conflict is consistently associated with poor child outcomes (Hetherington, Hagan, & Anderson, 1989). To summarize, boys in single-mother homes consistently appear to be at greater risk than girls.

In addition to gender, child temperament and personality are associated with single-parent family adjustment. Children with easy temperaments, as well as other positive characteristics such as intelligence, independence, internal locus of control, and self-esteem, and who also have adequate social support, seem to be quite adaptable to family transitions (Hetherington, Hagan, & Anderson, 1989; Rutter, 1979). Temperamentally difficult children are both more vulnerable to the stress of family transitions and more likely to be the elicitors and recipients of parental negativism. Difficult children also contribute to the social isolation of single parents. The incidence of divorce and desertion is high among families with an exceptional or difficult child (Allen, Affleck, McGrade, & McQueeney, 1984), and remarriage rates are lower for single parents with difficult children (Ambert, 1985).

Another critical mediator of children's adjustment in single-parent homes is the involvement of the noncustodial parent (in postdivorce single-parent families) and the interparental relationship. Children typically wish to have a relationship with both parents, and, in general, involvement between the noncustodial parent and child is beneficial, particularly for boys and noncustodial fathers (Hetherington, Hagan, & Anderson, 1989). The benefits to be derived from involvement with the noncustodial parent, however, are attenuated by the degree to which the co-parental relationship is conflictual. Children show fewer social and emotional problems when divorced parents control their anger and cooperate with one another. Perhaps not surprisingly, conflict between divorced parents predicts a gradual loss of involvement by the noncustodial parent, especially after the noncustodial parent remarries. Noncustodial mothers are more likely to remain in frequent contact with children than noncustodial fathers (Furstenberg, 1988).

Socioeconomic status is frequently more strongly associated with adverse consequences for children's development in single-parent homes than is parent absence. As noted earlier, single-parent homes are often characterized by financial strain. Furthermore, there is evidence that although maternal employment enhances the adjustment and independence of girls in single-parent homes, it may have deleterious effects on sons, particularly in stressful life situations (Hetherington, Hagan, & Anderson, 1989).

Given the financial and physical demands characteristic of the single-parent family life, social support can be critical to the success of children. Authoritative schools and daycare centers have been found to offset negative effects of family transitions (Hetherington, Cox, & Cox, 1982; Guidabaldi, Cleminshaw, Peery, & McGloughlin, 1983; Rutter, 1983).

Relatives also offer assistance with finances, childcare, and household tasks. Research has found that black children adjust better when residing with a grandmother and mother than with a single mother, and Caucasian boys adjust better when they have an involved grandfather (Hetherington, Hagan, & Anderson, 1989). Additionally, there is some evidence that siblings, particularly female siblings, may buffer the effects of unresponsive parents in single-parent homes (Hetherington, Hagan, & Anderson, 1989). However, as noted earlier, social support networks can create stress as well as support for single parents and their children.

In summary, children in single-parent homes are least likely to experience adverse effects if (1) they are female; (2) their custodial parent is confident, mentally healthy, educated, and authoritative; (3) the family is economically secure and resides in a community with resources oriented to the well-being of children; and (4) relationships between the single custodial parent and other family system members, including the noncustodial parent, are cooperative and nonconflictual.

Family Tasks

The essential family tasks that must be completed by single-parent families follow logically from the previous discussion of factors and mediators of children's adjustment in single-parent homes. These tasks may also serve to guide intervention with single parents and their children. Single-parent family tasks include the establishment of the following: (1) economic stability; (2) authoritative parenting; (3) adequate support for the custodial single parent such that optimal parenting can be established and maintained; (4) healthy and

cooperative relationships with extrafamilial members, including (in postdivorce) the noncustodial parent and his or her family; and (5) provision of supplemental support for the growth and development of children if the single-parent extended family or social network system is unable to provide adequate support.

Consistent with the "undermanned" nature of the single-parent family system, *support* is the key component of many of the family tasks. For the school psychologist intervening with single-parent families, support is best construed broadly with a view to all the possible sources of support for the child. Supplemental support of the child, for example, may include school and teacher selection, taking advantage of free lunch programs, enrollment in extracurricular activities, and developing a volunteer car pool such that children of employed single parents can engage in extracurricular activities. It is important to bear in mind, however, the research findings of Hetherington, Hagan, and Anderson (1989) regarding the inability of single parents to benefit from social support when they were most in need of it. Therefore, the critical groundwork for single-parent social support is empowerment of the single parent. In summary, assessment and intervention with the single-parent family should focus on the adequacy of support across the ecological niches of the child and the capacity of the single parent to create or utilize social support.

STEPFAMILY HOMES

Definitional Issues

The identity of stepfamilies is noteworthy for its variation and complexity. As with single-parent homes, the adjustment of children to stepfamilies will be characterized more by diversity than similarity. A stepfamily can be defined as one that is created by the marriage or committed partnership of two adults, one or both of whom have children (Crohn, Sager, Brown, Rodstein, & Walker, 1982).

Many varieties of stepfamilies exist, each with unique adjustment demands. Katz and Stein (1983) identify four types based upon marital patterns:

> Type 1: A previously married woman with children marries a man with no children
>
> Type 2: A previously married man with children marries a woman with no children
>
> Type 3: A remarriage where both spouses have children from previous marriages
>
> Type 4: A single-parent with children whose spouse remarries.

The unique family adjustment demands of each stepfamily type have been outlined in Carlson (1985).

In a study of the "linked family systems" most commonly experienced by children, Jacobson (1987) identified the following stepfamily types:

> Type 1: Child lives with a single mother and visits a remarried father
>
> Type 2: Child lives with a remarried mother and visits a remarried father
>
> Type 3: Child lives with a remarried mother and visits a single father
>
> Type 4: Child lives with a single father and visits a remarried mother.

Although children could also live with a remarried father and visit their single or remarried mother, this stepfamily type was quite uncommon.

In summary, the diversity of stepfamilies attenuates the clarity with which their effects on children can be ascertained.

System Properties and Adaptations

Stepfamily systems are notable for the complexity of family members' roles, for the necessity of communication links across households, and for the inclusion in households of members with varying degrees of emotional attachment. Regarding roles, stepfamilies can be considered "overmanned" family systems in that there may be two or more family members who are engaged in similar family roles (e.g., father, mother, sister, financial provider, social director). Although one might expect that this supplement of resources is enviable, given the undermanned condition of the single-parent home, the placement of multiple persons in similar roles appears to create considerable disequilibrium and distress in stepfamilies (Visher & Visher, 1988).

For children, stepparenting appears to fuel loyalty conflicts in which obedience to the stepparent is not possible because it would evidence disloyalty to the biological parent. For adults, the social and universal expectations associated with the family roles of mother and father appear to fuel pressure for stepparent involvement in child rearing equivalent to that expected of a natural parent and dissatisfaction when this expected parenting roles is not fulfilled.

The role difficulties of stepfamilies appear to stem, in part, from the lack of clearly defined and distinct social roles for stepparents, but also the critical role of attachment in family relationships. Stepfamilies are distinct from intact families in that the attachments or intense emotional bonds among family members are not uniform. In general within stepfamilies, the adults establish an attached, intimate relationship, which results in marriage and a reasonably strong marital subsystem;

however, few stepparents "court" their stepchildren with the same duration or intensity such that an attached parent-child relationship emerges. Furthermore, one might argue, given the biological origins of parent-child attachment, that stepparent-stepchild bonds can seldom be equivalent with biological bonds regardless of the adequacy of the stepparent-stepchild relationship.

Attachment theory, then, helps us understand the emotional difficulty stepparents and stepchildren can face in remarriage when they are asked to behave "as if" they were attached to one another and to their stepsiblings. Both research and clinical experience with stepfamilies finds that adjustment is enhanced by the *gradual* development of an attached stepparent-stepchild relationship and the acceptance by all family members of the differentiated roles that parents must play in child rearing as a result of differing emotional attachments (Hetherington, 1987; Visher & Visher, 1988).

In addition to a lack of clearly defined roles and differentiated emotional bonds, stepfamilies are distinguished by the necessity of frequent and continuous coordination of the schedules, rules, and expectations of multiple households. This characteristic of the stepfamily system demands a high level of interaction within and between households, often made more difficult by the emotional injury that frequently accompanies divorce and remarriage. Participation in multiple households also demands that each family system provide mechanisms, both emotional and physical, for the frequent absence and addition of family members. This aspect of stepfamilies underlies the "linked" family system view of Jacobson (1987), in which the child, as a member of two households, often serves as the major communication link, both overt and covert, between the systems. This can be expected to be a significant source of stress to the child, depending on the quality of the adult relationships within and across homes.

In summary, stepfamily systems are characterized by a complexity of roles and relationships across multiple households that vary in emotional attachment. Optimal stepfamily functioning depends on establishing clear relationship roles, rules, and boundaries. Furthermore, relationship roles are most likely to be successful if they conform with the level of emotional bonding between family members. This requires consistent and clear communication within and across households, a behavioral skill that may be difficult in the face of emotional injury. Stepfamilies further demand tremendous patience, faith, and commitment on the part of the adults, and particularly stepparents, that the emotional bonds and attachments that ease parenting stress will be forthcoming, given consistently warm and respectful parenting, albeit over a considerable period of time.

Child Outcomes and Mediating Variables

Research studies on the child outcomes associated with rearing in a stepfamily have produced inconsistent findings when children in stepfamilies are compared with children in intact homes. In his review of the research, Bray (1988) cites many studies that find children in stepfamilies to be less well adjusted, manifest more anxiety and withdrawal, exhibit more behavior problems, and have lower self-esteem than children from nondisrupted homes. In contrast, many research studies find no differences, differences only in clinical samples, or differences only in early remarriage (Ganong & Coleman, 1987). The most recent research, however, suggests a complex picture pointing to consistent sex differences in the behavioral outcomes and family relationship patterns of step- versus intact families, and in stepfather versus stepmother families (see Hethering-ton & Aratesh, 1988; Pasley & Ihinger-Tallman, 1987).

Multiple studies have found that girls, particularly between the ages of 9 to 12, exhibit difficulties following remar-riage in stepfather families, that were not evident when residing with single-parent mothers. Studies cited in Bray (1988) found girls in stepfather homes to have more problematic family and peer rela-tionships, to be more angry with their mothers, to exhibit more behavior prob-lems, and to perceive greater life stress and anxiety when compared with boys in step-father families, girls in intact homes, or girls in single-parent homes. The self-reported life stress of girls in stepfather homes, not surprisingly, was related to their internalizing and externalizing prob-lems, as well as to lowered school perform-ance (Bray, 1988).

In the most comprehensive investiga-tion of stepfamily processes to date, Hetherington (1987, 1989) found that following remarriage, both mother-daughter and stepfather-stepdaughter conflict and hostility is high. Stepdaugh-ters exhibit more demandingness, hostil-ity, coercion, and less warmth toward both parents than girls in single or intact homes. Furthermore, whereas mother-daughter hostility was found to ease over a two-year family transition period, stepfather-stepdaughter hostility remained high. Neither a positive marital relationship or positive behavior on the part of the step-father toward stepdaughters eased the conflictual stepfather-stepdaughter rela-tionship.

Thus, over the course of the remar-riage, stepfathers, who have already been found to be considerably less involved in parenting than biological fathers in intact homes (Furstenburg, 1988), were found to increase dramatically their disengagement from stepdaughters (Hetherington, 1987). Research has not found that noncustodial father involvement either positively or negatively affects girls' adjustment to re-marriage (Furstenburg, 1988).

Although stepfather homes appear more distressing for girls than boys, this does not suggest that remarriage is not an adjustment for both sexes. Compared with intact families, both boys and girls are re-ported to have more developmental prob-lems (Zill, 1988). Hetherington found that both preadolescent boys and girls exhib-ited higher rates of behavior and learning problems following remarriage; however, boys, but not girls, demonstrate improved adjustment over a two-year period (Heth-erington, Hagan, & Anderson, 1989). Fur-thermore, multiple studies have reported the long-term beneficial impact of step-father homes on boys, including improved social competence, intellectual perform-ance, and behavioral control (Bray, 1988).

Although the stepfather family sys-tem appears most difficult for girls, the stepmother family structure poses chal-lenges to both girls and boys, particularly in middle childhood. In a national survey, Zill (1988) found a higher incidence of be-havior and learning problems among chil-dren in stepmother homes when com-pared with intact homes as well with mother-headed and father-headed single-parent homes. Furthermore, contact with the biological mother in stepmother fami-lies was related to an increase in adjust-ment problems for children and greater conflict with stepmothers (Brand, Cling-empeel, & Bowen-Woodward, 1988; Zill, 1988).

How is one to interpret the complex gender-related child outcomes associated with stepfamilies? Bray (1988) and Heth-erington (1989) note that the differences in outcomes between boys and girls in stepfamilies appear to be related to the different processes that characterize the development of males and females. Cho-dorow (1978) has demonstrated that because girls do not need to pull away from their primary love object, the mother, their self is experienced primarily in relation to others. In contrast, because boys must pull away from their primary love object, the mother, in order to identify as a male, their self is experienced primarily in relation to achievement in arenas other than relationships.

Applied to the gender-related adjustment patterns of children in single-parent and remarried families, it would appear that boys and single-parent mothers are always at risk for developing a "too close" relationship, which compromises the self-development of the boy. This anxiety may trigger the acting-out behavior of sons. The entrance of a stepfather diffuses the anxiety of relational closeness to the mother. Boys, then, appear able to benefit from the increased emotional support and authority available in the stepfather home and to fare best in stepfather families characterized by emotional bonding, cohesion, and an involved stepfather (Bray, 1988).

In contrast, girls in single-parent mother-headed homes usually develop a close emotional bond with their mothers. Furthermore, given the lack of adverse consequences of single parenting on girls, it appears that mother-daughter closeness supports the development of daughters. For example, 85 percent of adult women report that their mother is a central source of emotional and logistical support (Josselson, 1987). Girls, in contrast with boys, appear to "lose a good thing" in remarriage, with the emotional support they received from the mother now "shared" with a stepfather. Furthermore, girls appear to be more sensitive to relational moods and changes than do boys (Fohl & Montemayor, 1989). Girls, then, have been found to adjust better in stepfather homes that are characterized by less cohesion.

One mediator of gender-related differential child outcomes associated with remarriage is developmental status (Hetherington, Hagan, & Anderson, 1989).

Younger children appear most able to form attachments with a stepparent, and thus are most likely to improve in adjustment over time with positive stepparenting. The impact of remarriage on older adolescents is inconclusive. Although the risk of sexual abuse is higher for stepfathers and stepdaughters when remarriage occurs in late childhood or adolescence, in general, older adolescents may find the entry of a stepparent to be less difficult, as their developmental focus is already shifting away from the family.

Early adolescents, particularly girls, appear to be at the greatest risk in remarriage. The unique developmental demands of this age with puberty, autonomy thrusts yet necessary reliance upon family resources and rules, intense emotional relationships with friends, adjustments to a larger social system (e.g., middle school), intense self-consciousness with the onset of formal cognitive operations, the accompanying lowered self-confidence, and the intensification of the identity-development process appear to increase the vulnerability, particularly of girls, to the introduction of a family member into the affective family system. In addition, the affectional displays between remarried partners may be particularly difficult for girls to handle during puberty when their own sexual urges are emerging.

In summary, children in stepparent homes are least likely to experience adverse effects if (1) they are male; (2) they are younger school-age or older adolescents; (3) they reside in stepfather homes, (4) in which the stepparent does not attempt to become a parent too quickly; and (5) the remarried biological parent does not expect the stepparent-stepchild relationship to replicate a biological parent-child relationship.

Family Tasks

The primary tasks for stepfamilies to accomplish, based on the previous discussion, include: (1) clarification of the roles, rules, and relationship boundaries both within and across families; (2) developing attachments; (3) accepting a process view of relationships; and (4) balancing cohesion and autonomy.

With the complexity of stepfamily relationships, clarity regarding the roles in the linked family system is critical to success. For example, are stepparents responsible for establishing and monitoring rules? Are they responsible for the emotional well-being and cognitive development of their stepchildren? To what degree are they financially responsible for stepchildren? These responsibilities have legal answers; however, legal decisions provide only the framework for parental roles, not the solutions to day-to-day decision making.

Given the tremendous variability that can be expected in the values, attitudes, motivation, and competence of stepparents, communication among family members, particularly the adults, regarding their short- and long-term expectations, for stepparent child rearing involvement becomes critical to the success of children. Based on the reports of stepfamily members, the process of establishing and clarifying roles is difficult, even in the best of circumstances. Stepfamilies appear to be at greatest risk when role expectations vis-à-vis role enactment within the family are quite discrepant, or when there is competitive role enactment across families.

A second task of stepfamilies is the formation of attachment bonds between family members. Critical to the formation of attachment is responsive parenting; however, responsive parenting will not create quick attachments. Since attachment reflects an intense emotional bond, this must be viewed as a process that occurs over time. Thus, a third related stepfamily task is the adoption by family members of a process view of relationships. A process view of relationships is one that recognizes that, although attraction may be im-

mediate, trust, shared interests, and intimacy, develop slowly.

The development of attachment bonds and the adoption of a process view of relationships may be particularly difficult for postdivorce stepfamily members who have previously experienced the anxiety and grief associated with breaches of trust and attachment. Stepfamilies are most likely to experience difficulty when adults expect the rapid formation of attachment bonds between stepparents and stepchildren or between stepsiblings. The development of attachment bonds is not only related to the characteristics of family members and their histories but also related to developmental stage and sex. The formation of close attachments is most feasible for stepfamilies who reconstitute with young children, and between boys and stepfathers. Close emotional attachments may be inappropriate to expect in families with adolescents.

In summary, the overlapping tasks of family formation—a task that demands cohesion, with individual development, a task that demands autonomy, particularly in adolescence—highlights the complexity of processes facing stepfamilies. Furthermore, the necessity of children maintaining associations and affectional loyalties with multiple households attenuates family cohesiveness. Thus, a final task for stepfamilies is the balancing of cohesive family relationships with family member autonomy and mobility. Stepfamilies are most likely to fail at this task when their social comparison norm is the cohesiveness characteristic of harmonious intact families.

ASSESSMENT AND INTERVENTION

School psychologists have many options from which to choose in working with children in single-parent and stepfamily homes. The choice of intervention will depend on the nature and severity of the presenting problem, the accessibility and motivation of persons involved with the child, and the resources available to the school psychologist. It is recommended that school psychologists evaluate the needs of single-parent and stepfamily children and their family members along the basic theoretical dimensions discussed: system organization, family developmental life-cycle stage, quality of parent-child relationship and affective bonding, adequacy of social support, and degree of stress and coping response. It is expected that all assessments would include a formal or informal evaluation of the competencies and vulnerabilities of the child.

There are multiple strategies and methods for gathering information on the noted theoretical dimensions. Guidelines for key family variables, methods, and intervention implications appear in Table 1. Key references for each of the theoretical variables appear in the table. For additional discussion of family assessment methods, the interested reader is referred to Carlson (1987b) and Grotevant and Carlson (1989). Interview guidelines, specifically for single-parent and stepparent

TABLE 1 Key dimensions in assessment and intervention with single-parent and stepparent families

Dimension	Key Variables	Methods	Interventions
System Organization (Minuchin, 1974)	Family Roles Family Rules Clarity of Above	Family Observation Parent/Family Interview Kinetic Family Drawing Family Apperception Test	Family Therapy
Family Life-Cycle Stage (Carter & McGoldrick, 1980, 1989; McGoldrick & Gerson, 1985)	Family Developmental Stage(s)	Genogram Parent/Family Interview	Parent Consultation Parent Education
Parent-Child Relationship (Steinhauer, 1983; Grotevant & Carlson, 1989; Sameroff & Emde, 1989)	Parenting Style Parenting Knowledge Quality of Attachment	Parent & Child Interview Self-Report Measures Kinetic Family Drawing Family Apperception Test	Parent Consultation Parent Education Family Therapy Supplemental Child Support
Family-Social Support (Hartmann, 1979)	Sources of Support Sources of Strain	Ecomap Parent/Family Interview	Parent Consultation Supplemental Support Parent & Child
Coping Style (Epstein, Schlesinger, & Dryden, 1988; Garmezy & Rutter, 1983; McCubbin & Figley, 1983)	Coping Style Cognitions	Parent/Family/Child Interview Self-Report Measures	Parent, Child, or Family Cognitive-Behavioral Therapy

families, are available in Carlson (1985) and Visher and Visher (1988). It is strongly recommended in completing an assessment of single-parent or stepparent children that mental health professionals interview the parental figures as well as the individual child, and preferably conduct a whole family interview. An excellent beginner's guideline for completing a family interview can be found in Weber, McKeever, and McDaniel (1985).

Optimally, choice of intervention should be made based on evaluation data that indicate successful outcomes have been previously obtained with the treatment; however, only a limited number of intervention programs have published evaluation data, and no studies were located that compared the effectiveness of different intervention programs. Moreover, there are a limited number of intervention programs specifically targeted to children in single-parent and/or stepfamily homes. Rather, the focus of most interventions is children's adjustment to divorce. A recent review of these programs found that prevention programs implemented early in the adjustment process demonstrated the most promise, particularly school-based, child-focused interventions and interventions to promote competence in parenting skills (Stolberg & Walsh, 1988).

Given that the major antecedent of single-parent and stepparent homes is divorce, the following discussion of intervention approaches will overlap with the divorce adjustment literature. Although the content of intervention should differ, the process of transition from one family form to another is likely to demand a similar reorganization of behavioral patterns, affective bonds, and cognitions on the part of the child. For greater discussion of divorce-related interventions, however, the interested reader is referred to Carlson (1987a), Kelly and Wallerstein (1977), Knoff (1987), Pedro-Carroll and Cowen

(1985), Stolberg and Garrison (1981), Stolberg and Walsh (1988), and Wallerstein and Kelly (1983). Although an ecological approach to intervention is considered optimal, in which the multiple niches of the child are concurrently targeted, for purposes of clarity, the following discussion is organized by the primary focus of intervention: child, parent, or school.

Child-Centered Intervention

The goal of child-centered interventions is to increase the individual competence of the child such that the child is maximally able to utilize available resources and maintain a realistic sense of self-efficacy. Child-centered interventions for children in single-parent and stepparent families may either be directly or indirectly targeted to the child's coping. Directly targeted interventions specifically address the problems faced by the child in each family constellation and would include such interventions as school-based individual or group therapy or bibliotherapy. In contrast, an indirect child-centered intervention would be defined as one that builds competencies in the child that are known to enhance adaptation to single-parent and stepfamily situations but are not directly an outcome of these family forms. These would include, for example, social skills groups, academic tutoring, assignment to particular classes and teachers, and involvement in supplementary activities.

Empirical studies find that school-based groups are beneficial for children of divorce (Cantor, 1977; Stolberg & Walsh, 1988; Wilkinson & Bleck, 1977). Two intervention projects, each designed to include opportunities for children to express their feelings as well as the teaching of social problem-solving skills, have been conducted and carefully evaluated. Results found improvements in anxiety on Pedro-Carrolls' Children of Divorce Project (Pedro-Carroll & Cowen, 1985; Pedro-

Carroll, Cowen, Hightower, & Guare, 1986) and increased self-esteem and social skills in Stolberg's Divorce Adjustment Project (Stolberg & Anker, 1983; Stolberg & Garrison, 1981). Although these school-based group interventions were not specifically designed for the transition to remarriage or for life in a stable single-parent family, the format and content are expected to be applicable with adaptation. Helpful audiovisual resources are identified by Kimmons and Gaston (1986) and Hausslein (1983).

The technique of bibliotherapy is another directly related child-centered intervention that may be helpful to children coping with family transitions. Bibliotherapy may be used by the school psychologist as an adjunct to individual child psychotherapy, an assignment in school-based groups, or in teacher consultation and curriculum development. Useful books for school-aged children are *My Other-Mother, My Other-Father* (Sobel, 1979) and *Two homes for Lynn* (Noble, 1979). Middle-school children would be able to read on their own *The Boys and Girls Book about One-Parent Families* (Gardner, 1978) and *The Boys and Girls Book about Stepfamilies* (Gardner, 1982). In addition, a list of relevant fiction references for adolescents in stepfamilies has been compiled by Coleman, Marshall, and Ganong (1986).

Excellent guides for additional books include *The Bookfinder: A Guide to Children's Literature about the Needs and Problems of Youth Aged 2–15* (Dreyer, 1977), *Children and Divorce* (Hausslein, 1983), the "Reading List for Children" in *Old Loyalties, New Ties: Therapeutic Strategies with Stepfamilies* (Visher & Visher, 1988, pp. 253–254), and the *Educational Materials Program* (Stepfamily Association of America). Bibliotherapy is expected to be well suited for the school setting as it requires minimal organizational support and is compatible with school educational/reading goals. No empirical support, however, for the

effectiveness of bibliotherapy was identified.

In addition to group interventions and bibliotherapy, individual child psychotherapy is always an intervention option available to school psychologists. Wallerstein and Kelly (1980, 1983), and Kelly and Wallerstein (1977) have developed a model of brief interventions for children following divorce. Robson (1982) provides a developmental model of treatment for children in remarriage. Given the time constraints of many school psychologists, it is anticipated that the more cost-beneficial school-based group approach may be preferable. School-based groups have the additional benefit of building supportive peer relationships that may be attenuated by the stress of family transitions. On the other hand, in cases of acute distress, individual psychotherapy will most likely be the intervention of choice.

In addition to child-centered interventions, which directly address difficulties associated with single-parent and stepparent homes, children in these family situations can also be expected to benefit from interventions that enhance their overall competence. For example, Nastasi and Guidabaldi (1987) found that good social-coping skills (self-efficacy, social problem solving, and social interaction) predicted academic success, popularity, conduct, and physical health in both postdivorce and control groups of school-aged children, and predicted fewer family transition problems in postdivorce children. These results suggest that an intervention that enhances social coping and social skills could be beneficial for children who are currently or have previously experienced a family transition.

It is expected that socially competent children will be more able to access social support from peers and teachers during times of family stress than children at risk. In addition to interventions that strengthen the competence of children in single-parent and stepfamily homes, attention to adequate models and opportunities for sex-role development would appear to be appropriate, especially for boys in single-parent homes (see Carlson, 1987). In summary, any intervention that enhances children's experience of success in school is likely to be beneficial to children who demonstrate adjustment difficulties related to the multiple transitions of separation, divorce, single parenting, and remarriage.

Parent-Centered Intervention

The quality of the parent-child relationship is critical for children's adjustment in both single-parent and stepparent homes. Although it is not within the mandate of the school to provide treatment to parents, schools, unencumbered by the stigma and financial burden attached to seeking therapy, have the opportunity to provide critical preventive and indirect mental health services via education, support, and consultation with parents.

Group approaches with single parents and stepparents are popular. Support groups for single parents have been described by Johnson (1986), Stolberg (Garrison, Stolberg, Carpenter, Mallonee, & Atrim, no date; Stolberg & Anker, 1983; Stolberg & Garrison, 1981), and Warren (Warren et al., 1984).

The program of Warren and associates (Warren et al., 1984) is a structured psychoeducational and support group for single parents and their children. Evaluation data indicated the program to be effective in changing parent-child interaction, with the strongest effects associated with the Family Education Component in which children and parents participated. The single parent program of Stolberg and associates (Stolberg & Walsh, 1988) contrasts with that of Warren in that the focus is on the development of participants as individuals as well as parenting skills.

Evaluation data found that adult adjustment was enhanced with the program, but improved adult adjustment did not generalize to the parent-child relationship or to children's adjustment. Thus, interventions appear to be most effective when they directly target the assessed problem (e.g., parenting skill, parent dysphoria).

In addition to the above mentioned postdivorce single-parent programs, which have been carefully empirically evaluated, the popular STEP (Systematic Training for Effective Parenting) program has been recently extended to address the concerns of single parents and stepfamily parents (Dinkmeyer, McKay, & McKay, 1987). Additional stepparent educational programs are noted by Visher & Visher (1988): *Learning to Step Together: A Course for Stepfamily Adults* (Currier, 1982); *Strengthening Stepfamilies* (Albert & Einstein, 1986); and *Banana Splits: A School-Based Program for the Survivors of the Divorce Wars* (McGonagle, 1985).

Although programs specifically designed to address the needs of single-parent and stepparents are optimal, parent education programs, in general, which have been evaluated to be effective, are also likely to be helpful (see Fine, 1980, for a review of programs). In particular, single mothers with sons, single fathers with daughters, stepfathers with daughters, stepmothers with sons, and/or stepparents who have not previously had children are most likely to benefit from education regarding parenting and child development.

Parent consultation offers a second intervention method for use with single parents and remarried parents. School personnel are frequently called on to engage parents in discussion of their children's progress, particularly when learning or behavioral difficulties are evident. Parent consultation provides an opportunity for assessment of parent competence, support regarding the challenging parent role, education about family and child processes associated with family transitions, and a reframing of the parents' cognitive beliefs and expectancies about the child, family, and school.

Parents, like children, are likely to benefit from books on single parenting and stepparenting. Excellent book and resource lists for parents have been provided by Greenwood (1983), Kimmons and Gaston (1986), and Visher and Visher, (1988). In addition, two national organizations compile a wealth of information for single parents and stepparents: Parents Without Partners and Stepfamily Association of America.

Most importantly, parent consultation provides the opportunity for the establishment of communication between the "linked" family and school systems of the child. As noted by Bronfenbrenner (1979), children's developing competence can be expected to be enhanced by involvement in multiple ecological niches when these environments have congruent expectations, mutual regard, and supportive communication.

School-Centered Intervention

Research studies find that schools make a difference in the adjustment of children to family instability (e.g., Guidabaldi, Peery, & Cleminshaw, 1984; Rutter, 1983). Specifically, schools that have high expectations, opportunities for success, structure, and supportive teacher-student relationships have been found to influence positively the development of children despite family stress. Thus, schools that are authoritative (that is, characterized by high expectations as well as responsiveness to individual children) provide the most supportive environments for children under family stress.

One direction of school-centered intervention, then, is the provision by school psychologists of "goodness-of-fit" between child characteristics and school environment. Rather than the more traditional random placement of children with teachers in classrooms, or the more stressful reshuffling of a child following a classroom failure, it is recommended that children who are more vulnerable due to family circumstances be thoughtfully placed in classroom environments that will provide structure and support.

Research also indicates that school personnel (as well as the population at large) hold negatively biased perceptions of children in single-parent homes (Santrock & Tracy, 1978) and children in stepfamilies (Coleman & Ganong, 1987), when compared with children in intact families. In these studies, boys were more negatively perceived than girls, although both differed significantly from children in intact homes. In addition, single parents and stepparents are viewed more negatively than their never-divorced counterparts (Coleman & Ganong, 1987).

What are the possible effects of these negative stereotypes? Negative stereotypes predispose persons to evaluate the stereotyped group less favorably no matter what behavior is observed (i.e., the "cognitive confirmation" effect) (Darley & Fazio, 1980), and to influence interaction in such a way that expected behaviors are elicited (i.e., the "behavioral confirmation" effect) (Snyder, Tanke, & Berscheid, 1977). Although these cognitive biases have not been investigated in school settings, the consistency of findings elsewhere suggests that the negative stereotyping of students from single-parent and stepfamily homes may be a concern.

Cognitive distortions can be altered with the presentation of didactic materials (e.g., information handouts, inservice training) and with collaborative problem-solving consultation in which consultees discover the inaccuracies of their thought processes (Epstein, Schlesinger, & Dryden,

1988). The traditional school psychology roles of teacher consultation and inservice training, then, provide fertile ground for sensitizing school personnel to the possible influence of negative stereotypes with children from nonnuclear families.

In summary, interventions targeted to the child, parent or family, and school are all likely to be appropriate for children from single-parent and stepfamily homes. As noted in Table 1, the target of intervention should reflect the differential assessment of the source of difficulties in the family or child system.

SUMMARY

Single-parent and stepparent homes continue to be the family form in which the majority of children in the United States will reside. These family forms place unique adjustment demands on children, parents, and schools. Understanding the dynamics of single-parent and stepparent families, and remaining conscientious about the distinctiveness, but not lesser quality, of these family types is the first step to effective school psychological practice with the children residing in these homes.

Single-parent and stepparent families are more characterized by diversity than similarity. However, commonalities exist both across and within these family types. Both single-parent and stepparent families are characterized by transformations of family roles and affective relationships, by emotional loss, and by an intensification of the biological or custodial parent-child relationship. Single-parent and stepparent families may differ in degree of family stress associated with lowered income and parent overload.

Children's adjustment to life in single-parent and stepparent families is highly variable and appears dependent on multiple variables including age, sex, and temperament of the child; the quality of the parent-child relationship; the quality of the parent-parent relationship; and the quality of extrafamilial social support (including school environment). In particular, boys residing in single-parent, mother-headed homes and early adolescent girls whose single-parent remarries appear to be at greatest risk. It is important to note, however, that the vast majority of children in single-parent and stepparent families do not evidence problems requiring intervention.

When children evidence adjustment difficulties associated with single parenting or stepparenting, school personnel have many choices available to them in assessment and intervention. A multidimensional approach to assessment has been recommended in which the key variables of family system organization, family life-cycle stage, quality of parent-child attachment, adequacy of child and family social support, and adaptive quality of parent and child coping responses are evaluated and linked with appropriate interventions.

References

Ahrons, C. R., & Wallisch, L. (1987). Parenting in the binuclear family: Relationships between biological and stepparents. In E. M. Hetherington & J. D. Aratesh (Eds.), *Impact of divorce, single parenting, and stepparenting on children* (pp. 225–256). Hillsdale, NJ: Erlbaum.

Albert, L., & Einstein, E. (1978). *Strengthening stepfamilies.* Circle Pines, MN: American Guidance Service.

Allen, D. A., Affleck, G., McGrade, B. J., & McQueeney, M. (1984). Effects of single-parent status on mothers and their high-risk infants. *Infant Behavior and Development, 7,* 347–359.

Ambert, A. (1985). Custodial parents: Review and a longitudinal study. In B. Schlesinger (Ed.), *The one-parent family in the 1980's: Perspectives and annotated bibliography, 1978–1984* (pp. 13–34). Toronto: University of Toronto.

Anderson, J. Z., & White, G. D. (1986).

An empirical investigation of interaction and relationship patterns in functional and dysfunctional nuclear families and stepfamilies. *Family Process, 25,* 407–422.

Beal, E. W. (1980). Separation, divorce, and single-parent families. In E. A. Carter and M. McGoldrick (Eds.), *The family life cycle: A framework for family therapy* (pp. 241–264). New York: Gardner.

Biller, H. B. (1982). Father absence, divorce and personality development. In M. E. Lamb (Ed.), *The role of the father in child development* (2nd ed.) (pp. 489–552). New York: Wiley.

Bowlby, J. (1988). *A secure base: Parent-child attachment and healthy human development.* New York: Basic.

Brand, E., Clingempeel, W. G., & Bowen-Woodward, K. (1988). Family relationships and children's psychological adjustment in stepmother and stepfather families. *Impact of divorce, single parenting, and stepparenting on children* (pp. 299–324). Hillsdale, NJ: Erlbaum.

Brassard, M. R. (1986). Family assessment approaches and procedures. In H. Knoff (Ed.), *The assessment of child and adolescent personality* (pp. 399–449). New York: Guilford.

Bray, J. H. (1988). Children's development during early remarriage. In E. M. Hetherington & J. D. Aratesh (Eds.), *Impact of divorce, single parenting, and stepparenting on children* (pp. 279–298). Hillsdale, NJ: Erlbaum.

Bretherton, I., & Waters, E. (Eds.) (1985). Growing points of attachment theory and research. *Monographs of the Society for Research in Child Development, 50* (1–2), Serial No. 209.

Bronfenbrenner, U. (1979). *The ecology of human development.* Cambridge, MA: Harvard University Press.

Burns, R. C., & Kaufman, S. H. (1970). *Kinetic Family Drawing (K-F-D): An introduction to understanding children through kinetic drawing.* New York: Brunner/Mazel.

Camara, K. A., & Resnick, G. (1988). Interparental conflict and cooperation: Factors moderating children's post-divorce adjustment. *Impact of divorce, single parenting, and stepparenting on children* (pp. 169–196). Hillsdale, NJ: Erlbaum.

Cantor, D. W. (1977). School-based groups for children of divorce. *Journal of Divorce, 1,* 183–187.

Carlson, C. I. (1985). Best practices in working with single-parent and step-families. In A. Thomas & J. Grimes (Eds.), *Best practices in school psychology* (pp. 43–60). Kent, OH: The National Association of School Psychologists.

Carlson, C. I. (1987a). Single-parent homes. In A. Thomas & J. Grimes (Eds.), *Children's needs: Psychological perspectives* (pp. 560–571). Washington, DC: The National Association of School Psychologists.

Carlson, C. I. (1987b). Family assessment and intervention in the school setting. In T. R. Kratochwill (Ed.), *Advances in school psychology* (Vol. VII). (pp. 81–129). Hillsdale, NJ: Erlbaum.

Carter, E. A., & McGoldrick, M. (1980). *The family life cycle: A framework for family therapy.* New York: Gardner

Carter, E. A., & McGoldrick, M. (1989). *The changing family life cycle* (2nd ed.). Boston: Allyn and Bacon.

Chodorow, N. (1978). *The reproduction of mothering.* Berkeley: University of California Press.

Clingempeel, W. G., Brand, E., & Segal. (1987). A multi-level-multivariable-developmental perspective for future research on stepfamilies. In K. Pasley and M. Ihinger-Tallman (Eds.), *Remarriage and stepparenting: Current research and theory* (pp. 65–93). New York: Guilford.

Coleman, M., & Ganong, L. H. (1987). The cultural stereotyping of stepfamilies. In K. Pasley & M. Ihlinger-Tallman (Eds.), *Remarriage and stepparenting: Current research and theory* (pp. 19–41). New York: Guilford.

Coleman, M., Marshall, S. A., & Ganong, L. (1986). Beyond Cinderella: Relevant reading for young adolescents about stepfamilies. *Adolescence, 21,* 553–560.

Crohn, H., Sager, C. J., Brown, H., Rodstein, E., & Walker, L. (1982). A basis for understanding and treating the remarried family. In J. Hansen & L. Messinger (Eds.), *Therapy with remarried families.* Rockville, MD: Aspen.

Currier, C. (1982). *Learning to step together: A course for stepfamily adults.* Baltimore: Stepfamily Association of America.

Darley, J. M., & Fazio, R. H. (1980). Expectancy confirmation processes arising in the social interaction sequence. *American Psychologist, 35,* 867–881.

Dell, P., & Appelbaum, A. S. (1977). Trigenerational enmeshment: Unresolved ties of single-parents to family of origin. *American Journal of Orthopsychiatry, 47*(1), 52–59.

Dinkmeyer, D., McKay, G. D., & McKay, J. L. (1987). *New beginnings: Skills for single par-*

ents and stepfamily parents. Champaign, IL: Research Press.

Dreyer, S. S. (1977). *The bookfinder: A guide to children's literature about the needs and problems of youth aged 2–15.* Circle Pines, MN: American Guidance Service.

Egeland, B., & Farber, E. A. (1984). Infant-mother attachment: Factors related to its development and changes over time. *Child Development, 55,* 753–771.

Emery, R. E. (1988). *Marriage, divorce, and children's adjustment.* Newberry Park, CA: Sage.

Epstein, N., Schlesinger, S. E., & Dryden, W. (1988). *Cognitive-behavioral therapy with families.* New York: Brunner/Mazel.

Erikson, E. H. (1950). *Childhood and society.* New York: Norton.

Fine, M. J. (Ed.) (1980). *Handbook on parent education.* New York: Academic.

Fohl, E. M., & Montemayor, R. (1989). *The impact of conflict, maternal adjustment, and parenting skills on children's behavior after divorce.* Paper presented at the Fourth Annual Summer Family Research Institute, National Institute of Mental Health, Cape Cod, MA.

Forgatch, M. S., Patterson, G. R., & Skinner, M. L. (1988). A mediational model for the effect of divorce on antisocial behavior in boys. In E. M. Hetherington & J. D. Aratesh (Eds.), *Impact of divorce, single parenting, and stepparenting on children* (pp. 135–154). Hillsdale, NJ: Erlbaum.

Fulmer, R. (1983). A structural approach to unresolved mourning in single-parent family systems. *Journal of Marital and Family Therapy, 9,* 259–269.

Furstenberg, Jr., F. F. (1987). The new extended family: The experience of parents and children after remarriage. In K. Pasley & M. Ihlinger-Tallman (Eds.), *Remarriage and stepparenting: Current research and theory* (pp. 42–61). New York: Guilford.

Furstenberg, Jr., F. F. (1988). Child care after divorce and remarriage. In E. M. Hetherington & J. D. Aratesh (Eds.), *Impact of divorce, single parenting, and stepparenting on children* (pp. 245–262). Hillsdale, NJ: Erlbaum.

Ganong, L. H., & Coleman, M. (1987). Effects of parental remarriage on children: An updated comparison of theories, methods, and findings from clinical and empirical research. In E. M. Hetherington & J. D. Aratesh (Eds.), *Impact of divorce, single parenting, and stepparenting on children* (pp. 94–140). Hillsdale, NJ: Erlbaum.

Gardner, R. A. (1978). *The boys and girls book about one-parent families.* New York: Bantam.

Gardner, R. A. (1982). *The boys and girls book about stepfamilies.* New York: Bantam.

Garmezy, N., & Rutter, M. (Eds.) (1983). *Stress, coping, and development in children.* New York: McGraw-Hill.

Garrison, K. M., Stolberg, A. L., Carpenter, J. G., Mallonee, D. J., & Atrim, Z. D. (no date). *Single parent support group: Leader's manual.* (DHEW Publication No. 1 RO1MH34462–02).

Gladlow, N. W., & Ray, M. P. (1986). The impact of informal support systems on the well being of low income single parents. *Family Relations, 35,* 113–123.

Glenwick, D. S., & Mowrey, J. D. (1986). When parent becomes peer: Loss of intergenerational boundaries in single parent families. *Family Relations, 35,* 57–62.

Greenwood, P. D. (1983). Contemporary family and human development materials. *Family Relations, 32,* 149–152.

Greif, G. L. (1985). *Single fathers.* Lexington, MA: Lexington.

Grotevant, H. D., & Carlson, C. I. (1989). *Family assessment: A guide to methods and measures.* New York: Guilford.

Guidabaldi, J., Cleminshaw, H. K., Peery, J. D., & McGloughlin, C. S. (1983). The impact of parental divorce on children: Report of the nationwide NASP study. *School Psychology Review, 12,* 300–323.

Guidabaldi, J., Cleminshaw, H. K., Peery, J. D., Nastasi, B. K., & Lightel, J. (1986). The role of selected family environment factors in children's post-divorce adjustment. *Family Relations, 35,* 141–151.

Guidabaldi, J., Peery, J. D., & Cleminshaw, H. K. (1984). The legacy of parental divorce: A nationwide study of family status and selected mediating variables on children's academic and social competencies. In B. B. Lahey & A. E. Kazdin (Eds.), *Advances in clinical child psychology (Vol. 7)* (pp. 109–151). New York: Plenum.

Haley, J. (1987). *Problem-solving therapy.* San Francisco: Jossey-Bass.

Hanson, S. M. H. (1986). Healthy single parent families. *Family Relations, 35,* 125–132.

Hartmann, A. (1979). *Finding families: An ecological approach to family assessment in adoption.* Beverly Hills, CA: Sage.

Hausslein, E. B. (1983). *Children and di-*

vorce: An annotated bibliography and guide. New York: Gardner.

Hernandez, D. J. (1988). Demographic trends and the living arrangements of children. In E. M. Hetherington & J. D. Aratesh (Eds.), *Impact of divorce, single parenting, and stepparenting on children* (pp. 3–20). Hillsdale, NJ: Erlbaum.

Hetherington, E. M. (1972). Effects of paternal absence on personality development in adolescent daughters. *Developmental Psychology, 7*, 313–326.

Hetherington, E. M. (1984). Stress and coping in children and families. In A. Doyle, D. Gold, & D. S. Moskowitz (Eds.), *New directions for child development: No. 24. Children in families under stress* (pp. 7–34). San Francisco: Jossey-Bass.

Hetherington, E. M. (1987). Family relations six years after divorce. In K. Pasley & M. Ihlinger-Tallman (Eds.), *Remarriage and stepparenting: Current research and theory* (pp. 185–205). New York: Guilford.

Hetherington, E. M. (1989). Coping with family transitions: Winners, losers, and survivors. *Child Development, 60,* 114.

Hetherington, E. M., & Aratesh, J. D. (Eds.) (1988). *Impact of divorce, single parenting, and stepparenting on children.* Hillsdale, NJ: Erlbaum.

Hetherington, E. M., Cox, M., & Cox, R. (1982). Effects of divorce on parents and children. In M. Lamb (Ed.), *Nontraditional families: Parenting and child development.* Hillsdale, NJ: Erlbaum.

Hetherington, E. M., Hagan, M. S., & Anderson, E. R. (1989). Marital transitions: A child's perspective. *American Psychologist, 44*(2), 303–312.

Hill, R. (1986). Life cycle stages for types of single parent families. *Family Relations, 35,* 19–29.

Ihinger-Tallman, M., & Pasley, K. (1987). Divorce and remarriage in the American family: A historical review. In K. Pasley and M. Ihinger-Tallman (Eds.), *Remarriage and stepparenting: Current research and theory* (pp. 3–18). New York: Guilford.

Jacobson, D. S. (1987). Family type, visiting patterns, and children's behavior in the stepfamily: A linked family system. In K. Pasley & M. Ihlinger-Tallman (Eds.), *Remarriage and stepparenting: Current research and theory* (pp. 257–272). New York: Guilford.

Johnson, B. H. (1986). Single mothers

following separation and divorce: Making it on your own. *Family Relations, 35,* 189–197.

Josselson, R. (1987). *Finding herself: Pathways to identity development in women.* San Francisco: Jossey-Bass.

Julian III, A., Sotile, W. M., Henry, S. E., & Sotile, M. (1988). *Family Apperception Test.* Feedback Services, Charlotte, NC (Distributor).

Kanoy, K. W., Cunningham, J. L., White, P., & Adams, S. J. (1984). Is family structure that critical? Family relationships of divorced and married parents. *Journal of Divorce, 8*(2), 97–105.

Katz, L., & Stein, S. (1983). Treating stepfamilies. In B. Wolman & G. Streicker (Eds.), *Handbook of family and marital therapy.* New York: Plenum.

Kelly, J. B., & Wallerstein, J. (1977). Brief interventions with children in divorcing families. *American Journal of Orthopsychiatry, 47*(1), 23–39.

Kimmons, L., & Gaston, J. A. (1986). Single parenting: A filmography. *Family Relations, 35,* 205–211.

Knoff, H. M. (1987). Divorce. In A. Thomas & J. Grimes (Eds.), *Children's needs: Psychological perspectives* (pp. 173–181). Washington, DC: National Association of School Psychologists.

Laosa, L. M. (1988). Ethnicity and single parenting in the United States. In E. M. Hetherington & J. D. Aratesh (Eds.), *Impact of divorce, single parenting, and stepparenting on children* (pp. 23–52). Hillsdale, NJ: Erlbaum.

Lewis, W. (1986). Strategic interventions with children of single-parent families. *The School Counselor, 33,* 375–378.

Lindblad-Goldberg, M. (1987). The assessment of social networks in black, low-income single-parent families. In M. Lindblad-Goldberg (Ed.), *Clinical issues in single-parent households* (pp. 39–46). Rockville, MD: Aspen.

McCubbin, H. I., & Figley, C. R. (Eds.) (1983). *Stress and the family, Vol. 1: Coping with normative transitions.* New York: Brunner/Mazel.

McGoldrick, M., & Gerson, R. (1985). *Genograms in family assessment.* New York: Norton.

McGonagle, E. M. (1985). *Banana splits: A school-based program for the survivors of divorce wars.* Ballstron Spa Central Schools, Ballston Spa, NY 12020.

McLanahan, S. S. (1983). Family structure and stress: A longitudinal comparison of two-parent and female-headed families. *Journal of Marriage and the Family, 45*(2), 347–357.

McLanahan, S. S., Wedemeyer, N., & Adelberg, T. (1981). Network structure, social support, and psychological well-being in the single parent family. *Journal of Marriage and the Family, 10,* 601–612.

Minuchin, S. (1974). *Families and family therapy.* Cambridge, MA: Harvard University Press.

Nastasi, B. K., & Guidubaldi, J. (1987). *Coping skills as mediators of children's adjustment in divorced and intact families.* Paper presented at the biennial meeting of the Society for Research in Child Development, April, Baltimore, MD.

Noble, J. (1979). *Two homes for Lynn.* New York: Holt.

Norton, A. J., & Glick, P. C. (1986). One parent families: A social and economic profile. *Family Relations, 35,* 9–17.

Pasley, K., & Ihinger-Tallman, M. (Eds.) (1987). *Remarriage and stepparenting: Current research and theory.* New York: Guilford.

Patterson, G. R. (1982). *A social learning approach: Vol. 3. Coercive family process.* Eugene, OR: Castalia.

Patterson, G. R. (1986). The contribution of siblings to training for fighting: A microsocial analysis. In D. Olweus, J. Block, & M. Radke-Yarrow (Eds.), *Development of antisocial and prosocial behavior* (pp. 235–262). Orlando, FL: Academic Press.

Pedro-Carroll, J. L., & Cowen, E. L. (1985). The children of divorce intervention program: An investigation of the efficacy of a school-based prevention program. *Journal of Consulting and Clinical Psychology, 53,* 603–611.

Pedro-Carroll, J. L., Cowen, E. L., Hightower, A. D., & Guare, J. C. (1986). Preventive intervention with latency-aged children of divorce: A replication study. *American Journal of Community Psychology, 14,* 277–290.

Robson, B. (1982). A developmental approach to the treatment of children with divorcing parents. In J. Hansen & L. Messinger (Eds.), *Therapy with remarried families.* Rockville, MD: Aspen.

Rollins, B. C., & Galligan, R. (1978). The developing child and marital satisfaction in parents. In R. M. Lerner & G. B. Spanier (Eds.), *Child influences on marital and family interaction* (pp. 71–106). New York: Academic.

Rutter, M. (1979). Protective factors in children's responses to stress and disadvantage. In M. W. Kent and J. E. Rolf (Eds.), *Primary prevention of psychopathology. Vol. 3.* Hanover, NJ: University Press of New England.

Rutter, M. (1983). School effects on pupil progress: Research findings and policy implications. *Child Development, 54,* 1–29.

Sameroff, A. J., & Emde, R. N. (Eds.) (1989). *Relationship disturbances in early childhood.* New York: Basic Books.

Sanik, M. M., & Maudlin, T. (1986). Single versus two parent families: A comparison of mothers' time. *Family Relations, 35,* 53–56.

Santrock, J. W., & Sitterle, K. A. (1987). Parent-child relationships in stepmother families. In K. Pasley & M. Ihlinger-Tallman (Eds.), *Remarriage and stepparenting: Current research and theory* (pp. 273–299). New York: Guilford.

Santrock, J. W., & Tracy, R. L. (1978). Effects of children's family structure status on the development of stereotypes by teachers. *Journal of Educational Psychology, 70*(5), 754–757.

Santrock, J. W., & Warshak, R. A. (1979). Father custody and social development in boys and girls. *Journal of Social Issues, 35*(4), 112–125.

Snyder, M., Tanke, E. D., & Berscheid, E. (1977). Social perception and interpersonal behavior: On the self-fulfilling nature of social stereotypes. *Journal of Personality and Social Psychology, 35,* 656–666.

Sobel, H. L. (1979). *My other-mother, my other-father.* New York: Macmillan.

Steinhauer, P. D. (1983). Assessing for parenting capacity. *American Journal of Orthopsychiatry, 53*(3), 468–481.

Stepfamily Association of America. 602 E. Joppa Rd., Baltimore, MD 21204.

Stolberg, A. L., & Anker, J. M. (1983). The cognitive and behavioral changes in children resulting from parental divorce and consequent environmental changes. *Journal of Divorce, 7*(2), 23–39.

Stolberg, A. L., & Garrison, K. M. (1981). *Children's support group: A procedures manual.* (DHEW Publication No. 1 R01MH 34462-02).

Stolberg, A. L., & Walsh, P. (1988). A review of treatment methods for children of divorce. In S. A. Wolchik & P. Karoly (Eds.), *Children of divorce: Empirical perspectives on adjustment* (pp. 299–321). New York: Gardner.

Terkelsen, K. G. (1980). Toward a theory of the family life cycle. In E. A. Carter & M. McGoldrick (Eds.), *The family life cycle: A framework for family therapy* (pp. 21–52). New York: Gardner.

Visher, E. B., & Visher, J. S. (1988). *Old loyalities, new ties: Therapeutic strategies with stepfamilies.* New York: Brunner/Mazel.

Wahler, R. G. (1980). The insular mother: Her problems in parent-child treatment. *Journal of Applied Behavior Analysis, 13,* 207–219.

Wallerstein, J. (1986). Women after divorce: Preliminary report from a ten-year follow-up. *American Journal of Orthopsychiatry, 56*(1), 65–77.

Wallerstein, J., & Blakeslee, S. (1989). *Second chances: Men, women, and children a decade after divorce.* New York: Ticknor & Fields.

Wallerstein, J., & Kelly, J. B. (1980). *Surviving the breakup.* New York: Basic Books.

Wallerstein, J., & Kelly, J. B. (1983). Children of divorce: Psychological tasks of the children. *American Journal of Orthopsychiatry, 53*(2), 230–243.

Warren, N. J., Grew, R. S. Ilgen, E. R., Konanc, J. T., Van Bourgondien, M. E., & Amara, I. (1984). *Parenting after divorce: Preventive programs for divorcing families.* Divorce Intervention Workshop, National Institute of Mental Health, Washington, DC.

Weber, T., McKeever, J. E., & McDaniel, S. H. (1985). A beginner's guide to the problem-oriented first family interview. *Family Process, 24*(3), 356–364.

Weiss, R. (1979a). *Going it alone.* New York: Basic.

Weiss, R. (1979b). Growing up a little faster: The experience of growing up in a single-parent household. *Journal of Social Issues, 35*(4), 97–111.

Wilkinson, G. S., & Bleck, R. T. (1977). Children's divorce groups. *Elementary School Guidance and Counseling, 11,* 205–213.

Zakariya, S. B. (1982). Another look at children of divorce: Summary report of the study of school needs of one-parent children. *Principal, 62,* 34–37.

Zill, N. (1988). Behavior, achievement, and health problems among children in stepfamilies: Findings from a national survey of child health. *Impact of divorce, single parenting, and stepparenting on children* (pp. 325–368). Hillsdale, NJ: Erlbaum.

13

The Abusive Family:
Theory and Intervention

MARLA R. BRASSARD

University of Massachusetts, Amherst

ILIA M. APELLÁNIZ

University of Massachusetts, Amherst

THIS CHAPTER EXAMINES the abusive family from an ecological, systemic orientation and advocates interventions guided by these principles. In this chapter we will describe maltreating families, present three ecological conceptualizations of child abuse, and describe a systemic/ecological approach for assessment and treatment of abusive families in school settings. The following case study serves to highlight a number of issues that arise in working with these families. The subsequent literature review further clarifies these issues.

CASE STUDY

The Cowens, an intact middle-class family with an 11-year-old son, Tim, and a 17-year-old daughter, Lily, were reported by their son's teacher to child protective ser-

vices (CPS) for emotional abuse. The teacher had observed the father publicly belittling the son for his poor schoolwork and conduct on parents' night at the school. In addition, Tim had drawn a picture of his father watching television and himself as a cockroach on the ceiling with the pictorial father saying, "You're just an insect!" to the boy/cockroach. She had also heard him saying to other kids, "I hate my parents and they hate me."

Although bright, Tim had a five-year pattern of starting strong in the first quarter with As and dropping to Cs by the end of the year. The teacher described him as highly distractible, needing constant teacher redirection to accomplish tasks, and unpopular with other children. Prior to the CPS investigation, his behavior had deteriorated. He had urinated on the restroom walls in front of other boys, made an obscene telephone call to a girl in the class, and constructed a penis and testicles out of clay during arts and crafts and then proceeded

The authors would like to thank George Barrett Litchford, Jr., Catherine Dimmitt, and Sally Carlton for their helpful comments on earlier versions of this chapter.

to taunt girls with his creation. The teacher followed her CPS report with a referral to the Committee on the Handicapped.

The CPS investigator reported serious concerns about the family but did not substantiate the case, partially because the family reported a willingness to seek help. The school psychologist was the first mental health professional to meet with the family after the CPS investigation. The mother called regarding the referral for evaluation and shared the information about the CPS report.

When the psychologist met with the family for an initial assessment, the family appeared to be isolated from the community and each other. The daughter, Lily, was the exception in that she had a group of school friends, a rather fast crowd, with whom she spent most of her time. The parents appeared distraught. They loved their children and were keenly aware of what they saw as their failures in parenting. Their daughter could not wait to leave home for college. Their attempts to improve their son's academic performance and conduct had not only been unsuccessful but he was seen by others as deviant, unpopular, and miserable. Distrustful of institutions and professionals, they were seeking help only out of despair. Tim alternated between sullen withdrawal and a disarming openness about his feelings.

After a two-session assessment to look at the family system, the psychologist met jointly and individually with the parents. Both had come from large alcoholic middle-class families that still continued to deny their problems. Neither had individuated from their families or dealt with the traumas of their childhood. As parents they continued dysfunctional patterns, undermining each others' efforts. For example, the stricter Mr. Cowen became with his son, the more indulgent Mrs. Cowen became, and, in reaction to this, Mr. Cowen insistently raised his standards.

A psychoeducational evaluation of Tim revealed above-average learning ability and academic skills. Behavioral ratings from both parents and teacher, along with classroom observations, revealed consistent attentional problems in group situations, no functional self-management or study habits, a pattern of negative interaction with peers that resulted in rejection, and a general appearance of being anxious and depressed. A detailed interview with Tim confirmed the impression of a boy who was isolated, depressed, socially inept, and who met the criteria for attentional deficit-hyperactive disorder.

Treatment focused on both individual therapy for Tim and therapy for Tim's parents. Couples therapy, parent skills training, and individual treatment to focus on family of origin issues were provided to the parents. Tim received individual therapy to enable him to come to terms with his own traumatization and to gain an awareness and control of his own aggressive and sexual impulses. Tim's treatment was complemented with social skills training.

In addition, the parents were referred to a local support group for adult children of alcoholic families. A tutor (an advanced student in school psychology) worked three times a week with Tim on classroom assignments, study habits, and cognitive skills training. The tutor served as a liaison between the parents and the teacher. The psychologist worked with Tim, the parents, the tutor, and the teacher on a behavioral program for setting weekly goals for assignment completion and classroom conduct. Tim was involved in selecting the home-delivered reinforcers for achieving the goals and the tutor monitored the program.

The Committee on the Handicapped classified Tim as emotionally disturbed and offered him weekly sessions with the school psychologist as a special service. His teacher was willing to keep him in the regular classroom if she received frequent consultations from the psychologist on the classroom behavioral program and the support of the tutor to keep Tim up with the class academically. With this enormous input of school and family resources, Tim made steady progress in academics and in conduct and was promoted with his class at the end of the year. He still is socially isolated but has made friends with another boy who has behavior problems.

Lily declined to be involved in treatment other than two sessions with the family and one individual session. She wanted to focus on enjoying and saying goodbye to her high school friends and not get reentangled in family crises at this point in her life.

The Cowens have made major strides in their ability to function as a consistent team in their parenting. They continue to work together on issues of identity, intimacy, and enjoying leisure time as a family.

DESCRIPTION OF ABUSIVE FAMILIES

Abusive families is the term we have chosen to describe families where any child maltreatment—physical, emotional, and sexual abuse, and/or physical and emotional neglect—is present. Although these categories of maltreatment have been separately addressed in many state laws and regulations, and in much of the clinical and some of the empirical literature, we are addressing them jointly for several reasons. First, we consider all forms of maltreatment to be primarily emotional or psychological in nature (Brassard & Gelardo, 1987; Garbarino, Guttmann, & Seeley, 1986; Hart & Brassard, 1987; Erickson & Egeland, 1987). Lack of emotional support is common to all forms of maltreatment and in virtually all cases the psychological consequences of maltreatment endure and become the focus of intervention.

Second, many families simultaneous-

ly perpetrate more than one form of abuse (Giovannoni & Becerra, 1979). In our experience, and that of other researchers working with a lower social class maltreatment population, the longer one knows a maltreating family the more likely one is to identify multiple forms of maltreatment (Flanzer, 1986; Erickson & Egeland, 1987).

Third, although some research suggests that family process and child behavior may be differentially related to particular forms of maltreatment, there is very little controlled research that has focused on forms of maltreatment other than physical abuse in lower class populations (Wolfe, 1988).

A description of abusive families is difficult because of their diversity and their similarity to other dysfunctional families. We only have information on families whose behavior is sufficiently conspicuous to come to the attention of community professionals. Maltreating families have high frequencies of substance abuse, spousal conflict and violence, and health problems. They tend to be multiproblem families. Clinical generalizations of maltreating families that repeatedly appear in the literature and parallel the case study are:

1. A pattern of isolation and limited openness to new information from the environment permits the maltreatment to occur by excluding comment by others, and makes maltreatment more likely because of the absence of support (Garbarino, 1977; Polansky, Chalmers, Buttenweiser, & Williams, 1981; Wahler, 1980). Furthermore, the lack of contact with other models of parenting or family relationships maintains the belief that abusive behavior is appropriate parenting, and that the abuse was the fault of the child (Kaufman, 1988; Spinetta & Rigler, 1972).

2. The unmet psychological needs of the adults in maltreating families serve as

obstacles to empathizing with and protecting their children (Erickson, 1988; Fraiberg, 1983). Whether conceptualized as transference issues (Fraiberg, 1983), dysfunctional representational working models of relationships (Bretherton, 1985; Sroufe & Fleeson, 1986), unresolved issues in parents' families of origin (Bowen, 1978), or a cognitive developmental immaturity (Ivey, 1987; Newberger, 1980), many maltreating parents are not psychologically able to assume the role of adult and parent because of unmet needs and concomitant delays in their cognitive and emotional development. These families tend to be undifferentiated, have role and boundary confusion between generations, and lack skills for solving the intra- and extrafamilial interpersonal and concrete problems of living.

The second national incidence study recently investigated the current national incidence and prevalence of child maltreatment in the United States (U.S. Department of Health and Human Services, 1988). Using a standard set of definitions, it sampled all child maltreatment cases recognized and reported to community professionals in a nationally representative sample of 29 counties during a three-month period. The study did not gather data on maltreatment known to neighbors, family members, victims, and perpetrators that was not reported, or on maltreatment that occurs but is not identified by the participants as maltreatment. Thus, the incidence figures represent minimal estimates.

In 1986, the report estimated that 16.3 per 1,000 (more than 1 million) children in the United States experienced maltreatment and suffered demonstrable harm at the hands of caregivers. When cases of endangerment were included, the total went to 25.2 per 1,000 cases (1.5 million cases). Only 46 percent of the cases were known to child protective services

(CPS) through official reports. The report noted that "the *vast majority* of [cases recognized by professionals] remain *unreported* and/or uninvestigated" (pp. 6–16).

Overall in this study, sex was not related to rates of maltreatment; however, when abuse and neglect were separated, females were found to be sexually abused at a rate four times that of males. Ethnicity and race were not related to type or severity of maltreatment. There was a positive relationship between age and physical abuse. Neglect in general was not related to age but educational and emotional neglect tended to increase with age. The authors speculated that age may relate less to abuse occurring than to abuse being recognized due to the increased involvement of children with adults outside the family as they grow older.

Family income was overwhelmingly the factor that was most related to risk status. Children from families with income under $15,000 per year had much higher rates of maltreatment than those from families with income over $15,000 (rates of 54.0 versus 7.9 per 1,000 cases). Patterns of maltreatment also differentiated between the two groups. The low-income group had equivalent rates of abuse (51 percent) and neglect (54 percent), whereas the higher income group had considerably more abuse (67 percent) than neglect (36 percent). In the higher income group physical abuse was the highest form of abuse reported (2.5 per 1,000 cases) followed by emotional and sexual abuse, which occurred at equivalent rates (1.2 and 1.1. per 1,000 cases, respectively).

SYSTEMIC CONCEPTUALIZATIONS OF ABUSE

Child maltreatment research and practice is currently influenced by three theoretical models, all of which support a systemic or ecological analysis of the problem of child maltreatment.

From a family systems perspective, child abuse should not be viewed as an end in itself but as a complex behavioral pattern symptomatic of a family in distress. It is not an isolated phenomenon, but part of a more general pattern of parent-child interaction that can only be understood in the context of the family system (Berger, 1985). Treating child abuse is not just a matter of fighting the symptom by blaming the abusive parent and victimizing the child, but of thoroughly examining and looking at which patterns of family interaction generate, maintain, and perpetuate the abusive behavior.

As in other dysfunctional families, the abusive family may display symptom formation in family members other than the identified "victim." Symptom formation may also be apparent in multiple family crises, structural disorganization, and impaired communication and problem-solving skills. This was certainly the case with the Cowen family (discussed at the beginning of the chapter).

Family systems theory has not produced research in support of their model with abusive families. However, there are two studies done by members of the organizational/attachment theory school mentioned below that have examined their findings from the family systems as well as the organizational perspective (Sroufe & Ward, 1980; Sroufe, Jacobvitz, Mangelsdorf, DeAngelo, & Ward, 1985). Examining the differential interaction patterns of seductive mothers with their male and female children, the authors provided inferential support for family systems models of dysfunctional interaction in abusive families. The authors are unaware of any controlled treatment studies using family therapy as an intervention. Family therapy is a promising treatment approach if one generalizes from the success of treatment of families with parent-child conflict (see Hazelrigg, Cooper, & Borduin, 1987, for a recent review).

The organizational approach to development (Cicchetti & Braunwald, 1984; Erickson & Egeland, 1987; Waters & Sroufe, 1983), which was derived from psychoanalytically oriented theorists (Bowlby, 1969, 1973, 1980; Erikson, 1963), holds that competence results from the child's successful resolution of stage-salient developmental tasks. The resolution of tasks during earlier stages of development forms the foundation for optimal adaptation during subsequent developmental periods. Parents play an important role in the resolution of tasks and adaptations by providing an environment that allows for success. When there is not a supportive environment for a child, and thus developmental tasks are not successfully negotiated, maladaptation may occur.

According to this model, a particularly critical caregiver function is to provide the context in which the child develops a model of interpersonal relationships and learns what to expect of the other and of the self in relationships. The research generated by this model has tied patterns of care giving (hostile, rejecting, psychologically unavailable caregiving) to impaired child competence at successive stages and the development of psychopathology. It has also demonstrated a relationship between a mother's emotional and environmental resources and her competence in parenting (Egeland & Farber, 1984) and a mother's childhood history of adequate or abusive care (as assessed retrospectively) to the quality and pattern of care she gives her children (Egeland, Jacobvitz, & Papatola, in press; Sroufe et al., 1985).

Miller (1983, 1986) presents a related position, based on psychoanalytic object relations theory. She posits that child maltreatment is the result of extreme forms of socially sanctioned child-rearing practices (e.g., training children to repress feelings of pain, exuberance, and early trauma) that result in repressed rage, depression, and inability to empathize with the sufferings of others. These intense feelings are displaced onto the next generation of helpless, dependent children when these children become parents.

Miller's theory is supported by independent findings of Fraiberg, a fellow psychoanalyst (Fraiberg, 1983), and Main, a developmental psychologist (Main & Goldwyn, 1984; Main, Kaplan, & Cassidy, 1985). They found that parents with unresolved childhood trauma often identify with their aggressive parents rather than with their needy children, thus maintaining the maltreating pattern across generations.

Treatment approaches developed from this perspective stress the importance of developing a long-term (at least a year) therapeutic relationship with the maltreating parent (usually the mother). Such treatment provides the parent with an opportunity to learn new ways of relating to another individual, work through some of the psychological trauma from his or her childhood that may serve as a barrier to providing a nurturant relationship with the child, and then work on additional skills that are important for successful functioning as an adult and parent in our society.

Fraiberg's (1983) clinical infant mental health program developed in Michigan, and the University of Minnesota's STEEP Project (Erickson, 1988) are two examples of interventions that appear to be successful in treating high-risk or abusive parents from this framework. However, a critical evaluation of their effectiveness is not yet available.

Social learning theory or behavioral analysis models have provided equally relevant models and data in support of their position. Examining abusive families at multiple levels—individual, family, and environmental/social—this model focuses on critical antecedents, important events in the history of the parent or development of the child, the nature of the maltreating act, consequences that may maintain the behavior, and the context (familial, community, and larger social system) in which the abuse occurs (Wolfe, 1988).

Research based on this model has been very promising in the area of building parenting skills, although few studies have conducted followup assessments for longer than a few months after treatment ended (Goldstein, Keller, & Erne, 1985; Wolfe, 1987). In the studies that did follow families a year or more after termination, treatment effects appeared to continue (Christopherson, Kuehn, Grinstead, Barnard, Rainey, & Kuehn, 1976; Lutzker, 1983; Wolfe, Edwards, Manion, & Koverola, 1988). Social learning approaches also appear to be successful in improving parents' control of anger and interpersonal skills. There is some evidence that this skills training approach may be most effective in a group training format (Goldstein, Keller, & Erne, 1985).

IMPLICATIONS FOR ASSESSMENT AND TREATMENT

Assessment and intervention in child abuse need to stem from a framework that incorporates a multiple systems (ecological) and a developmental perspective. An ecological framework is critical because effective intervention must address all the levels of systems that impinge on and contribute to the problem of child abuse—societal policies, ideologies of child rearing, institutions and their interconnections, the local community, the family, the parental/marital system, and the child. Intervening on only one level, such as at the parental level, is ineffective because parental behavior is so strongly influenced by other, collectively more powerful, levels.

Intervention must be systemic and developmental because maltreatment is interwoven into the life cycle of individuals, families, communities, and cultures. Cultures promote a pedagogy of parenting and have characteristic styles of child rearing (Miller, 1984; Rohner, 1975) that vary dramatically in the support and encouragement provided to children. Similarly, the resources available to families and the social support provided to them by society impacts on their performance as parents (Bronfenbrenner, 1979; Garbarino, Stocking, and associates, 1980). Their performance as parents in turn affects society.

Developmentally, at an individual level, a maltreated infant becomes an acting-out seven-year-old who harms other children, annoys the teacher, and who may eventually elicit maltreatment from other adults and peers. The seven-year-old may become a teen father who abandons his offspring with a resourceless teen mother who may abuse or neglect her children. And the cycle continues. Families proceed through developmental stages that correspond to individual stages (Carter & McGoldrick, 1980). Family and individual developmental levels are reciprocally influenced.

The goals of assessment and treatment are threefold: (1) prevent further child abuse; (2) prevent abuse by the "helping system" of the family; and (3) change the intra- and extrafamilial interactional patterns (within the family and without) that are maintaining the abuse, and begin to substitute patterns that will facilitate the child's (and hopefully the family's) social, emotional, and academic competence.

Some families cross the lines from adequate to borderline to maltreatment as a result of extreme situational stress. They may be helped by a crisis intervention approach that diffuses the situation, identifies stressors that can then be alleviated through reframing the situation and/or problem solving, and identifies supports. However, at least a third of Child Protective Service (CPS) cases are multiproblem families in chronic crises for whom short-term intervention is inappropriate (Faller, 1985). These families need a comprehensive treatment plan. We advocate systemic assessment and intervention on all levels with these multiproblem families: the community and its institutions, the family as a whole, the marital subsystem if relevant, and individual family members.

The most effective way to elicit accurate information for an assessment is to build a relationship of trust over time with a family. Unfortunately, the commonly used crisis intervention model may result in these families being dropped in six months if there have been no new reports of abuse (Faller, 1985). Families then tend to be assigned to a new caseworker when a new charge of maltreatment is substantiated. A relationship with a mature professional is crucial for establishing the trust necessary to conduct a valid assessment and obtain information useful for planning treatment. This relationship is just what CPS workers with their heavy caseloads are rarely in a position to offer. Psychologists working in the schools may be in a better position to either develop such a relationship or assist the family in finding someone who will.

One of the basic tenets of a systemic model is that problematic behavior serves some purpose and function in maintaining the balance within the family. A main task in understanding child abuse is to ask ourselves questions such as the following:

- How is child abuse functional to the family?
- What purpose does it serve?

• How does it help the abusive family keep its "balance" as it is?

Trying to disentangle the family members' views of the problem and the interactions that center around the abusive behavior can guide our search for answers to these questions. From a systemic point of view, we can assume that if the child abuse pattern is well established in the abusive family, predictable patterns of interaction may be identified. For example, we may assume that when the abusive parent tries to change his or her behavior, relational patterns in the family change and may need to be substituted by nonabusive behavioral patterns. To achieve this end, we may ask the family a series of circular questions (Penn, 1982) that illuminate family process and influence the family's perspective:

• Who will be most affected by the change?
• Who will talk most about the need for professional help?
• Who will have previously made an attempt to help the abusive parent/child?

In addition to circular questioning, family strengths and weaknesses can be assessed through interviewing, using standardized psychological measures, and observing the family or parent-child dyads interact over structured tasks in the home or laboratory. Wolfe (1988) recently presented a comprehensive model for assessing maltreating families that could be used in a modified form in school settings.

Areas of related parental functioning are also important to assess. A parent's personal resources such as intellectual ability, occupational achievement, practical problem-solving skills, mental status, and cognitive developmental level are all important to assess (Jones, 1987; Wolfe, 1987). Similarly, sources of parental support and stress, particularly from the marital relationship or its equivalent,

should be noted. Assessing the parents' knowledge of available community resources is also helpful. In addition, factors associated with increased danger to the child and poor prognosis in treatment are important to assess.

Jones (1987) identified the following factors as being related to negative treatment outcomes: (1) resistance to change and refusal of treatment; (2) substance abuse; (3) parental history of severe abuse coupled with denial, memory loss, or splitting of recall for those events; (4) parental lack of empathy for the child and failure to see the child's needs as separate from their own; (5) severe personality disorder, particularly when coupled with mental retardation; and (6) psychosis with delusions involving the child.

Assessment of the child victim is also important. Learning and developmental delays and behavior problems have been repeatedly cited in the literature on abused children (Brassard & Gelardo, 1987; Wolfe, 1987). The child's interpretation of the abuse and his or her role in it has important treatment implications and this needs to be assessed along with the child's patterns of coping and strengths.

Finally, systems issues are part of a comprehensive assessment. Family relationships with schools, CPS, other social agencies, the extended family, private institutions such as churches, and so forth all play a role in the conceptualization of the problem, its maintenance, and its resolution.

GENERAL CONCEPTS IN INTERVENTION

Much of the research on intervention programs with maltreating families suggests that these families are very difficult to treat and that efforts are often unsuccessful.

Cohn and Daro (1987) reviewed the findings of four-multiyear evaluation studies funded by the National Center on Child Abuse and neglect on the effectiveness of interventions with maltreating families. The majority of these interventions were model demonstration projects utilizing a casework, family support approach. The authors' conclusions are discouraging, as they stated that "child abuse and neglect continues despite early, thoughtful, and often costly intervention" (p. 440).

Programs demonstrating the most success focused on improved parental functioning (e.g., lay counseling, parent evaluation) and worked with parents charged with sexual abuse. Much success was reported in interventions with children. However, treatment of children did not seem to affect clinicians' ratings of future risk of abuse. Programs that attempted to halt or reduce the likelihood of continuing abuse with the more severe cases of physical abuse, neglect, and/or emotional maltreatment were relatively ineffective. Summarizing across these programs, 33 percent or more parents continued to maltreat during intervention, and over 50 percent were rated by staff as likely to abuse following termination from the program.

A major factor that seems to affect treatment outcomes is the degree to which the therapist is able to build and maintain a relationship with these high-risk and abusive families (Fraiberg, 1983; Greenspan, 1988; Lyons-Ruth, Botein, & Grunebaum, 1984). Maximizing continuity of care and reducing the number of individuals involved with a family is also helpful. Efforts to focus on outreach to families by offering them help with problems as they perceive them seem related to better outcomes.

Second, countertransference issues are particularly troublesome when treating abused individuals (Miller, 1984). All professionals need to be aware of their own childhood traumas, particularly when dealing with maltreated individuals. It is important for psychologists to affirm the pain and helplessness experienced by the parent or child by accessing one's own experiences of helplessness, hurt, and shame.

Finally, professionals working with maltreating families need supervision and peer support to work through the emotional reactions common when working with this population (Greenspan, 1988; Mann & McDermott, 1983). Covert rejection, early termination, the infantilization of clients, and rescue fantasies about children are a few of the responses professionals may have. Such issues must be worked through in supportive supervision to avoid tremendous repercussions for client families.

A systemic perspective with abusive families should look at the function of school in the life of the child. Psychologists in schools can effectively intervene on three levels: (1) consulting with schools to coordinate their interactions with child protective services and the school's internal structures and practices, (2) providing direct services to families and parents, and (3) providing direct services to maltreated children.

Services to School and Child Protective Services

Factors such as the nature of the referral, the objective of intervention, and the mission of the different agencies involved influence the manner in which a child abuse case is handled (Alexander, 1985). Lack of coordination among agencies working with abusive families is a serious concern. Although our experience in several states suggest that this is a serious problem among child protective services, the courts, the police, and mental health agencies, we are most familiar with the virtual absence of coordination between public schools and child protective services.

According to the second national incidence study, schools are the largest institutional reporters of maltreatment cases (U.S. Department of Health and Human Services, 1988). However, school personnel report only a quarter of the cases they are aware of to CPS. The reasons for the "ineffectiveness" of the school as a reporter are complex and merit further investigation.

Two studies in New York state offer some clarification. Alfaro (1985) surveyed 243 professionals in New York City, of which 131 were school personnel. For all professionals surveyed (including police and medical staff), doubts about the quality of CPS intervention was the highest ranked impediment to reporting. For school personnel, but not the other two groups, fear of reprisals was the highest ranked impediment to reporting. For the entire sample, experience with CPS made the professionals more willing to report future cases. The results of the second study were similar (Noyes, 1987).

However, school psychologists need to remember that poor interagency cooperation is certainly not onesided. From our experience, depending on the state in question, school personnel are often unaware of which students are under a protective service plan. Similarly, some state agencies are often unaware of the educational and mental health services provided to clients by schools. One of us (Brassard) has, on a number of occasions, been asked by CPS to evaluate children, only to discover in routine requests to the schools for academic and conduct information that the child in question was classified as handicapped, had a current psychoeducational evaluation on file, and was receiving counseling from either the school social worker or psychologist.

Viable suggestions for addressing this lack of cooperation and communication include (1) holding yearly cross-training workshops or conferences for CPS and school personnel as Jacksonville (Florida) and Burlington (Vermont) do; (2) placing a CPS member on the Committee for the Handicapped in relevant cases to ensure a coordination of services, as the states of New York and Massachusetts are considering; and (3) conducting intensive state-training seminars for school personnel together with CPS personnel, as Connecticut is doing.

Efforts to facilitate interagency cooperation are of primary importance since many maltreated children enter special education programs (Erickson & Egeland, 1987; Gelardo & Brassard, 1987) and are thus involved with school personnel over long periods of time as they move in and out of protective care. Maltreatment has also been implicated as a factor in many childhood learning and behavior problems, ranging from mental retardation (see Brassard & Gelardo, 1987, for a review) to suicide and substance abuse. Many of the children and adolescents with whom school psychologists already work come from abusive families.

School Structure and Procedures

In addition to fostering intersystem cooperation, there are ways to restructure classrooms that would be of help to maltreated children. Sroufe (1983) found that when several warm, skillful teachers of both sexes were available in a preschool class, maltreated children were able to form secure attachments to one teacher (often of the same sex). He suggests employing several teachers per classroom, particularly in the early grades. If this is not possible, a child should be moved to another classroom if a good relationship does not develop between a vulnerable child and his or her teacher. We agree with Sroufe that "all children deserve to be in a program where someone cares for them unconditionally" although "no teacher should be expected to unconditionally love every child" (p. 75).

Another suggestion is that we examine the current practices in many districts to take children out of the class for instruction. In first grade a child may be pulled out for up to five separate learning experiences a day. Often vulnerable children are pulled out more often than children who are succeeding. This practice undermines a child's ability to form a close relationship with a teacher and it reduces the marginal sense of predictability and control a child from a chaotic home may have.

Other school practices that limit or deny emotional development of children, as identified by Hart (1987), are the use of discipline and control through fear and intimidation of students, low quantity and quality of one-to-one human interaction, limited opportunities to develop competencies and self-worth, encouragement to be dependent, and denial of opportunities for healthy risk taking.

Staff Training

Psychologists can help prevent maltreatment by providing psychoeducational programs for professional staff that demonstrate the influence a positive educational environment can have on the effects of maltreatment. The often overlooked positive results of structured discipline, responsible and dependable adult role models, and a routine schedule are but a few of the helpful elements an educational environment can provide for abused children.

We can also help school staffs recognize what a powerful impact they have on children. This was an important part of the intervention in the Cowen case (discussed at the beginning of the chapter). If children have not received acceptance and warmth at home, it is very important that they compensate and get the attention from adults in other sectors of their life.

Research has shown that what separates vulnerable from invulnerable children (those who cope and are better adjusted as adults while others in the same adverse life circumstances do not) is an adult who took an interest, who made a commitment to the child, and who was available for support and encouragement (Egeland, Jacobvitz, & Sroufe, 1988; Featherman, 1989; Garbarino, Guttman, & Seeley, 1986). Frequently these individuals were teachers, coaches, other relatives, and therapists.

All young people need someone who is on their side, who is available, and who offers guidance and even love. Psychologists in the schools do not have the time to build this relationship with every needy child they encounter, but often they can help the child find another adult, such as a teacher, who is available and willing to fill this role.

We can also increase staff awareness of the powerful negative impact that they can have on children—an impact that is particularly devastating for children who are maltreated at home. Krugman and Krugman (1984) and Hyman (1985) report a few case studies of teachers who were emotionally maltreating children. These teachers exhibited a variety of maltreating patterns that included ridiculing children who did not do perfect work, making the class join in the belittling of one child, maintaining total classroom silence, restricting access to the bathroom, and taping children's mouths shut. The teachers' behaviors were only discovered after the children's reactions became serious enough to alarm parents. Children became fearful and adamant about not going to school; avoided unfamiliar men (in one case with a male teacher); developed nightmares, sleep difficulties, and headaches; and demanded that their parents review homework to make sure it was perfect.

The Citykids, a multiracial youth group in New York City, recently conducted a survey of teenagers and emotional abuse. As many adolescents reported being ridiculed by teachers at school as by parents at home (Citykids, 1987). Children of all ages look as much to teachers and other school personnel for feedback, encouragement, and attention as to parents. Verbal neglect or battering in the classroom can be as damaging and long-lasting as other forms of abuse. Through training, we can sensitize staff to the powerful impact they have on students.

Direct Services to Families

Maltreating families are dysfunctional families. They exhibit difficulties similar to those of other client families and require many of the same approaches and interventions. They often have multiple and more severe problems. Unlike most other families, they face a realistic fear that society threatens the integrity and survival of the family. This makes them reluctant to come for help, even when it is clear to them that they need it.

A powerful approach to intervention is one where the therapist joins with a family to identify troublesome issues, as well as factors and patterns that maintain problems. Working together, they can generate alternatives and solutions, and the family can try new behaviors and interactions with the therapists' support and feedback (Brassard, 1986; Dunst & Trivette, 1987; Fine, 1986).

Family systems theory's emphasis on positive connotation as an intervention may be particularly helpful for psychologists working with maltreating families. These families have not been shown to benefit from typical intrusive, punitive interactions with societal agents. Parents in maltreating families appear to benefit from supportive relationships with other adults who are nonjudgmental, available, and supportive (Schmitt, 1980). The Cowen family would not have stayed in

treatment without this positive, supportive approach to their difficulties.

Wahler (1980), working with lower class mother-child pairs with management problems, found that when mothers' positive social contacts outside the home increased, conflictual interactions with their children decreased. Most of these positive contacts were with friends. However, the nonfriend contacts, most of which were with human service workers or relatives, were considered aversive. Some of the comments about contacts with friends that they rated as positive were: "I don't know why but when she comes around I can just relax." "When she comes over, she's not come to borrow nothing. She likes me. I know that."

Comments about the contacts mothers rated as aversive were: "I tell you. She's not only a snoop, she expects me to be perfect" (said of a welfare worker). "It's pick at this and pick at that. I just wish she'd stay away" (said of a maternal grandmother). "We didn't want him in here. We know what's wrong. He don't need to keep reminding me" (said of a psychologist) (Wahler, 1980, p. 209).

As mentioned previously, parents' unresolved issues with their families of origin affect their own parenting. Parents abused as children need assistance in learning new models of relating and an opportunity to work through, cognitively and affectively, the painful experiences of childhood that prevent them from forming nurturant relationships with their children. As seen in the Cowen family, parents often need this individual attention and nurturance before the psychologist can begin working effectively with families as a whole or with subsystems.

When a relationship has been established and individual and family issues have begun to be addressed, the psychologist may want to offer parents assistance in acquiring important life skills such as parenting (child management, knowledge of child development and how to facilitate it); anger management; relationship forming and maintaining (communication, social skills, problem solving, perspective taking); empowerment (money management, assertiveness with welfare, hospitals, schools); leisure enjoyment; and personal enhancement. Behavior therapists have demonstrated the effectiveness of behavioral interventions with maltreating parents in these areas (Lutzker, 1983; Goldstein, Keller, & Erne, 1985).

Direct Services to the Child

There is a large and growing literature documenting the long-standing and serious damage children suffer as a result of maltreatment (Brassard, Germain, & Hart, 1987; Mann & McDermott, 1983). Thus, abused children require special handling. They have not had important psychological needs met by significant adults. Maltreatment is related to cognitive deficits, problems with aggression and self-control, and maladaptive peer relations. In addition, abused children are perceived by their mothers and teachers to be less socially and academically competent (Brassard & Gelardo, 1987). Like Tim Cowen, some of these children seem to encourage people to dislike them (Gelardo & Brassard, 1987; McNeill & Brassard, 1984; Sroufe, 1983) and some are irritatingly clingy and needy.

Since child maltreatment is usually seen as a symptom of parental dysfunction, most interventions have focused on changing parents or the home environment rather than on direct treatment of children (cases where a child is removed from the home and provided with treatment would be the exception). This approach rarely relieves the child's emotional response to the maltreatment and leaves the child vulnerable to repeating the pattern with his or her own children (Mann & McDermott, 1983).

Therapeutic work with children in general is still in its infancy (Kazdin, 1988) but there are promising models and findings that suggest that this is a fruitful area for exploration. Play therapy (see Mann & McDermott, 1983), developmental therapy (Ivey, 1987), and group therapy for children (Steward, Farquhar, Dicharry, Glick, & Martin, 1986) are several models that merit further evaluation.

Results of studies mentioned earlier by Main and Goldwyn (1984), Egeland, Jacobvitz, and Sroufe (1988), and Fraiberg (1983) suggest that if we can offer children an alternative model of relationships, support them while they work through their trauma, address areas of developmental delay, promote competence in areas of strength, and support them in their positive relationships, we can make a real and lasting difference in their lives.

However, not all psychologists are in a position to offer a therapeutic relationship to a maltreated child or adolescent. Abuse victims have many unmet needs. They need a therapist who can realistically make a long-term commitment to them and who has the capacity to tolerate their neediness and not to become overwhelmed. If a psychologist does not have the time, the interest, the therapeutic background and training, personal therapeutic experience, and other professionals to consult in times of crisis, he or she should not attempt to treat abused children and instead should assist them in finding other resources.

Once a relationship has been established, it is important never to underestimate what the relationship means to the child or adolescent. These children desperately need a dependable adult who will listen and accept, while not minimizing their feelings, rage, hurt, or ambivalence about their parents. Such clients can be difficult to treat because they often have a multitude of problems—depression, eating disorders (including obesity), suicidal ideation and behavior, borderline personality disorder, panic attacks, and substance abuse—that the psychologist may be unaware of until later in the treatment.

SUMMARY

Abusive families are difficult to describe and to treat because of their diversity and the range of problems that often co-occur with maltreatment. A systemic/ecological conceptualization of abuse—drawing on family systems, organizational/psychoanalytic theory and social learning theory—was presented. Psychologists working in schools are urged to view child abuse systemically, to assess the problem comprehensively, and to intervene on as many ecological levels (community, school, family, parental/marital, and child) as possible if positive change is to occur. A case example was cited to illustrate the complexities of treating these families in the schools.

References

Alexander, P. (1985). A systems theory conceptualization of incest. *Family Process, 24,* 79–88.

Alfaro, J. D. (1985). *Impediments to mandated reporting of suspected child abuse and neglect in New York City.* Paper presented to the Seventh National Conference of the National Committee for the Prevention of Child Abuse, Chicago.

Anthony, E. J., & Cohler, B. (Eds.). (1987). *The invulnerable child.* New York: Guilford.

Berger, M. (1985). Characteristics of abusing families. In L. L'Abate (Ed.), *Handbook of family psychology and therapy.* Chicago: Dorsey.

Bowen, M. (1978). *Family therapy in clinical practice.* New York: Jason Aronson.

Bowlby, J. (1969). *Attachment and loss (Vol. 1), Attachment.* New York: Basic Books.

Bowlby, J. (1973). *Attachment and loss (Vol. 2), Separation, anxiety, and anger.* New York: Basic Books.

Bowlby, J. (1980). *Attachment and loss (Vol. 3), Loss, sadness, and depression.* New York: Basic Books.

Brassard, M. R. (1986). Family assessment approaches and procedures. In H. N. Knoff (Ed.), *Assessment of child and adolescent personality* (pp. 399–449). New York: Guilford.

Brassard, M. R., & Gelardo, M. S. (1987). Psychological maltreatment: The unifying construct in child abuse and neglect. *School Psychology Review, 16,* 127–136.

Brassard, M. R., Germain, R., & Hart, S. N. (1987). *Psychological maltreatment of children and youth.* New York: Pergamon.

Bretherton, I. (1985). Attachment theory: Retrospect and prospect. In I. Bretherton & E. Waters (Eds.), *Growing points in attachment theory and research: Monographs of the Society for Research in Child Development, 50* (1-2, Serial 209). Chicago: University of Chicago Press.

Bronfenbrenner, U. (1979). *The experimental ecology of human development.* Cambridge, MA: Harvard University Press.

Carter, E., & McGoldrick, M. (1980). *The family life cycle.* New York: Gardner Press.

Christopherson, E. R., Kuehn, B. S., Grinstead, J. B., Barnard, J. D., Rainey, S. K., & Kuehn, F. E. (1976). A family training program for abuse and neglect families. *Journal of Pediatric Psychology, 1,* 90–94.

Cicchetti, D., & Braunwald, K. G. (1984). An organizational approach to the study of emotional development in maltreated infants. *Infant Mental Health Journal, 5,* 172–183.

Citykids. (1987). *Citykids speak against emotional abuse.* A public hearing presented on May 28, 1987, to Mrs. Matilda Cuomo and the New York State Commissioners. Testimony available from the Citykids Foundation, 99 Hudson Street, New York, NY 10013.

Cohn, A. H., & Daro, D. (1987). Is treatment too late: What ten years of evaluative research tell us. *Child Abuse and Neglect, 11,* 433–442.

Dunst, C. J., & Trivette, C. M. (1987). Enabling and empowering families: Conceptual and intervention issues. *School Psychology Review, 16,* 443–456.

Egeland, B., & Farber, E. (1984). Infant-mother attachment: Factors related to development and change over time. *Child Development, 55,* 753–771.

Egeland, B., Jacobvitz, D., & Papaola, K.

(in press). Intergenerational continuity of parental abuse. In J. Lancaster & R. Gelles (Eds.), *Biosocial aspects of child abuse.* San Francisco: Jossey-Bass.

Egeland, B., Jacobvitz, D., & Sroufe, L. A. (1988). Breaking the cycle of abuse. *Child Development, 59,* 1080–1088.

Erikson, E. (1963). *Childhood and society.* New York: Norton.

Erickson, M. F. (1988). *School psychology in preschool settings.* Paper presented at the annual meeting of the National Association of School Psychologists, Chicago.

Erickson, M. F., & Egeland, B. (1987). A developmental view of the psychological consequences of maltreatment. *School Psychology Review, 16,* 156–168.

Faller, K. C. (1985). Unanticipated problems in the United States child protection system. *Child Abuse and Neglect, 9,* 63–69.

Featherman, J. (1989). Factors relating to the quality of adult adjustment in female victims of child sexual abuse. Unpublished dissertation, University of Massachusetts, Amherst.

Fine, M. J. (1986). Intervening with abusing parents of handicapped children. *Techniques, 2,* 353–363.

Flanzer, J. (1986 August). *Group work: Treatment of choice for child neglect.* Paper presented at the biennial meeting of the International Society for the Prevention of Child Abuse, Sydney, Australia.

Fraiberg, S. (Ed.) (1983). *Clinical studies in infant mental health: The first year of life.* New York: Basic books.

Garbarino, J. (1977). The human ecology of child maltreatment: A conceptual model for research. *Journal of Marriage and the Family, 39,* 721–735.

Garbarino, J., Guttman, E., & Seeley, J. (1986). *The psychologically battered child: Strategies for identification, assessment, and intervention.* San Francisco: Jossey-Bass.

Garbarino, J., Stocking, H., & associates. (1980). *Protecting children from abuse and neglect.* San Francisco: Jossey-Bass.

Gelardo, M. D., & Brassard, M. R. (1987). *An ecological comparison of the psychological characteristics of physically abused primary grade children and matched classmates.* Paper presented at the biennial meeting of the Society for Research in Child Development, Baltimore, MD.

Giovannoni, J. M. (1988). Overview of issues on child neglect. *Child neglect monograph: Proceedings from a symposium.* Washington, DC: Clearing House on Child Abuse and Neglect Information.

Giovannoni, J. M., & Becerra, R. M. (1979). *Defining child abuse.* New York: Free Press.

Goldstein, A. P., Keller, H., & Erne, D. (1985). *Changing the abusive parent.* Champaign, IL: Research Press.

Greenspan, S. I. (1988). Fostering emotional and social development in infants with disabilities. *Zero to Three, 9*(1), 8–18.

Hart, S. N. (1987). Psychological maltreatment in schooling. *School Psychology Review, 16,* 169–180.

Hart, S. N., & Brassard, M. R. (1987). A major threat to children's mental health: Psychological maltreatment. *American Psychologist, 42,* 160–165.

Hazelrigg, M., Cooper, H. M., & Borduin, C. M. (1987). Evaluating the effectiveness of family therapies: An integrative review and analysis. *Psychological Bulletin, 101,* 428–442.

Hyman, I. (1985 August). *Psychological abuse in the schools: A school psychologist's perspective.* Paper presented at the annual meeting of the American Psychological Association, Los Angeles.

Ivey, A. (1987). *Developmental therapy.* San Francisco: Jossey-Bass.

Jones, D. P. H. (1987). The untreatable family. *Child Abuse and Neglect, 11,* 409–420.

Kaufman, K. (1988). Child abuse assessment from a systems perspective. Unpublished paper obtainable from the author at Children's Hospital, Department of Pediatrics, Ohio State University, Columbus, Ohio 43210.

Kazdin, A. (1988). *Child psychotherapy.* New York: Pergamon.

Krugman, R., & Krugman, M. (1984). Emotional abuse in classrooms. *American Journal of Diseases of Children, 138,* 284–286.

Lutzker, J. R. (1983). Project 12-Ways: Treating child abuse and neglect from an ecobehavioral perspective. In R. F. Dangel & R. A. Polster (Eds.), *Parent training* (pp. 260–297). New York: Guilford.

Lyons-Ruth, K., Botein, S., & Grunebaum, H. U. (1984). Reaching the hard-to-reach: Serving isolated and depressed mothers with infants in the community. In B. Cohler & J. Musik (Eds.), *Intervention with psychiatrically disabled parents and their young children.* New Directions for Mental Health Services, 24. San Francisco: Jossey-Bass.

Main, M., & Goldwyn, R. (1984). Predicting rejection of her infant from mother's representation of her own experience: Implications for the abused-abusing intergenerational cycle. *Child Abuse and Neglect, 8,* 203–217.

Main, M., Kaplan, N., & Cassidy, J. (1985). Security in infancy, childhood, and adulthood: A move to the level of representation. In I. Bretherton and E. Waters (Eds.), *Growing points of attachment theory and research: Monographs of the Society for Research in Child Development, 50* (1-2, Serial No. 209). Chicago: University of Chicago Press.

Mann, E., & McDermott, Jr., J. F. (1983). Play therapy for victims of child abuse and neglect. In C. Schaefer & K. O'Connor (Eds.), *Handbook of play therapy* (pp. 283–307). New York: Wiley.

McNeill, L., & Brassard, M. R. (1984). *The behavioral correlates of father-daughter incest with elementary school-aged girls and matched peers.* Paper presented at the International Society for the Prevention of Child Abuse and Neglect, Montreal, Canada.

Miller, A. (1984). *For your own good: Hidden cruelty in child-rearing and the roots of violence.* New York: Free Press.

Miller, A. (1986). *Thou shalt not be aware: Society's betrayal of the child.* New York: Meridian.

Newberger, C. M. (1980). The cognitive structure of parenthood: Design a descriptive measure. *New Directions in Child Development, 7,* 45–67.

Noyes, D. M. (1987). School professionals' knowledge and experience with child abuse and neglect: Impact on reporting. Unpublished dissertation, State University of New York at Stony Brook.

Penn, P. (1982). Circular questioning. *Family Process, 21,* 267–80.

Polansky, N. A., Chalmers, M., Buttenweiser, E., & Williams, D. (1981). *Damaged parents: An anatomy of child neglect.* Chicago: University of Chicago Press.

Rohner, R. P. (1975). *They love me, they love me not.* New Haven, CT: Human Area Relations File, Inc.

Schmitt, B. D. (1980). The prevention of child abuse and neglect: A review of the literature with recommendations for application. *Child Abuse and Neglect, 4,* 171–177.

Spinetta, J. J., & Rigler, D. (1972). The child abusing parent: A psychological review. *Psychological Bulletin, 77,* 296–304.

Sroufe, L. A. (1983). Infant-caregiver attachment and patterns of adaptation in preschool: The roots of maladaption and competence. *The Minnesota symposium on child psychology* (Vol. 16) (pp. 41–83). Hillsdale, NJ: Erlbaum.

Sroufe, L. A., & Fleeson, J. (1986). Attachment and the construction of relationships. In W. W. Hartup & Z. Rubin (Eds.), *Relationships and development* (pp. 51–72). Hillsdale, NJ: Erlbaum.

Sroufe, L. A., Jacobvitz, D., Mangelsdorf, S., DeAngelo, E., & Ward, M. J. (1985). Generational boundary dissolution between mothers and their preschool children. *Child Development, 56,* 317–325.

Sroufe, L. A., & Ward, M. J. (1980). Seductive behavior of mothers of toddlers: Occurrence, correlates and family origins. *Child Development, 51,* 1222–1229.

Steward, M. S., Farquhar, L. C., Dicharry, D. C., Glick, D. R., & Martin, P. W. (1986). Group therapy: A treatment of choice for young victims of child abuse. *International Journal of Group Psychotherapy, 36*(2), 261–269.

United States Department of Health and Human Services. (1988). *Study findings: Study of national incidence and prevalence of child abuse and neglect: 1988.* Washington, DC: National Clearinghouse on Child Abuse and Neglect.

Wahler, R. G. (1980). The insular mother: Her problems in parent-child treatment. *Journal of Applied Behavioral Analysis, 13,* 207–219.

Waters, E., & Sroufe, L. A. (1983). Social competence as a developmental construct. *Developmental Review, 3,* 79–97.

Wolfe, D. A. (1987). *Child abuse: Implications for child development and psychopathology.* Beverly Hills: Sage.

Wolfe, D. A. (1988). Child abuse and neglect. In E. J. & L. G. Terdal (Eds.), *Behavioral assessment of childhood disorders* (pp. 627–669). New York: Guilford.

Wolfe, D. A., Edwards, B., Manion, I., & Koverola, K. (1988). Early intervention for parents at risk of child abuse and neglect: A preliminary investigation. *Journal of Consulting and Clinical Psychology, 56,* 40–47.

14

Substance Abuse
and the Family

RAYMOND TRICKER
Oregon State University

JOHN POERTNER
University of Kansas

SUBSTANCE ABUSE as a problem for American society and two of its primary institutions, family and school, is no longer debated. Teachers, principals, social workers, parents, and counselors are constantly confronted with the devastating effects of substance abuse. In some cases, the abuser is a parent and school personnel experience the effects on the child whenever he or she is not functioning appropriately due to the emotional turmoil of living with a substance abuser. In other instances, the substance abuser is the child who does not effectively function emotionally, educationally, or socially. The major focus of interest for the addicted individual becomes the next chemical high instead of activities that promote health.

Why is it that one youth experiments with a substance and functions normally, while another becomes a slave to the substance? Why is it that some substance abusers come from apparently well-functioning families? Why is it that some families with multiple problems produce children who do not have substance abuse problems? These are just a few of the complex quest-

ions with which teachers, counselors, substance abuse professionals, and researchers are struggling.

Substance abuse is not a phenomenon that is attributable to a single or even a small number of causes. The reasons why a child engages in substance abuse are as varied as the range of substances available to abuse; as varied as the social, psychological, and biological makeup of the person who abuses; and are as varied as the families from which abusers come. Substance abuse is a problem of multiple interactions within and between systems. Perhaps the most important of these systems is the family. Regardless of the importance one places on biological, social, or psychological theories of substance abuse, it is the family in which all of these are transmitted, reinforced, or modified. It is the family in all its forms and complexity that is the primary caregiver of society's youth. It is the family as a complex system that must be recognized and addressed in our efforts to prevent or intervene in substance abuse problems.

Most members of the mental health

care profession would probably agree that the adage "an ounce of prevention is worth a pound of cure" is of significant importance, especially since the National Institute on Drug Abuse (1981) has recognized that a high proportion of drug abusers revert to their former abusive behaviors following treatment. The high rates of recidivism and considerable costs involved exemplify the need for preventing the early onset of drug abuse by children. This involves reducing the risks of long-term substance abuse in the school-aged population by at least delaying involvement with drugs for as long as possible through the teaching of accurate, unbiased information and encouraging effective life skills development at home to parents and children, and in the school environment.

It is important for counselors, school psychologists, social workers, and other mental health care professionals to examine continuously the many opportunities that exist for employing preventive and early intervention techniques. In recognizing the need for constant clarification of those important elements of a prevention-oriented approach to substance abuse, this chapter adopts less of a treatment-oriented approach and focuses more on the family as a framework for prevention and intervention. This focus considers the relationship of the family to abuse, and to school and family systems approaches toward preventing substance abuse. The chapter will also examine some issues related to what schools can reasonably be expected to do in conjunction with a family systems approach in dealing with the problem.

THE SUBSTANCE

Substance abuse is a broad label reflecting recognition that the range of objects of abuse is as varied as the substances that exist in our complex modern society. Forman and Randolph (1983) list 37 commonly used/abused drugs including depressants, stimulants, opiates, psychedelics, and inhalants.

Substance abuse can be regarded as the use of a chemical substance that causes physical, mental, emotional, or social harm to an individual or those close to him or her (National Institute on Drug Abuse, 1981). It is the harmful consequence of the use of a substance that is of concern. This naturally leads to the search for reasonable explanations for why alcohol or any other substance results in abuse and harm in some people, while it does not in other people.

THE FAMILY AS AN EXPLANATORY FRAMEWORK

The family perspective as it relates to chemical or substance abuse is important, particularly because the family is the primary institution for providing youth in our society with care, guidance, and preparation for independence. Until recently, attempts to explain why some youths become substance abusers, while others only experiment, and still others do not ever use have focused primarily on the individual. Explanations to these questions vary widely with frequently conflicting results that can seldom be resolved for a variety of methodological and logical reasons; however, there are persistent themes in the literature that seem to "make sense" to those involved with substance abusers. These explanations fit approximately into three categories.

In some cases, substance abuse is interpreted from primarily a *biological* perspective (Allinson, 1983; Goodwin, Schlesinger, Moller, Hermansen, Winkor, & Guye, 1974). This perspective supports a rationale that some biological/chemical process motivates the abusers and determines how they will react.

Another school of thought explains substance abuse from a primarily *psychological* perspective (Sutker, 1982; Brook, Gordon, Whiteman, & Cohen, 1986). Psychological theories of substance abuse vary as widely as the field of psychology; however, the major thrust of many theories is to distinguish the abuser from the nonabuser along some psychological construct such as sensation seeking, self-esteem, or impulsiveness. Many youth who have a substance abuse problem appear to feel inadequate and unloved (Roberts and associates, 1985). Since those are primary aspects of self-esteem, these theories seem to account at least in part for a number of substance abusers.

The third set of substance abuse explanations is primarily *sociological* in nature (Allinson, 1983; Kandler & Adler, 1982). From this perspective, the explanation of substance abuse focuses on the influence of a youth's peer group, the youth's family, or society's attitudes and values. A youth may come from a family that has not communicated effectively and does not set clear limits. The youth and the family exist in a society where chemical substances such as alcohol are marketed in conjunction with "the good life." This youth seeks to become a member of a peer group that requires abuse of a substance for membership, and the group teaches its members how to use the substance. This constellation is a powerful set of social factors that many school personnel face in relation to substance abuse by students.

What is needed is a framework that effectively accommodates all of the factors that are said to contribute to or explain substance abuse. The family system perspective is such an organizing framework. The strength of systems approaches is that they allow for inclusion of the myriad of variables needed to provide a richer explanation of any phenomenon. Consequently, a broader range of prevention and treatment approaches can be mounted that have a greater chance of showing a significant and positive impact on the problem.

As shown in Figure 1, the family can be conceptualized as a system with a particular structure and a set of processes and subsystems that provide cultural and ideological style (Turnbull, Summers, & Brotherson, 1984). The family operates through essential functions for family members and the family unit. Family structures, processes, and functions all change as the family goes through its own life cycle and historical changes. Family processes and products related to parenting an infant are vastly different from those family processes and products of a family with an adolescent. Each of the units in the family system will be briefly outlined with reference to the problem of substance abuse.

Family structure is, in a sense, the raw material with which the family begins to operate. This includes the makeup of the family and its cultural and ideological style. It is within this context that many of the insights into family history and the complex relationship between genetics, psychology, and anthropology can be accommodated. The intergenerational nature of some substance abuse is well documented (Hawkins, Lishner, Calolana, & Howard, 1986; Goodwin, 1985). What is less well understood is if this is due to genetics of some constellation of cultural and social learning variables. Again, both explanations are very likely to be correct for different abusers.

Substance abuse prevention or treatment programs from the family systems perspective must include explicit consideration of the family structure. The knowledge that a family has had individuals with substance abuse problems in each of several generations is critical in-

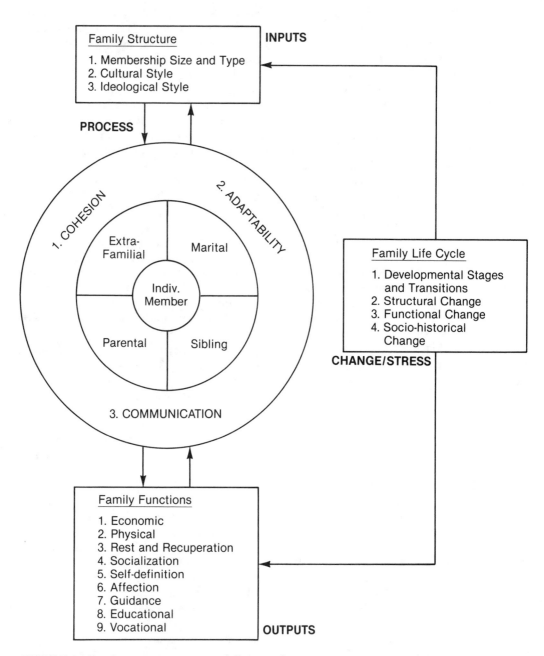

FIGURE 1   Family systems conceptual framework
Source: Turnbull, A. P., Summers, J. A., & Brotherson, M. J. (1983). *Working with families with disabled members: A family systems approach.* Lawrence: University of Kansas Research and Training Center for Independent Living.

formation for prevention or treatment programming. Intergenerational family norms about substance abuse and a particular substance such as alcohol are powerful forces operating on the youngest members of the current generation. The family's ideology in terms of democratic participation or autocratic dominance is an important determinant in a child's ability to bring concerns to the attention of adults. From a treatment or intervention point of view, these become critical areas for probing and discussing with the family or subsystem within the family. From a prevention standpoint, this suggests introduction of topics about which a young family member must receive information regarding outcomes, which derive from families with a history of substance abuse.

Family interactions or processes are those mechanisms through which the family functions on a day-to-day basis. The communication patterns, the degree to which members feel close to other members, and the ability to change and adapt are all primary family processes. Each of these has been connected in some way to substance abuse of youth. For example, Friedman, Utada, and Morrissey (1987) studied the dimensions of cohesion and adaptability of adolescent drug abusers and their parents, and found that these families categorized themselves as disengaged and rigid.

Substance abuse programs, whether prevention or treatment oriented, must include analysis and instruction in communication skills. Family members need to assess feelings of disengagement or connectedness. Young family members need the information and skills to develop independence yet remain a member of the family. Families need assistance in assessing and possibly modifying the established responses to those normal changes and stressors usually experienced by a family. In some situations, a young person may need help from a mental health pro-fessional when he or she is unable to find the stability and insights that are found in a family that sets fair limits and expectations.

The relationship between substance abuse and such characteristics of youth as peer influence (Jessor, Chase, & Donovan, 1980; Fors & Rojek, 1983); self-esteem (Guglielmo, Polak, & Sullivan, 1985), and school performance (Brook et al., 1986; Friedman, Glickman, & Utada, 1985) is well documented. However, few insights exist to explain clearly the dynamic structure that integrates and connects these variables to substance abuse. For example, does low self-esteem cause one to become an abuser or does abuse lower one's perception of self?

Efforts to prevent or treat substance abuse using a family systems approach should acknowledge that it is less important to know what the variables are and how they relate to abuse then it is to consider normal parameters of family functioning. Prevention and treatment programs need to focus on the family meeting the youth's needs in terms of affection, guidance, education, self-definition, socialization, and basic necessities of life. Prevention programs need to equip the child with the necessary skills of responsible adulthood. These skills include development and maintenance of self-esteem, decision making, refusal skills, confrontation, and coping.

The last component of Turnbull, Summers, and Brotherson's (1983) family systems perspective is the family life cycle. Families go through developmental changes in a manner similar to individuals. The structure of the family changes through birth, marriage, independence, death, and divorce. The functions change as the family acquires more or less economic resources as the needs of family members change due to normal life transitions. The family also exists in a sociohistorical context; the contextual circumstances that relate to substance abuse differ widely from those of 20 or more years ago. Therefore, prevention and treatment programs must recognize and accommodate the nature of family and societal changes within today's behavioral contexts. Intervention in a substance abuse problem requires analysis of recent changes within the family due to such factors as unemployment or employment changes, family relocation, divorce, or death. Possible relationships between these life factors and substance abuse should be explored and attempts should be made to develop alternative coping abilities.

However, the expectations for normal family life transitions can drastically change when a younger family member becomes involved in substance abuse. In this case, the abuse of a substance can often arise as a consequence of many other underlying elements within a family that now need to be modified or completely changed. This may involve addressing parental expectations of the child and increasing the flexibility of interpersonal family boundaries. Family policies and rules must sometimes undergo radical changes before a young family member can be effectively reintegrated back into the family network.

The benefits of a treatment program that focuses on alternatives, bolstering the child's self-esteem and sharing his or her needs, will be considerably enhanced if the child feels secure and cared for after returning to the family system. Therefore, it is important that mental health professionals help parents develop roles that support positive, prevention-oriented policies within the family in a restructured supportive home environment for the returning young member. Helping parents to feel responsible and in control of their parental roles can considerably enhance the future success the family will have for nurturing the child and avoiding any future involvement with substance abuse. To be more effective, the work that is accomplished within the home must also interface with the work of the school as a further positive behavioral reinforcement for the child.

SYSTEMS OF INTERVENTION FROM A FAMILY-SCHOOL PERSPECTIVE

Parents and schools face the problem of trying to keep their children from abusing drugs, but many adults do not fully appreciate the potential of their role for preventing their child's future use of drugs. Reports from many experts in the field indicate that prevention strategies should begin early in a child's life, both in the home and at school, especially because some children may have some drug knowledge in the fourth grade or earlier (Kansas ICC Subcommittee Report, 1986; "Your children and drugs," 1984). Therefore, most organizers of early childhood drug prevention programs support the philosophy that children, in general, derive benefits from well-designed, multifaceted early educational and parental interventions.

The diagram in Figure 2 illustrates the types of prevention and intervention that can be used during the pre-experimental stages and the regular drug use stage (Kansas Department of Social and Rehabilitation Services, 1986). Despite the critical importance of implementing early interventions and prevention, programs frequently meet with reluctance from parents, who often fail to acknowledge the involvement of their child with chemicals. Mental health professionals should recognize that many parents, fraught with anxiety about the self-destruction of their son or daughter, cou-

Primary Prevention/Intervention	Secondary Prevention/Intervention
Awareness promotion	Court/Juvenile programs
School team training	Student assistance programs
SADD, MADD	Family systems therapy
Education K–12 curricula	Substance abuse action
Community programs	Projects
Parent Education	Confrontation
Peer projects	Outreach—Public awareness
Wellness projects	
School drug counselor projects	
"Just Say No" clubs	

Nonuse of Drugs 1	Experimental Substance Use 2	Regular Substance Abuse/Use 3

FIGURE 2   Primary and secondary prevention and intervention and the continuum of substance abuse
Source: Adapted from the Kansas Department of Social and Rehabilitation Services (1986).

pled with their own self-doubts of failure as a parent, will often revert to extremes of denial and uncooperativeness, thereby blocking the potential effectiveness of a school prevention program.

The major objectives of school drug education programs are focused primarily within the "nonuse stage" on the substance abuse continuum. Ideally, these programs will include many of the important elements of accurate information, life skills training, examination of positive alternatives to drug abuse, policy, and constituency development as they apply to each grade level.

Many programs have focused on inoculation theory (Duryea, 1984), the development of self-esteem and coping skills (Iverson & Roberts, 1980; Botvin & Eng, 1986), teaching formulation of sound decision making (Botvin, Eng, & Williams, 1980; Smith, 1983), teaching stress management (McAlister, Perry, Killen, Slinkard, & Maccaby, 1980), teaching self-awareness and expression of feelings (Safford, Deighan, Corder, & Miller, 1975; Blizzard & Teague, 1981), and positive role modeling by older adolescents (Hurd, Johnson, Pechacek, Bast, Jacobs, & Luepker, 1980; Perry, Maccaby, & McAlister, 1980; Spizzeri & Jason, 1979). These school-based primary prevention programs represent a wide variety of approaches to substance abuse. Given the complexity of the family system and the problem of substance abuse, a variety of programs is needed.

From this perspective, what role can schools realistically be expected to play? Can parents honestly expect schools to succeed in preventing their offspring from becoming involved in drugs when the child has received a "double message" since birth from parents who have repeatedly driven an automobile after consuming alcohol, use chemicals to offset life stress, and regularly smoke cigarettes? Understanding the school's responsibility, operating in one area of a child's life, and how it can relate to families is important.

THE ROLE OF SCHOOLS IN INTERVENTION AND PREVENTION OF SUBSTANCE ABUSE

The school, as an extension of the family, has a unique function to help parents and students to clarify values and set standards for acceptable behavior. Therefore, the school should not be regarded as a substitute or surrogate parent, despite the attempt to act "in loco parentis." At best, the school should attempt to establish programs that are comprehensive and that include education, prevention activities, identification and intervention techniques, and create referral sources for students and families who need help.

The problem of substance abuse is a disorder within the total system (of school, home, and community) and affects every participant in the system. Thus, schools can hardly be expected to solve all of the chemical abuse problems of its students, although school-based efforts can assist in early detection and intervention and help to dissolve the serious complications that evolve when communities and parents deny that a chemical abuse problem exists.

Ideally, the objectives of an intervention should involve families, schools, and communities in cooperative ventures within the total prevention and intervention process, contributing to the solution instead of creating further problems. For example, a school counselor dealing with an uncooperative child may identify a communication block that is most obviously identified through aberrant behavior connected to substance abuse. In such a situation, the real source of the child's problem is embedded within the family, whereas the school merely receives the brunt of having to deal with truancy, tardiness, and violence when the child is under the influence of alcohol, marijuana, or other substances.

The role of the mental health professional involves working with the family to isolate the essential nature of the problem and facilitate the adjustment in family dynamics that can ameliorate the different effects each family member has on the other. Effecting this process of adaptation is not so much the school's responsibilty, although the school can provide an important supporting influence.

If schools were to focus solely on eradicating substance abuse altogether, they could be fighting a losing battle, use too much time in the attempt, and jeopardize greater amounts of time that are needed for teaching the academic skills that our society expects of today's child (Sheppard, 1984). Schools face multiple demands on the time available to educate children. Schools are increasingly seen as vehicles for teaching traditional academic skills in addition to providing solutions to societal problems such as sexual abuse, substance abuse, teen pregnancy, and AIDS. Given the multiple demands and limited time, many schools are reluctant and often unable to extend their roles and take on new efforts.

In providing primary assistance, schools can (1) implement programs of drug and alcohol abuse prevention, (2) be alert to behavioral changes in students and provide an early form of detection, and (3) establish a viable referral system for students who need the help of qualified professionals in the field of substance abuse.

Secondary intervention resources for persistently active drug-using students are provided by community treatment centers and residential treatment centers, and are beyond the responsibility of schools and most mental health professionals. Therefore, it is important to create an efficient system of detection and referral that is based on consultation between professionals who consider that a student's aberrant drug associated behaviors warrant the specific assistance of a drug counselor or rehabilitation specialist.

The schools in most states throughout the United States recognize that substance abuse is a serious and widely spread problem and now provide some form of drug education, often in addition to other intervention/prevention strategies and activities. The challenge is to design programs that recognize the complexity of the problem and the multiple demands placed on schools. The value of the family systems perspective is in providing a framework for balancing these demands. Programs should promote effective family interactions and functions, as well as recognize the diversity of input and the developmental changes that occur.

Since the initial appearance of drug education in the late nineteenth century, classroom activity has centered mainly on giving information about psychoactive substances and their use (Globetti, 1974). However, experience has shown that fear arousal (using "scare tactics") is unsuccessful in trying to prevent children from using drugs and in some cases exacerbates substance abuse (Bukoski, 1979; Kinder, Pape, & Walfish, 1980; Plant, 1980).

From the mid-1970s onward, a reconceptualization evolved toward drug education. This led to the formation of a different theoretical base focusing on life skills for students related to problem solving, decision making, values awareness, stress reduction, interpersonal communication, and refusal skills. However, although current efforts toward drug education attempts to serve many individual needs, parents may still wonder if these current approaches to drug education in schools actually are any more effective than the former methods used in preventing children from using drugs. Unfortunately, this remains open to conjecture, and research in this area has still not fully answered this question.

The interaction and influence of family home environment, peers, and other societal influence have not been accurately evaluated (Schaps, DiBartolo, Moskowitz, Pulley, & Churgins, 1981; Goodstadt, 1981). Hopefully, future efforts will more closely explain the interactive effects of the impact of parental influence, home background, individual characteristics, the school's influence, and the part these factors play in determining drug education's impact on children.

The extent of the current literature related to the effectiveness of school-based drug education is both extensive and inconclusive. Although more definite and conclusive evidence is needed, the general consensus among experts in the field reflects that the most appropriate solutions to the problem of substance abuse among children lay in education at home and in the school. However, educating children and parents about drugs involves more than giving information and theory.

Patton (1979) emphasized that methodology alone was inadequate, following a study of 22 compensatory drug education models in 158 school districts. The results indicated that the implicit effects of a program depended more on the degree and quality of the local circumstances (community and parental involvement) than on the model it employed. Other reports have also expressed a concern about the degree of involvement of teachers, administrators, and parents in the implementation process of drug programs (Tricker & Davis, 1987; Evans, Henderson, Hill, & Raines, 1979). As these reports indicate, the school plays an important part in preventing substance abuse, but the overall impact of a school program relies on the synergistic effects of other important factors such as home life and community support. The climate of change is best created when parents, families, schools, mental health professionals, and communities work together (Manatt, 1979).

The school mental health professional is ideally situated to play an important role in prevention program and treatment program development. Experience gained from counseling with the child, as well as other forms of professional consultation and assessment with families, parents, and school administrators, provide the raw material from which programs may be designed, modified, and developed. Important insights gained can be adapted to suit the framework of prevention and intervention programs within the particular contextual needs of the individual, school, and family.

Examples of School-Based Approaches to Intervention and Prevention of Substance Abuse

School-based approaches to addressing the problem of substance abuse vary within schools and school districts; these approaches and are too numerous to discuss adequately in this chapter. However, many drug and alcohol programs are currently in operation, and although they encourage varying degrees of parental involvement, they could be strengthened with a family-oriented component. Indeed, the absence of a family component could be the fundamental weakness of many programs that fail to provide an adequate and comprehensive approach to the problem of substance abuse in the schools. Hopefully, developers of future programs will incorporate a family-oriented component into the structure to strengthen the impact on children and parents.

The two programs described in this section are presented as examples of school-based educational intervention and prevention. The first program employed a school-based substance abuse counselor and can be regarded as prevention and intervention oriented. The second pro-gram is an example of a K–12 drug abuse prevention curriculum, which is taught in a classroom setting to children who come from a variety of socioeconomic backgrounds.

Substance Abuse Counselor Project (SACP)—Kansas City

The Substance Abuse Counselor Project (SACP) was funded by an industrial company in the area and established to develop the position of a substance abuse counselor in a high school specifically to provide counseling for students with drug problems (Shawnee Mission, 1985). The responsibilities of the counselor involved:

1. Providing intervention counseling for students while concurrently working with their parents and school personnel
2. Conducting in-house assessments and making appropriate referrals to community agencies for treatment
3. Conducting in-service training for counselors, other staff, and administrators within the school district
4. Providing services to students returning from treatment
5. Providing in-service and community programs.

The three basic components of the school-based prevention/intervention program included awareness and education (the school also implemented the "Here's Looking at You, Two" K–12 drug education curriculum [Roberts & associates, 1985]); identification and referral (students were self-referred and referred by administrators, teachers, parents, and other students); support groups; and activities to reinforce abstinence. A special abstinence group (SAG) of students referred for substance abuse was also established. Crowley (1984) has also reported the success of similar school-based intervention programs in the Minneapolis area.

A one-year followup evaluation of the Kansas high school SACP project indicated that many children with previously unnoticed substance abuse problems had received counseling. A significant improvement in grade point average, parental relationships, and attendance at school was recorded for the SAG students (Tricker & Beauford, 1986).

"Here's Looking at You, Two"
Drug Education Curriculum

The "Here's Looking at You, Two" (Roberts & associates, 1985) K–12 curriculum employs techniques with many participatory activities designed to emphasize the four components of enhancing self-esteem, improving decision making, coping, and providing information on alcohol and other drugs.

The guide includes an additional "yellow pages" section with supplemental information for teachers. Each grade level can be taught separately or as a sequence through the grades. Students have the opportunity to examine their personal attitudes about drugs and alchohol and the influences exerted by other people (parents, peers, etc.). The content, procedures, and materials for each lesson are outlined step by step with suggestions for integration into other subject areas. Lessons generally extend over a 20-hour period and cover four components in a one-semester course. This chapter is too brief for an extensive review of school substance abuse prevention programs. However, many drug and alcohol programs are currently in operation and while they encourage varying degrees of parental involvement, could probably be strengthened with a family-oriented component.

CHILDREN AND SUBSTANCE ABUSE: THE ROLE OF PARENTS AND FAMILIES

The reason how and why a child becomes involved in substance abuse are deeply rooted in a series of many and varied circumstances, and many parents face the challenge of trying to understand and hopefully change the circumstances that have contributed to their child's use of drugs. The family systems perspective provides a useful framework for introducing the information and skills required by family members to enable them to function adequately in today's society.

A program developed by the National Parent Teacher Association (1984) uses this perspective and stresses the importance of maintaining a high-quality parent/child relationship with honest and open communication, cooperating, learning how to be personally responsible, allowing a child to make judgments and decisions, spending quality time together, setting firm but fair limits, and learning how to give and receive love. The association has advised that children need positive reinforcement, nonauthoritarian guidance, and parental role modeling, which promote a positive, healthy, individual and family life style. Whereas these are desirable aspects of family life, their absence may contribute to drug use as an alternative form of gratification in the absence of a happy and fulfilling home life.

Unfortunately, the stresses on families caused by modern living often replace healthy positive family interactions. Consequently, communications among family members deteriorate in such circumstances and the early signs of substance abuse may go unnoticed. Furthermore, a child's violent mood swings may even be compatible with the "normal" family atmosphere instead of indicating warning signs of behavior patterns that are connected with drug abuse. In some families, parents may not wish to confront the child in the hope that, if the situation is ignored, things will improve in due course. In later stages, when relationships have deteriorated seriously, families may simply choose to ignore the situation altogether and cease trying to communicate with the child on any level.

"How do you get parents involved in communicating with their children about substance abuse education?" This is a common concern of mental health care professionals, educators, counselors, school administrators, and community groups, who face the challenge of trying to involve parents and families in substance abuse prevention and intervention programs. Laudeman (1984) has recognized that there are essentially four types of parents: "Apathetic," "Burned-Out," "Intimidated," and the "Resigned." Many support groups exist to help these parents to be more actively involved in helping their children lead healthier lives. When working with parents and parent support groups, mental health professionals should use a variety of encouragement and positive strategies for parents who may be hesitant in reaching out for help. Many group leaders are faced with overcoming numerous obstacles that are caused by parents who deny the circumstances that have contributed and now relate to the child's involvement with drugs. For example, in circumstances when a child has been removed from a family for treatment, parents can, with professional assistance, attempt to clarify their own values about their roles as parents, and then progress toward understanding the problems within the family system that connect to their child's substance abuse.

Fostering parent participation is a difficult task and involves both start-up and continuation activities. Many different approaches have been reported as more

and more parents demonstrate their sense of urgency related to substance abuse in children. Reports from Montana and Ohio (Crowley, 1984), and New York, Indiana, Florida, Georgia, Nebraska, Connecticut, Texas, and California (Manatt, 1979) provide strong evidence of the impact that parents can have when they work together on substance abuse issues. For example, parent pressure in southeastern Georgia, in collaboration with Georgia State University South East Drug Conference recommendations, in three years successfully reduced the total number of surveyed teenagers experimenting with marijuana from over 50 percent to 33 percent.

The adolescent age group poses a particular challenge for intervention, both in the family and in the school. Because the transition from childhood to adolescence often reflects the quality of an adolescent's earlier childhood experiences, the best way to prepare for adolescence is to begin in infancy; however, many unprepared parents feel powerless when belatedly trying to deal with an adolescent drug user in the family. Great pain and difficulty is experienced in accepting that their child uses drugs. Daroff, Marks, and Friedman (1986) have emphasized that this predicament, which is faced by many parents, is wrapped in the underlying belief that their child was raised with love, guidance, and support, and they wonder, "Where did I fail?"

Parents may need help in facing the existing substance abuse problem and in recognizing when their child needs help, but they are essentially unable to communicate the existing need. Many parents wonder, "How can I assess when or if my teenager is using drugs?" without developing their ability to communicate with the child and to encourage the child to reciprocate and communicate with them. While confronting many painful situations related to the child's substance abuse problems, parents may also recognize the need to more closely examine their own guilt and self-blame, and to work more on the ambivalent feelings they have toward their child (Daroff, Marks, & Friedman, 1986).

In particular, parents should be encouraged to feel that they are not alone, and that their child's substance abuse problem is not unique. Parents and school personnel who are interested in developing an improved perspective on parental feelings of isolation should examine the many encouraging reports described in *Parents, Peers, and Pot II: Parents in Action* (Manatt, 1979).

In seeking to discover family characteristics that may provide reasons why teenagers become involved in substance abuse, school psychologists, counselors, and other professionals can help parents to consider how the following important and internal family characteristics may predispose the early onset of substance abuse in a child. These factors pertain to:

> Negative interactions (put-downs, complaints, nagging)
> Massive parental denial of a problem
> Inconsistent or too lenient or too severe limit setting or structuring by parents
> Substance abuse as a means of gaining parental attention
> Drug use as a disinhibition to aid in expressing angry or violent behavior
> Difficulty in expressing anger between parents and children or no expression of any emotion
> Irrational parental expectations and failure of parents to perceive a child as a real person
> Unrealistic promises that cannot be believed (Barun & Boshe, 1988).

Although these predisposing factors can form a basis for intervention, they also clearly exemplify the complex nature of family interactions and provide support for a family systems approach to prevention and intervention. The issues related to adolescent substance abuse can often be traced back within the total framework of the family and does not necessarily result from a series of externally produced phenomena.

Families face an enormous challenge in trying to monitor the changes that take place from childhood to adolescence. This challenge is never greater than when parents seek despairingly to communicate with a child who is using drugs. Whenever possible, parents should exercise adequate control in parent/adolescent relationships, continuously attempt to more accurately identify the behavioral patterns in general related to drug abuse, and be prepared to observe and identify them in their own children (Crowley, 1984). Effective use of parental control within the family also involves knowing how and when to let go of the child, encouraging responsible independence while providing important guidance, and setting reliable, mutually acceptable limits.

Children who have had the opportunity to develop a mutually trusting relationship with their parents are more effectively prepared to make safer, more responsible decisions when confronted with drug-using situations (Grady, Gersick, & Boratynski, 1985). Therefore, parents need to develop a willingness to share the responsibility of problems in general with their children, including eliciting the child's insights on substance abuse issues. Parents should be encouraged to establish acceptable rules for all members of the family. Involving younger family members in decision making will encourage a level of self-responsibility, which will help them to cope personally with issues related to substance abuse (Grady, Gersick, & Boratynski, 1985; Family life skills, 1984).

SUMMARY

This chapter discussed the problem of substance abuse and the family from a predominantly preventive standpoint. Using a family systems framework as a basis for discussion, the problem of substance abuse among school children was addressed. Particular reference was given to inputs to the family structure, family functions, systems of intervention from a family-school perspective, the role of the schools in intervention and prevention of substance abuse, substance abuse prevention programs, and the role of parents and families.

The two programs described in this chapter were included as examples of well-designed, practical, and theoretically viable approaches to many of the problems that are associated with substance abuse. However, both programs mirror to some extent many of the programs currently in operation, which lack a strong family component. Therefore, this chapter stressed the need for a greater, more functional parental and family commitment, to encourage younger family members to deal positively and effectively with their personal concerns related to substance abuse.

References

Allison, R. (1983). *Drug abuse: Why it happens.* Lower Burrel, PA: Valley Publishing.

Barun, K., & Boshe, P. (1988). *How to keep the children you love off drugs.* New York: Atlantic Monthly Press.

Blizzard, R., & Teague, R. (1981). Alternatives to drug use. An alternative approach to drug education. *The International Journal of the Addictions, 2,* 371–375.

Botvin, G., & Eng, A. (1986). A comprehensive school-based smoking prevention program. *The Journal of School Health, 50*(4), 209–213.

Botvin, G., Eng, A., & Williams, C. (1980). Preventing the onset of cigarette smoking through life skills training. *Preventive Medicine, 9*(1), 135–143.

Brook, J. S., Gordon, A. S., Whiteman, M., & Cohen, P. (1986). Dynamics of childhood and adolescent personality traits and adolescent drug use. *Developmental Psychology, 22*(3), 403–414.

Bukoski, W. (1979). *Drug use prevention evaluation. A meta-evaluation process.* Presented at the annual meeting of the American Public Health Association, New York.

Carrol, J. (1986). Secondary prevention: A pragmatic approach to the problem of substance abuse among adolescents. In G. Beschner & A. Friedman (Eds.), *Teen drug use.* Lexington, MA: Lexington Books.

Crowley, J. (1984). *Alliance for change: A plan for community action on adolescent drug abuse.* Minneapolis, MN: Community Intervention, Inc.

Daroff, L., Marks, S., & Friedman, A. (1986). Adolescent drug abuse: The parents' predicament. In G. Beschner & A. Friedman (Eds.), *Teen drug use.* Lexington, MA: Lexington Books.

Dembo, R., & Miran, M. (1976). Evaluation of drug prevention programs by youths in a middle-class community. *International Journal of Addictions, 11*(5), 881–943.

Duryea, E. J. (1984, Jan./Feb.). An application of inoculation theory to prevention alcohol education. *Journal of Health Education,* 4–7.

Evans, R., Henderson, A., Hill, P., & Raines, B. (1979). Smoking in children and adolescents: Psychological determinants and prevention strategies. In *Smoking and Health: A Report of the Surgeon General.* Public Health Service. DHEW (Phs) 79-5006. Washington, DC: Supt. of Docs., U.S. Govt. Printing Office.

Family life skills: Training for drug abuse prevention. (1984). U.S. Dept. of Health & Human Services, Public Health Service, Alcohol, Drug Abuse and Mental Health Administration. Rockville, MD.

Forman, S. G., & Randolph, M. R. (1983). Children and drug abuse. *Children's Needs: Psychological Perspective.*

Fors, S. W., & Rojek, D. S. (1983). The social and demographic correlates of adolescent drug use patterns. *Journal of Drug Education, 13*(3), 205–222.

Friedman, A., Glickman, N., & Utada, O. (1985). Does drug and alcohol use lead to failure to graduate from high school? *Journal of Drug Education, 15*(4), 131–147.

Friedman, A. S., Utada, A., & Morrissey,

M. R. (1987). Families of adolescent drug abusers are rigid. Are these families either "disengaged" or enmeshed, or both? *Family Process, 26*(1), 131–147.

Globetti, G. (1974). A conceptual analysis of the effectiveness of alcohol education programs. In M. Goodstadt (Ed.), *Research on methods and programs of drug education.* Toronto: Addiction Research Foundation.

Goodstadt, M. (1981). Planning and evaluation of alcohol education programs. *Journal of Alcohol and Drug Education, 26,* 1–10.

Goodwin, D. W. (1985). Alcoholism and genetics: The sins of the fathers. *Archives of General Psychiatry, 6,* 171–174.

Goodwin, D. W., Schlesinger, F., Moller, N., Hermansen, L., Winkor, G., & Guye, S. B. (1974). Drinking problem in adopted and nonadopted sons of alcoholics. *Archives of General Psychiatry, 31,* 164–169.

Grady, K., Gersick, E., & Boratynski, M. (1985). Preparing parents for teenagers: A step in the prevention of substance abuse. *Family Relations, 34,* 541–549.

Guglielmo, R., Polak, R., & Sullivan, A. P. (1985). Development of self esteem as a function of familial reception. *Journal of Drug Education, 15*(3), 277–286.

Hawkins, J. D., Lishner, D. M., Calolana, R. F., & Howard, M. O. (1986). Childhood predictors of adolescent substance abuse: Toward an empirically grounded theory. In S. Griswold-Eyekaye, K. Kumpfer, Beckoslie, (Eds.), *Childhood and chemical abuse: Prevention and intervention.* London: Haworth Press.

Hurd, P., Johnson, C., Pechacek, T., Bast, L., Jacobs, D., & Luepker (1980). Prevention of cigarette smoking in seventh grade students. *Journal of Behavioral Medicine, 3*(1), 15–28.

Iverson, D., & Roberts, T. (1980). The juvenile intervention program: Results of the process, impact and outcome evaluations. *Journal of Drug Education, 10*(4), 289–300.

Jessor, R., Chase, J. A., & Donovan, J. E. (1980). Psychosocial correlates of marijuana use and problem drinking in a national sample of adolescents. *American Journal of Public Health, 70*(6), 604–612.

Johnson, L. D., Buchanan, J. G., & O'Malley, P. M. (1984). Period, age, and cohort effects on substance abuse among American youth (1976–82). *American Journal of Public Health, 74*(7), 682–688.

Kandler, N. B., & Adler, I. (1982, December). Socialization into marijuana use among French adolescents: Across cultural comparison with the United States. *Journal of Health and Social Behavior, 23,* 295–309.

Kansas Department of Social and Rehabilitation Services. (1986). *Kansas continuum of care for alcohol and other drug abuse services.*

Kansas ICC Subcommittee Report. (1986). *Alcohol and drug abuse prevention and intervention in Kansas schools: A road map for the future.*

Kansas SRS/ADAS. (1984). *Kansas schools teaming for substance abuse prevention and intervention.* Wichita Public Schools, Wichita.

Kinder, B., Pape, N., & Walfish, J. (1980). Drug and alcohol education programs: A review of outcome studies. *Int. Journal of the Addictions, 15,* 1035–1054.

Laudeman, K. A. (1984). Seventeen ways to get parents involved in substance abuse education. *Journal of Drug Education, 14*(4), 307–314.

Manatt, M. (1979). *Parents, peers, and pot II: Parents in action.* National Institute on Drug Abuse. U.S. Dept. of Health & Human Services, Public Health Service, Alcohol, Drug and Mental Health Administration. Rockville, MD.

McAlister, A., Perry, C., Killen, J., Slinkard, L., & Maccaby, N. (1980). Pilot study of smoking, alcohol and drug prevention. *American Journal of Public Health, 70*(7), 719–721.

National Institute on Drug Abuse. (1981). *Adolescent peer pressures: Theory, correlates, and program implications for drug and abuse prevention.* (DHHS Publication No. ADM 81-1152). Washington, DC: U.S. Government Printing Office.

Pagagiannis, G., Klees, S., & Bikel, R. (1982). Toward a political economy of educational evaluation. *Review of Educational Research, 52,* 245–290.

Patton, M. (1979). Evaluation of program implementation. In L. Sechrest (Ed.), *Evaluation studies review (vol. 4).* Beverly Hills: Sage.

Perry, C., Maccaby, N., & McAlister, A. (1980). Adolescent smoking prevention: A third year follow-up. *World Smoking and Health, 5*(3), 40–45.

Plant, M. (1980). Drug taking and prevention: The implications of research for social policy. *British Journal of the Addictions, 75,* 245–254.

Roberts and associates (1985). *"Here's looking at you, two," drug and alcohol curriculum.* South Seattle, WA: Author.

Safford, P., Deighan, W., Corder, L. K., & Miller, W. S. (1975). Training teachers for drug abuse prevention: A humanistic approach. *Journal of Drug Education, 5*(4), 335–349.

Schaps, E., DiBartolo, R., Moskowitz, J., Pulley, C., & Churgins, S. (1981). Primary prevention evaluation research: A review of 127 impact studies. *Journal of Drug Issues, 11,* 17–43.

Shawnee Mission substance abuse counselor project. (1985). Mohawk Instructional Center. Shawnee Mission Public Schools, Shawnee Mission, KS.

Sheppard, M. (1984). Drug abuse prevention education: What is realistic for schools? *Journal of Drug Education, 14,* 223–229.

Smith, T. (1983). Reducing adolescents' marijuana use. *Social Work in Health Care, 9*(1), 33–34.

Spizzeri, A., & Jason, L. (1979). Prevention and treatment of smoking in school age children. *Journal of Drug Education, 9*(3), 189–208.

Successful school drug prevention programs, stress, decision skills, coping, self image. (1982). *Drugs and Drug Education Newsletter, 13*(11), 1–10.

Sutker, P. B. (1982). Adolescent drug and alcohol behavior. *Review of Human Development Field.*

Tricker, R., & Davis, L. (1987). Implementing school drug and alcohol education programs: A descriptive evaluation. *Techniques: Journal of Remedial Education and Counseling, 3,* 281–293.

Tricker, R., & Beauford, K. (1986). *The impact of prevention and intervention strategies upon high school substance abuse.* Published in the proceedings of the AAHPERD convention, Las Vegas.

Turnbull, A. P., Summers, J. A., Brotherson, M. J. (1984). *Working with families with disabled members: A family systems approach.* Lawrence: University of Kansas Research and Training Center for Independent Living.

Your children and drugs and what parents can do. (1984). *PTA Today, 10*(3), 10–11.

15

Childhood Depression: Theory and Family-School Intervention

KEVIN D. STARK
University of Texas, Austin

CATHERINE SIMMONS BROOKMAN
University of Texas, Austin

INTEREST IN THE SYNDROME of depression during childhood has dramatically increased over the past decade. Psychometrically sound instruments have been developed for identifying and assessing depressive symptomatology in children (see Reynolds, 1984) and issues about how to most effectively assess depression in children have been empirically evaluated (Kazdin, Esveldt-Dawson, Unis, & Rancurello, 1983; Stark, Reynolds, Kaslow, Rehm, & Linn, 1988). The advent of this improved assessment methodology and the delineation of standard diagnostic criteria (APA, 1980) formed the foundation for a rapid growth in relevant research.

A great deal has been learned about the behavioral (e.g., Poznanski, Cook, Carroll, & Corzo, 1983), cognitive (e.g. Haley, Fine, Marriage, Moretti, & Freeman, 1985; Seligman, Peterson, Kaslow, Tanenbaum, Alloy, & Abramson, 1984), affective (e.g., Stark, Kaslow, Hill, & Lux, 1987), and physiological (e.g., Puig-Antich, Novacenko, Goetz, Corser, Davies, & Ryan, 1984) manifestations of depression in children. Recently, attempts have been made to develop and empirically evaluate treatment programs for depressed youths (Reynolds & Coats, 1986; Stark, Reynolds, & Kaslow, 1987). Although this research has advanced our understanding of depressive disorders during childhood, a critical piece of the puzzle has been overlooked. The missing piece is the family.

It will become apparent to the reader that there has been a paucity of family-related research. This void may be a reflection of the fact that much of the existing research on childhood depression has been guided by the theoretical models of depression in adults. It has been commonly assumed that since children manifest depression in a manner analogous to adults, the same models that apply to adults would apply to children (e.g., Kaslow & Rehm, 1983). The most widely investigated and cited models of depression in adults (e.g., Abramson, Seligman, & Teasdale, 1978; Beck, 1967; Rehm, 1977) are based on the premise that unipolar, nonpsychotic depression is primarily the result of intrapsychic, primarily cognitive disturbances, whereas bipolar and endogenous depressive disorders are primarily the result of biological and intrapsychic disturbances (see Stark, Best, & Sellstrom, in press).

Research does indicate that depressed children exhibit disturbances in information processing that are similar to those found among depressed adults (e.g., Kendall, Stark, & Adam, in press; Moyal, 1977; Seligman et al., 1984). However, the process through which these disturbed patterns of thinking about the self, others, the world, and the future develop has not been investigated.

Bandura (1977) has hypothesized that the rules an individual uses to understand himself or herself and the world, and to guide behavior are internalizations of the rules that are communicated to him or her through day-to-day interactions. Many of these rules, including those that guide interpersonal behavior both inside and outside of the family, are formed during childhood. The primary socializing agent for acquiring the rules is the youngster's family. It behooves researchers in the area of childhood depression to begin to explore the role of the family in the development of childhood depression.

Treatment outcome research, like the rest of the research in the area of childhood depression, has followed a path of borrowing heavily from the work with depressed adults (Stark, Brookman, & Frazier, in press). In the few existing treatment outcome studies (Butler, Miezitis, Friedman, & Cole, 1980; Stark, Reynolds, & Kaslow, 1987), depressed children were treated using downward extensions of

treatment programs for depressed adults. Thus, the children were treated independently from their families.

In the authors' most recent treatment outcome study (Stark, Kaslow, Rehm, & Reynolds, 1988), an attempt was made to integrate a group treatment for the children with a brief parent-training program and consultation with school personnel. Elsewhere (Stark, Brookman, & Frazier, in press), the authors have noted the need to explicate and evaluate a brief family therapy component that would be combined with the cognitive-behavioral treatment and school consultation. The portion of the treatment package that focuses on the individual child has been described in another manuscript (Stark, Brookman, & Frazier, in press).

Thus, in accord with the focus of this chapter, the authors will describe a brief family therapy procedure for families with a depressed youngster. This intervention will be illustrated through a case example in the final section of the chapter. However, we will first turn our attention to research into the relationship between depression and academic achievement and then to the interaction patterns of families with a depressed child. Finally, there will be a brief discussion of the impact of depression on peer relationships.

ACADEMIC ACHIEVEMENT AND CHILDHOOD DEPRESSION

Performance in school is likely to be affected by many of the symptoms of depression and especially difficulties in concentration, lack of interest and motivation, preoccupations, fatigability, and poor school attendance. To determine whether the school performance of depressed children differs significantly from that of nondepressed children, studies that directly investigated the relationship between academic achievement and depression will be reviewed (Puig-Antich, Lukens, Davies, Goetz, Brennan-Quattrock, & Todak, 1985a, 1985b; Strauss, Lahey, & Jacobsen, 1982; Tesiny & Lefkowitz, 1982; Tesiny, Lefkowitz, & Gordon, 1980; Vincenzi, 1987).

A variety of approaches have been used to investigate the relationship between depression and academic achievement. Several clinical-descriptive reports suggested that depression may be a contributing factor to poor academic performance (Glaser, 1967; Hollon, 1970; Connell, 1972). In two investigations that indirectly studied academic achievement, investigators obtained teachers' (Kovacs & Beck, 1977) and parents' (Leon, Kendall, & Garber, 1980) global ratings of the children's academic performance and ratings of the severity of children's depressive symptomatology. Results of their investigations indicated that there was an inverse relationship between academic achievement and severity of depressive symptomatology (Kovacs & Beck, 1977; Leon, Kendall, & Garber, 1980).

Results of a pair of early investigations that directly evaluated the relationship between depression and academic achievement were mixed. Tesiny, Lefkowitz, and Gordon (1980) found that ratings of the severity of depressive symptomatology (as assessed through peer nominations) among fourth- and fifth-graders was significantly correlated with standardized reading and math scores, and teachers' ratings of academic achievement and work/study habits. In contrast, Strauss, Lahey, and Jacobsen (1982) did not find a significant relationship between depression and reading and math achievement among second- through seventh-graders.

A couple of investigations have explored variables that might mediate the relationship between depression and academic achievement. Feshbach and Feshbach (1987) explored the relationship between teachers' and self-ratings of "depressive affectivity" and achievement test scores between two age groups (8–9 years old and 10–11 years old) of elementary school children. Results yielded somewhat stronger correlations than had been reported in previous investigations. In addition, age and gender differences were found. Teacher ratings were inversely related to achievement for the younger group but only for girls in the older group. Self-report did not correlate with achievement indices. In addition, teacher ratings predicted achievement scores two years later for girls only.

Vincenzi (1987) explored the relationship between depression, reading ability, and grade point average in reading, math, science, and social studies between two economically different groups of sixth-grade minority students. Severity of depressive symptomatology was based on a self-report measure, and academic achievement was assessed using teacher estimates of current reading level and standardized reading achievement test scores. When the effects of economic level were controlled, there was a weak negative relationship between depression ratings and teacher ratings of reading level, reading test scores, and grade point average.

In the four studies noted above, the relationship between depression and academic achievement was weak to nonexistent. This may be a function of the measures utilized to assess the severity of depressive symptomatology and the populations utilized. In all four studies, either peer nomination inventories and/or self-report measures were used to assess the severity of depression. Such assessment devices may be more of a measure of general psychopathology. A clinical interview of a child who is suspected of being depressed is a methodological imperative (Stark et al., 1987).

A second consideration is the fact

that the aforementioned studies all used normal school children as their subjects. Thus, it is very likely that these children, even those who were rated as depressed, were not actually depressed or only mildly to moderately depressed. The impact of depression on academic achievement is likely to be most evident in more severely depressed children.

Puig-Antich and colleagues (Puig-Antich et al., 1985a) completed an investigation of the effects of depression on academic achievement that used an improved methodology to assess depression but used mothers' ratings as their assessment of achievement. Children were diagnosed as having major depression either endogenous and nonendogenous subtypes, and a group of other neurotic disordered children was included as a control condition for the effects of psychopathology in general. In addition, a normal control condition was included.

Results of the study indicated that children in all three psychiatric groups were achieving at a significantly lower rate of performance than the normal controls. The endogenously depressed group was most severely impaired, followed by the psychiatric control group and then the nonendogenously depressed group. However, there were no significant differences between the three psychiatric groups. When specific areas of achievement including reading, spelling, and arithmetic were analyzed, a similar pattern of results was found. The authors concluded that the disturbance in academic achievement existed but was nonspecific to depression.

In the second study in this series, Puig-Antich and colleagues (Puig-Antich et al., 1985b) evaluated the change in academic achievement that followed the recovery from the depressive episode. Four months after the children had stopped exhibiting a diagnosable mood disorder, according to their mothers, there

was a significant improvement in academic achievement. In fact, they had improved to the point that they were rated similarly to the normal controls and significantly better than the nondepressed neurotic controls. When these results are considered in combination with the earlier results, they suggest that the academic performance of children is adversely impacted by an episode of major depression and that there is an improvement in academic performance following symptomatic relief. However, the adverse impact on academic achievement may be nonspecific to type of disorder.

It is important to note that while Puig-Antich and colleagues used an improved methodology in regard to the assessment of depression and selection of subjects, the results also were limited by the fact that the ratings of achievement were based on the mothers' perceptions of their children's performance in school. It was not based on actual, objective, and/or standardized measures of academic achievement. Such measures may have been more sensitive to differences and subject to fewer confounding biases.

FAMILIES AND CHILDHOOD DEPRESSION

The current empirical knowledge base about the nature of the interactions and relationships among families with a depressed child is in a preliminary state in which investigators are just beginning to address the very basic question of whether there is a difference between families with and without a depressed child. Important questions about causation and the specific nature of the disturbance, if it should exist, have yet to be addressed.

Our review of the existing literature indicates that there is a disturbance in the interaction patterns and relationships of families with a depressed child. In order to determine the nature of these differences, three areas of literature will be reviewed: clinical impressions (Arieti & Bemporad, 1980; Grossman, Poznanski, & Banegas, 1983; Kashani & Carlson, 1985; Kashani, Ray, & Carlson, 1984; Pfeffer, 1981); retrospective research (Abrahams & Whitlock, 1969; Blatt, Wein, Chevron, & Quinlan, 1979; Crook, Raskin, & Eliot, 1981; Jacobson, Fasman, & DiMascio, 1976; LaMont, Fischoff, & Gottlieb, 1976; LaMont & Gottlieb, 1975; McCranie & Bass, 1984; Munro, 1966; Parker, 1979, 1982; Raskin, Boothe, Reatig, & Schulterbrandt, 1971; Schwarz & Zuroff, 1979); and prospective studies (Amanat & Butler, 1984; Asarnow, Carlson, & Guthrie, 1987; Cole & Rehm, 1986; Kaslow, Rehm, & Siegel, 1984; Puig-Antich et al., 1985a, 1985b; Stark, Brookman, Vevier, & Jolley, 1988).

A few caveats about the nature of this literature are warranted prior to entering the review. Perhaps one of the most striking and disturbing characteristics of this body of literature is the partisan approach to conducting and interpreting the results of the research. It is not uncommon for investigators to brush aside or reframe contradictory results. In addition, some of the studies suffer from methodological shortcomings, some of which are inherent to the research methodology employed (e.g., retrospective), which limit the conclusions that can be drawn from the investigations. Furthermore, a number of investigators go beyond the data in hand when interpreting their results and conclude that they provide support for some inferred constructs that were not directly tested.

Thus, in the following review of the literature an attempt has been made to avoid fitting the findings into any preconceived theoretical scheme. However, due to space considerations there will be a very limited discussion of methodological concerns. In a later section of this chapter, a hypothetical model of the relationships and interactions of families with a depressed youth will be posited based on structural and strategic perspectives and the empirical evidence, which is both supportive and counterindicative, and will be integrated in the true spirit of science.

Clinical Impressions/Observations

A number of clinician-researchers have described their impressions and observations of the interactions and relationships of families with a depressed child. These articles appear to be a mix of theory and clinical experience. At times it is difficult to distinguish between the two, which is not surprising since the areas naturally color each other. A clinician is likely to conceptualize cases from a preferred theoretical perspective, which leads him or her to look for, see, and label psychological phenomena in a specific way. Likewise, through actual clinical experience an individual's theoretical scheme may be reinforced or altered.

Arieti and Bemporad (1980) paint a rather bleak and disturbing picture of the interactions of families with a depressed child. From their experiences, the power in the family typically lies with one dominant parent who is highly critical and intolerant of behavior that deviates from his or her norms. The dominant parent uses punitive and psychologically damaging means, such as guilt, shame, and threats of abandonment to enforce his or her rules and to coerce other family members into a submissive posture. Affection for a child is expressed contingently upon parental expectations for achievement and good behavior. Attempts by a child to seek extrafamilial contacts are suppressed. Finally, Arieti and Bemporad noted that more severe depression was associated with maternal dominance, whereas paternal dominance was associated with moderate levels of depression.

Grossman, Poznanski, and Banegas (1983) have described their observations of parent-child interactions during an unstructured time (lunch break) in a psychiatric clinic. A few of the families ($n = 5$) had a child who received a diagnosis of a mood disorder. In two of the families with a depressed child, the mothers were "oversolicitous" of their daughters, focusing the entire conversation on them. The authors also noted that in the case where both parents were present with the depressed child, the disturbance in the marital relationship was expressed openly in front of the child who appeared to be trying to split the parents apart both physically and emotionally.

In the most objectively written case studies, Kashani and coworkers (Kashani & Carlson, 1985; Kashani, Ray, & Carlson, 1984) described the environments and relationships of families with a depressed preschool-aged child. Depression is extremely rare among children this age (Kashani, Ray, & Carlson, 1984) and appears to be associated with family environments that are characterized by extreme chaos, neglect, abuse of the child and/or spouse, parental psychopathology, and drug or alcohol abuse by one or both parents. None of the children came from intact families. One of the depressed children clearly experienced the neglect of her basic needs and the other four may have experienced emotional neglect as a result of their parents' diminished functioning that stemmed from parental psychopathology.

Pfeffer (1981) described her observations and theoretical opinions about families with suicidal children. Although it is recognized that not all suicidal children are depressed and not all depressed children are suicidal, there is a fair amount of overlap in these two populations. Thus, there may be something to be learned about families with a depressed youth

from Pfeffer's years of experience with the families of suicidal children.

Pfeffer noted that the family system with a suicidal child was characterized by vaguely defined generational boundaries, serious marital conflicts, symbiotic parent-child relations, projection of parental feelings onto the child, and inflexibility in this pattern. The parents were self-indulgent in a regressive way that excluded the child's needs or desires. Change in the pattern was viewed as a threat to the survival of the family. On a more emotional level, the family interactions were often vague and hostile with little expression of empathy or support. Overall, this pattern of interactions, which was intense, fixed, and of long duration, prevented the children's progress toward individuation and autonomy.

Retrospective Investigations

Investigations that used a retrospective methodology to study the role of the family in the development of, or predisposition for, reacting with depression during adulthood also may contribute to our understanding factors that may lead to the development of depression during childhood. It is assumed by investigators employing this retrospective methodology that early childhood experiences are critical to the later development of psychopathology. Furthermore, it is hypothesized that the child's family relationships and interactions are critical influences during childhood. It may be as logical or perhaps more logical to assume that childhood experiences not only affect later mental health but also the psychological well-being of an individual during childhood itself.

In addition, if there was evidence that indicated that adults who experienced episodes of depression were also likely to have experienced depressive episodes during childhood, then it seems even more fruitful to explore this literature base. There is, in fact, some research (e.g., Simons, Garfield, & Murphy, 1984) that indicates that depressed adults were likely to have had depressive episodes during childhood.

Investigators who used a retrospective approach to study the family's role in the development of depression typically identified a population of adults who were depressed. These adults were asked to recall their childhood experiences and describe their relationships and interactions with their parents. This retrospective methodology is subject to a number of limitations, including the reliance on memory, which may be further confounded by the possibility that the rater's depression (negative style of perceiving self and the world) has negatively biased his or her perceptions of the past. Another limitation of simply looking at the rater's perceptions of parental behaviors and attitudes is that it fails to capture the reciprocal nature of the interactions of family members.

Thus, the impact of the subject's behavior on the parents' behaviors and attitudes is overlooked. A related concern is that since the investigators cannot objectively observe the family interactions, they have to use instruments that assess their preconceived notions about the nature of the family interactions. The questionnaires and structured interviews may miss valuable information and cannot capture the sequential nature of the interactions.

It is important to recognize that the degree to which the studies discussed below are subject to these and other limitations varies. A number of the investigators used highly creative methodologies to avoid some of the methodological limitations of this approach. However, it may prove most prudent to read this discussion with an eye for those results that were found consistently across investigators and especially those that were consistent with the clinical impressions discussed above

and the prospective studies reviewed in the next section.

Lack of Parental Affection

Depressed adults have reported that they experienced a bad, unsatisfactory, unhappy, or disturbed relationship with their parents during childhood (Abraham & Whitlock, 1969; Munro, 1966). The emotional tone of the parent-child relationship has been characterized by depressed adults (Blatt et al., 1979; Raskin et al., 1971) and psychiatric social workers (Crook, Raskin, & Eliot, 1981) as less warm and affectionate. The parents also were described as less caring (Blatt et al., 1979; Parker, 1979); less supportive, nurturant, and accepting; and less concerned (Blatt et al., 1979).

Parker's (1982) results would suggest that a lack of concern or care for the child was one of the primary contributors to the development of depression. When warm positive parental emotions were expressed, they appeared to be expressed either inconsistently or in a confusing fashion, or contingently on parentally sanctioned behavior (Crook, Raskin, & Eliot, 1981; McCranie & Bass, 1984; Schwarz & Zuroff, 1979). Not only were the parents described as expressing less positive, endearing emotion, they were also described as having expressed more negative affect toward the child, including criticism (LaMont & Gottlieb, 1975) and rejection (Crook, Raskin, & Eliot, 1981; Jacobson, Fasman, & DiMascio, 1976; LaMont, Fischoff, & Gottlieb, 1976).

Punitive, Controlling, and Constraining Environment

The family milieu during childhood has been described by depressed adults as punitive, depriving, and abusive (Jacobson, Fasman & DiMascio, 1976). There appears to have been less positive involvement of any kind on the parents' part (Raskin et al., 1971).

The parents were perceived as allowing the youngsters to attain a minimum of autonomy (Crook, Raskin, & Eliot, 1981; Jacobson, Fasman, & DiMascio, 1976; LaMont, Fischoff, & Gottlieb, 1976). However, this limiting of autonomy was not found when psychiatric social workers assessed the childhood experiences of depressed adults using information from sources other than the depressed adults (Crook, Raskin, & Eliot, 1981). In the studies that did find that parents limited their child's autonomy, attempts by the child to attain some autonomy from the parents were limited through overprotection by the child's mother (Parker, 1979) or both parents (Jacobson, Fasman & DiMascio, 1976).

The parents' means of controlling their youngsters' behavior have been characterized as strict (McCranie & Bass, 1984), negative (Raskin et al., 1971), and psychologically harmful (Crook, Raskin, & Eliot, 1981). The behavior management procedures were aimed at inducing submissive conformity to parental norms (McCranie & Bass, 1984). More specifically, the parents controlled the children's behavior through guilt (Crook, Raskin, & Eliot, 1981; LaMont & Gottlieb, 1975; Raskin et al., 1971), and hostile detachment and hostile control, which instilled persistent anxiety (Crook, Raskin, & Eliot, 1981). Fathers in particular were characterized as unloving disciplinarians who provoked hatred (LaMont, Fischoff, & Gottlieb, 1976).

Parental Dominance

Depressed adults remember their families as being dominated by one parent. Schwarz and Zuroff (1979) hypothesized that depression was caused by three factors, one of which was cross-sex dominance. Their results (Schwarz & Zuroff, 1979) provided support for this contention. However, McCranie and Bass

(1984) found that paternal dominance was not associated with depression among females. Rather, their results indicated that maternal dominance was associated with depression in women during adulthood.

Loss of a Parent

Central to the psychoanalytic formulation of depression is the loss of a parent during childhood. This loss leads to a disruption in the primary object relation. There are intense emotional feelings associated with this loss that may be reactivated by later trauma. The loss of a parent could stem from death, separation, or illness.

Retrospective research (Abrahams & Whitlock, 1969; Jacobson, Fasman & DiMascio, 1976; Munro, 1966) does not support the contention that loss of a parent during childhood causes depression in adults. A number of investigators (e.g., Jacobson, Fasman, & DiMascio, 1976; Munro, 1966) have found that although the loss of a parent was not an etiological factor in adult depression, it did appear to be a factor that was associated with the severity of depression when it occurred. Loss of a parent during childhood occurred more often among severely rather than moderately depressed adults. Abrahams and Whitlock (1969) reported contradictory results. They did not find a significant difference in the number of moderately and severely depressed adults who had experienced the loss of a parent during childhood.

Thus far, the discussion has focused on the parent-child relationship. The results of one retrospective investigation indicated that there was greater marital conflict during the childhoods of depressed adults when compared to normal controls (Schwarz & Zuroff, 1979). This topic will be further addressed in later sections of this chapter.

Prospective Investigations

A few investigators have explored the psychosocial milieu of families with a depressed child. Kaslow, Rehm, and Siegel (1984) made a preliminary attempt to determine whether there was a difference between children who endorsed elevated levels of depressive symptomatology and nondepressed children in their perceptions of their families. The children who endorsed elevated levels of depressive symptomatology, relative to normal controls, reported significantly more dysfunction in ther families on a brief, eight-item questionnaire. However, the nature of the dysfunction was not stated.

Preliminary results of one of our own investigations (Stark et al., 1988) shed some light on the nature of the family milieu. Depressed and nondepressed children from grades 4, 5, and 6 and their mothers were interviewed with the Schedule for Affective Disorders and Schizophrenia for School-Age Children-Present Episode (K-SADS-P) (Puig-Antich & Ryan, 1986) and they completed parallel versions of the Children's Depression Inventory (Kovacs, 1981) and the Family Environment Scale (FES) (Moos & Moos, 1981).

Children's ratings of the severity of depression were significantly related to a number of the subscales on the FES. As the severity of the child's depressive symptomatology increased according to self and mother's ratings, the family environment was rated by the children and their mothers as less supportive and open to self-expression, and more conflictual and chaotic. In addition, family members reportedly participated in fewer social and recreational activities. Two additional characteristics of the mothers' perceptions of the family environment were significantly related to the severity of their children's depression. As the emphasis on intellectual and cultural activities decreased, or the degree to which the family was run by set rules increased, the severity of depressive symptomatology increased.

The two aforementioned studies provide support for the preliminary conclusion that there is a disturbance in the milieu of families with a depressed youngster. However, the results of a study conducted by Asarnow, Carlson, and Guthrie (1987) suggest that this disturbance may not be specific to families with a depressed child. Rather, it may be nonspecific to psychological disorders and the disturbance may be most apparent among families with a child who exhibits a very severe psychological disturbance such as suicide.

Asarnow, Carlson, and Guthrie (1987) compared the perceptions of the family environment of impatient children who were diagnosed as suicidal, depressed, or experiencing some other nonpsychotic psychological disorder. The youngsters completed a portion of the FES. Results indicated that there were no significant differences between the perceptions of depressed children and children with other nonpsychotic disorders. In contrast, the suicidal children perceived their families as significantly less cohesive, higher in conflict, and less controlled.

A pair of studies conducted by Puig-Antich and colleagues (1985a, 1985b) indicates that there are disturbances in the relationships of members of a family in which there is a child with a neurotic disorder, and that there may be some disturbances that are specific to families with a depressed child. According to mothers' responses to a semistructured interview, the amount of impairment was greatest where there was an endogenously depressed child, followed by a neurotically depressed child, and then a control group of children with other neurotic disorders. The mothers of children with psychological disorders relative to those with normal children reported less communication with their disturbed child and the communication they did have was of lesser quality.

The affective tone of the mother-child relationship was characterized as cold, hostile, tense, and sometimes rejecting.

The mothers of disturbed children also reported subjecting their children to more severe punishment than that for normal children. The severity of the impairments in communication and the affective tone of the relationship were significantly worse for depressed children. In addition, mothers of depressed children reported doing significantly fewer activities with their children.

Mothers also rated the father-child relationship during a portion of the interview. In general, the results were similar to those of the mother-child relationship except the magnitude of the differences between groups was smaller and the differences appeared to be nonspecific to psychological disorders.

To determine whether the family relationships would change following remission of the child's depressive episode, Puig-Antich and colleagues (1985b) interviewed the mothers that participated in their first study, four months after their child's depressive episode had remitted. In general, the amount of improvement in a specific aspect of psychosocial relations was related to the severity of the disruption in that aspect of the relationship during the depressive episode. The more severe the disruption, the smaller the improvement following termination of the depressive episode. The aspects of psychosocial functioning that were most impaired during the episode either took longer to recover or only partially recovered. The most noticeable improvement was in the quantity and quality of communication between the mothers and children. The negative affect significantly decreased as did the severity punishment.

The authors concluded that a depressive episode in a child may act as a superimposed agent, producing or exacerbating deficits and distortions in the family relationships—especially the mother-child

relationships—that probably are reversible. The affective state of the depressed child may be the central contributor to many of the psychosocial difficulties.

The previous investigations relied on an individual's perceptions of the family to assess the family milieu, relationships, and interactions. A couple of investigators have recorded family interactions while engaged in contrived tasks. Amanat and Butler (1984) compared the interactions of families with a depressed or overanxious child while completing a decision-making task. Results of the observations revealed that the parents of depressed children, unlike the parents of the overanxious children, tended to be dominant and exerted nearly total control over the decision-making process. The children's attempts at self-expression and autonomy were suppressed by the parents of depressed children, forcing them into a submissive, helpless posture.

Cole and Rehm (1986) found that parents, and mothers in particular, of depressed children set high standards for their children's performance and only expressed positive affect when their children's performance reached these higher levels of achievement. In contrast, the mothers of normal children tended to express positive affect over a broader range of performance, including the lower and moderate levels.

Thus, it appeared as though the depressed children had to perform for longer periods of time without receiving any positive messages from their parents and they would only receive positive expressions of affect upon attainment of very high levels of performance. The authors noted that their results were in part a reflection of the fact that many of the depressed children had depressed mothers.

Marital Relationship

The health of the marital relationship is given a central role by structural and strategic therapists. Given the importance attributed to the marital relationship in theorizing and actual clinical practice, it seems as though it is important to review the research that addresses the nature of the marital relationship in families with a depressed youngster. Results of the existing research is mixed and does not allow one to come to a clear conclusion. This lack of consistency may be a reflection of varied research methodology as well as the fact that very few related studies have been completed. Thus, it is not possible to come to a clear empirically based conclusion with respect to this tenet as it relates to families with a depressed youth.

Amanat and Butler (1984) and Puig-Antich and colleagues (1985a, 1985b) did not find significant differences in the marital relationships between couples with a depressed child and couples with control group children. Amanat and Butler (1984) observed the interactions of parents and their depressed or anxious child while completing a decision-making task. The authors reported no significant differences in the parental coalition, hierarchy of power, or self-expression of the parents.

Puig-Antich and colleagues (1985a) explored the quality marital relationship in detail from the mother's perspective through an interview. The authors found no significant differences between parents with a depressed child or normal control child with respect to the following characteristics of the marital relationship: irritability, complaining, quarrels, activities together, whole-family activities together, affection, satisfaction, conversations together, problem-solving and decision-making styles, sharing of housework, global warmth, and hostility. The sole difference was that mothers with a depressed youngster reported significantly more disagreements with their spouse over discipline. The mothers completed the same interview four months after their child's depressive episode had remitted and reported no significant change in the quality of the marital relationship (Puig-Antich et al., 1985b).

Brookman (1988) analyzed the audiotapes of parents and their depressed or normal sixth-grade children while completing a family interaction task. Preliminary lag-sequential analysis of the verbal interactions revealed evidence of conflict in the marital dyad with a depressed child that was not evident in families with a nondepressed child. Parents with a depressed child reacted to disagreements initiated by their child by indirectly disagreeing between themselves. In contrast, the nondepressed children and their parents engaged in direct, sustained, and reciprocal disagreement.

PEER RELATIONSHIPS AND CHILDHOOD DEPRESSION

A few investigations indicate that depressed children experience serious social difficulties. Studies that have used sociometric ratings indicate that children who exhibited elevated levels of depressive symptomatology are less popular. Several investigators (Jacobsen, Lahey, & Strauss, 1983; Lefkowitz & Tesiny, 1985; Tesiny & Lefkowitz, 1982) have reported that children who are reported to exhibit elevated levels of depressive symptomatology are rated by their peers as more unpopular than their nondepressed counterparts.

Further support for the contention that depressed youths experience social difficulties can be found in the Puig-Antich studies (Puig-Antich et al., 1985a, 1985b). Mothers of depressed children reported significantly more peer-related difficulties for their children when compared to mothers' ratings of normal children. The depressed children also exhibited significantly more problems than both normal controls and neurotic controls in a few areas. Specifically, depressed children were less able to maintain a best friendship, were less capable of making and maintaining positive interpersonal relationships, and were teased more frequently by peers.

Following recovery from a depressive episode, the depressed children were rated as significantly improved in their peer relationships. In many areas they were similar to their normal peers and significantly better than the neurotic controls, and in other areas they were intermediate between the normal and neurotic controls. There were significant improvements in frequency of contacts with friends, number of children who had a best friend, less shyness, and less teasing by peers.

CONCEPTIONS OF FAMILY FUNCTIONING AND DEPRESSION IN CHILDREN

Although this body of family-related research is characterized by an overreliance on theoretical formulations of depression in adults, it underutilizes pertinent knowledge from another source. This source is the field of family research. For example, only two investigations (Asarnow, Carlson, & Guthrie, 1987; Stark, Brookman, et al., 1988) use an instrument that has been empirically validated to assess family functioning. It seems prudent to use relevant theoretical and therapy models from the field of family psychology as a resource. Those models that are based on systems theory are particularly relevant for investigating the family context of depression in children.

Family Systems Framework

The systems view of human functioning has had a major impact on the field of family research. Family systems theory has shaped concepts of family functioning and change. In their application of systemic principles to family functioning, family theorists (Bateson, 1972, 1979; Hoffman, 1981; Jackson, 1957; Haley, 1976; Minuchin, 1974; Satir, 1967; Watzlawick, Beavin, & Jackson, 1967) shifted the focus of analysis from the study of individual internal processes to the study of the system(s) of which the individual is an interdependent, contributing part. In this formulation, psychopathology is defined as a relationship problem (Haley, 1970).

Several derivative principles from a systems perspective include the following:

1. Individual behavior cannot be meaningfully isolated for study apart from the context in which the behavior is embedded.
2. Individual symptoms are multiply determined with multiple pathways of development and change. This is predicated on the tenet that family interaction patterns consist of recursive feedback loops with circular chains of influence (i.e., the family's response to an individual's distress is an important factor in maintaining symptomatic behavior).
3. Individual symptoms function to regulate the system in order to maintain a familiar equilibrium or homeostasis. Symptoms may be adaptive and functional to family homeostasis (e.g., by deflecting marital conflict through the child).

Questions

Consistent with a systems paradigm, the previous review raises questions about the family process and structure in families with a depressed child. Specifically, what is the function of the child's symptom within the family system and the regulatory power of that symptom within the system? Second, what is the nature of recurring interaction patterns between family members, particularly between parent(s) and the depressed child, parents and siblings, and spouses? Do these patterns define particular organizational and power structures?

Our approach is to examine models of family functioning, grounded in systems theory, whose theoretical and clinical focus provides an appropriate framework for generating and testing hypotheses. Two related theoretical approaches include Minuchin's structural family theory (Minuchin, 1974; Minuchin & Fishman, 1981) and Haley's strategic problem-solving approach (Haley, 1973, 1976). Both focus on identifying and modifying patterns of communication that maintain symptomatic behavior, but each model has particular emphases.

The structural model emphasizes the organizational structures of the system, whereas the strategic model focuses on the repetitive sequences in which structures are embedded. Since Haley's model integrates communication perspectives with structural principles, many of the constructs are the same. However, since Haley's is primarily a theory of change rather than an explanatory model of family functioning, his focus is on family variables (power and organization) that are important to effect change (Walsh, 1982).

In this section we will (1) briefly describe a rationale for applying structural and strategic models along with basic concepts and supportive research, (2) generate hypotheses, and (3) outline research directions.

Discussion of Models

Rationale

There are several reasons for applying Minuchin's structural paradigm to the problem of childhood depression. First, a substantial body of research, including both descriptive/etiologic studies of family functioning and treatment outcome studies, offers cogent evidence in support of its major tenets. It is one of the few family treatment approaches that has been empirically derived and validated. Second, the principles of the model are applicable to all social systems, including family, school, and community systems. This allows for an ecostructural approach to assessment and intervention that is useful with children in general and depressed children in particular (Carlson, 1987). In many cases of depression, multiple systems become involved, such as the school when the child evidences academic or behavioral problems or a psychiatric clinic when the child is taking antidepressant medication.

A third reason for applying the model is that it has empirically derived family characteristics associated with another type of child symptomatology that bears some similarity to depression—psychosomatic illness. Like depression, psychosomatic illness is characterized as an internalizing type of disorder (Achenbach & Edelbrock, 1978) where symptoms include somatic complaints, unhappiness, and fearfulness (Achenbach, 1982). This descriptor refers to individual differences in adaptive style that involves an introversive manner of dealing with stress and is manifested in overcontrolled, overinhibited, shy-anxious, and other behaviors expressed in a covert fashion.

The strategic model complements the structural model and includes concepts from the original communication model (Bateson, 1972; 1979; Jackson, 1957):

1. Its emphasis on the symptom and the patterns that support and maintain the symptom contributes to a deeper understanding of family communication processes.
2. Haley's concepts of power, organization, and flexibility augment those in Minuchin's model.

Another reason for including this model includes the implications for therapeutic change. Strategic principles are often used in combination with structural principles as tactics to augment an overall strategy suggested by structural theory (Stanton, 1981; White, 1979). The therapeutic aim of structural therapists is to change the family organization, whereas strategic therapists seek to reduce or eliminate the symptom.

Basic Concepts

The strategic model seeks to identify (1) what the symptom means functionally for the system and (2) repetitive sequences of behavior that function to support and maintain the symptom. From these interpersonal behaviors, rules that regulate interaction can be inferred. These rules about participation and authority define the organizational structure that is described in the structural family model.

Family structure can be observed in the repeated transactional patterns of communication that occur between family members and between the family and other systems. The major concepts of the structural model include subsystems, boundaries, alignment, power, and adaptation. Families carry out their functions through *subsystems,* membership of which is based on function, interest, age (spouse, parental, and sibling subsystems), or gender (female and male subsystems).

Boundaries are the "rules defining who participates, and how" (Minuchin, 1974, p. 53). These rules dictate family members' roles with respect to carrying out a particular function and serve to protect the differentiation of the whole system.

Alignment refers to the pattern of joining with someone to carry out an operation. Coalitions (joining against a third person) and alliances (joining together based on shared interests or goals) are included in this concept.

Power, or force, refers to the relative influence of a person or subsystem on the outcome of an activity (Aponte, 1976). Haley's formulation of power imbalances indicate that they occur when there is unclear and/or inadequate hierarchical organization.

Adaption refers to the concept of the functional fit (Aponte & VanDeusen, 1981) between the family's structure and life circumstances. The family's ability to adapt to new situations or stressors depends on the family's ability to shift structures to accommodate to change while maintaining continuity.

Review of Empirical Research

Most of the research using the strategic paradigm is treatment outcome research. However, structurally based researchers have conducted descriptive etiological studies of family characteristics associated with low income, multiproblem families (Minuchin, Montalvo, Guerney, Rosman, & Schumer, 1967), child psychosomatic illness (Minuchin, Rosman, & Baker, 1978), and adolescent substance abuse (Stanton & Todd, 1979).

Research with psychosomatic families (Minuchin, Rosman, & Baker, 1978) is most relevant. The relationship between symptoms (episodes of keoacidosis) and family interaction patterns was investigated in an extensive study of over 200 children with diabetes mellitus. The observation that family conflict seemed to precipitate the symptoms led to a series of investigations involving the collection of behavioral measures of family interaction and physiological measures of stress.

Four family interaction characteristics that differentiated psychosomatic families from the other groups were enmeshment, overprotectiveness, rigidity, and lack of conflict resolution. Four forms of parent-child transaction were identified: triangulation (each parent competing with the other parent in allying with the child), parent-child coalition (one parent allying with the child against the other parent), detouring supportive coalition (parents appearing united in their concern for the sick child), and detouring attacking coalition (parents appearing united in attacking or scapegoating the child for their problems).

Patterns of handling conflict also differentiated the families. Psychosomatic children tended to suppress and deny conflict, as indicated by expressions of instant agreement. Discussions tended to be unfocused and lacked closure. In addition, family members exhibited overprotectiveness, or a high degree of concern for each other's welfare (especially physical well-being), and rigidity or low adaptibility of the family interaction.

Application to Depression in Children

Depression is manifested through a complex and diverse symptomatologic picture. Different clusters of symptoms may be associated with different family patterns. The expression of the depressive symptoms changes as a function of development and life circumstances. In the discussion that follows, we have attempted to use a systemic perspective to develop a picture of the interaction patterns of families with a depressed child.

Given the limited state of our empirically based understanding of the interaction patterns among families with depressed youngsters, the many methodological shortcomings of the existing research, the contradictory results, and the fact that investigators have not directly evaluated systemic constructs as they pertain to families with a depressed child, the following discussion will, by necessity, be based on theory. Empirical results, both contradictory and supportive, will be integrated where possible. Thus, the following discussion should be viewed as consisting of a series of hypotheses that need to be tested prior to embracing or discarding them.

A. Subsystems

HYPOTHESIS: The marital subsystem is weak relative to other subsystems.

RATIONALE: Marital conflict was widely reported among the articles that were based on a mix of theory and clinical impressions (Arieti & Bemporad, 1980; Grossman, Poznanski, & Banegas, 1983; Pfeffer, 1981; Schwartz & Zuroff, 1979). Brookman's (1988) preliminary analyses of verbal interaction suggest covert marital conflict. However, contradictory results were reported by Puig-Antich and colleagues (1985a) and Amanat and Butler (1984).

B. Boundaries

HYPOTHESIS: Boundaries are diffuse between parents and the depressed child, defining an enmeshed relationship.

The enmeshed relationship is expressed through overprotective, oversolicitous, smothering behaviors that compromise the child's development of mastery (Carlson, 1987; Nichols, 1984). Because the child does not differentiate between his or her own feelings and those of the overinvolved parent, he or she may become overly sensitive to others' feelings and project his or her feelings onto others. Other symptoms include sleep disturbance, low self-esteem, guilt, fatigue, and other internalized symptoms.

At school, these children may overly rely on their teachers and may expect to have a special relationship with the teacher similar to the relationship that he or she has enjoyed with the overly involved parent. Because the child has failed to master developmentally appropriate tasks, the child actually needs the special relationship with the teacher. With peers, this may result in rejection or ignoring. The home-school relationship also would be enmeshed, with parents expecting the school to perform parental functions that are inappropriate. The parents may be competitive with school personnel, although they would avoid conflict.

In the context of this enmeshed, overinvolved relationship, the parent may withdraw support and affection or be critical and punitive. These critical, deprecatory, and detached behaviors, along with the enmeshment, may constitute a pattern of parental inconsistency. Unlike overprotectiveness, this pattern may be associated with anger and acting-out behaviors in combination with dysphoria and the other depressive symptoms. This pattern of hostile withdrawal may be most pronounced when the parent is depressed. Such inconsistency is associated with parental depression (Kaslow & Rehm, in press). The child's behavior also may be inconsistent with alternating self-blame versus other-blame.

At school the child may give mixed messages regarding self-reliance and self-esteem. This inconsistency interferes with the establishment and maintenance of relationships with teachers and peers. The home-school relationship would be alternately cooperative and openly conflictual.

RATIONALE: In the literature on psychosomatic children (Minuchin, Rosman, & Baker, 1978) and suicidal children (Pfeffer, 1981), there is a pattern of enmeshed parent-child relations. Moreover, other family researchers (Carlson, 1987; Nichols, 1984) have reported that children who are engaged in enmeshed relationships fail to develop a sense of mastery and independence. In the context of an enmeshed relationship with their children, parents may exert the kind of overcontrolling, overprotective, and stifling influence described in previous studies (Amanat & Butler, 1984; Jacobson, Fasman, & DiMascio, 1976; LaMont, Fischoff,

& Gottlieb, 1976; Parker, 1979; Raskin et al., 1971; Stark, Brookman et al., 1988).

We hypothesize that the combination of overprotectiveness and rejection is associated with more severe pathology in the child. The research cited in the previous sections of this chapter was quite consistent in indicating that families that are associated with depressed offspring are perceived to be more cold, hostile, and rejecting (Arieti & Bemporad, 1980; Blatt et al., 1979; Crook, Raskin, & Eliot, 1981; Jacobson, Fasman, & DiMascio, 1976; Kashani & Carlson, 1985; LaMont, Fischoff, & Gottlieb, 1976; Parker, 1982; Puig-Antich et al., 1985a).

C. Alignment and Power Imbalances

HYPOTHESIS: The family system of the depressed child has low levels of supportive alliance behaviors.

RATIONALE: Minuchin (1974) stated that low support leads to negative affective states. However, research conducted by Amanat and Butler (1984) did not find a disturbance in the parental subsystem or the power hierarchy.

HYPOTHESIS: The family systems of the depressed child has dysfunctional alignments, including:

1. *Stable Coalitions.* This configuration occurs when two family members are allied against a third and tends to produce symptoms of anxiety, such as hypochrondriasis, obsessions, phobias (Minuchin, 1974; Barragan, 1976), dependence, and gender-related peer difficulties (Carlson, 1987).

Dysfunctional parent-child coalitions may contribute to dysfunctional generational hierarchies. The child may be in an undesirable position of power relative to the nonaligned spouse. In a case example of a depressed child, Madanes (1983) described how the child was simultaneously in an all-powerful position and powerless position in the family. The child's depression expresses the power inversion between child and parent.

2. *Detouring Coalitions.* This occurs when parents detour or deflect their conflict through the child. A detouring-supportive coalition may be the most common configuration in which parents conceal conflict by being overprotective or oversolicitous toward a sick or special child, which may produce shyness, insecurity, and psychosomatic disorders (Minuchin, 1974; Barragan, 1976), along with dependence, immaturity, and other internalizing disorders (Carlson, 1987). A detouring-attacking coalition may also be present with the child who manifests both dysphoria and acting-out behaviors. This is the pattern in which parents conceal conflict by scapegoating the child and may produce behavior disorders, delinquency, learning difficulties (Minuchin, 1974; Barragan, 1976), and externalizing behaviors (Carlson, 1987).

RATIONALE: There is a minimum of research that addresses this issue. Grossman, Poznanski, and Banegas (1983), in their observations of the interactions of a few families with a depressed child, noted one case in which there was a detouring of the marital conflict through the child.

D. Adaptability

HYPOTHESIS: These families demonstrate little flexibility and alternative patterns in response to stress. This rigidity may represent helplessness. Rigid patterns may be particularly evident when the child reaches puberty because the child's moves toward increased autonomy threaten the family equilibrium.

RATIONALE: Such rigidity was noted by Pfeffer (1981). No other research has addressed this issue.

E. Symptom-Maintaining Sequences

HYPOTHESIS: There are deviation-countering feedback loops with the child's expression of individuality/instrumentality indicating the resistance of the system to tolerate the child's separateness and autonomy. Parental responses might include punishment, avoidance (nonresponsiveness), and overprotectiveness (you can do it but not without our help).

RATIONALE: Parents were described as being overly critical and to exhibit many negative behaviors (Arieti & Bemporad, 1980).

CASE STUDY

Background Information

In the following case example, a family with a depressed child will be described. The family had multiple problems; in fact, each member of the family exhibited some symptomatology. However, our discussion will be limited to Tina and her parents where possible.

Tina, an 11-year-old, fourth-grade girl, was identified by her school counselor as a child who needed psychological services possibly for depression. Tina's teachers reported that she was experiencing serious academic difficulties, she was alienating herself from her peers, and she had a very negativistic attitude. However, they noted that she was not a discipline problem. Tina's academic problems in school were not new to her teachers. She was retained in the fourth grade during the previous academic year. If policy did not dictate that a child could not be retained more than once in any given grade, her academic performance was bad enough that she would have failed fourth grade a second time.

On an initial administration of the CDI, Tina received a total score of 39. This score was over 4 standard deviations above the mean and more than double the recommended clinical cut-off score of 19. She reported an increase in the severity of symptomatology (total score of 46) on a second administration of the CDI that was completed one week later. Subsequently, both Tina and her mother were interviewed with the K-SADS-P. Results of the interviews indicated a relatively long-standing episode of dysthymic disorder of at least one year duration.

Tina reported a dysphoric mood that became somewhat worse in the evening. Once she felt sad, there was not much that could be done to cheer her up. Mixed in with the feelings of sadness were feelings of anger, which had parallel characteristics in terms of diurnal variation and reactivity to the environment. In addition to the disturbance in mood, she reported a moderate level of anhedonia and more severe levels of excessive guilt, hopelessness, fatigue, somatic complaints, negative self-image, and feelings of being unloved. She reported a mild level of psychomotor retardation that the interviewer did not detect and some mild initial insomnia. Tina reported some suicidal ideation that was situation-specific and no previous attempts; thus, there was no indication that she was a suicide risk.

Tina came from a chaotic home environment that was comprised of her biological mother, stepfather, biological brother, and a half brother. Tina's mother, who was 30 years old, had been married two previous times. Tina's mother and stepfather had been married for a year and a half. Both of her previous husbands abused alcohol and were physically abusive to her and the children. She worked full-time in a secretarial position. Tina's stepfather was 28 years old and had entered his first marriage. He worked a construction job that provided the family with a relatively stable although modest income. Tina's half brother was 3 years old and a product of the second marriage. The parents reported serious financial problems that resulted in items being repossessed from their mobile home.

Tina's mother was a bright, flirtatious woman who first married at the age of 18 years. Her parents were alcoholics and her father physically abused the mother and the children, and he sexually abused the children. Tina's mother experienced episodes of depression that coincided with her menstrual cycle. In addition, she reported a phobia of driving in heavy traffic and drove a roundabout trail to and from work each day.

Tina's stepfather was a soft spoken, gentle, good-natured man who was not abusive of anyone in the family and he did not abuse drugs or alcohol. His family of origin was a blended family that he described as rigidly run by the stepfather who was quite strict, although not abusive.

Tina's biological brother was an angry and aggressive 9-year-old boy. His bullying of the neighborhood children had led to his social isolation. He was continually grounded by his parents, and the neighborhood parents would not allow him to play with their children. He had been sexually abused by the first stepfather. He was delayed in his reading but very well behaved in school. He craved adult attention. The brother and half brother did not get along with each other. The half brother exhibited delayed speech development, had nocturnal enuresis, and slept with the parents.

Multilevel Family Assessment

Viewed from a systems perspective, Tina's behaviors will be described in the context of family and school relationships. We will examine how her problems are maintained in each system and the reciprocal influences of each system on each other and on Tina.

A. Subsystems

1. *Marital:* Marital conflict was covert. The spouses initially characterized their relationship as solid; however, over time it

became apparent that there was considerable unexpressed conflict. The wife felt as though the husband was not paying enough attention to her and complained about their sex life. The husband was basically satisfied but complained that his authority was undermined by his wife.

2. *Parental:* There was a weak parental subsystem, which would be expected to some extent due to the recent marriage (one and a half years old). It takes time for parents to coordinate and exercise their executive power in the family system. There was a significant lack of clarity regarding family rules, which resulted in a glaring lack of household organization.

3. *Sibling:* The sibling subsystem was fragmented. Relationships within this subsystem were inconsistent and conflictual. The youngest child occupied a favored position with both parents, with the older two vying with each other for attention and control.

B. Boundaries

1. *Parent-Child Relationships:* The boundaries between parent-sibling subsystems were extremely diffuse. Tina's relationship with her mother was enmeshed and her relationship with her stepfather was disengaged. Tina's brother was involved in a detoured-attacking relationship with the mother and father. Tina and her mother appeared to be sensitized to each other's distress. As her mother's emotional tension increased, the arousal appeared to be transmitted to her children and especially Tina. Tina internalized her anxiety and was symptomatic at school and at home, whereas her brother externalized his anxiety at home and in the neighborhood but not at school.

2. *Family-School Relationships.* The boundaries between school and family systems were rigid and relationships were generally disengaged. The school officials' attempts at communicating with the family fell on deaf ears. However, the school placed total blame on the family for Tina's academic problems.

3. *Child-School Relationships.*

a. *Child-teacher:* The parent-child-teacher relationship appeared to be the result of a displacement of the parent-child conflict to the teacher-child relationship. Tina's vulnerability in the family system was evidenced in her relationships with her teachers.

b. *Child-peer:* Tina's peer relationships at school were conflictual. She commonly fought with her peers about anything. Tina perceived other's behavior as personal affronts and thus would lash out at them. Tina was demanding, bossy, controlling, and possessive with peers. Tina was rejected by her peers.

C. Alignment and Power

Tina's involvement in a coalition with her mother against her father was a central feature of this system. This parent-child coalition blurred the boundaries between child and parent subsystems, placing her in an undesirable position of power relative to the father and her brother. This cross-generational coalition further provided the mother with an alternate support system, thus reducing the mother's motivation to deal with marital issues.

Because of the weak parental subsystem within the family, the school was placed in a position of authority. The school functioned as the parental subsystem to the family, which collectively functioned as a sibling subsystem. Tina retained power over the school because of her parents' defiance of the school. Intersystemic conflict between family and school obscured her problems, thereby maintaining her position of power in both systems.

D. Adaptation and Development

The developmental stage of this blended family included consolidating new structures. Another developmental consideration was the fact that Tina had entered puberty. As a consequence, she was beginning to seek some additional autonomy and privileges that were denied by her mother. Likewise, Tina appeared to vacillate between total dependence and a desire for some developmentally appropriate autonomy. The rigidity of the family's structures was revealed in the family's difficulty in adjusting to this developmental transition.

E. Symptom-Maintaining Sequences

The function of Tina's depressive symptoms was to test her mother's love for her and bring some order or focus out of the chaos in the family. Tina's inappropriate behavior was followed by her mother being oversolicitous and her stepfather ignoring things. Tina would escalate her misbehavior, followed by her mother and stepfather becoming punitive. Her mother attacked her father for being too strict and she would begin to feel guilty about punishing Tina and back out of her punishment. Additionally, her mother undermined the stepfather's authority. Tina successfully avoided the negative consequences for her misbehavior. She viewed her stepfather as the cause of any problems she had at home and as the individual who had split Tina and her mother apart. In a parallel manner, both the school and family scapegoated each other as being the cause of the problem.

Extrafamilial Relationships

The family was experiencing a significant number of external stressors including financial problems and their neighbors rejected them as a result of their children's misbehavior. Each parent had some acquaintances at work but neither did anything after work with any friends. The parents rarely did anything together outside of the home with other people. Their closest relatives lived too far away to provide much direct support.

Family-School Intervention

The intervention program was designed to: (1) reduce the chaos through the establishment of a routine, (2) strengthen the parental dyad, (3) reduce the mother-daughter enmeshment and engage the stepfather in Tina's life, and (4) establish a line of communication between the home and school.

The discrepancy between the children's generally appropriate behavior at school, daycare, and home was used as the rationale for creating additional structure and routine at home. Through the Socratic process, the parents were helped to see that their children behaved appropriately when there were clear, consistent rules set for their behavior and when they had to eat, sleep, change, and so on, on a preset routine. Education and problem solving were the primary techniques used within the sessions to develop a routine.

Family members were given homework assignments to collect relevant information and to develop and test routines. Since the stepfather was a slave to his routine, he was given the directive to take primary responsibility for the development of the family routine. This objective was achieved when the parents reported the development of a routine, exhibited it during the sessions, and were able to report that they could spontaneously modify it to fit new life circumstances.

Support, education, coaching, and corrective feedback were some of the procedures used to strengthen the parental subsystem as well as to obtain a change in the boundaries. The focus of much of this portion of the intervention was on the parents' acquiring more adaptive and positive approaches to managing their children's behavior. Contingent reinforcement of appropriate behavior and timeout for maladaptive behavior were emphasized, whereas physical punishment and yelling were discouraged.

In addition, the parents were encouraged to take more of an active parenting style that promoted prevention and the early termination of unacceptable child behaviors. Emphasis was placed on prompting the parents to utilize their new skills in response to spontaneous sequences and within-session enactments. Homework assignments were given to collect information to determine whether they were functioning as a team or whether one of them was undermining the other.

The therapists' observations suggested that the latter was the case. In fact, the parents concluded from their homework that they were not working in unison. Subsequently, they were educated about the confusion this created for the children and they were coached to work as an executive team during the sessions and corrective feedback was given when necessary. They were then asked to continue to monitor their support for each other during disciplinary actions. After a couple of weeks, the parents were functioning more as a pair in the sessions and reported that they had avoided undermining one another during disciplinary situations.

To reduce mother-daughter enmeshment and strengthen Tina's relationship with her stepfather, Tina and her stepfather developed plans to do enjoyable, low-cost activities together. Tina's stepfather also was placed in charge of helping Tina with her school work and he provided her with transportation to social events on weekends. Boundaries between parental and sibling subsystems were further defined by encouraging the parents to develop plans to be alone.

It became evident that the first three objectives were being met when the parents' spontaneously reported the development and implementation of their own behavior management plans. They had developed and followed through on plans to keep the youngest son out of their bed at night and to manage a number of additional problematic behaviors. The parents worked

out more time to be alone and to do things as a family. In addition, Tina began to call and refer to her stepfather as "dad" instead of calling him by his first name.

To improve the school-family relationship, meetings were held between school personnel and Tina's parents. In addition, one of the therapists consulted with Tina's teachers on a regular basis and set up a reward system for the completion of her homework.

SUMMARY

Although interest in childhood depression has increased dramatically over the past decade, researchers, theoreticians, and practitioners have approached this very serious clinical concern from an adult perspective. That is, they have treated depressed children like depressed adults and applied the existing adult models and treatment procedures. Typically this means that the focus is on the intrapsychic processes of the individual and much less attention is paid to the individual's family.

Research, although somewhat contradictory, suggests that the academic performance of children may suffer during an episode of depression. However, this impairment may be nonspecific to psychopathology and appears to improve following recovery from a depressive episode. It also appears as though there is some impairment in the social functioning of depressed children. Some aspects of this impairment are specific to depression. The most noticeable impairment is in quantity and quality of communication.

Clinical impressions and research suggest that there are disturbances in the interactions of families with a depressed child. The affective tone of the family relationships is negative and sometimes described as cold and hostile. There is a minimum of support and an excess of conflict. The families often are quite chaotic, experiencing many major life changes and other stressors. The child management techniques of the parents are characterized as punitive and in some cases abusive or neglectful. At the least, the parents manage their children's behavior through psychologically damaging procedures such as the inducement of guilt. The families appear to lock themselves into a maximum of exposure to this style of interaction by engaging in a minimum of social and recreational activities that might allow them a respite from these negative interactions.

Given the paucity of research that is based on systems theory, we proposed a model of family functioning that was based on systems theory and the research that was reviewed. The marital system was hypothesized to be weak and the parent-child boundaries as diffuse, defining enmeshed relationships. There may be two types of dysfunctional alignments—stable coalitions and detouring coalitions. Finally, this pattern of interactions was characterized as rigid and inflexible.

References

Abrahams, M. J., & Whitlock, F. A. (1969). Childhood experiences and depression. *British Journal of Psychiatry, 115,* 883–888.

Abramson, L., Seligman, M. E. P., & Teasdale (1978). Learned helplessness in humans: Critique and reformulation. *Journal of Abnormal Psychology, 87,* 49–74.

Achenbach, T. M. (1982). *Developmental psychopathology.* New York: Wiley.

Achenbach, T. M., & Edelbrock, C. S. (1978). The classification of child psychopathology: A review and analysis of empirical efforts. *Psychological Review, 85,* 1275–1301.

Amanat, E., & Butler, C. (1984). Oppressive behaviors in the families of depressed children. *Family Therapy, 11,* 65–77.

American Psychiatric Association (1987). *Diagnostic and statistical manual of mental disorders* (3rd ed.). Washington, DC: Author.

Aponte, H. J. (1976). Underorganization in the poor family. In P. J. Guerin (Ed.), *Family therapy: Theory and practice.* New York: Gardner.

Aponte, H. J., & VanDeusen, J. M. (1981). Structural family therapy. In A. Gurman & D. Kniskern (Eds.), *Handbook of family therapy* (pp. 310–360). New York: Brunner/Mazel.

Arieti, S., & Bemporad, J. R. (1980). The psychological organization of depression. *American Journal of Psychiatry, 137,* 1360–1365.

Asarnow, J. R., Carlson, G. A., & Guthrie, D. (1987). Coping strategies, self-perceptions, hopelessness, and perceived family environments in depressed and suicidal children. *Journal of Consulting and Clinical Psychology, 55,* 361–366.

Bandura, A. (1977). *Social learning theory.* Englewood Cliffs, NJ: Prentice Hall.

Barragan, M. (1976). The child-centered family. In P. J. Guerin (Ed.), *Family therapy: Theory and practice.* New York: Gardner.

Bateson, G. (1972). *Steps to an ecology of mind.* New York: Ballantine.

Bateson, G. (1979). *Mind and nature.* New York: Dutton.

Beck, A. T. (1967). *Depression: Clinical, experimental, and theoretical aspects.* New York: Hoeber.

Blatt, S. J., Wein, S. J., Chevron, E., & Quinlan, D. M. (1979). Parental representations and depression in normal young adults. *Journal of Abnormal Psychology, 88,* 388–397.

Brookman, C. S. (1988). A multimethod study of depression in children: Family process and perceived family environment. Unpublished doctoral dissertation, The University of Texas at Austin.

Butler, L., Miezitis, S., Friedman, R., & Cole, E. (1980). The effects of two school-based intervention programs on depressive symptoms in preadolescents. *American Educational Research Journal, 17,* 111–119.

Carlson, C. (1987). Eco-structural family therapy for school psychologists. *School Psychology Review, 16,* 457–468.

Cole, D. A., & Rehm, L. P. (1986). Family interaction patterns and childhood depression. *Journal of Abnormal Child Psychology, 14,* 297–314.

Connell, H. M. (1972). Depression in childhood. *Child Psychiatry and Human Development, 4,* 71–85.

Crook, T., Raskin, A., & Eliot, J. (1981). Parent-child relations and adult depression. *Child Development, 52,* 950–957.

Feshbach, N. D., & Feshbach, S. (1987). Affective processes and academic achievement. *Child Development, 58,* 1335–1347.

Glaser, K. (1967). Masked depression in children and adolescents. *Annual Progress in Child Psychiatry and Child Development, 1,* 345–355.

Grossman, J. A., Poznanski, E. O., & Banegas, M. E. (1983). Lunch: Time to study family interactions. *Journal of Psychosocial Nursing and Mental Health Services, 21,* 19–22.

Haley, G. M. T., Fine, S., Marriage, K., Moretti, M. M., & Freeman, R. J. (1985). Cognitive bias in depression in psychiatrically disturbed children and adolescents. *Journal of Consulting and Clinical Psychology, 53,* 535–537.

Haley, J. (1970). Approaches to family therapy. *International Journal of Psychiatry, 9,* 233–242.

Haley, J. (1973). Strategic therapy when a child is presented as the problem. *Journal of the American Academy of Child Psychiatry, 12,* 641–659.

Haley, J. (1976). *Problem solving therapy.* San Francisco: Jossey-Bass.

Hoffman, L. (1981). *Foundations of family therapy: A conceptual framework for systems change.* New York: Basic Books.

Hollon, T. H. (1970). Poor school performance as a symptom of masked depression in children and adolescents. *American Journal of Psychotherapy, 24,* 258–263.

Jackson, D. (1957). The question of family homeostasis. *Psychiatric Quarterly Supplement, 31,* 79–90.

Jacobsen, R. H., Lahey, B. B., & Strauss, C. C. (1983). Correlates of depressed mood in normal children. *Journal of Abnormal Child Psychology, 11,* 29–39.

Jacobson, S., Fasman, J., & DiMascio, A. (1976). Deprivation in the childhood of depressed women. *The Journal of Nervous and Mental Disease, 160,* 5–14.

Kashani, J. H., & Carlson, G. A. (1985). Major depressive disorder in a preschooler. *Journal of the American Academy of Child Psychiatry, 24,* 490–494.

Kashani, J. H., Ray, J. S., & Carlson, G. A. (1984). Depression and depressive-like states in preschool-age children in a child development unit. *American Journal of Psychiatry, 141,* 1397–1402.

Kaslow, N. J., & Rehm, L. P. (1983). Childhood depression. In R. J. Morris & T. R. Kratochwill (Eds.), *The practice of child therapy* (pp. 27–51). New York: Pergamon.

Kaslow, N. J., & Rehm, L. (in press). Conceptualization, assessment, and treatment of depression in children. In A. E. Kazdin & P. Bornstein (Eds.), *Handbook of clinical behavior therapy with children.* New York: Dorsey.

Kaslow, N. J., Rehm, L. P., & Siegel, A. W. (1984). Social cognitive and cognitive correlates of depression in children. *Journal of Abnormal Child Psychology, 12,* 605–620.

Kazdin, A. E., Esveldt-Dawson, K., Unis, A. S., & Rancurello, M. D. (1983). Child and parent evaluations of depression in psychiatric inpatient children. *Journal of Abnormal Child Psychology, 11,* 401–413.

Kendall, P. C., Stark, K. D., & Adam, T. (in press). Cognitive deficit or cognitive distortion in childhood depression. *Journal of Abnormal Psychology.*

Kovacs, M. (1981). Rating scales to assess depression in school-age children. *Acta Paedopsychiatrica, 46,* 305–315.

Kovacs, M., & Beck, A. T. (1977). An empirical clinical approach towards a definition of childhood depression. In J. G. Schulterbrandt & A. Raskin (Eds.), *Depression in childhood: Diagnosis, treatment and conceptual models.* New York: Raven.

LaMont, J., Fischoff, S., & Gottlieb, H. (1976). Recall of parental behaviors in female neurotic depressives. *Journal of Clinical Psychology, 32,* 762–765.

LaMont, J., & Gottlieb, H. (1975). Convergent recall of parental behaviors in depressed students of different racial groups. *Journal of Clinical Psychology, 31,* 9–11.

Lefkowitz, M. M., & Tesiny, E. P. (1985). Depression in children: Prevalence and correlates. *Journal of Consulting and Clinical Psychology, 53,* 647–656.

Leon, G. R., Kendall, P. C., & Garber, J. (1980). Depression in children: Parent, teacher, and child perspectives. *Journal of Abnormal Child Psychology, 8,* 221–235.

Madanes, C. (1983). *Strategic family therapy.* San Francisco: Jossey-Bass.

McCranie, E. W., & Bass, J. D. (1984). Childhood family antecedents of dependency and self-criticism: Implications for depression. *Journal of Abnormal Psychology, 93,* 3–8.

Minuchin, S. (1974). *Families and family therapy.* Cambridge, MA: Harvard University Press.

Minuchin, S., & Fishman, H. C. (1981). *Family therapy techniques.* Cambridge, MA: Harvard University Press.

Minuchin, S., Montalvo, B., Guerney, B., Rosman, B., & Schumer, F. (1967). *Families of the slums.* New York: Basic Books.

Minuchin, S., Rosman, B., & Baker, L. (1978). *Psychosomatic families.* Cambridge, MA: Harvard University Press.

Moos, R. H., & Moos, B. S. (1981). *Family Environment Scale Manual.* Palo Alto, CA: Consulting Psychologists Press.

Moyal, B. R. (1977). Locus of control, self-esteem, stimulus appraisal, and depressive symptoms in children. *Journal of Consulting and Clinical Psychology, 45,* 951–952.

Munro, A. (1966). Parental deprivation in depressive patients. *British Journal of Psychiatry, 112,* 443–457.

Nichols, M. P. (1984). *Family therapy: Concepts and methods.* New York: Gardner.

Parker, G. (1979). Parental characteristics in relation to depressive disorders. *British Journal of Psychiatry, 134,* 138–147.

Parker, G. (1982). Parental representations and affective symptoms: Examination for an hereditary link. *British Journal of Medical Psychology, 55,* 57–61.

Pfeffer, C. R. (1981). The family system of suicidal children. *American Journal of Psychotherapy, 35,* 330–341.

Poznanski, E. O., Cook, S. C., Carroll, B. J., & Corzo, H. (1983). Use of the Children's Depression Rating Scale in an inpatient psychiatric population. *Journal of Clinical Psychiatry, 44,* 200–203.

Puig-Antich, J., Lukens, E., Davies, M., Goetz, D., Brennan-Quattrock, J., & Todak, G. (1985a). Psychosocial functioning in prepubertal major depressive disorders I: Interpersonal relationships during the depressive episode. *Archives of General Psychiatry, 42,* 500–507.

Puig-Antich, J., Lukens, E., Davies, M., Goetz, D., Brennan-Quattrock, J., & Todak, G. (1985b). Psychosocial functioning in prepubertal major depressive disorders II: Interpersonal relationships after sustained recovery from affective episode. *Archives of General Psychiatry, 42,* 511–517.

Puig-Antich, J., Novacenko, H., Goetz, R., Corser, J., Davies, M., & Ryan, N. (1984). Cortisol and prolactin responses to insulin-induced hypoglycemia in prepubertal major depressives during episode and after recovery. *Journal of the American Academy of Child Psychiatry, 23,* 49–57.

Puig-Antich, J., & Ryan, N. (1986). Schedule for affective disorders and schizophrenia for school-age children (6–18 years)—Kiddie-SADS (K-SADS). Unpublished manuscript. Western Psychiatric Institute and Clinic, Pittsburgh, PA.

Raskin, A., Boothe, H. H., Reatig, N. A., & Schulterbrandt, J. G. (1971). Factor analyses of normal and depressed patients' memories of parental behavior. *Psychological Reports, 29,* 871–879.

Rehm, L. P. (1977). A self-control model of depression. *Behavior Therapy, 8,* 787–804.

Reynolds, W. M. (1984). Depression in children and adolescents: Phenomenology, evaluation and treatment. *School Psychology Review, 13,* 171–182.

Reynolds, W. M., & Coats, K. I. (1986). A comparison of cognitive-behavioral therapy and relaxation training for the treatment of depression in adolescents. *Journal of Consulting and Clinical Psychology, 54,* 653–660.

Satir, V. (1967). *Conjoint family therapy.* Palo Alto, CA: Science and Behavior Books.

Schwarz, J. C., & Zuroff, D. C. (1979). Family structure and depression in female college students: Effects of parental conflict, decision making power, and inconsistency of love. *Journal of Abnormal Psychology, 88,* 398–406.

Seligman, M. E. P., Peterson, C., Kaslow, N. J., Tanenbaum, R., Alloy, L. B., & Abramson, L. Y. (1984). Explanatory style and depressive symptoms among school children. *Journal of Abnormal Psychology, 93,* 235–238.

Simons, A. D., Garfield, S. L., & Murphy, G. E. (1984). The process of change in cognitive therapy and pharmacotherapy for depression. *Archives of General Psychiatry, 41,* 45–51.

Stanton, M. D. (1981). Strategic approaches to family therapy. In A. Gurman & D. Kniskern (Eds.), *Handbook of family therapy* (pp. 361–402). New York: Brunner/Mazel.

Stanton, M. D., & Todd, T. C. (1979). Structural family therapy with drug addicts. In E. Kaufman & P. Kaufman (Eds.), *The family therapy of drug and alcohol abuse.* New York: Gardner.

Stark, K. D., Best, L. R., & Sellstrom, E. A. (in press). A cognitive-behavioral approach to the treatment of childhood depression. In J. N. Hughes & R. J. Hall (Eds.), *Cognitive behavioral approaches in educational settings.* New York: Guilford.

Stark, K. D., Brookman, C., & Frazier, R. (in press). A comprehensive school-based treatment program for depressed children. *Professional School Psychology*

Stark, K. D., Brookman, C., Vevier, E., & Jolley, P. (1988). A comparison of the family environments of depressed and nondepressed children. Manuscript in preparation.

Stark, K. D., Kaslow, N. J., Hill, S. J., & Lux, M. G. (1987). Childhood depression as assessed with the Children's Depression Inventory and the Schedule for Affective Disorders and Schizophrenia for School-Age Children: Relationships to cognitive and affective variables. Manuscript submitted for publication.

Stark, K. D., Kaslow, N. J., Rehm, L. P., & Reynolds, W. M. (1988). A comparison of the relative efficacy of cognitive-behavioral and nonspecific therapies for the treatment of depression in children. Manuscript in preparation.

Stark, K. D., Reynolds, W. M., & Kaslow, N. J. (1987). A comparison of the relative efficacy of self-control therapy and a behavioral problem-solving therapy for depression in children. *Journal of Abnormal Child Psychology, 15,* 91–113.

Stark, K. D., Reynolds, W. M., Kaslow, N. J., Rehm, L. P, & Linn, J. D. (1988). Assessment of depressive symptomatology in school children: An exploration of variables that mediate rater variance. Manuscript submitted for publication.

Strauss, C. S., Lahey, B. B., & Jacobsen, R. H. (1982). The relationship of three measures of childhood depression to academic underachievement. *Journal of Applied Developmental Psychology, 3,* 375–380.

Tesiny, E. P., & Lefkowitz, M. M. (1982). Childhood depression: A six-month follow-up study. *Journal of Consulting and Clinical Psychology, 50,* 778–780.

Tesiny, E. P., Lefkowitz, M. M., & Gordon, N. H. (1980). Childhood depression, locus of control, and school achievement. *Journal of Educational Psychology, 72,* 506–510.

Vincenzi, H. (1987). Depression and reading ability in sixth grade children. *Journal of School Psychology, 25,* 155–160.

Walsh, F. (1982). *Normal family processes.* New York: Guilford.

Watzlawick, P., Beavin, J., & Jackson, D. (1967). *Pragmatics of human communication: A study of interactional patterns, pathologies and paradoxes.* New York: Norton.

White, M. (1979). Structural and strategic approaches to psychosomatic families. *Family Process, 19,* 303–314.

16

School Refusal and
Family System Intervention

NICHOLAS C. ALIOTTI
Family Enrichment Center
La Mesa, California

OVER FIFTY YEARS AGO Broadwin (1932) described school phobia as a problem emanating from the family system. In particular, he noted a characteristic of the school-phobic child was the tendency to stay with the mother or near the home, a factor that purportedly distinguished the school-phobic child from the truant. Although investigations of school phobia have distinguished between *school phobia* and *truancy,* with the former term associated with separation anxiety, and the latter associated with delinquency, from a family systems perspective, the distinctions may be more ephemeral than real. Viewing the problem from a family perspective provides for a more open process that entertains other possible interpretations. For example, Davidson (1961) described these children as "mother phobes" rather than "school phobes" and viewed the problem as a family problem rather than a diagnosis.

In planning strategic family interventions with such children, assessment of the family context plays a paramount role. Consistent with the family systems perspective, the term *school refusal* rather than *school phobia* fits best within a systemic framework and is utilized in this chapter. *School refusal* is a more open term and does not have the connotation of focusing on a feared stimulus or *reaction* exclusively within the child. Furthermore, *school refusal* reflects the *intentional, instrumental* aspects of the behavior rather than the retrospective, circumscribed viewpoint of a condition ascribed to the child. Occasional usage of the term *school phobia* in this chapter reflects the historical context of how this school problem has been described.

Minuchin (1984) has commented specifically on a family system perspective in treating this disorder:

> If a child is referred to treatment because of a school phobia, the 1966 Group for the Advancement of Psychiatry report states: "The child has unconsciously displaced the content of his original conflict onto . . . a situation in the external environment that has symbolic significance for him. . . . Thus the child avoids those situations that revive or intensify his displaced conflict. . . ." (p. 232)

The focus of this diagnosis does not take into account the environment of the child or the target of the phobia. But looking at the child with school phobia in his or her current life context broadens possible points of entry. The problem and/or an area available to therapeutic interventions might be found in the school, the home, or the interval between school and home.

Minuchin (1984) adds:

> In exploring the school context for possible points of entry, the therapist would look at the child's perception of himself as a learner and his performance as a student. He would explore the child's position in the peer group and his self-perception as a member of this peer group, his relationship with the teacher and the ways he perceives the teacher as similar to or different from other significant adults, the teacher's view of the child and how correct and differentiated that view is, and how the child and the teacher work together. (p. 450)

Waldfogel's (Waldfogel, Tessman, & Hahn, 1959; Waldfogel, Collidge, & Hahn, 1957) characterization of school phobia further explicated the multifaceted nature of school phobia and strongly suggested the need for a systems approach in treating this problem. The sequence he observed is especially instructive:

1. The child displays and expresses an acute fear that is associated with the school.
2. He or she tends to report a variety of somatic symptoms, including nausea, gastrointestinal distress, and headaches.
3. The somatic complaints are used as a device to justify staying at home.
4. The child resists all attempts at reassurance, reasoning, or coercion by the family and school personnel.
5. As the problem continues, the potential exists for establishing an equilibrium or stalemate, which, from the perspective of the school and family, becomes a disabling disorder of childhood or adolescence.

Without a successful intervention, a vicious circle may develop where the longer the child stays out of school, the more severe are the social and educational impairments and the more difficult is the problem of treatment.

From a systemic view, school refusal behavior also typically elicits the involvement of other subsystems in the community. These can include the juvenile system, the medical system (a course of hospitalization or a 24-hour school may be suggested in extreme cases), or other subsystems that interface between the child, the family system, and society. In San Diego county, for example, students can be referred to the SARB (School Attendance Review Board), which meets monthly and includes representatives from the school district, the County Department of Education, the San Diego County Juvenile Probation Office, and the San Diego County Sheriff's Department. Parents can be enjoined under penalty of fines to assure school attendance, an attendance contract can be developed, subsistence payments can be eliminated, or the child can be placed on probation and ordered by the court to attend a probation school.

Traditional consultation approaches to school refusal have typically followed one of three models: behavioral, psychoanalytic, or mental health approaches.

BEHAVIORAL APPROACHES

Behavioral consultants view school refusal from the perspective of social learning theory. The focus of school consultation is on the students' dysfunctional symptoms, which are seen as directly related to the interactions between antecedent events and consequences. School consultants seek to control the environment by arranging reward and nonreinforcement events. Usually, but not exclusively, the phobic child is viewed as the primary focus of treatment.

Since schools typically focus on the offending symptoms such as nonattendance, tardies, visits to the nurse, out-of-bounds behavior, academic failure, and the like, these symptoms are typically measured to obtain a baseline prior to instituting a treatment. This leads to a paradigmatic intervention involving baseline measurements, behavioral interventions, and a return to a baseline or nontreatment stage. Behavioral consultants seek to reduce or eliminate the students' presenting problem behaviors by working with school staff and the parents in using shaping, incentive programs, response cost, and so on to "motivate" the child and thereby increase school attendance.

PSYCHOANALYTIC APPROACH

Psychoanalytic approaches view school phobia as a specific neurosis where anxiety is partly relieved by the child's or adolescent's attachment of these feelings onto an object, person, or situation in order for the individual to keep intact his or her personality functioning. Differential diagnosis is likely to consider whether other psychiatric syndromes may account for the symptom of school phobia. These could include hysteria, obsessional states, depressive states, and psychosis. The treatment focus is directed to the underlying psychiatric disturbance and not to the symptom of school phobia.

Psychoanalytic approaches tend to view motivational states of school phobia as mostly determined by the child's intrapsychic functions. Systemic family approaches would stress the ongoing sequential interactions that preceded and continue to maintain the school phobia. Framo (1982) is critical of this psychoanalytic perspective. He writes:

One gets the curious feeling, in reading in the psychoanalytic literature, that the patient lives in a vacuum, that the intra-psychic world is a closed system, that life stops when one is in analysis, and that the environment is largely treated as a constant.

Framo further notes that psychoanalytic theory functions from "the assumption that it is not the environment that makes people sick but that people do it to themselves via fantasy and intrapsychic work and the elaboration of what goes on inside."

Framo (1982) argues for a theoretical position that melds the relationship between intrapsychic and transactional phenomena. He states, "The creative leap of the family system theory was recognition of the interlocking, multi-personal motivational system whereby family members collusively carry psychic functions for each other."

MENTAL HEALTH CONSULTATION

Traditional mental health approaches (Caplan, 1970) see the goal of consultation as helping the teacher, counselor, and others who work with the child to gain insight into normal and abnormal emotional development and personality dynamics. This model assumes that by this increased understanding, the school staff can create a healthier emotional climate for children. Typically, this model did not include the child or the family. Clients and families were not viewed as part of the treatment plan. One of the questions of this model is whether or not increasing understanding of the child's feelings and perspective would really change his or her school-refusal behavior.

THE TWO SUBSYSTEMS: FAMILY AND SCHOOL

Nicholas Hobbs's (1966) keynote address to the 74th Annual Meeting of the American Psychological Association stressed the need for the family system and school system to work effectively to further the emotional development of children. He emphasized the need to view the child or adolescent from the perspective of a large ecological system where each aspect of the child or adolescent's life is interrelated. Essentially, the child's or adolescent's parents work as collaborators to provide their offspring with an environment that works harmoniously on their behalf. The goal is for the school and family system to work effectively as one functional unit.

Green (1985) has described the school and family systems and their interface. For example, entering a junior or senior high school presents a variety of new roles and behaviors for students and their families. An influx of new people, ideas, situations, and challenges must be confronted. In addition, the adolescent period itself, with its concomitant physical changes, identity issues, and the like, influences the student as well as the parents.

As the adolescent struggles for individuation and social competence in the school system, the family system must necessarily flex and become more elastic. Social and role boundaries may need to accommodate to other subsystems, including school organizations such as the band, athletics, and school social events. In this process, the transition is eased and facilitated when there is collaboration between the school and family systems.

When functioning in one or both systems deteriorates, the adolescent may begin to show dysfunctional behavior, including school refusal. To thoroughly understand school refusal, it is necessary to view how adolescents are dealing with this normal adolescent phase, how families negotiate the required increase of experiences and times away from the family and its influence, and how the adolescent develops the social skills and identity consolidation that will result in a well-developed ego, social competence, and appropriate relationships with authority figures. The school system is but one of several systems in which the adolescent must develop competencies in successfully coping with a system. Students who do not cope successfully in the school system invariably find it difficult to cope with their own family systems, the work system, the military system, and other social systems of which they will later be a part.

AN OVERVIEW OF SCHOOL PHOBIA

Since school-refusal behavior typically activates the school and family systems into some form of interaction, family system consultants need to be cognizant of what is known about school-refusal behavior.

Interested readers are referred to Marks (1969), Kahn and Nursten (1968), and Goodwin (1983) for reviews of school phobia. This disorder includes the following features. The first signs of school phobia take the form of physical complaints or simple school refusal. This is particularly true for younger children. Older students will attribute their concerns, which the school system labels as school phobia, to a variety of aspects of school life. They may complain of teachers, dressing for gym, aggressive peers, and the like. This is often accompanied by vague physical symptoms.

Percipitating factors often include level changes in the educational system or family life events. In a sample of 50 cases, Hersov (1960) reported a peak age of onset at 11 to 12 years, a period coincident with the period in England when most children move from a primary to a secondary school. Similarly, a break in school attendance following a weekend, new term, holiday, or illness has been associated as a precipitant.

Family life events that have been observed include a death in the family, birth of a sibling, and financial distress. In attempting to understand the problem, the family and school systems posit a variety of reasons of what the feared objects or events might be in the school environment. As the child's or adolescent's complaints increase, the parents' anxiety about the child increases and a covert or overt agreement eventually often developed in which one or both of the parents believe the child should stay at home. Since school attendance is mandatory in most states, the school system soon intervenes and this usually results in the referral.

One of the first tasks of school-based consultation in family system intervention is assessment of the family (see Chapter 2 of this volume) Paget (1987) and others have described a variety of assessment procedures elsewhere. In particular, school and family system consultants should be sensitive to particular constellations of symptoms, which will be discussed next.

ASSESSMENT OF SCHOOL REFUSAL

The Dependency-Attachment Dyad

A hallmark symptom complex that is often encountered in cases of school refusal is the dependency-attachment dyad. Hersov (1960) and others have reported that parental attitudes in cases of school refusal are often significantly unusual. In Hersov's sample, half the mothers were noted to be overly indulgent and the students to be dominated by their mother, whereas a quarter experienced the opposite and had parents who were severe, demanding, and controlling.

A related finding, with significant implications for family systems approaches, is the fact that the parents' close dependence on and from their children may be masking in many mothers unsatisfactory marital or personal relationships. Often these mothers also report histories of unhappy relationships with parents in their family of origin. Careful interviewing designed to elicit transgenerational information in these areas often provides important clues to understanding school-refusal behavior.

Projective Distortion

In assessing transactional processes in the family that may be maintaining school refusal, it is very important for the school-based consultant to assess the projective distortions that may be occurring between family members. Kramer (1987) suggests that "one way of assessing these projective processes is to focus on the affectively charged issues that are being expressed. Often the most emotionally charged situations have to do with the projective phenomenon."

Thus, according to Kramer, a father who is critical of his son for being weak and becomes exasperated and outraged when his son becomes weak may be reflecting the father's "vulnerable-weaker side" that he cannot tolerate in himself. When this occurs as a pattern in encounters with family members, it may be helpful to obtain historical accounts of the family's origin and to document the father's need to separate from his consciousness his more "weaker-vulnerable side."

Similarly, the parent with low self-esteem may attempt to keep from his or her own child the parent's weaker-vulnerable side. The parent may have great anxiety regarding the child's ability to achieve competency in the school system with its demands for academic and social adequacy. The parent may also fear the inherent competition that exists in functioning in a social system. In assessing the family system, school psychologists, family therapists, and school-based consultants should be mindful of these family perceptions of school.

Kahn and Nursten (1968, p. 105) describe a case study in which a projective distortion by the parents played a critical role in understanding and treating the phobia.

CASE STUDY 1

Graham is an 11-year-old boy of middle-class parents. His mother was a teacher and the father held a clerical post. He has one older brother, 12 years his senior. At the time of the referral, Graham had not attended school for six months and was spending most of his time in bed. Initially, his symptoms were so severe he had to be seen in his home. His symptoms, which included dizziness and altered perceptions, had begun following the graduation ceremony of the older brother.

Graham claimed he was unable to get out of his bed but he ate meals normally, read school books and fiction, and played with his toys. Although he seemed highly intelligent with mature interests for his age, his play was often at an infantile level. Interestingly, his older brother, living in a dormitory away from home, had simultaneously given his parents news of his success in his degree examination and notice of his intent to be married. The marriage was arranged to take place two weeks after the ceremony of the conferring of his degree. The brother never returned to his home as a single young man.

This case, representative of a psychodynamic team approach, involved two sessions a week in the home by the treating psychiatrist for six months, followed by a course of treatment as an outpatient in a child guidance clinic. A social woker also maintained collateral contacts with the family and school. Play therapy (involving drawing) in the home finally provided a clue that led to a family systems hypothesis, which proved to be essential in treating the problem. Asked to draw something he had dreamed of, Graham produced a tram car. When asked to describe it, he said it was a black one that could be used for "an important occasion—such as a wedding."

After some inquiring, the psychiatrist asked what Graham's feelings were when he and his family learned that his older brother would be marrying and not return to the home, and whether they felt they had lost him. Graham was loud in his protestation that this was not the case. However, independent parent interviews with both parents by the social worker confirmed both the parents' pride and their feeling of dissatisfaction with the older son. Furthermore, as pacifists, they had great difficulty expressing anger. For example, Graham's parents stated that when Graham had to be carried to the clinic by his father, struggling, punching, and kicking, "he could not really have known what he was doing."

In understanding Graham's behavior from a family systems perspective, it is noteworthy that a significant breakthrough in therapy came when the therapist understood the school-refusal behavior as the child's way of complying with "the parents need for reassurance that *he* was still with them," despite the fact they had lost an older treasured son "as a result of the freedom given by academic success."

In effect, the members of the family system had a covert pact to maintain the school-refusal behavior as a collusive means of coping with their own projections of anxiety and anger regarding the possibility of losing a second son to the academic process. The resistance of the family to change was reflected in the anger directed toward the treatment team. The conscientiousness of the family members to keep their appointments, however, served to keep them in treatment.

Graham eventually completed secondary school and, following treatment, successfully completed requirements for university entrance. What is most significant from a treatment perspective is the possibility that earlier intervention based on an assessment from family systems theory may have significantly reduced the considerable time and effort expended by the treatment team.

The need to involve the noncustodial parent in a family systems approach to school refusal was reported by Green (1985).

CASE STUDY 2

Sally was referred for therapy at the beginning of seventh grade due to her refusal to attend school. Her parents were divorced when she was 4 years old. Her father had been remarried for two years, and the mother had never remarried. Sally lived with her mother and older brother. Although Sally's father and stepmother lived within walking distance, Sally and her brother had only minimal, sporadic contact with their father. Sally's mother had a history of unemployment, often coincident with Sally's history of school refusal; her father was a local businessman with steady employment.

In addition to school-refusal history, Sally had a variety of maladaptive behaviors, including physical aggression toward her mother, immaturity, and a long history of physical illnesses and complaints. She had also been seen by at least five therapists. Sally's older brother functioned as the responsible child with adequate social and academic behavior, but had an intensely rivalous relationship with Sally.

In assessing the family system and school systems, it was determined that neither the school nor the family had been contacted about Sally's current and past difficulties. Both the school and the family appeared locked into an enmeshment pattern of some duration. Sally and her mother still shared a bed, and the daughter still sat in mother's lap at meetings. Both the school and Sally's mother seemed frustrated and helpless in working with Sally.

Following a meeting with Sally, her mother, and brother, and a telephone consultation with her school counselor, Green posited the following hypothesis:

It was hypothesized that Sally's school refusal protected mother from seeking and maintaining gainful employment and that it served to keep the family locked in the developmental stage of Sally being a young child, which she was at the time of the divorce. It also served to provide mother with sufficient material on which to focus her anger and resentment at her husband for leaving her and inhibited full emotional resolution concerning the divorce. In addition, it prevented mother and father from joining together in a collaborative parenting relationship. (p. 200)

In terms of power, the situation represented an inverted hierarchy in which Sally was clearly in charge. Role boundaries between mother and daughter were also diffuse, as the mother would always call on the assistant principal for help—an action that excluded the father. These communication patterns proved so mystifying to the school that the family's goals and the school's responsibility were obscure.

Green posited the need to involve Sally's father in an appropriate way with both systems in order to mitigate the enmeshment pattern present in both systems. Green's goals were to establish a functional hierarchy with the adults in charge of Sally in a collaborative, nonsabotaging manner. It was felt that Sally's educational issues could only be addressed when the school and family established clear boundaries.

A series of meetings involving differing subsets of members of both subsystems were held. A plan was devised where the parents would work as partners to get Sally out of bed and into a car if she refused to go to school. School personnel agreed to assist the parents as needed. Anticipating the possibility of the mother sabotaging the plan, the issue was indirectly addressed by a paradoxical intervention. Since the mother had linked going back to work as being dependent on Sally's school attendance, it was suggested that this would probably not be possible and that the mother should be prepared for additional years of battling with Sally to attend school.

The school also cooperated in the paradox by noting the high school was not prepared to continue the level of assistance previously provided and by indicating that the mother would be left on her own to deal with Sally. The parents and school also agreed that the weather conditions were justifiable reasons for Sally to stay at home and presented them to Sally.

The combination of assigning the noninvolved parent with his ex-wife to strategically monitor their daughter, the paradoxical message to the mother supported by the school, and the school taking an appropriate assistant role was sufficient to elicit regular attendance within two weeks. Once a pattern of attendance was established, other interventions were instituted that resulted in additional collaborative efforts between the parents and the school. Sally was also found to have significant learning disabilities, which en-

abled the school to offer academic support through Public Law 94–142.

Conoley's (1987) case study of school refusal in a school-aged child utilized both standard school-based strategies and strategic family interventions, and contrasted traditional school-based consultation and family interventions in assisting the child and her family.

CASE STUDY 3

Shannon, a fourth-grade girl, was referred for services due to school refusal. Her school-refusal behavior would begin in the evening when she announced her intentions not to attend school, take a bath, go to bed, fix her lunch, or prepare her school clothes. Initially, in the first two weeks, her parents physically carried her and drove her to school, and then had her taken from them by the school principal. She spent the first period in class crying, but by the end of the hour she would be positively engaged in classroom activities.

A baseline procedure was instituted to collect frequency counts on a number of behaviors. Both the school counselor and parents kept logs of Shannon's school- and home-refusal behaviors. Extensive interviewing at school did not reveal any remarkable characteristics—she was performing well academically and had developed adequate peer relationships. At the time of her referral she was receiving significant positive attention from peers and teachers. To eliminate the positive attention Shannon was receiving for her crying and clinging, her parents were instructed to bring her to school 15 minutes early to reduce the peer audience. Shannon was also placed in a private area while she cried and was instructed that she could reenter the classroom when she was ready. Teachers also stopped all noncontingent attention. Using this behavioral intervention, no clinically important change resulted.

A series of strategic interventions were then implemented that involved the parents in a direct confrontation with the presenting behavior. Conoley hypothesized the problem could be solved by focusing on the symptom. In the strategic interventions, the parents were instructed to cling to the child after school and sit very close to her when her friends were visiting, to hold onto her when she attempted to go out and play, and to carry her to school and sit close beside her for the entire day if she engaged in any two of her school-refusal behaviors. Additionally, in the evenings before school, Shannon was to be assisted with her bathing by her mother and have her father pick out her clothes and fix the lunch. The parents were further instructed to make as many "mistakes" as possible while doing these tasks (i.e., mismatch the clothes, use the "wrong' shampoo, etc.).

The first strategic intervention prescribed the symptom; that is, it provided Shannon with an exaggerated form of what she appeared to want. Conoley commented, "Shannon's morning school refusal was interpreted to her as a request for closeness with parents. Then subsequent behaviors were not punishing but only the result of her needs for closeness."

In the second strategic intervention, Haley's (1984) suggestion to make keeping the target behavior more trouble than giving it up was utilized. This strategy is based on the understanding that school refusal may be reinforced by parents and that it may reflect their own projection of their anxiety concerning the need to separate—the child separating from them. Thus, the child's school refusal should become very inconvenient for parents who may be unwittingly maintaining the behavior. Although

the directives were very time consuming, they appealed to the parents as, Conoley suggests, "perhaps as a way to punish her (Shannon) according to the 'doctor's prescription.' "

Following implementation of the family intervention, a dramatic decrease in all refusal behavior occurred. A nine-month followup revealed no reappearance of the school-refusal behavior, with the exception of one instance where Shannon failed to lay out her school clothing.

Madanes (1981, p. 104) reported a case of school refusal that utilized metaphor as a strategic intervention.

CASE STUDY 4

Mary was the youngest of six children. Her mother had died when she was 5 years old. She was raised with the help of an older sister, who was now attending college in a nearby city. Her father, a construction worker, was currently not on speaking terms with the older sister because he had discovered she was living with a young man.

The therapist arranged a school meeting with the father and Mary. Subsequent to the meeting, the father was instructed to take Mary to class and stay with her, if necessary. As soon as Mary arrived at school, she pulled away from the father and ran away. The school psychologist reported Mary was well liked, had good grades, and had mentioned to him she did not want her father to get married.

In consultation with her supervisor, the therapist hypothesized Mary's behavior was a metaphor for being like a wife to her father. Rather than attend school, Mary was opting for staying at home and keeping house for her father, as a mother would. Interestingly, the school-refusal behavior was occurring at a time that the older sister, who had the position of wife and mother and had helped raise Mary, was estranged from her father.

An intervention strategy based on the metaphor posited was planned, involving the following components:

1. Praise by the father for having successfully raised so many children
2. Raising the issue of remarriage and deserving the companionship of a woman
3. Discussing the limited work opportunities for young adults without an adequate education
4. Mentioning the possibility of fines for nonattendance since the therapist could not testify the child was emotionally disturbed
5. Suggesting, in view of the situation, that the father should marry, and enumerating the benefits of this to Mary and her dad

In an interview, the possibility of visiting her sister if Mary would attend school regularly and cheerfully was proposed by the therapist. The following day, Mary attended school. A followup one year later indicated that Mary was attending school regularly and was doing well academically. Her father had reconciled with her sister and had not remarried.

In understanding the metaphor as an intervention, Madanes (1981) stresses the need for the therapist to get the child to give up the disturbed behavior and to give up a system that had a useful, but maladaptive function in the family. To do this, Madanes suggests that the counselor discover the metaphor and prescribe a plan that confronts the metaphor directly. In assessing the family system, Madanes also suggests that the counselor listen carefully for statements of similarity between the behaviors, fears, failures, and the like of the parent and child. This duplicity of emotional feeling may underlie diffuse role boundaries, which are often seen in referrals of students for school-refusal behavior.

Aliotti (1987) reported a case of school refusal in a high school student, which illustrated a family system approach combined with referral to a family therapist.

CASE STUDY 5

Robert, a transfer student from a private school, was referred to the school psychologist for special education services by the school counselor. He had a history of very poor attendance and difficulty in maintaining academic performance. In addition, his math skills, written expression, and spelling were very weak. He also had severe allergies and a history of frequent contacts with the school nurse.

In interviews, Robert presented as a tense, anxious, passive, and obese adolescent. As he described his situation, he projected a great deal of blame for his situation onto the school. He reported that in kindergarten "some of the kids were not your best," elementary school as "a pain," and he did not make it into first grade because "the teacher was not much of a teacher." Therefore, his mother pulled him out.

Robert provided a whole litany of complaints with collusion and support from his family to not attend school. He explained that his lack of attendance in elementary school resulted because his parents "didn't put him through the whole school." Later, in a private school, his poor school performance and social skills were in marked contrast to those of his academically conforming classmates. There he felt a great deal of pressure and stated that the students represented "one big family."

In assessing the family, a structural assessment was undertaken. This point of view stressed the here-and-now sequential behaviors, social transactions, and maintenance of the family system via feedback loops. A significant source of anger and conflict was identified when Robert communicated that he was under a lot of pressure from his parents "to get his education." This represented a significant distortion since the parents' actions and emotional responses, particularly those of the mother, were to disparage past teachers and support nonattendance. When Robert was questioned about what his parents had done to help him attend school, he was vague and evasive.

In general, there was a great deal of enmeshment in this family, particularly between Robert and his mother. Robert seemed to be intensely involved with his family, with little sense of autonomy. In interviews where the mother was present, Robert's mother would speak for him. In separate interviews with Robert, the examiner often felt he was speaking to his mother. Robert would often parrot back statements of explanations that the school counselor had reported were made by the mother. In conjoint interviews, Robert's mother related to him as a peer or much younger child.

It was hypothesized that the family system was dysfunctionally organized to maintain Robert's passivity, his school refusal, and his attachment. In terms of the power structure of the family, although Robert felt powerless, guilty, and defeated, his passivity provided some measure of control of his family. Viewing his school-refusal behavior from a family systems perspective, his relationship to his parents represented an inverted hierarchy (Haley, 1987) whereby his parents had less power than he in school interactions. He could exert control over his parents and thereby manipulate the family system by acquiescing to school and home efforts to get him to attend. Alternatively, he could threaten not to attend and use these threats to his advantage. This, in fact, occurred as in the past he demanded his parents purchase video games as a condition of school attendance.

Robert's role in the family was that of the martyr. In effect, he stated, "I am angry and I am going to be passive and then my parents will have to try their hardest to be better parents." Robert's school refusal and negative problems also served to perpetuate the stage of childhood and served to prevent his transition into manhood. His presence in the home also had the further effect of meeting his mother's affectional needs.

As understanding of the family increased, a two-pronged treatment plan was developed. Since Robert was seriously decompensating in the home and the family was being overwhelmed, the mother consented to an outside referral to a family therapist. It was explained that a combination of efforts involving school and home intervention would result in the most effective treatment of the problem. Releases of information were obtained and the parents were informed that close contacts would be maintained with this trusted family therapist. Following consultation with the family therapist, a meeting involving Robert, his counselor, and his mother was arranged to discuss a school program to get Robert back into a pattern of school attendance.

At the meeting, the problem was reframed in a different perspective. It was explained that Robert's somatic complaints, anxieties, and depressions were a *consequence* of not attending school, not the *cause* of his problems. In effect, his chronic history of nonattendance had denied him the opportunity to develop comfort and competency in the role of a student. Furthermore, the resulting social isolation served to create intense anxiety for him in the classroom setting.

In the light of this new interpretation, in a conjoint session, Robert's mother was engaged in a strategy that addressed the parents' competency and related it to the child. Since both mother and father were competent and responsible employees, no less should be expected of their son. In effect, the intent of the interview was to *empower* the parents and to return legitimate authority to them.

A specific plan to address the issue of school attendance was formulated. A paradoxical intention strategy was presented, which served several purposes: First, it fostered additional passivity vis-à-vis the parents, which would hopefully create an opposite reaction in Robert (i.e., individuation or autonomy). Second, it placed the focus of the problem on school attendance and not health issues. (Consultation with his physician had documented the limited extent and role of his medical issues and this was made very concrete with his parents.) Third, it attempted to stablize a more normal hierarchy in which the parents could assert their legitimate authority and establish appropriate boundaries.

The parents were instructed to take Robert with them in the morning and, if necessary, physically place him in the car. If Robert complied and agreed to attend school without objection, he would be allowed to leave the school parking lot and attend his classes. If he complained and resisted in any way, his mother was to accompany him to each class and sit next to him until he felt comfortable and was ready to attend. Robert's mother found this suggestion quite reasonable. In contrast, Robert, who had said little during the meeting, suddenly balked at this plan and stated he could motivate himself to go to school.

The communication that Robert hope-

fully heard was "you are a very passive person." By prescribing the symptom (passivity) to Robert as part of the treatment, it lost all its power. Robert was put into a position where he could choose not to be a party to a plan to having his passivity used by the school psychologist as a school treatment. This was done with the hope that he would retreat from passivity and begin to attend school.

In this strategy, it was critical to assess the family system carefully. This is what led to a psychological hypothesis that formed the basis for the school intervention.

Even with a great deal of student assessment and contact, if school-based consultants do not really understand the psychological functioning of the family, when consultants develop recommendations, they may not be well received by the family. In this case study, information had to be presented in a paradoxical way so that this dysfunctional family would receive the message.

Additionally, in working with this family, the school psychologist and the family therapist were able to combine in a complementary fashion two types of structural interventions. Elsewhere, Carlson (1987) has discussed these strategies in the context of school-based interventions. Structural interventions are said to fall into two broad categories: *restructuring* and *redefinition* (Aponte & VanDeusen 1981; Minuchin & Fishman, 1981). Restructuring interventions typically seek to alter the family systems structure by blocking recurrent patterns and unbalancing structure by joining existing alignments and coalitions and the like.

In working with this family, the family therapist reduced the mother-son enmeshment and increased the involvement of the father by encouraging the father to bring the son for his therapy sessions, work with him on a hobby, and accompany the son to sports events. The school psychologist reinforced a redefinition of the problem by suggesting that the student's discomfort for school was caused by his lack of attendance.

Treatment considerations need to develop from a careful assessment of the family. The way information is presented can have very important implications regarding the parents' receptivity to school recommendations. In fact, the interventions described did appear to have a positive effect. At a special education meeting held four weeks later to review the placement, Robert had been attending school regularly and, when he attended, his teacher reported he did his work with no problems. In view of his age and lack of high school credits, Robert later enrolled in an adult school program.

A FAMILY SYSTEM MODEL FOR TREATING SCHOOL-REFUSAL BEHAVIOR

Like other disorders reported in this book, the development of treatment models for school-refusal behavior following a family systems approach is still in the early stages of development. The following five-step program is proposed.

Assess the Family

The family systems perspective would stress structural analysis of the relationship of the referred child to all other members of the immediate family as well as an analysis of the parents' family of origin. The child and family's attitudes and perception vis-à-vis the school system would also be a central part of the assessment. Similarly, the child's relations with peers and authority figures would be assessed as well as all of the various relationships in the child's immediate family.

Interview sessions should avoid diagnostic labels that would explain the problem as something residing in the child. School-refusal behaviors would be reframed into terms that are likely to attain more acceptance from the family. A family interview would be prognostic, future oriented, focused on problem solving, and presented in concrete terms utilizing the family's own language. At the same time, the family consultant will need to be sensitive to seriously dysfunctional family members who may be alcoholic, depressed, or psychotic, and who will need to be referred to private practitioners or non-school agencies to address their specific issues as they operate in the family system.

Determine the Metaphor

School-based family consultation of school-refusal behavior will likely require more thinking and interpretation of family dynamics than action, particularly in the early stages of treatment. A primary focus should search out the dysfunctional metaphor that, in its basic elements, may provide a broad generalization of the core problem. In this respect, the target of the dysfunctional behavior should be ascertained by positing a family systems hypothesis. Following this careful analysis, a series of interventions can be planned to address the problem areas. If need be, the hypothesis can be modified or discarded.

Develop Strategic Interventions

Assuming the appropriateness of a family systems approach, the school-family consultant should consider what approaches best fit the needs of the problem situation. Dysfunctional characteristics of the child and the family system should be carefully considered and possible strategic interventions explored. These should be viewed as part of a comprehensive treatment plan. Strategies can include establishing appropriate family hierarchies, setting appropriate school and family boundaries, prescribing the symptom, making a target behavior more trouble than giving it up, discovering the metaphor, reframing the behavior, and the like.

These concepts and strategies have been reported in this chapter as well as others in this volume. They are illustrative of possibilities and should be viewed as options for further evaluation, consideration, and development.

Establish Therapeutic Alliances

In the case studies presented, the establishment of therapeutic alliances among the family-school consultant, private therapist, school system, and family system figured prominently in the family systems intervention. Family members as well as school members recognize the intuitive logic of such alliances but rarely are they invited to problem solve in a mutual manner to address school-refusal behavior.

There are also indications that the public would welcome family systems interventions and view them as viable options for addressing school problem behaviors such as school refusal.

Parade Magazine, for example, recently reported a school program that was clearly similar to a paradoxical intention (Ryan, 1987). Parents of students showing maladaptive classroom behaviors were invited by the principal to sit next to these students and assist them in their work. The young principal described his brainchild idea as follows:

A kid came into my office whom I had seen a number of times for minor discipline problems—talking in class, being late, not bringing materials, driving the teachers crazy. I just got fed up and said, "The next time I see you, we're going to have your mother come in and see what we have to put up with all day." The reaction I got from him was, "Do anything you want, but don't have my mother come in."

I'd never had this reaction from a kid before—and we've had kids arrested for drugs, suspended, and expelled. He begged me not to have his mother come in. Something lit up in my head.

The threat of this type of parent involvement was often sufficient to result in positive changes in a student's behavior. Building on this concept, the principal developed the Parent Involvement Program in which parents were invited to spend a day in school with their child. The principal also encouraged teachers to make phone calls—positive or negative—to students' homes each week. This served to encourage the family system to join the school.

Collaborate with Family Systems-Oriented Mental Health Professionals

School-based mental health consultants must also recognize that in dysfunctional families, individual members as well as the family unit will require mental health services that are well beyond the scope, time commitments, and mission of school-based consultants. Attempts should be made to learn about agencies and private practitioners whose expertise and interests are consonant with family systemic thinking. Parents and other family members with significant emotional issues that extend to past generations will not be adequately served by the school-based consultant and will require appropriate referral.

Mindful of the resistance to change often encountered by school psychologists and school-based consultants, Braden and Sherrard (1987) provided guidelines for effecting a referral as well as consideration of when a family should be referred for family systems therapy. They suggest the following indicators:

1. Abrupt changes in the child's behavior that appears to have no specific cause

2. Behavioral changes in the child that coincide with known changes in the family system (e.g., illness in the family, divorce, unemployment, separation)
3. Problem behaviors in which the family appears to support the child's misbehavior
4. Distortions or denial of the child's problem by the family.

These indicators seem to be particularly relevant to school-refusal behavior as reflected by the case studies reported in this chapter.

SUMMARY

The application of family systems theory to school-refusal behavior has not been systematically investigated. Most of the data are based on experiential applications reported in occasional case studies that have been published. Nevertheless, several case studies in the literature suggest innovative approaches to this traditional school problem. Key concepts from family systems theory contribute to a more meaningful reinterpretation of the phenomena associated with this psychological disorder. Several case studies were presented to illustrate how the key concepts can help to understand this problem. A model for treating school-refusal behavior from a family systems perspective was presented, based on a review of case studies reported in the literature.

Further research and additional case studies will doubtlessly contribute to a clearer understanding of how most effectively to utilize family systems interventions for school-refusal behavior. In terms of clinical applications, the area of school-family systems interventions would seem to parallel the initial applications of behavior modification techniques in school settings. The development of treatment modalities, however, will require additional research and dissemination of such approaches in professional journals.

References

Aliotti, N. C. (March 1987). *School-based family assessment*. Paper presented at the Annual Meeting of the National Association of School Psychologists, New Orleans.

Aponte, H. J., & VanDeusen, J. M. (1981). *Structured family therapy*. In A. S. Gurman & D. P. Kniskern (Eds.), *Handbook of family therapy* (pp. 310–361). New York: Brunner/Mazel.

Braden, J. P., & Sherrard, P. A. D. (1987). Referring families to nonschool agencies: A family systems approach. *School Psychology Review, 16*(4), 513–518.

Broadwin, I. T. (1932). A contribution to the study of truancy. *American Journal of Orthopsychiatry,* 253–259.

Caplan, G. (1970). *The theory and practice of mental health consultation.* New York: Basic Books.

Carlson, C. (1987). Resolving school problems with structural family therapy. *School Psychology Review, 16*(4), 457–468.

Conoley, J. C. (1987). Strategic family interventions: Three cases of school-aged children. *School Psychology Review, 16*(4), 469–486.

Davidson, S. (1961). School phobia as a manifestation of family disturbance, its structure and treatment. *Journal of Child Psychology and Psychiatry, 1*(4), 270–287.

Framo, J. L. (1982). Symptoms from a family transactional viewpoint. In N. Ackerman (Ed.), *Explorations in marital and family therapy: Selected papers of James L. Framo.* New York: Springer.

Goodwin, D. W. (1983). *Phobia: The facts.* New York: Oxford University Press.

Green, B. J. (1985). Systems intervention in the schools. In M. P. Mirkin & S. L. Koman (Eds.), *Handbook of adolescent and family therapy.* New York: Gardner.

Haley, J. (1978). Ideas which handicap therapists. In M. M. Berger (Ed.), *Beyond the double bind* (pp. 67–82). New York: Brunner/Mazel.

Haley, J. (1984). *Ordeal therapy.* San Francisco: Jossey-Bass.

Haley, J. (1987). *Problem solving therapy.* San Francisco: Jossey-Bass.

Hersov, L. A. (1960). Persistent non-attendance at school. *Journal of Child Psychology and Psychiatry, 1,* 130–136.

Hersov, L. A. (1960). Refusal to go to school. *Journal of Child Psychology and Psychiatry, 1,* 137–145.

Hobbs, N. (1966). Helping disturbed children, psychological and ecological strategies. *American Psychologist, 21,* 1105–1115.

Kahn, J. H., & Nursten, J. P. (1968). *Unwilling to school: School phobia or school refusal a medico-social problem* (2nd ed.). New York: Pergamon.

Kramer, S. Z. (October 1987). Family therapy corner: Family systems evaluation, psychodynamic intergenerational perspective. *Newsletter Academy of San Diego Psychologists.*

Lewis, M. (1987). SARB crusades against student dropouts. *District Dialogue* (Grossmont Union High School District), *2*(2), 1, 6.

Madanes, C. (1981). *Strategic family therapy.* San Francisco: Jossey-Bass.

Marks, I. M. (1969). *Fears and phobias.* London: William Heineman Medical Books.

Minuchin, S. (1974). *Families and family therapy.* Cambridge, MA: Harvard University Press.

Minuchin, S. (1984). Structural family therapy. In R. J. Green & J. L. Framo (Eds.), *Family therapy: Major contributions.* New York: International University Press.

Minuchin, S., & Fishman, H. C. (1981). *Family therapy techniques.* Cambridge, MA: Harvard University Press.

Paget, K. D. (1987). Systemic family assessment: Concepts and strategies for school psychologists. *School Psychology Review, 16*(4), 429–442.

Ryan, M. (January 10, 1987). How one school straightens out students who act up. *Parade Magazine.*

Waldfogel, S., Collidge, J. C., & Hahn, P. B. (1957). The development, meaning, and management of school phobia. *American Journal of Orthopsychiatry, 27*(4), 754–780.

Waldfogel, S., Tessman, E., & Hahn, P. B. (1959). Learning problems: A program for early intervention in school phobia. *American Journal of Orthopsychiatry, 29,* 324–332.

17

Family-School Intervention: A Family Systems Perspective

EDWARD W. BEAL

Oak Leaf Center, Bethesda, Maryland

LYNN S. CHERTKOV

Oak Leaf Center, Bethesda, Maryland

THIS CHAPTER REFLECTS the efforts of the authors to conceptualize the family and school as systems within themselves and family-school interaction as a function of these two systems. In general, family-school interaction is almost always child focused. At its best, with mature individuals and low levels of stress, this interaction is beneficial for children. At its worst, with immature individuals and high levels of stress, family-school interaction can be detrimental to the functioning of children.

The authors' frame of reference relies heavily on the Bowen Family Systems Theory (Bowen, 1978) and its application to the treatment program that has evolved at the Oak Leaf Center in Bethesda, Maryland. The Oak Leaf Center is an outpatient community mental health center that offers therapy and special programs (including therapeutic daycare) to children, adolescents, and their families. Most referrals to the Center are made by public school personnel who suggest counseling to help resolve a child's school difficulties.

Families produce children, send them to school for formal education, and, together with the school system, launch them into society to carry out society's work. Children carry the benefits and the burden of being not only the future of society but the future of each family. There are many ways to characterize the growth and development of children from birth to maturity as well as ways to characterize all the forces that impinge on that process.

Bowen Family Systems Theory (Kerr & Bowen, 1988) proposes that in human relationships there are two counterbalancing forces influencing growth and development: a force for individuality or autonomy in relationships and a force for togetherness or fusion in relationships. The degree of integration and balance between these two forces can be evaluated by an examination of the emotional attachment between spouses and between a child and a parent. The balances of these forces is also reflected in the nature of the family-school interaction.

CONCEPT OF EMOTIONAL ATTACHMENT (DIFFERENTIATION)

All family relationships maintain an emotional balance or equilibrium, but not all families experience the same degree of intensity in the emotional postures that prevail among their members. The intensity of these emotional attachments reflects the integration of two broad processes that are present in all families. One process leads in the direction of individuality and emotional autonomy—that which an individual defines as important for self. The other leads toward emotional fusion and dependency among individuals—that which a family defines as important for its members. The balance within an individual of these two processes, individuality versus togetherness, is one measure of the level of differentiation of self.

The concept of differentiation can be viewed as a continuum and refers to one important way in which humans differ from one another. At the higher end of the continuum, where individuality predominates over togetherness, family members can be effective team players within the family as well as well-defined individuals in their own right. At the lower end of the continuum, where togetherness predominates over individuality, people are often very good team players but are much less effective as individuals in their own right.

Although the concept of differentiation is complex and there are many ways to measure it, the importance of describing it here is in understanding the response of families to stress. In general, families whose members maintain a higher level of differentiation have a greater repertoire of responses to stress, and are more adaptive and less vulnerable to symptom development (Kerr, 1981; Kerr & Bowen, 1988).

The concept of differentiation can assist in the understanding of a family's response to the development of a school-related problem in one of its members. Each parent-child relationship falls somewhere on the continuum between emotional autonomy and emotional fusion. The greater the fusion between the two, the more one person's attitudes, beliefs, and behavior are emotionally influenced by the other. The degree to which a child is inappropriately emotionally influenced by a parent reflects the degree to which a child loses self-direction in his own life. A child whose emotional attachments are more autonomous is likely to negotiate the separation from family and the developing peer relationships with a minimum of stress (Beal, 1979).

STRESS AND THE USE OF COMPENSATORY MECHANISMS

Stress affects the characteristics of family relationships. In general, the greater the stress, the more intense the relationships; the more intense the relationships, the stronger the tendency toward emotional fusion and therefore the more emotional influence among family members (Beal, 1989). As individual family members are stressed, compensatory mechanisms begin to operate, which reestablishes the balance of emotional forces in the relationships. Acute stress can produce temporary changes in the nature of family relationships; chronic stress may produce longer lasting changes.

In describing the processing of stress and anxiety in human relationships, Family Systems Theory (Kerr & Bowen, 1988) focuses on triadic as opposed to dyadic relationships. Systems thinking states that in an anxious emotional field, a two-person relationship is basically unstable and that the more uncomfortable person will seek to "resolve" the relationship anxiety by engaging a third person. If the more anxious one is successful in engaging that third person, then the less anxious member of the original twosome becomes an outsider to the new dyad. Depending on the level of anxiety in the emotional field, the outsider can be either relieved or distressed by his or her position.

If the tension is mild to moderate, it may be contained within the central family triangle. If the tension is high yet continues to be contained within the central triangle, the classic scapegoating pattern may ensue wherein the one member who is most chronically and persistently focused on by the other two becomes the identified patient. School problems are but one of the examples of this process where stress activates the family relationship patterns leading to a reaction pattern in one member who becomes labeled as the identified patient.

The patterns of family interaction contained within the concept of the emotional triangle can be thought of as homeostatic mechanisms. Therefore, the presence of an identified patient within a family indicates the end result of increased stress within the family relationship process. From a systems perspective, the labeling of an individual as impaired, troubled, or ill allows the family to contain the tension within its own boundaries. This labeling process keeps the family intact but to some extent at the expense of compromising the functioning of one of its members. When the school system and family system join together to focus on a child, they may cooperate in resolving the stress or collude in the intensification of the family relationship processes.

Clinical observations of triangular family relationship patterns have been noted with such frequency and regularity that the basic patterns have been formulated in the concept of the nuclear family emotional system (Kerr, 1981). When families exchange information or work at resolving differences, tension is often generated. The greater the differences or the more traumatic or emotionally toxic the information, the greater the potential anxiety elicited.

According to Family Systems Theory, the management of stress-related interaction within a nuclear family involves use of four basic relationship patterns: individuals are in conflict with one another, individuals distance themselves emotionally or physically from one another, one of the pair adapts or compromises his or her own functioning in order to preserve relationship harmony, or the twosome can join together over a common concern.

In response to acute stress, all four of these patterns may be present to some degree in all families. With chronic stress, one pattern may come to be used excessively or repeatedly; such a process can then lead to the problems about which families commonly complain: marital conflict, emotional or physical distance between family members, dysfunction in one spouse, or problems with a child.

Each of these patterns or mechanisms operates to preserve stability within an individual or to preserve the existing organization within the family. Yet, the stability of a system or of one individual may come to be preserved at the expense of another's functioning. Marital conflict of moderate intensity may preserve the emotional bond between the spouses, albeit in a negative fashion, but it may do so at the expense of their own functioning. Compromising one's functioning to preserve relationship harmony can thus be a way to keep the marriage or family intact, but at the expense of one individual. A conflictual couple uniting together over the mutual concern for a child may preserve the marriage, but, over time, it may place undue responsibility on that child for continued marital preservation (Beal, 1989).

Conflictual marriages are relationships of intense emotional character in which each spouse's affective reactivity is focused on the other spouse. The multitude of specific issues introduced as causes of the disharmony are not as critical as the emotional intensity of the conflictual process itself. Therapeutic focus on reducing the intensity or the automatic reactivity of the conflictual process itself will reduce the symptoms.

Emotional Distance

Emotional distance is used by couples who seek to preserve a sense of autonomy in an intense relationship or to avoid the anxiety or discomfort associated with too much emotional closeness. This mechanism is based on automatic responses that lead one to avoid speaking to, looking at, being near, or thinking about another individual. This style of adaptive coping can be maintained externally by physical avoidance or internally by denial mechanisms (Beal, 1979).

Spouse Dysfunction

Stress between marital partners can be reduced by means of one spouse giving in to or adapting to the other. The dominant spouse often feels he or she knows best, and the adaptive spouse may want to avoid the responsibility of decision making. Compromises based on which of the spouses has the best judgment and expertise in a certain area are quite functional. However, emotionally determined compromises continue to be functional for both spouses only so long as the stress in the system remains within manageable limits. If the stress is sustained and/or reaches high levels, the overfunctioning/ underfunctioning pattern may gradually impair the ability of one of the spouses to function.

THE COMPENSATORY MECHANISM OF CHILD FOCUS

The previously mentioned mechanisms refer to the manner in which the immaturity and reactivity of the spouses are contained within the marital relationship or absorbed by one spouse. Alternatively, however, emotional reactivity between spouses can be detoured by a parental emotional focus on one or more of their children. Such a child focus is a mechanism that allows family members to deal with stress by means of focusing their anxiety on one or more of the children.

In general, all of the siblings present in the same family are not likely to be equal recipients of parental anxieties or conflict. To the extent that one child becomes the more salient focus of parental anxieties, he or she converts to a more "relationship-oriented" rather than "task-oriented" child. That is to say, the child's energy is diverted away from the developmental tasks appropriate to his or her age; instead, that energy is invested in the parent and the parent's problems.

When the parental anxiety that is shared with the child increases, the parent-child relationship comes to be defined around mutual concern and worry. The parent's emotional energy and stress is typically matched by an approximately equal amount of emotional energy devoted to worry on the part of the child; the child is thus made vulnerable to a variety of symptoms, including school failure and physical illness.

Children who are the recipients of strong parental emotional investments (i.e., who are the primary targets of a child-focused family) are therefore most likely to be highly relationship oriented and less task oriented. They are also likely to have more difficulty coping with parental distress. Because these children cannot emotionally separate themselves from their parents and their parents' problems, parental anxiety regarding such issues as divorce is added to the children's own anxiety and fears about their parents' marriage.

This, then, is the emotional fusion view of the underlying process in the etiology of childhood mental problems. When parents are confronted with a problem in their child, their automatic emotional reaction is to seek to repair the difficulty. This, however, may lead to a level of activity or emotional focus on the child that, in the long run, can add stress to a vulnerable child's stress and promote his or her dysfunction.

For both professionals and parents it is difficult to balance overinvolvement/underinvolvement in providing an impaired child with the appropriate degree of professional and personal intervention. Within Family Systems Theory, child focus is a concept that underscores the idea that the intensity of the intervention process is a significant factor in the outcome of the provision of services to impaired children (Beal, 1979).

FAMILIES WITH A MILD DEGREE OF CHILD FOCUS

The authors will address developmental tasks managed first by families with a mild child focus, then by families with a severe child focus. Family-school interaction is child focused, but with relatively mature individuals and low levels of stress this interaction can be of benefit to the child. It automatically creates a triadic relationship between child, parent, and school.

Flexibility, maturity, and responses that decrease the levels of stress can often quickly resolve a school problem within this triad. Family and school systems where there is a higher level of differentiation will have a variety of choices as they re-

spond to a child's school tasks and will be able to produce support for the child in their interaction. The individuals within the family system with a mild degree of child focus will be able to call on their problem-solving skills rather than being emotionally reactive to the tasks and to other family members, therefore further complicating the resolution of a school-related issue.

Throughout the life of a family there are events that increase stress on individual family members and the relationships within the family. A family with a child beginning school and a new infant compensates by becoming somewhat more child focused. Tension may become so great that it can no longer be contained within the central family triangles, which have shifted with the birth of a new child. The following case examples are offered.

CASE STUDY 1

Michael refuses transportation to school and demands instead that he be accompanied to school by his mother. He has difficulty separating from her to enter the classroom. The triangle between new baby, son, and mother is stressed to the point that this five-year-old is unable to separate appropriately from his mother and must be pushed into the classroom and held by the teacher.

The mother has shifted her investment of emotional energy from Michael and father to the baby. As a result of this shift, Michael is experiencing separation anxiety after having earlier taken considerable pleasure in school. The parents are stressed by the birth of their child, and now their son is having difficulty at school. This couple might consult with mental health professionals or, perhaps using their own resources, they could respond to their son's school difficulty by modifying family relationship patterns to decrease the emotional reactivity.

In addition to adjusting to the birth of a sibling, Michael is responding to the stress his mother is experiencing in the morning along with the absence of his father as he leaves for school. The father has been leaving for work earlier since the birth of the baby, saying that he can better maximize his work time with an early departure. In fact, he may well be feeling on the outside of the mother, baby, father triangle, while Michael feels further displaced in relationship to both his mother and father. There is some resolution of the problem when the father shifts his schedule and escorts his son to the bus each morning before he leaves for work.

All of the compensatory mechanisms are in play in response to the stress of the birth of a new baby. There is more conflict between the parents, the mother feels inadequate to her added responsibility, the father is tending to distance himself, and the system becomes child focused around Michael's refusal to ride the school bus. However, more mature individuals who are not experiencing chronic external and internal stress can respond with flexibility, using the interaction around their son's school attendance to promote the higher functioning of each individual family member despite the stress generated by the birth of the baby.

The parents are able to work with the teacher as she provides reassurance and understanding to Michael while they give him added support at home to overcome his anxiety. An anxious or reactive response from the classroom teacher to either mother or child would serve to increase the pressure on Michael. Teachers, administrators, and support personnel who are able to maintain a supportive but not overindulgent position with Michael will encourage this family's process of healthy realignment around the birth of another child.

CASE STUDY 2

The Miller family has moved from the midwest to a large eastern city, away from both the maternal and paternal grandparents. They have three children, all of school age, and though the couple is pleased by job promotion for the husband, the wife has not yet located employment as a classroom teacher. The children are enrolled in the neighborhood elementary school where Brian, the middle child, is having some difficulty mastering the shift from printing to script writing. This skill training had not yet been introduced in his former school but had been emphasized last year with his current classmates.

The parents attend a regular school conference where it is suggested that their son receive some resource support. This family is stressed by the move, loss of grandparent support, and the mother's failure to find a job. There is tension between the parents about the husband's busy work schedule.

In a mildly child-focused family, the stress of the relocation might well increase the intensity of response to the son's school problem. This mother could attempt to rescue Brian both in response to her husband's distance and to establish her competence as a teacher and parent. The problem could increase conflict between the parents as they became critical and accusing of one another about the effects of the move on the family.

A family system that has some flexibility in response, where family members can offer one another support rather than intense emotional attachment and fusion with the child's problem will provide the child with messages that allow him to master this learning task. The mother will allow Brian to receive resource support in order to bring his writing skills to the required level. She recognizes her own anxiety about finding a teaching position as separate from her son's problem. The father will help Brian with his homework rather than the mother, who is aware of the risk of using his performance as a measure of her teaching abilities.

The school is required only to recognize the task to be mastered and provide the educational support for the child. They are able to communicate the problem in a regularly scheduled conference so as to not heighten the parents' anxiety. The teacher is aware of the parents' move to the community as well as the mother's concern for employment as an educator. Thus, the task of teaching this writing skill is performed within the school setting and not shifted to the mother, thereby encouraging reactivity between parent and child.

In families that maintain a mild level of child focus, the children are able to move more autonomously through their educational tasks. They can be aware of family stress and participate in resolution of difficulties as they assist a sibling or increase their responsibility within the household, while at the same time they have the freedom to work on their own life tasks. As a result, they are more able to differentiate a response from that of their parents during a stressful time. The next brief case summary illustrates these observations.

CASE STUDY 3

Lisa, 15 years old, lives with her mother and brother. Her parents have been separated for only two months. She is a child who is active and high achieving both academically and socially. Lisa recently auditioned for a large part in a high school drama production but was given only a small role. One day, she complains of a headache to her mother and asks that she be allowed to stay home from school because she thinks she is coming down with the flu. The mother, preparing to leave for work, begins shouting that she does not need any more problems. She complains that she just finished helping her son, age 12, deliver newspapers because he was tired from the fishing trip with his father over the weekend. The mother insists that her daughter dress and prepare for school immediately.

As the two of them drive toward the school, Lisa demands that her mother "get off her case." She says that sometimes her mother acts as if everything is falling apart when she is feeling upset. She argues that her brother can manage his newspaper delivery quite adequately on his own and that he did not need to be babied. She states that she has taken her temperature and has a fever so that staying from school is appropriate.

Lisa is able to recognize and identify the source of the stress as the separation and impending divorce. Though angry with her mother, she can communicate her needs, reflect on those of her brother, and comment on her mother's distress. She is functioning maturely and independently while being an observing and participating family team player. The mother hears these observations and wonders with her daughter about the lesser role she will play in the school drama production. There is enough flexibility in this nuclear family's emotional system so that perspective is regained and individuals within the family are encouraged toward age-appropriate roles and tasks.

Brief Commentary on Families with a Mild Degree of Child Focus

These three examples of family-school interaction illustrate the potential for problem resolution when the family system has a fairly high level of differentiation. In all three instances, family members were able to choose from a number of options in response to developmental tasks in the life of the family. Individuality predominated over a reactive, enmeshed response and the child's problem was addressed. The child focus triggered by the school difficulty did not serve to focus the families' anxiety on the child, as it might when the emotional fusion is more intense. If the child focus is more severe, the reactivity in the system as it relates to the child can instead heighten the difficulties.

FAMILIES WITH A SEVERE DEGREE OF CHILD FOCUS

A large number of families who seek outpatient mental health treatment do so at the suggestion of the school where their child is experiencing moderate to severe adjustment problems. They approach treatment with a severe degree of child focus. Treatment from a family systems perspective requires assessment of the nuclear family emotional system, the intensity of emotional attachment, reactivity levels, the overlapping triangular relationships, and the use of compensatory mechanisms in response to stress.

Intervention with this orientation can prevent overinvolvement with the child and a labeling process that may only further compromise the child's functioning. Otherwise, mental health agencies can unwittingly collude with the family and school to further intensify a family relationship process that is focused on the "problem child."

The greater the emotional fusion of family members, the more limited will be their ability to support the child's resolution of the school problem. Intervention with these severely child-focused families includes family assessment, provision of supports such as therapeutic groups for the child, and a treatment approach that shifts the family emotional process toward one that allows for a more autonomous and less fused or child-focused response to stress.

The preceding section examined situations occurring in mildly child-focused families. When similar problems arise in severely child-focused families, the result is often a child-focused referral for mental health treatment for a highly symptomatic child. Drawing from case material at the Oak Leaf Center, a nonprofit community mental health center serving families with varied socioeconomic backgrounds, it is apparent that problems like those presented in the three earlier cases have a far different outcome in severely child-focused families. The authors will present clinical material, along with family systems applications and intervention strategies with these families.

CASE STUDY 4

Mr. Smith contacts an agency at the suggestion of the school principal. He reports that his 5-year-old son, David, is refusing to go to school and that when forced to do so he has tantrums for long periods in the classroom. Since the winter holiday break, David has refused to use language with the teacher and peers at school, although he is quite verbal with both mother and father.

An appointment is arranged for an initial family evaluation to include members of the nuclear family system. Mr. and Mrs. Smith, David, and 5-month-old Alice attend the initial session where the current school problems are discussed and an assessment of family relationship patterns begins. The forces of individuality and togetherness are observed as they operate in the relationship between Mr. and Mrs. Smith, and between David and his parents, as well as between their new baby, Alice, and David and the parents. Mr. and Mrs. Smith are asked about their families of origin, and as data are collected the intensity of emotional attachment is explored in a multigenerational perspective.

Mrs. Smith, Alice, and David sit together on the couch as Mr. Smith moves into a chair and begins to describe David's problem with school. He states that David has always had some problem staying with baby-sitters and has seemed like a "real mommy's boy." He wishes Mrs. Smith would be firmer with him and indicates that they argue frequently about how to manage this problem. Mrs. Smith feels that David's teacher is too harsh and thinks a classroom change might resolve the problem, whereas Mr. Smith thinks David should be forced to go to school. Similar conflict occurs at home about bed time when David insists that his mother lie on his bed with him until he falls asleep. David awakens during the night whenever the baby cries and again demands the presence of his mother in the bed. Mrs. Smith complains of exhaustion and lack of support from her husband, whom she feels responds to the demands of his work but not of the family.

The marital relationship is described as always having been somewhat conflictual, especially around their difficulties about child rearing. Mrs. Smith was raised as an only child who was indulged by both parents, and Mr. Smith is a middle child in a family where "children were seen and not heard." A pattern of extreme conflict about David's difficulty separating from his mother

seems to alternate with one where the father retreats into his work and the mother becomes more and more isolated, angry, and depressed. It appears that on the continuum between emotional autonomy and emotional fusion, David is reacting to his mother's isolation and depression by fusing with her and withdrawing from age-appropriate school behavior. The parent relationship does not presently have the flexibility of responses that allows for problem solving; instead, the parents are reactive to the positions of the other in a push-pull manner that reflects an intense, negative attachment.

Intervention with this family occurs on several levels. In response to David's immediate school problem, a plan is devised where Mr. Smith will take David to school each morning. David will also attend an activity therapy group where he will receive support in interaction with both peers and adults. The parents will begin a course of therapy that will acknowledge their child focus but also try to lower their reactivity to the school problem by encouraging them to explore relationship patterns in their families of origins. This will allow Mr. and Mrs. Smith to be less reactive to one another and more able to problem solve around the needs of their children. As they begin to define themselves and their individual relationship styles in the therapy sessions, the emotional process becomes less intense and the parents experience less conflict and distance in their relationship. Mrs. Smith begins to feel more competent and David has an increasing ability to invest himself in school.

CASE STUDY 5

The Andrews family initiates therapy soon after relocating from the midwest. They want treatment for their middle child, Paul, who has a history of learning and emotional problems. The move came about because of a job opportunity for Mr. Andrews, and this area was chosen because of the educational resources available to Paul in the local schools. It has required a separation from the maternal grandparents, who have been an active resource for this family. The parents are seeking group therapy for their son so that he might improve his social skills both with peers and adults. He is currently oppositional with adults and aggressive with peers. Mrs. Andrews is formerly a classroom teacher but is not seeking employment because she feels she must be available to her children and especially for the special needs of Paul.

Both parents indicate little difficulty managing the children at home. They describe with pride the achievements of their older son, who, like the father, is academically oriented. The youngest child, a girl, is described as well adjusted and happy. During the initial evaluation session, the older son joins with his father and mother to describe his grandparents and extended family, while Paul sits quietly on the couch between his two parents and the youngest child plays contentedly on the other side of the room with the dollhouse. When the daughter is asked to draw a picture of her family, it shows her older brother and father watching a football game, the mother preparing dinner while Paul does his homework at the kitchen table, while she plays alone in her room with a kitten. The drawing, like the family's seating pattern in the therapy session, shows the pairing between older son and father, mother and middle child, and the isolation of the youngest child.

There is a high degree of emotional attachment between the mother and Paul, with increased emotional distance in the marital relationship. It is possible to speculate that because of the intensity of emotional reactivity in this family, Paul's symptoms might fail to respond positively to either educational or mental health intervention. Resources will probably not be supportive of this child's growth and development when they are part of a process that further focuses the family emotional reactivity on his disability.

Mrs. Andrews has already established regular contact with Paul's teacher. She is a room mother and teacher's aide in the classroom. She is becoming active in the local association for children with learning disabilities. The school is delighted to have such an active and involved volunteer, and Mrs. Andrews is pleased to have found a circle of friends as an outgrowth of her involvement in finding resources for her son.

Intervention with this family might well include peer group therapy for Paul, but a focus must be maintained with the parental dyad in order to shift the emotional process of this family away from its focus on this child's dysfunction. Mr. and Mrs. Andrews begin a family therapy process to include sessions with the children where parenting and relationship styles are identified. Gradually, the focus shifts to the relationship between the parents, with the therapist encouraging a thinking rather than a wholly emotionally based communication process.

Mrs. Andrews begins to write to her parents regularly, reestablishing the intergenerational support system in a different but no less meaningful way. She also resumes her career with substitute teaching. Mental health treatment provides support for Paul, but in the context of addressing the overall relationship patterns in the whole nuclear family emotional system.

The previous section discussed a family where a teenager was able to respond autonomously and with insight into the needs of other family members even in the midst of the stress of a separation and divorce. In contrast, another severely child-focused family comes to the attention of an outpatient clinic.

CASE STUDY 6

Amy, a teenager who is the youngest of four children, is referred by the school psychologist because of symptoms of depression, suicidal ideation, and her developing tendency to avoid school since her recent breakup with her boyfriend. She attends a highly competitive high school in a high-income community where there have been several student suicides in the past two years.

Mother, father, and Amy attend the first appointment. The three older siblings are attending college and away from home. The parents report that they are not like other parents who suffer with an "empty nest" but that they are delighted to be free of the confusion of so many teenaged children at home. They are openly resentful of their daughter's "overreaction" to breaking up with her boyfriend. They define her problem in terms of the school, which they describe as overly competitive for their daughter whom they see as an underachiever, though the school reports that she is of average ability and working up to her potential.

The parents indicate a history of high blood pressure and early death of parents on both sides of the family. They deny any concern about this problem, though they both suffer symptoms of high blood pressure. The parents are resistant to any discussion of the importance of the older children's absence from the home as a factor causing family stress, and are especially annoyed that their daughter expressed concern during the evaluation about their health.

They are interested in short-term counseling for their daughter, as they feel that things work very well in their family—unlike many others they point to that are single-parent families or families where parents are too busy to spend time with their children. They want to get their daughter "back on track" so that she can forget her boyfriend and stop all this talk about killing herself. They wonder if a school change would be helpful, since it would get her away from the boyfriend as well as a school environment where academic success is a matter of "life or death."

Immediate intervention occurs to encourage communication between Amy and her parents. She begins to express feelings of loss as her siblings have left home. The parents are encouraged to recognize that their emotional distancing and denial is a response to the stress on their relationship created by the children's move away, the deaths of their parents, and their own health problems. Rather than providing support for Amy, their anxiety about her functioning leads to emotional distance. The break-up with her boyfriend and her siblings' move away from home leaves her isolated. The therapy process includes individual sessions with Amy to support her refocus on school and friends, while her parents explore their relationship patterns with each other, their children, and their families of origin.

The parents are highly reactive to Amy's discussion of her losses, secondary to their difficulty in handling their own issues of loss with both their parents and their older children. The parents are able to reduce their reactivity and listen to their daughter so that the anxiety is contained within the family. As the chance of suicide is reduced, there is a lowering of the school's reactivity, allowing Amy to resume task-directed behavior.

Brief Commentary on Severely Child-Focused families

Each of these severely child-focused families responds to family stress and/or the developmental tasks of their children with relationship patterns that serve to intensify the dysfunction of the child. Assessment and intervention from a family systems perspective can avoid exacerbation of the child's school difficulty. The authors will summarize this therapy approach in the next section.

HOW FAMILY THERAPY OPERATES

A family systems viewpoint of symptomatic families suggests that important emotional attachments occur within an entire network of the nuclear and extended family. This perspective conceptualizes symptoms as distortions of emotional attachment or as imbalances in the system of family relationships. If symptoms are conceptualized in this manner, then therapy requires thinking about the family as a unit to modify the management of relationships, attachments, and symptoms.

Family therapists begin their work by asking those questions that will identify relationship patterns and family emotional processes. Their first task is to define the symptoms in the context of the overall family emotional system. After identifying family patterns of emotional attachment, the therapist attempts to identify the part each individual plays in establishing and maintaining these overall patterns. The focus is on helping each person to change himself or herself, rather than on encouraging the family members to try to change each other.

The therapist relates to the family but remains outside of the family's emotional field, so that he or she can provide feedback to the family on how their interactional patterns lead to specific dysfunctions in each family member. The unique aspect of family therapy is its emphasis on emotional attachment as it is reflected in emotional distance and conflict between individuals, emotional or physical dysfunction within an individual, child focus, and the multigenerational origins of these processes.

A frequent approach in family therapy, therefore, is to try to decrease the intensity of emotional focus on the child and to shift the parental focus to the marital relationship or to each spouse's relationship to his or her own family origin. In mildly child-focused families, this shift may be relatively easy. In severely child-focused families, the problem may be of sufficient intensity that little can be accomplished beyond reducing anxiety and relieving some of the pressures on the child.

A family therapist is likely to encourage parents to examine their overinvolvement and underinvolvement with their child's school difficulty toward clarifying expectations for the child, educators, and themselves. The therapist is not likely to intervene directly with the school but instead to support the parents and child in obtaining appropriate educational resources.

The greatest potential for modifying family problems occurs if there is a shift away from child focus for both parents. This shift can be accomplished most easily if parents can learn to view the child as an extension of the marital dyad and cease to see the family as an extension of the child. For example, in the severely child-focused families described earlier, life events such as the relocation of the family, illness or dysfunction of a family member, birth of another child, or a shift in the family constellation will trigger or intensify school problems. Therapy would address the parents, both directly and indirectly, as the decision makers in the family. The therapist would clearly convey to the parents how the stress of these family transitions was intensely child focused and therefore contributing to their child's anxiety and symptoms. This therapeutic viewpoint is predicated on the assumption that the more responsibly the parents can act toward the children and the more they can decrease the child-focus process, the greater the chance of symptomatic improvement in the child.

In mildly child-focused families, keeping the emotional focus away from the children can often be accomplished most easily by leaving the children out of the therapy sessions. Accomplishing this shift depends on the therapist's concept of the problem and his or her skill in keeping the family involved in the therapeutic process. In severely child-focused families, the same basic strategies are available, but it is more likely that the child would be seen separately at times and at times with the parents in order to shift emotional focus away from the children. Treatment options that support the autonomous growth and development of the child (e.g., peer group therapy) are often a useful adjunct to the family therapy process. This approach does not undermine an approach that defocuses attention on the child but at the same time it addresses the risk of a temporary increase in the child's symptoms as a secondary consequence of a change in the balance of parental emotional investment in the child (Beal, 1979).

SUMMARY

The developmental tasks of family life are ones through which emotional attachments are established, modified, and may be resolved. The counterbalancing forces that influence the growth and development of individuals within the family are conceptualized as those for inviduality and those for togetherness in relationships. The degree and manner in which children and parents maintain a balance of these two forces influences the interaction between family and school. This chapter focused on the concepts of emotional attachments in general and child focus in particular, suggesting that the family's own emotional equilibrium is an essential component in the process of family-school intervention and the resolution of a child's school problems.

The intensity of the intervention process in a child's school problem is discussed particularly as it relates to families with a mild degree of child focus, as compared with families with a severe degree of child focus. Case material illustrates that families with a lesser degree of child focus may realign and adjust to a child's school problem more easily. These families adjust to the stress of family developmental tasks or life events with more flexibility toward resolution of the child's school problem using school resources, while not over-focusing anxiety around the child's difficulty.

Families with a severe degree of child focus frequently respond with relationship patterns that intensify the child's school dysfunction. Case material illustrates both how family emotional process and the balance of forces of togetherness and individuality can interact with school systems to intensify the focus on the child's difficulties. Assessment and intervention from a family systems perspective can minimize focus on the child's problems as well as reduce stress and disequilibrium both within the family and family-school relationships.

References

Beal, E. W. (1979). Children of divorce: A family systems perspective. *Journal of Social Issues, 35,* 140–154.

Beal, E. W. (1989). Family therapy. In American Psychiatric Association (Ed.), *Treatments of psychiatric disorders* (pp. 2566–2578).

Washington, DC: American Psychiatric Association.

Bowen, M. (1978). *Family therapy in clinical practice*. New York: Jason Aronson.

Kerr, M. (1981). Family systems theory and therapy. In A. Gurman & D. Kniskern (Eds.), *Handbook of family therapy* (pp. 226–264). New York: Brunner/Mazel.

Kerr, M., & Bowen, M. (1988). *Family evaluation*. New York: Norton.

18

Family-School Intervention Using a Structural Model

MARIAN C. FISH
Queens College
City University of New York

SHASHI JAIN
City University of New York

RECENT LITERATURE has emphasized the usefulness of a systems orientation to family-school assessment and intervention (Carlson, 1987; Conoley, 1987; Fine & Holt, 1983; Hobbs, 1978; Tittler & Cook, 1981). The importance of incorporating the systems relevant to the child into both assessment and intervention is widely acknowledged, though there is little empirical evidence to support this position (Carlson & Sincavage, 1987).

Of interest is whether school personnel are actually using systems approaches in their daily practice. In a survey by Carlson and Sincavage (1987) that explored the use of family-oriented school psychology practice, results indicated that 60 percent of school psychologists utilize information about the family in their psychological assessment of the child; however, only 41 percent collect such information on their own. The majority of this information is gathered from clinical interviews with the mother. The clinical interview with the whole family is still one of the least used methods of assessment. In their family intervention practices, 67 percent of the sample indicated that they conducted child and family intervention in their practice; however, most of these interventions were individual, with the mother or child alone, rather than with the whole family.

There was also a considerable discrepancy in the sample in their perception of the etiology of behavior versus learning problems. Family factors were seen as most influential in behavioral problems, whereas school factors such as classroom environment and learning history were seen as most influential in learning problems. These results suggest that assessment and intervention of school psychologists remain child centered despite the professed interest in a systems approach. To perceive the etiology of learning and behavior problems as dichotomous is not truly seeing them from a systemic point of view.

Eno (1985) suggests that children's learning problems are viewed too narrowly and that they often can have problems with learning that may or may not relate to problems with teachers or peers. Similarly, to gather information only from the mother does not provide a comprehensive picture appropriate for a systems analysis. The importance of understanding the family and school is not because they may be "causing" the problem but because they provide the resources for change (Eno, 1985, p. 152).

There are a number of reasons why the use of systems approaches in school practice is still limited. First, it appears that the school setting may interfere with a systems orientation. For example, in the Carlson and Sincavage (1987) survey, time constraints and lack of administrative support for parent and family interventions were reported. This suggests that, as with all systems, schools are resistant to change and want to maintain the status quo. Second, there seems to be a lack of understanding of what a systems orientation means as opposed to a more general family-school orientation. As mentioned, it is not enough for a school psychologist to have a conference with the mother of a child having a problem. A broader perspective is required.

Third, though increasing, there are still relatively few programs providing systems training for school psychologists. Fagan (1985) indicates that only 5 of 58 doctoral programs in school psychology offer a specialization in family-oriented practice. Brassard and Anderson (cited in Carlson & Sincavage, 1987) have reported a lack of family training among school psychology professors. Fourth, the lack of empirical research may be slowing the introduction of family systems training into some of the graduate programs (Fine & Holt, 1983).

Fifth, although systems constructs and theory may appear rather straightforward and easy, in reality, systems approaches are complicated, difficult to implement, and require extensive training (Fine & Holt, 1983; Fish & Jain, 1988).

Finally, school psychologists are part of the school system, which may create inherent difficulties in the application of this approach.

Despite the difficulties inherent in integrating a systems approach into school settings, there are, indeed, a number of advantages to its use. In particular, structural theory (Minuchin, 1974) is especially appropriate for application when dealing with children's problems.

The purpose of this chapter is (1) to provide a rationale for using structural theory in the schools; (2) to explain the major constructs of structural theory as they apply to family and school systems, and to provide some empirical support; and (3) through a case example, to illustrate intervention techniques and strategies based on structural theory that can be used by the school psychologist to facilitate change.

THE USE OF STRUCTURAL THEORY IN SCHOOLS

The advantages of structural theory for use in school settings have been enumerated by a number of authors (e.g., Aponte, 1976; Carlson, 1987; Fish & Jain, 1988). Nichols (1984) suggests that structural theory presents the most clearly explicated constructs of the major systems theories. It provides a model of normal family development as well (Fish & Jain, 1988). The theory is empirically based and tested in diverse economic and sociocultural settings with a variety of problems (e.g., Carlson, 1987; Minuchin, Baker, Rosman, Liebman, Milman, & Todd, 1975; Minuchin, Montalvo, Guerney, Rosman, & Schumer, 1967; Perosa & Perosa, 1981). This is important because "schools, like families, are ubiquitous yet highly variable" (Eno, 1985, p. 152).

Applications of structural theory to

interfaces between family and school have been encouraged and found effective (Aponte, 1976; Green & Framo, 1981). Because structural intervention approaches are brief and action oriented, they are conducive to use in school settings (Carlson, 1987). Finally, compared to traditional approaches to children's problems in the schools (e.g., psychodynamic, behavioral), the nature of a structural approach is that it not only deals with the symptom but it also builds competency into the system to manage problems better and to prevent future problems.

A STRUCTURAL MODEL OF THE FAMILY AND SCHOOL

As with other systemic approaches, structural theory considers every problem in its context and views all parts of the system as reciprocally interacting. Minuchin (1974) describes the family as an open system in transformation, which goes through several developmental stages depending on the ages and needs of its members. Moving through these developmental stages requires restructuring within the system. The family also adapts to changed circumstances so as to maintain continuity and enhance the psychosocial growth of each member. When families do not adapt, however, dysfunctional patterns or pathology may arise.

The model has been formulated based on clinical interviews with effectively functioning families. Based on this conceptual schema, the three main components of the model are described below: matrix of identity, structure, and adaptation. These components are also applicable to other systems such as schools and classrooms, and thus useful to school personnel.

Matrix of Identity

"Human experience of identity has two elements: a sense of belonging and a sense of being separate. The laboratory in which these ingredients are mixed and dispensed is the family, the matrix of identity" (Minuchin, 1974, p. 47). A sense of belonging means the child learns to accommodate to the family group and to understand the rules and behaviors of the family. The sense of separateness and autonomy, on the other hand, is promoted by the accommodation of the family to the child's individual needs.

In the case of a learning disabled child, for example, the child will develop a sense of belonging and feel secure if he or she is fully accepted as a member of the family (i.e., not rejected or over protected) and treated like any other member of the family. Acceptance of the child is believed to promote a sense of belonging. Accommodation of the family to the child's needs acknowledges the child's individuality. Structural theory would suggest that a learning disabled child who experiences cognitive and/or behavioral deficits would require more accommodation and support from the family in order to develop a sense of separateness and autonomy.

Thus, the basic tasks of the family provide a matrix for forming identity by the child. Through acceptance and promotion of autonomy in the child, the family fulfills this task. The specific tasks given depend on the developmental stages of the family (Carter & McGoldrick, 1980). What is required for parenting a 2-year-old may be totally different than for a 5-year-old or a 14-year-old.

Although certainly not as critical as the family to matrix of identity, the school is also a system where the development of belonging and autonomy occurs. The child learns to accommodate to the school and classroom rules and regulations. As a member of the school population, the child understands the code of behavior in the school and classroom. Schools differ greatly in how they define inappropriate behavior and the consequences for it. At the same time, the school and classroom promote autonomy by providing skills and experiences to meet the child's needs to become more self-sufficient. As the child advances in school, demands become greater, requiring increased autonomy.

Structure

Family structure is clearly the most elaborated component in Minuchin's structural model. It pertains to the organization of the family, which encompasses internal hierarchies, roles, and responsibilities of each member. A family is a system that operates through transactional patterns, which, when repeated, establish patterns of how, when, and to whom to relate. For instance, when a mother tells her son to put his shoes away and he obeys, this interaction defines who she is in relation to him and who he is in relation to her, in that context, at that time. Recurrent interpersonal behaviors constitute a transactional pattern.

Minuchin introduces concepts of subsystems and boundaries as essential aspects of family structure.

Subsystems

Families are differentiated into subsystems of members who join together to perform various functions. Individuals are subsystems within their family, as are dyads (e.g., husband-wife, mother-child). Subsystems can be formed by age, gender, and/or common interests. In each subsystem, an individual has different levels of power and learns differentiated skills. A man can be a son, husband, father, older brother, younger brother, and nephew,

depending on the subsystem, and in different subsystems he enters into different complementary relationships.

Boundaries

Individuals, subsystems, and whole families are demarcated by interpersonal boundaries. The boundaries of a subsystem are the rules defining who participates and how. For example, the boundary of a parental subsystem is defined when a mother tells her older child, "You are not your sister's parent." If the parental subsystem includes a parental child (a child who is given temporary parental power), the boundary is defined by the father's telling the children, "While I'm gone, your brother is in charge." The function of boundaries is to protect the differentiation of the system. For proper family functioning, the boundaries of subsystems must be clear; the clarity of boundaries is used as a parameter to evaluate family functioning.

Interpersonal boundaries vary from being rigid to diffuse. Rigid boundaries are overly restrictive and allow little contact between systems or outside the system, resulting in disengagement. If parents are disengaged from their child, they will be slow to notice and react when the child is experiencing trouble and needs support and guidance.

In those families where the interpersonal boundaries are diffuse, subsystems are enmeshed. Help and support is offered abundantly by the parents, but this may be at the expense of autonomy and independence in the children. For example, a mother does homework for a child, so that the child doesn't get into trouble with the teacher. A task that clearly belongs to the child is taken over by the mother. The child in this case does not do what he or she is supposed to do nor does the child learn responsibility. "The lack of subsystem differentiation discourages autonomous exploration and mastery of problems. In children particularly, cognitive-affective skills are thereby inhibited" (Minuchin, 1974, p. 55).

All family systems have enmeshed and disengaged boundaries at some time. For example, when the children are infants, the mother and father may be highly enmeshed with the child or the mother and child may be so enmeshed as to make the father peripheral. As the child grows older, however, and is capable of doing more, parents tend toward disengagement, giving more and more autonomy to the child. It is the inflexibility of boundaries that indicates areas of possible problems in the family. An effective family needs a structure with subsystems having clear boundaries, with parents at a level of authority, and with parents having complementary roles.

Schools and classrooms have definite structures of their own. Schools are systems whose members are organized into hierarchies and have roles and responsibilities. Though varied, schools have specific functions that they perform.

Several authors have discussed the similarities between family and classroom structure (e.g., Conoley, 1987; Pfeiffer & Tittler, 1983). Generic subsystems exist in schools (e.g., administrators, teachers, and students) and within classrooms (e.g., teacher, gifted students, reading groups). There are idiosyncratic systems such as "jocks" or "punks," or social misfits. As in the family, the transactional patterns define the relationships among the members. Again, rules giving teachers power over the students are generally in place, with exceptions; for example, when the teacher asks a student to be a monitor during lunchtime.

As with families, dysfunctional structure in a school or classroom may occur when there is diffusion among subsystems or when there are inflexible boundaries and transactional patterns. For example, when a principal overrules a teacher's decision in front of the class, there is a diffuse boundary between the administration and teacher subsystems. At the heart of a well-functioning school or classroom system are clear subsystem boundaries, strong teacher authority, and flexible transactional patterns.

Adaptation

A family is subject to inner pressures coming from developmental changes in its own members and subsystems and to outer pressures coming from external demands. Responding to these demands from within and without requires a constant transformation of the position of family members in relation to one another so they can grow while the family system maintains continuity. "Inherent in this process of change and continuity are the stresses of accommodating to new situations" (Minuchin, 1974, p. 60).

Having a child with a handicap creates an idiosyncratic stress on the family, which requires accommodations from each of its subsystems and the family as a whole. For example, a mother who has been taking care of a learning disabled child may require extra support from her husband when their child enters school and needs more help with homework. This would require changes within the parental subsystem. The individual child's difficulties can be exacerbated or perpetuated if the family as a whole does not change its transactional patterns according to the needs of the child (or maintains a rigidly enmeshed or disengaged pattern of transactions).

Just as the family adapts to the pressures from within the child and from external sources, the school too must adapt to these demands. By recognizing developmental changes in the child as well as new societal trends that impinge on the school, such as single-parent households or two working parents, the school system can respond with flexibility. When the school system is slow or reluctant to recognize and adapt to societal changes, it creates incongruity between the two subsystems, which can be a source of conflict for the child. For example, if the school does not provide early morning or evening time for conferences with working parents, this can create a distance between the school and the family.

Minuchin (1974) has provided a conceptual schema of effective family functioning. The three components of matrix of identity, structure, and adaptation can be used to identify specific facilitating structural and interactional processes both in the family and school or classroom.

RESEARCH FINDINGS

Research based on the structural model of the family includes both descriptive and treatment studies. The focus of these studies have been primarily dysfunctional, clinically symptomatic families. Five types of clinical families have been described in studies appearing to date: the low socioeconomic family (Minuchin et al., 1967), the psychosomatic family (Minuchin, Rosman, & Baker, 1978), the alcoholic family (Davis, Stern, & Van Deusen, 1977), the addict family (Kaufman & Kaufman, 1979; Stanton, Todd, Kirschner, Kleinman, Mowatt, Riley, Scott, & Van Deusen, 1978; Ziegler-Driscoll, 1979), and the family with a learning disabled child (Perosa, 1980). A study by Minuchin, Rosman, and Baker (1978) provides an example of how the three components described above are useful in assessment and intervention.

Minuchin, Rosman, and Baker (1978) studied the characteristics of families with children who suffered from either diabetes, asthma, or anorexia nervosa. The focus of their study was to identify the family processes that maintained the problems of the child. They found that the family did not accept and accommodate to the child's problems and that these adolescents did not have a sense of autonomy or feel competent. The subsystems in the families were enmeshed and the boundaries were diffuse. As a result, parents did not carry out executive functioning and children often took the parental role in the absence of a clearly defined and effective parental collaboration. The families were not successfully adapting to the idiosyncratic and developmental needs of the child.

To reiterate, the major components of a healthy functioning family system are that these families provide a matrix of identity, have a cohesive structure, and are flexible in their adaptation. These three components can also be used as a framework to evaluate and intervene in the school and classroom system. Now, through case example, it is essential to examine the application of the structural model to school intervention.

APPLICATION OF THE STRUCTURAL MODEL WITHIN THE SCHOOL

Working from within the System

Much of the literature on family-school intervention has been written from the perspective of a clinician external to the school. These consultants belong to neither system and therefore are viewed as objective by both the school and the family. As mentioned above, school psychologists are part of the school system, placing them at a disadvantage because their objectivity may be viewed with skepticism. Further, the school psychologist may not have the same authority or power as an outside clinician because he or she is an employee of the same system and a colleague of some staff who are contributing to the maintenance of the child's problem.

Generally, power with the family is limited as well because unlike the outside therapist, school psychologists seek out the family rather than the family approaching them. On the other hand, school psychologists have some advantages as part of the school system; they are the first ones that the child is referred to within the child's home-school context. They also have easier access to the child/teacher than an outside clinician. They can enter the class and school systems more easily than an outside person. Finally, they have a realistic understanding of how the school functions (Eno, 1985).

At the outset, due to the special position of the school psychologist just described, it may be necessary for the school psychologist to take a "meta-position." Dowling (1985) warns the clinician in dealing with home-school problems that the therapist should remain "meta" to the system in order to be free to intervene effectively. A close or permanent alliance with either of the systems can trigger off resistance and apprehension on the part of the other system. School psychologists have built in belongingness to the school systems. Therefore, they need to be very cautious so as to join with the family as well. An ideal situation may be where the school psychologist can enlist both the school's and family's assistance in exploring how a particular problem in the child is maintained.

Approaching the Problem

The purpose of intervention based on a structural model is to change the system that maintains the problem in the individual. The main techniques used to attain these goals are joining and restructuring. *Joining* refers to creating an active affiliation with the system (Fish & Jain, 1988). *Restructuring* is designed to make changes in the organization of the system, for example in roles and boundaries (Sherman & Fredman, 1986). Minuchin and Fishman (1981) elaborate on these techniques by focusing on varied aspects of joining and restructuring.

In order to identify and map where the child's problems lie, the school psychologist must observe the child in context. The family's contribution to the child's problem cannot be decided simply from the information obtained from the developmental history of the child, or by having a single interview with the mother and child, excluding other members of the family. Whether the family thinks and conveys that the child's problems are caused by the school, or the school sees the family causing the problem in the child, or both school and family contribute to the child's problems, to the child's inner pathology, a systems-oriented school psychologist would focus on how, not why, the problem is maintained in the child by observing the child in both home and school contexts before making an intervention plan.

Whether the child has a learning problem or a behavior problem, a school psychologist would enlist both systems not only to determine how and if these two systems maintain the child's problem but to investigate how each can help and to see what resources they can provide. The family's support for an academically poor child is just as essential as the contribution of the school's supportive structure for eliminating behavior problems in the child. Minuchin (1974) says:

If a child is having trouble in school, the problem may be related basically to the school. If the therapist's assessment indicated that the family is supporting the child adequately, the major intervention will be directed toward the child in the school context. He may act as the child's advocate, arrange a transfer or arrange tutoring. But if the child's problems in school seem to be an expression of family problems, the therapist's major intervention will be directed towards the family. Both types of intervention may often be necessary. (p. 65)

CASE STUDY

Joe, a third-grader, was referred by his teacher. Joe soils himself several times a day during school. This youngster does not show any deficits in any of the academic skills but frequently does not bring back completed homework. The teacher was able to contact the mother after several attempts. Although Joe's mother was apologetic about his behavior, she did not know what to do. She said that the problem occurs at home as well. Both she and her husband have tried to talk with Joe as well as reprimand him, but to no avail. The mother also conveyed to the teacher that at their last visit to the pediatrician, the physician found nothing physically wrong with Joe to explain his problem.

Classroom System Assessment

It is good to begin the intervention from the origin of the referral. Plas (1986) recommends that it is better to adapt a conservative approach and initially focus only on those components of the systems related to the problem—that is, child referred (Joe) and the person doing the referring (the teacher).

Joining

Joining and accommodation are the first steps in forming a therapeutic system. Unless the therapist can establish a therapeutic system, restructuring cannot occur (Minuchin, 1974). *Joining* pertains to

creating a milieu in which the members involved feel nonthreatened and understood by others. In the process of joining, the school psychologist needs to determine both Joe's and the teacher's formulation of the problem (e.g., he's lazy, he's disobedient, he has emotional problems), what possible solutions they have applied and planned, and what has been successful and not successful in the past.

In addition to the focus on the specific problem, the school psychologist needs to determine the relationship boundaries that may exist between Joe and his teacher. Is the classroom system accepting of Joe and giving him a sense of belonging? How is the classroom system promoting his autonomy? For example, if the teacher becomes embarrassed and accompanies Joe to the bathroom after he soils, this would suggest enmeshed boundaries between these two subsystems. However, if she is oblivious to his discomfort and embarrassment, this suggests disengaged boundaries.

The second step in the systemic approach is to define the problem in interactional terms. Since interactions and transactional patterns cannot be determined in a vacuum, enactment or creating an analog to the problematic situation and observing the sequence of behaviors in that situation is employed. The school psychologist, in this case, observes the child, teachers, and peers in the classroom, on the playground, in the lunchroom, and in the gym. She observes that Joe sits quietly in the back of the class. He seems somewhat fearful in answering questions. His teacher does not give him any positive feedback when he does try to answer. On the playground, Joe seems forlorn. A few of his peers laugh at him; one of the children even tries to make him trip. Joe remains quiet and moves away from these children. When Joe is questioned about his soiling, he does not know why this happens; it just does. His teacher had reminded him to go to the bathroom, reprimanded him when he soiled, and sent him to the principal's office on several occasions, but this did not seem to help him. The teacher sees Joe as lazy. She is also critical of the family for not being organized or doing something about this.

Classroom System Intervention

After viewing these interactions and looking for transactional patterns, the school psychologist creates a map as to where Joe's symptom fits into the class. How is the classroom situation maintaining the symptom and how does it help? The school psychologist also reviews the boundaries, autonomy-belongingness, and adaptability of the system. In this case, she finds that the boundaries between the classroom teacher and Joe are rigid where the teacher is not supportive of the child. She observed Joe isolated from peers, and expressing helplessness in doing something about his problem.

The formulation of this problem in interactional terms is crucial to the decision as to what strategy or intervention to use and to the goal of the intervention. Dowling (1985) claims that this formulation need not be final, just a starting point that will help identify the repetitive and interactional sequences. It will also provide an opportunity to measure the flexibility of the system—that is, the degree to which the teacher and/or school are willing to change in order to help the child.

Systemic interventions help clarify boundaries, get the system unstuck, and maneuver the system in such a way that autonomy and belongingness are facilitated, that the competency of each individual member is emphasized in achieving the desired goal. In this situation, the goal is to make Joe feel more in charge of his body and more effective within the classroom situation.

The intervention in this case would focus on softening the teacher's view of Joe's problem (he is lazy), making her more supportive of him, while at the same time giving Joe a sense of competency. This intervention might come about by using direct, indirect, or paradoxical techniques aimed at modifying how Joe and his teacher relate to one another. It is better to use simpler techniques that create the least amount of stress on each party as well as emphasize the competency of each person involved. Following are some examples of least intrusive techniques resulting in restructuring.

Reframing

Reframing refers to changing the meaning of events and behavior and presenting it in a more positive light. Joe's soiling behavior might be reframed, for example, as a plea for attention (peers laugh at him, teacher reprimands and sends him to office). Joe also needs to feel competent. The teacher at this point might see Joe in a different light than lazy and change her behavior accordingly.

Boundary Marking

Once the structure and boundaries of a given system are identified and problems are reframed, the task of the school psychologist is to modify the systems boundaries, reinforcing appropriate and modifying inappropriate ones. Because Joe's teacher is somewhat disengaged, it may be a good idea to move Joe from the back of the class to the front where he is in closer physical proximity to the teacher. The school psychologist may also focus on enhancing clear boundaries between Joe and peers.

Task Setting

The purpose of giving an assigned task for the system to carry out in the absence of the therapist is to reinforce the newly created boundaries and new structure and make the members of the system relate to each other in different ways. Since the classroom teacher is not a client, but a colleague of the school psychologist, it is crucial that the school psychologist involve the teacher in selecting a task that would achieve the purpose identified previously—in this case, raising competency in Joe so he feels in charge. Ideas to raise Joe's competency should emanate from the teacher rather than the school psychologist (e.g., the teacher may create a star chart for Joe to reinforce him for appropriately using the bathroom). She also assigns Joe to teach some simple math skills to another peer who is weak in that subject and reinforces Joe for doing a good job.

If the system is stuck and the teacher refuses to change her views, the school psychologist may have to enlist the assistance of other members from the hierarchy or extended family of the school system. For example, if the teacher in this case is bent on getting Joe out of her class and into a school for the emotionally disturbed and remains inflexible in her view of Joe, the school psychologist may have to bring in other members of the Child Study Team to strengthen his or her position, or transfer Joe to another class where the teacher may be more willing to have him.

Family System Assessment and Intervention

Usually when school problems do not get resolved in the classroom system and continue in spite of the intervention in the classroom, the child's family system may be contributing to the existing problem. In Joe's case, the problem is serious enough that the family's help needs to be sought immediately. The teacher's view of the family also points out the existing distance and hostility between the teacher and mother. Using the structural family therapy techniques, school psychologists can take similar sequential steps in making interventions with the family.

One of the caveats Eno (1985) suggests for clinicians entering the school system is "gentle leaning"; that is, making gentle minimal interventions within the school system because clinicians are not part of the school system and are not there to counsel teachers or classrooms. Similarly, school psychologists need to take the approach of "gentle leaning" while working with families. The school psychologist does need to join with the entire family and observe the family itself in enactment and then formulate plans for intervention. In Joe's case, the school psychologist invites the family to investigate how the family can help Joe to feel more in control of himself. She observes that the mother is the spokesperson of the family. She is more articulate than her husband, who did not finish high school.

Joe is the second of three children, the youngest of whom is 2 years old. The oldest child constantly interrupts and moves around during the family conference. Joe quietly plays, and every once in a while he tries to get his parents' attention, but the other two children are overwhelming for the parents. Joe is more or less neglected. The school psychologist further observes that the father is the active person who tries to control and manage the children. The mother does not help but does criticize the father's handling of the children.

The family lost one child in a fire two years ago. The mother blames the father for that. She also does not trust her husband to be a good provider for the family, as the father keeps changing jobs and the family has to turn to the mother's parents for food and shelter occasionally. Even though the chaos and multiproblems of this family are obvious, the school psychologist does not need to point out at the outset the marital issues.

In this situation, the school psychologist joins with the father for his efforts and energy in managing three active children. She joins the mother through her pain of losing a child and still having strength to run the family and keep it together. The school psychologist holds the baby on her lap and asks the family how the older brother is doing in school. She suggests that the older boy is so agile that he could belong to a soccer team. Then she raises Joe's status in the family by saying that he is beginning to coach another peer in math in his school. She further asks the family about their perception of Joe's problems. The family members either blame Joe or seem disengaged from Joe's problem or needs. His problem is viewed by the parents as one more extra stress.

Joe's autonomy and competency are both undermined because of his parents' underinvolvement with him. The school psychologist in this case empathizes with the family and at the same time elaborates on their strengths. She tries to restructure the system by assigning tasks to the family where Joe would be given attention individually by both the mother and father. She also suggests to the parents that they have several painful issues to deal with in the future. She would be willing to help them deal with these issues if they so desire or refer them to an outside clinic. In this way, in spite of joining, the school psychologist respects the boundaries between the family and school and works on changing the system on behalf of the child.

School-Family System Assessment and Intervention

A child is a connector of both family and school systems. At times when he or she experiences difficulties in one system, it may spill over to the other system. The child's difficulties—developmental, behavioral, or academic—are handled smoothly if both of these systems take on complementary roles.

DiCocco (1986) discussed progressive stages that family-school relationships go through, depending on the degree and nature of the child's problem. Initially, the teacher and the parents bear responsibility for the child in their respective settings. If the problem worsens, parents are asked to step in and help the child's school difficulty. DiCocco further said that it is important that the child believes and sees these two (parent/teacher) are working collaboratively and agree on the appropriate actions to take.

In Joe's situation there is a negative sequence of blame and feeling of resentment on the part of both teacher and parents. The parents do not realize the teacher's situation and the teacher does not realize the overwhelming situation of the parents. Like a child in a divorced family of two conflicting adults, Joe bears the burdensome role of primary communicator between home and school, carrying information and messages between the two systems.

Tucker and Dyson (1976) have pointed out that the role of messenger may take a heavy toll on the child physically, emotionally, and/or academically. Dowling and Pound (1985) suggest that while facilitating collaboration between home and school is the mainstay of successful intervention, the school psychologist needs to strengthen and clarify boundaries between school and home by creating an atmosphere of friendliness and mutual support before a meeting between teacher and family takes place. Further, the joint resources of teacher and parents should be used to try to find solutions rather than to dig for causes of the trouble, which can be experienced as blaming or scapegoating (Dowling & Pound, 1985).

For Joe, the school psychologist makes the teacher aware of the parents' appreciation of her taking an interest in Joe. Similarly, she makes the family aware of the teacher's appreciation of the family's difficulties and attempts to work on the problem. In the case where the hostility or distance between home and school is not too entrenched and rigid, usually setting a positive tone and identifying competency of each system's participation in the problem solving is enough to make the systems move to a common goal. However, if the systems are too far apart, breaking the contact between school and family may be an appropriate intervention (Lusterman, 1984). Lusterman proposed interventions that decrease the intensity of communication when the systems are both rigid, and interventions that increase the pressure for action when the systems are both chaotic.

SUMMARY

In reviewing the work on structural family therapy, numerous interventions, techniques, and strategies are suggested. However, it is critical that the techniques be applied only with a clear theoretical understanding of what the technique is for and what it will accomplish. Considering the position of the school psychologist and the realities of working in a school setting, it is generally best to use the simplest and most parsimonious intervention approaches. For example, school psychologists should be cautious about using techniques such as unbalancing, raising intensity, and introducing paradox. Approval from school authorities might be necessary for these interventions.

As described above, Minuchin's structural orientation is a very viable approach for use in the school setting. It is essential, of course, that the school psychologist receive training and supervision in the implementation of such an approach.

References

Aponte, H. (1976). The family-school interview: An ecostructural approach. *Family Process, 15,* 303–311.

Carlson, C. I. (1987). Resolving school problems with structural family therapy. *School Psychology Review, 16,* 457–468.

Carlson, C. I., & Sincavage, J. M. (1987). Family-oriented school psychology practice: Results of a national survey of NASP members. *School Psychology Review, 16,* 519–526.

Carter, E. A., & McGoldrick, M. (1980). *The family life cycle.* New York: Gardner.

Conoley, J. C. (1987). Schools and families: Theoretical and practical bridges. *Professional School Psychology, 2,* 191–203.

Davis, P., Stern, D., & Van Deusen, J. (1977). Enmeshment-disengagement in the alcoholic family. In F. Seixas (Ed.), *Alcoholism: Clinical and experimental research.* New York: Grune & Stratton.

DiCocco, B. E. (1986). A guide to family/school interventions for the family therapist. *Contemporary Family Therapy, 8,* 50–61.

Dowling, E. (1985). Theoretical framework—A joint systems approach to educational problems with children. In E. Dowling & E. Osborne (Eds.), *The family and the school: A joint systems approach to problems with children* (pp. 5–32). London: Routledge & Kegan Paul.

Dowling, J., & Pound, A. (1985). Joint interventions with teachers, children and parents in the school setting. In E. Dowling & E. Osborne (Eds.), *The family and the school: A joint systems approach to problems with children* (pp. 91–111). London: Routledge & Kegan Paul.

Eno, M. M. (1985). Children with school problems: A family therapy perspective. In R. L. Ziffer (Ed.), *Adjunctive techniques in family therapy* (pp. 151–180). New York: Grune & Stratton.

Fagan, T. (1985). Best practices in the training of school psychologists. In A. Thomas & J. Grimes (Eds.), *Best practices in school psychology* (pp. 125–142). Kent, OH: National Association of School Psychologists.

Fine, M. J., & Holt, P. (1983). Interventions with school problems: A family system's perspective. *Psychology in the Schools, 20,* 59–66.

Fish, M. C., & Jain, S. (1988). Using systems theory in school assessment and intervention: A structural model for school psychologists. *Professional School Psychology, 3,* 291–300.

Green, R. J., & Framo, J. L. (Eds.) (1981). *Family therapy: Major contributions.* New York: International Universities Press.

Hobbs, N. (1978). Families, schools and communities: An ecosystem for children. *Teachers College Record, 79,* 756–766.

Kaufman, E., & Kaufman, P. (1979). From a psychodynamic orientation to a structural family therapy approach in the treatment of drug dependency. In E. Kaufman & P. Kaufman (Eds.), *The family therapy of drug and alcoholic abuse*. New York: Gardner.

Lusterman, D.-D. (1984, June). *School and family as ecosystem: An application of Olson, Sprenkle and Russell's Circumplex Model*. Paper presented at the meeting of the American Family Therapy Association, New York.

Minuchin, S. (1974). *Families and family therapy*, Cambridge, MA: Harvard University Press.

Minuchin, S., Baker, L., Rosman, B., Liebman, R., Milman, L., & Todd, T. (1975). A conceptual model of psychosomatic illness in children. *Archives of General Psychiatry, 32,* 1031–1038.

Minuchin, S., & Fishman, H. C. (1981). *Family therapy techniques*. Cambridge, MA: Harvard University Press.

Minuchin, S., Montalvo, B., Guerney, B., Rosman, B., & Schumer, F. (1967). *Families of the slums*. New York: Basic Books.

Minuchin, S., Rosman, B., & Baker, L. (1978). *Psychosomatic families*. Cambridge, MA: Harvard University Press.

Nichols, M. P. (1984). *Family therapy: Concepts and methods*. New York: Gardner.

Perosa, L. M. (1980). The development of a questionnaire to measure Minuchin's structural family concepts and the application of his psychosomatic model to learning disabled families. Unpublished doctoral dissertation. State University of Buffalo, New York.

Perosa, L. M., & Perosa, S. L. (1981). The school counselor's use of structural family therapy with learning disabled students. *The School Counselor, 29,* 152–155.

Pfeiffer, S. I., & Tittler, B. I. (1983). Utilizing the multidisciplinary team to facilitate a school-family systems orientation. *School Psychology Review, 12,* 169–173.

Plas, J. M. (1986). *Systems psychology in the school*. New York: Pergamon.

Sherman, R., & Fredman, N. (1986). *Handbook of structured techniques in marriage and family therapy*. New York: Brunner/Mazel.

Stanton, M. D., Todd, T., Kirschner, S., Kleinman, J., Mowatt, D., Riley, P., Scott, S., & Van Deusen, J. (1978). Heroin addiction as a family phenomenon: A new conceptual model. *American Journal of Drug and Alcohol Abuse, 5,* 125–150.

Tittler, B. I., & Cook, V. J. (1981). Relationship among family, school and clinic: Towards a systems approach. *Journal of Clinical Child Psychology, 10,* 184–187.

Tucker, B. Z., & Dyson, E. (1976). The family and the school: Utilizing human resources to promote learning. *Family Process, 15,* 125–141.

Ziegler-Driscoll, G. (1979). The similarities in families of drug dependents and alcoholics. In E. Kaufman & P. Kaufman (Eds.), *The family therapy of drug and alcoholic abuse*. New York: Gardner.

19

The Use of Systemic Provocation in Family Therapy for School Problems

ROBERT N. WENDT
University of Toledo

THIS CHAPTER PRESENTS a model for family intervention based primarily on the work of Maurizio Andolfi and others in Rome, Italy. Although the focus of this chapter will pertain to problems of children in school, the principles involved are applicable to all levels of family intervention and, to a lesser extent, systems consultation.

The principles and techniques in this approach evolved from working with very rigid families. They emphasize the use of self, ranging from an involved creative manner to a separated distant position. In addition, simultaneous support and intrusion that often involves systematic provocation will create pressure for change. Entry into the family is often through the symptom, and the school frequently provides the initial pressure for change. This approach, which provokes systemic change, often includes multiple generations and the use of metaphors and metaphorical objects.

The chapter begins with a discussion of the historical and theoretical aspects pertaining only to this approach (more comprehensive theoretical discussion is provided in other chapters of this book). The principles and techniques are presented, beginning with the therapist's role

and use of self in terms of creativity, pressure, and use of symptoms. This is followed by a discussion relative to transgenerational involvement and use of metaphorical objects. The issues relative to therapist-school collaboration are presented and, finally, a general summary and discussion is provided.

Two cases are presented throughout the chapter that illustrate the concepts and techniques employed. These are cases of the author and they reflect a fair representation of systemic provocation. In examining the cases, many theoretical influences or approaches can be noted, although discussion of these influences is beyond the scope of the chapter.

THEORETICAL DEVELOPMENT

The Istituto di Terapia Familare in Rome was developed primarily by Maurizio Andolfi, Carmine Saccu, Anna Nicolo-Corigliano, and Paolo Menghi. Today, in the United States, the work of Maurizio Andolfi is best known for its use of provocation with rigid families. However, his work relative to training therapists and helping families has continually evolved into levels of complexity that encompasses not only the family system but the creative use of self as a therapist.

This model of therapy began with Salvador Minuchin in terms of observing interactions and analyzing relationships existing in the present between individuals and their interactional system. From this point, the paradoxical thinking of Watzlawick and the creative developments of Haley and Selvini-Palazzoli and her colleagues stimulated clinical applications with more difficult psychotic families, particularly regarding roles and tasks that the family system assigns its members. Carl Whitaker has more recently influenced Andolfi relative to the use of metaphors, metaphorical objects, and creative imagination in the use of the therapist's self to facilitate change in the family system.

One aspect to consider theoretically is the level at which the therapist chooses to work with the family. Watzlawick, Beavin, and Jackson (1967) distinguished between logical levels relative to both human communication and a systemic approach to human reality. Human communication occurs at several different levels and the differences between these levels allow for concrete, literal work with families and also playful fantasy and creativity. These levels of communication are basic to all families, and difficulties at either level can lead to symptom formation within the family, particularly in children. But each level also forms the basis for entry by the therapists in a psychotherapeutic manner that will effect productive change (Batson, 1972).

Although one might choose to examine human communication or behavioral sequences of children in the system created in the school and the family, the plurality of logical levels inherently limits the effectiveness and concrete interactions of these approaches (Watzlawick, Beavin, & Jackson, 1967). The here and now are

distinctly different from the logical level of systemic rules that are inevitably established by human interactions. The family, of course, provides the most powerful set of rules; however, rules of subsystems within the culture (e.g., school) also have considerable impact upon the child.

The distinguishing of logical levels differentiates between the systemic approach, behavioral approaches (that emphasize transactions), and psychodynamic approaches (with conceptual formulations of intrapsychic psychopathology). It allows the notion that intervention with the family needs to be seriously considered. Selvini-Palazzoli, Cecchin, Prota, and Boscolo (1978) point out that the family is a human group with a history and is a system with implicit rules that all members unconsciously obey and that all members help to define. This premise also leads to a transgeneration perspective and the need to work with three generations when dealing with the complexities of the family.

Therefore, on the one hand, human systems are characterized by energy, emotional intensity, and entrophy, which provide the power and influence on the individual; whereas on the other hand, a logical level of rules are present that provide an order and structure to the group. The first level provides observable, circular patterns of behavior and communication. The second level of systemic rules provides the homeostatic redundancy and the symptom "dance" within the family or classroom.

It was the rigidity of the symptom dance that moved the Rome group into using redefinition, provocation, and metaphors and metaphoric objects in therapy (Andolfi, Angelo, Menghi, & Nicolo-Corigliano, 1983; Andolfi, Angelo, & DeNichilo, 1989). The therapeutic system demands that the therapist continuously provides a redefintion or reframing of the problem in order to disturb the patterns of interaction. This forces the family to modify its relationships and interactions. When one relationship changes, the consequences of that change affect all other relationships.

Clinicians who have worked with rigid families and rigid teachers or administrators are also well aware of the remarkable ability of people to assimilate new input into their old patterns. Thus, it is up to the therapist to change the redefinition or amplify the complexity to the extent to maintain an imbalance so that new relationships can evolve (Whitaker, 1975). Redefinition can be at both the explicit (verbal) level and implicit (nonverbal) level.

Provocation in effect induces a crisis in the family. Many families experience tension and anxiety; however, the tension is so well channeled amongst the system that it is used to maintain an acceptable level of homeostasis. In spite of the problem (e.g., the child), the family basically fears unbalancing the equilibrium and renegotiating rules. Thus, the implicit message from the family is to fix the child and leave us intact. The therapist is expected to manage the tension and solve the problem in a manner that leaves the relationship and the definition of the problem the same.

The more severe the problem, the greater the need the family has for stability, and the greater the need for intensity in the therapeutic intervention. The inducement of instability and creating a family crisis is related to the intensity of the intervention, which in turn is related to the rigidity of the system. In fact, families often can be aggressive and provocative in their communication with each other, creating the need for the therapist to counterprovoke the family. Andolfi and colleagues (1983) point out that:

> if the family provokes the therapist and controls the therapeutic system through the identified patient, the therapist too, must try to provoke the family and to control the therapeutic system using the same channel. . . . In this way the perception of the problem and the therapist-family relationship would be radically redefined by an intense and disorienting provocation to the entire family system. The definition then becomes an integrating element and final outcome of the provocation. (p. 51)

More recently, Andolfi clarified this concept in a more general sense. He pointed out the need to connect with the family before the provocation. When heavy stress is induced, the therapist needs to intrude in a nonprotective manner and yet contain the suffering and pain of the family. If the therapist is too scared, too protective, or too positive, the family will only stabilize and prolong therapy (Wendt, 1987).

One method of containing the pain and reducing the resistance is to use metaphor and metaphoric objects. For example, we know that symptoms of children can be a metaphor for a relational problem between the parents or the parent(s) and grandparent(s). Even more specifically, individuals develop their own personal set of metaphoric symbols in order to capture reality and the multiple meanings of events. Thus, the therapist's use of metaphorical images moves beyond the client's concrete level of definition (and resistance) into the symbolic level to provide a different contextual framework of experience for the client.

Thus, the metaphor enables the creation of an image of the emotions related to behaviors, basic character, or the relationships within a system. The use of objects such as toys provide for the client a crystallized concrete externalization of an abstract process. The use of objects provides the basis for redefining relationships among the family members and between them and the therapist (Angelo, 1981). The use of toys or other objects comes from material observed at the logical level in family interactions, relies on the creativity of the therapist, and also allows the therapist to withdraw from the center. In effect, the object becomes the co-therapist.

Bianciardi and Galliano (1987) believe this approach to family therapy is essentially carried out at the logical rather than the rule level of intervention. The therapist is highly active and emotionally intensive in a dramatic and often humorous fashion. The therapist uses energy or emotions in a very conscious way, often using "memesis" in connecting with the functions of the family. The use of self serves as a counterprovocation to the system. While connecting with the individuals through the pain, the therapist provokes not individuals but rather the system, using materials and information given by the family.

Therefore, what began as an interactional approach (Andolfi, 1979) has evolved into a methodology whereby ambivalence is induced in order to avoid looking for truth, which is believed only to mire the family in their homeostasis. In this approach humor is very important.

We play with issues, with toys, and verbal language which defies understanding by the family. If you are understood they will retreat into passivity and lose the energy to struggle with family issues. One of the main goals is to take the passivity of the family upon entering therapy and transform them into the main actors in the drama. (Wendt, 1987, p. 155)

USE OF SELF

Looking at the therapist's role in the therapeutic process has been a focus of study for all major approaches to psychotherapy. Although to a lesser degree in the consultation process, the use of self appears to be most crucial when working with systems. In a review of studies of deterioration of marital and family therapy

cases, Gurman and Kniskern (1978) point out that the bottom-line crucial element in therapy is the alliance with the family. However, despite the alliance, treatment may fail because of passivity and lack of assertiveness on the part of the therapist. It might be concluded that while therapists and consultants need to have basic relationship skills that allow them to connect with empathy, other ranges of behaviors, especially assertiveness, are critical elements for success. The development of behaviors that allow for active intervention in creative manners is a complex challenge for trainers, supervisors, and professionals themselves.

Batson (1979) and, more recently, Maturana have advocated an epistemological shift from the role of the professional observing and assessing objectively the "observed system" to the understanding that the "observer" is indeed part of the system. Therefore, according to this viewpoint, it is impossible to be a part without being involved, and involvement of the professional is in itself crucial to what happens in the system.

Minuchin and Fishman (1981) also believe that the therapist has to become part of the system and advocate the flexible use of self. Families and teachers have expectations of the therapist's role. He or she needs to be sensitive and perceptive of these expectations so that behaviors can be adapted in order to provide simultaneously acceptance and rejection of the expectations.

These constructs have powerful implications for therapists. A debated point of neutrality versus provocation, with the Milan approach (Selvini-Palazzoli et al., 1978) of neutrality vs. the Rome approach of provocative involvement, has been debated extensively in workshops and presentations over the last several years. The involvement position means that it is critically important for therapists to use their own personal affective responses often involving their own moods, images, and symbolic interpretation as initiating the therapeutic process.

Probably the best examples of the intuitive conscious process in action are found in the work of Milton Erickson (Haley, 1973). More specifically, Haber (1990) delineates two central aspects of using oneself "(a) the external position or contact-boundary between the therapist and client system *and* (b) the internal work of images, kinesthetic reactions, intuitive flashes, past experiences, and crazy thoughts of the therapists" (p. 376).

However, when using oneself, it is critical that the therapist adapts oneself to the needs of the system and does not force the system to adapt to the professional. More succinctly, the belief that the professional needs to operate solely from a philosophical rationalistic base, consistent with his or her own personality and style of functionality, will lead only to limited effectiveness, which will be a narrow range of clients that are able to respond to that particular approach. To summarize, in order to become involved, the professional needs to adapt oneself to the system, work with one's internal self in order to have available a wide range of behaviors, and connect with the family while simultaneously taking risks to effect change.

INTRUSION AND SUPPORT

The therapist is an intruder by virtue of being a change agent moving into a rigid system anchored by the symptom of the identified patient (IP). For the purposes of this chapter, the IP will initially be the child experiencing problems at school. Thus, the presence of the therapist is felt by both the family and the school.

Intrusion to provoke systemic reactions without support is often interpreted as callousness or not caring; therefore, the supportive element is crucial to whatever level or style the therapist chooses to adopt when entering the system. Support is essentially given by connecting with the pain or distress in the IP, the parents, the family, or the teacher, often nonverbally as well as verbally discussing the "problems." With the connection, the therapist then is often able to intrude to a level of discussion that the family cannot or is too embarrassed to discuss, or to provoke action that people do not want to take to create change. To clarify, intrusion means moving with support into levels of hesitancy, embarrassment, and discomfort because it is only at these levels that meaningful change can occur.

The following case study illustrates the "embarrassment disease." The initial phase of this case will be presented here and continued in a later section because of the relevance to concepts presented later in the chapter.

CASE STUDY 1

The Smith family* consists of the father (John), the mother (Susan), and a six-year-old son (Carl). The family physician referred the family because of problems with Carl.

Carl, who was quite small and frail, was literally losing patches of hair. His school had reported the family to Children's Services for investigation because of concerns about physical and emotional neglect. Carl was having difficulties in school, being retained in kindergarten. He generally was withdrawn and openly refused to do assigned work. Prior to the referral for investigation, the school psychologist, principal, and teacher went to the home. The

---

*The co-therapist with the Smith family was Virginia Whitmire, Ph.D.

father refused to talk to them and slammed the door in their faces. When the Children's Services worker interviewed the parents, Susan panicked and turned to the family physician for support relative to Carl's physical appearance. The physician indeed believed that Carl's physical frailties were biological in origin. He also accurately assessed the emotional problem and referred the family for therapy.

The previous year had been devastating for the family. John had been unemployed for five years and the family was living in a low-income housing project and was supported by welfare. Susan had a rare form of lymphatic cancer. She was hospitalized extensively the past year, several months at a time, and at one point it was clear to everyone that death was imminent. The oncologist felt her remission and absence of tumors was "unbelievable" and the family was now optimistic about her recovery even though it was only about four months since her release from the hospital. During this time, Carl was totally in John's care. It was quickly apparent that Susan was angry at John, and John was angry at the pressure from the school, Children's Services, and Susan.

During the first several sessions with the family, Susan did most of the talking, while Carl appeared negative and refused to listen to both parents. John was sullen, avoided eye contact, and expressed only anger at everyone, including us (the therapists).

We worked hard at expressing concern for the family and Carl, agreeing that Carl indeed was having problems. We connected with Susan's cancer and listened to her feelings of being mistrusted and abused by the insensitivities of the school. While we heard her frustration with John, we kept the focus on Carl, primarily because we kept hearing from John, in almost a whine, that he didn't want help nor did he want to come to therapy.

Throughout all phases of therapy, it is important that while moving from the symptoms of the child to the symptoms of the system, guilt is not created in the parents. John was hearing from Susan and his family of origin how inept and neglectful he was in most areas of life, and he was convinced we would be critical and that we were "out to get him." Despite our attempts, John remained adamant, and after the third session he refused to return.

We had a session with Susan and Carl to find out what was happening and sensed Susan's desperation and fear. What would happen to Carl if she got sick again? The marriage was an nonexistent relationship with two parents/children living together with a great deal of yelling and anger between John and Susan over the pressure of John's unemployment, lack of money, their being together all the time, and over Carl's problems. We felt connected to Susan's pain. John continued to refuse to believe anything we said and had completely shut us out. We knew we had to take a risk in order to engage him in therapy, and after careful deliberation we decided to write him a letter.

Dear Mr. and Mrs. Smith:

Based on John's questions regarding length of treatment, we have reviewed your case. We have consulted with the Family Counseling Staff, who have also reviewed your assessment information. They feel your problems may be so severe that therapy is not worth our time. We disagree with them. We have a 100% success rate in helping cancer patients and we will continue to work with Susan. John's not staying in the last session was helpful to Susan and our success rate. However, we are concerned that in the long run, John may also lose Carl.

Sincerely,

Robert and Virginia
Family Therapy Team

The letter was provocative. We wanted to set a tone of professional arrogance and concern, and to provoke fear and curiosity. The professional arrogance was to create the aura that we were competent professionals despite John not allowing us that position; our concern for his child was made in order to connect with his concern, which had been evident through his reacting in an angry disciplinary manner in the sessions to Carl's every behavior. We needed to add more pressure through that concern and create enough fear that he might lose the child (which could have happened) because Carl was his only real connection to anyone in his life. We also wanted him confused by being ambiguous and curious about what we had to offer him.

The letter proved effective. Susan called and indicated that John was upset upon receiving the letter and wanted to be at the next session. At the session we told John quite frankly that considering Susan's condition and the mood of the school, he could lose Carl if Susan should die. We then moved to join with him to help the family deal with the school, who was seen as an enemy, and to help the teacher deal with Carl.

We then proceeded to contact the school psychologist and the teacher. We indicated that we were working with the family and we stated our belief that no abuse was present in the home (although John was very harsh with Carl). We further agreed that retention should be considered for Carl.

After several more sessions, one involving the interpretation of the psychological report to the parents, they, including John, felt we had something to offer and became committed to therapy. What we had in store for us were two difficult years of therapy with a father who was unemployed, resisting job training, and had previously been diagnosed as paranoid-schizophrenic by a psychologist. In addition, we had a mother who may or may not be terminal, was considerably overweight, and was very unhappy with the marriage. And we had a frail child who was pulling out his hair, defiant, and not achieving in school. Further aspects of this case will be discussed later in the chapter.

Essentially, the therapists used themselves at several levels to connect with the family, increase pressure, and then join the family in order to engage them in therapy. The connection was with the fears, which were discussed openly, about Susan dying and John losing Carl to Children's Services and with their intense concern about Carl. Because the therapists demonstrated the ability to handle fear and anger, the family felt safe to allow them to continue to work with them.

The letter and the pressure exerted on the father within the session produced the crisis that was simmering below the surface. By increasing the stress and anxiety, the therapists were able to deal openly with the issues confronting the family yet contain the pain. Therefore, an alliance was allowed to be formed, which the family lacked because both extended families were unable to deal with or support them in a meaningful manner.

The author's background as a school psychologist was also particularly helpful in dealing with the school and convincing the parents of the therapists' ability to handle the school personnel for them. Another issue involves the therapists' level of risk taking and moving beyond their own fear of creating anger and rejection in order to work effectively with families. Andolfi has stated that there are no resistant families, only resistant therapists. Although the letter does not reflect either therapist's personal philosophy, what is important is not the therapist but rather the family, and to what extent therapists will go to in order to be successful.

THE ROLE OF THE SCHOOL-BASED SYMPTOM

Other chapters of this book have clearly established the isomorphic qualities (parallel process) between what is happening in school and what is symptomatic in the family. The school symptom can be placed within the larger context of the teacher-pupil interaction, the classroom system, the school, and the community system. Of course, the same is true for the isomorphic nature of the symptom within the family in terms of the nuclear family, the extended family (including all three generations), and the community.

As the school symptom provides the entry for work within the context of the school, the symptom provides the nodal point for pressure to provide entry into the family system. The symptom at school provides embarrassment for the family, and the pressure exerted by the school often pushes the anxiety of the family about the symptom into taking action, such as engaging the therapist to reduce the anxiety within the family. Although it is often difficult for the family to accept the school problem as a family problem, the anxiety and pressure become so intense within the family that, despite the risk of being "at fault" or "to blame" for the problem, the family will do almost anything to change the child and reduce the pressure.

PRESSURE

It is important for therapists to view symptoms as allies rather than enemies and to utilize pressure to induce change. In the previous case study, the symptoms within Carl caused the school to exert pressure on the family, which induced fear and overwhelming anxiety. Rather than using the pressure to eliminate the symptom, the therapists used the symptom to create

additional systemic pressure to engage the family. In the next case study, the opposite process was employed. The pressure was applied to the identified patient to eliminate the symptom, which had interesting results on the rest of the system.

CASE STUDY 2

The Kane family has two children, Tim, age 12 and in the sixth grade, and Amy, age 15. Tim and the family were referred for therapy because of Tim's repeated absences from school and lack of achievement, especially regarding completion of assignments. The father is an engineer and the mother is a secretary. Psychological testing by the school psychologist revealed an IQ in the average range (WISC-R, Full Scale 104), and achievement (WRAT-R) scores of 8th grade in word recognition, 6th grade in spelling, and 5th grade in arithmetic computation. Adequate functioning was present in perceptual-motor and language; however, projective testing displayed withdrawal, psychosomatic complaints, and impulsivity, with depressive features. Apparently Tim talked about suicide to the mother.

The school personnel met and considered the results of Tim's psychological testing his pattern of low achievement, and his absences of over 90 days over the last several years. They decided to retain him in sixth grade. Moreover, they filed a complaint of truancy with the court and referred the family for family therapy.

In the first session, the father appeared hesitant, the mother was concerned and self-assured, and Amy was attractive, bright, and high achieving in school. The family expressed concern about Tim and were at a loss as to how to handle the situation inasmuch as he was defiant and argumentative at home—traits only passively displayed in school. The most clear picture of the family dynamics was provided by Amy, and it became apparent that both parents were ineffectual. The father was prone to outbursts of anger and clearly was not involved with Tim, although he would support the mother with discipline. The mother complained that Tim would not get out of bed in the morning nor respond to discipline.

In the second session, after learning that Tim had begun the absences in fourth grade, which also coincided with the death of the mother's mother, it was determined that the best course of action would be to apply pressure on Tim to change, and to work from a brief therapy context. In order to reduce guilt, blame, and pressure on the parents, it was pointed out that the mother was depressed for a year or more after her mother's death (which she confirmed and stated that it was difficult for her to get out of bed for that period). As a result of the father's work schedule and concern for the mother, he too was unavailable to Tim. As a result, Tim also had become concerned about his mother. By redefining the context of the problem, the pressure was off the parents, allowing the pressure to be placed on Tim.

In a strong, emotional, definitive tone, Tim was told that he was still a fourth-grader, and that as a fourth-grader he could not have succeeded in seventh grade, nor could he succeed even in repeating sixth grade. The parents were informed that, as a fourth-grader, Tim could not make decisions. Thus, the parents needed to treat him like a fourth-grader in terms of going to bed, getting up in the morning, and not giving reasons beyond what a fourth-grader could understand.

This move created confusion within Tim, clarity for the parents, and the opportunity to increase pressure on Tim to change. It was also discussed how dumb fourth-graders acted and how far behind the sixth-graders they were. The position was even pushed further when discussing what Tim would be like at age 16, thinking and acting like a dumb fourth-grader, and at age 25 and 40 (Dad's age).

In one sense, this may have been paradoxical in that the therapist was taking the stance that Tim would fail, thereby having Tim state that he wanted to be a sixth-grader. Taking a skeptical stance, the following assignments were made based on data elicited in the sessions. When asked what his sixth-grade friends did that he admired, Tim talked about bike trips. After considerable discussion, Tim was told to plan a 20-mile bike trip with his father. They were to lay out a course and measure it in the car. He was also told to have three temper tantrums the next week so that his parents could practice dealing with a fourth-grader. The parents were told not to let Tim interrupt their conversations (which is a common problem in this and many families). Tim was also told to order his father two times to do something for him to test his father's willingness to say no without anger.

The third session showed a marked decrease in the immature behaviors; however, neither the father nor Tim planned the trip. In discussing why, it was decided that 20 miles is more like a seventh- or eighth-grade trip, and 14 miles would be more appropriate. The parents indicated they had stopped Tim's interruptions, and Tim was instructed by the therapist to deliberately test them one time the next week. Dad was to yell when he was not angry, and Mother was to cut Tim off.

The fourth session still had Tim not asking his Dad to plan the trip. However, school attendance had improved remarkably, as the parents, particularly Mother, would insist he attend despite his complaints. Tim was told to deliberately fake a headache. Referral was also made to the reading teacher for a more thorough diagnosis relative to reading comprehension and speed to see if problems in these areas were affecting his academic performance.

This was a move to involve the school personnel in a cooperative manner with the parents as well as to lessen the pressure on the parents. At this point, Tim's stubbornness appeared to become a factor.

However, at the next session, Tim had asked his father to assist him in planning a trip to a friend's house, and Tim promised he would take the trip the following weekend. Tim was assured that planning the trip, listening to his parents, and attending school was an indication that he was no longer frozen as a fourth-grader.

Two weeks later, the parents reported everything was going extremely well for Tim and they were getting very positive reports from the teacher about his academic effort and his not missing school once in the last six weeks. However, the mother indicated to the father that she had been having an affair for the last year and was unsure about the future of the marriage.

The therapy for the next five months moved into marital therapy with the couple. Details of this process are beyond the scope of this chapter; however, several aspects of the intergenerational dynamics are relevant to understanding Tim's difficulties. Although the fusion between the mother and her mother was the same as the fusion between Tim and Mother, the father had never been able to separate emotionally from his grandmother who raised him from the age of 6 after his mother left him in her care in order to pursue her own life. He never really reconnected with his mother, and the grandmother was a critical, stern, religious, and moralistic woman whose values he adopted when dealing with his wife over the affair.

Essentially, the parents were unable to separate from their "mothers," and because of this and the difficulties created in his work setting related to his "grandmother's" style, the father had been as equally withdrawn and depressed as the mother. The mother had been attending seances and communicating with her deceased mother as a means of achieving separation, but the father had been blind to his level of fusion. The pressure from the therapist switched to the father in order to move him from a pouting, moralistic, angry spouse to dealing with the pain and his wife's ambivalence in a more adult and mature manner. Rituals were assigned relative to the father and his grandmother, and finally the couple were able to grieve jointly about the affair. This was done by having a "funeral" and taking a coin given to the mother by the "other man" and burying it in a particularly beautiful place. It was a very emotional and moving experience for the couple.

Throughout the five-month period, both children were aware of the affair and discord between the couple, especially when the father would inform them angrily that everything was their mother's fault, and what she had done was immoral and wrong. Tim and Amy continued to do well in school, but almost immediately after the ritual Amy threatened suicide and Tim broke his finger and complained about his pain and didn't attend school. Amy was seen individually for a session where it was determined that she was not suicidal. Her stomach pains and anger were diagnosed to her as a delayed stress reaction. Basically, she was well adjusted and did not need therapy. In essence, it appeared that the children were testing the healthiness of the family by intensifying the fusion between generations. Amy insisted on knowing everything about the "funeral" assignment and continually kept track of her parents' relationship and whereabouts.

In the next session, it was interpreted to the parents that the children were in collusion to make the father strong and stand up to the mother more appropriately, while the mother had been married to the children. Selvini-Palazzoli's (1978) invariant prescription was assigned, whereby the parents were to leave the home unannounced, come home at a late hour, and refuse to tell the children where they had been or what they had done. The parents were very apprehensive because they always let both children know about such things, and there would be a storm of anger when they returned. The assignment worked extremely well, and the actions induced created for the parents the impetus to establish firmly the generational boundaries between themselves and the children. The last report was the family had stabilized and was doing well.

To summarize, this case illustrated the need to apply pressure on the person displaying the symptoms with the symptom being the entry into the family. In other situations the pressure might be diffused away from the child (IP) and spread around the system. Continued redefinitions were utilized, along with rituals and metaphors, although of equal importance was the three-generational perspective.

TRANSGENERATIONAL INVOLVEMENT

Both cases in this chapter were examples of indirect involvement within the therapy process of the third generation. Whittaker (1975) and Andolfi, Angelo, and De-Nichilo (1989) believe in the direct involvement of three generations as quickly as possible (like the Kanes). They believe that three generations are part of the problem and a key to the solution, and direct involvement is more powerful than indirect or lack of involvement.

Certainly, the three-generational perspective is necessary. If, in the Kane situation, the third generation had still been alive, they would have been brought into the therapy room. However, images, metaphors, and rituals needed to be used

to deal with "ghosts" rather than real people. In the Smith case, the adult children's parents were never called in, which in hindsight was a clinical mistake because it prolonged treatment and intensified the need to deal with the grandparents by using action and metaphorical techniques.

METAPHORS AND METAPHORICAL OBJECTS

Metaphors are the vehicle by which we can reproduce and reconstruct reality and relationships in our lives. Often, events, objects, and relationships are associated with intense emotional affect related to past experiences. Andolfi and colleagues (1983) believe that a metaphor will

readily lend itself to use by family members in expressing states of mind or relational situations, as well as by the therapist in his effort to analyze and restructure the family system. Metaphor seems to spring from our need to stop the continuous flow of reality, in order to possess it, to recapture what we lose of our everyday experience by means of something that resembles it. (p. 93)

The metaphoric image can come from either the family through verbal representation or nonverbal interactions, or from the internal processes of the therapist. The use of metaphor is to condense observations made of the family into a concrete image that provides for the family the opportunity to loosen the emotional intensity and gain new perspectives.

In order for this to occur, the therapist needs to have available toys, objects, and so on in the room to draw upon during the course of therapy. The objects represent behaviors, relationships, interactions, or rules of the family. The therapist must listen carefully to the language pattern and interactions of the family; the redundancies observed provide the basis for searching the therapist's internal self for images.

It is also important to watch for complementarities. When one side is predominant, such as anger, the therapist needs to surface another side (e.g., love). The metaphoric object can represent either side, although most commonly the predominant side provides the entry for the therapist. If this fails to occur, direct solicitation from the family or individual members can be helpful (e.g., What kind of animal does he remind you of?). Using one's own internal process is part of using oneself, in terms of one's personality, mode of acting, androgony, and own emotional processes.

When the metaphor is not correct, often the family will spontaneously offer a new metaphor, and, when using the family's own metaphor, the family will react with a higher level of affective intensity.

CASE STUDY 1, CONTINUED

The work with the Smith family was difficult, particularly with John's thinking process that included a great deal of craziness. He initially believed we were with the "C.I.A. or something" and were spying on him. He also believed the country would be attacked soon by Iranians, and that a good job for him would be a U.S. Senator, Supreme Court Justice, or even President. He also had an intense desire to become a police officer (which was scary considering his lack of impulse control) and an astronaut. During the course of therapy, he actually applied to NASA from an address in one of Carl's first-grade books.

We continually dealt with John's ideation with absurdity, by first agreeing with his premise and then carrying it one or two steps further. For example, we would agree that being President was appropriate, but that ruler of the solar system would give him even more power, or that we were really members of a super secret world intelligence organization and he was our most important assignment. After about eight or nine months of continually playing with his ideation, John learned to laugh at himself. Ultimately, we taught him to appreciate his craziness and playfulness and to keep his mouth closed to outsiders, especially employers, about his silly ideas.

During this time, Carl was placed in a behavior disorders class and was beginning to progress well in that environment. Susan's cancer was in remission. However, the emotional climate at home, with John unemployed and living in a public housing development on welfare, continued to be intense and angry. John's parents, especially the mother, were critical and crazy. John had a brother who died when John was 10 years old. His mother believed it would have been better if John had died. The brother's room, 20 years later, was still intact. Our decision was not to include his parents, but rather to teach John how to distance himself from his mother as she would berate him over the phone or in person. This was minimally effective until, after a year, we designed a ritual for John.

We finally told John that we had misdiagnosed him and that he was suffering from an "embarrassment disease." He was a very sensitive man, and his yelling at Carl, not going to apply for jobs, and not having friends was because of embarrassment; when he was embarrassed, he turned into a monster, similar to the "Hulk" on the television series. We pointed out how he inherited the disease from his mother and we talked about the similarity of behaviors. We discussed at length the implication of having a cure, especially in regard to his relationship with his parents and immediate family. John was instructed to go to a store to buy a small plastic model of the "Hulk." After looking in many stores, John came in with a facsimile, which was used to demonstrate the connection of John's anger with embarrassment, especially with Carl.

John's assignment for the cure was to wear the toy around his neck at home and in public (in full view) for two weeks, after which time we would give him a final cure. The next session was held in front of a team of five therapists to whom we and John discussed his "embarrassment disease," something he never could have previously done. As a final gesture, we had John smash the toy with his foot to everyone's applause and congratulations.

Six months later, John found employment for the first time in seven years. He is doing extremely well, and the marriage has stabilized with an appropriate distance to John's parents. During that time Susan's mother died of cancer and we assisted her with the grieving process. John was told by his boss on his maintenance job that he was a model employee (he worked nights and alone) and the family is now off welfare. According to the teacher, Carl is making "excellent progress" and will eventually move back into regular education.

Although the complexities of this case were not completely presented, it is our judgment that the major changes occurred through systemic provocation with the use of the metaphor and toy object. By relabeling the problem and using an object to represent John's symptoms within the context of the symptom, the family was able to mobilize themselves to engage in new behaviors and relationships.

THERAPIST-SCHOOL COLLABORATION

The emphasis in this chapter has been on the concepts involved in working with families. These constructs are also applicable to the interactive process between the therapist and the school. Two aspects of the consultation process will be analyzed. The first involves the therapist entering the school as a consultant about an individual case, whereas the second involves the school personnel attending the family session as a consultant to the therapist.

Therapist in the School

By the nature of the school system itself, when a therapist goes into the school, this action becomes an intrusive process. Before the school personnel will listen, they need to sense that the therapist is there to support the teacher. When intrusion takes place without connection and support, the therapist is viewed with mistrust, which results in resistance by the school. Therapists with prior experience working in schools have a distinct advantage over clinicians without this experience because they can more quickly adopt the language and style of communication, and communicate understanding more quickly and efficiently. Nonetheless, it is important to listen and look for ways of connecting while intruding into the system.

Consistent with working with rigid families, redefinition of the symptom(s) from a school context to a family context creates new perspectives, less pressure on the teacher and/or principal, and openness to try new ideas for intervention. At other times, however, the therapist may need to increase pressure, most often on the teacher or principal. Although the symptoms displayed by the child provide the entry, pressure (involving social, legal, and community sources in addition to the therapist) may need to be employed to induce change within the school.

Effective collaboration takes place within the context of connection with the school's concern about itself and the child. This also includes creativity for solutions resulting from the collaborative effort and the appropriate increase and decrease of pressure. With a knowledge about the family and the understanding of the systemic context of the problem, the therapist should be able to redefine and assist the school in developing alternative solutions. After this occurs, it then becomes important for the therapist to separate the work with one person as a liaison relative to further contacts.

School in the Therapy

Another aspect of consultation for consideration involves having the school come into the therapy session. This might be the teacher, principal, counselor, or some other significant individual. By enlarging the therapeutic system, pressure is increased within the session and the therapist can use the pressure to create a more collaborative relationship between the family and the school.

A number of additional benefits can be gained. First, roles of various helpers can be clearly defined, eliminating cross-purposes of helping the family, and the power of the helpers relative to the family can be delineated. Second, communication between all parties can be enhanced. Third, the information supplied by the school can be used in the redefinition process. Each benefit allows the therapist greater flexibility for finding connections and for intrusion.

These types of consultations are normally for one or two sessions, and seem to be most powerful when three generations of the family are involved in the sessions. As in most sessions, the school person can be used to increase pressure on the IP or distribute the pressure to include the school as well as the family.

SUMMARY

Like most therapeutic endeavors, to provoke is dependent on the personal charac-

teristics and skills of the therapist. What may be different about this approach is that although skills are considered to be the result of theoretical knowledge, supervision, and clinical experience, the evolving self of the therapist is equally important. When the therapist removes personal handicaps and conflicts that impede the use of self in therapy, the clients' own resistance and embarrassment is minimized, resulting in accessing creative processes. In order to utilize provocation effectively, all aspects of the self need to be available to the therapeutic process.

What has not been discussed in this chapter is the need for the therapist to provide not only intensity and power but also coolness and impotence. This is achieved through the process of connection and separation. Andolfi believes that the degree to which therapists are able to connect is also the degree to which therapists can separate. Therapists learn how to connect, but when the connection is not real then the therapist cannot separate and become emotionally fused with the family or problem. Separation from the family can often be used to increase or decrease pressure and is just as powerful as connection. One without the other, however, is unreal and ineffectual in helping families to change.

The use of objects and toys can be used not only as metaphoric images but also as an aid for the therapist in the separation process. For example, by handling, examining, and focusing on the object, the therapist achieves separation. In essence, the object becomes the co-therapist.

An interesting thought to consider is that this approach may appeal more to therapists who enjoy the connection and find they have the ability to connect. In contrast, therapists who enjoy separation and observation may prefer an approach that places them in a more neutral position.

For those who find this approach appealing and effective, the challenge becomes one of finding one's own handicaps and conflicts, and moving beyond them in order to have as complete an access to one's internal self as possible. This becomes a challenge not only for the therapist but also for trainers and supervisors. However, the more effectively we rise to the challenge, the more effective and powerful the therapy.

References

Andolfi, M. (1979). *Family therapy: An interactional approach.* London: Plenum.

Andolfi, M., Angelo, C., Menghi, P., & Nicolo-Corigliano, A. M. (1983). *Behind the family mask.* New York: Brunner/Mazel.

Andolfi, M., Angelo, C., & DeNichilo, M. (1989). *The myth of Atlas: Families and the therapeutic story.* New York: Brunner/Mazel.

Angelo, C. (1981). The use of the metaphoric object in family therapy. *American Journal of Family Therapy, 9,* 69–78.

Batson, G. (1972). *Steps to an ecology of mind.* London: Chandler.

Batson, G. (1979). *Mind over nature.* New York: Dutton.

Bianciardi, M., & Galliano, M. (1987). Hypothesizing or provocation: A comparative analysis of two Italian schools of family therapy. *The American Journal of Family Therapy, 15,* 3–13.

Gurman, A. S., & Kniskern, D. P. (1978). Deterioration in marital and family therapy. *Family Process, 17,* 3–20.

Haber, R. (1990). From handicap to handy capable: Training systemic therapists in use of self. *Family Process, 29,* 375–384.

Haley, J. (1973). *Uncommon therapy: The psychiatric techniques of Milton H. Erickson, M.D.* New York: Norton.

Minuchin, S., & Fishman, H. C. (1981). *Family therapy techniques.* Cambridge, MA: Harvard University Press.

Selvini-Palazzoli, M., Cecchin, G., Prota, G., & Boscolo, L. (1978). *Paradox and counterparadox.* New York: Aronson.

Simon, R. (1987). Good-by paradox, hello invariant prescription: An interview with Maria Selvini-Palazzoli. *The Family Therapy Network, 11,* 13–16.

Watzlawick, P., Beavin, J. H., & Jackson, J. J. (1967). *Pragmatics of human communication.* New York: Norton.

Wendt, R. (1987). Interview with Maurizio Andolfi. *Australian-New Zealand Journal of Family Therapy, 8,* 153–157.

Whitaker, C. (1975). Psychotherapy of the absurd with a special emphasis on the psychotherapy of aggression. *Family Process, 14,* 1–16.

Whitaker, C., & Keith, D. (1981). Symbolic-experiential family therapy. In A. Gurman & D. Kniskern (Eds.), *The handbook of family therapy.* New York: Brunner/Mazel.

20

Solution-Focused Brief Therapy: Applications in the Schools

RON KRAL

School District of Elmbrook, Brookfield, Wisconsin

THE FIELD OF psychotherapeutic intervention has continued to change with the introduction of systems theory. This paradigm has resulted in a new methodology—family therapy—which works from the premise that an individual's behavior must be viewed from the context within which it occurs. This concept has much to offer educators, as their world is definitely interpersonal (Johnston & Fields, 1981). Children learn within a group setting—the classroom. Also, a student's success or failure in school can be viewed as a family issue since the child is representing the family in the world. Therefore, the concepts and methodology of family therapy can be applied within the school context in several ways: (1) to provide a framework within which to conceptualize problems and solutions, (2) to give an educator assistance in understanding and intervening with family-school issues, or (3) to offer a menu of techniques for intervention within the school.

The field of family therapy, however, cannot be viewed as a single entity with a distinct theoretical basis with specific therapeutic techniques. Rather, family therapy is more like the start of a marathon race, with runners dodging and weaving amongst the crowd, each "running his or her own race" based on training, experience, and beliefs about running. All have their eyes on the goal and all run within the confines of the course. However, for some, completing the race is enough; for others, winning is most important.

Family therapists also go their own ways to approach the task of creating change while staying generally within a path called "systems therapy." Brief therapy, particularly the described by de Shazer, Berg, Lipchik, Nunnally, Molnar, Gingerich, and Weiner-Davis (1986) and de Shazer (1985), offers a useful model for intervening in the problems that children experience in the context of school. This model offers the advantages of systems thinking as well as providing an unique theory of change that is complementary with the constraints and needs of the school environment.

Solution-Focused Brief Therapy is based on the work of Milton H. Erickson and the thinking of Gregory Bateson (de

Shazer, 1985). It proceeds from a non-pathological view of human problems, which is expressed in the assumptions implicit in the model. The following discussion clarifies these assumptions.

Human problems result from patterns of interaction within a system.

Although this point of view is rather widely accepted within the family therapy community, it may represent a shift in thinking for school personnel. For the most part, schools look at student problems from a linear, individual focus. From this perspective, something is wrong with the pupil, which results in problems within the classroom or on the playground. A clear cause-and-effect relationship is assumed and remedial approaches proceed from this premise. Acceptance of the systems principle, however, would challenge the thinking and actions of schools in response to student problems. No longer is the child to be blamed, but rather the patterns of interaction within the child's life (teacher-child, child-child, teacher-parent, parent-child, etc.) need to be examined.

Individuals have within them the necessary resources to resolve their problems.

People are seen from a position of strength and optimism rather than deficiency. Quite often students who are experiencing difficulty are doing so because they have not applied alternative approaches that they already possess to the situation. It is through a creative use of a student's, teacher's, and/or parent's underlying strengths that successful change can be accomplished. By identifying the ability and building on it, the focus of treatment is positive and encouraging rather than negative or hopeless.

A small change within the system can have large results.

Based on the premise that everyone within a system is interconnected and that the behavior of one individual influences the behavior of others, intervention may be effective even if it is only directed at one part of the system. Similarly, a small change can escalate into a larger, more significant improvement as it "reverberates" throughout the system. Therefore, the therapist needs to be conscious of doing as little as necessary, allowing the system to adjust in its own idiosyncratic fashion.

The therapist also has a choice of which to change first—behaviors (observable actions) within the system, perceptions (individual thoughts, cognitions, world views) of members of the system, or both. For example, a teacher's perception of a child as a hard worker with limited ability elicits one set of teacher behaviors (support, reassurance, patience, etc.), whereas the belief that a particular student is very capable and lazy often results in an entirely different set of teacher reactions (nagging, anger, diminishing interaction, etc.).

In this example the therapist can choose to address the teacher's perceptions by offering information about the student's "learning blocks," or an intervention directed at the student's behaviors such as reinforcement for assignments completed on time can be attempted. Either approach may result in the desired end (an increase in student participation and learning), but a restructuring of the student's personality or elaborate behavior modification scheme may not be necessary. Instead, a small intervention geared at how the student and teacher interact may suffice.

The goal of intervention is the solution.

Quite often the emphasis of most mental health and educational training programs is on what is not working. This problem focus actually reduces the clinician's ability to define clearly and/or create a solution since a great deal of time and energy is used on rehashing undesirable behaviors. This type of discussion often prevents clients and therapists from focusing on available strengths and resources.

When solutions are identified, however, they typically tend to be overly optimistic conceptions of the situation as it should or could be and may not reflect what the situation realistically can be.

Solution-Focused Brief Therapy emphasizes the solution side of the problem-solution equation, utilizing clearly defined and realistic solutions that are mutually developed with the client. The question, How will you know when the problem is solved?, is often used to clarify a definition of the solution. This process works to enhance the business of change through the use of positive expectations and self-fulfilling prophecies.

All "rules" have exceptions.

People who experience problems, whether personal or with others, maintain a position that the difficulty occurs all of the time. Yet, upon closer inspection, most problems occur often, but not as consistently as the client believes. There are times when the problem could have occurred but did not or incidents when the problem was resolved more effectively than on other occasions. These exceptions are valuable diagnostic data and useful starting points for intervention. Clients are usually more capable than they can admit and often need to be made aware of their abilities. For example, consider the child who is fearful about going to school. At closer examination, it is usually true that the child is less anxious on some days compared to others. By identifying these patterns, the direction of invervention can quickly be determined by prescribing those elements that are present on the "less anxious" days. Consequently, the goal of intervention often is to increase the occurrence of things that do happen already rather to initiate whole new patterns of action.

People cooperate in therapy.

Much has been written relating to a system's resistance to change or homeosta-sis. Similarly, clients have been described as resistant to therapy. The model assumes that clients cooperate in therapy (de Shazer, 1982). The style of cooperation can vary in several ways, making it the therapist's responsibility to cooperate with the client in a useful fashion. Also, based on the exceptions assumption above, systems are more flexible than the homeostasis concept might predict. There is flux and changeability within a system that can be capitalized on to promote variations. In this fashion, the therapist is able to utilize the client's resources rather than attempt to introduce something new and foreign to the world view of the client.

The idea of utilization is a keystone in the work of Milton Erickson, who was particularly skillful and creative in using what a client brought into therapy to resolve the complaint (de Shazer, 1985, O'Hanlon, 1987). In the school setting, counselors, psychologists, and social workers often forget the wide range of students most teachers have successfully taught. At times, a simple remark like, "How have you best handled similar problems in the past?" can be a powerful intervention.

There is more than one way to skin a cat.

Inherent in Solution-Focused Brief Therapy is the notion that there is no one right way to do things. Part of the richness of life is the wide assortment of variations in living. Therefore, no single concept of "mental health" or "adjustment" is held. Individuals have behaviors, background experiences, and unique ways of looking at the world that may be useful in arriving at a useful solution. Therefore, it is the responsibility of the therapist to work within the world view of the client to develop a creative solution rather than to attempt to fit a client into a preconceived notion of what is "right." The issue is what is useful for the client and how well does it work within the context of the situation.

These assumptions create a system of operating that is inherently optimistic and pragmatic where doing less rather than more is valued. Individuals are viewed with respect and the therapist needs to remain alert to a rather clearly defined division of labor. The therapist works to create a relationship with the client where change is not only possible but expected (O'Hanlon, 1987) and the therapist strives to understand the client's world view (values and concept of how things are and should be), while the client is expected to provide data about exceptions and do the actual work of changing. People are not "forced" to change, just as a client is not expected to learn "psychologese" in order to benefit from the interaction. Additionally, little value is placed on traditional insight. A person does not need to understand "why" he or she has been doing something. Rather, the person is seen as needing to be able to define what he or she wants to be doing instead and what it takes to do that. This learning, which is the goal of Solution-Focused Brief Therapy, does not need to be conscious in the sense that a client can describe it in words. Rather, understanding based on what the client *does* is what is necessary.

THE PROCEDURE OF BRIEF THERAPY

Although several excellent descriptions of the procedure of brief therapy are available (de Shazer, 1985; de Shazer et al., 1986; de Shazer, 1988), a short description of how Solution-Focused Brief Therapy is implemented at the Brief Family Therapy Center in Milwaukee should help the reader understand the process. Generally, each case is seen by a team of therapists utilizing a one-way mirror, although a therapist working alone can successfully use this model. The family is interviewed for 30 to 40 minutes. During this time, the therapist elicits the family's view of the problem, any patterns of behavior around the com-

plaint, useful exceptions to the pattern, and a definition of what will be an acceptable solution.

Following this a 10-minute consulting break is taken. The therapist leaves the room to consult with the team or to work alone. During the break a series of positive compliments about the family are designed and an intervention, typically in the form of a task, is composed. The therapist then returns to the family and delivers the message. Another appointment, if necessary, is then scheduled.

At the start of the next session the therapist inquires about the task or asks a general question about what the family has done or observed that has been "good for them." If there are any noted differences, the therapist continues the interview, underscoring changes in the direction toward solution. The consulting break is taken in every session.

Sessions are initially scheduled at weekly intervals until positive changes are occurring. At this point, sessions are spread out over several weeks. At times, particularly in child-focused cases, parents and children can be seen separately for one or more sessions. This helps to strengthen parent-child boundaries and provides for the use of more strategic interventions.

Naturally, this format for sessions is very impractical within the school setting. However, a great deal of intervention can be accomplished in informal contacts, parent and/or teacher conferences, or doing counseling alone without the assistance of the team/mirror/video setup. Counselors or school psychologists can still take breaks to think over the material from the interview or a teacher can be seen the next day after the consultant has had an opportunity to consider things over night. In some instances students can be given a note with an intervention message, or parents could receive a followup call after a conference. The stance of the therapist, however, remains the same following the assumptions described above and the techniques listed below.

TECHNIQUES OF SOLUTION-FOCUSED BRIEF THERAPY

One of the strengths of brief therapy is the individualization of tasks and messages for each case, but the use of standard or invariant tasks has also proven very effective. de Shazer and Molnar (1984) and Molnar and de Shazer (1987) describe a number of useful interventions that can be applied across a number of cases and the conditions under which they should be used. Classes of these approaches will be described below.

Client Roles

As the therapist encounters the various individuals involved in a problem situation, it is essential to identify who's who. Three possibilites exist: visitor, complainant, or customer (de Shazer, 1988).

A *visitor* is someone who is there because he or she has to be; consequently, a visitor is not interested in change. This position most often defines the student who is sent to the school psychologist, counselor, or social worker so he or she can "get help." The student usually does not see things as a problem and often is described as "resistive" because he or she fails to see the wisdom of accepting help. Some families also are in this situation as they do not have difficulties with their children at home as a result of different norms at home, a lack of parental interest in school, or factors unique to the child's classroom.

The therapist's primary functions when dealing with a visitor are the following:

1. Avoid the temptation to try to make the visitor do something, as this will prove to be fruitless and impede further opportunities to effectively intervene.
2. Develop a positive relationship with the visitor by seeing his or her point of view ("Ain't it awful you had to come and see me?") and by complimenting him or her on all of the positives that can be identified ("I am impressed that you care enough about your daughter that you took time out to come in").
3. Enlist the visitor's assistance by taking a "one down" (Fisch, Weakland, & Segal, 1982) position ("It was helpful to me to learn how well you handle Angela's temper at home").

A *complainant* is someone who admits to a problem and wants to talk about it but is not yet willing to take action. The therapist is advised to give a complainant tasks that require thinking in order to learn more about the situation. Again, it is important to listen and give compliments. Another task may be to ask the complainant *not* to do anything (Fisch, Weakland, & Segal, 1982; de Shazer & Molnar, 1984). This can result in a difference as he or she now has to do something to stay the same. The focus of treatment with complainants is on their perceptual, cognitive view.

A *customer* responds to a more direct approach. He or she comes in with a problem and wants to *do* something about it. A behavioral task designed to interrupt an existing pattern or to initiate a new pattern is most often the strategy to use with a customer. For example, a student is a customer if she is irritated with the relationship between her and her teacher and is eager to follow through on certain tasks.

The following case study demonstrates how these roles are not static and how a complainant may change to a customer with initial intervention by the therapist.

CASE STUDY 1

Mr. and Mrs. Scott brought their daughter, Justine, for therapy because of their concern that she would be referred for Special Education. Justine had been retained in 4-year-old kindergarten due to behavior difficulties. Now, Justine was scheduled for 5-year-old kindergarten and the Scotts were worried that there would be more problems. (This case was seen in a private clinic and represents the type of situation where treatment through the schools may not prove effective since the therapist was able to be flexible in initially siding with the family "against" the school.)

In the first two sessions the Scotts complained about the school and had few, if any, complaints about Justine's behavior at home. In order to address the parents' worries that Justine had "underlying problems," the therapist requested psychoeducational testing. The results of this evaluation were interpreted to the Scotts in light of their initial concerns. The testing "showed" that Justine did have difficulties accepting limits. The Scotts were told that Justine was bright enough to challenge limits verbally, but developmentally needed to know where the limits were. The negative "Don't do that" approach that they had tried was good for older kids, but was too sophisticated for someone at Justine's level. She could understand that she needed to stop whatever it was she was doing, but she was too immature, cognitively, to know what to do instead.

Therefore, Justine's parents had to "catch" her doing the right things. Justine was to receive a "happy face" on the refrigerator everytime she complied with a parental request *but* Mr. and Mrs. Scott could not tell Justine why she received the reward. After one week, Justine had not only figured the system out but she was reminding her parents that she was following their directions!

The second stage of therapy was to explain to the Scotts that since they understood Justine's "style" of behaving, they needed to share this with her teacher so that she could also take advantage of the information. A parent-teacher conference was held where the testing and "experimental data" were shared. The therapist took the role of "positively blaming" (Kral, 1986) the parents for seeking out help, trying something new, and asking for the teacher conference. This process entailed assigning the responsibility for positively influencing the girl on her parents. The teacher was told how "catching her being good" had positive results at home. This served to challenge the teacher to try something new and lead to a new working relationship between home and school as they both were told what to do by a professional.

In this case, the parents' concern about school became a way of motivating them to "do something different." This, in turn, was used to inform and challenge the teacher to try a new approach with Justine. Both adult systems were modified and no direct treatment with the child (other than testing) was necessary. Initially the Scotts were not customers. They did not report any problem other than the belief that their daughter had gotten a lousy teacher. Certainly they did not need to do anything different. The therapist was able to accept this position as he was not acting as part of the school system. The testing was used to create the hypothesis that Justine needed positive reminders and this was used to enlist the parents' help in getting "ammunition" to use with the teacher. Once they accepted this new definition of the situation, they became customers—individuals who wanted to *do* something to convince the teacher that there was nothing wrong with Justine but that she just needed to be handled differently.

Reframing

Bowman and Goldberg (1983) describe the school psychologist's use of reframing within the context of the school. Reframing is a tool that anyone within the school setting can and quite often already does use. Milton Erickson described reframing by stating, "I go over the possibilities and pick out a nice one" (Haley, 1985, p. 71). As described above, one of the focal points for intervention is an individual's belief or perception about a situation. Reframing is the principal technique in addressing perceptions. Hyperactive behavior can be reframed as "busy," "involved," or "widely focused." Depression can be seen as the state of being "overwhelmed" (Kral, 1986). In most problem situations, the participants see things from a negative, pessimistic point of view. By offering a new, positive interpretation of the problem, the therapist is able to intervene significantly in the system. An example of a simple use of reframing is provided below.

CASE STUDY 2

Marvin was presented at a child study team meeting because of his increasing level of noncompliant and oppositional behavior in his Exceptional Education class placement. Marv was in a program for emotionally disturbed students for 57 percent of his school day and was mainstreamed into a regular sixth-grade program for the remainder. In the ED class, Marv was a challenge. He was rude to his teacher, negative toward other students, and would often deliberately break classroom rules. In his mainstream classes, however, he was able to maintain a level of behavior that was tolerable to his regular education teacher.

During the meeting the building prin-

cipal asked the study team the question, "If you were treated as a 'crazy kid,' wouldn't you act weird, too?" This simple and apparently innocent comment changed the views of the staff, who were moving toward a placement in an alternative setting for emotional disturbed children. As a result, the team tried a trial placement outside of the Exceptional Education program altogether.

Although Marvin continued to be a challenge to his teacher, the intensity of his behaviors was reduced to the point where he passed the sixth grade. The principal inadvertently "reframed" Marvin's behavior as not only appropriate for the EEN program but also as "expected" within that context.

Conceptualizing Problems and Solutions

Problems can be viewed from a variety of perspectives, but most useful to the therapist is the one presented by the Brief Therapy Center at the Mental Research Institute. This group conceptualizes problems as arising from the attempted solutions applied to a difficulty (Fisch, Weakland, & Segal, 1982).

An example of this type of difficulty is the parent who is faced with a crying child. The child may be crying for any number of reasons; a favorite toy may have broken, the child may have been frightened by lightning, or she or he may simply be overtired. Often, the first solution attempted is to threaten the child sternly with physical punishment if he or she does not stop crying. In some cases, this may be successful. Most often, however, the child becomes more frightened at the prospect of the punishment and may actually begin to cry more. This reaction is met with increased threats and intimidation on the part of the parent, followed by additional (and possibly justified) fear and crying on the part of the child. In the end, either the parent "does something different" or the child's fears come true. The solution (threats) becomes the problem (the impetus for further crying).

This type of pattern can be played out over and over in relation to a particular problematic situation. The therapist needs to identify the pattern and then recognize that this is exactly what had *not* worked. Instead, the pattern needs to be broken. This may most easily be accomplished through the application of a "do something different" prescription. The underlying thought is that a chain of behaviors can develop within a system that not only results in the problematic situation but may even cue the problem to occur. The parents' threats act as signals that the child may soon be experiencing pain on the behind. This cue can intensify the problem behavior and a negative feedback loop is established. By "doing something different," the pattern can be interrupted and new, adaptive behaviors can fill the subsequent void.

Behavioral tasks that ask the client to *do* something have proven to be particularly useful in these situations. The behavioral pattern can be disrupted through the use of competing actions on the part of someone within the system. This contrasts with the more cognitive approach addressed by reframing, which deals primarily with perceptions rather than specific actions. By acting "differently" within the context of a behavioral sequence, a new sequence can be established. In this model, "different" means more than simply "something else"; it implies a second-order change (Watzlawick, Weakland, & Fisch, 1974). Instead of substituting a spanking for yelling at a child, the spanking would be replaced with Mom going into the bathroom for 20 minutes or Dad giving a kiss and hug. The "different" ac-

tion is a behavior that does not "fit" based on the prevailing logic of the situation. The following case will demonstrate this concept.

CASE STUDY 3

The Bryant family came to the school counselor as a result of concerns that Mrs. Bryant expressed to her son's teacher. Jimmy was, at times, disrespectful, belligerent, and argumentative to his mother in particular. The counselor saw Mr. and Mrs. Bryant, Jimmy (age 10), and Claire (age 6), together. In the sessions it became clear that Mr. Bryant was not particularly worried about Jimmy's behavior since "boys will be boys." Claire was generally noninvolved and appeared to be reasonably well adjusted for her age. Jimmy contended that the problem was not a "big deal." Mrs. Bryant, however, was quite upset about the situation.

The counselor saw the Bryants for six sessions, with the goal of "teaching" Mr. and Mrs. Bryant good parenting techniques. Mrs. Bryant was interested but she learned very little because she had been attending a parent education program through her church. Mr. Bryant "listened" attentively but failed to change his approach with Jimmy. He was clearly taking the "visitor" role (as described earlier). Thus, the therapist decided to work primarily with the mother at this point since she was a "customer."

The school year ended so the counselor discontinued her meetings with the family. Over the summer she had the opportunity to consult with a family therapist at a workshop on brief therapy. The therapist gave her some advice about the Bryant family. Several weeks later she received a call from Mrs. Bryant, who was still concerned about Jimmy. In desperation, the counselor shared with Mrs. Bryant the interpretation provided by the family therapist, the "famous Dr. Schmoo."

What the therapist had said was that Jimmy recognized his mother's position. She had given up a potentially successful career to raise her children and she was feeling somewhat stifled in her current position. So, he discovered that by misbehaving, his mother had some excitement in her life and she was making new social contacts through her involvement in the parent training classes and frequent trips to the school about his behavior. The counselor said that she did not really understand it, but in some way Jimmy thought he was being helpful to his mom by acting out. Mrs. Bryant responded by saying that this really did not make sense to her either.

Several weeks later Mrs. Bryant called back and told the counselor that she had often thought about what the counselor had told her. In fact, every time Jimmy misbehaved she remembered it and couldn't stop herself from laughing. Jimmy had picked up on it and laughed too. Therefore, the problems between the two of them had subsided to a remarkable degree.

A month after Mrs. Bryant's call, the counselor received a call from Mr. Bryant, who said that the idea of Jimmy "helping" his mom was the most ludicrous concept that he had ever heard. He was calling, however, because it seemed to have made a difference. The conflicts between Jimmy and his mom had noticeably diminished and there was a lot more peace in their home. In fact, he was so pleased that he and his wife wanted to take the counselor out to lunch.

The act of "doing something different" in the face of Jimmy's belligerent behavior, which in this case was to laugh a little and not take it seriously, resulted in a significant change in Jimmy's response patterns. Mrs. Bryant was able to do this because the counselor's reframe regarding the helpfulness of Jimmy's behavior allowed her to be creative. She was not facing "disturbed" but only "disturbing" behavior; therefore, she was free to try new things.

APPLICATIONS WITHIN THE SCHOOLS

This way of working has numerous applications within the school setting, outside of the more limited idea of counseling or therapeutic intervention. In many ways this model represents a "way of thinking" rather than a specific methodology. It can be viewed as a "metamodel" that organizes the change agent's ideas about what needs to be done and then presents techniques or processes taken from other ways of intervening such as neuropsychology, cognitive behavior modification, learning styles research, Adlerian counseling, reality therapy, family systems therapy, and the like. What follows are examples of the use of this model across several common situations within the school setting.

Parent Conferences

Parents are called into the school regularly for various reasons. Quite often the parents are faced with a litany of complaints about their child. Equally as often the school personnel have little or nothing of a constructive nature to provide to the family. Usually parents are summoned at that point, when the school does not know what to do next or the family is blamed for the problem (DiCocco, 1986).

From the point of view of the Solution-Focused Brief Therapy model, this situation can be problematic. Parents need to be included as a part of the solution instead of the problem. Following the format of the treatment session (de Shazer et al., 1986), a sense of the parents' view of the problem needs to be identified and the teacher/counselor/administrator needs to construct some idea of what would be helpful in the situation. The parents are then complimented and may be advised of something they could do that would be helpful to the school in solving the problem their child is presenting.

This method tends to run contrary to the "typical" school conference where the parent is deluged with all of the problems their child is having and usually not provided with much of an opportunity to speak. In this model the parents' opinion is sought in an effort to discover "what *you* have done that works with this child." In this fashion the parents are placed in the "expert" role where their experience with the child is valued and sought. The final result is new information about something that may work with this student and a working relationship with the parents is fostered.

CASE STUDY 4

As the result of an all-school survey on drug and alcohol abuse, Tim Williams came forward as concerned about his father's drinking problem. In discussing the situation with Tim, it became apparent that he was in need of help but he refused to participate in the school's educational group for Concerned Others. A conference was scheduled with Tim's mom to consider other alternatives. The school psychologist who had interviewed Tim met with Mrs. Williams. The meeting started with the psychologist complimenting Mrs. Williams on Tim's ability to express himself clearly and openly and his concern for the family. This was directly attributed to the quality of parenting he had received from both his parents.

Mrs. Williams was then asked if she had noticed any signs of concern on Tim's part. She said that he was not doing as well in school as she thought he could. The mother was then told that Tim was worried about his father, and, as a result of an educational program at school, Tim felt that his father had a drinking problem. Mrs. Williams agreed that Tim was worried about his dad and so was she. However, she did not realize that he was so concerned that he would be willing to discuss it with people at school. Tim's reluctance to talk in a group was described and Mrs. Williams agreed. She said that she had attended an Al-Anon meeting but disliked it because there were so many people there, so she never went back. A referral was made for Tim to see a counselor who specialized in treating children of alcoholics on an individual basis.

In this case, the mother was provided with a point of view that did not attack the family or her husband and yet provided the impetus to take specific and direct action. The school psychologist worked to facilitate appropriate action without trying to do therapy in the usual sense. The resources and concerns of the family were utilized to make a difference.

Teacher Consultation

Approaches with teachers do not significantly differ from those used with parents. Each is in the position of a caregiver who has authority and responsibility for the child. In some ways, though, the teacher is in a better position because he or she has had more experience with a wider range of student behaviors and problems. This previous learning needs to be accessed and utilized for the benefit of the student. Reframing a pattern interruption tasks can be considered.

One useful starting tactic is a modification of the fixed first session task, described by de Shazer and Molnar (1984). This task asks a family to make note of "what is going on in the family that they would like to see continue to happen." The family members need to notice positives that are already occurring but may (or may not) have been in their awareness. Similarly, teachers can be asked to keep an anecdotal record, for a limited period of time, of what the child does that they would like to see continue.

A followup interview is conducted to identify what has been noted and to ask, "Was this different?" Next, whether this is what the teacher is looking for is examined. Finally, what the teacher might do to make this happen again and/or more frequently is identified. If something is found that makes the situation better, then the teacher is instructed to do more of that.

Another approach in teacher consultation would be to provide a new interpretation of a student's behavior that falls within the range of "solvable problems" for a particular teacher. Some teachers work well with students who are nervous or frightened but balk at students labeled with an "anxiety disorder." The range of reframes is countless, but the consultant needs to remember that the new label needs to fit the observable facts in order to be effective and believable.

Pattern interruption tasks simply mean that the teacher does something different that is out of the ordinary for a particular situation. Asking a student to take a note to the office when he is beginning to get fidgety is an obvious and often used tactic. Calling on a student to answer an easy question when she is beginning to act out is similar. Reinforcing other students for proper behavior while ignoring poor behavior is yet another. Each requires that the teacher recognize what he or she usually does and if it does not work, then to try a different response to the student's behavior.

CASE STUDY 5

Alex was referred because of severe attention-seeking behavior in his third-grade class. He had transferred from a school in a rough neighborhood and his parents had hoped he would do better in the new school. Even during his first day Alex acted out and was belligerent to his teacher, Mrs. Delancy. The teacher immediately contacted the school counselor and asked that Alex be considered for a class for students with emotional disabilities. The counselor investigated the situation by reviewing Alex's record and talking to his mom on the phone for a few minutes. She came back to Mrs. Delancy and stated that it appeared to her that Alex was scared as he often was the victim in his previous school. So, in order to put up a "tough front" that would put other kids off and protect him, he was acting out in class.

This reframed Alex's behavior but offered little as a solution to Mrs. Delancy's concerns. The counselor went on, however, and stated that what Alex needed was the sense that he was safe in the new school. Mrs. Delancy could best provide this by showing Alex that no one, not even he, could get away with misbehaving in her class. This required Mrs. Delancy to be firmer with Alex and use a system of rewards and consequences that she had used earlier, but disliked. She did do it, though, because she wanted Alex to feel "safe." In a few weeks, Alex's behavior had settled remarkably.

Parent Consultation

There are times when parents will seek assistance from the school rather than look to a private practitioner. Coppersmith (1982) lists advantages and disadvantages to providing family therapy services from within the public school. Golden (1983) also describes the utility of the school providing "brief family therapy" when certain conditions are met. These include the stability of the family and the severity of the symptom as defined by how long the problem has been occurring. The brief therapy model can be quite useful in many such situations, as the focus is positive and intervention is kept to a minimum while the strengths of the family are emphasized. The concepts of cooperation, reframing, doing something different, and emphasizing solution as opposed to problems all apply in this situation as well. The following case example will demonstrate these points.

CASE STUDY 6

Mrs. Jarvis consulted the school social worker because her son, Doug, was giving her a great deal of trouble. He could be quite argumentative and would have angry temper tantrums, which frightened her because, at age 14, he was physically capable of hurting her or the other children in the family. Doug started out every day in a foul mood, arguing with his mother about getting up and going to school. He would do reasonably well in school and was generally reasonable when he came home after his paper route in the evening. The major problem seemed to be the mornings. Mrs. Jarvis reported that Doug was very responsible when it came to the route and he expressed some concern about earning a detention after school.

In the morning Mrs. Jarvis felt compelled to nag Doug about getting up, even though she knew that this would provoke a fight. The therapist asked her to "do something different" in the morning in order to find out what effect this may have on Doug's behavior. This was presented to her as an "experiment" (Kral, 1986, p. 58) to help in deciding the "depth" of Doug's problems. She was asked to call Doug only once in the morning and then to leave the house to take the younger kids to school. She was next to go out for breakfast and to come home after the time when Doug was supposed to leave for school. She agreed that Doug would not want to miss school since he would get a detention, which would interfere with his paper route.

Due to her reluctance to try this "experiment," Mrs. Jarvis was asked to try it only once over the next week. Since this was a time-limited task, she was more willing to try it rather than feel "condemned to a life sentence" of this activity. At the end of three days, Doug had gotten up on time every day *and* he had gone to bed earlier than usual on the last day. The early bedtime was extremely unusual, as Doug's bedtime had long been a point of contention.

Mrs. Jarvis continued this for several weeks and the frequency of the early-morning fights diminished significantly. In addition, Doug began to sleep longer by going to bed sooner. This increase in sleep correlated with a more "positive attitude" and a decrease in fighting at home. He continued to do well in the classroom and Mrs. Jarvis was quite satisfied with this "new" situation.

Student Counseling

A number of considerations are important when counseling students (Kral, 1988). Students are the least powerful parts of the system; therefore, more work is necessary to effect a significant and lasting change by working with an individual student. However, children are often the most therapeutically available member of a system, as teachers and parents alike will send a child to a counselor, school psychologist, or school social worker to "get fixed." These professionals need to take special care to avoid a "more of the same" situation where they are only repeating to the child what the parent, teacher, or principal has already said. Instead, the child's view of the situation needs to be understood and accepted. Goals for counseling may need to be "How can we get your teacher off your back?" rather than "What will it take for you to pass seventh grade?" The basic principles of Solution-Focused Brief Therapy continue to apply, however, as the following case will demonstrate.

CASE STUDY 7

Melissa, an eighth-grader, was referred for testing by the school psychologist because she was "underachieving." She attended a small, private school known for its accelerated curricula. The school psychologist reviewed Melissa's record and noted that she functioned solidly within the average range on nationally normed group tests—a performance level that was considerably below her peers at school. He recommended that Melissa's parents consider enrolling her in the public school where she would be more competitive academically.

Upon entering the public school, Missy's parents were worried because she continued to show a lack of investment in her studies. The school psychologist saw her individually because her parents refused parent sessions and the public school staff did not see her as a significant problem. In session, Missy stated that she wanted to do well and had done so for several weeks but was falling a bit behind currently. The psychologist absentmindedly commented that this was understandable because Missy was probably unable to apply herself for any length of time. Actually, he thought aloud, it would be a good bet that she would be falling further and further behind as time went on. In fact, this was such a good bet that he would be willing to put up a Coke that she would continue to fall behind. Melissa took the challenge and asked if she could drink the Coke in school, which was against policy, when she won. The psychologist said that this could be arranged—at great difficulty.

Missy won the bet and three subsequent ones as well. Each time she drank her Coke in the psychologist's office during the school day after he "smuggled" it in to her. The case is notable in that it shows an awareness on the part of the psychologist of several points. First, Missy was not expected to do anything she had not already done. She had a usable "exception" in that she had done well in the new school for five weeks. Second, the obstinate nature of an eighth-grade student was utilized in a playful manner to maintain the changes that were already present. The Coke was not a reinforcer in the usual sense, as it was of little value. Missy had as much Coke as she wanted outside of school. It was powerful because it represented a challenge to authority, on which many adolescents thrive. Finally, this strategy worked because Missy said it would. She asked *when* she succeeded (not *if*), if she would be able to drink the Coke at school. Without this commitment, the psychologist would have won a Coke and then used an entirely new approach.

Psychoeducational Testing

This solution-focused model overlaps well with the use of psychological and psychoeducational testing. Various tests are used quite routinely within the school setting in order to classify students and to determine appropriate instructional strategies. Within the framework presented above, tests can be used in several ways to develop and/or maintain positive changes. The first principle is that no one is ever "cured" by being given a test. Rather, the interpretation and subsequent use of the test results are where the true value of psychometric data lies.

Second, tests generally command a certain amount of "mystique" and therefore power. That is, if a teacher is told that a student is "bright" based on an IQ test, there is a greater chance that this information will be viewed as accurate than if the teacher is told that the student is "bright" based on an interview or clinical impression. It is as if the school psychologist, armed with test results, has an "expert witness" along who can testify to the validity of the psychologist's claims.

Finally, a flexible interpretation of test data allows for the generation of a variety of "reframes" that can then be selected based on the fit between collateral facts and the interpretation of the data (Ziffer, 1985). In this way an examiner may be able to broaden the range of possible meanings and then select one that offers a positive direction and/or potential solution. Therefore, a student's strengths should be delineated based on the testing data and then utilized in the change process. This differs from the more traditional, problem-focused approach applied in psychological assessment.

In order for psychological testing to be useful in the development of a solution, several additional factors need to be considered. The examiner needs to be able to identify a solution to the presenting problem. For example, consider an "underachieving" student. This is a child viewed as working below her "potential." A multitude of solutions are possible: (1) she could have limited ability for school suc-cess relative to mental retardation, learning disabilities, or some other intrinsic condition; (2) she may be reacting to some psychosocial stressor such as divorce, abuse, or drug addiction; or (3) she may lack a sense of "contact" with the traditional school context relative to social problems. Unfortunately none of these conditions can be significantly changed. Instead, alternative realities need to be developed for the complainant or customer. These alternatives may include a "slower rate of learning," a unique "learning style" that requires concrete presentations of material or demonstration approaches, or a need to develop greater involvement of the student in the learning process through the use of high-interest materials. Finally, concepts that will bridge the customer's view of the current situation and the therapist's desired frame must be created. The following case demonstrates this approach.

CASE STUDY 8

Christopher was referred for a psychological evaluation to determine eligibility for placement in a program for emotionally disturbed children. The test results yielded a pattern of better-developed skills on the performance as opposed to the verbal scale of the Wechsler Intelligence Scale for Children—Revised (WISC—R). Additional information indicated that Chris tended to act out in the classroom during oral presentations. At the same time, he was seen as having problems with fighting. The teacher's response to Christopher's inappropriate behavior was to scold him or lecture him in front of the class. Following the application of this "discipline," his behavior usually became even more problematic.

In the followup meeting, the school

psychologist suggested that, based on the elevated performance score on the WISC—R, this student was easily overwhelmed with verbal stimulation (reframe) and tended to be *more* physical in his style of learning and responding than other children. Therefore, what was needed (prior to trying a special class placement) was to use concrete consequences with a minimum of discussion. The teacher was to point out to Chris, in short and simple terms, what the problem was and then to give him one more chance before a time out was used (doing something different within the context).

ADDITIONAL CONSIDERATIONS

The use of Solution-Focused Brief Therapy can take many forms and can be widely applied across a variety of functions within the context of the school. Several factors, however, need to be considered in the application of any therapeutic methodology, particularly one associated with family therapy. There are a number of concerns to be addressed in the provision of family therapy services within a school setting. On the plus side, it would be beneficial for schools to begin to conceptualize a child's problems from a new perspective, viewing the symptom as a result of interactions within a system rather than from "within" a child.

Second, since referrals for school-oriented problems come from the school, it may be easier to treat them within the school rather than involving the mental health system with its more negative connotations. This way families may be more open to intervention than if they had to seek therapy elsewhere. Third, the maintenance of problems is due, in part, to the actions of the school. By treating the symptoms from the vantage point of the school, these problem-maintaining patterns can be more effectively changed. Finally, it could be beneficial to provide family therapy services within the school since the school and family systems are the two most powerful influences in a child's life. Therefore, when these two systems work together, the dangers of negative triangulation (Okun, 1984) can be addressed and avoided.

There are equally powerful pitfalls to the provision of family therapy from the school, however. An emphasis on family therapy may, in many cases, put the focus of the problem on the family rather than the ecology of the school where many problems are maintained. After all, "family therapy will not . . . teach children to read" (Coppersmith, 1982, p. 271). Second, therapy within the schools may violate a family's confidentiality, dealing with issues within the family that are not the business of the school. Third, intervention from the school continues the "one-up" position of the school, which can be an issue in itself with the school dictating what parents should do, thereby widening the gap between home and school. Finally, the school may become overly involved with the concerns of the family, thereby hampering the family's ability to resolve independently their own concerns. This could inhibit the family's ability and/or willingness to deal with similar problems on their own in the future.

Foster (1983) adds several other potential blocks to this approach. These include the additional time constraints on already stressed pupil service workers in the schools. And, as a further complication, school employees would have to work very hard to maintain a position of neutrality between the family and the school, usually without the benefit of support of other practitioners coming from the same point of view.

With these cautions in mind, can family and/or systemic therapy be successful in the schools? Several of the concerns listed above can be addressed through the use of the Solution-Focused Brief Therapy model. The model is systemic in its focus, taking advantage of the strengths of each of the elements within the system. The teacher, parent, and/or student may easily be seen as the focal point for intervention. The student is not viewed as the problem. In fact, interest in any problem is short lived, as the emphasis of intervention is focused toward a solution. In this manner involvement with the student's family becomes positive and nonintrusive.

The goal of the contacts is to discover "exceptions" to the rule or to define actions that have proven successful with the student rather than to underscore problems or failures. Similarly, behavior is viewed on an equal footing with internal dynamics, so changing the behavior is viewed as addressing and changing the dynamics of the individual as well. Therefore, the intrusiveness of more traditional forms of therapy that rely on history is missing. Psychological as well as behavior changes can be made by addressing the behavior and/or perceptions, which result in new patterns.

Finally, Solution-Focused Brief Therapy attempts to build on the strengths and resources of the system and in this way develops independence so that future intervention may not be necessary. The school and the family are viewed as equals, each as a part of the "solution" rather than the "problem." By developing a working relationship, these two powerful systems begin to learn to work together for the best interest of the child.

SUMMARY

Solution-Focused Brief Therapy represents a model of change and intervention that is uniquely suited to the school context. Although psychotherapy is not a traditional role for the school or for school personnel, this approach offers numerous avenues for application within the school setting. Its emphasis on the strengths and resources of the individual and family provide for the development of a powerful working relationship between the home and school. Intervention strategies are designed to be minimal in order to allow for the natural forces of the system to maintain positive changes. This also serves the school, which is faced with limited resources. Finally, the ability of these principles to be applied across a wide variety of situations and settings makes it flexible and pragmatic—two elements necessary for the schools.

References

Bowman, P., & Goldberg, M. (1983). "Reframing": A tool for the school psychologist. *Psychology in the Schools, 20,* 210–214.

Coppersmith, E. I. (1982). Family therapy in a public school system. In A. S. Gurman (Ed.), *Questions and answers in the practice of family therapy, volume 2.* New York: Brunner/Mazel.

de Shazer, S. (1982). *Patterns of brief family therapy: An ecosystemic approach.* New York: Guilford.

de Shazer, S. (1985). *Keys to solution in brief therapy.* New York: Norton.

de Shazer, S. (1988). *Clues: Investigating solutions in brief therapy.* New York: Norton.

de Shazer, S., Berg, I. K., Lipchik, E., Nunnally, I., Molnar, A., Gingerich, W., & Weiner-Davis, M. (1986). Brief therapy: Focused solution development. *Family Process, 25,* 207–222.

de Shazer, S., & Molnar, A. (1984). Four useful interventions in brief family therapy. *Journal of Marital and Family Therapy, 10,* 297–304.

DiCocco, B. E. (1986). A guide to family/school interventions for the family therapist. *Contemporary Family Therapy, 8,* 50–61.

Fisch, R., Weakland, J. H., & Segal, L. (1982). *The tactics of change: Doing therapy briefly.* San Francisco: Jossey-Bass.

Foster, M. A. (1983). Schools. In M. Berger & G. Jurkovic (Eds.), *Practicing family therapy in diverse settings.* San Francisco: Jossey-Bass.

Golden, B. (1983). Brief family interventions in a school setting. *Elementary School Guidance and Counseling, 17,* 288–293.

Haley, J. (Ed.). (1985). *Conversations with Milton H. Erickson, M. D., Volume 3: Changing children and families.* New York: Triangle Press.

Johnston, J. C., & Fields, P. A. (1981). School consultation with the "classroom family." *The School Counselor, 29,* 140–146.

Kral, R. (1986). Indirect therapy in schools. In S. de Shazer & R. Kral (Eds.), *Indirect approaches to therapy.* Rockville, MD: Aspen.

Kral, R. (1988). *Strategies that work: Techniques for solution in the schools.* Milwaukee, WI: Brief Family Therapy Center.

Molnar, A., & de Shazer, S. (1987). Solution-Focused Therapy: Toward the identifica-

tion of therapeutic tasks. *Journal of Marital and Family Therapy, 13,* 349–358.

O'Hanlon, W. (1987). *Taproots: Underlying principles of Milton Erickson's therapy and hypnosis.* New York: Norton.

Okun, B. (1984). Family therapy and the schools. In B. Okun (Ed.), *Family therapy with school related problems.* Rockville, MD: Aspen.

Watzlawick, P., Weakland, J., & Fisch, R. (1974). *Change: Principles of problem formation and problem resolution.* New York: Norton.

Ziffer, R. L. (1985). The utilization of psychological testing in the context of family therapy. In R. L. Ziffer (Ed.), *Adjunctive techniques in family therapy.* Orlando: Grune & Stratton.

School and Family Consultation:
A Language-Systems Approach

LYLE J. WHITE
Southern Illinois University, Carbondale

MARY LUE SUMMERLIN
Deer Park Indpendent School District
Deer Park, Texas

VICTOR E. LOOS
Deer Park Independent School District
Deer Park, Texas

EUGENE S. EPSTEIN
Center for Social Theory
Bad Wimpfen, West Germany

THIS CHAPTER PRESENTS a language-systems approach to consulting with schools, families, and problem children. The language-systems approach differs from other systemic and structural models of consultation in a number of important areas, including identification of the relevant system for consultation, diagnosis and definition of the consultation problem, and development of the consultant's roles and goals within the school system. The chapter describes the challenges of implementing language-systems ideas in a districtwide consultation program in a metropolitan public school setting. A case example is used to illustrate how these ideas inform the consultant's thinking throughout the consultation process.

SCHOOL AND FAMILY CONSULTATION

Consultation as a method of providing psychological services to schools has be-

This chapter was written while the first author was a postdoctoral fellow and the other authors were senior faculty members at the Galveston Family Institute. Special appreciation is extended to Harold A. Goolishian, Ph.D., and Mary Lue Summerlin, Ed.D., for directing the School Consultation Project, and to Ms. Lynn Hale, Superintendent of Deer Park Independent School District, for her openness to the project and for her commitment to developing quality psychological/consultation services in a school setting.

come increasingly popular during the last 25 years (Curtis & Meyers, 1985; Witt & Elliot, 1983). School psychologists have also come to recognize the importance of taking a systems perspective in consultation (Curtis & Meyers, 1985) and to include the family system in their psychological assessments (Elliot & Erchul, 1987; Paget & Nagle, 1986; Wilson, 1986).

In our discussion of school and family consultation we will describe the theoretical constructs of a language-systems approach developed at the Galveston Family Institute (GFI) (Anderson & Goolishian, 1988; Goolishian & Anderson, 1987, 1990). To help clarify this approach, we will (1) compare and contrast the language-systems approach with another recently suggested model for providing psychological services to schools, (2) describe how the language-systems approach has been implemented within a school district, (3) provide a case study to illustrate language-systems consultation and address practical issues, and (4) identify potential pitfalls in consulting to schools and families around youth with school problems.

Consultation and systems models contain assumptions regarding the role of the consultant, the client, and the social systems in which they operate. These assumptions dictate to a large degree the way the consultant thinks and works. For example, inherent in the medical model of consultation is the assumption that the consultant has the expertise for solving problems.

This assumption has been frequently challenged by supporters of other models (e.g., Curtis & Meyers, 1985; Schein, 1969). In its place a more collaborative relationship between the consultant and the client has been suggested in order to help the client retain the major ownership of the problem. In addition, it is often the client, not the consultant, who has more information and understanding of what is possible to change within the system (Curtis & Meyers, 1985; Schein, 1969). It has also been suggested (Argyris, 1970) that it is the consultants' primary task to increase the problem-solving skills of those with whom they work.

Several models of consultation have been proposed as alternatives to the medical model for working within schools: mental health (Caplan, 1970), behavioral (Bergan, 1977), organizational (Schmuck & Runkel, 1985), meta (Gallessich, 1985), and systems (Curtis & Meyers, 1985). Some family therapists have suggested that the principles of systems thinking found in the various schools of family therapy have direct application to school systems (e.g., Fisher, 1986; Grossman, 1989; Silvestri, 1989). Others (Merkel & Carpenter, 1987), however, have cautioned against the overgeneralization of family therapy principles to larger systems such as schools without consideration for the underlying assumptions and their implications for consultation with other systems. In this discussion we will offer another alternative to consulting within a school system—one that does not depend on assumptions regarding systems structure (Epstein & Loos, 1989a) or a priori definitions of systems based on sociological constructs (Parsons, 1951).

A LANGUAGE-SYSTEMS APPROACH

Several theoretical assumptions underlie a language-systems approach to school consultation (Anderson & Goolishian, 1988; Goolishian & Anderson, 1987):

1. Human systems are meaning-generating systems.
2. Meaning is generated in language as we interact with others.
3. A consultation system is one kind of meaning-generating system.
4. A consultation system generates meaning around a problem (i.e., it is

both "problem-organizing" and "problem-organized").

5. Consultation occurs through a process of ongoing conversation.
6. The goal of consultation is the "dissolving" of the problem through dialogue.
7. The role of the consultant is to create a space for dialogue and to manage the conversation with all relevant persons.

The assumptions outlined above have some direct implications for the practice of school consultation. To highlight these implications, three questions will be discussed in detail.

> With whom does the consultant work?
>
> How does the consultant define or diagnose the problem or problems?
>
> What is the role of the consultant or relevant domain for consultation?

If one holds to the constructivist belief that "realities" are generated locally by persons in communication (Braten, 1986, 1987; Epstein & Loos, 1989a; Gergen, 1985; Goolishian & Anderson, 1987; Rorty, 1979), then consultation may be seen as the "management of conversation" with persons who are connected by their active communication about someone or something that is being described as problematic. Problems in this approach are not viewed as the result of some faulty or dysfunctional system (i.e., the child's emotional disturbance, the family's dysfunction, or the poor school system). They are not seen as empirically testable conditions or "facts" that can be discerned by the trained professional.

Rather, "problems" are constructed realities in language, which are fluid and changing. Each involved person has different notions and ideas about what is problematic and how to correct it. Hence, the consultant must work to engage with all persons in active communication around the problem. The members of this "problem system" may cut across the boundaries of socially defined systems such as families, schools, social service agencies, and may include other persons as well (Anderson & Goolishian, 1988; Goolishian & Anderson, 1981). For instance, the problem system may include the peers of a student, a concerned neighbor, a physician, the school bus driver, a baby-sitter, a lunchroom aide, or a school nurse. The consultant must try to understand as completely as possible the perceptions of all of these people and must develop a workable problem or diagnosis that does not violate any one of their ideas.

The diagnosis, in our sense of the word, is a process—one that is fluid and evolving as long as the consulting conversation continues. A diagnosis always involves the making of distinctions, and the act of diagnosing always changes the diagnosis. It is not a process of narrowing down to the "correct" perspective but rather a broadening of perspectives that opens up new possibilities. Once a diagnosis becomes fixed and static, the range of options becomes indelibly limited.

For instance, if the consultant were to think solely about the kinds of "deficits" inherent within the neurology of psychology of the child that are "causing" that child's disruptive behavior in the classroom, this might limit the consultant to diagnose the child as "learning disabled" or "emotionally disturbed." Once done, this diagnostic label would point toward the infusion of special remedial services for the child, but might preclude the possibility of examining the effects of other factors such as the classroom "climate," the teacher's personal style and instructional methods, the school "ethos," and the child's living situation (Brookover, Beady, Flood, Schweitzer, & Wisenbaker, 1979; Hamilton, 1983; Hargreaves, 1976; Rutter, 1983; Rutter, Maughan, Mortimore, Ouston, & Smith, 1979). The unique operational style, ethos, values, and social climate of a particular school exert influence on whether children are identified as problematic, which children are identified, and in which ways they are then treated (Galloway & Goodwin, 1979; Rutter, 1978).

The consultant must develop a diagnosis that respects the positions of all the relevant members of the system. For instance, he or she must seek to understand how the teacher who initially complained about this child understands the behaviors in question. Likewise, he or she must be sensitive to the perspectives of all of the people who have been involved in working with or complaining about this child's behavior.

A diagnosis should serve to amplify the uncertainty surrounding the problem. Uncertainty guides us to seek new ideas and new meanings and thus provides a context for change to develop, whereas certainty closes down options. For example, a teacher referring a disruptive student for consultation, may be convinced that the child's actions are intentional and malicious. If the teacher can be engaged in a collaborative quest to "more clearly understand" when and why the child misbehaves in class, it is possible for the teacher's ideas and, hence, his or her behaviors toward the child to change.

Consultants and consultees create a reality, or meaning system, together in dialogue (Loos & Epstein, 1989). Both are viewed as active "co-conspirators" in the creation of that reality. The consultant contributes his or her own ideas, values, and prejudices toward the construction of that reality, as do the consultees.

The act of labeling a child's behavior as "problematic" makes a value judgment about the meaning of that behavior, but does little to describe that behavior (Galloway, Ball, Blomfield, & Seyd, 1982). The act of labeling tells more about the assumptions and attitudes of the labeler with regard to normative and pathological functioning than it tells about the particular problem. The consultant, in our view, is an active participant in this process, not a passively objective observer.

For instance, researchers have found a variety of discrepancies in the identification and assessment of learning disabilities and severe emotional disturbance by school professionals (Algozzine & Ysseldyke, 1983; Gerber & Semmel, 1984; Ostrander, Colegrove, & Schwartz, 1988). In our view, the "facts" of a particular case are but a reflection of the values and prejudices of those persons describing that situation (Epstein & Loos, 1989b).

It is through those very descriptions that we develop agency (i.e. take action) concerning an issue. How one described a "problem" delimits the range of actions to be taken around that problem. The language of pathology and pathological systems leads one to view symptoms as inherent within the mind of a student, or reflective of a dysfunctional family or inadequate school system. These normative views concerning the structure of systems limit the range of possibilities available to the consultation system.

To further illustrate the theoretical and practical implications of this approach to consultation with schools and families, we will compare and contrast the language-systems approach to a recently developed systems consultation model—a model that represents many of the ideas that have become associated with consulting over the last 25 years.

Comparison of a Systems Model and Language-Systems Approach

Curtis and Meyers (1985) have suggested nine basic assumptions of an effective systems approach to consultation. These assumptions contrast sharply with the medical or clinical model and represent commonalities from the mental health, behavioral, and organizational models of consultation. In order to contradistinguish a language-systems approach to this model, we will provide a brief summary of each of their assumptions. The reader is encouraged to refer to Curtis and Meyers (1985) for a more comprehensive presentation of these ideas.

Assumption 1: Participants in Consultation

SYSTEMS MODEL. There are three participants in the consultation process: the consultant, who provides assistance; the consultee, who is the caregiver; and the client, who is the ultimate beneficiary of the consultation. The consultant and the consultee roles are not fixed but can shift (e.g., the school teacher could also be a consultant for the school psychologist).

LANGUAGE-SYSTEMS APPROACH. The participants in the consulting process are not distinguished by their particular roles in the consultative process. Rather, the participants are delineated according to their views and ideas regarding the problem being discussed. Those included in the consultation system are those persons who are struggling (i.e., in language or conversation) around what is being labeled a problem. The participants may vary greatly between problem situations (i.e., they are not bound to a predefined social system such as family or school) and may vary at different temporal points in the consultation process. The "problem" determines the constituents of the system.

Assumption 2: Collaborative Relationship

SYSTEMS MODEL. A nonhierarchical collaborative relationship exists among those involved in the problem-solving process. Both the consultant and consultee have knowledge and skills necessary to resolve the problem. The consultee develops

a sense of "ownership" and may be the primary implementer of the intervention plan. Ideas generated by the consultee deserve equal consideration with those of the consultant as long as they do not appear to have "detrimental implications" for the client. Consultant and consultee discuss ahead of time what information is shared outside the consulting relationship.

LANGUAGE-SYSTEMS APPROACH. Everybody who is in conversation around a problem has a unique and equally valid perspective compared to others in that language system. Consequently, all those in conversation are responsible for their own views and the actions they take with regard to those views. Thus, the consultant is not bound to create a sense of ownership with any one person in that system or to attempt to change any one person in that system. The only thing the consultant can change is the way he or she manages the conversation so that new ideas can be generated.

Ideas are not generated by any one individual, but are cocreated with others who are in conversation around the problem. There is no relevance in determining whose view is right or even better, but whether the reality or narrative that is created out of the conversation is one with which all parties in dialogue can live.

Issues around confidentiality become less problematic as ideas that are generated by the language system become the most important part of the conversations rather than individually owned values and points of view. These may lead to differing points of view. The goal of the consultant is not to reach consensus but to appreciate and understand the differences among the positions.

Assumption 3: The Need for Confrontation

SYSTEMS MODEL. Indirect and direct approaches to confrontation are possible and maybe useful in a systems model. Both types of confrontation are designed to be nondestructive, tentative, and devoid of hostility. To illustrate, Curtis and Meyers (1985) have provided examples of indirect (e.g., "Be careful how you deal with Johnny because *he* has difficulty dealing with authority figures," [p. 82]) and direct confrontations (e.g., "Do you think it implies that one important issue may have to do with your own ambivalence about being an authority figure to the students?" [p. 83]).

LANGUAGE-SYSTEMS APPROACH. Confrontation, either direct or indirect, is not viewed as a useful technique by the language-systems consultant. Rather, the language-systems consultant views any attempt to convince, coerce, or confront the consultee as a sign of hubris. It is critical for the consultant to believe that every position in the consultative system is correct within the individual's domain of existence and to work toward understanding the correctness of that point of view. It is in that never-ending process of attempting to understand the other that thinking changes and acceptable options evolve.

For example, take the illustrations of indirect and direct confrontation noted above. Rather than confronting, a language-systems consultant would attempt to gain information and understand the correctness of a point of view by asking questions similar to "I wonder what ideas you might have about how to deal with Johnny, given he shows difficulty dealing with authority figures" or "As I was thinking about this, I was puzzling about what you might think about your role as a teacher in managing students." Questions ask for information without implying the incorrectness of a point of view.

Assumption 4: Indirect Services

SYSTEMS MODEL. The consultant works primarily with the consultee rather than the client, but may work directly with the client to gather additional information to use in the consulting relationship with the consultee.

LANGUAGE-SYSTEMS APPROACH. There is no distinction between direct and indirect services. The consultant works with those in the system who are troubled by someone's behavior. During the course of the consultation, those in direct conversation with the consultant may change as will the individual conversations.

Assumption 5: Responsibility for Client

SYSTEMS MODEL. The consultee is primarily responsible for the client, although the consultant must also assume "some level of responsibility."

LANGUAGE-SYSTEMS APPROACH. The consultant's responsibility is to manage the conversations and interactions such that new alternatives are developed and the problem dissolves (i.e., the issue is no longer being described as a "problem" by those people involved in it). The consultant is responsible for his or her participation in and contribution to the evolving narrative around what is described as a problem.

Assumption 6: Work-Related Focus

SYSTEMS MODEL. Consultation is differentiated from therapy in that the focus of consultation is always on work-related concerns and not on the consultee's feelings, except to create a productive consulting relationship.

LANGUAGE-SYSTEMS APPROACH. As the process of consultation evolves, the definition of the problems may change from those initially presented. The co-evolving of these new narratives may focus on different members of the system. Limiting the consultant's conversations to those initial "work-related" problems reduces the consultant's maneuverability. The range of issues to be discussed in the consultation is bounded only by the relevance of those topics for the participants in the conversation.

Assumption 7: Goals of Consultation

SYSTEMS MODEL. The goals of consultation are to resolve the problem and to improve the consultee's ability to respond to similar problems in the future.

LANGUAGE-SYSTEMS APPROACH. The goal of the consultant is not to resolve problems but to manage and continue the conversations around the problem until new meanings are co-evolved and the problems dissolve or dissipate. The consultant does not endeavor to teach problem-solving skills to others because to do so suggests that the consultant is the most knowledgeable of the problem solvers—a position that would negate a truly "collaborative" relationship wherein ideas are co-created.

Assumption 8: Systems Theory

SYSTEMS MODEL. Interactions within the system are reciprocal in their relationship; that is, a change in one part of the system has the tendency to change other parts of the system. This concept implies that the consultative process is affected by interactive variables (including characteristics of the consultant) and that the child is only one component of an interacting system.

LANGUAGE-SYSTEMS APPROACH. In a language-systems approach, changes in one part of the system may induce changes in another. Yet, changes and the direction or shape they may take cannot be predetermined. The language system is not static or closed in its membership, as implied by a priori defined social systems (e.g., family, school) but is fluid and open

in its membership and how each talks about the organizing problem. Hence, changes may or may not affect various members of the consultation system. Changes may affect persons outside the consultation system as well as those within, since the boundary of that system is only a "boundary" in language. Changes may be viewed differently by different members of the consultation system.

Assumption 9: Affective/Cognitive Components to Consultation

SYSTEMS MODEL. The consultant needs to have four areas of expertise to fulfill the requirements of the affective (i.e., the interpersonal consultive relationship) and cognitive (i.e., how the consultant views the problem) aspects of consultation. The four areas of expertise are (1) establishing a positive working relationship with the consultee, (2) having a strong foundation in the content area of the problem, (3) being an expert in problem solving and facilitating the problem solving process, and (4) having knowledge of systems theory.

LANGUAGE-SYSTEMS APPROACH. The expertise of the consultant is not divided into cognitive and affective aspects; rather, it is to be a participant manager of conversation.

IMPLEMENTATION OF THE LANGUAGE-SYSTEMS APPROACH IN A PUBLIC SCHOOL DISTRICT

The Galveston Family Institute (GFI) School Consultation Project was established to provide a wide range of psychological services to the students and school personnel of a small suburban school district in the greater Houston area.

Following an initial planning meeting with the district superintendent, a needs survey was conducted by the five-member psychology team from GFI at each of the 12 schools in the district. At these assessment meetings, counselors, diagnosticians, principals, and teachers were encouraged to provide input as to the type of program they felt would best meet their needs and those of the students. This survey was considered to be an ongoing phase of the project. Monthly meetings were held with the counselors and diagnosticians in order to keep the conversation going around issues involving the implementation of the program.

After the initial meetings with school district personnel, the GFI team developed a language-systems approach for school consultation. The approach developed as a collaborative effort between the school district personnel and the GFI staff. Two major components, training and direct services, were considered essential in developing a unified districtwide philosophy of psychological services.

The training component of the project included several facets. A weekly intensive school externship program was established for six counselors and diagnosticians. The participants formed an active treatment group and were encouraged to bring their own difficult cases for live consultation and ongoing treatment. The participants observed from behind a one-way mirror and operated as a team. Additional time was spent on assigned readings, theoretical issues, case consultation, and observation of live clinical interviews.

A week-long course in systemic and family therapy was offered for six other counselors and diagnosticians. This format provided an accelerated introduction to the concepts and practices of a language-systems approach for therapy. Special focus was given to the concept of problem-organizing systems and the ways in which the therapeutic conversation defines the focus and direction of therapy. The course included relevant readings, participant dialogue, theoretical discussion, and live case observation. Counselors and diagnosticians who did not participate in the externship program or the week-long training course were given the opportunity to do so the following school year.

All counselors and diagnosticians were involved in monthly inservice training meetings. Topical inservice programs were developed around the ideas evolved out of the ongoing needs survey. Evaluation of the program was conducted at regular intervals, with changes being implemented as needed.

Small group consultation teams were formed with the counselors and diagnosticians to meet once a month for case consultation and live case observation. Since the school system had installed a one-way mirror and observation room, the groups were able to work together as consultants or ongoing treatment teams for difficult cases from each of their respective schools.

The other major component of the project consisted of direct services by the GFI team to the teachers, administrators, counselors, diagnosticians, students, and families. For psychological evaluations, the GFI staff implemented an ongoing series of conversations about the child in question with all members of the relevant system, as described earlier (rather than conducting evaluations from a traditional testing method).

We see the language-systems approach as being consistent with state and federal guidelines (e.g., Public Law 94–142); however, this approach goes beyond attempts to assess accurately the child's individual disability toward a systemic understanding of the problem. (This thinking has important implications for evaluating learning as well as emotional problems. These issues are beyond the scope of this chapter.)

CASE STUDY

Janie, a new sixth-grade student in junior high, was referred to the counselor during the second week of school. Her teachers reported that she was constantly crying and was "throwing up" several times a day. She was spending most of her time in the nurse's office. In talking with her, the counselor learned that on the third day of school, she had collided with another sixth-grader on a bicycle and had broken her arm. Janie would not, or could not, explain the reasons for her distress, saying only that she wanted to be home with her mother.

Janie's mother was called to the school. She explained, in Janie's presence, that Janie had always been a timid and conscientious child. Even though her grades had been average in elementary school, her mother felt that she had to struggle constantly to keep up with her classmates. Her previous testing in elementary school indicated average intelligence, with achievement scores being approximately six months behind her grade placement. Her mother reported that since her arm had been broken, Janie was unable to take notes, complete written assignments on time, or open her locker in time to make it to class before the bell had rung. (The right arm, her dominant one, was in a cast up to her shoulder.) She explained that Janie was too shy to ask for help and instead tried to do everything with her left hand.

The mom emphasized that Janie was very fragile and needed extra attention even when not handicapped by the cast on her arm. The counselor explained to the mother that he would talk to Janie's teachers about her special needs and assign a locker to her that could be easily manipulated with one arm. He tried to reassure the mother that the school personnel could handle the situation and encouraged the mother to try to allow Janie to become more independent. The counselor briefly discussed the case with the psychologist in a typical "hallway consultation."

At this point, the following people appear to be involved in the communicative system regarding Janie: Janie, teachers, nurse, junior high counselor, mother, and peripherally the school psychologist. The psychologist's tentative thoughts about their positions around the problem are:

> *Teachers' Position:* We are worried about Janie but don't know what to do. We believe this is probably separation anxiety, and not school phobia.
>
> *Nurse's Position:* This child is making herself throw up so that she can be home with her mother.
>
> *Janie's Position:* I'm scared and overwhelmed and just want to be with my mother.
>
> *Mom's Position:* Janie is very fragile and needs extra attention.
>
> *Counselor's Position:* Janie does need extra attention and extra help but we need to help her to do this on her own.
>
> *Psychologist's Position:* I need to avoid becoming wedded to each or any of these positions. How can I avoid getting locked into one particular view? What questions can I ask that will create new options for those involved and maintain my flexibility with them?

The next morning the mother, accompanied by her neighbor, went to the principal and requested an appointment. The principal would not allow the neighbor to join the mother in the office discussion, even the mother emphasized that the neighbor had been her best friend for 15 years and knew Janie's needs better than anyone else.

During the discussion, the mother explained that she and the neighbor had decided, after much debate and discussion, that the best solution would be to move Janie back to the elementary school and place her in fifth grade. They had decided that another year in elementary school would allow her to gain confidence and catch up on her achievement levels. The principal felt this option was not the best and said Janie needed to "toughen up" and needed to learn to deal with junior high pressures. He reiterated that discussions regarding Janie's academic difficulties would have to involve the mother and *not* the neighbor.

During the next few days, Janie continued to miss classes, cried constantly, and vomited regularly. The counselor talked to her several times a day and tried to reassure her.

The therapeutic system has evolved to encompass others communicating about Janie's difficulties. Clearly, both the principal and the neighbor are invested in finding a solution. The psychologist's tentative thoughts regarding the language system are: Although the school—especially the counselor—has tried to be responsive and sensitive to Janie's needs, it appears that the mother has felt that her position has not been heard. She went straight to the principal.

> *Counselor's Position:* Tell me what to do and I'll do it.
>
> *Janie's Position:* Junior high is too hard. My mother tells me to tell my counselor that I want to go back to fifth grade.
>
> *Mother's Position:* I really don't know what is best for Janie, but my long-time friend and neighbor has helped me to see that Janie needs to be placed back in elementary school to gain more confidence.
>
> *Neighbor's Position:* Janie's mother has difficulty explaining herself to others. Like Janie, she is shy and timid, and does not express her needs directly. She needs help in talking with the school, and especially in explaining to them why Janie needs to be placed back in elementary school.
>
> *Principal's Position:* This child is like all other children entering junior high. She needs to learn how to handle the pressures of junior high school, and the best way to do that is to keep at it. To place her back in elementary school would only cause her to regress. Furthermore, because of confidentiality and ethical issues, I cannot allow the neighbor to participate in any of the academic discussions.
>
> *Psychologist's Position:* This poor child has experienced more stress than she can handle at one time. We need to find some way to relieve the pressure on her. But wait a second—what are the implications of my thinking this way? I'm thinking only from the child's perspective. Am I in danger of siding with the child and neglecting the other's positions? And certainly, since the neighbor has known the mother for 15 years, she is important to this language system and I must include her. The pressure is mounting to act. How can I generate options rather than dictate action? I need to find a way to understand the perspectives of the other members more fully. Questions I might ask: "How do the mother and the neighbor explain Janie's condition?" "What ideas do they have about why they haven't been able to convince the school of this position?" "Why is all of this occurring right now?" "With all this pressure I feel to act, who's pressuring me to act in which ways?"

Three days later, the mother and neighbor made an appointment with the assistant superintendent and again requested that the school district do something. The assistant superintendent referred them immediately to the school psychologist. In fact, he brought them in person to the psychologist, requesting that the psychologist rearrange her schedule to handle this urgent case.

The system now included administrative personnel. The psychologist's role has changed from indirect consultation with the counselor to direct participation. The position of the mother and the neighbor again seemed to be that their concerns were not heard. The assistant superintendent's position seemed to be "It is not my job to be providing counseling to students and families. The school psychologist should handle this immediately."

The psychologist saw the neighbor and mother immediately and requested that Janie come in for an appointment that afternoon. During these sessions, the psychologist learned that Janie had refused to attend school for the past three days and had cried and thrown up each morning. They had taken her to her pediatrician, and he had referred them to a psychologist for family therapy. The mother and neighbor appeared quite frantic and offered numerous explanations as to why Janie was experiencing such difficulties.

The mother explained that she had recently told Janie for the first time that she had two half-sisters from a previous marriage. The mother had divorced the sisters' father when they were two and three years old and had not had contact with them in the intervening years. She had married Janie's father two years later, but subsequently divorced him when Janie was two years old. She married her current husband when Janie was four years old and described the current marriage as difficult. She stated that Janie rarely saw her natural father and was not close to her stepfather.

The neighbor did most of the talking. She expressed great concern over Janie's situation and explained that the only viable solution was to move her back to fifth grade. She told how she had always been available to help the mother with Janie.

As the problem and the problem system continue to evolve, the concerns of the members in the system become more clearly articulated.

Janie's Position: I'm scared. I want someone to help me.

Pediatrician's Position: This mother and daughter are too close. The child is developing physical symptoms because of separation anxiety on the part of both daughter and mother. They clearly need family counseling.

Mother's Position: Janie is afraid I will abandon her like I did her sisters. I should have never told her about them. But I'm confused. Maybe she is just immature and needs another year in elementary school to gain confidence.

Neighbor's Position: Janie's mother needs my help in parenting. Janie is just shy and immature. It is clear that Janie is not ready for junior high because she has no interest in boys, doesn't wear makeup, and she still wears socks instead of hose. Returning her to fifth grade is the solution. Nobody is listening to our concerns.

Psychologist's Position: The neighbor, perhaps the most intensely involved person, is an integral part of the system. Therefore an apriori structural view of systems that restricts system membership to particular social structures is clearly inadequate. What position can I take that accounts for the numerous and varied explanations? This is too complicated. I need to do something to help get some perspective and to help me attend to elements in the system that I seem to be overlooking. I will request consultation from one of my colleagues. Dialoguing with colleagues seems to be a primary way for me to maintain flexibility.

The psychologist recommended that mom, neighbor, and Janie meet with her and a colleague. The elementary school counselor and the junior high counselor were both asked to attend. The stepfather was also invited to the session but was unable to attend. Both counselors expressed concern about moving Janie back to elementary school and suggested several ideas designed to help reassure her as she adjusted to junior high. The junior high counselor offered to set her up with a buddy to walk her to class. Her mother was invited to come walk through the school at night, and to come up to the school for lunch and eat with Janie.

The next day Janie appeared at the counselor's office first period crying and asking for her mother. After several unsuccessful attempts to get her back to class, he reluctantly called the mom to pick her up. He called the psychologist and another appointment was arranged for the following afternoon for the family, the neighor, both counselors, and both psychologists.

One of the primary goals of the joint sessions was to interview the persons involved in such a way that new understandings and new options could emerge. Special emphasis was placed on the "diagnoses" and proposed "treatment plans" of each person. A number of responses were developed. All were jointly developed in the session and all were designed to address the mother's concerns about Janie's timidity. By talking with the mother, the neighbor, Janie, and both elementary and junior high counselors, the psychologist was trying to connect with the relevant therapeutic system.

The next morning, the mom and the neighbor arranged an appointment with the superintendent of the school district. The superintendent called the psychologist at home and stated, "We need to do something fast or we will have a full-blown school phobic on our hands."

The previously scheduled session was held that afternoon, and it was decided that Janie would be placed in fifth grade for a trial period. The neighbor emphasized that family therapy was needed for Janie, her mother, and her stepfather.

The next morning Janie entered the elementary school crying and throwing up. The counselor talked with her and then went to her classroom to prepare the other students for her arrival while Janie waited in her office. Janie was escorted to class by the counselor. The counselor gave her a decorated coffee can and kleenex, in case she get sick, and encouraged the teacher to have her remain in class if possible. Although Janie cried and whimpered throughout the day, spitting up in the painted canister, she stayed in the class.

The next day, Janie entered class crying, but stayed at school for the entire day without getting sick. Another session was held with the mom, the neighbor, both counselors, and the two psychologists. The elementary counselor reported that Janie was adjusting slowly. Janie was going regularly to drill team, and even though she spit up periodically, she did not ask for her mother. Most of the session centered around the mother's marriage difficulties and her thoughts about getting a job. She had not worked in five years, primarily so she could be available for Janie.

The therapy system has now expanded to include the elementary counselor and the potential classmates of Janie. The psychologist is actively involving them in the consultative planning. It also appears that the mother's concerns have shifted to managing her own life. The psychologist is aware that this shift is possible partly because (1) the mother has begun to feel that her concerns are being heard and (2) the neighbor has been invited to play an active, ongoing role in the consultation process.

At this point, the case was presented to the 30 counselors and diagnosticians in one of the ongoing, districtwide inservice meetings. The counselors were invited to help the psychologists examine (1) who is involved in the consultative system (i.e., who should the psychologists be paying attention to, who has been overlooked, what does the consultative system look like); (2) the positions of each of the persons in the system (especially, in what ways have the psychologists presumed to understand too quickly); and (3) what position the consulting psychologist should be taking regarding the problem and regarding each person in the system. The inservice was not a demonstration by experts of a "successful" case, but rather an invitation to the counselors to participate in a yet-to-be-completed case that required constant reassessment.

Several new ideas were developed with the counselors. The elementary counselor was identified as the person who was the most concerned about Janie at that point in time. She felt that most of the pressure to help Janie had fallen on her shoulders, with little support from others. It was also noted that the stepfather's position was unknown and might be relevant to the future development of the case. He might be blaming the mother or he might be thinking that the most important thing is to get Janie in school no matter where. A debate emerged as to whether placing Janie back in fifth grade was the "correct" thing to do, whether Janie's diagnosis should be "school phobia" or "separation anxiety," and who should be considered the source of the problem (Janie, mother, neighbor, school, etc.).

Psychologist's Position: This inservice was designed to give the counselors a chance to participate in generating new perspectives for the consulting team on this particular case and to outline the implications of a language-systems approach to consulting in general. It seems to have been successful on both accounts. This inservice has certainly has given me many new things to think about and it has highlighted a number of crucial issues: (1) normative models of consultation are often unhelpful precisely because they localize blame for problems at certain points in the system, (2) the consultant needs to be constantly open to new ways of viewing the problem and the positions, and (3) if diagnostic categories were restricted to DSM-III-R categories, many of the positions of relevant persons would have been ignored.

A session was scheduled for the following week with the mother, the neighbor, Janie, and the two psychologists. Several days later, the mom called the psychologist to cancel the session, saying she had found a job as a secretary and that she loved working. She reported that Janie was going to school and gaining confidence. Another appointment was scheduled for the following week. The mother again called to cancel. She apologized for the cancellation, but said she felt the situation had been resolved.

At a six-month followup, Janie was regularly attending class and was not complaining of physical symptoms. Mother was satisfied with work and school. The family had not entered family therapy, although they talked periodically with the neighbor about the possibility of counseling outside of the school. On the phone, the psychologist talked with the mother about the importance of closely monitoring Janie's progress and of making plans for the transition to junior high next year. The mother agreed to talk with the junior high counselor, who was concerned about repeating the same experience next year. At this point, the discussion was now around preventive and developmental issues rather than urgent crisis resolution.

A number of issues are highlighted by this case. The consultative system is not structurally defined by an a priori systemic model; rather, it is composed of those who have been organized by the problem—those actively involved in communication around the child's school difficulties. The system changed as the problem evolved. The question, then, of who the consultant should treat becomes a moot issue. The consultant works with all those involved in the system. There are a variety of interpretations of the events not limited to DSM-III-R categories. The interpretations that are the most important are the ones belonging to those who are most concerned and most actively involved. The psychologist asked questions, not to get at the underlying "truth" of the situation but to open up possibilities for people to work together. The problem changed, as did the problem system.

SUMMARY

The language-systems approach to consultation with schools and families breaks from the more traditional models of psychological consultation to schools, as well as from Parsonian structural ideas regarding social systems that underlie current family therapy models. These differences center on (1) the definition of the relevant systems for consultation, (2) how problems

are diagnosed and defined, and (3) the role and goals of the consultant within schools.

We believe that the relevant system for consultation is defined only by the membership of those who are actively participating in the conversations around the problem. The action system is *not* related to any particular social structure. This means that the consultant is *not* simply applying family therapy to a broader system (i.e., school system). It is only through conversation with those struggling around the problem that the relevant system for consultation emerges.

We believe that diagnosis is a fluid and evolving process. The problem changes as people change the way in which they talk about it. People organize their behaviors around their diagnoses and are always in the process of acting on the linguistic distinctions they make. Diagnosis, then, involves action and is not simply a cognitive denotation in the head of one or more observers. The consultant must work together with the relevant system to develop diagnoses that broaden perspectives and open up new possibilities for thinking and behaving. This is a joint process and is not a matter of attempting to find the single correct perspective.

We believe the role of the consultant is to manage the conversations of the participants in an attempt to understand each person's definition of the problem, and to develop diagnoses that are respectful of all persons within the consultation system. The expertise of the consultant is in maintaining multiple conversations around the issue, not in diagnosing dysfunctional systems, rectifying defective social structures, or even providing corrective experiences. The goal of consultation is simply to talk with those struggling around the problem so that what was originally defined as a problem is no longer considered problematic. As Anderson and Goolishian (1988) have noted, the job of the consultant is not to *solve* problems, but to converse so that problems *"dis-solve."* We believe that the most effective way to generate fresh alternatives and to create new possibilities for the problem being confronted is to assume the role of conversation-manager. Managing the conversation entails facilitating who talks to whom about what. It also assumes the consultant is an active and respectful participant in the evolving meaning system. Through conversation and dialogue the diagnosis evolves, the consultative system changes, and the problem dissipates.

References

Algozzine, B., & Ysseldyke, J. (1983). Learning disabilities as a subset of school failure: The over-sophistication of a concept. *Exceptional Children, 50*(3), 242–246.

Anderson, H., & Goolishian, H. (1988). Human systems as linguistic systems: Preliminary and evolving ideas about the implications for clinical theory. *Family Process, 27*, 371–393.

Argyris, C. (1970). *Intervention theory and method.* Reading, MA: Addison-Wesley.

Bergan, J. R. (1977). *Behavioral consultation.* Columbus, OH: Charles E. Merrill.

Braten, S. (1986). The third position: Beyond artificial and autopoietic reduction. In F. Geyer & J. van der Zouwen (Eds.), *Sociocybernetic paradoxes: Observation, control and evolution of self-steering systems.* London: Sage.

Braten, S. (1987). Paradigms of autonomy: Dialogical or monological? In G. Teubner (Ed.), *Autopoiesis in law and society.* New York: EUI Publishers.

Brookover, W. B., Beady, C., Flood, P., Schweitzer, J., & Wisenbaker, J. (1979). *School social systems and student achievement: Schools can make a difference.* New York: Prager.

Caplan, G. (1970). *The theory and practice of mental health consultation.* New York: Basic Books.

Curtis, M. J., & Meyers, J. (1985). Best practices in school-based consultation: Guidelines for effective practice. In A. Thomas & J. Grimes (Eds.), *Best practices in school psychology* (pp. 79–94). Kent, OH: National Association of School Psychologists.

Elliott, S. N., & Erchul, W. P. (1987).

Mini-series on family systems assessment and intervention [Special issue]. *School Psychology Review, 16*(4).

Epstein, E. & Loos, V. (1989a). Some irreverent thoughts on the limits of family therapy: Towards a language-based explanation of human systems. *Journal of Family Psychology, 2,* 405–421.

Epstein, E. & Loos, V. (1989b). The ethics of language and the language of ethics. *Journal of Family Psychology, 2,* 426–429.

Fisher, L. (1986). Systems-based consultation with schools. In L. C. Wynne, S. H. McDaniel, & T. T. Weber (Eds.), *Systems consultations: A new perspective for family therapy* (pp. 342–356). New York: Guilford.

Gallessich, J. (1985). Toward a metatheory of consultation. *The Counseling Psychologist, 13,* 336–354.

Galloway, D., Ball, T., Blomfield, O., & Seyd, R. (1982). *Schools and disruptive pupils.* London: Longman.

Galloway, D., & Goodman, E. (1979). *Educating slow-learning and maladjusted children: Integration or segregation?* London: Longman.

Gerber, M. M., & Semmel, M. I. (1984). Teachers as imperfect test: Reconceptualizing the referral process. *Educational Psychologist, 19*(3), 137–148.

Gergen, K. J. (1985). The social constructionist movement in modern psychology. *American Psychologist, 40,* 266–275.

Goolishian, H., & Anderson, H. (1981). Including non-blood related persons in family therapy: Who is the family to be treated. In A. Gurman (Ed.), *Questions and answers in family therapy.* New York: Brunner/Mazel.

Goolishian, H., & Anderson, H. (1987). Language-systems and therapy: An evolving idea. *Journal of Psychotherapy, 24,* 529–538.

Goolishian, H., & Anderson, H. (1990). Understanding the therapeutic process: From individuals and families to systems in language. In F. Kaslow (Ed.)., *Voices in family psychology* (pp. 91–113). Newbury Park, CA: Sage.

Grossman, N. S. (1989). Family psychology and the schools. *The Family Psychologist, 5,* 3–4.

Hamilton, S. F. (1983). The social side of schooling: Ecological studies of classrooms and schools. *Elementary School Journal, 83,* 313–334.

Hargreaves, D. H. (1976). The real battle for the classroom. *New Society, 35,* 207–209.

Loos, V., & Epstein, E. (1989). Conversational construction of meaning in family therapy: Some evolving thoughts on Kelly's sociality corollary. *International Journal of Personal Construct Psychology, 2,* 149–167.

Merkel, W. T., & Carpenter, L. J. (1987). A cautionary note on the application of family therapy principles to organizational consultation. *American Journal of Orthopsychiatry, 57,* 111–115.

Meyers, J. (1975). Consultee-centered consultation with a teacher as a technique in behavior management. *American Journal of Community Psychology, 3,* 111–121.

Ostrander, R., Colegrove, R., & Schwartz, N. (1988). Legislative ambiguity and the accurate identification of seriously emotionally disturbed. *Journal of School Psychology, 26*(1), 77–85.

Paget, K. D., & Nagle, R. J. (1986). A conceptual model of preschool assessment. *School Psychology Review, 15,* 154–165.

Parsons, T. (1951). *The social system.* New York: Free Press.

Rorty, R. (1979). *Philosophy and the mirror of nature.* Princeton, NJ: Princeton University Press.

Rutter, M. (1978). Family, area and school influence in the genesis of conduct disorders. In L. Hersov, M. Berger, & D. Schaffer, (Eds.), *Aggression and anti-social behaviour in childhood and adolescence.* Oxford: Pergamon.

Rutter, M. (1983). School effects on pupil progress: Research findings and policy implications. In L. Shulman & G. Sykes (Eds.), *Handbook of teaching and policy* (pp. 3–41). New York: Longman.

Rutter, M., Maughan, B., Mortimore, P., Ouston, J., & Smith, A. (1979). *Fifteen thousand hours: Secondary schools and their effects on children.* Cambridge, MA: Harvard University Press.

Schein, E. (1969). *Process consultation: Its role in organization development.* Reading, MA: Addison-Wesley.

Schmuck, R. A., and Runkel, P. J. (1985). *The handbook of organizational development in schools* (3rd ed.). Palo Alto, CA: Mayfield.

Silvestri, K. (1989, January/February). Need to widen school context. *Family Therapy News,* p. 5.

Wilson, C. C. (1986). Family assessment in preschool evaluation. *School Psychology Review, 15,* 166–179.

Witt, J. C., & Elliott, S. N. (1983). Assessment in behavioral consultation: The initial interview. *School Psychology Review, 12,* 42–49.

22

Ecosystemic Treatment of Family-School Problems: A Private Practice Perspective

DON-DAVID LUSTERMAN

Private Practice, Baldwin, New York

THE PRIVATE PRACTICE of family therapy is in a sense a paradox. Born together with the age of television, nurtured in the era of Sputnik with its worship of technology and teamwork, family therapy thinking and training are radically different from the traditional image of therapy as an intensely private and intimate dialogue. Most of us trained as members of a team. We learned behind the one-way mirror, "bug" in the ear, telephone close at hand. Afterwards, like football players, we sat down with our teammates and coach to study the video replays. Perhaps we never even imagined that some of us would one day set up our own shops and, teamless and televisionless, ply our trade.

As such a private practitioner, I have been particularly concerned with ecosystemic issues, where two or more systems organize around an apparently dysfunctional person who plays a role in each system. One such situation occurs when a child is doing poorly at school and neither family or school alone seems able to effect positive change. Auerswald, a pioneer in ecosystemic thinking (Ferber, Mendelsohn, & Napier, 1972, p. 699) says, in describing a particular ecosystemic intervention:

It was necessary that the situation be confronted by a delivery system made up of people with a mix of skills who were not locked in time and space into an appointment system in an office or into a vertical organizational and departmental system that limited the field in which they could think and act. (p. 699)

However, few private practitioners are free of time or fee constraints, nor do they function as members of a multi-disciplinary "swat team," ready to jump into action as crises occur. On the other hand, because they operate outside of an institutional frame, they are not locked into an organization and departmental situation that limits thought and action. How can the private practitioner use this particular combination of strengths and potential weaknesses to help correct school-family problems?

ECOSYSTEMIC INTERVENTION

Any intervention that is undertaken with an understanding that it may have impact on the ecosystem is considered to be an ecosystemic intervention. Systemic thinking is a way of conceptualizing a problem. It is not a rigid "method" of treatment. In the same sense that a family-systems-oriented therapist may choose to intervene with a unit as small as one member of a system or as large as a trigenerational system, so may an ecosystems-oriented therapist choose to work with only one subsystem or with several. This decision should be made on the basis of an educated guess about how the subsystems constituting the ecosystem are interacting. This educated guess takes the form of a tentative description, which may be thought of as an *ecomap*. Based on this ecomap, the therapist decides whom to include in the treatment process and how to intervene.

I find it useful to think of ecosystemic intervention as a continual cycle of description, prescription, and redescription. The prescription may take many different forms. Ecosystemic intervention is an integrative position. It is useful to imagine the therapist possessing a quiver with many arrows. Each arrow represents a skill or a theoretical concept. The particular arrows depend on the therapist's training and knowledge, and use of self. It is the therapist's responsibility to choose an appropriate arrow for the target at hand. This requires knowledge of many theoretical positions and good training in both individual and systems therapeutic approaches. A case is considered successful when the ecosystem is described as functioning well, thus necessitating no further prescription.

For example, a school may be very concerned about the work and behavior of a child, and a number of school personnel may be writing and/or calling to tell the parents how poorly the child is doing. Despite these efforts on the school's part, the child's behavior may fail to improve. After interviewing the family, the therapist may decide that the parental response to the school's contacts is somehow worsening the situation. The therapist will design an intervention to alter the interaction between school and family and then track the success or failure of the intervention.

If the parents make extravagant and often unfulfilled threats, they will be asked to try some new behavior. The therapist might suggest that they stop threatening the child, and instead write a note to the teacher indicating that they have shared the school's concern with the child and would now like the teacher and the child to speak together about it. Thus, the parental behavior of threatening punishment may be curtailed, the child encouraged to take greater responsibility for his or her own actions, and the child and teacher may be drawn together in a potentially problem-solving manner. This intervention may bring about positive change in the relationship between school and family, although it directly involves only the home. On the other hand, it may be unsuccessful, in which case an intervention directly including school personnel might be devised. In either event, it is the first step in the cycle of describing, prescribing, and redescribing.

CONSTRUCTING AN ECOMAP

An ecomap is a description of both the interaction within each subsystem and the interaction between subsystems. It may be a verbal description or it may be accomplished through a more formal evaluative procedure. I find it helpful to organize the therapist's perceptions of family function through an adaptation of Olson's (1986) Circumplex Model. After studying the variables used by a number of systems theorists, he isolated three major variables, originally called *cohesion, adaptability,* and *communication.*

Cohesion, for which Olson now prefers the term *closeness,* is measured on a continuum from *disengaged* to *enmeshed.* The midpoint of this continuum is described as ranging from *separated* to *connected.* Adaptability is now referred to as a "change" variable. Families are rated on this continuum as *chaotic, flexible, structured,* or *rigid.* Cohesion and adaptability are curvilinear variables and can be easily mapped on a circular format (see Figure 1). For example, a family characterized by erratic discipline, lacking parental leadership, and evidencing little closeness would be rated as *chaotically disengaged.* The third variable, communication, is a linear variable, running from low to high. Communication is evaluated in terms of listening skills, speaker's skills, self-disclosure, clarity, continuity, and respect.

Olson has devised two evaluative systems—one to be completed by members of the family, and the other, called a Clinical Rating Scale (CRS), by the clinician. I have described elsewhere (Lusterman, in press) an adaptation of the CRS for the evaluation of the school, team which is organized around the dysfunctional child. It is used to evaluate the team's internal structure and communication, as well as its communication with the family. Once both the family and the school have been described, a good first picture of how the ecosystem is currently operating can be obtained, and changes in their interaction and internal organization can be clearly followed.

Beyond the importance of mapping as a tool for describing change, it is also of value in developing strategies. For example, the system may include a mother who is enmeshed with her children, and a disengaged father. If it is the school's policy to contact the mother when problems arise, the therapist might suggest that the school arrange to contact the father next time. Such a small change may have important consequences for both the family and the school.

OBTAINING INFORMATION FROM THE SCHOOL

The primary means of diagnosing family interaction is direct observation. However, much important information is often gathered during the course of therapy about the extended family, friendship networks, and other systems with which the family interacts. It is more difficult to diagnose the school-family ecosystem, because it is not possible to observe directly the many interactions that occur within the school team and between school and family.

There are basically two means of developing a picture of how the school team is functioning, and how it is interacting with the parents and child. One, obviously, is by collecting information from the family about the various school personnel who work with the child and have contact with the parents, and asking parents and child about the quality of the interaction. The second is through direct involvement with school personnel. Generally speaking, I find that this work can be done by telephone.

In some instances the school makes the initial contact with the therapist. The manner in which the referral is framed is a useful place to begin a map of the school's system. For example, a counselor who calls and says that family therapy is advisable because "Johnny is a sweet kid with two very disturbed parents" may be hypothesized as taking a child-advocating position—one that is parent-blaming and possibly blind to what contribution the school environment maybe making.

In any event, in speaking with the

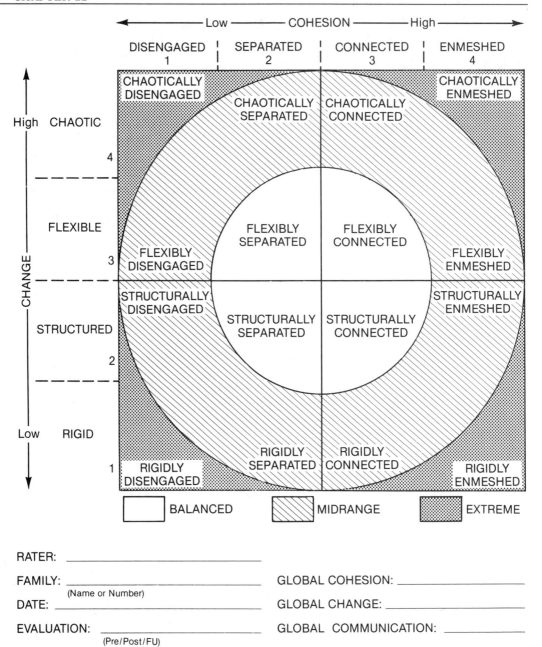

FIGURE 1 Circumplex model: Sixteen types of marital and family systems
Reproduced with permission from David Olson, Ph.D., Family Social Services, University of Minnesota.

initial school contact, I would inquire about how the child is functioning in class, what teachers have shown either positive or negative interest, and whether other school personnel, such as a psychologist, social worker, nurse, or administrator, have been involved with the child. When the school contact precedes my first telephone contact with the parents, I inform them that I have had contact with a member of the school team and would like permission from them to have further contact with other school personnel as well.

Sometimes the referred family calls before I have heard from the school. At other times, I do not become aware of school problems until other family problems have been explored. In cases like these, I begin by asking the family what school personnel they have been involved with and requesting their permission to contact them. Whether I begin contact with the school or with the family, I find it important to indicate from the outset that therapy will be more effective if I am free to maintain contact with both systems. In some instances, the family, or at least some member of the family, is extremely suspicious of contact between school and therapist. I treat these misgivings courteously and with respect, but I indicate that my effectiveness will be greatly reduced without such contact. Generally, once a trusting relationship is established with the family, permission is forthcoming.

THE TELEPHONE AS A NETWORKING TOOL

Once contact with the school is initiated, a working relationship with the school team organized around the child is developed through telephone contact. I have found it invaluable to maintain a "hotline" number, by means of which I can be available to teachers and other school personnel during their very busy day. This line rings directly into my office. I answer it during sessions. If the conversation can be kept brief, I conduct it in the presence of whomever I am treating, being careful to conceal the identity of the person about whom I am speaking. This not only facilitates rapid communication but also models for the family in the treatment room the idea of openness of communication and a problem-solving approach.

Most families are very comfortable with this interruption. In fact, on occasion a family that has resisted the idea of contact between the school and the therapist becomes more amenable to the idea when they see it in action. Of course, there are occasions when a conversation will be too time consuming, in which case I arrange a time when we can speak together at greater length. Teachers will often call on their own time, including weekends and evenings. They are usually happy to be included and most cooperative. During these brief conversations, I am gathering more information about how the school team is operating, and we will often work out some new approach to the child, which we then agree to review by telephone in about a week.

Careful notes are made of these conversations. For example, in talking with a teacher, she might describe how angry a particular child can make her, and that she finds herself becoming sarcastic. I might point out that the child's mother is now learning that when she tells him clearly what is bothering her without sarcasm, she gets better results. Such an observation may help the teacher to fashion a new approach.

Sometimes problems within the school are aired. A teacher may feel that the school counselor is too soft on a child, and that her classroom discipline is thereby undermined. I will then arrange to talk to the counselor and begin to explore whether there is some way of bringing the two into a more unified position.

Telephone interventions are rapid, inexpensive, and powerful. One advantage of the telphone is that it places the recipient of the call in a one-up position, in that it is easy enough to terminate the call in a socially acceptable manner. This can be quite useful, for example, in dealing with a building principal who is considered to be autocratic. Such a person might not welcome a formal meeting, but be willing to speak briefly by telephone. Such an intervention may avoid some of the hierarchy problems that can arise in a school-family meeting, where the principal might be threatened by the presence of an outside "expert," and consequently maintain a formal and bureaucratic stance that inhibits communication.

The use of the telephone may produce dramatic results. A woman called me at the suggestion of her son's guidance counselor, who had told her that I should be contacted for family therapy. She told me that her family consisted of herself, her son, and a young daughter. I inquired about her husband and she informed me that she was divorced. I said that I would like to meet with him as well, and she told me that this was impossible, since she knew that he would refuse.

In a divorce, one party frequently asserts that the other is not interested in helping the child. This attitude is often a replication in the divorce situation of the problems that were inherent in the marriage. It is unwise to accept this information at face value. For that reason, I asked if she knew where I could reach him at the moment, and she gave me a number. I told her that I had a conference calling system, and that, if she would hold on for a moment, I could patch the three of us in. I did, and after a few minutes of three-way conversation, he agreed to come in with her to discuss the boy's problems. His presence at some of the family meetings proved to be of great value. It later developed that the boy had a serious illness that troubled both the parents and the school. Telephone contact with the physician and a school nurse, both important elements in this ecosystem, greatly facilitated treatment.

CONFIDENTIALITY

As one moves away from the notion of therapy as a dialogue and toward the idea of therapy as a means of facilitating systemic change, the concept of confidentiality becomes increasingly complex. There is at present no uniform standard among family therapists. Most family therapists will at times see one member of the family alone. Some tell their patients that in such an event they will feel free to share what they have learned with the family in order to avoid complicity in family secrets. Some say they will use their discretion about what to reveal and what to withhold. Still others hold that anything that is discussed with one family member alone is to be held in confidence. It is my belief that any standard of confidentiality can work, as long as the therapist clearly informs all parties of his or her approach and gains their agreement.

I have found it helpful to think of confidentiality as if it were a wall around the communication between the therapist and the particular part of the system being worked with at the moment, but that it is a wall with a door. If an adolescent speaks with me alone and shares her despair about the way her father tries to get her on his side in his frequent arguments with his wife, I will inquire at the end of the session whether I may feel free to disclose this to the parents at a subsequent meeting or whether this should be considered a confidence.

My rules about confidentiality are

made clear at the very first meeting with a family. They are told that any information will be considered confidential unless there is agreement that it be shared. The sole exceptions are where the therapist is legally bound to reveal information, such as concrete threats of suicide or homicide, or where there is evidence of abuse.

There are, of course, dangers in keeping confidences of one part of the system from another. When a commitment to maintain a confidence is made, it must be strictly held. An inadvertent lapse on the therapist's part will severely shake the family's trust. Once the parameters of confidentiality are defined, people feel quite comfortable in exploring touchy subjects that might otherwise remain hidden from the therapist. It is not rare that an issue that is explored under confidentiality is subsequently revealed spontaneously, not by the therapist but by the people themselves.

In one instance, it became apparent during a family therapy session that the parents were under some extreme stress, which they avoided talking about in the children's presence. Toward the end of the session, the children were dismissed, and confidentiality rules were reestablished for the couple. They revealed that they were very burdened because their family business appeared to be failing. They feared that speaking about it with the children would frighten them, or that they might talk to other children about it, thus further endangering the business because of rumors. They also feared sharing information with the school.

They agreed to a full session just for themselves the following week to talk more about their own feelings. They felt relieved after this meeting, but still very conflicted about letting the children in on what was happening. Following this meeting, they decided to share the information with both their children and the guidance counselor, although they were at no point

pressured to do so. They subsequently reported that this had relieved some of the tension at home and had given them confidence that, if further trouble erupted, they would have good backup for the children at school.

In another case, parents were enraged at the irrational behavior of a particular teacher toward their child. The principal revealed to me in confidence that this teacher would be fired within a month, but that under no circumstances could he let the parents know this until action was taken. After the teacher was fired, the parents told me that they realized that I must have known in advance and they appreciated my refusal to discuss it. If anything, they felt it made them feel safer in revealing confidences in therapy that they did not want shared with the school.

PSYCHODIAGNOSTIC EVALUATION AND THE ECOSYSTEM

As mentioned earlier, an ecosystemic viewpoint must take into account a wide range of factors. In some instances, diagnosis of the family-school system is not sufficient, making it necessary to arrange a psychodiagnostic and/or psychoeducational evaluation of the child. A review of major journals of systems therapy (Lusterman, 1987) revealed not a single article in the preceding five years devoted to the integration of psychodiagnostic evaluation into systems therapy. Thus, guidelines have not been established for the systemic use of this information. I will present a method that has proven useful in integrating diagnostic input into the ecosystem.

When ecosystemic intervention is not producing change, the issue should be raised with the family that additional information about the child might be of help. The nature of such a evaluation is carefully described, and it is explained to the parents that the therapist will meet with them after the evaluation in order to share it with them in understandable language, and with time to answer whatever questions they have. It is explained to the child that, once the parents have been informed, a time will be set aside when the therapist will speak with him or her alone as well, so that the information can be explained in an understandable way, and to answer his or her special questions.

Often, adolescents complain that they want to hear the results first. They are told that there may be upsetting information, and it would be unethical to send them home to parents who are not prepared beforehand so that they can help them with any uncomfortable feelings they might have. If it is believed that testing may reveal important dynamic information that the parents need to understand but may not wish to share with the school, it is wise to arrange for an external evaluation. However, it is made clear at this time that all relevant information will be shared with the school.

I have described elsewhere (Lusterman, 1987) a relevant case example.

CASE STUDY

The parents of four children, ranging in age from seven years to eight months, were referred by the school because of their extremely punitive and angry reaction to their eldest son's poor performance in school. He was frequently expelled from class, spending considerable time in the principal's office. The parents were of working-class background but were highly upwardly mobile. They had done poorly in school and were eager that their children would excel academically, in line with the expectations of the upper-middle-class community in which they now lived. It was noted early in therapy that Mother tended to take the more angry and punitive role, and Father was protective of the boy and critical of his wife. Even as the parental situation emeliorated, Billy continued to perform poorly. When the school sent home a negative report, the cycle would begin anew, even if there had been a period of relative calm. At this point, it was suggested that a psychodiagnostic evaluation might determine why Billy was not improving, even though his parents had become somewhat more supportive. Testing revealed a WISC Verbal IQ of 135, Performance of 114, and a Full-scale IQ of 127. The Bender did not reveal visual-motor problems, but there were emotional indicators of impulsivity, short attention span, and anxiety. Projective testing revealed signs of guilt and anxiety over his poor performance, and a fear of consequent parental rejection.

The evaluator recommended the continuation of family therapy, but also suggested remedial therapy from a well-trained learning-disability teacher, rather than the tutor they were using, who unwittingly joined the parents in pressuring the child for improved performance. They expressed relief when it was explained to them that the discrepancy between Billy's verbal and performance abilities led adults to expect more of him than he could deliver at the time. They were also surprised to learn that he felt guilty and anxious about his failures, since they believed that he was simply rebellious and willful. Billy was relieved to understand something of why he was having so much trouble in school and at home.

His performance did improve over the next few months, with much cooperation among the school, family, remedial therapist, and the family therapist (pp. 513–514).

POWER AND HIERARCHY ISSUES

In some instances communication between school and family becomes so intense that it begins to take on the quality of a nulcear meltdown. Each interaction seems to further an increasingly bitter and nonproductive interaction between home and school. An ecosystem functioning in this manner is enmeshed. In other cases the exact opposite appears to occur. Both home and school seem to have lost control of a troubled child, whose escalating misbehavior is denied and neglected. This type of ecosystem is disengaged. Diagramming the ecosystem on the circumplex map reveals that in these instances, family and school lie fairly close together at an extreme point on one of the quadrants.

I have found that these extreme cases require particularly well-structured interventions that invariably involve both family and school. Both the parents and the school team have lost their hierarchical positions, and neither is able to exert appropriate and benign power to facilitate the child's growth and achievement. It is in these situations that the therapist must take a very powerful position for a period of time, until both school and family are reeempowered to operate at a more autonomous level. I will now describe strategies to deal with these two situations.

Interdiction

In some situations, intense and frequent contact between school and parents only seems to worsen an already difficult situation. This is often the case if the home is functioning in a chaotically enmeshed way. A family of this sort shows no clear parental leadership, a lack of well-defined generational boundaries, very high involvement, and, above all, parental inability to control children's behavior effectively. Such parents alternate unpredictably between endless negotiation with the children and sudden and impulsive threats and punishments.

When the school bombards such parents with negative information about their child, they can only do more of what they are already doing. Now the ecosystem itself is becoming chaotically enmeshed. This causes the child to become increasingly more disorganized and unmanageable.

In these cases, the therapist's first responsibility is to interdict direct contact between the parents and the school. This model entails the following steps (Lusterman, 1985):

1. Complete disengagement: The family therapist separates out the home problems from the school problems, defining the child's responsibility to the school (and vice-versa) and the child's responsibility to the family (and vice-versa).

2. The therapist contracts an agreement beween the parents and the school, stating that, for a period of time, the school will not contact the parents in case of difficulties at school, but will contact the therapist instead, who will work together with school personnel to create more effective educational interventions. the family agrees to a temporary-hands-off policy.

3. The therapist works with the family to correct non-school-related problems such as bedtimes, curfews, marijuana and/or alcohol abuse, sibling problems, etc.

4. As the therapist sees some improvement in the home situation, s/he gradually reintroduces parent-school involvement, with very careful coaching of the family and coordination with the school.

5. The therapist withdraws as more appropriate and productive contact between school and family is established. (p. 25)

The most frequent question about the use of therapeutic interdiction is whether the school will risk not informing the parents of continuing failure. It is important to gain agreement from the family that they are willing to let the school impose the normal consequences on the child. This means that if the child's behavior warrants repeating the grade, expulsion, or removal to a more restricted educational setting, they agree to accept this. This relieves the administration of the fear of subsequent parental accusations that they were not kept informed and were unaware that failure was imminent. The parents generally express great relief at the halt in communication, because they are tired of the constant bombardment. Finally, it puts responsibility for change in the child's behavior in his or her own hands, thus strengthening appropriate boundaries and increasing autonomous behavior.

Intensification

In some cases, we find a child who is lost in the cracks, so to speak, between a chaotically disengaged family and a poorly organized school setting. These families exhibit extreme emotional separateness, spend little time together, and have little control over their children. If their children attend poorly organized, chaotic schools, they tend to become either increasingly passive and uninvolved in school, or increasingly caught up in uncontrolled acting out and truancy.

In such a situation, the therapist must find ways of mobilizing the school and the home to take strong, clear action. Frequently the parents in such a family feel totally immobilized. They invariably come with a strong attitude of child blaming, and expect the therapist to fix him or her up, preferably in a hurry. They seem utterly incapable of helping their child to change, and if they become engaged in the task, it quickly degenerates into a battle of wills. The child often conforms to a diagnosis of oppositional disorder, at least on the surface.

Because these systems are so lacking in any cogent hierarchical structure, it is frequently valuable to introduce some new element that quickly creates a sense of accountability for both family and school. In New York state the family court system includes a quasilegal process called a PINS petition. This acronym stands for "Person in Need of Supervision." If a child is out of control, the parents, the school, or both may request that a hearing be arranged to determine if the child is appropriate for this classification. If there is a positive finding, a probation officer is assigned to the case, and the child is reportable to the officer. If there are "violations" of the probation (for example, violence, drug abuse, failure to obey basic parental rules, truancy, and the like), the probation officer may bring the child before a judge for a formal warning. Eventually some action may be taken, such as a weekend lockup or, in extreme cases, placement in an adolescent residential treatment setting.

It should be noted that the PINS petition is a type of double message. It is not only an open admission that the child is out of control but also an admission of failure of the parents and the school to provide appropriate supervision. This bind may have dramatic results. Parents as well as child are now reportable to a higher authority. Rather than engage in endless negotiation with the child, they now tell him or her that they will be forced to speak honestly with the probation officer, but truly don't want to report things that may result in the child's removal from the home. For the first time, realistic goals of accountability may be set forth. The school also is frequently mobilized, because an external agency is monitoring its activity.

Now the therapist's task becomes helping all concerned to create a better environment that promotes more healthy and autonomous behavior on the child's part. It is often important to link these parents to a parent support group as well. It is not infrequent that as parents in a chaotically disengaged system see progress in the child, they request marital therapy as well. This generally betokens a movement away from disengagement and toward a more organized and congenial home life. The knowledge that they have been able to experience success with their child seems to empower them to begin to work on their own relationship. This in turn reinforces their improved interaction with the child.

CONCLUSION

I have focused here on the particular problems encountered by the therapist in private practice who works with ecosystemic issues. Implicit in this manner of working is the idea that the therapist is also part of the ecosystem, and thus also perhaps part of the problem, in that he or she may become locked in power and hierarchy issues.

It is my hope that the adoption of an ecosystemic approach, with its emphasis on reaching out and bringing together many elements of the ecosystem, will increase the therapist's sensitivity to his or her own position within the ecosystem and relieve to an extent the isolation that so often char-acterizes private practice. Contact with teachers, counselors, school psychologists, and social workers and other professionals provides necessary feedback to the therapist and enables the therapist to gain some distance on his or her own role in the larger system. In this sense, work with coprofessionals encourages an informal opportunity for peer supervision and provides the pleasure that comes from collegiality, so often lacking in the private practitioners' life.

References

Ferber, A., Mendelsohn, M., & Napier, A. (1972). *The book of family therapy.* New York: Jason Aronson.

Lusterman, D-D. (1984). The family therapist's role in school consultation. *American Journal of Family Therapy, 12,* 67–68.

Lusterman, D-D. (1985). An ecosystemic approach to family-school problems. *American Journal of Family Therapy, 13,* 22–30.

Lusterman, D-D. (1987). The use of psychodiagnostic evaluation in systems therapy. *Psychotherapy, 24,* 511–515.

Lusterman, D-D. (1988). Family therapy and the schools: An ecosystemic approach. *Family Therapy Today, 3*(7), 1–3.

Lusterman, D-D. (in press). School-family interaction and the circumplex model. *Journal of Psychotherapy and the Family.*

Olson, D., & Killorin, E. (1985). *Clinical rating scale for the circumplex model of marital and family systems.* St. Paul, MN: Family Social Science, University of Minnesota.

Olson, D. (1986). Circumplex model VII: Validation studies and FACES III. *Family Process, 25,* 337–351.

23

Family Therapy's Contributions to Parent Education

MARVIN J. FINE
University of Kansas

JIM JENNINGS
The Family Tree, Overland Park, Kansas

PROVIDING EDUCATION for parents has a long history in the United States. Over 300 years ago, maternal associations in New England met regularly to discuss such important topics as "breaking the will" of the child (Brim, 1965). Of more recent vintage but still over 60 years ago, the National Society for the Study of Education (1929) published a yearbook on parental education. Despite its extended history in this country, only in the last two decades has parent education assumed the proportion of a national movement.

In 1976, it was estimated that just one popular organized program had trained over 8,000 instructors and 250,000 parents (Brown, 1976). Today, most communities of any size typically offer a range of parent education activities through churches, mental health clinics, public schools, medical settings, and private organizations. The programs focus mainly on information sharing, skill building, and problem solving. They use different theoretical models, including a child development, behavioral, Adlerian, communication theory, and Rogerian approaches. The leaders vary from educators, clinicians, clergy, nurses, to "uncredentialed" individuals, all with presumed expertise in parenting.

Populations being served also vary greatly. Many participants are simply parents wishing new information or assistance with fairly benign concerns such as "How do I get Freddy to do chores without complaining?" Some parents are directed into parent education programs by social service and court agencies because of more serious difficulties or inappropriate parental behavior. The burgeoning literature on the impact of growing up in alcoholic or otherwise dysfunctional families underscores how many adults may not have had adequate role models and assumed necessary survival behaviors in their families. These experiences may have impaired their subsequently assuming a healthy parenting role.

The efficacy literature, although of questionable quality, does present the case for parents generally benefiting from involvement in parent education programs of almost any kind (Medway, 1989). This is hardly surprising since one would expect that parents voluntarily choosing to join a parent group would be fairly motivated learners and consequently would report positive gains in almost any dimension examined. Well-controlled studies comparing programs, identifying specific changes, and following up participants are in short supply (Fine, 1980; Croake & Glover, 1977; Medway, 1989; Clarke-Stewart, 1981). Dropouts are a common problem with many parent programs, and can contaminate research results. One prediction is that needier parents are more inclined to terminate, whereas healthier parents will stay to the end, feeling good about their parenting experiences.

Despite a great deal of enthusiasm for the parent education movement, a number of problems have been identified (Fine, 1980; Fine & Brownstein, 1983; Clarke-Stewart, 1981; Fine & Henry, 1989). On the assumption that parent education is valuable and potentially beneficial to many, some unanswered questions are: Once parents get involved, how can they be encouraged to continue in programs and not to drop out? How can the generalizability of what is learned at a meeting be extended to the home? How can the likelihood be increased that if parents attempt to generalize or extend new skills and behaviors to their actual families, they will continue to do so?

There are concepts, activities, and techniques that derive from the field of family therapy that can be incorporated into parent education programs and have the potential for (1) reducing dropouts, (2) increasing applications in the home of what is learned in the parent education program, and (3) increasing the longevity of the new parent behaviors following termination of the actual parent program. These desirable outcomes can be expressed as hypotheses and lend themselves to manageable research designs. However, what will be presented in this chapter are not the results of formal studies but the ideas and experiences of the writers as generated through their training and practice as family therapists and their active involvement in parent education.

It may be somewhat pretentious to identify family therapy per se as the origin of these concepts since their antecedents also include learning theory, group dynamics, and even organizational theory. In addition, the human potential movement, with its rich legacy of actively involving persons in examining themselves and their relationships in experiential ways, definitely contributed to the range of concepts and techniques used by family therapists.

It should also be clear from the onset that the authors are not proposing a new kind of parent education program. There are already ample programs in use, some prepackaged (Dinkmeyer & McKay, 1976; Hall, 1978; Gordon, 1980; Popkin, 1989) and many others put together from different sources. The writers' position is that activities from family therapy can be selectively introduced to enrich any parent education program.

This chapter will discuss several areas of concern related to the extension of family therapy concepts and techniques into parent education. This seems necessary in order to clarify our objectives, to present a conceptual framework, and to highlight some professional/ethical issues.

FAMILY LIFE EDUCATION VERSUS PARENT EDUCATION

There are similarities as well as differences between family life education and parent education. The point of discussing and differentiating the two areas is that the proposed inclusion of family therapy activities invites the extension of parent education into family life education, which is not the intent of this chapter.

As one traces the roots of parent education, the emphasis on improving the quality of family life is evident. The work of Jane Addams over 50 years ago at Hull House in Chicago centered on helping immigrant families adapt to America and to improve the overall quality of their lives (Addams, 1942). Even more recently, the dream of Head Start was not just to separate children from their families for a stimulating preschool experience but to actively involve parents in the education of their children and, through related programs, to enhance the quality of family life (White, 1980; Dunlop; 1980).

Family life education, with the explicit goal of strengthening families beyond simply improving specific parenting skills, is a contemporary and growing force. One reflection of the interest in this area is in a number of popular books that describe healthy family functioning and encourage readers to examine their own family patterns (Lewis, 1979; Roman & Raley, 1980; Fine, 1979; White, 1980). Catchy titles like *Your family is good for you* (White, 1980) and *How's your family?* (Lewis, 1979) convey the books' themes very readily to the prospective reader. The annual National Symposium on Building Family Strengths at the University of Nebraska produces a yearly text on the conference. These volumes present a panorama of concepts and programs dealing with the enhancement of family life and make clear that this is a national phenomena.

Contemporary parent education, however, has been more narrowly defined than family life education. A definition that covers many of the available parent education programs is "parent education . . . refers to a systematic and conceptually based program, intended to impart information, awareness, or skills to the participants on aspects of parenting" (Fine, 1980, pp. 5–6). The popular approaches to parent education include Parent Effectiveness Training (Gordon, 1980), behavioral approaches (Simpson, 1980; Hall, 1978; Becker, 1971), and the Adlerian emphasis (Christensen & Thomas, 1980; Popkin, 1989; Dinkmeyer & McKay, 1976; Dreikurs & Soltz, 1964). Other conceptual bases for parent education have been presented by Ginott (1965, 1969) and Transactional Analysis (Babcock & Keepers, 1976; James, 1974).

Although parent educators can choose to ignore the broader picture of the family, the family structure is necessarily influenced by and, in turn, influences attempts by parents to behave differently. The recognition of the systemic nature of families is one basis of the rationale for the selective inclusion of family therapy concepts and skills. Increased awareness by parents of what they bring to their parenting role, how their own family backgrounds influence current family makeup, and how their contemporary family has developed its own structure can lead to greater discrimination by parents of changes they wish to make and of the implications for needed family involvement.

The family is a network of interconnected relationships functioning in such a manner as to enhance or maintain its functioning as a system. Efforts to change the behavior of an acting-out or withdrawn child can end in frustration because of the positive function the child's behavior serves in the family system. At other times, significant modification of a child's behavior may be accomplished only for the family to fall back to their "old ways" and for the problem behavior to reemerge.

A family systems model can potentially provide the family with a broader picture and a clearer vision of the linkages of the behavior of family members to each other and how generational histories affect the immediate family. It is through this sense of connectedness that families can evaluate the advantages and disadvantages of the status quo as well as any changes they may be contemplating.

Parent education programs need to be aware of the variety of family styles that constitute healthy or well-functioning families (Lewis, Beavers, Gossett, & Phillips, 1976; Stinnett & DeFrain, 1989). In particular, what patterns of communication, problem solving, control, and affection characterize these families? In what ways will specific parenting skills support or detract from the dynamics of a healthy family? If parents are trained to become more effective controllers of their children's behavior but do not "mend" poor communication patterns and existing resentments, then what will be the short- and long-term psychological costs of the improved control skills?

An important consideration is that effective parent education programs should contribute toward the enlightenment of family life and not detract from the quality of family relationships. Yet family life education or family enrichment programs are likely to be considerably broader in scope than parent education and the two kinds of programs are indeed different.

FACILITATING CHANGE

Participation in a parent education program does not guarantee change. What is often ignored is that parents differ in their attitudes toward and readiness to actively involve themselves in a parent education experience (Clarke-Stewart, 1981). Some parents attend a program in hopes of getting reassurance that they are doing things right and that change is not needed. Not every parent who attends a program believes that there is a problem at home for which they are seeking a solution. Some parents attend for the social aspects or with the intention of intellectually reacting to the ideas, much as one might do at a political lecture, and without the intention of changing beliefs or behaviors. The group leader needs to be sensitive to and accepting of these different postures.

Parent education programs often assume that current problems exist with children because parents lack knowledge and/or skill in parenting. It is then assumed that with new knowledge and skills, parents will change their behavior and, in turn, the child will change his or her behavior. However, it may be that knowledge and skill are only minimally connected with the identified problem and how the parents are reacting to it. For example, the family dynamics might require the maintenance of a problem to distract the parents and/or others from more volatile issues.

Yet participation in a parent education program does open up the possibilities for constructive attitude and behavior changes to occur. Borrowing from the literature on change in therapy, it seems important to get the parent to try new behaviors (Goldfried, 1980; Alexander & French, 1946; Strupp, 1976). One view of change is that behavior change can lead to personality change (Wheelis, 1973). Also, from a systemic viewpoint, parents who change and maintain the change in personal attitudes and behavior will necessarily affect change in their network of family relationships.

A framework for viewing change that seems applicable to parent education programs was presented by Watzlawick, Weakland, and Fisch (1974). According to this framework, first-order change occurs when parents change their behavior within a family system that remains unchanged, whereas second order change refers to a change in the system.

An example of a first-order change would be parents who continue to view their teenage son as a "bad kid" while hoping to learn additional control techniques in a parenting class. The parents may change their behavior via new control techniques, but the family system remains the same with the son viewed as a bad boy needing to be controlled. In effect, the parents are applying more of the same kind of intervention.

If the parents' perception of a situation is accurate and constructive and if in fact they simply need help refining or acquiring skills, then first-order change seems appropriate. For example, if a child is perceived as testing limits, the parents may need information regarding the importance of consistency in their attempts to set limits.

As already noted, a second-order change would occur when the system changes. For example, the parents of a teenage boy gain some insight through a parent education experience as to how they have been projecting their own parent-child values and expectations from 30 years ago onto their son. They shift from viewing him as a "bad kid" to someone struggling to establish a sense of identity and individuality. From this new perspective, parent behaviors are likely to change, but, more importantly, the family system that had been organized to do battle with this rebellious teenager will have changed. New supportive relationships are likely to emerge from the parents' changed view of themselves and their son.

The kinds of activities and concepts that this chapter will present can assist parents to understand their families better and to view behavior more constructively. In these ways, the activities increase the likelihood of second-order change occurring. Although some parents enter a parenting program with the goal of seeking techniques to "fix" or "control" a child, the parenting program has the potential of shifting their focus and to fostering more effective family relationships.

This is not to ignore that parents may indeed need to acquire some basic skills in terms of communication, setting limits, and problem solving. But in addition or in relation to the acquisition of those skills, parents can benefit from being able to assess behavioral patterns within the system, the roles and relationships that different family members have assumed, how certain individuals have become "scapegoated," how dysfunctional alliances may have developed, and how love, control, and communication can occur in healthy, functional ways.

Such an approach or orientation helps the parents to view behavior as feedback loops rather than simple cause-effect events. Family members are not just acted upon by other family members. Each person is in a reciprocal relationship with each other family member, and all together form a system, characterized by roles and relationships, communication patterns, rules, and predictable behavioral sequences. Real change in terms of attitudes, beliefs, and behaviors is more likely to occur when the parent educator incorporates this frame of reference into the parent education experience.

PROFESSIONAL ISSUES

A number of published parent education programs, according to the authors and/or publishers, can be readily used by almost any person who can read the instructor's manual. There are arguments on behalf of training and supervision in becoming a parent educator (Fine & Henry, 1989). Only a very naive leader would believe that there was one correct way for parents to function. There are many cultural and value issues that will come up in parent groups. The leader should be acquainted with information on variances in child development and on the breadth of normal behavior so as not to lead the group in a dogmatic, "true believer" fashion.

Behavioral parent programs seem quite vulnerable to ethical problems because of their frequent directiveness, the inherent view that they are training parents, and the focus on methodology. Sapon-Shevin (1982) has addressed several problem areas including potential conflicts between parent's/childrens' rights, the use of punishment, conflicts between parents and researchers, and the level of training offered parents who are expected to develop behavior modification programs with their children.

An important professional issue emerges because of the ease with which an educational program can shift into a pseudopsychotherapy program (Fine & Henry, 1989). Once parents get involved in discussing and sharing about their children, it is a short next step to begin disclosing about their families and about home problems. Group discussions on the value of parents working together in a supportive fashion can prompt disclosures of spouse conflicts that are quite personal in nature.

The untrained leader may not have a clear sense of what is appropriate and inappropriate material to be publicly processed, and may move (or be pulled) into an advice-giver or side-taker role with the needy parent. Attempting to advise on disturbed family relationships may be destructive in terms of consequences for the parents. There is a "protection" function that a leader needs to assume in relation to detouring parents eager to "tell their story." The protection is both for the parent and for the rest of the group whose time would be more productively spent on task.

The possibility of some parents attempting to precipitate a therapy-like experience would be increased as a parent education group becomes experientially and activity oriented. The inclusion of the activities that follow would then seem to increase the need for the instructor to be a mature, well-trained individual. This person should have a clear sense of boundaries, have the ability to discriminate between therapy and experiential learning, and possess enough presence and skill to intervene as needed in both a protective and leadership manner.

THE ACTIVITIES

The several activities being described derive from different sources in the family therapy literature and have been adapted by the writers for application in parent education programs. These are just a limited and illustrative sampling of activities. Their selection and integration into a coherent parent education program would require, as discussed, judgment by the parent educator.

Family-of-Origin Sharing

Purpose: To assist participants in gaining a multigenerational perspective of their families. To establish a tool and perspective that will enable them to identify and observe patterns within their family system.

Group Size: Size of group is not critical; however, individual participation is likely to be higher with group size not exceeding 14 to 16.

Materials: 18″ × 24″ (or larger) newsprint sheets for each participant. Participants are encouraged to bring pictures and other mementos. Scissors, paste, and tape.

Space: Sufficient space (preferable at a table) for participants to work with their materials.

Time: Construction portion will take 20 to 30 minutes. Group discussion time will vary with size and interest of group (allow 10 to 15 minutes per participant).

Procedure: The participants are instructed on how to construct genograms and are asked to prepare a family history through three generations for the following week's session. If there are materials that help to depict the family, such as pictures or other mementos, they are asked to bring them. Some additional information and questions are given about families to help them organize their perceptions and recollections of their family background and growing-up experiences:

1. What was happening in your family at the time of your birth and what was the meaning of your birth to the family?
2. What role(s) did you take on in the family and how was your role(s) related to your birth positon?
3. How easy or difficult is it to be an "individual" in your family?
4. How did family rules and expectations change as the children got older?
5. Who made decisions in your family? Was it clear all the time as to who was in charge? How was it determined who was in charge?
6. What kinds of alliances (partnerships) and coalitions (2 against 1) existed among the children and parents (e.g., Mom and Billy against Dad; the oldest and youngest children versus the middle child) and what purposes seemed served by them?
7. In what ways are you still emotionally connected to your family?

Presenting this assignment to a group of parents encourages them to understand the family as a system. The leader, as with all tasks and assignments, needs to be sure that communication is occurring, which at times will require rewording and presenting illustrations. The assignment can also be elaborated upon or reduced in complexity depending on the leader's judgment of the sophistication of the parents.

The sharing can occur the following week in small groups of three or four. If the participants really get involved, then each person might need 20 to 30 minutes. Some rules can be presented regarding how others are to respond. For example, the other participants can ask questions of clarification, but must respect the "story teller's" right to privacy and to share only as much as he or she wishes.

Detriangulating Activity

Purpose: To assist parents in developing a greater awareness of how sequences of behavior occur, how people get pulled into predictable dysfunctional responses, and how parents can avoid those pitfalls.

Group Size: Since this is mainly a "homework" assignment to be followed-up by group discussion, the actual size of the group is not important. As with other activities, the subsequent group discussion could occur in a subgroup of four to six—small enough to ensure participation.

Materials: None.

Space: Nothing special is required beyond enough space for small discussion.

Time: This activity is assigned in one session and processed in the subsequent session, typically one week later. The discussion time is usually 30 to 40 minutes in total.

Procedure: Parents can get caught up in the conflict sequences within their family. Once involved, the nonproductive transactions can be understood via the concept of triangulation, which is a phenomenon through which the family's dysfunction is often expressed. A basic example is how, when the two children begin to argue, a parent moves in and takes sides. By being instructed to assume a "curious observer" role, the parent can become more aware of the sequences of events, how people get pulled in, and how the situation ends in a predictable fashion. The catalyst for being pulled into the sequence as a "player" is the emotional gravitation that the parent feels. The act of observing others (making some notes on paper or mentally) and then sharing in group session with other parents can help to dissipate the emotional pull, in essence serving to detriangulate the parent from the dysfunctional relationships. The discussion should also focus on strategies for staying out of the dysfunctional sequence.

Parental Projection Task

Purpose: To understand the strong emotional responses, positive or negative, that parents have at times toward specific behavior of their children. To become more self-aware and in turn to view their relationship somewhat more objectively.

Group size: Size of group is not critical; however, individual participation is likely to be higher with a group size not exceeding 14 to 16.

Materials: None.

Space: For the discussion portion of this exercise, participants should be arranged in a circle.

Time: Allow 10 to 15 minutes for the sentence completion activity. Allow 10 minutes per participant for the discussion.

Procedure: The leader can use the following specific instructions:

Here is an exercise that can be fun and also helpful to us in our desire to function effectively as parents. Complete the following statements about one of your children. It is important that in completing the task you complete the whole sentence as I am, adding your child's name, and then the behavior. You can do this for each of your children.

What I like about _____ is his/her _____ and his/her _____.

What I don't like about _____ is his/her _____ and his/her _____.

Now make the statement, What I like about me is my _____ and my _____, but use the same two characteristics you used regarding your child. Next, do the same thing for the statement, What I don't like about me is my _____ and my _____.

The instructor asks persons to volunteer to say their statements (both about their children and self) aloud. The person is then asked if the statement is generally true about himself or herself. Usually, most persons will agree that it is generally true. If this does not seem to be working, the instructor can ask the participants to think of a synonym and try it in the statement. This usually brings into agreement a few of those who earlier disagreed.

Following the activity, the participants can process the experience and their thoughts on how parents project their feelings regarding children.

Family Sequences and Triangles

Purpose: To broaden the participants' view and perspective of transactions that occur within the family. To enable the participants to see the linkages that exist between behavioral episodes. To increase the participants' understanding of triangles and the triangulation process in the family.

Group Size: 8 to 16 participants.

Materials: Paper and pens (or pencils) for each participant. Participants can use their own genogram as a reference.

Space: Sufficient space so that subgroups can talk without detracting each other. All group discussion should use circle arrangement.

Time: Subgroup phase takes about 30 to 40 minutes. All group discussion should allow 5 to 10 minutes per participant.

Procedure: The instructor asks participants to prepare a list of three acceptable behaviors and three unacceptable behaviors that one of their children engages in on a regular basis (Note: *Regular* does not necessarily mean *frequent*—only that it repeats over time.)

The instructor elicits some examples of both acceptable and unacceptable behaviors from the group, helping them to clarify the difference between behaviors and attitudes.

Example: John is a good boy!

Instructor:. What does John do that you see as good?

Participant: He is always polite.

Instructor: What does John do or say that you call polite?

Participant: He always says thank you.

Once the instructor is satisfied, the participants are asked to bring their lists with them to the next meeting.

Participants are divided into groups of four (separating spouses), which are then divided into dyads.

Dyad members are told to help each other describe the sequence of events preceding, during, and following one acceptable and one unacceptable behavior. (Note: Sequencing may cover minutes, hours, days, weeks, or even longer; however, the longer the time frame of the sequence the more difficult it will be to identify.) It has proven helpful for participants to organize the sequence of events in five categories. These can be set up on a sheet of paper in a circular fashion or simply as a connected sequence. The five categories are: (1) the preceding event or circumstance; (2) the child's behavior; (3) the parent(s)' reaction; (4) the child's response to the parent(s); and (5) other family members' reactions to (2), (3), and (4).

The dyads then return to their groups of four partners and share their behavioral sequence. Each member of a dyad will share his or her partner's sequence and not his or her own with the group of four. This helps to detach people emotionally from their own sequence and allows them to view their family's behavior

more objectively. Discussion can also focus on how the parent(s) could behave differently so as to break the pattern.

As an option, following the group-of-four discussion, the entire group could come back together to roleplay a few of the sequences. Volunteers can be recruited to play the part of family members. The participant whose family is being roleplayed will coach the players in their roles. (Note: The instructor may want to give spouses a chance to collaborate about the decision to volunteer since the revelation will undoubtedly involve both spouses.)

The roleplaying will then be followed by a discussion on the sequence pattern, function or functions it might serve the family, identification of triangles, and roles various members serve in the family system. Some optional ways that the cycle could be broken and more appropriate behaviors substituted should also be considered.

Exploring Similarities and Differences

Purpose: To increase awareness of the projection process.

Group Size: 6 to 16 participants.

Materials: Each participant's own genogram. For variation, question sheet for each dyad.

Space: Sufficient space for dyads to talk without distracting other dyads. All group discussion should use circle arrangement.

Time: Allow 20 to 30 minutes for dyad sharing. Allow 5 to 10 minutes per participant for group discussion.

Procedure: Participants are asked to identify an extended family member from their family of origin whom they feel has held or holds a special place in the family network. Participants form nonspousal dyads. Each participant shares with his or her partner about that extended family member, the kind of person he or she is (or was), and the function or role he or she serves (or served) in the family system.

Using their family genograms, participants then attempt to identify others within the family that serve the same or similar function in the family system.

VARIATION: Participants are asked to identify which extended family member from the previous generation with whom they have the most in common (who are they most like or similar to). To assist participants, the instructor should encourage them to recall statements made by parents or other family members when they were children that in effect said, "You're just like your Uncle Joe (or Aunt Mary or Grandpa Jones)."

Participants then generate two lists. The first list contains those characteristics (both physical and behavioral) that they hold in common with this extended family member. The second list is those characteristics that are dissimilar (both physical and behavioral). Participants should be in groups of four to six to discuss the above tasks.

To facilitate discussion, participants may be provided with the following guide questions:

1. Did you learn/discover or rediscover anything about yourself or the extended family member?
2. Do you agree with your family members' assessment as to similarity?
3. Was the similar characteristic(s) you possess seen as an asset or liability? Do you view it the same or differently?
4. Would you change it?

End with an all-group discussion.

SUPPLEMENT: This exercise can be repeated with the family member the participant is least like.

SUMMARY, SYNOPSIS, AND AFTERTHOUGHTS

A family is a living dynamic organism and what happens in one part has a ripple effect through all parts of the system. Just as the loss of a limb by an individual requires adaptation of the entire organism, including the psyche, so a family as an entity must and will adapt and adjust to changing circumstances of each of its members.

Within the life cycle of the family, individual behaviors that would otherwise be seen as aberrant take on a positive and a purposeful meaning. Helping parents understand the issues common to the life cycle transitions (e.g., adolescents leaving home, death of members of the oldest generations, births, etc.) provides a context in which to interpret behavior.

It is not unusual for a child to be labeled as bad or a problem child. The family frequently comes to believe that the source of its problems in life is the child or at least the source of the problems she or he appears to create. It can be more useful to be able to place such behavior in a broader context that enables the parents to see the child's attempt to provide a solution to a family issue through the presentation of a problem. How enlightening it would be for the parents to learn that such a child is indeed attempting to accomplish precisely the same goal (albeit via a different strategy) as the "good" child. It could be quite enlightening for the parents to learn that both children are probably equally troubled and in need of parental help and support.

The primary potential value of a family systems perspective in parent education is the elimination of fault or blame. In some parent education programs the child may be explicitly identified as the cause of the problem or the problem; that is, the problem lies within the child and the parents need to learn how to modify the child's behavior. Implicitly the parents may feel that they are being identified as the culprits, because they are the ones held responsible for their children. Such an approach is less likely to provide a positive incentive or motivation for participation on the part of parents. Some parents feel progressively guiltier and inadequate as the program proceeds, then eventual dropout is predictable.

However, when the epistemology is a systemic one then the participants are seen as making efforts to add to or maintain family functioning and not to detract from it; some of these efforts are helpful, other efforts are not helpful, and still others may be counterproductive. From this perspective parents are not at fault, but can see themselves caught up in behavior patterns or sequences that are simply counterproductive. Parents can then experience a sense of growing competency and empowerment as they initiate changes to break old patterns and increase family health.

The preceding activities and exercises can be a significant contributor to parents' increased self-awareness and awareness of family dynamics of which they are a part. Accordingly, they may be better able to "unhook" from old patterns and find gratification in their parenting roles. The ones described in this chapter were submitted as examples. Individual instructors can select additional exercises or even develop their own for inclusion in standard programs.

This chapter has included a number of cautions, many revolving around instructor competence and sensitivity. The parent education field, as perhaps a component of a broader family studies curriculum or sequence, could benefit for specific instructor training and supervision components. There are many ethical considerations of which instructors need to be aware. Experiential components, such as those described, can prompt participants into disclosures more appropriate for therapy groups. Instructors have a very important role in presenting material, guiding discussion, and offering participants adequate protection.

References

Addams, J. (1942). *Twenty years at Hull House*. New York: MacMillan.

Alexander, F., & French, T. (1946). *Psychoanalytic therapy*. New York: Ronald.

Babcock, D., & Keepers, T. (1976). *Raising kids OK*. New York: Grove Press.

Becker, W. (1971). *Parents are teachers*. Champaign, IL: Research Press.

Brim, O. (1965). *Education for child rearing*. New York: Free Press.

Brown, C. (1976). It changed my life. *Psychology Today, 10*, 47–57, 109–112.

Christensen, O., & Thomas, C. (1980). Dreikurs and the search for equality. In M. Fine (Ed.), *Handbook on parent education*. New York: Academic Press.

Clarke-Stewart, K. (1981). Parent education in the 1970s. *Educational Evaluation and Policy Analysis, 3*, 47–58.

Croake, J., & Glover, K. (1977). A history and evaluation of parent education. *The Family Coordinator, 26*, 151–158.

Dinkmeyer, D., & McKay, G. (1976). *Systematic training for effective parenting*. Circle Pines, MN: American Guidance Services.

Dreikurs, R., & Soltz, V. (1964). *Children: The challenge*. New York: Meredith Press.

Dunlop, K. (1980). Child care and parent education. *Education and Urban Society, 12*, 175–191.

Fine, M. (1979). *Parents versus children: Making the relationship work*. Englewood Cliffs, NJ: Prentice-Hall.

Fine, M. (1980). The parent education movement: An introduction. In M. Fine (Ed.), *Handbook on parent education*. New York: Academic Press.

Fine, M., & Brownstein, C. (1983). Parent education and the school social worker. *Social Work in Education, 6*, 44–55.

Fine, M., & Henry, S. (1989). Professional issues in parent education. In M. Fine (Ed.), *The second handbook on parent education: Contemporary perspectives*. New York: Academic Press.

Ginott, H. (1965). *Between parent and child.* New York: MacMillan.

Ginott, H. (1969). *Between parent and teenager.* New York: MacMillan.

Goldfried, M. (1980). Toward the delineation of therapeutic change principles. *American Psychologist, 35,* 991–999.

Gordon, T. (1980). Parent effectiveness training: A preventive program and its effects on families. In M. Fine (Ed.), *Handbook on parent education.* New York: Academic Press.

Hall, M. (1978). *The responsive parenting program.* Lawrence, KS: H and H Enterprises.

James, M. (1974). *Transactional analysis for moms and dads.* Reading, MA: Addison-Wesley.

Lewis, J. (1979). *How's your family? A guide to identifying your family's strengths and weaknesses.* New York: Brunner/Mazel.

Lewis, J., Beavers, W., Gossett, J., & Phillips, V. (1976). *No single thread: Psychological health in family systems.* New York: Brunner/Mazel.

Medway, F. (1989). Measuring the effectiveness of parent education. In M. Fine (Ed.), *The second handbook on parent education: Contemporary perspectives.* New York: Academic Press.

National Society for the Study of Education. (1929). *Twenty-eighth year-book: Preschool and parental education.* Bloomington, IL: Public School Publishing.

Popkin, M. (1989). Active parenting: A video-based program. In M. Fine (Ed.), *The second handbook on parent education: Contemporary perspectives.* New York: Academic Press.

Roman, M., & Raley, P. (1980). *The indelible family.* New York: Rawson, Wade Publishers.

Sapon-Shevin, M. (1982). Ethical issues in parent training programs. *The Journal of Special Education, 16,* 341–357.

Simpson, R. (1980). Behavior modification and child management. In M. Fine (Ed.), *Handbook on parent education.* New York: Academic Press.

Stinnett, N., & DeFrain, J. (1989). The healthy family: Is it possible? In M. Fine (Ed.), *The second handbook on parent education: Contemporary perspectives.* New York: Academic Press.

Strupp, H. (1976). The nature of the therapeutic influence and its basic ingedients. In A. Burton (Ed.), *What makes behavior change possible.* New York: Brunner/Mazel.

Watzlawick, P., Weakland, J., & Fisch, R. (1974). *Change: Principles of problem formation and problem resolution.* New York: W. W. Norton.

Wheelis, A. (1973). *How people change.* New York: Harper & Row.

White, H. (1980). *Your family is good for you.* New York: Berkeley Books.

24

A School-Based Divorce Intervention Program

SUSAN R. BERGER

Newton Public Schools, Newton, Massachusetts

ROHNA SHOUL

Newton Public Schools, Newton, Massachusetts

SUSAN WARSCHAUER

Newton Public Schools, Newton, Massachusetts

EACH DAY all over the United States children arrive in school with their books, completed homework, snacks, and whatever emotional baggage encumbers them. More than 1.5 million children under age 18 are affected each year by family breakups (Diamond, 1985), and nearly half the children born in 1980 will live in single-parent families at some point before they turn 18 (Glick, 1979).

Although the school's primary mission is to educate, it must deal with the implications of this situation. Unless school children are psychologically available while they attend school, the learning process will be severely impaired. This availability is affected by the amount of emotional turmoil children are experiencing and by the stability of the adults on whom they depend (Guidabaldi, Cleminshaw, Perry, & McLouglin, 1983; Guidabaldi & Perry, 1985).

Opinions regarding the role of schools in dealing with family issues may vary, but the very presence of children in classrooms ensures that some role will evolve. Classroom behavior that interferes with learning cannot be ignored if teaching is to take place (Holzman, 1982). School is very often the one stable factor in the lives of children experiencing family instability, particularly for children at the elementary level (Shoul, 1985). Therefore, we feel that schools have a responsibility to address both the educational and the emotional needs of children. This approach represents an ecological perspective that recognizes the many systems that make up a child's world—family, school, and community (O'Connor & Lubin, 1984; Plas, 1986).

This chapter addresses the emotional and developmental issues that confront children and how schools can best respond to the concerns and changes that divorce precipitates. Its organization reflects our participation (as a psychologist, a social worker, and a classroom teacher) in a systemwide Divorce and Separation Committee formed in 1980 by the Newton, Massachusetts, public school system.

In seeking to understand how children are affected by divorce, we will examine emotional issues and variables of age and sex, the important roles of the classroom teacher and the classroom environment, school policies and family communications, administrative support, and school-based models of intervention. Because the classroom teacher assumes the greatest ongoing responsibility in working with children from divorced families and generally receives little support and few resources, we will include a model program developed by one of the authors (Warschauer) that can be incorporated into a general curriculum. We will focus on the elementary school because parents, teachers, and administrators most frequently interact with children in that setting.

Also, we have included a survey of the process that our Divorce Committee underwent. This produced a school/community model applicable to any concerned school system. We have also put these parts into a systems framework that considers a holistic view and recognizes that the environment of the school or the classroom reflects more than the sum of its individual classes or students. There is a circular connectedness between individual student, family, teacher, classroom, and school.

WHAT IS DIVORCE?

Divorce is a process, not an event. When a divorce occurs, the parents experience the loss of a dream, and the children are confronted with a parental loss (Visher & Visher, 1988) and a restructuring of their lives that they have not chosen. In families with children, the decision to divorce rarely occurs by mutual consent (Wallerstein & Kelly, 1980). The disruption of divorce challenges a child's capacity to cope, both immediately and in the future. Children will experience stress even when the parents process the decision to divorce reasonably well. The loss of the family as it was creates a stress and all subsequent family interactions are affected. Children have to deal with a transition in the family system that will, by necessity, require coping with alliances and loyalties.

It is valuable to take a family life-cycle perspective regarding divorce. Such a perspective views symptoms and dysfunctions in relation to normal functioning over time. Current problems can be placed within the course the family followed in its past, the tasks it is trying to master, and the future toward which it is moving (Carter & McGoldrick, 1988). If one connects the family life-cycle perspective with family systems theory, the transition of divorce becomes a modal point in time that affects all members of the family circularly. In other words, divorce disrupts the family equilibrium—the experience of one family member will affect the functioning of another family member, and by definition, the entire family.

Carter and McGoldrick (1988) conceptualized the stages of the family life cycle, paying particular attention to dislocations that require additional steps to restabilize and proceed developmentally in the divorcing and postdivorce family as well as in the remarried family. Montalvo (1979) defined a *dislocation* as the experience of having lost one's place in relation to other people. The dislocation or disruption is the result of fractured relationships, of major shifts in the ties among the people on which one depends.

To deal effectively with the experience of dislocation in children, it is necessary to understand the triangular arrangements in which children exist (Montalvo, 1979). Bradt and Bradt (1986) described a *triangle* as the smallest unit of both process and structure in the alliancing-skirmishing-loyalty processes of family life. Children will have to deal with the divorce by nature of their being members of a family system, and cope with the shift in the triangular alliances and loyalties.

As personnel working within a school system, we view the system of the school and the system of the family as being simultaneously independent and interactive. When parents are in the process of divorce, the child is affected with divided loyalties and reshifting alliances. The way the child moves through this dislocation will affect the way he or she relates in a classroom, and the stability of the classroom and school will further influence his or her transition at home.

Ideally, the mental health professional in a school system has an opportunity to build an alliance and join with the subsystem of the child to create a supportive environment while the parents work through the necessary transitions in the parental system. Although the family is a system in continual process of change in various subsystems and reciprocal interrelationships, we maintain the position of focus on the child.

Impact of Separation and Divorce

Emotional and Behavioral

A significant body of research has carefully documented the emotional impact of family dissolution on children (Wallerstein & Blakeslee, 1989). The divorce process affects all phases of children's lives, including their lives in the classroom. Not all such children bring serious problems to school. For some of them, the divorce is a solution that lessens stress and turmoil. Those who manifest problems, however, can be considered in two general groups: those who withdraw and those who act out (Wallerstein & Kelly, 1980).

The withdrawn student has difficulty in peer activities and can become shy and noncommunicative. The relationship with the teacher can show regressive behavior such as clinging or excessive demanding of attention. The acting-out student also seeks extra teacher time, but in a demanding manner. This child is often disruptive and noisy. Frequently, the behavior antagonizes other children, creating numerous problems in peer relationships. Interestingly, there can be real contrasts in home and school behavior. The child may be obedient and hard working at home and disruptive in school, or the opposite may be true.

Mediators of Adjustment

Research has also shown that the response to divorce is closely related to age and sex (Guidabaldi et al., 1983; Kurdek, Bilsk, & Siesky, 1981; Wallerstein & Kelly, 1980).

The life cycle in family systems does not always proceed uninterruptedly from marriage until the death of both partners. The frequency of divorce and remarriage creates significant changes in family organization, personal adjustment, and treatment issues (Nicholas & Everett, 1986).

The reactions of preschool and kindergarten children include regression, guilt, fantasy, denial, aggression, and increased emotional need. Young school-aged children experience fear, disorganization, yearning, anger, and conflicts in loyalty. Older school-aged children deal with profound underlying feelings of loss and rejection, helplessness, and loneliness.

Some reach out to adults for help, whereas others keep very busy trying to distract themselves from thinking about divorce or separation.

Somatic symptoms or alignment with one parent are common reactions. Adolescents often become disengaged from peers and family, worry about sex and marriage, and express loyalty conflicts. This failure to cope can interfere with entry into adolescence. On the positive side, following divorce the adolescent's participation in the family may change. Adolescents in single-parent homes often develop a more realistic view of money, greater maturity, and moral growth (Jellinek & Slovik, 1981).

Gender

Age-related factors can become affected by sex differences. Until recently it was thought that divorce affected boys more seriously than girls. Although first-grade girls also indicated problems related to divorce, it appeared that unlike those of their male peers these did not generally become more serious as the girls matured (Guidabaldi et al., 1983; Knoff, 1987). There is still strong evidence that boys initially demonstrate many more problems from divorce than girls on all levels: socially, emotionally, academically, and intellectually (Guidabaldi & Perry, 1985; Kurdek, 1981; Wallerstein & Kelly, 1980). In the 1989 study by Wallerstein and Blakelee, reference to the "sleeper effect" is introduced. This indicates that although girls' initial adjustment to divorce seems less stormy that that of boys, their entry into young adulthood precipitates serious relationship problems. As Carlson (1987a) suggested, this information about children's divorce-related adjustment can help guide classroom placements. For example, placement of at-risk boys with a male teacher may be helpful. Hiring practices at the elementary level might consider outreach to role-model professionals.

The Ecology of the School

Role of the Teacher

When the home cannot give the customary emotional and general support in divorce situations, we believe the school can play a significant role in responding to the student's needs. Schools can provide: (1) stability within the classroom, (2) kindness and understanding coupled with firm and realistic expectations, and (3) extra support and recognition of learning accomplishments, especially if the student appears to be self-deprecating.

Friendly and accepting peer relationships become crucial at this time, and teachers can structure activities and opportunities to create this atmosphere. The child needs to experience school as a stable, nonchanging aspect of his or her daily life. If possible, a mental health professional within the school will be available so that the child can share feelings and thoughts. This availability should extend to all members of the separated or reconstituted family.

In our experience, if a climate of trust exists in a school, parents are more likely to inform their child's teacher about an impending separation or divorce. How sensitively teachers and the school community handle this information can be critical in enabling students and their families to manage this time of family upheaval. Respecting confidentiality, not giving unsolicited advice, and reassuring parents they are not alone are helpful guidelines for school personnel to observe (Diamond, 1985).

When there is a nurturing relationship between teacher and student, help in coping with home problems very often takes place (Allers, 1980; Whitfield &

Freeland, 1981). For some teachers who have a special sensitivity in working with children of divorced parents, the teacher checklist devised by Drake (1981) may be useful.

Research indicates that teachers with personal experience of divorce are more likely to encourage involvement by the school (Green & Schaefer, 1984). Psychiatrists have confirmed the value of placing a child involved in divorce with a teacher who has been through the process (Diamond, 1985). In the videotape, "When Divorce Comes to School" (Holzman, 1982), one of the authors (Warschauer) commented:

> I've made it a point to let the children know that I'm divorced. I think it's important for them to know that not only their parents are going through this, but other people have gone through it. They've survived, they're happy, they're functioning, and that it's OK. It's another way of living in this world.

If a teacher has coped well, the child sees a positive role model and the stigma of the experience has lessened. If the child has a close relationship with the teacher, resentment toward the parents may be decreased. Placing a child in a classroom where there are other children going through the experience may also be helpful.

Teachers who in conversation openly communicate what is happening in their families and what is important to them encourage children to do the same. This involves a great deal of thought and knowledge of the personal circumstances of the children who are in their classrooms. Mature, experienced teachers who are comfortable with affective education (Jones, 1968) will incorporate this approach as part of their teaching style. Unfortunately, schools of education devote very little time in their teacher-training programs toward helping students acquire these skills (Shea,

1982). Teacher characteristics are a potentially important factor in mediating students' adjustment to divorce.

School Policies/Family Communications

The U.S. Family Education Rights and Privacy Act is clear about the rights of both parents to have equal access to school records unless a court order removes that right from either parent (Newton Public Schools, 1986). The legal issues must be clearly understood by all personnel who have direct contact with children, particularly those involved with the dismissal of a child to the care of someone other than the custodial parent, or if a custody suit is in progress (Punger, 1984).

School events, parent conferences, and PTA/PTO meetings are areas that can be adjusted to meet the special circumstances of single-parent families (National Committee for Citizens in Education). Being aware of different surnames between parent and child, the role of stepparents (Diamond, 1985), and conferring with parents separately are further areas to which school personnel must be sensitive.

School librarians are in a unique position to provide helpful information to pupils, teachers, and parents. Displays, reading lists, newsletters, storytelling, discussion groups using bibliotherapy techniques all represent opportunities to address the issue of separation and divorce (Pardek, 1985; Winfield, 1983).

Appropriate mental health professionals (counselors, social workers, psychologists) should provide workshops for school personnel to sensitize staff to the various needs of pupils and their families (Burns & Brassard, 1982; Drake & Shellenberger, 1979; Hill, Brent, & Mathews, 1983; Newton Public Schools, 1986; Summak, 1984). Concrete, practical suggestions that demonstrate the school's concern about changing families without creating additional burdens on the school system can emerge.

A school secretary might ask parents to provide enough addressed, stamped envelopes so that notices could be mailed to the absent parent without excessive extra work. Some teachers have written to a non-custodial parent living elsewhere and have had the child keep a special folder of classroom work. This was sent at regular intervals along with copies of report cards and other pertinent information.

Periodic updating of family information on school registration forms (Diamond, 1985) helps in understanding some of the issues children may be dealing with and helps school personnel to respond appropriately. The increasing availability of computers in schools simplifies the collection of data in creating student and classroom profiles. This facilitates development of appropriate interventions.

A SCHOOL-BASED MODEL OF INTERVENTION

Rationale

The magnitude of the problem of family dissolution and its impact on children raises the issue of where intervention can most effectively take place. In our view, a school-based program develops from the theoretical base of a systems perspective. Divorce or separation is a complex process that relates to cultural, ethnic, religious, social, legal, economic, and psychological factors. Children bring all of these, in some way, to school.

Many of these environmental factors influence the choice of which support systems might minimize the severity of children's adjustment problems (Kurdek,

1981). As Knoff (1987) indicated, mediating factors or variables facilitate the long-term adjustment that children make to the divorce process. One factor is the school environment (Kurdek, 1981). Facilitative school characteristics are smaller populations, environments emphasizing structure and orderliness, and proximity to the home. In our view, although these factors may be relevant, the sensitization of administration and teaching staff to the issues and concerns that children have following divorce are of primary importance and factors over which there is some control.

Knoff (1987) suggested that single parents, to a greater extent than intact families, are likely to expect schools to augment their role as child socializers. From a systems theory perspective, any proactive school system that supports the individual child, by definition, also supports the family, school, and community. The school environment may be seen as the single most important institution in the life of the child.

Other sources of support for children include friends, siblings, teachers, classmates, grandparents, cousins, neighbors, and parents of good friends (Beal, 1979; Wallerstein & Kelly, 1980). These researchers noted, however, that children did not readily turn to friends, teachers, or classmates and that siblings were generally of little help. They suggested that children's help seeking is a generalized trait in that children who turned to parents for assistance were also likely to turn to friends and teachers. Children who seek help are likely to tap a variety of resources, whereas children who do not seek help are apt to be psychologically stranded. Although these findings need to be replicated and supplemented by future research (particularly regarding the role of siblings), they nevertheless provide a rationale for the design of child-oriented community or school-based intervention programs that might offset the short- and long-term effects of stressful family relations (Cantor, 1977; Hetherington, 1979). Children whose parents are divorced often find that other children in similar situations are helpful in dealing with divorce-related concerns (Kurdek, 1981). Group-intervention techniques can capitalize on these findings.

The Newton Model

The Newton Model evolved as the result of a challenge from a divorced father who had not been informed of his son's high school graduation. He wanted the school system to review its policies of communication with noncustodial parents. The first decision was to offer staff members an educational program relating to the legal issues of divorce and how these impact on schools. These were examined with a probate judge (Ginsburg, 1979), and the interface became clear when he explained the importance of school reports in helping to shape custodial decisions. The Divorce and Separation Committee, which functioned actively for four years, grew directly from this consciousness-raising experience. The committee's work resulted in two distinct models: community involvement and in-school programming.

Community involvement entailed:

1. A conference of school and social agency personnel to identify mutual concerns of service delivery to families experiencing disruption
2. A meeting with a single-parent group to explore the responsiveness of school policies to their needs (i.e., daycare, school opening times)
3. Development of a resource brochure for school and agency personnel as well as parent use
4. A cooperative effort with a local cable station to produce a film (entitled "When Divorce Comes to School"; see Holzman, 1982).

In-school programming began with a survey of the staff to determine:

1. How the issue was perceived
2. What efforts were already in place
3. What kind of help teachers and support personnel could use

Of the respondents, 90 percent indicated a need for staff training that would include (1) the emotional and academic effects experienced by students, (2) curriculum ideas, (3) when to make appropriate referral to social work/psychological/counselor staff, and (4) knowing the laws and regulations governing child custody (Shoul, 1985). In response to these expressed needs, staff workshops were conducted using curriculum materials developed during a summer workshop (Newton Public Schools, 1986) and the film "When Divorce Comes to School." The following list illustrates the evolution of the Newton Model and demonstrates the type of interventions conducted and the subsystems targeted.

Intervention	Subsystem Target
Legal issues seminar	Administration/ pupil personnel/ faculty
Establish divorce and separation committee	Pupil personnel and faculty
Survey	School
Support groups	Children/parent
Film/cable/community meetings	Child/family/school
Divorce curriculum	Teacher/workshop
Inservice training	Teacher/pupil personnel
Resource brochure	Community/school

The original concept envisioned a followup community conference for parents that would help in developing responsive programs by the schools and social agencies. However, budget cuts resulting in the loss of personnel severely restricted follow-through. However, faculty who participated in the workshops brought an increased awareness to their schools, and staff continue to lead support groups for children. Because parents generally are not available during the day, any effort to organize support groups for them requires evening meetings. Staff receive no compensation for this. Groups that do exist are generally sponsored by a religious group, social agency, or center specializing in divorce-related issues. However, without the originally envisioned approach that would have involved the family, the benefits to the children are diminished.

Because most school systems are controlled at the local level, programs relating to the impact of divorce on school-aged children will be erratic in implementation. To rectify this, legislation has been introduced in the Massachusetts legislature that would establish an Office for Family Education. This would provide training and education to school personnel regarding the psychological and legal aspects of divorce and its effect on school-aged children. This is a result of research done by the Special Commission Relative to Divorce (State of Massachusetts, 1986), established by the Legislature in 1984.

Groups for Children

Despite a 50-year history of group psychotherapy for children, using groups as interventions for children whose parents have divorced is a new procedure (Goldstein, 1985; Kalter, Pickar, & Lesowitz, 1984). From numerous reports in the popular media and at professional meetings, it is clear that new efforts in this direction are considerably more widespread than the professional and scientific literature indicates (Kalter, Pickar & Lesowitz, 1984). Kalter also suggested that the schools offer an excellent opportunity to reach and engage a substantial percentage

of children of divorce. The structure already present can serve to facilitate the intervention. In the familiar context of the school, the professionally facilitated peer group can also begin the process of normalizing the divorce experience.

Several configurations of child and parent groups deal with divorce issues: (1) those led by school-based mental health professionals (Berger, 1987); (b) those led by mental health professionals from the community within the schools (Kalter, Pickar, & Lesowitz, 1984); and (3) community-based preventative programs, such as The Divorce Adjustment Project (Stolberg & Cullen, 1983). We feel that those who select school-based groups will have the most productive home-school communication, which always benefits the child.

Children's support groups may be preventive for children who are not experiencing severe distress or psychopathology. Several school-based, divorce-related adjustment groups can serve as models (Berger, 1987; Cantor, 1977; Stolberg & Garrison, 1981; Wilkinson & Bleck, 1977). Group formats tend to provide support by encouraging the expression of thoughts and feelings about the divorce and a skills-building function by teaching adaptive coping strategies such as problem solving and anger control (Carlson, 1987b).

Groups conducted in the schools provide therapeutic support, are often limited in time, and involve little cost. The effort of a school providing a forum for a PTA evening or a series of meetings for parents or children promotes good will and becomes cost effective because of the potential decrease in use of in-school pupil personnel services. The formation of groups will reflect the demographics of the particular school community, how the problem is perceived by the teachers and administration, and what is seen as most acceptable to the parents. Groups may be initiated by a counselor, psychologist, or social worker.

Although the duration and format of groups may vary, the group members rarely deviate from issues pertinent to the topic of being in a single-parent or divorced family. If the leaders of these groups are able to create the critically needed atmosphere of caring, confidentiality, acceptance, and understanding, the children will see themselves as "not the only one" and see each other as resources (Berger, 1987).

Parent Groups

The school system serves as an important support system for parents who are separated or divorced. Very often single parents seek out a mental health professional in a school as a way of gaining support and feeling less isolated, or they may be referred by their child's teacher or principal. If we hope to ameliorate the plight of children who are involved in a divorce process, the obvious source of support is the family system.

A mutuality of concern joins the school and the family in the common goals of the child's education and socialization. Support groups for parents can be initiated in a school where organizations such as Parents Without Partners do not exist in the community. The goal is to provide a forum for the mutual support and information sharing of the participants, an opportunity for parents to depathologize the experience of divorce, and to increase parents' availability to their children in providing emotional and academic support. Fine (1980) is a good resource for the development of such groups. Although the group may be initiated and facilitated by a school professional for a time-defined interval, the group could become self-sustaining. Enhancing parental information and support will be of mutual benefit to children, parents, and school staff.

Not all school mental health professionals are experienced in leading groups, and some may be resistant. If they lack this expertise administrative support should provide for inservice training, or encourage released time for professional development, and provide adequate supervision. Mental health professionals must be in charge of such groups. Groups are not intended to be casual "club-like" meetings; they should be working, productive discussions in which serious issues about feelings and family functioning are considered (Berger, 1987; Sonnershein-Schneider & Baird, 1980). This view contrasts with Knoff's assertion that group interventions should focus on ways to minimize the school-related social-emotional and academic-intellectual effects of the divorce (Knoff, 1987).

Issues do arise spontaneously in both child and parent groups. These need to be addressed sensitively, and can be handled confidentially by a skilled mental health professional, who will also be able to make a referral to the appropriate community agency or private practitioner when more intensive individual therapy is required. Groups with children require the approval of the appropriate parent, who should also understand what the format will be, how family issues will be handled, and what kind of communication will take place.

Teacher-Conducted Classroom Meetings

In addition to the divorce groups led by mental health professionals, teachers can plan many activities for all the children, not just those going through trauma (Newton Public Schools, 1986). A classroom-based activity sequence developed by one of the authors (Warschauer) sensitizes children to others' expression of feelings and the variety of family configurations represented in the class. The goal is to provide a base of trust among the children and their teacher around issues of separation and divorce. It is important that a comfortable, confidential, voluntary, and nonjudgmental climate be established regarding disclosures, expressing of feelings, and discussion of family styles. Four or more class meetings provide a sequential process from generalized expression and recognition of feelings to the feelings specific to divorce and separation.

Format for Teacher-Conducted Classroom Meetings

The first group meeting takes about 30 minutes and focuses broadly on feelings. Group rules are established to enhance listening skills. The children write a feeling on a slip of paper such as "anger," "shyness," or "fear." Responses are listed on the board and the children are encouraged to give examples of their feelings. A discussion centering on appropriate ways to deal with these feelings is recommended. The second meeting, which also lasts about 30 minutes, deals with sibling relationships. Below are five questions that are to be answered in written form (children in kindergarten through second grade may need to have verbal responses in a circle format).

1. My place in the family is the _____ child. (youngest, oldest, etc.).
2. I would like my place in the family to be_____.
3. The best part about being where I am in the family is_____.
4. The worst part about being where I am in the family is_____.
5. I wish_____.

(After completing the five statements, children are encouraged to share their responses and discuss them in the meeting.)

The third group meeting, lasting about 40 minutes, deals with relationships in all types of families. The children are asked to draw a picture of their family in the place where the family gathers most often. In the discussion that follows, the children describe who is in the pictures and what the family is doing. The teacher can stress the variety of lifestyles represented in the pictures, such as single parent, extended family, stepparents, combined families, grandparents, or other adults sharing the household. This needs to be handled carefully and sensitively, without value judgments.

The fourth meeting, which may require two or three sessions, deals directly with divorce and separation. The suggested activity is to read a story about these issues to the whole class to stimulate class discussion. Books for this purpose can be found at a school or local library (Newton Public Schools, 1986; Pardek, 1985; Winfield, 1983). After the books have been read, a class discussion is easily initiated by the teacher and should deal directly with issues regarding separation and divorce. Some teachers feel more comfortable having a counselor, social worker, or school psychologist present for these discussions. Communication can also be stimulated by presenting some type of questionnaire as the following:

Mark *A* if you agree or *D* if you disagree:

— Parents should not get a divorce until their children grow up.
— Sometimes when parents divorce it is the fault of the children.
— It is better not to tell anyone if your parents divorce.
— Once people marry they should never get a divorce.

(Other similar statements can be elicited from the children.)

Curriculum Areas

In addition to the four class meetings, other important curriculum areas can deal directly with divorce and separation issues.

Creative writing can be quite helpful in allowing children to express feelings and release tensions. Assignments should be broad to allow all pupils to write about issues that have emotional meaning for them and yet specific enough to allow children involved in the divorce process to feel supported in expressing their feelings. Possible topics might include "Things I'd Like to Tell My Family," "Dear Abby," "Happiness Is . . . ; Sadness Is . . . ," or "Once Upon a Time There Was a Loving Stepmother." It is important for children to know that their writing need not be shared with others.

Similarly, *art* allows children to express emotions as well as talent. Animals and imaginative characters can depict many easily identifiable real-life situations. Family activities portrayed in paint or other media often reveal far more than the factual event.

Dramatics puts children in touch with their own feelings. It can be a full-fledged play, a reenactment of a happening, roleplaying, or pantomime. Materials that could be used as bases for dramatization might include an actual problem conveyed by a child, an external source such as an incomplete story with alternative endings, a short story, a poem, or a story written by the teacher for a specific purpose. The emphasis should be on feelings and relationships. Pantomime might be used to increase awareness and accurate perception of body language and other nonverbal communication. The sequence might progress from pantomime to role playing.

When selecting the actors, teachers should ask children to play roles that will help them gain personal insight or empathy for others. Children can benefit from playing roles with which they identify or that are opposite to those with which they identify. A teasing child might be asked to play the role of the teaser and another time that of the victim. It is important that all actors be willing participants; a

role should never be forced on a child. A discussion of the impact of the acting experience should follow immediately. This sharing must be heard nonjudgmentally by children and teachers.

Studying *literature* in the classroom is another way for children to begin to understand their own feelings. Exploring the emotions, needs, interpersonal relationships, and social problems of literary characters is often much safer psychologically for children than exploring their own personal struggles. Through sensitive discussions about the emotions of characters in a story, followed by listening to the feelings of individuals identifying with the characters because of similar experiences, the children are better prepared for free and articulate communication in class meetings and for social problem solving.

By its very nature, *poetry* sensitizes children and helps them to express thoughts and emotions they might previously feel hesitant about. This can occur through both reading and writing.

Although not formally a part of the curriculum, divorce is often a very real element within the contemporary classroom. By acknowledging its reality and including related activities within the curriculum, a sensitive treacher can alleviate the stress not only of those children directly involved but also of all the others who cannot help being affected.

SUMMARY AND DISCUSSION

Because divorce is such a common life crisis in contemporary society, it influences children from intact as well as nonintact families. We have discussed various possibilities of intervention to ameliorate these harmful influences of divorce. These suggestions have all been made from a systems perspective. This ecological systems approach ensures that the entire process of planning for a community is rooted in the reality and needs of that community (Auerswald, 1966). When the community is a school system and programs will be designed to address the effects of divorce, considering the various subsystems of the school structure (e.g., administration, individual school, individual classroom, family, teacher, principal, and student) makes it possible to intervene more effectively.

To plan for effective use of resources, to streamline existing programs, and to develop new ones, administrators should view these various subsystems according to the way they interface. They can also be considered as pivotal links at which educational pressure could be brought to bear to effect change. The focus of administrators and school staff should be on what Auerswald (1966) called the "transactional arena of each interface" (p. 212) which, by definition, ultimately informs and suggests which parts of the system need to be changed. This philosophy connects to Bateson's (1979) view that the whole is more than the sum of its parts.

Plas (1986) described a liaison approach similar to Auerwald's conceptual framework, in that it is grounded in ecological, transactional, and systems theory. According to Plas (1986), the liaison specialist in the school follows a seven-stage process: (1) entering the system, (2) mapping the ecology, (3) assessing the ecology, (4) creating the vision of change, (5) coordinating and communicating, (6) reassessing, and (7) evaluating (p. 140). In this way there is a cost-effective as well as creative utilization of current and projected services.

In creating a vision of change, school administration and pupil personnel specialists conceptualized a circular, rather than linear, process of causality, ultimately influencing the thrust of the intervention. The committee viewed the unit of child/family/community as interlocking and focused on a preventive approach within the school system which impacted on all system members. A similar approach was reported at the National Conference of Social workers (McGann & Strauss, 1985).

Our program attempted to appreciate the family systems background while also recognizing that the child within the system might be emotionally needy and should legitimately be the focus of the direct service. Ideally, meetings with the child and his or her reconstituted family would be offered by mental health professionals in the context of the school.

Our experience as members of the Divorce and Separation Committee has confirmed the original concept that school personnel must view the epidemic divorce rate as it affects the system (i.e., child, parent, teacher, staff, administration, and community). If school personnel acknowledge that they have a preventive role in ameliorating stress and thereby increasing learning, then the choice to intervene is obvious. It then becomes an issue of what interventions to initiate and implement. We believe that if components of a system communicate and interact, each will enrich the other and the overall system. A proactive school system forges a bond between family and school, which will have a circular effect in many areas beyond the focus of divorce.

References

Allers, R. (1980). Helping children understand divorce. *Today's Education, 69,* 26–29.

Auerswald, E. (1966). Interdisciplinary versus ecological approach. *Family Process, 7,* 202–215.

Bateson, G. (1979). *Mind and nautre.* New York: Dutton.

Beal, E. (1979). Children of divorce: A family systems perspective. *Journal of Social Issues, 35,* 140–154.

Berger, S. (1987, January). School-based support groups: Help for divorced children. *The Boston Parents' Paper,* p. 4.

Bradt, J. O., & Bradt, C. M. (1986). Resources for remarried families. In M. A. Karpel (Ed.), *Family resources: The hidden partner in family therapy* (pp. 272–284). New York: Guilford Press.

Burns, C., & Brassard, M. (1982). A look at the single parent family: Implications for the school psychologist. *Psychology in the Schools, 19,* 478–494.

Cantor, D. (1977). School based divorce groups for children of divorce. *Journal of Divorce, 1,* 183–187.

Carlson, C. (1987a). Children and single parent homes. In A. Thomas & J. Grimes (Eds.), *Children's needs: Psychological perspectives* (pp. 560–571). Washington, D.C.: National Association of School Psychologists.

Carlson, C. (1987b). Helping students deal with divorce-related issues. In *School-based affective and social interventions* (pp. 121–138). New York: Haworth Press.

Carter, B., & McGoldrick, M. (Eds.). 1988. *The changing family life cycle: A framework for family therapy.* (2nd ed.). New York: Gardner Press.

Diamond, S. (1985). *Helping children of divorce.* New York: Schocken.

Drake, E. (1981). Helping children cope with divorce: The role of the school. In I. Stuart & L. Abt (Eds.), *Children of separation and divorce: Management and treatment* (pp. 147–173). New York: Van Nostrand Reinhold.

Drake, E., & Shellenberger, S. (1979). Children of separation and divorce: A review of school programs and implications for the psychologist. *School Psychology Review, 10,* 54–61.

Elmore, J. (1986). *The teacher and the child of divorce.* Paper presented at the Annual Families Conference, Ogden, UT, September 12. (ERIC Document Reproduction Service MFOI/PCOI.)

Fine, M. (1980). *Parent education.* New York: Academic Press.

Gardner, R. (1977). *The parents' book about divorce.* New York: Doubleday.

Ginsburg, E. (1979). In the interests of children: A view from the bench. *Boston Bar Journal, 23,* 21–24.

Glick, P. (1979). Children of divorced parents in demographic perspective. *Journal of Social Issues, 35,* 176.

Goldstein, A. (1985). *Establishing a group counselling program for elementary school children who have experienced parental divorce.* Practicum Paper (043) Project Description (141) Nova University Journal Announcment: RIEDEC85.

Green, V., & Schaefer, L. (1984). The effects of personal divorce experience on teacher perceptions of children of divorce. *Journal of Divorce, 8,* 107–110.

Guidabaldi, J., Cleminshaw, H. K., Perry, J., & McLoughlin, C. S. (1983). The impact of parental divorce on children: Report of the nationwide NASP study. *School Psychology Review, 12,* 300–323.

Guidabaldi, J., & Perry, J. (1985). Divorce and mental health sequelae for children: A two year follow-up of a nationwide sample. *Journal of the American Academy of Child Psychiatry, 24,* 531–537.

Hetherinton, E. (1979). Divorce: A child's perspective. *American Psychologist, 34,* 851–858.

Hetherington, E., Cox, M., & Cox, R. (1978). Effects of divorce on parents and children. In M. Lamb (Ed.), *Nontraditional families: Parenting and child development* (pp. 233–288). Hillsdale, NJ: Erlbaum.

Hill, B. M., Brent, & Mathews (1983). *Effective child guidance: An educator's guidebook.* Nova University. (ERIC Document Reproduction Service No. ED 258-702.)

Holzman, T. (Producer). (1982). *When divorce comes to school* (videotape). Riverwoods, IL: Film Ideas.

Holzman, T. (1984). Schools can provide help for children of divorce. *American School Board Journal, 171*(5), 46–47.

Jellinek, M., & Slovik, L. (1981). Current concepts in psychiatry. Divorce: Impact on children. *New England Journal of Medicine, 305,* 557–560.

Jones, R. (1968). *Fantasy and feeling in education.* New York: University Press.

Kalter, N., Picker, J., & Lesowitz, M. (1984). School based developmental facilitation groups for children of divorce: A preventive intervention. *American Journal of Orthopsychiatry, 54,* 613–623.

Knoff, H. (1987). Divorce. In A. Thomas & J. Grimes (Eds.), *Children's needs: Psychological perspectives* (pp. 173–181). Washington, DC: National Association of School Psychologists.

Kurdek, L. (1981). An integrative perspective on children's divorce adjustment. *American Psychologist, 36,* 856–866.

Kurdek, L., Blisk, D., & Siesky, A. (1981). Correlates of children's long-term adjustment to their parents' divorce. *Developmental Psychology, 17,* 565–579.

McGann, J., & Strauss (1985, January).

Building a network for children of divorce. Paper presented at the annual meeting of the National Association of Social Workers. New Orleans, LA.

Montalvo (1979). Source unknown.

Newton Public Schools. (1986). *Divorce: Guidelines for teachers.* (Available from Department of Pupil Services and Special Education, 100 Walnut St., Newtonville, MA.)

Nichols, W. C., & Everett, C. A. (1986). *Systemic family therapy: An integrative approach.* New York: Guilford Press.

O'Connor, W., & Lubin, B. (Eds.). (1984). *Ecological approaches to clinical and community psychology.* New York: Wiley.

Pardek, J. (1985, January). *Helping children cope with the changing family through bibliotherapy.* Paper presented at the annual meeting of the National Association of Social Workers, New Orleans, LA.

Plas, J. (1986). *Systems psychology in the schools.* New York: Pergamon.

Punger, D. (1984). The non-traditional family: Legal problems for schools. *School Law Bulletin, 15*(2), 1–6.

Shea, C. (1982). Schools and non-nuclear families: Recasting relationships. (ERIC Document Reproduction Service MFOI/PCO2.)

Shoul, R. (1985). *Mobilizing a school system to address the issues of divorce and changing patterns of family living.* Newton, MA: Newton Public Schools.

Sonnenshein-Schneider, M., & Baird, K. (1980). Group counseling children of divorce in the elementary schools: Understanding process and technique. *Personnel and Guidance Journal, 59*(2), 88–91.

State of Massachusetts. (1986). *Interim report of the Special Commission Relative to Divorce.* (Available from Special Commission on Divorce, State House, Boston, MA 02133.)

Stolberg, A. L., & Cullen, P. M. (1983). Preventive interventions for families of divorce: The Divorce Adjustment Project. In L. Kurdek (Ed.), *Children and divorce* (pp. 71–82). New Directions for Child Development, No. 19.

Stolberg, A., & Garrison, K. (1981). Children's support group: A procedures manual. (DHEW Publications No.: 1 ROI MH 34462-02.)

Summak, S. (1984). *An annotated bibliography of the literature dealing with the effect of divorce on school age children and how schools can meet their needs.* (ERIC Document Reproduction Service No. MFOL/PCO3.)

Visher, E. B., & Visher, J. S. (1979). *Stepfamilies: A guide to working with stepparents and stepchildren.* New York: Brunner/Mazel.

Visher, E., & Visher, J. S. (1988). *Old loyalties, new ties: Therapeutic strategies with stepfamilies.* New York: Bunner/Mazel.

Wallerstein, J., & Blakeslee, S. A. (1989). *Second chances—Men, women, and children: A decade after divorce.* New York: Ticknor & Fields.

Wallerstein, J., & Kelly, J. (1980). *Surviving the breakup: How children and parents cope with divorce.* New York: Doubleday.

Whitfield, E., & Freeland, K. (1981). Divorce and children: What teachers can do. *Child Education, 58*(2), 88–89.

Wilkinson, G., & Bleck, R. (1977). Children's divorce groups. *Elementary School Guidance and Counseling, 11,* 205–213.

Winfield, E. (1983). Books for changing families to read and share. *PTA Today, 8*(7), 22–23.

25

Family Therapy in the Schools: The Pragmatics of Merging Systemic Approaches into Educational Realities

MARLENE A. MERRILL
Harvey County Special Education Cooperative
Newton, Kansas

ROBERT J. CLARK
Topeka Public Schools, Kansas

CHERI D. VARVIL
Topeka Public Schools, Kansas

CAREY A. VAN SICKLE
Topeka Public Schools, Kansas

LAURA J. McCALL
East Central Kansas Cooperative in Education
Baldwin City, Kansas

HISTORICALLY, clinical services in the schools have focused on providing programs that ultimately enhance the education of children. In today's complex and socially changing world, school-based mental health services have come to include traditional psychological diagnostic or social work asessments as well as individual and family counseling. In U.S.D. 501, Topeka Public Schools, a unique opportunity has occurred in the delivery of mental health services. Participants in what we affectionately call "Family Therapy Seminar" have become providers of family therapy. This chapter describes the background of this group, the model of family therapy used, the working structure of the group, and the efficacy of our approach. This model is based on a commitment to supervision, a reliance on staff referrals, and what we believe is strong administrative credibility and support even with the budgetary realities of the 1990s.

Family Therapy in the Context of the Schools

Because the school and the family have a mutual interest in the education of a child, it has been inevitable that the school, the child, and the family are linked together in an interchangeable systemic ecology. Systems theory (Bateson, 1971) has been useful in the analysis of home-school dysfunctioning because it considers the individual in all of the systems where he or she participates and evaluates the individuals in the system's interactions. One avenue of intervention derived from a systems view has been where the school and family were brought together in a joint interview. Here, a structured strategy was utilized to discuss expectations and to clarify communication patterns in order to develop a remediation plan for the student (Aponte, 1976; Friedman, 1969; Fine & Holt, 1983; Plas, 1986).

The child participates in a network of contexts, which is defined as an *ecosystem* (Hobbs, 1966, Fine, 1985; Gilmore & Glatthorn, 1982). Friedman (1973) states there is a correlation between a family's dysfunctional patterns and the child's school problems. The connection between school and home systems is a significant factor in the success of an educational program.

When a child is not successful at school, one of the first areas to receive "blame" is the home system. At times, parents who are in pain with regard to their child's behavior or progress in school will reach out for answers from school staff. One traditional response is to refer the family to a mental health resource rather than considering the parents' concern as the purview of the schools.

The contributions from family therapy theory place school-based clinicians in a powerful position to utilize the family as change agent where the child is presenting behavior problems (DiCocco, 1986; Okun, 1984; Conoley, 1987b; Haley, 1976). Clinicians trained in variations of a family therapy model are able to gain strategic entry into addressing family problems.

The literature has presented a wide range of problems where family therapy has proven effective. The reader is referred to Chapter 28 in this book by Agnes Donovan, which discusses the broad applications of family systems intervention.

When family therapy was first considered as a school intervention, psychology and school social work literature gave little support to this notion of school personnel providing family therapy services (Petrie & Piersel, 1982; Shellenberger, 1981). In fact, this literature talked more about methods to increase the number of kept appointments than suggesting a role as family therapist (Zins & Hopkins, 1981).

Many staff members of the Topeka Public School System felt there was a need for family therapy to be available in the school. The need to provide family therapy was not due to the lack of community resources. In fact, the Menninger Foundation, through consultations with our special services staff, encouraged us to provide a wide range of direct services; they validated our feelings that we were on the front line of observed need and that many families would use the schools with which they were familiar rather than go to a outside agency (E. Jansen, personal communication, 1978).

OUR ECOSYSTEM

Topeka Public Schools serves a fairly typical midwest urban center. As in most urban areas, declining enrollment is straining the tax base, and cuts in student services have been the focus of more than one board of education meeting. Presently serving slightly over 15,000 students, Topeka Public Schools has three distinct departments serving the emotional needs of its students: counseling department, school psychologists, and school social workers.

The counseling department, under the administration of student support services in regular education, presently has 6 elementary counselors serving 26 schools, 7 middle school staff serving 5 schools, and 11 counselors serving our 3 high schools. Within special education are administered 17 MSW level school social workers and 22 Ed.S. or equivalent school psychologists. The state of Kansas provides reimbursement for these special education staff without the requirement that they work solely with handicapped students, though a significant number of staff are assigned to specific special education programs. In general, our social workers and psychologists work throughout our school district and provide a wide variety of services.

Any discussion of an ecosystem within a large bureaucracy requires recognition of the need for administrative support. The family therapy program exists within Topeka Public Schools because the program garnered administrative support. Initially the program formalized its contract with the administrator in charge in a manner similar to the establishment of a professional inservice training program. Topeka Public Schools has continued to support additional services such as family therapy because the program offers another alternative for interventions directed to children's needs. In addition, Topeka Public Schools appreciates the connections to families this intervention offers to the school system.

For staff, the family therapy program provides inservice experience in addition to, not in place of, normal job responsibilities. We have attempted to take the "sting" out of working longer or working evening hours by providing some flexibility in our work day. Currently a plan is now in place to allow for substitution of clinical services for a portion of, for instance, evaluation service.

EVOLUTION—THE FIRST FIVE YEARS

The program to be described is now in its ninth year. It evolved during the years 1982 to 1987. Five of the original eight people continue to participate in the family therapy program. Participants initially entered the program primarily to gain professional knowledge and to increase clinical skills. These benefits appear to offset the fact that learning family therapy takes a great deal of time and intensive effort. The mean length of participation has been 2.47 years in a range of 1 to 5 years of participation. Approximately 30 percent of the support services staff have participated at various times in the seminar.

The original structure consisted of eight "trainees" and one supervisor/ coordinator. Because there was a strong conviction among the group that supervision and mutual support were necessary to learn and practice a clinical service such as family therapy, the structure included reading and group discussion, supervision for each co-therapy team, and active practice of family therapy. Each of four co-therapy teams treated a minimum of two families the first year. The seminar group was used for lectures on the family therapy concepts by the supervisor/coordinator, to discuss reading, and for case presentations. During the second year, the structure remained basically the same, with two exceptions: "trainees" could choose to do therapy alone and all participants began to take more responsibility for presenting content from the literature during seminar sessions.

Although the supervisor/coordinator

has always maintained a strong leadership role, the group as a whole has been involved in decisions about the direction the program should take. In the fourth year of the program, we experimented with peer supervision and the supervisor began taking a less active role. This effort was not successful and the group began to lose the cohesiveness we felt necessary to continue. As a result, a decision was made at the end of that year for the supervisor to take more control again.

In the fifth year we had a influx of several new members and we had to develop a method of presenting basic materials to them. This was done by the supervisor in a separate group meeting, which doubled the time the supervisor spent in seminar meetings. This added workload was a significant strain. Presently the original participants are sharing in the supervision caseload with the supervisor/coordinator acting as consultant in case supervision. New members are receiving basic content instruction in a separate seminar where the teaching load is now shared among the original seminar participants.

Although the literature we have studied has concentrated on the "classics" of family therapy, such as Minuchin (1974), Haley (1976), Bowen (1978), Papp (1977), and Ackerman (1966), we have endeavored to study current topics such as Palazzori's invariant prescription (Simon, 1987; Boscolo, Cecchin, Hoffman, & Penn, 1987), therapeutic rituals (Imber-Black, 1988), solution-focused therapy (Molnar & de Shazer, 1987), school interventions (Conoley, 1987a; Carlson, 1987; Power & Bartholomew, 1987; Paget, 1987), and the future of family therapy (Fish & Piercy, 1987; Nichols, 1987; Dell, 1986a, 1986b; Duhl, 1986).

Late in the fifth year, in order to address questions concerning effectiveness and practicality of the program, the group developed and administered surveys to all therapists who had participated in the seminar, referral sources, and a sample of participating client families. The therapist survey gathered information about the program components of the seminar, a cost/benefit analysis of the staff use, and therapist views of the client families' course of treatment and outcome.

This survey was returned by all therapists who had participated with the seminar longer than one year for a return rate of 79 percent (n = 19). Additionally, 17 client families were surveyed by phone to obtain their perceptions of the treatment and their rating of the outcome. Due to the small numbers of families that were contracted to respond to the survey, the results were unreliable and told us little about client satisfaction. This problem was a direct result of inadequate record keeping.

DESCRIPTION OF PROGRAM

The description of our present program consists of its administrative structure, the referral process, logistics, seminar, and the model for therapy.

Administrative Structure

The supervisor/coordinator facilitates the family therapy program. Administrative sanction was sought and work time was provided for family therapy program activities. The supervisor/coordinator organizes the seminar's instructional contract. As referral coordinator, the supervisor/coordinator assigns participants to cotherapy teams and presents intake cases for discussion during seminar meetings. After the cases are assigned, the coordinator facilitates supervision contacts with the therapists assigned to the family. Interestingly enough, the number of cases referred to the family therapy program has never outweighed the number of cases the program could successfully serve in any given year.

Working within a school system has required us to develop a public relations grapevine to generate family referrals each school year. This process has been successfully accomplished through a series of events. Initially, at the beginning of each school year, the supervisor of our group has sent out a memo announcing our existence and desire to work with families.

At the beginning of the 1983–84 school year, four members of the seminar presented at a Special Education Orientation Inservice. The presentation, "Family Therapy Used to Address School Problems", served many purposes:

1. It introduced our group to special education personnel (teachers, social workers, psychologists) as a viable alternative to referring families to outside agencies.
2. It focused on the manifestation of problems in the classroom.
3. It provided a general description of family therapy.
4. It explained how referrals could be made.
5. It demonstrated our support from administration.

Since this presentation, most of our efforts to tell people about our group have come through our daily contacts with parents, students, and staff as a function of our jobs as school social workers and psychologists.

Referral Process

A core group of colleagues (school psychologists, social workers, principals, and counselors) refer families to the Family Therapy Program. In most circumstances, referrals begin when a parent relates having problems with his or her child and wants treatment. Other times, when completing comprehensive evaluations and formulating recommendations, referrals for therapy are made. The staff person will recommend our group as a possibility. (The fact that, as patrons of Topeka Public Schools, they can get family therapy at no cost can be enticing.) With their permission, the staff person contacts the supervisor/coordinator of the group. The referring person provides basic information—a description of the problem, the names of family members, and the school(s) their children attend. The referring person is then asked to call the family and tell them who to contact. The assumption behind this step is that there is therapeutic power in calling and asking for help.

When the family calls, in-depth information is collected. The contact person attempts to obtain a detailed description of the family, each of its members, the nature of the problem, whether they have had therapy before, and when the family will be available to meet. This is also an opportunity to explain rules to the potential client. The entire family is expected to attend therapy. A team of therapists will work with the family. Families are videotaped and the tapes are used for training purposes.

The issue of record keeping was clearly brought before the group as we proceeded to gather information for this chapter. The referral information about the family and information about treatment interventions and progress was previously maintained by the case therapists. Since there was no standard method to maintain information, it was difficult to retrieve treatment information on previously treated family therapy cases. The seminar participants have now developed a computerized data tracking system for all current family therapy cases. This system will maintain a record of family identifying data, what the referring concern was, the family's problem list, duration of treatment, termination outcome, as well as names of the therapists and their supervisors.

To ensure educational and therapy quality control, only a limited number of cases are accepted. Cases are selected carefully to ensure they might be appropriately treated with our model and time frame. The same model of therapy is basically utilized for all the cases we accept.

Many factors have contributed to the success of our referral system. We have a strong following of colleagues who believe in what we are doing and are continuing to send us families. Our school system has provided the daily flexibility that allows us to serve families beyond our regular work hours. We have ensured that we have a strong and supportive leader. These factors and a supportive administration have provided an atmosphere that has motivated us to continue learning about and treating families.

Logistics

Families have been seen in a variety of different school facilities. In the beginning, a large conference room in the Special Education Support Center was used because it housed offices for many of the seminar's members. The video camera and equipment was stored there as well, so it was quite convenient. Eventually, a one-way mirror was installed in a seminar room within this area. This was used for live supervision and served its purpose well. Unfortunately, our offices have since been moved and we have inherited a family conference room not as well equipped as the last, but it is functional. We hope to install another one-way mirror in the future.

Families are sometimes seen in their homes as a strategic move to, for example, engage a key family member who would not or physically cannot get to sessions elsewhere. We also have chosen to see families in schools for convenience sake and to give us visibility to those to whom we are accountable.

Seminar

The literature from family training centers generally suggests that programs either present a hodgepodge of readings or focus on the work of a single well-known therapist (Kniskern & Gurman, 1980). We have attempted to present a single, integrated approach as problem-solving family therapy and this has been a strength of our program. The instructional component has been perceived to be very important by therapist participants, and most participants rated themselves to be more active than passive in their learning (mean was 2.47 on a 5-point scale).

To ensure the quality and support of our work, we maximized the use of a group learning model. The group has provided us with a positive learning environment, and we gave each other feedback and encouragement.

The first step in our group training model is to collectively negotiate the contract. A clear and explicit agreement is as important as the goal of developing a cohesive group. We meet bimonthly for two hours (using one hour of our lunch time) and attempt to reschedule if any member has a conflict. The application of the seminar contract between participants parallels the application of our model of therapy.

Initially the supervisor/coordinator took the responsibility for developing a reading list and didactic materials. The starting point is a clear, concise presentation of the use of the model. The model was *not* developed by the group and was not open for negotiation. This procedure ensured that the model retains its integrity. Co-therapy teams presented videotapes of their work and requested specific and/ or general feedback.

At the seminar meeting, an ongoing agenda item is the discussion and the assignment of all new cases. The information obtained about each family is shared and the contact person is questioned. The therapists who are interested in a case may request it or it may be assigned to a team that needs a family. It is the team's responsibility to contact the referral source with information about who the family is to call. When the family calls for the first appointment, it is the team's responsibility to reiterate the rules and negotiate appointment time and place.

The amount of time it takes to do family therapy varies. The seminar has allowed for individual needs to be met. According to the 1987 survey, seminar participants spend an average of five hours per week in seeing two to three families, preparing for sessions with their co-therapist, receiving supervision, and additionally reading and attending seminar meetings.

The structure of the seminar's instructional component includes group discussion, readings, lectures, roleplaying, and relating work skills to therapy skills. Lectures and readings have formed the basis of the learning or instructional component of the training program. The supervisor/coordinator has developed lectures to assist in participant assimilation of family therapy concepts and therapist skills necessary to practice family therapy.

Although each participant entered the family therapy program with a high level of clinical skills, these skills have been refined and participants have increased their expertise as therapists. Participation in the group instruction has been rated as being very important (mean was 1.60 on a 5-point scale). Seminar participants ranked their preferences regarding methods of instruction as viewing tapes, verbal discussion, reading, lecture, and roleplaying.

MODEL FOR THERAPY

Theoretical Assumptions

The family is a system with individual members who function in certain roles. The family functions through a series of patterns of behavior that Haley (1976) calls *sequences*. These patterns change over time, depending on a wide range of factors such as lifestage of family members (Carter & McGoldrick, 1980), history of family, stresses or demands on the family, and community or school impact. Life patterns can be functional at one point in time and become dysfunctional as the family system need evolves to a different level of functioning.

Minuchin (1974, 1985) proposed a structural assessment of a family's functioning. In particular the relevant structural components are boundaries, alignment, and power (Aponte & Van Deusen, 1981; Hoffman, 1981; Carlson, 1987) in assessing the family's relationships, rules for participation, and family roles (Coopersmith, 1985; Rosenberg, 1983). Through observing repeated patterns of interaction, the structure of the family is revealed (Paget, 1987).

A particular family sequence can be functional or dysfunctional over time. Clearly, family life patterns and the quality of life that individuals in the family system experience vary. In addition, ways in which a family learns vary. Using Bateson's (1971) theory about levels of change (Hoffman, 1981), we analyze how a family learns. One of our tenets is to avoid making decisions on what is good or bad, healthy or unhealthy, or what might be wrong for the family. The task is to assist the family members to decide what *their* problems are from *their view* and what particular life pattern would more successfully deal with their problem areas. This process of family choices is made through a series of assignments. Prior to the assignment phase of therapy, each individual family member's view of the problem is thoroughly explored.

The Process of Therapy

The first step the therapist must take is to involve as many relevant family members as possible in the therapy process. Various strategies are used to ensure that all members attend (i.e., the therapist may directly contact and ensure the hesitant party that he or she is important to this process). If a significant family member still decides not to attend, the therapists examine the potential for success without this particular family member. In starting therapy without a significant family member, therapists always make clear to the family their doubts of success but state their willingness to explore the possibilities for therapy.

As with almost all other therapy modalities, the therapeutic relationship with the family is very significant for the success of family therapy. This relationship starts from the first phone call and spans the entire therapeutic process. During the first session the engagement process continues. Initially, there is a phase of socialization that is very important in making the family feel comfortable.

Problem analysis also starts with the first session. No interventions are made until a clear contract of problems the family wants to address exists. Paying close attention to the language used by individuals in the family enhances an understanding of what family members are expressing with regard to their specific problem.

For example, a mother says she is frustrated and has a problem with her 18-year-old daughter sneaking out of the house every night at 10:30. One might assume that this mother wants her daughter safely tucked in bed each evening instead of out about town. When this mother clarified her view, however, the real problem was that her daughter was leaving by the window and not the door.

It is critical to avoid restating a family member's view in any different form than the way the statement was made originally. Actual key words that the family members have used to describe problems are important for the therapist to use for establishing rapport, but, more importantly, specific language is a tool the therapist uses to gain a clearer understanding of the family system without interpreting or making assumptions about what has been said.

Development of the problem list is similar to the format suggested by Watzlawick, Weakland, and Fisch (1974). *Each family member is asked the following:*

1. Describe how he or she would like the family changed through the family therapy process.
2. List some small specific indicators that the family is improving.
3. List the solutions they have tried.

These questions take a great deal of clarification to ensure the therapist understands each person's view. Small children may be asked the first question with a twist—If you had a magic wand, what would you change about your family? The answers are unique to the problems that a particular person is experiencing within the family system. A mother says she wants her son to complete his homework. The father wants the homework done and wants his son to respect him. The sister wants her brother to stay out of her room. The son with the problem identifies his sister's teasing him as a problem. All problems are noted and listed to be used in future sessions.

Each family member contributes his or her view of what would have to happen for him or her to know things were improving. A mother might want less fighting. Rather than having 10 fights a week, the mother could tolerate 5 fights a week. Parents can easily list the solutions that they have tried to remedy the problem—grounding, loss of allowance, spanking, and so on. This information is gathered so the therapist can be informed of the solutions that were tried, but failed, so they subsequently will not suggest unworkable solutions, Also, the therapist may establish a set of solutions that he or she can then utilize.

Taking a Baseline

Family members are asked to take a baseline in one or more problem areas. Specifically, the family is asked to count how many times that particular behavior occurs. Frequently, different family members discuss the same problem area but emphasize a different facet of the problem. It is important not to allow other family members to influence the reporting of problems by a particular family member. The therapists are sensitive to someone saying "what she really means" and attempt to return the focus to what the first person actually said.

Let's say, for example, that a teenaged boy says, "I am tired of my mother being on my case about taking out the trash." The boy is asked to count how many times his mother is "on his case." The mother is told clearly and sincerely not to change her behavior. A measure of current functioning is important to measuring improvement. This process helps the therapist discover how this particular family completes an assignment. It also starts the family in joining with the therapist in a process of successful therapy.

Families and/or family members have different learning styles. The learning styles of a family is noted and used for developing assignments. For example, some family members may learn best from the set of alternatives that the family has already utilized. Another family may have to experience a newly sequenced set of behaviors in order to change a family pattern (Bateson, 1971). An assignment generally needs to have enough impact to create a new experience (Haley, 1976; Madanes, 1981; Weeks & L'Abate, 1982).

The series of assignments starts by focusing on a problem from the list that is *not* the most serious problem. It is important to start with a less powerful problem in order for the family to learn how to be successful. This means starting in the middle or lower end of a prioritized problem list. It is important to select a problem in which the family will be invested but not be motivated to sabotage the therapist's efforts.

After the baseline measurement is taken, the second assignment is to make the easiest change either from the family's set of alternatives or from outside, depending on the best guess as to family style. This is followed by a series of assignments geared toward helping a family explore a variety of sequences surrounding a particular problem area. This exploration forces a family to select an alternative sequence that creates a more comfortable life pattern. If a family does not complete an assignment in one week, the assignment is reassigned after the therapists explore whether a small change might ensure completion of that assignment.

The pattern of giving assignments is repeated for each problem on the priority problem list. Typically, a family can develop a style of learning how to change sequences regarding a problem after three or four problems and feel successful about therapy and their problem list. After this process, the family moves to the natural process of termination of therapy. An important component of the model is an open-door policy. Families are always welcome to return to therapy.

SUPERVISION

Garfield (1977) and Kniskern and Gurman (1980) state that the therapist gains the most instruction on "how to be" a therapist in supervision. The literature suggests that techniques of supervision processes vary widely and are highly influenced by the supervisor's own theoretical and therapeutic orientation (Kniskern & Gurman, 1980). Everett and Koerpel (1986) conclude that the level of research regarding family therapy supervision lacks a consistent theoretical basis, lacks sophistication of research methodology, and lacks abundant research interest.

Supervision is perceived as an important component of the Topeka Public Schools model, and most therapist participants in the seminar have supervision in alternate sessions. Initially, the supervisor was tyically consulted after each session. Supervision is a strength of our program conponent because it is perceived as a positive experience where ideas are exchanged objectively, new skills are learned, and accountability for the therapy is provided.

It has been our experience and was stated by Cross and Brown (1983) that beginning therapists value more directive supervision, whereas more advanced therapists value a less directive and less structured supervisory relationship. It appears that the supervisee's perception of effective supervision is based on the supervisor's expertise and interpersonal trustworthiness (Heppner & Handley, 1982; Friedlander & Snyder, 1983; Worthington, 1984a, 1984b).

It also appears that supervision under our model differentiates between be-

ginning trainees and more experienced trainees, with more responsibility in providing therapy and assisting in supervision of others, unlike the findings of Kersey (1982) and Fisher and Embree (1980). We believe that the strength of the supervision component is what helps our model endure.

In the survey, respondents were asked to rate the importance of supervision as a program component. On a 5-point scale (1 being Very Important and 5 being Not At All Important), the supervision component was rated a mean score of 1.20. Another way of assessing importance is the frequency of use of each component. Respondents were asked to rank how frequently they use supervision (1 being Every Session and 5 being Never). The mean response was 2.40 and no one responded Never. Generally seminar participants sought supervision every other or every third session with the family. In an open-ended question the benefits of supervision were stated by participants as: the importance of learning new clinical skills, the opportunity to obtain another perspective, and help in generating ideas and intervention possibilities, as well as solving problems and helping with co-therapist issues. The only problem noted was difficulty in scheduling supervision sessions.

CO-THERAPY

The program has relied heavily on the use of co-therapy for learning to practice family therapy (Keith & Whitaker, 1983). The stages of co-therapy relationships were studied in order to utilize the relationship in an effective manner. Co-therapists are paired by similar experience levels. The supervisor/coordinator of the group originally supervised all the cases. The co-therapy team would come together in supervision with the material on a case and then, through the supervision process, would map out the appropriate steps for the model (Dimalanta & Hightower, 1986). We frequently struggled with how cost effective it was to have two therapists treat a family. At times, it was clear that two therapists helped with the balance of different family member's needs; in other cases, the co-therapy relationship was more of a benefit for the therapist's education than for the family.

Co-therapy has been important as a program component. As a learning aid, participants rated it 1.56 on a scale ranging from very important (1) to not at all important (5). Records kept by participants showed that a co-therapist was used 90.8 percent of the time.

Co-therapy has several advantages and some disasvantages as seen by seminar participants. Benefits of co-therapy included more effective and objective therapy implementation, increased creativity in strategies, two views of the family, and more accountability. Difficulties reported were scheduling, double staff time, issues from obtaining mutual agreement, different styles and paces among the therapy team, and the stage of pseudomutuality of the therapists.

DESCRIPTION OF CLIENT FAMILIES

From August 1982 until June 1987, the family therapy seminar staff from Topeka Public Schools saw 137 families. Each therapist has seen two to three families per year. Only ten families were seen only once. Most families were seen an average of eleven times (mean = 10.9, S.D. = 7.1). Considerations that were important in determining whether to refer to the seminar group versus a community agency included financial reasons, the family's comfort with school-based services, and type or severity of the problem.

Therapists in the Topeka seminar group during the last five years report treating a great variety of presenting concerns. The eight most common presenting problems the group has treated are (1) parent-child conflict (27 percent), (2) poor school performance (22 percent), (3) oppositional behavior (13 percent), (4) family communication difficulty (13 percent), (5) stepfamily formation (5 percent), (6) drug or alcohol concerns (4 percent), (7) antisocial behavior (4 percent), and (8) immature behavior (4 percent). Similar results were shown in a recent survey by Rait (1988).

CONSENT AND CONFIDENTIALITY

The client family needs to be provided with sufficient information in order to make an informed decision about whether or not to participate in family therapy (Aradi & Piercy, 1985). The family should be aware of the potential risks and benefits of their participation in therapy and have agreed to participate voluntarily. Informed consent is a component of being a responsible provider of direct intervention services.

It has been our rule, based on familiarity with the consultation and psychotherapy literature, never to share specific information received in a situation in which confidentiality has been assured either explicitly or implicitly. This statement creates an ethical issue when others, such as the teacher or administrator, try to get information from the family therapist who is also a school employee. However, generalizations may be shared with other school officials if the information is essential to their understanding the client's difficulty.

RECOMMENDATIONS

In the development of the model we have described, we have attempted to practice family therapy in a way that meets the needs of our school system, our client families, and seminar participants from the perspective of therapists and students of family therapy. During this process, several issues have become apparent that relate to time, learning, and effectiveness. Some of these issues relate specifically to applying the model to our district, whereas some relate generally to applying family therapy in the schools.

Recommendations are divided into categories: ideas to improve our own program and ideas to consider for others who may wish to provide family therapy in a school setting.

It is clear that the focus of our efforts has gone toward the development of a family therapy program that concentrated on both providing and teaching family therapy. Future research on the efficacy of our intervention may also offer a better understanding of the kinds of families that might better be referred elsewhere. Perhaps some new collaborative arrangement with a community agency could emerge. We need to look at ways to conceptualize and measure change. Better followup and improved accuracy of our outcome judgments could be achieved through implementing a more efficient record-keeping system. The new record-keeping system now in place will allow an assessment of change through a comparison of the family's original problem list with treatment outcomes and followup. We now have limited data and many personal impressions of our successes.

Other recommendations relating to training include: (1) participants in the program need to make a commitment of more than one year, (2) the program must continue to expand the supervision base, and (3) the program must continue to promote professional growth and development. In order to maintain our focus and emphasis on excellence in the provision of family therapy services in the schools, the program must always seek new ideas or innovations that will keep our program enriched and energized.

Final thoughts are ideas for the establishment of a family therapy program in other districts. The first three recommendations are ideas that are essential to the implementation of a successful and enduring family therapy program. So important are these first three recommendations that we would suggest that a program not be initiated unless all three recommendations are present. The other recommendations should assist newer programs to further develop a quality family therapy service.

1. At least one person should be available as a supervisor. This person should have strong training and experience in family therapy supervision.
2. *One* model should be implemented. It is important that all therapists need to practice the same model. We have found the problem-solving model particularly applicable to a school setting.
3. The administration should sanction and support staff time, money for equipment, and training/learning materials. The school district where the program is to be placed must have a belief in the role of clinical services in the schools.
4. A strong core of motivated and skilled professionals should become involved in the program.
5. A study component should be implemented to support the practice of family therapy, including a forum for presenting cases and a therapist support group.

6. Systemized record keeping should be implemented from the beginning.

7. Co-therapy should both enhance the learning of family therapy by involved professionals and support the process of dealing with difficult families.

References

Ackerman, N. (1966). *Treating the troubled family.* New York: Basic Books.

Aponte, H. (1976). The family-school interview: An eco-structural approach. *Family Process, 15,* 303–311.

Aponte, H. J., & Van Deusen, J. M. (1981). Structured family therapy. In A. S. Gurman & D. P. Kniskens (Eds.), *Handbook of family therapy* (pp. 310–361). New York: Brunner/Mazel.

Aradi, N. S., & Piercy, F. P. (1985). Ethical and legal guidelines related to adhenence to treatment protocols in family therapy outcome research. *American Journal of Family Therapy, 13,* 60–65.

Bateson, G. (1971). *Steps to an ecology of mind.* New York: Ballantine Books.

Bascolo, L., Cecchin, G., Hoffman, L., & Penn, P. (1987). The crying boy. *Family Therapy Networker, 11,* 34–41.

Bowen, M. (1978). *Family therapy in clinical practice.* New York: Jason Aronson.

Carlson, C. J. (1987). Resolving school problems with structural family therapy. *School Psychology Review, 16,* 457–468.

Carter, E. A., & McGoldrick, M. (1980). *The family life cycle.* New York: Gardner Press.

Conoley, J. C. (1987a). Schools and families: Theoretical & practical bridges. *Professional School Psychology, 2*(3), 191–203.

Conoley, J. C. (1987b). Strategic family intervention: Three cases of school-aged children. *School Psych. Review, 16,* 469–486.

Coopersmith, E. I. (1985). Teaching trainees to think in triads. *Journal of Marital and Family Therapy, 11,* 61–66.

Cross, D. G., & Brown, D. (1983). Counselor supervision as a function of trainee experience: Analysis of specific behaviors. *Counselor Education and Supervision, 22,* 333–341.

Dell, P. F. (1986a). Can the family therapy field be rigorous? *Journal of Marital & Family Therapy, 12,* 37–39.

Dell, P. F. (1986b). On the need for conversation in the family therapy field. *Journal of Marital & Family Therapy, 12,* 25–30.

DiCocco, B. E. (1986). A guide to family/school interventions for the family therapist. *Contemporary Family Therapy: An International Journal, 8*(1), 50–61.

Dimalanta, A. S., & Hightower, N. A. (1986). The use of self in cotherapy with families. *Family Therapy, 13,* 153–162,

Duhl, B. S. (1986). On stalking the wild questions. *Journal of Marital & Family Therapy, 12,* 31–36.

Everett, C. A., & Koerpel, B. J. (1986). Family therapy supervision: A review and critique of the literature. *Contemporary Family Therapy: An International Journal, 8*(1), 62–74.

Fine, M. J. (1985). Intervention from a systems-ecological perspective. *Professional Psychology: Research & Practice, 16,* 161–270.

Fine, M. J., & Holt, P. (1983). Intervening with school problems: A family systems perspective. *Psychology in the Schools, 20,* 59–66.

Fish, L. S., & Piercy, F. P. (1987). The theory & practice of structural & strategic family therapies: A Delphi study. *Journal of Marital & Family Therapy, 13*(2), 113–126.

Fisher, B. L., & Embree, T. (1981). *Supervision of beginning & advanced marital and family therapists: A comparative study.* Unpublished paper presented at the annual meeting of the American Association of Marriage & Family Therapy, San Diego.

Friedlander, M. L., & Snyder, J. (1983). Trainee's expectations for the supervisory process: Testing a developmental model. *Counselor Education & Supervision, 22,* 342–348.

Friedman, R. (1969). A structural family interview in the assessment of school learning disorders. *Psychology in the Schools, 6,* 162–171.

Friedman, R. (1973). *Family roots of school learning and behavior disorders.* Springfield, IL: Charles C. Thomas.

Garfield, S. (1977). Research on the training of professional psychotherapists. In A. Gurman & A. Razin (Eds.), *Effective psychotherapy: A handbook of research* (pp. 63–83). New York: Pergamon Press.

Gilmore, P., & Glatthorn, A. A. (Eds.). (1982). *Children in and out of school.* Washington, DC: Center for Applied Linguistics.

Haley, J. (1976). *Problem-solving therapy.* San Francisco: Jossey-Boss.

Heppner, P. P., & Handley, P. (1982). The relationship between supervisory behaviors & perceived supervisor expertness, attractiveness, or trustworthiness. *Counselor & Supervision, 22,* 37–46.

Hobbs, N. (1966). Helping disturbed children: Psychological & ecological strategies. *American Psychologist, 21,* 1105–1115.

Hoffman, L. (1981). *Foundations of family therapy: A conceptual frame work for systems change.* New York: Basic Books.

Imber-Black, E. (1988). Celebrating the uncelebrated. *Family Therapy Networker, 12,* 60–66.

Keith, D. V., & Whitaker, C. A. (1983). Co-therapy with families. In B. B. Wolman & G. Stricker (Eds.), *Handbook of family and marital therapy* (pp. 343–358). New York: Plenum Press.

Kersey, F. (1982). Supervisory process & focus applied in the development & training of marriage and family therapists. Unpublished doctoral dissertation, University of Iowa, Iowa City.

Kniskern, D. P., & Gurman, A. S. (1980). Research on training in marriage and family therapy: Status, issues & directions. In M. Andolfi, & I. Zwerling (Eds.), *Dimensions of family therapy* (pp. 221–238). New York: Guilford Press.

Madanes, C. (1981). *Strategic family therapy.* San Francisco: Jossey-Bass.

Minuchin, S. (1974). *Families & family therapy.* Cambridge, MA: Harvard University Press.

Minuchin, S. (1985). Families & individual development: Provocations from the field of family therapy. *Child Development, 56,* 289–302.

Monlar, A. & de Shazer, S. (1987). Solution-focused therapy: Toward the identification of therapeutic tasks. *Journal of Marital & Family Therapy, 13*(4), 349–358.

Nichols, M. (1987). The individual in the system. *Family Therapy Networker, 11,* 32–40.

Okun, B. (1984). Family therapy and the schools. In J. C. Hansen & B. Okun (Eds.), *Family therapy with school-related problems.* Rockville, MD: Aspen.

Paget, K. D. (1987). Systemic family assessment: concepts & strategies for school

psychologists. *School Psychology Review, 16,* 429–442.

Papp, P. (Ed.). (1977). *Family therapy: Full length case studies.* New York: Gardner Press.

Petrie, P., & Piersel, W. C. (1982). Therapy 2: Family therapy. In C. R. Reynolds & T. B. Gutkin (Eds.), *The handbook of school psychology* (pp. 580–590). New York: Wiley.

Plas, J. M. (1986). *Systems psychology in the schools.* New York: Pergamon Press.

Power, T. J., & Bartholomew, K. L. (1987). Family-school relationship patterns: An ecological assessment. *School Psychology Review, 16*(4). 498–512.

Rait, D. (1988). Survey results. *Family Therapy Networker, 12,* 52–56.

Rosenberg, J. B. (1983). Structural family therapy. In B. B. Wolman & G. Stricker (Eds.), *Handbook of family and marital therapy* (pp. 159–186). New York: Plenum Press.

Shellenberger, S. (Ed.). (1981). Services to families and parental involvement with interventions. (Special Issue). *School Psychology Review, 10*(1).

Simon, R. (1987). Good-bye paradox, hello invariant prescription: An interview with Mara Selvini Palazzoli. *Family Therapy Networker, 11,* 16–33.

Watzlawick, P., Weakland, J. H., & Fisch, R. (1974). *Change: Principles of problem formation and problem resolution.* New York: W. W. Norton.

Weeks, G. R., & L'Abate, L. (1982). *Paradoxical psychotherapy: Theory & practice with individuals, couples, & families.* New York: Brunner/Mazel.

Worthington, E. L. (1984a). Empirical investigation of supervision of counselors as they gain experience. *Journal of Counseling Psychology, 3*(1), 63–75.

Worthington, E. L. (1984b). Use of trait labels in counseling supervision by experienced & inexperienced supervisors. *Professional Psychology: Research & Practice, 15*(3), 457–461.

Zins, J. E., & Hopkins, R. A. (1981). Referral out: Increasing the number of kept appointments. *School Psychology Review 10*(1), 107–111.

26

Professional and Ethical Issues and Problems in Family-School Systems Interventions

JOHN P. QUIRK
Indiana University of Pennsylvania

MARVIN J. FINE
University of Kansas

LINDA ROBERTS
Kansas City Public Schools, Kansas

AS SHOWN IN the previous chapters, the range of school-related problems that can be addressed through a family-school systems orientation is quite varied. A diversity of therapeutic and consultation strategies has evolved from a systemic perspective that have been carried out by both mental health and educational professionals. Although a family-school systems approach has shown much promise, it is not without its limitations. Any theoretical orientation, when applied to a new real-life setting, will be confronted by unanticipated institutional, professional, and ethical stumbling blocks. These should be expected but should not discourage the practitioner who sees the need to include both the family and school subsystems when developing interventions for a child with school-related problems.

In this chapter, the professional issues and ethical concerns that may arise when using a family-school systems intervention in school settings or with school-related problems will be discussed. Whenever possible, resolutions to these concerns will be suggested.

CHARACTERISTICS OF FAMILY-SCHOOL INTERVENTIONS

In order to understand fully the potential professional and ethical issues related to family-school systems interventions, it is important to discuss them in light of several major dimensions: type of intervention, source of service, and focus of intervention. These characteristics interact in subtle ways to determine how successfully interventions will be received or implemented.

The type of intervention selected is the first dimension that can give rise to specific professional concerns. The issues confronted vary considerably, depending on whether the intervention involves a family-school systems consultation, a systems-oriented family therapy, or a combination of both. Each of these interventions brings with it a set of expectations as to treatment time requirements, client(s) participation, therapeutic focus, and a range of acceptable techniques. Intervention strategies and formats that can be appropriate in a clinic, such as paradoxical technqiues or family therapy groups, may pose some greater ethical or legal concerns if carried out in a school setting.

Second, professional issues may also be viewed differently or present unique problems according to who provides the service. It makes a difference whether the service is provided by school-based personnel or by a community-based family therapist. Mental health professionals, in contrast to educators, may have different attitudes about what constitutes appropriate behavior for children, parents, and teachers in a school environment. It has also been noted (Alpert, 1976) that teacher perceptions of consultants can differ, depending on whether they come from inside or outside the system. Similar interventions undertaken by different professionals may thus involve a conflicting set of expectations on the part of both the givers and receivers of service.

A final aspect of family-school systems interventions that must be considered when discussing professional and ethical contraints is the focus of treatment. This question of clientage has received considerable and at times heated discussion (Pantaleno, 1983; Hyman, 1983). Who is being treated—the child, the family, the teacher, or the school system itself? In a systems-oriented intervention, all subsystems are considered to be involved in some way in the problem and are, therefore, targets of treatment. But, as will be seen, not all of the subsystems may want or expect to be included in the treatment plan. Advocacy issues may come into play here in that the practitioner must decide who is the primary receiver of service. When a conflict occurs between the interests of the school and those of the parents, on whose behalf should the practitioner most vigorously pursue a solution? Moreover, many of the assumptions upon which consultation strategies are based can be called into question when a teacher becomes the target for change.

The primary strength of a systems model is its wholistic or integrative approach to understanding and resolving problems. But as the scope of the problem is broadened to include the family as well as the school, and causality is viewed as circular, the complexities of intervening greatly increase. Recommendations for change must take into account the subtle interplay of the subsystems involved, one of which is the practitioner himself or herself and the techniques that are to be used. Most of the existing family systems strategies have their origins in mental health settings and have been adapted for use in the school. Their "goodness of fit" has yet to be fully determined.

The remainder of the chapter will discuss this interplay in more detail. The first section will look at professional limitations and conflicts with existing theoretical models. The last section will focus on the ethical implications of using a family systems approach in a school setting.

PROFESSIONAL ISSUES AND PROBLEMS

Of greatest concern to professionals interested in addressing school-related problems from a family systems approach are those factors that would restrict their ability to use certain interventions or compromise their effectiveness when implemented. Constraints due to traditional school structure and role expectations, incompatibility of value systems between consultant and consultee, conflicts with theoretical models of treatment, and issues of professional advocacy all fall into this category. A review of these limitations will suggest that some of them can be addressed by thoughtful adjustments in clinical practice, whereas others may be beyond the control of the family practitioner.

Compatibility of Family-School Systems Interventions with the Public Schools

Before any form of family-school systems intervention can be implemented, consideration must be given to how it will affect the traditional goals and structure of the public schools. Public education has not traditionally thought of itself as a source of mental health service to the community. As school psychologists and counselors have broadened their influence, the psychological well-being of the child has received acceptance by some as a legitimate responsibility of the schools. It should be noted from the onset, however, that school mental health workers have had great ambivalence over the years as to how to conceptualize working effectively with parents and families (Fine, 1984a). Now that community-based as well as school-based practitioners are trying to more actively include the family subsystem when intervening with school problems, it is reasonable to expect some additional resistance to this wider focus.

Accommodation to change has not always come easily to institutions like the public schools. The resistance to a family orientation in the public schools seems to come primarily from administrators (Carlson & Sincavage, 1987; Durrell, 1969;

Raasoch & Laqueur, 1979), but is also found among teachers (Lightfoot, 1978) and even mental health professionals within the school (Fine, 1984a). Administrators concerned about the efficient use of educational resources may balk at agreeing to have school personnel engage in relatively time-consuming activities that could involve the school in sensitive family issues such as divorce, parent-child conflicts, or even substance addictions. It is reasonable to ask if the public schools should be the source of such a broad range of human services. This is particularly true in urban areas where there are many public and private community agencies to fill these needs. In rural settings, a better case can be made for an expanded role, as school psychologists and counselors are often the most highly trained mental health professionals available.

Although resistance to the adoption of a family-school systems approach is less likely to come from teachers, there are situations where it may come into play. Teachers have always been able to recognize the role that home factors play in the problems of children in school. However, if the subsystem boundaries between home and school authority are not clear, and it is perceived that too much influence for school decisions is given to the parents, resistance may arise with some teachers. This is where knowledge of the school's power structure, historical ways of making decisions, and the individual personalities involved could be very helpful. Family-systems consultants from within the school may have an advantage in this regard.

Time Constraints

Anyone who has worked within the public schools knows that the time required to carry out routine professional responsibilities frequently seems inadequate. Those taking a family systems approach within the school must consider the issue of time as it relates to their other professional responsibilities as well as to parent and family availability for service. Considerable time is needed for an extensive family systems assessment and this may also be the case for a family-focused intervention. The number of sessions are likely to extend beyond the time per case of a more psychometric approach to the problem.

When both parents work, their availability during the school day is often not a realistic expectation. Parents with professional jobs may be able to make time for meetings, but many other workers often cannot take time off during the day for school conferences without a significant pay loss. This kind of hardship will understandably make them reluctant to participate in such meetings.

A family-school systems intervention requires a comprehensive assessment of the interactive qualities of the family and the school environment. The typical psychological evaluation that assesses the personality characteristics of a child does not generally give much insight into family communication patterns (Gottman, 1979). Petrie and Piersel (1982) suggest that this may also be true for understanding the systemic nature of the school. To get such information requires assessment instruments specially designed for that purpose, or the opportunity to directly observe the family interaction or the classroom.

Classroom observations are routine to school-based psychological assessments. Parental input into a traditional assessment, on the other hand, frequently involves one parent, usually the mother, being interviewed briefly in person or over the phone. In order to understand the relational patterns within the family system, all members of the nuclear family need to be observed interacting during one or more interviews (Fine & Holt, 1983; Aponte, 1976). Setting up such meetings with the entire family can be a scheduling nightmare. Fathers often play a limited role in monitoring their children's education and do not see the need for participating in a school interview.

To observe a family interact and discuss issues directly related to school achievement can reveal very useful information as to the subtle ways parents communicate expectations to their children and influence their motivation for learning (Friedman, 1969; Fine & Holt, 1983; Aponte, 1976). The circular interview, which emphasizes relationship questions, may enable the family to grasp the interrelated nature of each member's behavior and the identified problem (Aponte, 1976; Fine & Holt, 1983, Selvini, Boscolo, Cecchin, & Prata, 1980). The overall goals of this kind of interview are to encourage the family to view their difficulties from a systemic frame of reference (Paget, 1987), as well as to give the mental health professional a vehicle for both understanding and intervening with the family system and family-school relationship.

Through one or more family interviews a wide range of systemic information can come to light. Since the time necessary to arrange and carry out these interviews can be a significant stumbling block, self-report measures of family functioning, which could be filled out independantly by parents, would seem to be a likely alternative. There are many good ones on the market, some of which have been suggested for use in school settings and with school-related problems (Brassard, 1986). However, the most widely used family and marital assessment instruments have been developed for clinic settings and contain items that could be interpreted by some parents as not being educationally relevant or being excessively intrusive into marital or family life. For this reason, self-report measures, as they now exist, can best be used only after a certain degree of rapport has been established with parents during or after a family interview (Brassard, 1986).

The development of family assessment instruments and strategies designed for use in the schools would appear to be a crucial need. Being able to evaluate family interaction patterns in a time-efficient fashion, and in a way that is sensitive to expectations of parents as to what is appropriate to disclose in a school setting, would be a major contribution to family-oriented practice in the schools.

As can be seen, a family orientation to school interventions by school-based personnel will require adjustments in caseload requirements and work schedules. The reader is referred to Chapter 25 in this book by Merrill and associates that describes such workload adjustments. The willingness to do evening work is essential, as is administrative support in the form of compensatory time or pay. Donating one's evenings is occasionally necessary, but the enthusiasm of even the most ardent family systems practitioners will be dampened if they have to sacrifice personal time on a regular basis. Moreover, judicious and innovative use of existing assessment techniques will also be necessary until alternative strategies specially geared for school use are developed.

Conflicts with Consultation Theory

The coequal status necessary in a truly collaborative relationship is potentially undermined by the systems-oriented consultant's view of the teacher's participation in problem formation and maintenance. After all, it is the teacher who initially identifies the child as having a problem and who presumably has unsuccessfully attempted to modify the situation. There is a literature that argues that the majority of teacher concerns in consultation are related to lack of knowledge or lack of skill (Gutkin, 1981).

Under these circumstances, the consultant should be able to respond collaboratively through the sharing of his or her expertise, taking into account the teacher's instructional expertise. But when the consultant actually views the teacher as in some way a part of a dysfunctional system, then the teacher, along with the child and involved others, becomes the client system. This shifting of the teacher from consultee to client has some ethical implications, as will be discussed, and is also a violation of a basic tenet of collaborative consultation.

The particular techniques that the consultant might use can range from fairly explicit and obvious to more "devious" and manipulative interventions. In a paper discussing the integration of structural and strategic components in consultation (Fine, 1984b), it was pointed out that in instances where the teacher is indeed open and receptive, the consultant can be fairly straightforward. But where the teacher is so involved or enmeshed in the system as to lack objectivity and is seen as part of the problem and resistant to change, then the consultant may need to utilize some more covert or indirect kinds of interventions. These could include paradoxical techniques, strategic reframing of behavior, and specific kinds of instructions given to the teacher.

It is important to stress that being an active participant in a dysfunctional system does not mean that one is to blame for the dysfunctionality. The implication for the consultant, however, is that the teacher's lack of objectivity and enmeshment with a dysfunctional system make it difficult to interact collaboratively with the teacher. The ensuing consultative strategies will be predicated on the view of the teacher as a part of the client system. Hughes (1986) referred to paradoxical recommendations as being highly manipulative and involving overt deception; she also recognized the inconsistency between the tenets of collaborative consultation and such deceptive techniques.

In discussing the ethics of strategic therapy, Haley (1976) made the point that a person hires him for his expertise and that he takes on certain prerogatives in terms of what he needs to do. He does not feel that he needs to explain or justify his manipulations as long as they are used to the end of achieving the desired results. These techniques can indeed accomplish what the therapist intended and in a short period of time (Papp, 1984), but the question of whether the means justifies the end remains answerable only by the individual employing such an intervention.

If the consultant feels that establishing a trusting relationship with the consultee is essential and that the way to test this is by being open and honest about his or her motives, then the use of manipulative techniques would represent a breach between one's ethical principles and one's concern with expediency.

Goldenberg and Goldenberg (1980) discussed two assumptions that therapists subscribe to when using such interventions. First, the therapist assumes the client is manipulative and thus the therapist must outmanipulate his or her client. Second, clients are resistant to change or help and a power struggle between helper and helpee usually results. Thus, manipulative strategies are employed as a means for the therapist to be in charge and direct what is happening. If the consultant from a systemic posture subscribes to these assumptions and sees the teacher as an active part of a dysfunctional system, his or her choice of intervention would likely include strategic techniques. But if the consultant also values collaborative consultation that requires an egalitarian relationship with open, honest communication and where power and influence are nonauthoritarian and noncoercive, the

consultant would encounter both conceptual and ethical dilemmas.

Somewhat of an extension of the point that the teacher may be a part of the problem is the attribution of the consultant for cause and resolution of the problem (Brickman, Rabinowitz, Karuza, Coates, Cohn, & Kidder, 1982). For example, in a Rogerian approach to therapy, key assumptions are that not only does the client have the problem but the client has the capacity to develop a better understanding of himself or herself and to work toward resolving the problem. The therapist's role is to create the necessary and sufficient conditions of empathy, congruence, and positive regard (Rogers, 1969).

Such an optimistic viewpoint may not be held by the systems-oriented consultant who sees the teacher as caught up in the system and unknowingly participating in the development and maintenance of the "problem"; accordingly, the teacher would likely be seen as unable to resolve the situation alone. As was mentioned earlier, the teacher would not be seen as the "perpetrator" of the problem, but instead as a participant in a sequence of behaviors that are reciprocal with the behaviors of others and in such a way as to maintain the "problem." From this viewpoint, the consultant is then in a position of believing that he or she needs to take charge of the intervention process and to control the flow of activity in order to shift perceptions and behaviors in a positive direction.

This raises the issue of problem ownership. From the viewpoint of collaborative consultation, problem ownership mainly belongs with the teacher or others, such as the parents, all of whom are concerned about the child. Through active participation the consultant may appear to share in problem ownership, but if proper boundary setting has occurred, the limits of ownership will have been established

(Fine, Grantham, & Wright, 1979). This is less the case with the systems-oriented consultant who is actively analyzing and attempting to intervene in the systemic nature of relationships. The systems-oriented consultant is an interventionist who moves more actively into the realm of at least shared problem and solution ownership.

The concept of coequal status also poses a problem when parents are the consultees. The family systems practitioner assumes that a broad range of children's learning and behavior problems are attributable to marital or family dysfunction. Parents are rarely, if ever, seen as objective partners in the treatment process. At best, they are sometimes viewed as victims of uncaused stress, such as in the case of a child with a severe developmental disorder.

In addition, a parent without professional training cannot be expected to have sufficient technical expertise to contribute equally to an intervention plan. Legally, PL 94–142 has given parents equal status in the process of educational planning for their child. This may be more an illusion than reality. Parents frequently feel intimidated or threatened in educational conferences and tend to be only passive partners in the decision-making process (Turnbull & Leonard 1981). Many of the same theoretical conflicts arise with parent consultation as occur when working with teachers. But one difference should be noted. Parents have been taught by our culture that they are responsible for their child's problem and therefore are less likely to resist at least token involvement as part of the solution. With teachers, this may not be the case.

Whether the consultation is with parents or teachers, it seems to be the consultee's perception of consultant empathy more than equality that influences the effectiveness of an intervention. When a consultee feels understood and appreci-ated, he or she is usually more willing to work with the consultant in a cooperative effort at problem solving.

The Objectivity and Shared Values of the Subsystems

The potential effectiveness of a family systems intervention increases as the consultant is able to communicate sufficiently similar values and attitudes to those held by the members of the respective subsystems in order to allow the "joining" process to occur (Minuchin & Fishman, 1981; Fine, 1985). The therapist-client match and its implication for treatment success has received some attention in the literature (Hunt, Carr, Dagadakis, & Walker, 1985; Mas, Alexander, & Barton, 1985; Kaplan, 1985). The compatibility of therapist-client gender, modes of expression, and cognitive style are some of the factors shown to impact treatment success. Therapist-client differences in expectations for treatment have also been shown to be influential (Feifel & Eells, 1963).

Family-school systems consultation in the schools is also influenced by these factors. The consultant's preconceived notions concerning appropriate parent or teacher attitudes invariably influence his or her ability to empathize with the consultee's concerns. Community-based mental health professionals may at times consult with schools without a full understanding or acceptance of the unique structure and problems faced in educational environments. Family therapists can get caught up in the parents' blaming attitudes toward the school (Eno, 1985) and are susceptible to getting triangulated in home-school conflicts. They sometimes cannot understand why educational administrators or staff will not accept suggestions for major accommodations in programming or management tactics to benefit a given child and may slip into siding with the family and child against the school. School personnel generally consider the broader implications of any recommendation to overall classroom, school, or school system functioning.

A problem of a given child must be solved in a way that not only takes the needs of the child into account, but the total educational and political reality of the school. Without understanding this, a community-based family systems consultant will have difficulty being effective. When there is infrequent contact between clinicians in the mental health community and school professionals, this kind of misunderstanding is more likely to happen (McDaniel, 1981).

Conversely, school personnel sometimes identify so strongly with school system values that they cannot be empathic to parental concerns. Parents caught up in what can be at times overwhelming personal or financial concerns may be labeled neglectful if they do not invest what is considered adequate time and interest in their child's education. Parents who question the educational decisions of the school may be viewed as uncooperative or troublemakers. A family-school interventionist must have a balanced view of both subsystems in order to empathize with the unique problems facing each and, in essence, to maintain a posture of neutrality (Selvini et al., 1980).

As school psychologists and counselors include family-focused interventions as a regular part of their practice, they will have to become more sensitive to cultural variations in family functioning. Defining what is normal or problematic within an ethnic family context can be very difficult (McGoldrick, 1982). For example, children of American Indians show less problems with dysfluent speech because the family is less demanding of precise speech at home. The more accepting attitudes of black families towards pregnancy out of wedlock has been well documented (Rainwater,

1966; Furstenberg, 1970). The clinican needs to be aware that a family's interpretation or reaction to problematic events might be quite different from his or her own.

Ethnicity can also influence the degree of receptivity a family will show to a proposed intervention. Cultural differences in the way people are comfortable in addressing problems will be reflected in how they react to a recommendation of family counseling or the types of issues focused upon during family interviews (McGoldrick, 1982). The ethnic groups to which this applies are not limited to cultural minorities, but can be found across the spectrum. An example would be Irish Americans, who assume that problems are a private matter to be kept within the family. They tend to be embarrassed to seek help and are not comfortable with therapies that emphasize the expression of feelings (McGoldrick & Pearce, 1981). Circumscribed, problem-focused, strategic techniques would probably be most effective with Irish American families.

An understanding of the influences of culture on family functioning is only beginning to find its way into the family therapy literature. It would be important for clinicians experiencing difficulty implementing a family-school systems intervention to look for cultural explanations before attributing the resistance to the personal characteristics of family members.

ETHICAL ISSUES

Professional Preparation

A fundamental issue related to the ethics of taking a family systems approach toward school problems involves the question of training and preparation. The application of a family systems orientation requires some subtleties of thinking and a high level of skill. It is doubtful if very many training programs for school psychologists or counselors give serious attention to training and supervised practice in this area. The experienced practitioner needs to be willing to seek out additional training opportunities before taking on this kind of role. Chapter 25 of this book illustrates the importance of preparation and ongoing supervision.

Confidentiality of Information

Working with the multiple subsystems of families and schools in assessing, planning, and implementing interventions requires a reconsideration of views related to the maintenance of confidential information. Schools, unlike mental health facilities, have not traditionally placed a strong emphasis on maintaining confidentiality. All kinds of problems of students are freely discussed during informal gatherings of educational staff. As the focus of school-based interventions expands to parents and families, a greater sensitivity to how and when family-related information is shared becomes important. Parents who hear that their personal problems were the topic of conversation in the teachers' lounge have a legitimate reason to be upset. The potential political fallout for administrators, counselors, and psychologists within the schools can be significant.

Mental health specialists have been trained to function under a code of ethics of their specialty, which always includes the careful protection of confidential information. When working from a family-school systems perspective, there are times when a practitioner will be working collaboratively with educational professionals who are not used to handling sensitive information on a regular basis. Even though an ethical family practitioner will always be discrete in sharing information when engaging in family-school systems con-

sultation, principles that guide disclosure may become clouded in a school setting.

In any form of consultation, information about the consultee is not shared with anyone (Hughes, 1986). But, as discussed earlier, when working from a broad systems perspective, who is the consultee—the parents, the teacher, or the administrator? When working with multiple consultees, can you be effective with one if you greatly limit disclosing relevant information about another? Can there be a coequal or collaborative status if a consultant does not trust the professional discretion of the consultee enough to be completely open with him or her? If an internal or external family consultant does share sensitive information with a teacher, can he or she expect the same discretion that would be anticipated from a mental health colleague? Given the differences in training and experience of educational staff, great care must be exercised in disclosing family data.

The multidisciplinary team (MDT) approach to special education program planning may pose additional problems of confidentiality. Although group problem solving in the form of staffings has long been a part of the mental health field, it has only come into education as a regular practice since the enactment of PL 94–142. Multidisciplinary teams, as suggested by Pfeiffer (1981), should have several key qualities: a common purpose, cooperative problem solving by different professionals who possess unique skills and perspectives, and coordination of activities. The assumption is that group decision making is superior to individual decision making; however, there is little hard evidence to support this assumption. (Kaiser & Woodman, 1985).

Research on MDT meeting efficiency has reported problems related to member role relationships, task structure, and member participation (Kaiser & Woodman, 1985). The kinds of information introduced at a meeting, or avoided because of the group nature of the process, has not been directly addressed. As part of a family-school systems assessment, data or impressions of teacher effectiveness, family dysfunction, and/or marital dysfunction may be gathered.

An important issue is how this kind of information should be introduced at a MDT meeting where the teacher in question or parent may be present (Quirk & Worzbyt, 1983). Can it be censored or totally avoided by the consultant without compromising the validity of the decisions made? Will the decision-making process be distorted if data about one or another subsystem is not made available? From a systemic point of view such distortions would occur under these circumstances. Interventions planned on the basis of selective and limited information cannot hope to be very effective. But presenting feedback that implicates teachers or parents in the origins and maintenance of a child's problem is difficult enough to do in a private meeting, much less in a group of colleagues or relative strangers.

The possibility exists that there are no totally satisfactory solutions to these two problems of confidentiality in the schools. Inservicing of teachers and administrators to sensitize them to the importance of confidentiality may help. Using positive "reframes" when presenting information about parents or teachers that could be construed as critical may blunt the negative impact. A third alternative might be to change from the typical pathology-oriented approach for the analysis of family problems to a family resource model where the identification of strengths to build upon in treatment becomes the primary focus.

Karpel (1986) conceptualizes family resources as "those individual and systemic characteristics among family members that promote coping and survival, limit destructive patterns, and enrich daily life" (p. 176). All families must cope with stress and move toward the attainment of group and individual goals. Even dysfunctional families do this successfully to some degree and/or in some areas.

Karpel (1986) goes on to suggest that helping family members recognize personal resources like hope, tolerance, self-respect, humor, and playfulness, and systemic qualities like loyalty and mutual respect can give them a sense of potency for dealing with problems. Moreover, talking about families and teachers in terms of strengths could greatly reduce the conerns about confidentiality being breached outside of school. Additionally, it would establish a more positive, less threatening image for the family-school systems consultant, which could reduce consultee resistance in the future.

A third situation where confidentiality becomes an issue is when a school-based family intervention is done in groups. Dombalis and Erchul (1987) review the applicability of multiple family group therapy to the schools. Its time and cost efficiency would clearly be an advantage. However, how could confidentiality be assured? Meyer and Smith (1977) indicate that the difficulty of assuring confidentiality in any kind of group therapy can present legal problems as well as reduced treatment effectiveness. Their data suggest that the inability of the therapist to assure the participants that revealed information would be held in confidence by all members of the group "would be likely to lessen the effectiveness of the group therapy process because of both an inclination to avoid entering therapy and a loss of substantial information to the group" (p. 640).

If we put group therapy within a public school context, we further complicate the issue. Schools are places where families meet and interact around a variety of child-related activities (e.g., the PTA and sports events). Moreover, schools are frequently tied to neighborhoods, so the likelihood of families coming in contact in the community is great. Under these conditions, it seems likely that many parents would be reluctant to join a group or feel comfortable being fully open in discussing family problems if the group were comprised of acquaintances or neighbors.

Multiple family group therapy may be appropriate in a mental health setting where clients are drawn from a wider geographic area and brought together only for the purpose of dealing with family problems. Schools, on the other hand, require family involvement for multiple purposes. Thus, there may be a limit to the range of techniques that can be adapted for use in the public schools. Even in the more acceptable context of parent education groups, concern has been expressed that without sensitive and skilled leadership, sessions can shift into a group therapy mode that encourages destructive personal exposure (Fine & Henry, in press).

Right of Privacy

As school psychologists or counselors choose to place an emphasis on the family and school systems, they must take into consideration the desires for privacy of noninvolvement on the part of consultees. Parents come to schools with the preconceived notion that schools are child focused and educationally oriented. When responding to a teacher referral of their child, parents might be quite willing to participate in the assessment and educational planning process, as long as it does not involve intrusion into family or marital affairs. A mother may have a very tenuous relationship with her husband and not want anything to disrupt the fragile status quo. Does the school-based consultant have

the right to probe into family relationships or therapeutically manipulate a consultee into accepting a broader definition of the problem? Should a parent be labeled resistant if he or she is not interested in such self-disclosure or broad-based involvement?

It is one thing for a community-based family practitioner, whose role and orientation is clearly understood, to assume a tacit approval for the exploration of family issues when a family seeks service. It does not seem reasonable to make the same assumption when parents come to the public schools.

The relationship of the parent with the school-based family systems consultant is usually not voluntary. School-initiated referrals, particularly related to behavior-disorder children, carry with them subtle or direct pressure for parents to do something about the problem. The goals of treatment, and what constitutes acceptable school behavior, are set by the school. Should the range of issues addressed in treatment also be determined by the school staff? Without the choice of "shopping around" to seek a service delivery model with which they are comfortable, undue pressure to accept a family-school systems approach seems questionable.

Respecting the rights of privacy of consultees should include allowing them to choose the level at which they want to deal with a problem. Family-school systems consultants need to be flexible enough to restrict their focus without letting this negatively color their perceptions of the consultee. This may mean gently exposing a parent to the possible relationship of family dysfunction to the school problem, but without coercive intent. It would be important, then, to accept with the same enthusiasm their choice to refuse family involvement, as would be the case if they were fully cooperative.

Some of the difficulties associated with including the teacher as part of a dysfunctional system have already been discussed in regard to consultation theory. Other problems are related to the issue of the teacher's rights to privacy. When a teacher refers a child for psychological services or agrees to collaborate with a consultant, is he or she giving implied consent to be included as a target of evaluation?

Hughes (1986) rightly contends that a consultant should avoid asking questions that would be unnecessarily intrusive into a teacher's private life. But what if it is suspected that stress in a teacher's private life is interfering with his or her ability to teach effectively? It could be argued that the responsibility of the consultant may be dictated by the degree to which the teacher is incapacitated. In cases where significant damage to students is likely to occur, the consultant must intervene to protect the child. In situations where the consequences to students are judged to be less severe, the prerogative to get involved may rest with the teacher.

With a systems perspective it is difficult not to explore any subsystem that seems to impact on the problem. In schools, though, teachers and sometimes parents enter into a consultation relationship with the understanding that the process will focus on the child and his or her educational programming, not the consultees' personal lives. Attempts to expand the focus without prior agreement could be a violation or privacy rights. A competent consultant will use his or her powers of persuasion to enable a family or teacher to see the interrelationship of their subsystem with the presenting problem.

The honest, open use of referent power to increase a family's or teacher's willingness to discuss personal issues is professionally appropriate. The use of covert or manipulative strategies to elicit a commitment seems highly questionable in school settings. Not only is it problematic from an ethical standpoint but such an approach could backfire on a school-based consultant's ability to function.

School psychologists and counselors need to consult with the same staff on repeated occasions and their success depends heavily on being trusted. Teachers who feel that their personal privacy has been violated or their behavior manipulated will resist future contact with the consultant. Informal contact with their teacher colleagues could lead to others also being reluctant to collaborate. With both parents and teachers, a delicate balance must be struck between exposing them to the value of taking a broad systemic perspective toward a problem and communicating an acceptance of their freedom to choose an intervention approach with which they are comfortable.

SUMMARY

The application of family systems thinking to a school-based intervention holds much promise but also presents a number of ethical and professional problems. As with any other "new" orientation to service, the mental health professional will have to gauge the issues carefully and exercise good professional and ethical judgments.

Although issues have been identified and caution has been encouraged, the authors of this chapter nonetheless recognize the potential value of a family systems orientation. Hopefully, future publications will continue exploring the issues and constraints associated with the approach so as ultimately to increase the sensitivity of clinicians and the effectiveness of their interventions.

References

Alpert, J. L. (1976). Conceptual basis of mental health consultation in the schools. *Professional Psychology, 74*, 619–625.

Aponte, H. (1976). The family-school interview: An ecostructural approach. *Family Process, 15,* 303–311.

Brassard, M. R. (1986). Family assessment approaches and procedures. In H. M. Knoff (Ed.), *The assessment of child and adolescent personality.* New York: Guilford.

Brickman, P., Rabinowitz, V. C., Karuza Jr., J., Coates, D., Cohn, E., & Kidder, L. (1982). Models of helping and coping. *American Psychologist, 37,* 368–384.

Carlson, C. I., & Sincavage, J. (1987). Family oriented school psychology practice: Results of a national survey of NASP members. *School Psychology Review, 16*(4), 519–542.

Dombalis, A. O., & Erchul, W. P. (1987). Multiple family group therapy: A review of its applicability to the practice of school psychology. *School Psychology Review, 16*(4), 487–497.

Durrell, V. G. (1969). Adolescents in multiple family group therapy in a school setting. *International Journal of Group Psychotherapy, 19,* 45–52.

Eno, M. M. (1985). Children with school problems: A family therapy perspective. In R. L. Ziffer (Eds.), *Adjunctive techniques in family therapy.* Orlando, FL: Grune & Stratton.

Feifel, H., & Eells, J. (1963). Patients and therapists assess the same psychotherapy. *Journal of Consulting Psychology, 27*(4), 310–318.

Fine, M. J. (1984a). Integrating structural and strategic components in school-based intervention: Some cautions for consultant. *Techniques: A Journal for Remedial Education and Counseling, 1,* 44–51.

Fine, M. J. (1984b). Parent involvement. In J. Ysseldyke (Ed.), *School psychology: Blueprint for the future.* Minneapolis, MN: National School Psychology Inservice Network.

Fine, M. J. (1985). Intervention from a system ecological perspective. *Professional Psychology: Research and Practice, 16,* 262–270.

Fine, M. J., Grantham, V. L., & Wright, J. G. (1979). Personal variables that facilitate or impede consultation. *Psychology in the Schools, 16,* 533–539.

Fine, M. J., & Henry, S. (in press). Professional considerations in parent education. In M. J. Fine (Ed.), *The second handbook on parent education: Contemporary perspectives.* New York: Academic Press.

Fine, M. J., & Holt, P. (1983). Intervening with school problems: A family systems perspective. *Psychology in the Schools, 20,* 59–66.

Friedman, R. (1969). A structural family

interview in the assessment of school learning disorders. *Psychology in the Schools, 6,* 162–171.

Furstenberg, F. (1970). Premarital pregnancy among black teenagers. *Transaction, 7,* 52–55.

Goldenberg, I., & Goldenberg, H. (1980). *Family therapy: An overview.* Monterey, CA: Brooks/Cole.

Gottman, J. M. (1979). *Marital interaction: Experimental investigations.* New York: Academic Press.

Gutkin, T. (1981). Relative frequency of consultee lack of knowledge, skill, confidence, and objectivity in school settings. *Journal of School Psychology, 19,* 57–61.

Haley, J. (1976). *Problem solving therapy.* San Francisco: Jossey-Bass.

Hughes, J. N. (1986). Ethical issues in school consultation. *School Psychology Review, 15*(4), 489–499.

Hunt, D. D., Carr, J. E., Dagadakis, C. S., & Walker, E. (1985). Cognitive match as a predictor of psychotherapy outcome. *Psychotherapy, 22*(4), 718–721.

Hyman, I. (1983). We are here for the kids: A reply to Pantaleno. *Journal of School Psychology, 21,* 115–117.

Kaiser, S. M., & Woodman, R. W. (1985). Multidisciplinary teams and group decision-making techniques: Possible solutions to decision-making problems. *School Psychology Review, 14*(4), 457–470.

Kaplan, A. G. (1985). Female or male therapists for women patients: New formulations. *Psychiatry, 48,* 111–121.

Karpel, M. (1986). *Family resources: The hidden partner in family therapy.* New York: Guilford Press.

Lightfoot, S. (1978). *Worlds apart: Relationships between families and schools.* New York: Basic Books.

Mas, H. C., Alexander, J. F., & Barton, C. (1985). Modes of expression in family therapy: A process study of roles and gender. *Journal of Marital and Family Therapy, 11*(4), 411–415.

McDaniel, S. H. (1981). Treating school problems in family therapy. *Elementary School Guidance and Counseling, 15*(4), 214–222.

McGoldrick, M. (1982). Normal families: An ethnic perspective. In F. Walsh (Ed.), *Normal family processes.* New York: Guilford Press.

McGoldrick, M., & Pearce, J. K. (1981). Family therapy with Irish Americans. *Family Process, 20.*

Meyer, R. R., & Smith, S. R. (1977). A

crisis in group therapy. *American Psychologist,* *32*(8), 638–643.

Minuchin, S., & Fishman, C. (1981). *Family therapy techniques.* Cambridge, MA: Harvard University Press.

Paget, K. D. (1987). Systemic family assessment: Concepts and strategies for school psychologists. *School Psychology Review, 16*(4), 429–442.

Pantaleno, A. (1983). Parents as primary clients of the school psychologist; Or, why is it we are here? *Journal of School Psychology, 21,* 107–113.

Papp, P. (1984). The treatment of a child's underachievement in school using a paradoxical approach with the family. In C. E. Schaefer, J. M. Briemeister, & M. E. Fitton (Eds.), *Family therapy techniques for problem behaviors of children and teenagers.* San Francisco: Jossey-Bass.

Petrie, P., & Piersel, W. C. (1982). Family therapy. In C. R. Reynolds & T. B. Gutkin (Eds.), *The handbook of school psychology.* New York: Wiley.

Pfeiffer, S. T. (1981). The problem facing multidisciplinary teams: As perceived by team members. *Psychology in the Schools, 18,* 330–333.

Quirk, J. P., & Worzbyt, J. C. (1983). *The assessment of behavior problem children: A systematic behavioral approach.* Springfield, IL: Charles C. Thomas.

Raasoch, J., & Laqueur, H. P. (1979). Learning multiple family therapy through simulated workshops. *Family Process, 18,* 95–98.

Rainwater, L. (1966). Some aspects of lower class sexual behavior. *Journal of Social Issues, 22,* 96–108.

Rogers, C. (1969). *Freedom to learn.* Columbus, OH: Merrill.

Selvini, M., Boscolo, L., Cecchin, G., & Prata, G. (1980). Hypothesizing-circularity-neutrality: Three guidelines for the conductor of the session. *Family Process, 19,* 3–12.

Turnbull, A. P., & Leonard, J. (1981). Parent involvement in special education: Emerging advocacy roles. *School Psychology Review, 10,* 37–44.

27

The Delivery of Special Services in Schools: Implications of Systems Theory

YVONNA S. LINCOLN
Vanderbilt University

IN THE SHIFT from agricultural to industrial to postindustrial society, the western world has undergone a concomitant shift in perspective around the *images* of society. Considering the terms *feedback loop, hardware, sexual revolution, collective unconscious, bioengineering, peripheral,* and *cybernetics* ought to give the reader some notion of the startling images, symbols, and associations that shape our worldview and are now a part of everyday usage. The common reference to terms like *systems theory, systems engineering,* and *systems analyst* is part of this restructuring of the guiding metaphors and language of a technical-rational model of the world.

Notions of "systems" antedate the work of Bertalanffy (1968), although it is Bertalanffy who is credited with the creation and explication of general systems theory. The work of Mary Parker Follett (1937) Max Weber (1946), and Frederick Taylor (1967), for instance, could be viewed as attempts to understand, disaggregate, order, and systematize technical, administrative, and production aspects (respectively) of industrial society.

Although Bertalanffy built his work on biology, in an effort to see how living systems interact to survive, the technical-production model was already strongly entrenched as an image that had power to compel loyalty, belief, and action.

The work of Bertalanffy provided the root metaphor for the system as organism (Morgan, 1986), although the now-famous Hawthorne studies (Mayo, 1947) and the work of persons such as Argyris (1957), Maslow (1954), and Herzberg (1966) elaborated many concepts relevant to this model as organizational theorists.

In retrospect, it is easy to see how powerful the tenets of systems theory are to a scientifically oriented society. In Bertalanffy's (1968) model, molecules become connected into cells, cells make up complex organisms, organisms may be divided into more or less complex species, and all survive within an appropriate ecology. In organizational theory, molecules may be viewed as individual units, cells are groups (such as work or task groups), complex organisms are organizations, species are populations of organizations (e.g., schools are a special population of organizations), and ecology becomes social and cultural ecology (Morgan, 1986). So far, so good.

The metaphor undergirding general systems theory has many strengths to commend it. It points out that life in an organization—such as a school—is essentially life in an open (versus closed) system. It suggests that the ecology of a school is a socially interactive set of processes that results in the creation of "shared futures" (Morgan, 1986). It stresses the idea of biological adaptivity and the success of organic forms in innovating to survive. The metaphor forces us to view our environment as, among other things, interactive and in the process of being created by each of us, singly and in groups (Morgan, 1986).

There are, however, two weaknesses to systems theory as it is currently formulated. One of those weaknesses is the inherent limitation of the metaphor (an organism) itself. The other has been its virtually wholesale merger with a counterproductive *mechanical model* of the universe.

Internal limitations to adoption of general systems theory are several. One limitation is that the organism metaphor leads people to conclude, wrongly, that the world is far more concrete than it is. Nature, organizations, and the social world are attributed a larger objectivity and more steadfast and concrete reality than actually exists. Second, the organism-as-model also makes it appear that individuals and the organization (school) are much more dependent on the external environment than they in fact are. There is a tendency to overemphasize the functional unity of schools, at the expense of seeing and coping with pluralism, conflict, and multiple socially constructed realities. The possibility that unity and harmony such as that found within a single organism might also be found within a sociopolitical organization such as a school is slight to nonexistent. Finally, Morgan (1986) cautions that there is the danger of adopting the metaphor as an ideology, wherein the rigid assignment of individuals to a "slot" on the biological or psychological hierarchy essentially denies them rights, autonomy, and agency over their own lives.

The second and more pressing limitation on systems theory has been its ideological takeover by a machine-like model of the world. The machine metaphor is exquisitely expressed by bureaucratic theories of organization. Mechanistic models of production and reproduction (e.g., General Motors, Ford), social regulation (e.g., municipal governments, the Department of Transportation), and service delivery (e.g., social security, the Veteran's Administration, Medicare) abound. Rather than providing the help for which they were originally created, they serve only to alienate individuals from the organizations supposedly created to contribute to the public welfare. Machine-like models of the social world operate more to frustrate and deny than to serve and affirm. Such models have as guiding principles the impersonalization or depersonalization, routinization and standarization of work and work life. Schools, the army, and prisons, as examples of classical coercive bureaucracies (Silver, 1983), share more characteristics than might be initially apparent or than many of us would want to see.

This mechanistic model of the world draws additional support and reinforcement from the model that has guided most of educational and psychological research—logical positivism (Lincoln & Guba, 1985). Traditional scientific paradigm research, operating in a closed system, tends to presume a natural (and, by extension, social) hierarchy of forms, and therefore a hierarchical and aggregationist stance toward knowledge and the acquisition of knowledge. This hierarchical posture toward knowledge—the image of the great clock ticking, with its many gears, flywheels, and pistons—strongly encourages hypothetico-deductive stances toward knowledge over induction and abduction, demands propositional knowledge statements when tacit knowledge and intuition might serve better, favors proofs over understanding, and imposes causal structures that bear little relationship to how individuals interact in their social systems or how individual and system engage in mutual influence and shaping.

Thus, the biological metaphor has been overtaken by a more powerful but less appropriate mechanical model, and reinforcement for this overthrow of an organic model has been supported by the dominant paradigm for research, evaluation, and practice of social and special services, particularly in schools.

THE PROBLEM

A major difficulty with this dominance of a research and service delivery/practice paradigm has been its lack of utility, its lack of match with the reality experienced by deliverers of special services in schools, and its sheer counterintuitiveness. It has served, in the first instance, to narrow unreasoningly the focus of service delivery. The imposition of a certain simplistic posture toward service delivery has left new practitioners with few hints as to the subtlety and nuance of their roles, and has left experienced practitioners with a sense of frustration at the discrepancy between their training and the realities of the roles they undertake.

In the second instance, it has created an expectation that the delivery of special services should be straightforward, comprehensible, and rational (as indeed the mechanical models of system and the dominant paradigm for research are expected to be), readily understood by school personnel, by special services personnel, and, mostly, by parents of special services children. When it has been none of those things, it has created anger and alienation rather than a sense of cooperation and control. And in the third instance, the nagging doubts experienced by all concerned with special services delivery have their basis in experience and reality: What personnel have been trained to do is very often the least "right" thing to be done in the situation, save in a legal sense.

POSSIBLE ALTERNATIVES TO MECHANISTIC MODELS FOR SERVICE DELIVERY

There are several ways in which special services delivery can break out of the typical training and delivery/practice models. One of the most productive among those ways is the adoption of a metaphor or guiding image that "fits" the social experience of service delivery more naturally. A competing paradigm for research, development, evaluation, policy analysis, and (potentially) service delivery exists. It is gaining a foothold among the academic disciplines generally, and reestablishing itself in psychology particularly. It is built on a phenomenological philosophy and constructivist psychology, and depends on a set of principles—or axioms—that deny the mechanistic models guiding most current practice and most discussions of systems theory. A brief review of the axioms might serve to introduce the reader to the worldview that might guide service delivery in schools and systems theory in particular more usefully.

Axioms of the Naturalistic Paradigm

There are five axioms in the naturalistic paradigm. These correspond to the generally accepted five axioms of the conventional, or scientific, inquiry paradigm. They are: (1) the axiom on reality, (2) the relationship of the inquirer to those who are respondents, (3) the axiom on generalization, (4) the axiom on causality, and (5) the relation of values to inquiry. Some additional explanation is probably in order, and then I shall try to make the connection between this particular worldview and a somewhat less constraining model for systems theory.

In the meantime, for those who argue that epistemological debates are unnecessary wastes of time, I would like to argue for the opposite position. What one believes about the world shapes the kinds of questions one can ask about the world, limits the answers to the questions that one might find, and constrains the search for answers to what one believes, fundamentally, to be knowable. A given model of the world carries within it assumptions regarding what it could find acceptable as "truth," what the nature of "evidence" for that truth might be, and implications for where one might look to find such evidence. Patton (1975) stated:

[A paradigm is] a world view, a general perspective, a way of breaking down the complexity of the . . . world. As such, paradigms are deeply embedded in the socialization of adherents and practitioners telling them what is important, what is *legitimate*, what is *reasonable*. Paradigms are normative; *they tell the practitioner what to do without the necessity of long existential or epistemological considerations.* (p. 9) (italics added)

Thus, beliefs about the nature of the world both permit and constrain *directionally* the actions of those who would act on it. Under one set of beliefs, certain actions would be seen as efficacious and proper, whereas under another set of beliefs, the same actions would appear misguided and foolish. The extent to which beliefs about the nature of service delivery influence the service delivery itself is correspondingly large. Consequently, the exploration of a contending worldview has merit, if only for allowing one to see possibilities not permitted by the dominant worldview.

The naturalistic axiom on reality, unlike the conventional paradigm's explanation, asserts that reality has no concrete existence, but rather is a social construction wherein actors agree to the rules and conventions (and language) that determine social and organizational behavior. Any focus on reality would be a focus on *multiple realities*, each socially constructed by individuals and groups, each resting on particular belief systems and personal and group values.

Hence, inquiry of whatever sort cannot converge on a single, "best" reality, as it is expected to do in conventional science (and in a court of law), but rather diverges, as many layers of meaning are explored, revised, and elaborated. Reality cannot be fragmented into small pieces (called variables) and studied; to do so would be to do violence to a person's experiences of the world. Rather, realities are made of whole cloth, and understanding them involves understanding the whole person, the whole situation or context, and understanding that *takes into account the context.* Understanding cannot be achieved hierarchically, but must rather be achieved heterarchically, organically, and holistically.

The second naturalistic axiom states that the subject and object of a given inquiry are not and cannot be separate. Conventional inquiry demands "objectivity" and distance, and requires a dualism that is not only impossible to achieve (and therefore artifically contrived) but that often gives rise to extreme measures, including deception, which robs individuals of their rights to informed consent and freedom from manipulation.

Naturalistic inquiry asserts that when knower and would-be-known are human beings, reactivity is to be expected. This interaction, far from being a drawback to research or practice, as conventional inquiry would construe it, provides enormous opportunity for the roles of teacher and learner to be exchanged any number of times. Recognition of the *interdependence* of known and knower, of service delivery personnel and families, and reliance on that interdependence to create understanding and knowledge and to devise strategies designed with the family in mind, are paramount to this worldview.

Third, this particular paradigm denies the possibility of generalization. In conventional mechanical models of inquiry, generalizations take the form of laws that purportedly govern the natural (and by extension, the social) world and human behavior. Such laws are made from the stuff of similarities, with dissimilarities written off insofar as possible as chance or statistically insignificant outliers. Conversely, the focus of naturalistic inquiry on dissimilarities as well as similarities makes the creation of nomothetic or lawlike statements extremely difficult, if not impossible. The focus here is on the impact of time and context in the shaping of human behavior, and the denial that rules for social life and behavior could be found or written for all time—or even for a generation or two. To paraphrase Lee Cronbach, most generalizations are more history than science anyway.

Fourth, the naturalistic worldview takes a rather dim view of more traditional notions of causality. Since the time of David Hume, most conceptions of causality have focused on a linear relationship, with the cause (A) being prior to, or concurrent with, the effect (B). Causes were either precedent to or temporally simultaneous with their effects. Clearly this linear view of causality is in harmony with a mechanical model of the universe (and consequently, with a mechanical model for understanding human behavior and guiding inquiry into it). The naturalistic model asserts, on the other hand, that causes are, at best, very difficult to sort out in the maze of human behavior.

A more productive stance might be to think of Kaplan's "pattern theories"—theories that attempt to explain situations without reference to causality, focusing instead on the webs or "patterns" of social interaction in which individuals live and work (Kaplan, 1964). Rather than attempting to ascribe causality to persons and situations, persons operating within this paradigm might instead—as systems theory suggests—try to understand the context that gave rise to the problem, behavior disorder, family dysfunction, and the like, and operate on the many connections within that framework.

Finally, conventional inquiry demands of both the researcher and the practitioner a clinical "distance," a stance of putative value-freedom, both in the inquiry process and in the service delivery process. But naturalistic inquiry forces both researcher and practitioner to recognize and own the roles that values play in service delivery and research on service delivery. This particular model requires ethical service delivery persons to state their value positions at the front of the delivery process, and to take into account, honor, and safeguard the value positions of the family during the whole process. The model demands that negotiation take place between the values of a given school, family values, professional values, and community standards, and that this negotiation take place between equals in the process. Values are acknowledged as inhering in social and familiar contexts, and they become an open and avowed part of the service delivery process.

The foregoing paragraphs are certain to strike responsive chords in many of those reading them, and the reasons might be intuitively or consciously clear. The phenomenological perspective on service delivery has three strong advantages: (1) it exhibits a great fit to the phenomenon (i.e., to service delivery in schools); (2) it demonstrates the fit to the earlier metaphor of systems theory, that of an ecological perspective on the role of context and the significance of social interdependence; and (3) it provides a fit to the lived experiences of school psychologists and other school special services personnel.

CONGRUENCE OF THE ALTERNATIVE PARADIGM TO SCHOOL SERVICE DELIVERY

A phenomenological and naturalistic worldview tends to exhibit greater fit to the world of special services delivery for the simple reason that it makes no demands about sorting until one reaches the "real" reality. Presupposing that social life is constructed of multiple, often divergent, sometimes conflicting, and always interactive realities allows special service delivery persons to operate in a Gestalt mode, helping to shape and restructure realities until negotiations are satisfactory to all parties involved: children, school personnel, and parents.

Without the constraint of having to agree on a single "story" regarding some particular case, the special services person may take into account multiple "stories," helping to fit and adjust each, acting as a mediating portrayer between parties as consultation gets underway in dealing with a specific problem. Rather than being forced to look for "the truth," school psychologists (or any other special services personnel) may examine multiple truths in an effort to get affected parties talking to each other about how the problem is seen by each of them.

The focus on multiple realities allows the psychologist or others to avoid deciding who is "right" or "wrong," who is to "blame," whose "story" best fits the situation, or who will prevail in the service delivery. Instead, in the best phenomenological fashion, naturalism allows special services personnel to concentrate on why each participant or client constructs his or her world in this particular way, and consequently, gives a view into the emotional world of the child, parents, teachers, and administrators.

Further, the fit to the earlier metaphor of an ecological system is ultimately more comfortable, since it focuses on biological, developmental, interactive, and interdependent aspects of service delivery in schools. The mechanical version of systems theory has as part of its root metaphor the implication that all "products" of the "system" will be fairly uniform; the biological version focuses on differentiation and specialization. In the mechanical metaphor, much store is set by an assembly-line system that can deliver standardized, uniform, and utterly homogeneous widgets. Not surprisingly, much of public school itself has depended on this uniform product concept.

The metaphor by extension leads us to believe the children—all children except perhaps the mentally disabled—should be able to complete certain kinds of mathematical calculations upon graduation, should be able to spell so many words correctly from a given list, should be able to read at such-and-such a grade level, should be able to handle certain straightforward technical material, and the like. Much of the current debate surrounding back-to-basics concerns itself with whether or not the "product" (children who have graduated from high school) is sufficiently uniform to make it in the world of work and civic life. Thus, we are not unfamiliar with the implications of mechanical models of schooling itself.

What we do know is that children are not machines, nor are they products (except in the broadest sense). And we know, too, that schools treated as factories are alienating to students and teachers alike.

Finally, experienced school psychologists intuitively understand that their job is made more difficult, if not impossible, by the efforts to construct a *single* reality, based on a single model, from which they might base the delivery of services. Even when special services personnel are thoroughly grounded in contemporary research traditions and trained in systems theory, their experience belies the rigid, linear, mechanistic models that have shaped much of research and practice in this generation. Most practitioners instinctively carry with them Jung's (1933) judgment, "The shoe that fits one person pinches another; there is no recipe for living that suits all cases. Each of us carried his own life-form—an indeterminable form which cannot be superseded by any other" (p. 57). Experience only confirms that service delivery cannot proceed along the lines of an assembly model; it has to be tailor-made to the individuals involved.

In addition, it becomes clearer and clearer as practitioners deliver such services that the process within schools is fraught with political considerations. Those political considerations, in an arena where most of us have been conditioned to think that politics is or should be absent, create tensions, disequilibrium, inequity, and confusion when they intrude—as they must—on the diagnostic and delivery process. Traditional and conventional research methodologies (and models of practice) would have us believe that research and the delivery of services resulting from that research is value free. But in fact, all human organizations, including schools, carry with them the pluralism of human value systems, and therefore are deeply ingrained with politics and political considerations. As a result, the diagnosis, prescription, and service delivery processes themselves are political acts, sometimes riddled with great conflict arising from multiple and competing value systems.

Thus, we have several reasons to question traditional systems theory as a respectable guiding principle for special services delivery. It exhibits little congruence with the social situation to which it has been applied; and there is little theoretical, practical, or metaphoric "fit." Systems theory itself has abandoned (or been torn from) its earlier roots in biology and ecosystems, losing sight of the root metaphor as it has been captured by time-and-motion researchers and production engineers.

And finally, it fails to capture the professional experiences of special services persons themselves. Opting for less traditional and more emergent models for research and practice, grounded in phenomenology, could, however, enable practitioners to feel some link between what they do and what they are taught about the nature of the world. But that conflict leaves us with the choice of abandoning systems theory as a useful tool for analyzing or understanding special services delivery, or returning it to its biological metaphoric roots.

If systems theory were to be returned to its biological metaphor, what would be the implications for practice? I believe there are several implications that have not been considered fully: the nature of the language and conceptions of the role of special services persons; the necessity to cope with the child's reality; the necessity of coping with the realities of family members; the necessity of coping with the reality of public schools; and the processes of altering, reconstructing, and negotiating new realities between child, parents, and school.

COPING WITH CONSTRUCTED, INTERACTIVE REALITIES

Language and Its Mandates

Feminists are quite correct when they move to alter the way in which we speak about persons (unisex rather than *he*), and naturalists are equally adamant regarding the forgoing of language that is shaped to the dominant paradigm (for instance, words like *variable, causal, dependent,* and the like). The power of words to shape how we think and feel about things is well known. The *names* we give to things create unconscious expectations regarding the "correct" nature of the world and our place in it. A chair*man* of the board is a male; a *variable* is a chunk of reality that can be ripped off, manipulated, studied for its presumably causal relationships to other chunks of reality, and returned (when our research is complete) to the larger reality from which it was originally separated.

It is the same with metaphors. Beginning with a metaphor of psychic prisons for organizations, for example, will force one to see Freudian implications in virtually all organizational activity (Morgan, 1986). In the same way, holding to a metaphor that is machine-like will lead to production and factory-like images, which in turn shape the language used to talk about some process. For instance, thinking of systems theory in a mechanical manner results in the title of this chapter (suggested by the editors): "The Delivery of Special Services in Schools." Goods and raw materials get *delivered* to factories. Finished products are delivered to warehouses, then to showrooms. Electricity and water are delivered to urban and suburban homes. But can human growth and development be *delivered*? The machinery model suggests a straight line input-throughput-output set of processes, much as pig iron becomes high-stress steel. Lunch, mail, grades, supplies, and parcels are delivered, but ought human interaction to be delivered? Doubtful at best.

A biological metaphor would suggest a vastly different view of the world. It would suggest minimal intervention (as in the case of the National Parks System plan to return wilderness areas to the natural, and therefore balanced, state for some period of time); it would suggest great care and delicacy (as in keeping pipeline off the permafrost in Alaska); it would suggest attention to seeing that appropriate nutrients (sun, rain, shade, food) for all organisms are available; and it would suggest the great power of nature to heal itself, given sufficient time and concern. It would suggest less of intervention and more of gentle facilitation, less of manipulation and more of egalitarian interaction. Rarely would it suggest delivery, with its attendant image of trucks and trains; more often it would suggest negotiation and diplomacy.

The tacit and propositional images that language carries with it are powerful to shape the way in which we view ourselves and others. One implication of switching metaphors is that we can "construct" ourselves, and therefore others, in new and different ways.

The Child's Reality

It is often the case that children, particularly those who are disruptive, destructive, or personal behavior problems in school, have little to say about the outcomes of services that are supposedly designed for them. Their options have included loyalty (going along with the services) or exit (leaving school or running away), but they have little "voice"—their constructions of the world have rarely been fully sought or honored. Moving to a new model of the world would allow the child's or adolescent's voice to be heard equally in the process of special services delivery. It is, after all, often her or his personal adjustment that is "out of tune" with that of the larger organization's.

A biological metaphor basis for systems theory would construct the child as not only part of the larger (disrupted) social system but would attempt to come to grips with the rather unique role that this "specimen" has to perform in the larger system. It would look as much to his or her contribution as to the flaws in balance in order to determine what is out of kilter. The process of diagnosing, prescribing, and delivery of services would seek to honor the construction of the child, taking into account the child's lack of sophistication relative to adults, and the genuine possibility that the system may be out of order. (This remark is not meant altogether lightly, since Marxian analysis of schooling would affirm that schools are repressive places for some children, and structural analysts would conclude that the system is geared more for indoctrination than for teaching.) In an emergent worldview, the child would have some equal say in designing a program or prescription for himself or herself.

Family Members' Realities

Systems theory operating from a biological, developmental metaphor, and from a phenomenological philosophy, would likewise carefully seek out, honor, and incorporate the values and constructions of family members in dealing with the problems between child and school. Family systems therapy is one recognition that families are part of a problem when children have problems; rarely, however, has this unit been seen as the major therapeutic solution, too. Thus, most textbooks concentrate on "treating" the family unit rather than on facilitating that unit's discovery of a solution to become more functional. Rather, the focus has been on the superior tools of the therapist in helping the family to "see" as useful what the therapist designs as the "treatment," and gaining the family's cooperation in trying out various solutions that the therapist wishes to see implemented.

A new paradigm for practice would direct attention to uncovering constructions of the family members' world that are in conflict with each other (or that mutually reinforce each other), and move the therapist or special services delivery person into the role of mediator, arbitrator, negotiator, portrayer, and guardian of the unit. The skills of the therapist would be exactly the same; only the construction of roles would be different. It would be different in that therapists would no longer see themselves as the most skilled, or even the most knowledgeable, in situations with problem children. Rather, they would see themselves as simply one person (or persons) who can aid the family in sorting out what it ought to do next. Special services delivery would become special services facilitation, taking on the air of a negotiation or arbitration, attempting to help design strategies for the future behavior of all parties, utilizing all parties' inputs.

The School's Realities

Schools are perhaps the most mechanical portion of the special services delivery equation. They are mechanical not because of the persons who inhabit them, although this is also sometimes the case, but because they are bureaucracies, and primary principles undergirding bureaucracies are uniformity of service delivery, depersonalization, routinization, standardization, and systematization of work. In organizations built on such principles, it is difficult and sometimes impossible to engage in human development work that is humane, authentic, fully and openly negotiated, interactive, and dialectic in intent.

Bureaucracies deem such person-to-person interactions as a waste of time and unproductive. And yet the reality—the climate, organizational press, atmosphere, and culture—of the school must be taken into account in the process of designing special services. This reality, or set of realities, for there might be organizational conflict in the school's culture, must also have its voice. However undemocratic schools tend to be, they are a chosen vehicle for perpetuating the culture, and the delivery of special services in schools mandates that the schools have a say in what services are delivered, to whom, how often, and under what circumstances.

Typically, schools have had the largest say, and the final say, in how special services are delivered. This is inappropriate. But a new model for services delivery recognizes the importance of the entire ecosystem, and finds evidence of fit between individual and organization wherever possible.

ALTERING, RECONSTRUCTING, AND NEGOTIATING REALITIES

I have argued elsewhere that evaluation has come through three generations and has moved into a fourth—negotiation (Guba & Lincoln, 1986). I would argue, by extension, that special services delivery is in exactly the same position. That is, it is now time for the special services delivery in schools to move to a position where the chief operational mode is one of negotiation. The role of such professionals would be that of mediating between the organism (child and family) and the larger ecosystem (school and community), relinquishing the position of expert and embracing the position of facilitator, caregiver, advocate, guarantor of equity, and mediator between and among realities. The chief description for such a position would be the ability to aid in the alteration and reconstruction of realities. The mode would be both dialectical and Gestalt oriented. The major skills needed would be the classical skills of active listening, and the more important skill of re-presenting various realities and interpreting the undergirding values to various parties to the service delivery.

The ability to represent faithfully the

realities uncovered, and to help various clients and audiences come to an enlarged understanding of the undergirding values and conflicts in others, would serve several powerful purposes. It would serve to leave each party to the negotiation with greater sophistication regarding others' constructions, and it would lend a sense of agency and empowerment in solving problems and creating ownership of solutions. Since one cannot fully understand the position of another without having oneself be changed in the process, the service delivery person (e.g., the school psychologist) in effect acts as a change agent, facilitating a mutual and noncoercive resolution while at the same time being only one party to it. The reconstruction of realities remains a highly idiographic process, but at the same time becomes a set of interactive agreements to which all parties can agree.

The final formal element in the process becomes the achievement of group consensus on what the problem is, and how all parties will handle the solution. Lest this sound very much like the current individualized education plan (IEP) process now in operation in most schools in the country, please note that rarely are all parties to such a process given equal standing to the negotiations and final agreement. Sometimes parents do not even fully understand what the school's "experts" have decided to do with their children. And the impact of that lack of understanding is that parents do not have a powerful say in what happens to their children in the process of schooling.

Under an emergent worldview, such deliberations would be taken as evidence of disenfranchisement and loss of agency. It would not be tolerated in a naturalistic worldview, since negotiations between persons who are not equals are accordingly unequally unbalanced. The implications of such a view are that parents could no longer be disenfranchised, but must rather be given the information they need to make informed decisions regarding their children. Further, if they do not understand the language of the professionals who are charged with service delivery, they must be tutored in the full implications of those decisions. Consent is not informed if all parties are not acting with equal information.

Clearly, this represents a major shift in the power alignments within schools and between schools, children, parents, and professionals. Such power realignments will be resisted by some, feared by others, and initially embraced by few. It means that some will have to relinquish power and some must be trained to exercise it. But the long-range impact is to continue moving schools away from the Rube Goldbergian mechanical models that have dominated schooling since the Industrial Revolution. It represents the empowerment of parents in the school process, the modeling of democratic and civic behavior to children and adults alike, and the agency of the schools' citizens in the decision making that affects them.

CONCLUSION

I have argued that schooling in general and the delivery of special services in particular has been dominated by an unexamined model called *systems theory*. Although systems theory in its original form was biologically based and developmentally modeled, the machine-like models of production soon overtook the biological format. The pervasive influence of both assembly-line-like efficient studies and growing interest in cybernetics came to dominate systems theory. Over time, an organismic metaphor become more concrete, less social, less interactive, and more mechanical. The focus on an external reality and a linear process model has left most persons with a more mechanical image in

their minds that is either appropriate or useful. The mechanical metaphor for systems theory has been buttressed by the dominant paradigm for inquiry and research, which is itself a closed-system model heavily reliant on a realist ontology and a dualist epistemology.

A major competitor to such linear view of reality and the research and practice deilemma is a phenomenologically oriented worldview. Such a view sees realities as social constructions—sees causality in terms of webs, influences, and patterns of human interaction instead of linear relationships; denies the possibility of generalization from one human situation to another because of the impact of time and context; confronts the interactive nature of human beings and accepts reactivity as a teaching-learning situation rather than an irritating research or practice dilemma; and accepts the powerful role of values in shaping and mediating behavior, including the service process (Lincoln & Guba, 1985). Such a philosophical system is entirely consonant with the biological/ organic metaphor for systems, but entirely incongruent with a mechanical systems model (e.g., PPBS, MBO, PERT). Furthermore, the emergent worldview brings about psychic "fit" with the phenomenon of special services delivery and "fit" with the everyday experience of school psychologists and other service professionals.

The implications of such a model—a return to the biological metaphor and the adoption of a model for inquiring into practice that exhibits resonance with that biological model—are legion. It means a change in the fundamental languages used to talk about special services in schools. It means a search for and an explication of the values undergirding the multiple realities that have an impact on service delivery: students, parents, schools, and professionals involved in the process. It means, too, that "experts" can no longer deliver diagnoses and prescriptions. Proposals for services and activities would be negotiated in good faith with all parties concerned, and this means that parents and children alike might well be involved in the design and delivery of such services. Most importantly, it would mean special services professionals would have the opportunity to rethink their roles and reconstruct the nature of the work they do, restructuring the institutions in which they work toward more productive and humane ends.

References

Argyris, C. (1957). *Personality & organization.* New York: Harper & Row.

Bertalanffy, L. V. (1968). *General systems theory: Foundations, development, applications.* New York: George Braziller.

Follet, M. P. (1937). The process of control. In L. Gulick & L. Urwick (Eds.), *Papers on the science of administration.* New York: Institute of Public Administration.

Guba, E. G., & Lincoln, Y. S. (1986). The countenances of fourth-generation evaluation: Description, judgment and negotiation. In D. S. Cordray & M. S. Lipsey (Eds.), *Evaluation studies review annual, 11.* Newbury Park, CA: Sage.

Herzberg, F. (1966). *Work and the nature of man.* New York: World.

Jung, C. G. (1933). *Modern man in search of a soul.* New York: Harcourt Brace.

Kaplan, A. (1964). *The conduct of inquiry.* Scranton, PA: Chandler.

Lincoln, Y. S. (Ed.) (1985). *Organizational theory and inquiry: The paradigm revolution.* Newbury Park, CA: Sage.

Lincoln, Y. S., & Guba, E. G. (1985). *Naturalistic inquiry.* Newbury Park, CA: Sage.

Maslow, A. H. (1954). *Motivation and personality.* New York: Harper & Row.

Mayo, E. (1947). *The social problems of an industrial civilization.* Cambridge, MA: Harvard University Press.

Morgan, G. (1986). *Images of organization.* Newbury Park, CA: Sage.

Patton, M. Q. (1975). *Alternative evaluation research paradigm.* Grand Forks: University of North Dakota Press.

Silver, P. (1983). *Educational administration: Theoretical perspectives on practice and research.* New York: Harper & Row.

Taylor, F. (1967). *The principles of scientific management.* New York: Norton Library. (Original edition, 1911.)

Weber, M. (1946). Bureaucracy. In H. H. Gerth & C. W. Mills (Eds. & translators). From Max Weber. *Essays in sociology* (pp. 196–264). New York: Oxford University Press.

28

The Efficacy of Family Systems Intervention: A Critical Analysis of Research

AGNES DONOVAN

Teachers College, Columbia University

EFFECTIVE FAMILY INTERVENTION practices are of increasing importance to school psychologists. Witness the substantial active membership of the Family Interest Group of the National Association of School Psychologists (NASP), three recent special issues of the *School Psychology Review* devoted to the topic of families (Erchul, 1987; Guidubaldi, 1980; Shellenberger, 1981), a chapter in *The Handbook of School Psychology* on family therapy (Petrie & Piersel, 1982), an edited book entitled, *Family Therapy with School Related Problems* (Hansen, 1984), and a number of recent articles, papers, and dissertations that articulate family-oriented roles for school psychologists (Anderson, 1983; Donovan, 1985; Fine & Holt, 1983; Graden, Brassard, Carlson, & Christenson, 1987; Lombard, 1979; Loven, 1978; Phillips, 1981; Quirk, Carlson, Kral, Fine, Aliotti, & Donovan, 1987; Smith, 1978; Wendt & Zake, 1984).

Historically, school psychologists recognized the importance of family life to students' school functioning (Dockrell, 1964; Gurman, 1970; Pollaczek, 1964;

Sells & Roff, 1965). Nonetheless, the ways in which families were involved by school psychologists largely reflected an individual child-focus to the practice of psychology in the schools. For example, school psychologists routinely involved families in an exchange of information when a child was referred for psychological assessment (i.e., school psychologists collected from parents the child's developmental history, documented the parents' perception of the student's functioning in the home and community environments, ascertained the parents' perception of the child's school-related problem, and, finally the school psychologist interpreted the results of psychological evaluation to parents). Largely, information from families was used to support or disaffirm the differential diagnosis suggested by test data and observational information gathered at school.

The present interest in family systems intervention diverges from past individual child-focused practices and coincides with a broader emphasis in school psychology on the applications of systems theory to practice (Hannifin & Witt, 1983; Rosenthal, Ellis, & Pryzwansky, 1987; Snapp & Davidson, 1982; Taplin, 1980). A call within the field for a more comprehensive family-oriented role for school psychologists is one example of this interest in the application of systems theory to the practice of school psychology (Anderson, 1983; Conoley, 1987; Green & Fine, 1980; Lombard, 1979; Loven, 1978; Pfeiffer & Tittler, 1983; Wendt & Zake, 1984). With the purpose of providing guidance for the development of effective systems-oriented applications to school psychology, empirically based family systems intervention literature will be critiqued in this chapter as a means of addressing the following questions: First, is there evidence that family systems intervention is an effective psychological intervention? More specifically, has family systems intervention been shown to be effective in treating students' school-related problems? Second, do models of family systems intervention exist which are particularly applicable to the practice of school psychology?

CRITERIA FOR SELECTION OF STUDIES

Studies selected for inclusion met four basic criteria. First, only studies with an empirical basis are included. There is a proliferation of "clinical" papers, case studies, and program descriptions that report the use of specific family intervention strategies. These reports are useful in suggesting areas for further research, but for obvious reasons cannot be considered in a comparative analysis of outcome. In 1983 Fine and Holt noted that "there is an absence of data-based research supporting the efficacy of a (family) systems approach within the schools" (p. 64). This situation has not markedly changed in the past few years. Therefore, this chapter draws more broadly from the mental-health literature.

Second, in the practice of psychology in the schools, children most often are the "identified patient" and the student's problem is the motivating force behind the teacher's and/or family's involvement with psychological services. Therefore, studies were included only if at least one treatment outcome measure focused on student change. It is possible that the use of this criterion has introduced some unknown differential bias, as some family researchers assess the outcome of family interventions only in terms of family functioning (e.g., Minuchin, Montalvo, Guerney, Rosman, & Schumer, 1967).

Third, in order to ensure a consistent use of the term *family systems intervention* and to focus clearly on the relationship between family systems intervention and child outcome, only studies using conjoint family therapy (at least one parent and child involved in treatment) and therapeutic strategies consistent with the assumptions of systems theory are included. This criterion excludes parent training or education, marital counseling, group counseling for parents, concurrent child and parent therapies, and home-school programs of behavioral contracts designed to improve student functioning, all of which are, broadly speaking, "family interventions" that can be directed at changing a child and/or the child's family environment. Their exclusion reflects no negative value judgment by the author as to the merits of these forms of intervention but merely the necessity to isolate studies of family systems intervention for the purposes of analyzing its effectiveness. A comparison of family systems interventions with other forms of family interventions and individual child and parent therapies deserves attention.

Last, studies were excluded from consideration if indications of brain damage, psychosis, and/or hospitalization were evident in the client population (either child or parent).

Studies meeting these four basic

criteria were identified from previous reviews by Dewitt (1978), Gurman and Kniskern (1978), Masten (1979), Olson (1970), and Wells, Dilkes, and Trivelli (1972), in addition to subsequent works that could be located through searches of psychological and educational abstracts and journals.

Studies meeting the above criteria can be categorized by the characteristics of the identified child/adolescent patient. These children and adolescents represent five distinct student populations familiar to school psychologists: (1) adolescent status offenders and juvenile delinquents, (2) adolescent alcohol and/or drug abusers, (3) nondelinquent adolescents with family problems, (4) students enrolled in special education programs for the emotional disturbed, and (5) nonhandicapped students with behavioral and/or attitudinal problems at school.

ADOLESCENT STATUS OFFENDERS AND JUVENILE DELINQUENTS

The first population of students considered are adolescents whose behavior brought them to the attention of the courts. Status offenses are crimes committed by a minor. These crimes are not acts of violence; rather, they are violations of the adolescent's socially prescribed roles in the school or family system and include transgressions such as noncooperation with parents, truancy, running away from home, and so on.

Beal and Duckro (1977) reported on the effects of a family intervention program for status offenders. At the adolescents' first contact with the legal system they were offered short-term family counseling as an alternative to the traditional services offered by a probation officer. The program was strictly voluntary and 44 families elected to participate. The family intervention was conceptualized as a two-phase process, lasting six to eight sessions.

Initially, crisis intervention strategies were used to deal with the family's anger and to recast the problem from a systems perspective. Family intervention techniques were then employed to modify pathological family interaction patterns. Successful outcome was defined as closure of a case without court action. By this measure, the experimental group was successful 85 percent of the time. Retrospective data collected for a group of families provided traditional probationary services the previous year indicated a success rate of 35 percent.

Although family intervention was effective in successfully diverting the majority of adolescents who received this intervention from further involvement in the legal system, no measures were taken of changes occurring within the family. Such an assessment of change in the family system is necessary in order to understand what it is that facilitated successful families in regaining an ability to monitor its own members' actions. Cautious interpretation of these results is necessary, for the results are undoubtedly inflated by the fact that all of the families involved in the family intervention program selected family intervention over the traditional probation services offered by the court system. At present, no followup studies have been undertaken to replicate these data.

Klein, Alexander, and Parsons (1977) extended earlier work with families with a delinquent adolescent (Alexander, Barton, Schiavo, & Parsons, 1976; Alexander, & Parsons, 1973). Their previous research demonstrated that short-term, behavioral, family systems intervention modified family interaction patterns and significantly reduced recidivism of the delinquent adolescent at 6 and 18 months postintervention.

Klein, Alexander, and Parsons (1977) contended that if systems theory was the theoretical basis for the family intervention program and "the family systems approach (had) modified the nature of the family interactions to produce a more effective problem-solving unit, (then) it would be expected that the siblings of the initially referred delinquents receiving the treatment would demonstrate fewer subsequent juvenile court contacts" (p. 471).

To test this hypothesis, Klein reviewed court records of families with a delinquent adolescent who were randomly assigned to an experimental group (short-term, behavioral, family systems intervention), two comparison treatment groups (client-centered family therapy and an eclectic-dynamic approach to family therapy), and a no-treatment control group, at two-and-a-half and three-and-a-half years from the time of the original treatment. Sibling contact with the courts for families who received short-term behavioral family therapy was one-half to one-third lower then in any other group. Additionally, a post-hoc analysis of family process measures for families with no sibling court contact (independent of treatment condition) revealed that these families demonstrated significantly more clarity, precision, and reciprocity in communication, and greater use of social reinforcement at treatment closure than did families whose siblings had court contact.

A report of a series of three replications (Barton, Alexander, Waldron, Turner, & Warburton, 1985) of the use of short-term, behavioral, family systems intervention provide further support for its effectiveness. Expanding on previous research on the use of behavioral, family systems intervention with adolescent status offenders (Alexander, et al. 1976; Alexander & Parsons, 1973; Klein, Alexander, & Parsons, 1977), Barton and colleagues (1985) report the use of these strategies of family intervention with two new client groups (i.e., families requesting child protective services and hard-core delinquents).

Following a one-week training workshop in family systems intervention, also described as Functional Family Therapy (FFT), two Utah state caseworkers for the division of protective and family services decided to implement FFT in their casework and to evaluate its effectiveness unbeknownst to their supervisors or the workshop trainers. They collected data to assist themselves in professional decision making and case management.

An analysis of the data lends support for the use of FFT with this population of families. A comparison of the pretraining and posttraining rates of utilization of foster care placement in all cases of parent-referred youth revealed a significantly lower posttraining rate of utilization when compared both with the pretraining rate of utilization by the same caseworkers and a time-yoked comparison of the rate of utilization by fellow caseworkers not employing FFT. It was concluded that training in functional family therapy provided caseworkers with effective and appropriate tools for dealing directly with intrafamilial stress, and an alternative clinical strategy to out-of-home placements for children. Furthermore, the data indicated that the number of units of service required for families was cut in half following the implementation of FFT, suggesting greater efficiency in the provision of services.

Although the report supports the use of family systems intervention in response to parent-identified family needs, generalizing from these findings is not advised. All cases considered by this report were family self-referrals for services. Neither the level of commitment or skill of the case workers, nor the preintervention level of family functioning was reported or controlled in assessment outcome. Additionally, the lack of outcome data other than of foster care placement/no placement limits severely the interpretability of these data. Although the study reported dramatic reduction in placements for the "experimental" group, the validity of placement as a measure of the efficacy of family intervention is questionable. No other objective measures of treatment effects, such as change in child or parent behavior, family interaction patterns, or quality of the perceived family environment, were available to substantiate what may have been a clinical judgment not to place the child outside the family.

A second replication applied FFT to 30 hard-core delinquents (adolescents incarcerated in a state training school for serious and repeated offenses). In addition to family intervention the FFT group was also provided supportive services such as remedial education, job training and placement, and school placement. The alternative treatment comparison group were placed in group homes with 24-hour treatment programs and received support for finding jobs and were encouraged to avail themselves of educational opportunities. The two dependent measures used to assess treatment effects were frequency of offenses and recidivism during a 15-month posttreatment period. The FFT group did have significantly fewer recidivists, and among the FFT group who did commit subsequent offenses the number of offenses was significantly fewer per youth (though not less severe) when compared with the alternative treatment group.

These results represent a significant improvement over the outcome associated with continued incarceration for adolescent offenders. Nonetheless, the results are more modest than those reported for adolescent status offenders. Alexander and colleagues (1976) state that in the identification of youths for the FFT program "the determining factor . . . was whether or not, in the workers' judgments, the youth were returning to an in-terpersonal environment which would lend itself to any kind of commitment to maintain the youth in the home" (p. 22). The FFT and alternative treatment groups were not matched on this highly salient variable. The discrepancy in selection criteria for the experimental and comparison groups enters considerable unspecified variance into the results, which is neither controlled for in the analysis nor explained.

Emshoff and Blakely (1985) evaluated the effectiveness of a diversion program for 73 adolescent delinquents who had committed serious misdemeaners or nonserious felonies. Status offenders were not accepted into this diversion program. Youths were randomly assigned to experimental and control conditions. Furthermore, youth assigned to the experimental projects were randomly assigned to one of two intervention conditions—either a services plan that focused on the family (Family Condition) ($N = 24$) or a model for services that focused on a wide range of areas critical to behavior and development (e.g., school peers and employment) (Multi-Focus Condition) ($N = 23$). The control group received a traditional formal or informal probationary period ($N = 26$). Nonprofessionals were trained as service providers for the project.

Both the Family and Multi-Focus groups provided the same amount of intervention, but differences in the services were documented. Intervention for youth assigned to the Family Condition were characterized by greater parental involvement and a higher level of contracting activities between volunteers and youth. By comparison, intervention for the Multi-Focus group was provided in a wider variety of settings, specifically at work, home, and school. Additionally, the Multi-Focus group increased intervention activities in the school over time, whereas the Family group was shown to decrease its level of activities.

As is customary for program evaluations, outcome measures included standard police data, self-reports of the youth, and school data. For all conditions (Family, Multi-Focus and control), youth decreased the frequency and seriousness of their contacts with police and the courts. The experimental conditions were clearly superior in assisting youth in avoiding further incarceration. Interestingly, all groups showed a decrease in school performance over time, (i.e., higher absenteeism and dropout rates and lower grade-point averages). The Multi-Focus Condition, however, showed the least deterioration in the youth's school functioning.

ADOLESCENT SUBSTANCE ABUSERS

The second population of students considered are adolescent substance abusers. In an analysis of the role of the family in the etiology of drug abuse, Friesen (1983) identified consistent familial relational patterns in families with a drug-abusing member. Based on a review of 17 articles, his report presents addict families as characterized by a long-standing emotionally conflicted relationship between parents, an ineffectual and/or distant parent, a dominating and infantilizing parent, a crisis-oriented feeling tone in the family, blurring of generational boundaries, and a family history of using and/or promoting the use of drugs/alcohol as a method of coping with bad events and feelings.

Using a developmental perspective, Haley (1980) suggested that for the addict family the problem lies not "in" the youthful drug abuser but in the failure of the family system to negotiate successfully the stage requiring mutual disengagement of parent and young person. Similarly, Reilly (1984) described the family of the adolescent drug abuser as having a defect in the

normal family "launch sequence" by which the adolescent is prepared for gradual disengagement and separation from the family of origin.

Programs of prevention and intervention have arisen throughout the nation to respond to the needs of alcohol/drug-abusing adolescents and their families, some of which have been systematically evaluated (e.g., Conner, 1984; Spiegel & Mock, 1977; Szapocznik, Lasaga, & Scopetta, 1976). However, there are almost no carefully controlled studies of family intervention with this population. The work of Szapocznik and colleagues is a notable exception. In a study (Szapocznik, Kurtines, Foote, Perez-Vidal, & Hervis, 1983) of 62 Hispanic families with a drug-abusing member, ages 12 to 20, the authors proposed to assess the relative efficacy of conjoint family therapy (CFT) with one-person family therapy (OPFT) in the treatment of a drug/alcohol-abusing adolescent. Adolescents were randomly assigned to one of the two treatment modalities (i.e., CFT or OPFT).

Prior to assignment, all families indicated a willingness to come for either treatment modality. In conjoint family therapy the entire family was present for most sessions; comparatively, one-person family therapy was conducted with only the adolescent. Both treatments were developed within the conceptual framework of Brief Strategic Family Therapy, which adheres to a family-systems approach. The treatments were time-limited and designed to achieve their goals within 12 sessions. An analysis of preintervention data indicated that the groups were comparable with few exceptions: Parents of adolescents assigned to OPFT reported higher level of pathology in the adolescent on two scales of the Behavior Problem Checklist, and a marginally significant difference was found between CFT and OPFT groups (with the OPFT group reporting more severe drug abuse).

A comparison of the total number of sessions for each group indicated that the OPFT group attended significantly more sessions. In the CFT group five families received between four and seven sessions, whereas all adolescents in the OPFT received eight or more treatment sessions. Results indicated that both time-limited therapeutic interventions were highly effective at termination and at followup (6 to 12 months following termination). Furthermore, OPFT was as effective as CFT in bringing about improvement in both family functioning and symptom reduction in the drug-abusing adolescent as measured by all the clinical scales. OPFT was somewhat more effective than CFT in maintaining continued improvement, especially in the adolescent's symptomology.

The authors conclude that their research findings and clinical experience suggest that OPFT is preferred over CFT in cases where there is particular difficulty scheduling the whole family, where one family member requires a great deal of strengthening, or where family members are unwilling to participate in the therapeutic process. The combination of both modalities in treatment was recommended most strongly.

A followup study (Szapocznik, Kurtines, Foote, Perez-Vidal, & Hervis, 1986) of 35 families provides further evidence for the effectiveness of one-person family therapy in the treatment of adolescent drug abuse for both individual and family functioning. One-person family therapy appeared to be somewhat better than conjoint family therapy at sustaining the improved functioning of families at followup.

NONDELINQUENT ADOLESCENTS WITH FAMILY PROBLEMS

A third population considered were nondelinquent adolescents who reported family problems. Everett (1976) reported on the development of a short-term (five sessions) Family Assessment and Intervention model designed for use by a community mental health center staff serving troubled teens and their families. The center's caseload consisted of a broad range of typical adolescent referral problems.

The Family Assessment and Intervention model involves a team of two therapists working with each family. During the first two sessions the parents and adolescents meet separately with "their" own therapist; the remaining three sessions are conjoint. The therapists collaboratively analyze the family problem presented, considering both the adolescents' developmental needs and family dynamics. Intervention, although time limited, is viewed as more comprehensive than traditional crisis intervention, since the goal of treatment is to evolve alternative family interaction patterns through the identification of new roles for family members or the development of new problem-solving skills. By the fifth session, the therapists are prepared to make informed, specific recommendations for the continuation of treatment.

Everett (1976) has preliminary data on the implementation of this model that suggest that it is well received by families referred for treatment. Significantly fewer clients missed or cancelled appointments, or withdrew from treatment, than with a comparison group receiving "traditional" treatment prior to the implementation of this model. Everett's results are encouraging, but the investigation is of a preliminary nature.

STUDENTS ENROLLED IN SPECIAL EDUCATION PROGRAMS FOR THE EMOTIONALLY DISTURBED

Two studies by Garrigan and Bambrick (1975, 1977) report the use of short-term family intervention with families who had a student attending a school for emotionally disturbed children. These studies are characterized by careful standardization of treatment method. Zuk's (1966, 1972) therapeutic strategy, described as the go-between process, was employed by all therapists who ere similarly trained and supervised. In the first study (1975), a relatively small sample size of nine included white, two-parent, middle-class families with boys. Families were assigned to an experimental or no-treatment control group. Groups were matched on student age and IQ, but not on the problem characteristics of the student. Treatment for the experimental group lasted for six weeks. The results reported were modest. Students indicated that they perceived improvement in the interpersonal functioning of their families. However, no significant change was found on a pre- and postteacher rating of student classroom behavior. Also, no significant difference was found on student's pre- and posttreatment report of self-concept.

Garrigan and Bambrick's second study (1977) was improved by the random assignment of 28 families to family intervention or no-treatment control groups. The inclusion of girls, numbering nearly 36 percent of the total sample size, made the samples more closely representative the actual population of students in classes for the emotionally disturbed. The duration of treatment was increased in the second study from six to ten sessions, which were held within a 16-week period.

The results of the family intervention reported were impressive. Independent observer ratings indicated significantly improved classroom behavior for students of families who completed treatment in the experimental (family intervention) group. Further, of the 12 students whose families were assigned to the family intervention treatment group, 5 were returned to regular classroom settings and, at six-month followup, 4 of these students were adjusting adequately. By comparison, only 1 student in the control group was returned to a mainstreamed situation. The authors suggested that "the primary significance of these findings is that beneficial effects of family therapy extend outside of the family into the school" (p. 86).

In addition to the changes noted in the child's school adjustment, parents judged family adjustment to have improved significantly. Students, however, did not share their parents' perception of positive change in family relations. As in the previous study (Garrigan & Bambrick, 1975), family intervention did not result in change on a measure of student self-concept. Additionally, there was less agreement among raters inside and outside the family system (mother, father, and independent rater) for female students than male students. Parents of female adolescents appeared less able to view the positive direction of changes that occurred in treatment. Mothers and fathers reported that things appeared "to be getting worse," while at the same time information provided by independent observers indicated that the girls' behavior was indeed improving outside the family. It appears that the sex of the student may be related to the ways families interpret and allow for change.

Family intervention did not affect a significant, positive change in all of the student behaviors and attitudes targeted for change. Neither parents nor independent raters noted changes in bizarre thinking, emotional distance, or hyperactivity. The identified students, themselves, reported no change in self-concept or anxiety.

CHILDREN WHO HAVE PROBLEMS AT SCHOOL

The last population considered are students enrolled in public schools. Hardcastle (1977) addressed the behavioral and/or attitudinal problems of third-, fourth-, and fifth-graders with a family treatment approach that appears to be based on a blend of systems theory and "training as treatment" concepts. Students were referred by school personnel to the Family Skills Program. Only mothers and the identified child participated in nine sessions lasting one-and-one-half to two hours. Counselors working in pairs were each assigned two family groups. Participating family members had the responsibility of teaching other family members the principles taught during the sessions.

The program was didactic in nature and emphasized three primary areas: (1) during initial sessions participants analyzed and discussed what it felt like to live in their own family; (2) communication skills and the impact of positive interaction on self-esteem and family atmosphere were considered; and (3) skills in the identification and renegotiation of family rules were taught.

Positive, significant gains were made on all posttreatment measures when compared with a no-treatment control group. The areas in which positive change was noted included parents' perception of satisfaction with their family, their level of congruence with each other, and their estimate of the degree of family integration.

The McMaster Family Therapy Outcome Study (Santa-Barbara, Woodward, Levin, Goodman, Streiner, & Epstein, 1979) is the report of an exploratory study designed to provide information concerning variables that relate to successful and unsuccessful family systems intervention treatment outcome. A homogeneous group of families were included in the study. To be considered for inclusion, one of the family's presenting problems had to involve academic and/or behavioral difficulties of the child at school. Data were collected on a large sample ($N = 279$), with information taken from a variety of sources (i.e., family, school, therapist, and research staff). Pre-post measures were taken and a followup assessment was completed at six months. Treatment was delivered at the regional Cheroke-McMaster Child and Family Center. The center followed a specific treatment philosophy and the family therapy provided was described as "brief [the mean number of sessions was nine], pragmatic, systems-oriented and focusing on the here and now" (p. 306). Entire families were seen for assessment and most often for treatment.

Goal attainment scaling was employed "to tap both the uniqueness of the problems presented by each family as well as family interactions" (p. 313). A minimum of three goals were articulated at the onset of the family intervention, and at least one goal had to assess changes in the child's academic and/or behavioral performance. By this method, children's disruptive school behavior showed a significant reduction between the onset of treatment and treatment closure. In addition, 79 percent of the families were rated by their therapists to have improved moderately or greatly, and 45 percent were given a good or excellent prognosis at treatment closure.

At a six-month followup evaluation, 79 percent of the families said that the original presenting problem was better or much better. And 88 percent of the families requested no further mental health services. Some 64 percent of the families had attained or exceeded the goals set for them.

The McMaster outcome study tested the "assumption that change in the family system, as a result of family therapy, will lead to changes in other areas, e.g., school performance and behavior" (p. 321). The findings support, but only partly confirm, this assumption. Children's disruptive behavior, both at home and at school, was amenable to change through family systems intervention. However, academic performance was not directly effected within a short time frame by this treatment method.

The results of this research are consistent with studies of the impact of Project Re-Ed (which follows an ecological systems treatment model) on the adjustment of emotionally disturbed children. Re-Ed is a short-term (four to six months) residential program that focuses on working with the child's entire ecological system—the family, school, church, neighborhood, and so on. Evaluation studies consistently show positive change in the areas of family and school adjustment (Gamboa & Garrett, 1974; Kirby, Wilson, & Short, 1977; Weinstein, 1969). However, although academic motivation and school behavior were significantly improved for Re-Ed graduates, the project was not able in four months to close the gap in the child's deficient academic skills.

Summary

The practice of family systems intervention is still largely guided by theory. Ideally, school psychologists should be able to recommend and implement the most appropriate psychological assessment and intervention procedures for students referred for services. The choice of the psychological procedures or strategies employed should be based on the salient variables in the case, such as the referral problem, presence of symptoms, psychological assessment and intervention alternatives, available professional time, and psychological expertise both within the school psychological staff and the larger mental health community. Progress toward this goal in the practice of school psychology requires that studies be undertaken that systematically vary and control for such variables. To establish the family systems interventions as an alternative or preferable psychological intervention for many or any of the problems en-

countered in children/adolescents by psychologists in the schools, controlled outcome studies are needed. This analysis of the family systems intervention literature is based on this perspective.

This chapter underscores the fact that an emerging body of family systems intervention research does exist. A critical analysis of the findings to date suggests that tentative generalizations can be drawn that impact on practice, and suggest new, untested hypotheses that need to be studied. Final conclusions on the practice of family systems intervention are premature in a developing field.

EFFICACY

The family systems intervention research analyzed generally supports the use of short-term family systems intervention. Table 1 summarizes the effects of family systems intervention in the treatment of the five distinct child/adolescent problems considered in this chapter.

Research to date indicates that a planned systemic family intervention is not only significantly more effective than traditional probationary programs in reducing the recidivism of adolescent juvenile delinquents but also that family systems intervention is more effective than other forms of family intervention (namely, insighted-oriented family therapy and didactic family group discussions on attitudes and feelings about family relationships) in improving the clarity, reciprocity, and precision of communication among family members and ultimately in reducing the recidivism of adolescent juvenile delinquents.

Additionally, there are suggestions that an ecologically based intervention is at least as effective with juvenile delinquents as family systems intervention in reducing recidivism. It is important to note that both

TABLE 1 Effectiveness of family systems intervention in addressing five referral problems

		Study Characteristics			Results	
			Dependent Variable(s)			
Study	Length of Treatment	Level of Therapist Training	Measure	Research Design	Child/ Adolescent	Family

Adolescent Status Offenders and Juvenile Delinquents

Study	Length of Treatment	Level of Therapist Training	Measure	Research Design	Child/ Adolescent	Family
Beal & Duckro (1977)	6–8 sessions	Counselors with training and supervision	Case termination without court action	T_1 family intervention T_2 retrospective comparison-probation services	T_1 83% cases closed with no court action T_2 65% cases closed with no court action	NR
Alexander & Parsons (1973)	12–15 sessions	Students with training	Within-family variations in amount speech, amount silence, frequency and duration of interruptions Recidivism	T_1 behavior, family systems T_2 client-centered family T_3 eclectic-dynamic family T_4 no treatment	T_1 significantly superior to T_2, T_3, T_4 Recidivism rates by group: T_1=26% T_2=59% T_3=73% T_4=50%	T_1 significantly superior to T_2 and T_3 on all measures; T_2 significantly to T_3
Klein, Alexander, & Parsons (1976)	12–15 sessions	Students with training	Sibling with courts	T_1 behavior, family systems T_2 client-centered family T_3 eclectic-dynamic family T_4 no treatment	Rate of sibling court referral: T_1=20% T_2=59% T_3=63% T_4=40%	

Study	Duration	Staff	Measures	Conditions	Results
Barton et al. (study III) (1985)	30 hours of service	NR	Recidivism and number of offenses	T_1 placement with family functional family treatment T_2 placement in group home and 24-hour treatment regimen	Recidivism: $T_1=60\%$ $T_2=93\%$ Number of offenses significantly decreased in frequency for T_1
Barton et al. (study I) (1985)	$x = 10.3$ sessions	Undergraduate with 32 hrs. of training & supervision	Recidivism	T_1 functional family treatment	Recidivism rate 26%; significantly lower than base rate of 51% for juvenile court district
Emshoff & Blakely (1983)	18 weeks	Trained undergraduate volunteers	1. Delinquent Behavior: —court records contact with legal system/incarceration —self-reported interview data on delinquent behavior 2. School performance—attendance, grades, credits earned	T_1 family condition T_2 multi-focus T_3 probation (control)	1. T_1 & T_2 had significantly fewer youth incarcerated and lower rate of self-reported deliquent behavior 2. No effect for group; main effect for time—decrease in performance in time

TABLE 1 *(continued)*

	Study Characteristics				Results	
Study	Length of Treatment	Level of Therapist Training	Dependent Variable(s) Measure	Research Design	Child/ Adolescent	Family
Adolescent Substance Abusers						
Szapocznik et al. (1983)	OPFT 8 sessions CFT 4 sessions	Social worker with training in structural or family therapy	Psychiatric Status Schedule Behavior Problem Checklist Structural Family Task Ratings Family Environment Scale	T_1 conjoint family treatment (CFT) T_2 one-person family treatment (OPFT)	Pre-post: Significant improvement for T_1 and T_2 on all clinical measures of family functioning and symptom reduction in IP. T_1 IP's symptom reduction was slightly greater at followup in several areas than T_2	
Szapocznik et al. (1986)	NR	Social worker with training in structural family therapy	Psychiatric Status Schedule Behavior Problem Checklist Structural Family Task Ratings Family Environment Scale	T_1 conjoint family treatment (CFT) T_2 one-person family treatment (OPFT)	Pre-post: Significant improvement for T_1 and T_2 on all clinical measures of family functioning and symptom reduction in IP. T_1 IP's symptom reduction was slightly greater at followup in several areas than T_2	

Adolescent with Family Problems

Everett (1976)	5 weeks	Professionals	Appointments missed	T_1 experimental group T_2 retrospective comparison group	Missed appointments: $T_1=2.5\%$ $T_2=28\%$ Withdrew from treatment: $T_1=6\%$ $T_2=30\%$	Students reported significantly improved family adjustment T_1 parents reported greater empathetic understanding and congruence in marital relationship

Students Enrolled in Special Education Programs for the Emotionally Disturbed

Garrigan & Bambrick (1975)	6 sessions				No significant difference in behavior problems at home or school or self-concept	
Garrigan & Bambrick (1977)	10 sessions	Professional with training in go-between process	Family Concept Q Sort Relationship Inventory Piers-Harris State-Trait Anxiety Inventory Devereux Adolescent Rating Scale	T_1 family intervention T_2 no treatment	T_1 significantly greater reduction of classroom and home behavior problems No significant difference in students' bizarre thoughts, emotional distance, hyperactive-expansive behavior, self-concept, or anxiety experienced in school	

TABLE 1 *(continued)*

		Study Characteristics			Results		
			Dependent Variable(s)				
Study	Length of Treatment	Level of Therapist Training	Measure	Research Design	Child/ Adolescent	Family

Students with Academic/Behavioral Problems in School

Hardcastle (1977)	9 sessions	Counselors		T_1 family skills program T_2 no treatment	T_1 decrease disruptive behavior	T_1 mothers & fathers reported significantly greater satisfaction congruence with each other, perceived family integration, and number of positive statements among family members
Santa Barbara et al. (1979)	$x = 9$ sessions	Professionals and trained students	Shipley Inst. of Living Scale WISC-R WRAT Gilmore Oral Reading Test Ottawa School Behavioral Checklist Treatment Goals	T_1 systems-oriented family therapy	Significantly less disruptive school behavior reported by teacher No changes on WRAT or Gilmore Oral Reading Test	Parents indicated family problems were better

family systems intervention and an ecological intervention emerge from a systems perspective on behavior. The differences, however, are that the ecological intervention has as its focus for change not only the family but also the adolescent's community, school, and work environments. It is therefore not inconsistent, and interesting, to find similar results when these two forms of intervention are employed.

The studies considered here also indicate that positive changes in family functioning and improvement in the reported symptoms of the child/adolescent can be attained even when all family members are not present for treatment. The ability to realize such positive therapeutic outcomes in the absence of all the family members participation and/or investment in the therapeutic intervention is congruent with the assumptions regarding behavior change that are central to systems theory. Such findings are also important for they may, if replicated, herald greater flexibility in the design of effective family systems intervention strategies and programs. Nonetheless, these results also raise serious ethical questions for practitioners that have not, to date, been adequately addressed.

Impact on Family Functioning

In addition to the observed changes in family functioning that have been reported, families themselves perceived family systems intervention to have resulted in greater family cohesiveness and integration, a higher level of expressiveness among members (of which a greater percentage of the interchanges among members were positive), and a less conflictual family environment than prior to treatment. Additionally, parents reported improved marital relationships (i.e., greater empathic understanding between partners and congruence in the marital relationship). The children and adolescents who

were the identified patients concurred with these positive assessments of change in family life. When asked, they perceived generally better adjustment in the family following intervention.

Szaprocznik and colleagues (1983, 1986) and Santa-Barbara and colleagues (1979) assessed the degree to which behavior change was maintained following termination of family intervention. In both studies the positive effects of the intervention either remained stable or showed continued improvement at a ten-week or six-month followup assessment, respectively. The number of studies that included followup assessments are too few from which to generalize; however, the trend is a positive one, which stands in sharp contrast to studies of treatment outcome for individual therapy that repeatedly show that the desired outcome is short-lived after treatment termination (Bergin & Suinn, 1975; Liberman, Frank, Hoehn-Saric, Stone, Imber, & Pande, 1972; Sloane, Staples, Cristol, Yorkston, & Whipple, 1975).

Impact on Student's School Functioning/Academic Performance

There is support for the hypothesis that family systems intervention is effective in treating students' behavioral, but not academic, problems in school. In those studies that specifically assessed students' behavior in school as an outcome variable, both teachers and independent observers noted less disruptive behavior following intervention. Clinically meaningful differences were found (e.g., more than 40 percent of the students in one study who were enrolled in special education programs for the emotionally disturbed were placed in regular education classes following the family intervention). The majority of students so placed adjusted adequately in this new setting.

An exception to these findings was in

a study that assessed treatment outcome after only six sessions. The brief duration of intervention was thought by the authors to have decreased the possibility of realizing all treatment effects, including improved school behavior. To date, studies have not been carried out comparing the efficacy of family systems intervention strategies in reducing undesired behavior at school, when controlling for the frequency and length of treatment, and level of family involvement. Such studies would add to present knowledge regarding family systems intervention.

The results of the research reviewed indicate that some student behaviors seemed impervious to family systems intervention. For example, no differences were found on pre- and postintervention measures of the levels of students' bizarre thoughts, hyperactive-expansive behavior, self-concept, emotional distance, or anxiety associated with school. Systematic research studies are needed to identify the problems children and adolescents experience in the educational context for which a family focus for intervention is the treatment of choice.

The expectation of improved academic performance subsequent to family intervention needs further investigation. As the authors suggest, there are many possible explanations for the lack of immediate improvement in children's academic performance. The tests used to measure change may not be sufficiently sensitive, or change in academic performance may indeed lag behind improvement of school behavior. If such a sequence of change is plausible, the assessment of academic functioning should follow, by six months or one year, the initial followup assessment of behavioral change. It seems that the ability of short-term, systems-oriented, family intervention to effect an increase in academic performance needs further exploration.

Prevention Function of Family Intervention

Klein, Alexander, and Parsons (1977) tested the hypothesis that a family systems intervention would serve a prevention function for siblings of an identified adolescent whose behavior problem (status offenses) first brought the family for treatment. The results indicated that those families who were exposed to a family systems intervention had siblings with significantly fewer court contacts than families who received nonsystems-oriented family interventions. If findings such as this can be replicated, a family systems approach to intervention may well reconceptualize the notions of prevention and intervention. Unlike individual treatment and family interventions designed on a psychodynamic perspective, prevention is an implicit aspect of any family systems intervention. There are indications that family systems intervention, at one point in time, has positive effects not only on the behavior of the targeted child but also on the subsequent adjustment of siblings.

APPLICABILITY TO SCHOOLS

Two concerns most frequently raised by school psychologists regarding the use of family systems intervention strategies in the schools are the perceptions that (1) intervention with families is time consuming and (2) school psychologists (who typically have a minimum of 60 hours of specialized graduate training including extensive supervised practicum and internship experiences [Bardon & Walker, 1972; Brown & Minke, 1986; Cardon & French, 1968/69; French & McCloskey, 1980]) do not have adequate training and skills to work effectively with families.

The literature suggests that neither

of these concerns is necessarily an insurmountable barrier to the practice of family systems interventions. The studies documented in this chapter employed interventions with families that ranged from 4 to 18 weeks in length. Many parent education and child-focused psychological interventions presently carried out by school psychologists are comparable in length. Furthermore, the evidence, to date, suggests that family systems interventions are efficacious, whether carried out by professionals with extensive training and experience in working with families or by students (undergraduate and graduate) with specific but limited family systems intervention training and ongoing supervision.

One study (Barton et al., 1985), which compared the relative efficacy of family intervention in producing positive child outcomes when controlling for the level of therapist training, found no differences in the rates of positive outcome for three groups of therapists: undergraduates with 16 hours of training and ongoing supervision, graduate students with training, and experienced professional therapists. A survey to collect data on the type and extent of family intervention training presently available to students in school psychology graduate programs across the United States is in progress (Donovan, in preparation). These data should help define the projected level of family intervention skills of future school psychologists, and identify available resources for training current practitioners in family systems intervention.

The evidence reported here should encourage a reanalysis of the use by school psychologists of family systems interventions. Although it is not the role of schools to provide general mental health services to families, family systems intervention may indeed be a more productive and economical intervention for some school-related problems of students than many of the intensive child-focused interventions presently employed. Additionally, family systems intervention has the attractive feature of mobilizing the child's/adolescent's natural support network and reinforcing the alliance between schools and families. The issue of adequate training for school psychologists may well be addressed "in-house." For it is clearly plausible that professional school psychologists with expertise and experience in family system intervention could provide training and supervision to other staff school psychologists interested in expanding their repertoire of skills. School divisions without such expertise available from personnel on staff might hire a consultant for training.

Models of family systems intervention, such as Everett's (1976) Family Assessment and Intervention, are appropriate for use in schools. The model outlines a method for assessing family problems and providing short-term family intervention, which may culminate in resolution of the child's school-related problem and therefore termination of the family intervention, or in a specific recommendation for further treatment outside the schools. Families may welcome short-term assistance in addressing their child's school problem from the school psychological staff who initially diagnosed the problem, who established a productive working relationship with the family, and who has special knowledge of child development, the ecology of schools, and the relationship between a child's school performance and his or her family's functioning.

It has been noted that families often do not make the transition successfully from a school mental health worker to a community agency or private practitioner when referred for treatment to address their child's school-related problem (Conti, 1973). For those families who require more extensive involvement with mental health services, the employment of this model may make the referral process more effective by providing families with the necessary motivation for treatment and support for movement between service providers.

METHODOLOGICAL ISSUES

The present family systems intervention literature reveals several unresolved methodological issues. Table 2 summarizes the design characteristics of the studies considered.

Control Groups

In nearly half of the studies reported in Table 2 either no control group was used or a retrospective comparison group was employed. An accurate interpretation of findings reported in studies lacking control/comparison groups is seriously compromised by such a weakness in research design. The careful construction of appropriate comparison and control groups is essential to future research assessing the impact of family intervention. In addition, the exploratory nature of these studies is emphasized by the fact that in only three of the studies reported were families randomly assigned to treatment and control conditions. Generally, family intervention was provided as an alternative to more traditional services, and families were given the option to choose the program they preferred. Self-selection, such as this, creates an unknown amount of variance in the response to treatment. Future research needs to employ experimental designs that control more completely for potential sources of bias.

Evaluation of Treatment Outcome

There is an indication that the gender of the identified child is related to the degree to which parents perceive positive change as a result of treatment (Garrigan & Bambrick, 1977). In their study of emotionally disturbed adolescents, Garrigan and Bambrick (1977) found that the ratings of independent observers did not correspond to parent ratings of behavior change for girls. The authors suggest that parent perceptions, and ultimately their ratings evaluating treatment outcome, may reflect some systematic gender bias. An alternative interpretation of these findings not put forward by the authors might suggest that early adolescent emotionally disturbed girls and boys do not respond similarly to family therapy intervention. Such findings highlight the necessity for the use of multiple measures to assess treatment outcome. Such a compilation of measures should represent a balance of subjective measures (such as parent, student, and teacher ratings) and objective measures (such as videotaped family problem-solving vignettes and structures observations of behavior by an independent rater). Both approaches to the assessment of change in families is necessary for an understanding of observable changes in the behavior of family members, and the "meaning" that the family assigns to such change.

Need for Cross-Sectional and Longitudinal Research Designs

All of the studies reviewed in Table 2 (with the exception of two) report the effects of family intervention on samples of families with an early to mid-adolescent school-age child (11 to 18 years). Such a restricted age range excludes the possibility of understanding the differential effects of this form of intervention over the life cycle of the family. Further research is needed to document the effectiveness of family intervention for problems of children at all ages—preschool, early school age, and early and late adolescence. The obvious lack

TABLE 2 Methodological characteristics of family systems intervention research

Study	Random Assignment to Group(s)	Prospective Comparison/ Control Group(s)	N	Multiple Measures	Pre-Post Assessment	Followup
Alexander & Parsons (1973)	X	X	86	X	X	X
Barton et al. (1985) Study I			27	X	X	
Barton et al. (1985) Study II			109			
Barton et al. (1985) Study III		X	74	X	X	X
Beal & Duckro (1977)	X		98	X	X	
Emshoff & Blakely (1983)	X	X	73	X	X	X
Everett (1976)		X	50	X	X	
Garrigan & Bambrick (1975)		X	18	X	X	
Garrigan & Bambrick (1977)	X	X	28	X	X	
Hardcastle (1977)			28	X	X	
Klein, Alexander, & Parsons (1977)	X	X	86	X		X
Santa-Barbara et al. (1979)			279	X	X	X
Szapocznik et al. (1983)	X	X	62	X	X	X
Szapocznik et al. (1986)	X	X	35	X	X	X

Research Methods

of longitudinal research with populations of families with children who have problems of delinquency, school and home adjustment, and emotional adaptation limits our understanding of how positive change in families supports, over time, child functioning both at home and at school.

Changing Conceptions of the Family

Throughout the literature the term *family* is used without further definition. It is unclear whether the use of this term to describe client populations has resulted in similar samples of families. Often the image that tends to leap to mind most rapidly when the word *family* is used is a stereotypic, and now frequently inaccurate, image of a home with two parents and their biological children. This, at best, describes only 25 percent of U.S. families. The studies reported do not make clear the characteristics of the families they study, nor do they analyze the results they report by such salient family characteristics.

Future studies need to reflect the reality of family life today by assessing the relative benefits of family intervention for two-parent, single-parent, adoptive and foster-parent families; large and small families; and the like, while taking into consideration the resources and needs of each family group.

IMPLICATIONS

An examination of the outcome research on family systems intervention suggests directions for future investigation. Implications of the present research for future study include the following:

1. There is a need for studies to specify more carefully the nature of the family intervention strategy, in terms of its theoretical orientation, therapeutic techniques, and the duration and frequency of treatment, in order to better assess the relative merits of different approaches to outcome.

2. There is a need to replicate and extend present research (Garrigan & Bambrick, 1977) that discriminates among the problems of children and families for which family systems intervention is the treatment of choice.

3. More long-term followup (three to five years) of short-term, family systems intervention is needed to document the notion of prevention as an implicit aspect of systems intervention.

4. Subjective ratings by parents and the identified patient are often used as outcome measures. There is sufficient indication in the research presently reviewed (Garrigan & Bambrick, 1977; Santa-Barbara et al., 1979) that such measures are open to bias. Further investigations of the validity of these measures is necessary.

5. There is a need for future research to design studies that can not only document the general effectiveness of family intervention but also identify the changes in family structure, roles, responsibilities, and interaction patterns that are most closely associated with positive outcomes for the child/adolescent, parents, and siblings. Such knowledge can ultimately direct family assessment practices, the prioritization of treatment goals, and the selection of appropriate strategies for use in family systems intervention programs.

CONCLUSIONS

The relationship between schools and families has changed dramatically over the years. It is clear that new and more varied approaches are needed by school psychologists for the productive involvement of families in resolving their child's school-related problems. Furthermore, school psychologists' repertoire of intervention strategies needs expansion from useful, but limited, child-focused strategies. There are indications in the literature critiqued that a family systems perspective to the practice of school psychology has merits.

References

Alexander, J. F., Barton, C., Schiavo, R. S., & Parsons, B. V. (1976). Systems-behavioral intervention with families of delinquents: Therapist characteristics, family behavior, and outcome. *Journal of Consulting and Clinical Psychology, 44*(4), 656–664.

Alexander, J., & Parsons, B. (1973). Short-term behavioral intervention with delinquent families: Impact on family process and recidivism. *Journal of Abnormal Psychology, 81*(3), 219–225.

Anderson, C. (1983). An ecological development model for a family orientation in school psychology. *Journal of School Psychology, 21,* 179–189.

Bardon, J. I., & Walker, N. W. (1972). Characteristics of graduate training programs in school psychology. *American Psychologist, 27,* 652–656.

Barton, C., Alexander, J., Waldron, H., Turner, C., & Warburton, J. (1985). Generalizing treatment effects of functional family therapy: Three replications. *American Journal of Family Therapy, 13*(3), 16–26.

Beal, D., & Duckro, P. (1977). Family counseling as an alternative to legal action for the juvenile status offender. *Journal of Marriage and Family Counseling, 3,* 77–81.

Bergin, A., & Suinn, R. (1975). Individual psychotherapy and behavior therapy. *Annual Review of Psychology, 26,* 509–555.

Brown, D. T., & Minke, K. M. (1986). School psychology graduate training: A comprehensive analysis. *American Psychologist, 41,* 1328–1338.

Cardon, B. W., & French, J. L. (1968/69). Organization and content of graduate programs in school psychology. *Journal of School Psychology, 7,* 28–32.

Conner, D. G. (1984). Multi family educational groups in juvenile court settings with drug/alcohol offenders. *Journal for Specialists in Group Work, 9,* 21–25.

Conoley, J. C. (1987). Schools and families: Theoretical and practical bridges. *Professional School Psychology, 2*(3), 191–203.

Conti, A. (1973). A follow-up investigation of families referred to outside agencies. *Journal of School Psychology, 11,* 215–222.

Dewitt, K. (1978). The effectiveness of family therapy: A review of outcome research. *Archives of General Psychiatry, 35*(5), 549–561.

Dockrell, W. B. (1964). Society, home and underachievement. *Psychology in the Schools, 1*(2), 173–178.

Donovan, A. M. (1985). *Maternal perception of family stress and ways of coping with adolescents: A comparison study of mothers with autistic, mentally retarded, and non-handicapped adolescents.* Unpublished doctoral dissertation, University of North Carolina at Chapel Hill.

Donovan, A. M., Holland-Beasley, K., and Kugler, L. (in preparation). A national survey of the pre-service education and training of school psychologists in family assessment and intervention skills.

Emshoff, J., & Blakely, C. (1983). The diversion of delinquent youth: Family-focused intervention. *Children and Youth Services Review, 5,* 343–356.

Erchul, W. (Ed.). (1987). Family systems assessment and intervention. *School Psychology Review, 16*(4).

Everett, C. (1976). Family assessment and intervention for early adolescent problems. *Journal of Marriage and Family Counseling, 2,* 155–165.

Fine, M. J., & Holt, P. (1983). Intervening with school problems: A family systems perspective. *Psychology in the Schools, 20,* 59–66.

French, J. L., & McCloskey, G. (1980). Characteristics of doctoral and nondoctoral school psychology programs: Their implications for the entry level doctorate. *Journal of School Psychology, 18,* 247–255.

Friesen, V. I. (1983). The family in the etiology and treatment of drug abuse: Toward a balanced perspective. *Advances in Alcohol and Substance Abuse, 2,* 77–89.

Gamboa, A., & Garrett, J. (1974). Re-education: A mental health service in an educational setting. *American Journal of Orthopsychiatry, 44,* 405–453.

Garrigan, J., & Bambrick, A. (1975). Short term family therapy with emotionally disturbed children. *Journal of Marriage and Family Counseling, 1,* 379–385.

Garrigan, J., & Bambrick, A. (1977). Family therapy for disturbed children: Some experimental results in special education. *Journal of Marriage and Family Counseling, 3,* 83–93.

Graden, J., Brassard, M., Carlson, C., & Christenson, S. (1987). *Family Assessment and Intervention in the Schools: Guidelines for Appropriate Actions.* A paper presented at the 19th Annual Convention of the National Association of School Psychologists, New Orleans.

Green, K., & Fine, M. J. (1980). Family therapy: A case for training school psychologists. *Psychology in the Schools, 17,* 241–248.

Guidubaldi, J. (Ed.). (1980). Families: Current status and emerging trends. *School Psychology Review, 9*(4).

Gurman, A. (1970). The role of the family in underachievement. *Journal of School Psychology, 8*(1), 48–53.

Gurman, A., & Kniskern, D. (1978). In S. Garfield & A. Bergin (Eds.), *Handbook of psychotherapy and behavior change: An empirical analysis* (2nd ed.). New York: Wiley.

Haley, J. (1980). *Leaving Home: The therapy of disturbed young people.* New York: McGraw-Hill.

Hannafin, M. J., & Witt, J. C. (1983). System intervention and the school psychologist: Maximizing interplay among roles and functions. *Professional Practice: Research and Practice, 14*(1), 128–136.

Hansen, J. C. (Ed.) (1984). *Family therapy with school related problems.* Rockville, MD: Aspen Systems.

Hardcastle, D. (1977). A mother-child, multiple family counseling program: Procedures and results. *Family Process, 16,* 67–74.

Kirby, T., Wilson, C., & Short, M. (1977). A follow-up study of disturbed children treated in a Re-Ed program. *Hospital and Community Psychiatry, 28,* 694–697.

Klein, N., Alexander, J., & Parsons, B. (1977). Impact of family systems intervention on recidivism and sibling delinquency: A model of primary prevention and program evaluation. *Journal of Consulting and Clinical Psychology, 45,* 469–474.

Liberman, B., Frank, J., Hoehn-Saric, R., Stone, A., Imber, S., & Pande, S. (1972). Patterns of change in treated psychoneurotic patients: A five-year follow-up investigation of the systematic preparation of patients for psy-

chotherapy. *Journal of Consulting and Clinical Psychology, 38,* 36–41.

Lombard, T. J. (1979). Family-oriented emphasis for school psychologists: A needed orientation for training and professional practice. *Professional Psychology, 10,* 687–696.

Loven, M. (1978). Four alternative approaches to the family/school liaison role. *Psychology in the Schools, 15,* 553–559.

Masten, A. (1979). Family therapy as a treatment for children: A critical review of outcome research. *Family Process, 18,* 323–335.

Minuchin, S., Montalvo, B., Guerney, B., Rosman, B., & Schumer, F. (1967). *Families of the slums: An exploration of their structure and treatment.* New York: Basic Books.

Olson, D. H. (1970). Marital and family therapy: Integrative review and critique. *Journal of Marriage and the Family, 32,* 501–538.

Parsons, B., & Alexander, J. (1973). Short-term family intervention: A therapy outcome study. *Journal of Consulting and Clinical Psychology, 41,* 195–201.

Petrie, P., & Piersel, W. C. (1982). Family therapy. In C. R. Reynolds and T. B. Gutkin (Eds.), *The handbook of school psychology.* New York: Wiley.

Pfeiffer, S. I., & Tittler, B. I. (1983). Utilizing the multidisciplinary team to facilitate a school-family systems orientation. *School Psychology Review, 12,* 168–173.

Phillips, B. N. (1981). School psychology in the 1980s: Some critical issues related to practice. In T. R. Kratochwill (Ed.), *Advances in School Psychology: Volume I.* (pp. 19–43). Hillsdale, NJ: Lawrence Earlbaum.

Pollaczek, D. P. (1964). The school psychologist considers parent education. *Psychology in the Schools, 1*(3), 279–282.

Quirk, J., Carlson, C., Kral, R., Fine, M., Aliotti, N., & Donovan, A. (1987). *Is family therapy compatible with the public schools or should they be divorced?* A paper presented at the 19th Annual Convention of the National Association of School Psychologists, New Orleans.

Reilly, D. M. (1984). Family therapy with adolescent drug abusers and their families: Defying gravity and achieving escape velocity. *Journal of Drug Issues, 14,* 381–391.

Rosenthal, S., Ellis, J., & Pryzwansky, W. (1987). *Systems theory and school psychology: Current applications in practice.* Manuscript submitted for publication.

Santa-Barbara, J., Woodward, C., Levin, S., Goodman, J., Streiner, D., & Epstein, N.

(1979). The McMaster family therapy outcome study: An overview of methods and results. *International Journal of Family Therapy, 1,* 304–323.

Sells, S. B., & Roff, M. (1965). Family influence as reflected in peer acceptance rejection resemblance of siblings as compared with random sets of school children. *Psychology in the Schools, 2*(2), 133–137.

Shellenberger, S. (Ed.). (1981). Services to families and parental involvement with interventions. *School Psychology Review, 10*(1).

Sines, J. D. (1987). *Relations between children's home environment and school behavior.* A paper presented at the 19th Annual Convention of the National Association of School Psychologists, New Orleans.

Sloane, R., Staples, F., Cristol, A., Yorkston, N., & Whipple, K. (1975). *Short-term analytically oriented psychotherapy versus behavior therapy.* Cambridge, MA: Harvard University Press.

Smith, A. H. (1978). Encountering the family system in school-related behavior problems. *Psychology in the Schools, 15*(3), 379–386.

Snapp, M., & Davidson, J. L. (1982). Systems interventions for school psychologists: A case study approach. In C. R. Reynolds and T. B. Gutkin (Eds.), *The handbook of school psychology.* New York: Wiley.

Speigel, R., & Mock, W. L. (1977). *A model for a family systems theory approach to prevention and treatment of alcohol abusing youth.* (Clearinghouse Accession No CG 013 238). Cleveland, OH: Alcoholic Services of Cleveland, Inc. (Eric Document Reproduction Service No. ED 166 624).

Szapocznik, J., Kurtines, W. M., Foote F. H., Perez-Vidal, A., & Hervis, O. (1983). Conjoint versus one-person family therapy: Some evidence for the effectiveness of conducting family therapy through one person. *Journal of Consulting and Clinical Psychology, 51,* 889–899.

Szapocznik, J., Kurtines, W. M., Foote F. H., Perez-Vidal, A., & Hervis, O. (1986). Conjoint versus one-person family therapy: Further evidence for the effectiveness of conducting family therapy through one person with drug-abusing adolescents. *Journal of Consulting and Clinical Psychology, 54,* 395–397.

Szapocznik, J., Lasaga, J. I., & Scopetta, M. A. (1976). *Culture specific approaches to the treatment of Latin multiple substance abusers: Family and ecological intervention models.* (Clearinghouse Accession No. UD 020 859). Coral Gables, FL: University of Miami, Department of Psychiatry. (ERIC Document Reproduction Service No. ED 193 371).

Taplin, J. R. (1980). Implications of general system theory for assessment and intervention. *Professional Psychology, 11*(5), 722–727.

Weinstein, L. (1969). Project Re-Ed schools for emotionally disturbed children: Effectiveness as viewed by referring agencies, parents and teachers. *Exceptional Children, 35,* 703–711.

Wells, R., Dilkes, T., & Trivelli, N. (1972). The results of family therapy: A critical review of the literature. *Family Process, 11,* 189–207.

Wendt, R. N., & Zake, J. (1984). Family systems theory and school psychology: Implications for training and practice. *Psychology in the Schools, 21,* 204–210.

Zuk, G. (1966). The go-between process in family therapy. *Family Process, 5,* 162–178.

Zuk, G. (1972). *Family therapy: A triadic based approach.* New York: Behavioral Science.

Author Index

465

Subject Index